Economic Control of Quality of Manufactured Product

DEDICATION

by

W. Edwards Deming

People who are interested in serious study of quality control will welcome the reprinting of Dr. Shewhart's great work, *The Economic Control Of Manufactured Product,* long out of print. This book did more than lay a foundation; it touched quality control in all aspects—specifications, problems with inspection of incoming materials and with inspection all along the line, improvement of the process, operational definitions, problems in the definition of quality. The consumer, to Shewhart, was the most important part of the production-line. Without the consumer, production ceases.

Quality aimed at, to meet the needs of the consumer, must be stated in terms of specified quality-characteristics that can be measured. It is necessary to predict what quality-characteristics of a product will produce satisfaction in use. Quality, however, to the consumer, is not a set of specifications. The quality of any product is interaction between the product, the user, his expectations, and the service that he can get in case the product fails or requires maintenance. The needs of the consumer are in continual change. So are materials, methods of manufacture, and products. Quality of a product does not necessarily mean high quality. It means continual improvement of the process, so that the consumer may depend on the uniformity of a product and purchase it at low cost. Chapters IV and XVIII in Shewhart's book are a masterpiece on the meaning of quality.

To Shewhart, quality control meant every activity and every technique that can contribute to better living, in a material sense, through economy in manufacture. His book emphasizes the need for continual search for better knowledge about materials, how they behave in manufacture, and how the product behaves in use. Economic manufacture requires achievement of statistical control in the process and statistical control of measurements. It requires improvement of the process in every other feasible way. The cost and inadequacy of inspection are well known. The ultimate aim of quality control should accordingly be elimination of inspection except for small samples for assurance of continuation of statistical control and for comparison of measurements between vendor and purchaser, manufacturer and customer, etc.

As the Japanese learned in 1950, productivity moves upward as the quality of process improves. One requires only 4th grade arithmetic to see this. If action of the process (as by introduction of operational definitions for a quality-characteristic) decreases defectives from 8% to 4%, any schoolboy can understand that this means at least 4% greater productivity. Waste is cut to half. It is important to note that this gain is accomplished with no outlay for new equipment. Besides, there is the long-run benefit that better quality achieves in the market-place, plus improvement in morale of the work-force. The next step is further improvement of the process for further reduction of the proportion defective, and further gain in productivity.

Tests of variables that affect a process are useful only if they predict what will happen if this or that variable is increased or decreased. It is only with material produced in statistical control that one may talk about an experiment as a conceptual sample that could be extended to infinite size. Unfortunately, this supposition, basic to the analysis of variance and to many other statistical techniques, is as unrealizable as it is vital in much experimentation carried out in industry, agriculture, and medicine.

Statistical theory as taught in the books is valid and leads to operationally verifiable tests and criteria for an enumerative study. Not so with an analytic problem, as the conditions of the experiment will not be duplicated in the next trial. Unfortunately, most problems in industry are analytic.

The needs of industry for something better from statisticians always bothered Shewhart. No wonder. As he often said, the requirements of industry are more exacting than the requirements for research in pure science. Industry requires statistical methods that are efficient. Good data are costly. Why waste information that can help to improve a process when efficient methods are known and are simple?

The scientific importance of controlled measurements in research has led Dr. Heihachi Sakamoto of Keio University to classify the problems of statistics into three types: enumerative, analytic, and methods by which to achieve statistical control.

Anyone who has tried to draw random samples of poker chips from a bowl, as Shewhart tried, and as Tippett tried, or anyone who has tried to bring use of a simple instrument into statistical control, can and should raise questions about how one can use some of the statistical methods taught today. It was in fact Tippet's difficulties with home-made cards that led him, at the suggestion of Karl Pearson, to construct his well known table of random numbers, and be rid of cards and poker chips forever.

Chapters XII and XIII form an excellent text on statistical methods. For example, the formula

$$\text{Opt } n_2 = \frac{\sigma_E}{\sigma_T}\sqrt{\frac{a_1}{a_2}}$$

for the optimum number of measurements to take on a selected unit is on page 389. Here σ_E is the standard deviation between measurements, σ_T the standard deviation between units, a_1 is the cost to select a unit and make it available for measurement, a_2 the cost of each measurement. Curiously, Tippett published the same formula, the same year, in his book *The Methods of Statistics,* now in the Wiley statistical series. The power of statistical theory is well illustrated by the uses made of this formula by these two authors: Shewhart was sampling wire; Tippett was sampling soils in England.

Although considerations of probability and distributions are basic to the control chart, Shewhart perceived that control limits must serve industry in action. A manufacturing process, even in statistical control, wavers. Control limits can thus not be associated with any exact probability of looking for trouble (an assignable cause) when there is none, nor with failure to look for trouble when an assignable cause does exist. It was for such reasons that he used 3-sigma limits. Experience of 50 years shows how right he was.

Another contribution from Shewhart is his recognition of the need for operational definitions. An operational definition is one that is communicable. How can an operator carry out his job if he does not know what the job is? How can he know what the job is if what he produced yesterday was right, but the same thing is wrong today? Inspection, no matter whether the operator inspects his own work or relies on someone else to do it for him, must have operational definitions of quality-characteristics. A system of measurement, whether by machine or visual, must exhibit statistical control. Otherwise, production can only remain in chaos.

An operational definition translates a concept (round, random, safe, conforming, good) into a test and a criterion—yes, it is sufficiently round, sufficiently safe, or it is not. The test-method and the criterion to have meaning for business or legal purposes can only be stated in statistical terms: likewise a standard for safety, reliability, or performance.

There was never before greater need for statistical methods in industry and in research. The whole world is talking about safety in mechanical and electrical devices (in automobiles, for example), safety in drugs, reliability, due care, pollution, poverty, nutrition, improvement of agricultural practice, improvement in quality of product, break-down of service, break-down of equipment, tardy busses, trains, and mail, need for greater output in industry and in agriculture, enrichment of jobs. The consumer requires month by month ever greater and greater safety, and he expects better and better performance of manufactured articles. The manufacturer has the same problems in his purchases of materials, assemblies, machines, and use of manpower. He must, in addition, know more and more about his own product. What is due care in manufacturing?

These problems cannot be understood and cannot even be stated, nor can the effect of any alleged solution be evaluated, without the aid of statistical theory and methods.

Study of Dr. Shewhart's great book will assist production and will bring better living to people the world over. It is fitting and proper that the American Society for Quality Control should reprint this monumental work.

June 1980

Economic Control of Quality of Manufactured Product

By

W. A. SHEWHART, PH.D.

Member of the Technical Staff

BELL TELEPHONE LABORATORIES, INC.

NEW YORK

D. VAN NOSTRAND COMPANY, INC.

250 FOURTH AVENUE

1931

Library of Congress Cataloging-in-Publication Data

Shewhart, W.A., 1891-1967
Economic control of quality of manufactured product / by W.A. Shewhart.
Published/Created: Milwaukee, Wis.: American Society for Quality Control, 1980.
Description: xiv, 501 p.: ill.; 24 cm.
Notes: "50th anniversary commemorative reissue"--T.p. verso.
Reprint. Originally published: New York : Van Nostrand, 1931.
Includes bibliographical references and indexes.
ISBN: 0-87389-076-0
1. Factory management. 2. Statistics—Graphic methods.
3. Quality control—Statistical methods.

TS155 .S47 1980

658.5/62 20

10 9 8 7 6 5 4

ISBN 0-87389-076-0

ASQ Mission: The American Society for Quality advances individual and organizational performance excellence worldwide by providing opportunities for learning, quality improvement, and knowledge exchange.

Printed in the United States of America

Printed on acid-free paper

ASQ
AMERICAN SOCIETY FOR QUALITY™

Quality Press
600 N. Plankinton Avenue
Milwaukee, Wisconsin 53203
Call toll free 800-248-1946
Fax 414-272-1734
www.asq.org
http://qualitypress.asq.org
http://standardsgroup.asq.org
E-mail: authors@asq.org

"When numbers are large, chance is the best warrant for certainty."

A. S. Eddington,
The Nature of the Physical World

"A situation like this merely means that those details which determine the future in terms of the past may be so deep in the structure that at present we have no immediate experimental knowledge of them and we may for the present be compelled to give a treatment from a statistical point of view based on considerations of probability."

P. W. Bridgman,
The Logic of Modern Physics

ABOUT THE AUTHOR

The father of modern quality control, Walter A. Shewhart (1891 – 1967) brought together the disciplines of statistics, engineering, and economics in a simple but highly effective tool: the control chart. These techniques, and the principles behind it, have played key roles in economic developments from the 1940s to the present.

A strong background in the sciences and engineering prepared Shewhart well for a life of accomplishments. Shewhart graduated from the University of Illinois with bachelor's and master's degrees, received his doctorate in physics from the University of California – Berkeley in 1917, and also taught at both universities.

Most of Shewhart's professional career was spent at Western Electric as an engineer from 1918 to 1924 and at Bell Telephone Laboratories from 1925 until his retirement in 1956. In addition, he served for more than 20 years as the first editor of the Mathematical Statistics Series published by John Wiley & Sons.

Called upon frequently as a consultant, Shewhart served the War Department, the United Nations, and the government of India. Shewhart was an honorary member of England's Royal Statistical Society, the Calcutta Statistical Association, and the American Society for Quality Control. He was a fellow and officer of the Institute of Mathematical Statistics, American Association for the Advancement of Science, and American Statistical Association; a fellow of the Econometric Society, the International Statistical Institute, and the New York Academy of Science; and a member of numerous other advisory committees and professional and technical groups.

In 1948, the American Society for Quality Control established the Shewhart Medal and presented Shewhart with the first medal struck. Comments made by the chairman of that first award committee perhaps best sum up the character of Walter A. Shewhart:

> *"...the art of awarding the medal focuses the spotlight of public attention on the recipient, revealing in clear light the qualities that have won for him the esteem of his peers. What are the qualities that lead us to so honor a person to give them a medal? First of all, he must have intellectual ability, enabling him to clear away a little of the dark cloud of ignorance that always surrounds us. Second, he must have the generosity of spirit that leads him to so express and restate his pioneering ideas that other members of his profession may benefit from them. And finally, he must have that warmth of human feeling that marks the true educator, endearing him to his students or disciples, even those who learn from him only remotely. All of these qualities are eminently personified in Dr. Walter A. Shewhart."*
> (Industrial Quality Control, *May 1949, p. 26.)*

PREFACE

Broadly speaking, the object of industry is to set up economic ways and means of satisfying human wants and in so doing to reduce everything possible to routines requiring a minimum amount of human effort. Through the use of the scientific method, extended to take account of modern statistical concepts, it has been found possible to set up limits within which the results of routine efforts must lie if they are to be economical. Deviations in the results of a routine process outside such limits indicate that the routine has broken down and will no longer be economical until the cause of trouble is removed.

This book is the natural outgrowth of an investigation started some six years ago to develop a scientific basis for attaining economic control of quality of manufactured product through the establishment of control limits to indicate at every stage in the production process from raw materials to finished product when the quality of product is varying more than is economically desirable. As such, this book constitutes a record of progress and an indication of the direction in which future developments may be expected to take place. To get as quickly as possible a picture of the way control works, the reader may find it desirable, after going through Part I, to consider next the various practical illustrations given in Parts VI and VII and in Appendix I.

The material in this text was originally organized for presentation in one of the Out-of-Hour Courses in Bell Telephone Laboratories. Since then it has undergone revision for use in a course of lectures presented at the request of Stevens Institute of Technology in its Department of Economics of Engineering. Much of the work recorded herein is the result of the cooperative effort of many individuals. To a considerable extent the experimental data are such as could have been accumulated only in a large industry.

On the theoretical side the author wishes to acknowledge the very helpful and suggestive criticisms of his colleague Dr. T. C. Fry and of Mr. E. C. Molina of the American Telephone and Telegraph Company. On the practical side he owes a great debt to another colleague, Mr. H. F. Dodge.

The task of accumulating and analyzing the large amount of data and of putting the manuscript in final form was borne by Miss Marion B. Cater and Miss Miriam S. Harold, assisted by Miss Fina E. Giraldi. Mr. F. W. Winters contributed to the development of the theory. The Bureau of Publication of the Laboratories cooperated in preparing the manuscript for publication. To each of these the author is deeply indebted.

The author is particularly indebted to R. L. Jones, Director of Apparatus Development, and to G. D. Edwards, Inspection Engineer, under whose helpful guidance the present basis for economic control of quality of manufactured product has been developed.

W. A. Shewhart.

Bell Telephone Laboratories, Inc.
New York, N. Y.
April, 1931.

TABLE OF CONTENTS

Part I

Introduction

275-277

Chapter XX

Chapter XXI

Part VII

Quality Control in Practice

Chapter XXII

Chapter XXIII

Chapter XXIV

PART I

Introduction

Fundamental Concepts of Statistical Control and an Outline of Five Economic Advantages Obtainable through Statistical Control of Quality of Manufactured Product

CHAPTER I

Characteristics of a Controlled Quality

1. *What is the Problem of Control?*

What is the problem of control of quality of manufactured product? To answer this question, let us put ourselves in the position of a manufacturer turning out millions of the same kind of thing every year. Whether it be lead pencils, chewing gum, bars of soap, telephones, or automobiles, the problem is much the same. He sets up a standard for the quality of a given kind of product. He then tries to make all pieces of product conform with this standard. Here his troubles begin. For him standard quality is a bull's-eye, but like a marksman shooting at a bull's-eye, he often misses. As is the case in everything we do, unknown or chance causes exert their influence. The problem then is: how much may the quality of a product vary and yet be controlled? In other words, how much variation should we leave to chance?

To make a thing the way we want to make it is one popular conception of control. We have been trying to do this for a good many years and we see the fruition of this effort in the marvelous industrial development around us. We are sold on the idea of applying scientific principles. However, a change is coming about in the principles themselves and this change gives us a new concept of control.

A few years ago we were inclined to look forward to the time when a manufacturer would be able to do just what he wanted to do. We shared the enthusiasm of Pope when he said "All chance is but direction thou canst not see", and we looked forward to the time when we would see that direction. In other words, emphasis was laid on the *exactness* of physical laws. Today, however, the emphasis is placed elsewhere as is indicated by the following quotation from a recent issue, July, 1927, of the journal *Engineering*:

> Today the mathematical physicist seems more and more inclined to the opinion that each of the so-called laws of nature is essentially statistical, and that all our equations and theories can do, is to provide us with a series of orbits of varying probabilities.

The breakdown of the orthodox scientific theory which formed the basis of applied science in the past necessitates the introduction of certain new concepts into industrial development. Along with this change must come a revision in our ideas of such things as a controlled product, an economic standard of quality, and the method of detecting lack of control or those variations which should not be left to chance.

Realizing, then, the statistical nature of modern science, it is but logical for the manufacturer to turn his attention to the consideration of available ways and means of handling statistical problems. The necessity for doing this is pointed out in the recent book [1] on the application of statistics in mass production, by Becker, Plaut, and Runge. They say:

> It is therefore important to every technician who is dealing with problems of manufacturing control to know the laws of statistics and to be able to apply them correctly to his problems.

Another German writer, K. H. Daeves, in writing on somewhat the same subject says:

> Statistical research is a logical method for the control of operations, for the research engineer, the plant superintendent, and the production executive.[2]

The problem of control viewed from this angle is a comparatively new one. In fact, very little has been written on the subject. Progress in modifying our concept of control has been and will be comparatively slow. In the first place,

[1] *Anwendungen der Mathematischen Statistik auf Probleme der Massenfabrikation*, Julius Springer, Berlin, 1927.

[2] "The Utilization of Statistics," *Testing*, March, 1924.

it requires the application of certain modern physical concepts; and in the second place, it requires the application of statistical methods which up to the present time have been for the most part left undisturbed in the journals in which they appeared. This situation is admirably summed up in the January, 1926 issue of *Nature* as follows:

A large amount of work has been done in developing statistical methods on the scientific side, and it is natural for anyone interested in science to hope that all this work may be utilized in commerce and industry. There are signs that such a movement has started, and it would be unfortunate indeed if those responsible in practical affairs fail to take advantage of the improved statistical machinery now available.

2. *Nature of Control*

Let us consider a very simple example of our inability to do exactly what we want to do and thereby illustrate two characteristics of a controlled product.

Write the letter *a* on a piece of paper. Now make another *a* just like the first one; then another and another until you have a series of *a*'s, *a*, *a*, *a*, *a*, ... You try to make all the *a*'s alike but you don't; you can't. You are willing to accept this as an empirically established fact. But what of it? Let us see just what this means in respect to control. Why can we not do a simple thing like making all the *a*'s just alike? Your answer leads to a generalization which all of us are perhaps willing to accept. It is that there are many causes of variability among the *a*'s: the paper was not smooth, the lead in the pencil was not uniform, and the unavoidable variability in your external surroundings reacted upon you to introduce variations in the *a*'s. But are these the only causes of variability in the *a*'s? Probably not.

We accept our human limitations and say that likely there are many other factors. If we could but name all the reasons why we cannot make the *a*'s alike, we would most assuredly have a better understanding of a certain part of nature than we now have. Of course, this conception of what it means to be able to do what we want to do is not new; it does not belong exclusively to any one field of human thought; it is commonly accepted.

The point to be made in this simple illustration is that we are limited in doing what we want to do; that to do what we set out to do, even in so simple a thing as making *a*'s that are alike, requires almost infinite knowledge compared with that which we now possess. It follows, therefore, since we are thus willing to accept as axiomatic that we cannot do what we want to do and cannot hope to understand why we cannot, that we must also accept as axiomatic that a controlled quality will not be a constant quality. Instead, a controlled quality must be a *variable* quality. This is the first characteristic.

But let us go back to the results of the experiment on the *a*'s and we shall find out something more about control. Your *a*'s are different from my *a*'s; there is something about your *a*'s that makes them yours and something about my *a*'s that makes them mine. True, not all of your *a*'s are alike. Neither are all of my *a*'s alike. Each group of *a*'s varies within a certain range and yet each group is distinguishable from the others. This distinguishable and, as it were, constant variability *within limits* is the second characteristic of control.

3. *Definition of Control*

For our present purpose *a phenomenon will be said to be controlled when, through the use of past experience, we can predict, at least within limits, how the phenomenon may be expected to vary in the future. Here it is understood that prediction within limits means that we can state, at least approximately, the probability that the observed phenomenon will fall within the given limits.*

In this sense the time of the eclipse of the sun is a predictable phenomenon. So also is the distance covered in successive intervals of time by a freely falling body. In fact, the prediction in such cases is extremely precise. It is an entirely different matter, however, to predict the expected length of life of an individual at a given age; the velocity of a molecule at a given instant of time; the breaking strength of a steel wire of known cross section; or numerous other phenomena of like character. In fact, a prediction of the type illustrated by forecasting the time of an eclipse of the sun is almost the exception rather than the rule in scientific and industrial work.

In all forms of prediction an element of chance enters. The specific problem which concerns us at the present moment is the formulation of a scientific basis for prediction, taking into account the element of chance, where, for the purpose of our discussion, *any unknown cause of a phenomenon will be termed a chance cause.*

CHAPTER II

Scientific Basis for Control

1. *Three Important Postulates*

What can we say about the future behavior of a phenomenon acting under the influence of unknown or chance causes? I doubt that, in general, we can say anything. For example, let me ask: "What will be the price of your favorite stock thirty years from today?" Are you willing to gamble much on your powers of prediction in such a case? Probably not. However, if I ask: "Suppose you were to toss a penny one hundred times, thirty years from today, what proportion of heads would you expect to find?", your willingness to gamble on your powers of prediction would be of an entirely different order than in the previous case.

The recognized difference between these two situations leads us to make the following simple postulate:

> *Postulate 1—All chance systems of causes are not alike in the sense that they enable us to predict the future in terms of the past.*

Hence, if we are to be able to predict the quality of proauct even within limits, we must find some criterion to apply to observed variability in quality to determine whether or not the cause system producing it is such as to make future predictions possible.

Perhaps the natural course to follow is to glean what we can about the workings of unknown chance causes which are generally acknowledged to be controlled in the sense that they permit of prediction within limits. Perhaps no better examples could be considered than length of human life and molecular motion. It might appear that nothing is more uncertain than life itself, unless perhaps it be molecular motion. Yet there is something certain about these uncertainties. In the laws of mortality and distribution of molecular displacement, we find some of the essential characteristics of control within limits.

A. *Law of Mortality*

The date of death always has seemed to be fixed by chance even though great human effort has been expended in trying to rob chance of this prerogative. We come into this world and from that very instant on are surrounded by causes of

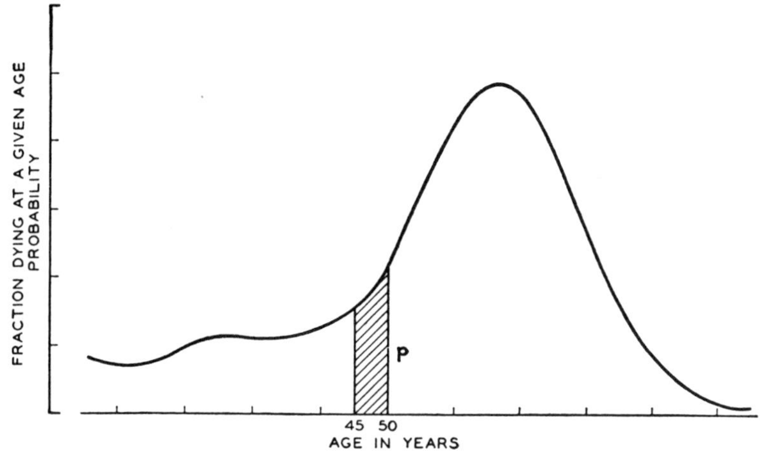

FIG. 1.—LAW OF MORTALITY—LAW OF FLUCTUATIONS CONTROLLED WITHIN LIMITS.

death seeking our life. Who knows whether or not death will overtake us within the next year? If it does, what will be the cause? These questions we cannot answer. Some of us are to fall at one time from one cause, others at another time from another cause. In this fight for life we see then the element of uncertainty and the interplay of numerous unknown or chance causes.

However, when we study the effect of these chance causes in producing deaths in large groups of individuals, we find some indication of a controlled condition. We find that this hidden host of causes produce deaths at an average rate which does not differ much over long periods of time. From such observations we are led to believe that, as we approach the condition of homogeneity of population and surroundings, we approach what is customarily termed a "Law of Mortality" such as indicated schematically in Fig. 1. In other words, we believe that in the limiting case of homogeneity the causes of death function so as to make the probability of dying within given age limits, such as forty-five to fifty, constant. That is, we believe these causes are controlled. In other words, we assume the existence of a kind of statistical equilibrium among the effects of an unknown system of chance causes expressible in the assumption that the probability of dying within a given age limit, under the assumed conditions, is an objective and constant reality.

B. *Molecular Motion*

Just about a century ago, in 1827 to be exact, an English botanist, Brown, saw something through his microscope that caught his interest. It was motion going on among the suspended particles almost as though they were alive. In a way it resembled the dance of dust particles in sunlight, so familiar to us, but this dance differed from that of the dust particles in important respects,—for example, adjacent particles seen under the microscope did not necessarily move in even approximately the same direction, as do adjacent dust particles suspended in the air.

Watch such motion for several minutes. So long as the temperature remains constant, there is no change. Watch it for hours, the motion remains characteristically the same. Watch it for days, we see no difference. Even particles suspended in liquids enclosed in quartz crystals for thousands of years show exactly the same kind of motion. Therefore, to the best of our knowledge there is remarkable permanence to this motion. Its characteristics remain constant. Here we certainly find a remarkable degree of constancy exhibited by a chance system of causes.

Suppose we follow the motion of one particle to get a better picture of this constancy. This has been done for us by several investigators, notably Perrin. In such an experiment he noted the position of a particle at the end of equal intervals of time, Fig. 2. He found that the direction of this motion observed in one interval differed in general from that in the next succeeding interval; that the direction of the motion

FIG. 2.—A CLOSE-UP OF MOLECULAR MOTION APPEARING ABSOLUTELY IRREGULAR, YET CONTROLLED WITHIN LIMITS.

presents what we instinctively call absolute irregularity. Let us ask ourselves certain questions about this motion.

Suppose we fix our attention on the particle at the point *A*. What made it move to *B* in the next interval of time? Of course we answer by saying that a particle moves at a given instant in a given direction, say *AB*, because the resultant force of the molecules hitting it in a plane perpendicular to this direction from the side away from B is greater than that on the side toward B; but at any given instant of time there is no way of telling what molecules are engaged in giving it such motion. We do not even know how many molecules are taking part. Do what we will, so long as the temperature is kept constant, we cannot change this motion in a given system. It cannot be said, for example, when the particle is at the point B that during the next interval of time it will move to C. We can do nothing to control the motion in the matter of displacement or in the matter of the direction of this displacement.

Let us consider either the x or y components of the segments of the paths. Within recent years we find abundant evidence indicating that these displacements appear to be distributed about zero in accord with what is called the normal law.[1]

Such evidence as that provided by the law of mortality and the law of distribution of molecular displacements leads us to assume that there exist in nature phenomena controlled by systems of chance causes such that the probability dy of the magnitude X of a characteristic of some such phenomenon falling within the interval X to $X + dX$ is expressible as a function f of the quantity X and certain parameters represented symbolically in the equation

$$dy = f(X, \lambda_1, \lambda_2, \ldots, \lambda_m)dX, \tag{2}$$

where the λ's denote the parameters. Such a system of causes we shall term *constant* because the probability dy is independent of time. We shall take as our second postulate:

> *Postulate 2—Constant systems of chance causes do exist in nature.*

To say that such systems of causes exist in nature, however, is one thing; to say that such systems of causes exist in a

[1] That is to say, if x represents the deviation from the mean displacement, zero in this case, the probability dy of x lying within the range x to $x + dx$ is given by

$$dy = \frac{1}{\sigma\sqrt{2\pi}} e^{-\frac{x^2}{2\sigma^2}} dx, \tag{1}$$

where σ is the root mean square deviation.

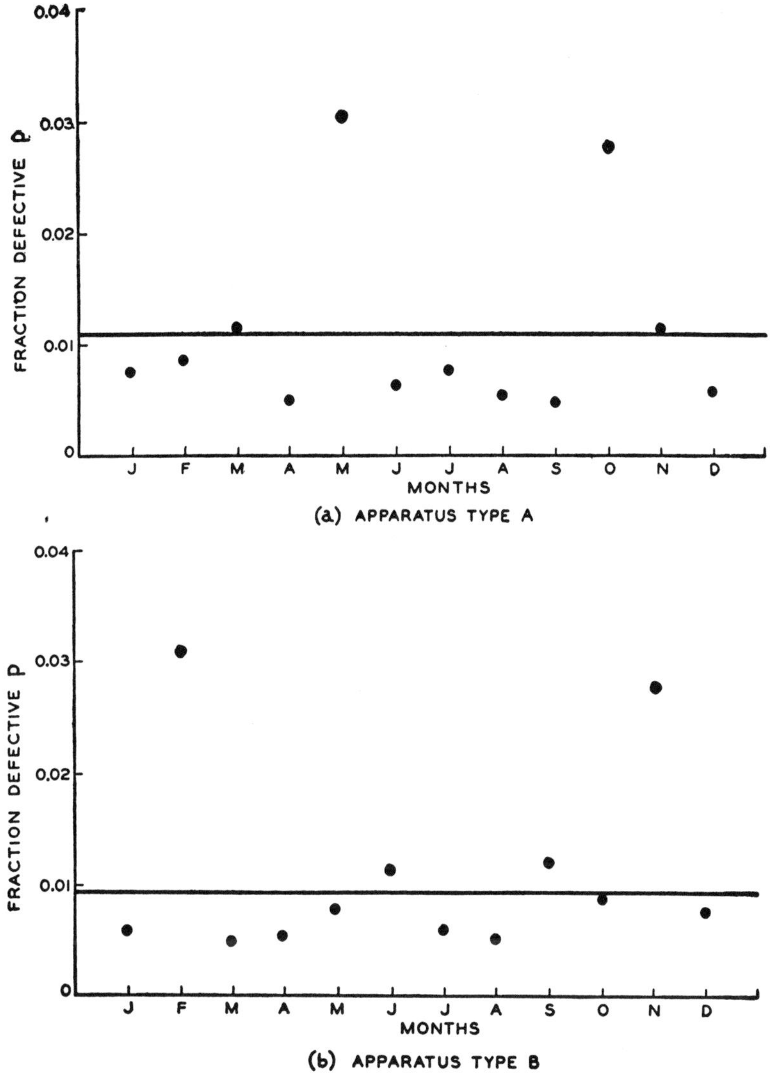

FIG. 3.—SHOULD THESE VARIATIONS BE LEFT TO CHANCE?

production process is quite another thing. Today we have abundant evidence of the existence of such systems of causes in the production of telephone equipment. The practical situation, however, is that in the majority of cases there are unknown causes of variability in the quality of a product which do not belong to a constant system. This fact was discovered very early in the development of control methods, and these causes were called *assignable*. The question naturally arose as to whether it was possible, in general, to find and eliminate such causes. Less than ten years ago it seemed reasonable to assume that this could be done. Today we have abundant evidence to justify this assumption. We shall, therefore, adopt as our third postulate:

Postulate 3—Assignable causes of variation may be found and eliminated.

Hence, to secure control, the manufacturer must seek to find and eliminate assignable causes. In practice, however, he has the difficulty of judging from an observed set of data whether or not assignable causes are present. A simple illustration will make this point clear.

2. *When do Fluctuations Indicate Trouble?*

In many instances the quality of the product is measured by the fraction non-conforming to engineering specifications or, as we say, the fraction defective. Table 1 gives for a period of twelve months the observed fluctuations in this fraction for two kinds of product designated here as Type A and Type B. For each month we have the sample size n, the number defective n_1 and the fraction $p = \frac{n_1}{n}$. We can better visualize the extent of these fluctuations in fraction defective by plotting the data as in Fig. 3-*a* and Fig. 3-*b*.

What we need is some yardstick to detect in such variations any evidence of the presence of assignable causes. Can we find such a yardstick? Experience of the kind soon to be considered indicates that we can. It leads us to conclude that it is feasible to establish criteria useful in detecting the presence of assignable causes of variation or, in other words, criteria which when applied to a set of observed values will indicate whether or not it is reasonable to believe that the causes of variability should be left to chance. Such criteria are basic to any method of securing control within limits. Let us, therefore, consider them critically. It is too much to expect that the criteria will be infallible. We are amply rewarded if they appear to work in the majority of cases.

Generally speaking, the criteria are of the nature of limits derived from past experience showing within what range the fluctuations in quality should remain, if they are to be left to chance. For example, when such limits are placed on the fluctuations in the qualities shown in Fig. 3, we find, as shown in Fig. 4, that in one case two points fall outside the limits and in the other case no point falls outside the limits.

TABLE 1.—FLUCTUATIONS IN QUALITY OF TWO MANUFACTURED PRODUCTS

Apparatus Type A				Apparatus Type B			
Month	Number Inspected n	Number Defective n_1	Fraction Defective $p=\frac{n_1}{n}$	Month	Number Inspected n	Number Defective n_1	Fraction Defective $p=\frac{n_1}{n}$
Jan.	527	4	0.0076	Jan.	169	1	0.0059
Feb.	610	5	0.0082	Feb.	99	3	0.0303
March	428	5	0.0117	March	208	1	0.0048
April	400	2	0.0050	April	196	1	0.0051
May	498	15	0.0301	May	132	1	0.0076
June	500	3	0.0060	June	89	1	0.0112
July	395	3	0.0076	July	167	1	0.0060
Aug.	393	2	0.0051	Aug.	200	1	0.0050
Sept.	625	3	0.0048	Sept.	171	2	0.0117
Oct.	465	13	0.0280	Oct.	122	1	0.0082
Nov.	446	5	0.0112	Nov.	107	3	0.0280
Dec.	510	3	0.0059	Dec.	132	1	0.0076
Average	483.08	5.25	0.0109	Average	149.33	1.42	0.0095

Upon the basis of the use of such limits, we look for trouble in the form of assignable causes in one case but not in the other.

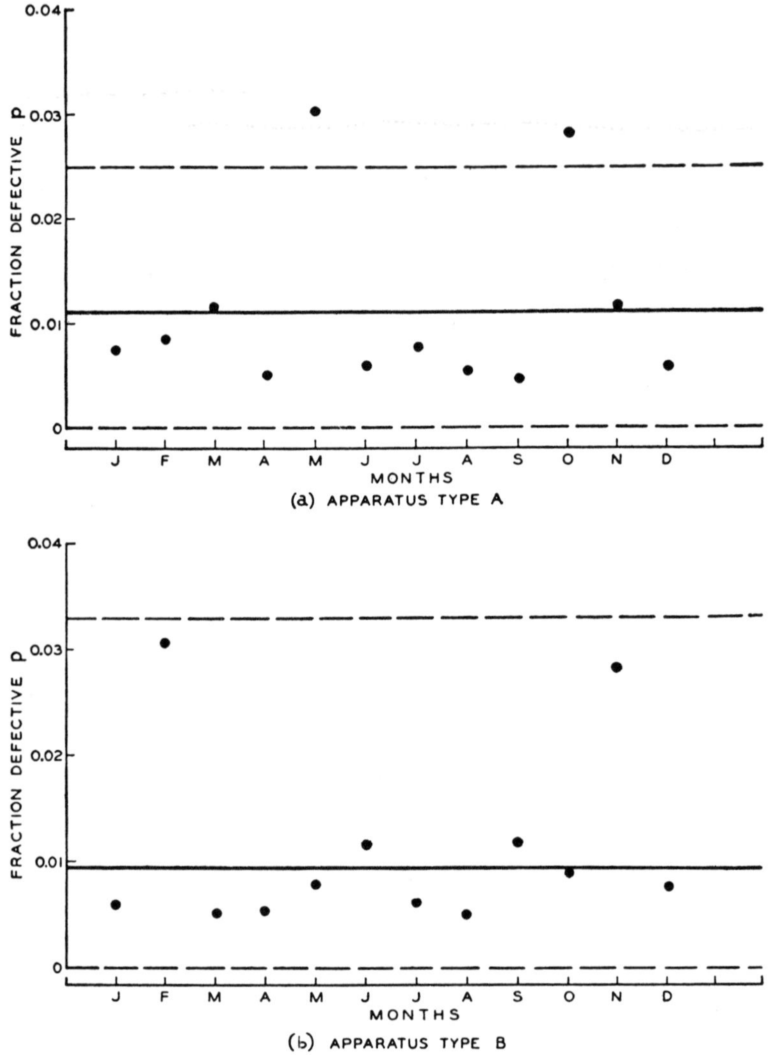

Fig. 4.—Should These Variations be Left to Chance?
a—"No." *b*—"Yes."

However, the question remains: Should we expect to be able to find and eliminate causes of variability only when deviations fall outside the limits? First, let us see what statistical theory has to say in answer to this question.

Upon the basis of Postulate 3, it follows that we can find and remove causes of variability until the remaining system of causes is constant or until we reach that state where the probability that the deviations in quality remain within any two fixed limits (Fig. 5) is constant. However, this assumption alone does not tell us that there are certain limits within which all observed values of quality should remain provided the causes cannot be found and eliminated. In fact, as long as

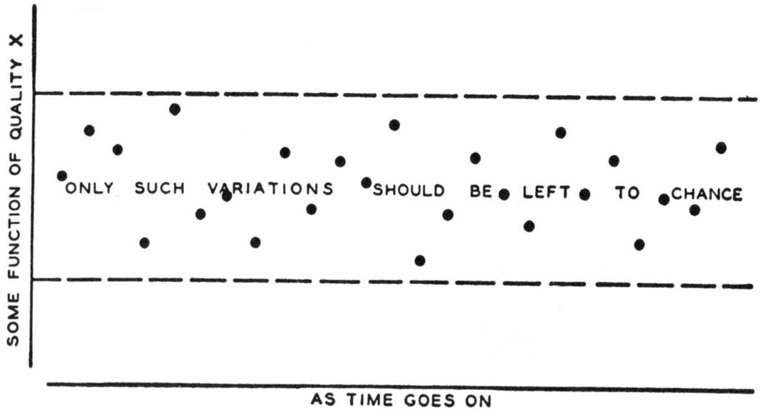

FIG. 5.—JUDGMENT PLUS MODERN STATISTICAL MACHINERY MAKES POSSIBLE THE ESTABLISHMENT OF SUCH LIMITS

the limits are set so that the probability of falling within the limits is less than unity, we may always expect a certain percentage of observations to fall outside the limits even though the system of causes be constant. In other words, the acceptance of this assumption gives us a right to believe that there is an objective state of control within limits but in itself it does not furnish a practical criterion for determining when variations in quality, such as those indicated in Fig. 3, should be left to chance.

Furthermore, we may say that mathematical statistics as such does not give us the desired criterion. What does this situation mean in plain everyday engineering English? Simply this: such criteria, if they exist, cannot be shown to exist by any theorizing alone, no matter how well equipped the theorist is in respect to probability or statistical theory. We see in this situation the long recognized dividing line between theory and practice. The available statistical machinery referred to by the magazine *Nature* is, as we might expect, not an end in itself but merely a means to an end. In other words, the fact that the criterion which we happen to use has a fine ancestry of highbrow statistical theorems does not justify its use. Such justification must come from empirical evidence that it works. As the practical engineer might say, the proof of the pudding is in the eating. Let us therefore look for the proof.

3. *Evidence that Criteria Exist for Detecting Assignable Causes*

A. Fig. 6 shows the results of one of the first large scale experiments to determine whether or not indications given by

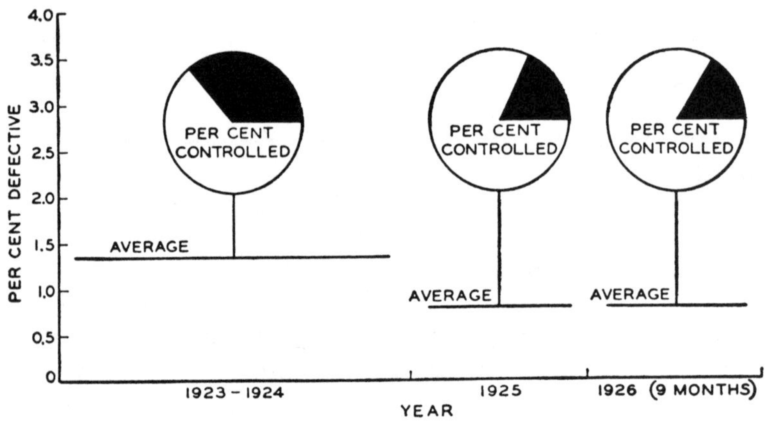

Fig. 6.—Evidence of Improvement in Quality with Approach to Control.

such a criterion applied to quality measured in terms of fraction defective were justified by experience. About thirty typical items used in the telephone plant and produced in lots running into the millions per year were made the basis for this study. As shown in this figure, during 1923–24 these items showed

68 per cent control about a relatively low average of 1.4 per cent defective.[1] However, as the assignable causes, indicated by deviations in the observed monthly fraction defective falling outside of control limits, were found and eliminated, the quality of product approached the state of control as indicated by an increase of from 68 per cent to 84 per cent control by the latter part of 1926. At the same time the quality improved; in 1923–24 the average per cent defective was 1.4 per cent, whereas by 1926 this had been reduced to 0.8 per cent. Here we get some typical evidence that, in general, as the assignable causes are removed, the variations tend to fall more nearly within the limits as indicated by an increase from 68 per cent to 84 per cent. Such evidence is, of course, one sided. It shows that when points fall outside the limits, experience indicates that we can find assignable causes, but it does not indicate that when points fall within such limits, we cannot find causes of variability. However, this kind of evidence is provided by the following two typical illustrations.

B. In the production of a certain kind of equipment, considerable cost was involved in securing the necessary electrical insulation by means of materials previously used for that purpose. A research program was started to secure a cheaper material. After a long series of preliminary experiments, a tentative substitute was chosen and an extensive series of tests of insulation resistance were made on this material, care being taken to eliminate all known causes of variability. Table 2 gives the results of 204 observations of resistance in megohms taken on as many samples of the proposed substitute material. Reading from top to bottom beginning at the left column and continuing throughout the table gives the order in which the observations were made. The question is: "Should such variations be left to chance?"

No *a priori* reason existed for believing that the measurements forming one portion of this series should be different from those in any other portion. In other words, there was

[1] Jones, R. L., "Quality of Telephone Materials," *Bell Telephone Quarterly*, June, 1927.

no rational basis for dividing the total set of data into groups of a given number of observations except that it was reasonable to believe that the system of causes might have changed from day to day as a result of changes in such things as atmospheric conditions, observers, and materials. In general, if such changes are to take place, we may readily detect their effect if we divide the total number of observations into compar atively small subgroups. In this particular instance, the size of the subgroup was taken as four and the black dots in Fig. 7-*a* show the successive averages of four observations in the order in which thev were taken. The dotted lines are the

Table 2.—Electrical Resistance of Insulation in Megohms—Should Such Variations be Left to Chance?

5,045	4,635	4,700	4,650	4,640	3,940	4,570	4,560	4,450	4,500	5,075	4,500
4,350	5,100	4,600	4,170	4,335	3,700	4,570	3,075	4,450	4,770	4,925	4,850
4,350	5,450	4,110	4,255	5,000	3,650	4,855	2,965	4,850	5,150	5,075	4,930
3,975	4,635	4,410	4,170	4,615	4,445	4,160	4,080	4,450	4,850	4,925	4,700
4,290	4,720	4,180	4,375	4,215	4,000	4,325	4,080	3,635	4,700	5,250	4,890
4,430	4,810	4,790	4,175	4,275	4,845	4,125	4,425	3,635	5,000	4,915	4,625
4,485	4,565	4,790	4,550	4,275	5,000	4,100	4,300	3,635	5,000	5,600	4,425
4,285	4,410	4,340	4,450	5,000	4,560	4,340	4,430	3,900	5,000	5,075	4,135
3,980	4,065	4,895	2,855	4,615	4,700	4,575	4,840	4,340	4,700	4,450	4,190
3,925	4,565	5,750	2,920	4,735	4,310	3,875	4,840	4,340	4,500	4,215	4,080
3,645	5,190	4,740	4,375	4,215	4,310	4,050	4,310	3,665	4,840	4,325	3,690
3,760	4,725	5,000	4,375	4,700	5,000	4,050	4,185	3,775	5,075	4,665	5,050
3,300	4,640	4,895	4,355	4,700	4,575	4,685	4,570	5,000	5,000	4,615	4,625
3,685	4,640	4,255	4,090	4,700	4,700	4,685	4,700	4,850	4,770	4,615	5,150
3,463	4,895	4,170	5,000	4,700	4,430	4,430	4,440	4,775	4,570	4,500	5,250
5,200	4,790	3,850	4,335	4,095	4,850	4,300	4,850	4,500	4,925	4,765	5,000
5,100	4,845	4,445	5,000	4,095	4,850	4,690	4,125	4,770	4,775	4,500	5,000

limits within which experience has shown that these observations should fall, taking into account the size of the sample, provided the variability should be left to chance. Several of the observed values lie outside these limits. This was taken as an indication of the existence of causes of variability which could be found and eliminated.

Further research was instituted at this point to find these

causes of variability. Several were found, and after these had been eliminated another series of observed values gave the results indicated in Fig. 7-*b*. Here we see that all of the points lie within the limits. We assumed, therefore, upon the basis of this test, that it was not feasible for research to go much further in eliminating causes of variability. Because of

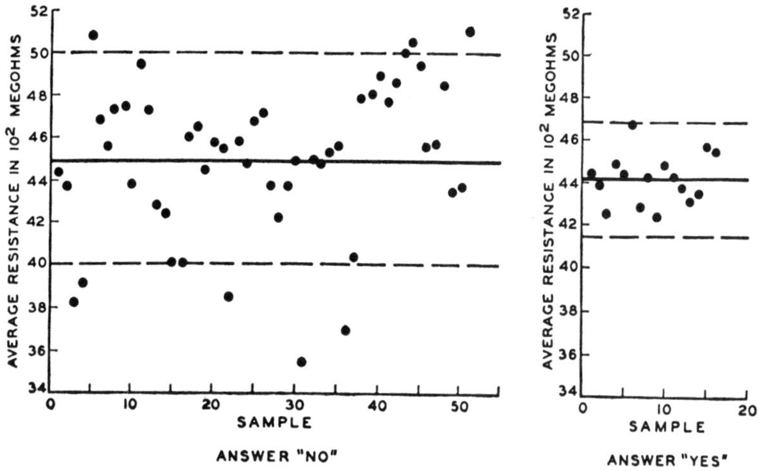

FIG. 7.—SHOULD THESE VARIATIONS BE LEFT TO CHANCE?

the importance of this particular experiment, however, considerably more work was done, but it failed to reveal causes of variability. Here then is a typical case where the criterion indicates when variability should be left to chance.

C. Suppose now that we take another illustration where it is reasonable to believe that almost everything humanly possible has been done to remove the assignable causes of variation in a set of data. Perhaps the outstanding series of observations of this type is that given by Millikan in his famous measurement of the charge on an electron. Treating his data in a manner similar to that indicated above, we get the results shown in Fig. 8. All of the points are within the dotted limits. Hence the indication of the test is consistent with the accepted conclusion that those factors which need not be left to chance had been eliminated before this particular set of data were taken.

4. *Rôle Played by Statistical Theory*

It may appear thus far that mathematical statistics plays a relatively minor rôle in laying a basis for economic control of quality. Such, however, is not the case. In fact, a central concept in engineering work today is that almost every physical property is a *statistical distribution*. In other words, an observed

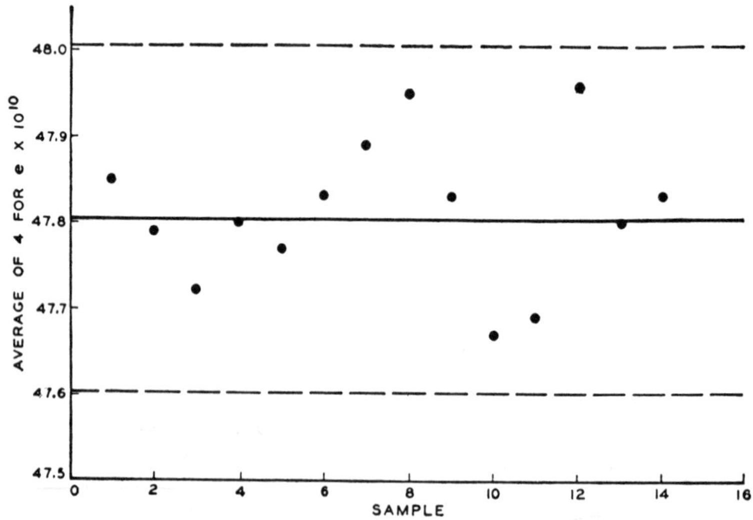

FIG. 8.—VARIATIONS THAT SHOULD BE LEFT TO CHANCE—DOES THE CRITERION WORK? "YES."

set of data constitutes a sample of the effects of unknown chance causes. It is at once apparent, therefore, that sampling theory should prove a valuable tool in testing engineering hypotheses. Here it is that much of the most recent mathematical theory becomes of value, particularly in analysis involving the use of comparatively small numbers of observations.

Let us consider, for example, some property such as the tensile strength of a material. If our previous assumptions are justified, it follows that, after we have done everything we can to eliminate assignable causes of variation, there will still remain a certain amount of variability exhibiting the state of control. Let us consider an extensive series of data recently published by a member of the Forest Products Laboratories,[1] Fig. 9. Here we have the results of tests for modulus of rupture on 1,304 small test specimens of Sitka spruce, the kind of material used extensively in aeroplane propellers

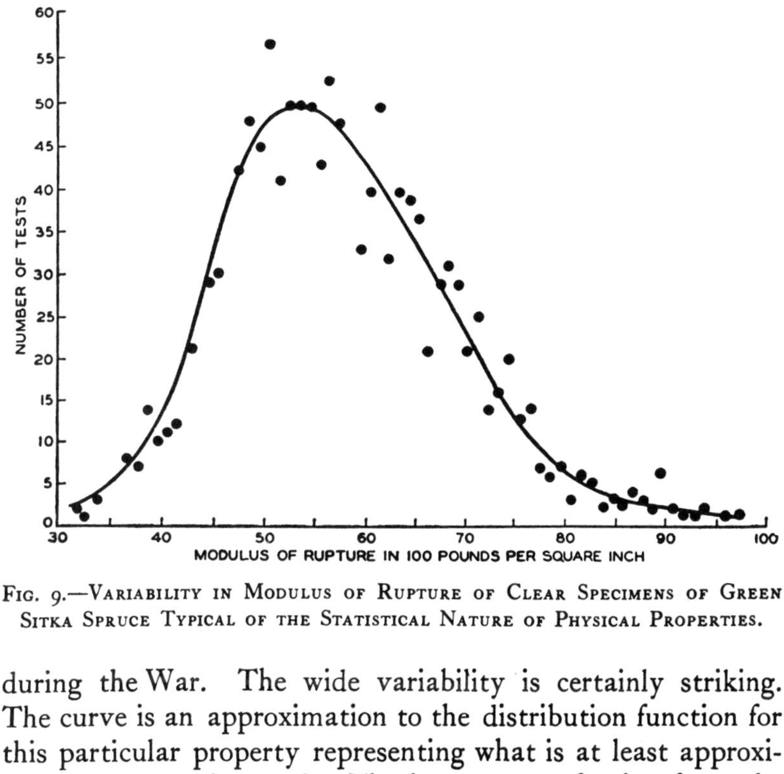

FIG. 9.—VARIABILITY IN MODULUS OF RUPTURE OF CLEAR SPECIMENS OF GREEN SITKA SPRUCE TYPICAL OF THE STATISTICAL NATURE OF PHYSICAL PROPERTIES.

during the War. The wide variability is certainly striking. The curve is an approximation to the distribution function for this particular property representing what is at least approximately a state of control. The importance of going from the sample to the smooth distribution is at once apparent and in this case a comparatively small amount of refinement in statistical machinery is required.

[1] Newlin, J. A., *Proceedings of the American Society of Civil Engineers*, September 1926, pp. 1436–1443.

Suppose, however, that instead of more than a thousand measurements we had only a very small number, as is so often the case in engineering work. Our estimation of the variability of the distribution function representing the state of control upon the basis of the information given by the sample would necessarily be quite different from that ordinarily used by engineers, see Fig. 10. This is true even though to begin with we make the same kind of assumption as engineers have been

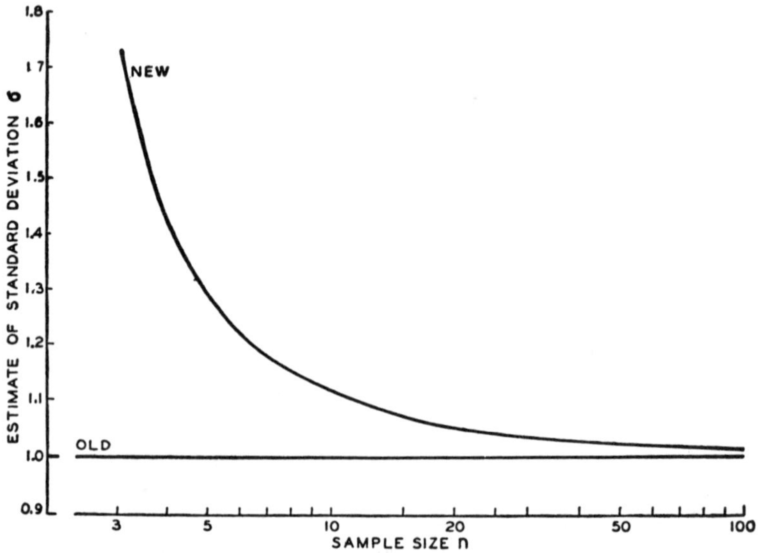

Fig. 10.—Correction Factors Made Possible by Modern Statistical Theory are Often Large—Typical Illustration.

accustomed to make in the past. This we may take as a typical example of the fact that the production engineer finds it to his advantage to keep abreast of the developments in statistical theory. Here we use *new* in the sense that much of the modern statistical theory is new to most engineers.

5. *Conclusion*

Based upon evidence such as already presented, it appears feasible to set up criteria by which to determine when assignable causes of variation in quality have been eliminated so that the product may then be considered to be controlled within limits. This state of control appears to be, in general, a kind of limit to which we may expect to go economically in finding and removing causes of variability without changing a major portion of the manufacturing process as, for example, would be involved in the substitution of new materials or designs.

CHAPTER III

Advantages Secured through Control

1. *Reduction in the Cost of Inspection*

If we can be assured that something we use is produced under controlled conditions, we do not feel the need for inspecting it as much as we would if we did not have this assurance. For example, we do not waste our money on doctors'

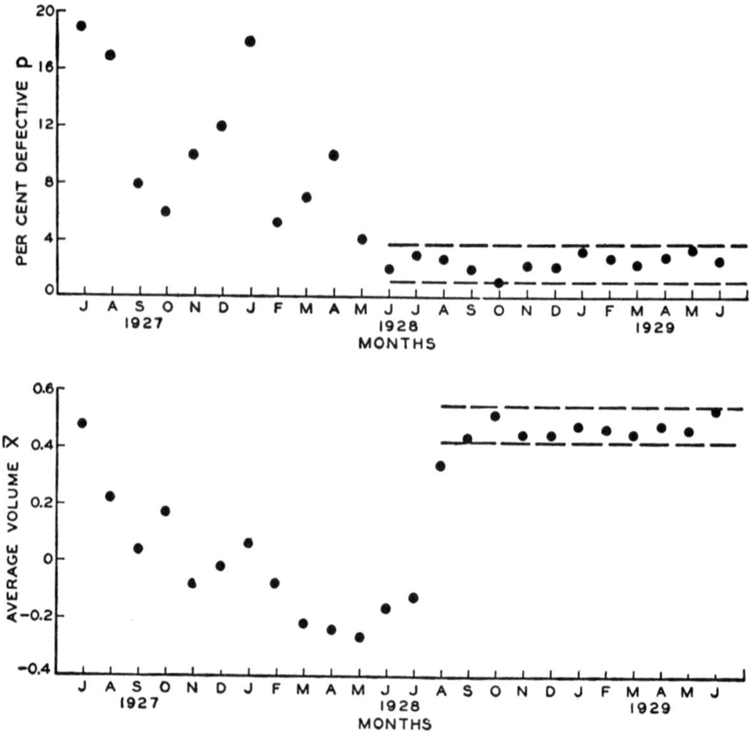

Fig. 11.—Approach to Stable Equilibrium or Control as Assignable Causes are Weeded Out, thus Reducing the Need for Inspection.

bills so long as we are willing to attribute the variability in our health to the effects of what in our present terminology corresponds to a constant system of chance causes.

In the early stages of production there are usually causes of variability which must be weeded out through the process of inspection. As we proceed to eliminate assignable causes, the quality of product usually approaches a state of stable equilibrium somewhat after the manner of the two specific illustrations presented in Fig. 11. In both instances, the record goes back for more than two years and the process of elimination in each case covers a period of more than a year.

It is evident that as the quality approaches what appears to be a comparatively stable state, the need for inspection is reduced.

2. *Reduction in the Cost of Rejections*

That we may better visualize the economic significance of control, we shall now view the production process as a whole. We take as a specific illustration the manufacture of telephone equipment. Picture, if you will, the twenty or more raw materials such as gold, platinum, silver, copper, tin, lead, wool, rubber, silk, and so forth, literally collected from the four corners of the earth and poured into the manufacturing process. The telephone instrument as it emerges at the end of the production process is not so simple as it looks. In it there are 201 parts, and in the line and equipment making possible the connection of one telephone to another, there are approximately 110,000 more parts. The annual production of most of these parts runs into the millions so that the total annual production of parts runs into the billions.

How shall the production process for such a complicated mechanism be engineered so as to secure the economies of quantity production and at the same time a finished product with quality characteristics lying within specified tolerances? One such scheme is illustrated in Fig. 12. Here the manufacturing process is indicated schematically as a funnel, at the small end of which we have the 100 per cent inspection screen to protect the consumer by assuring that the quality of the finished product is satisfactory. Obviously, however, it is often more economical to throw out defective material at some of the initial stages in production rather than to let it pass on to the final stage where it would likely cause the rejection of a

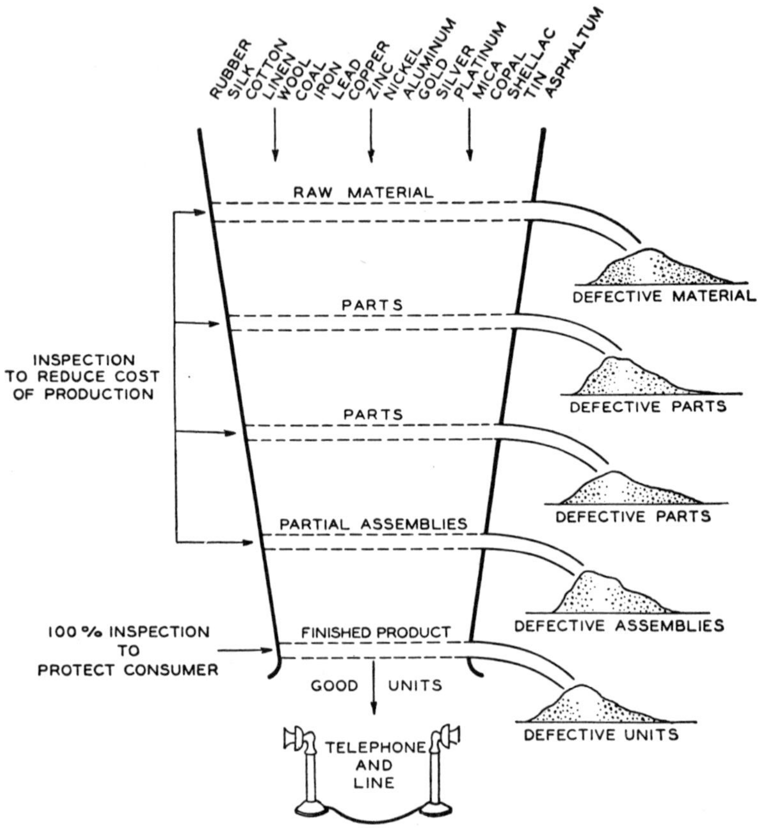

FIG. 12.—AN ECONOMIC PRODUCTION SCHEME.

finished unit of product. For example, we see to the right of the funnel, piles of defectives, which must be junked or reclaimed at considerable cost.

It may be shown theoretically that, by eliminating assignable causes of variability, we arrive at a limit to which it is feasible to go in reducing the fraction defective. It must suffice here to call attention to the kind of evidence indicating that this limiting situation is actually approached in practice as we remove the assignable causes of variability.

Let us refer again to Fig. 6 which is particularly significant because it represents the results of a large scale experiment carried on under commercial conditions. As the black sectors in the pie charts decrease in size, indicating progress in the removal of assignable causes, we find simultaneously a decrease in the average per cent defective from 1.4 to 0.8. Here we see how control works to reduce the amount of defective material. However, this is such an important point that it is perhaps interesting to consider an illustration from outside the telephone field.

Recent work of the Food Research Institute of Stanford University shows that the loss from stale bread constitutes an important item of cost for a great number of wholesale as well as some retail bakeries. It is estimated that this factor alone costs the people of the United States millions of dollars per year. The sales manager of every baking corporation is interested, therefore, in detecting and finding assignable causes of variation in the returns of stale bread if by so doing he can reduce this loss to a minimum.

Some time ago it became possible to secure the weekly record of return of stale bread for ten different bakeries operating in a certain metropolitan district. These observed results are shown graphically in Fig. 13. At once we see that there is a definite lack of control on the part of each bakery. The important thing to note, however, is that the bakery having the lowest percentage return, 1.99 per cent, also shows better control than the other bakeries as judged by the number of points falling outside the control limits in the 36-week period.

3. *Attainment of Maximum Benefits from Quantity Production*

The quality of the finished product depends upon the qualities of raw materials, piece-parts, and the assembling process. It follows from theory that so long as such quality characteristics are controlled, the quality of the finished unit will be controlled, and will therefore exhibit minimum variability. Other advantages also result. For example, by

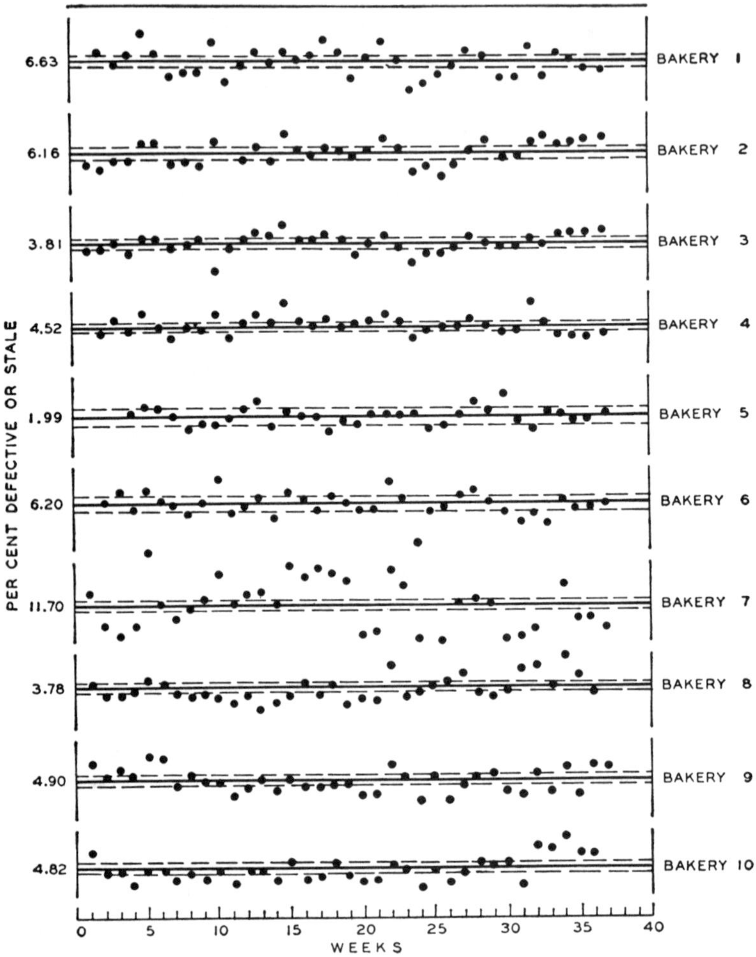

FIG. 13.—RESULTS SHOWING HOW CONTROL EFFECTS A REDUCTION IN THE COST OF REJECTIONS.

gaining control, it is possible, as we have already seen, to establish standard statistical distributions for the many quality characteristics involved in design. Very briefly, let us see just how these statistical distributions representing states of control become useful in securing an economic design and production scheme.

Suppose we consider a simple problem in which we assume that the quality characteristic Y in the finished product is a function f of m different quality characteristics, $X_1, X_2, \ldots,$ X_m, representable symbolically by

$$Y = f(X_1, X_2, \ldots, X_m). \tag{3}$$

For example, one of the X's might be a modulus of rupture, another a diameter of cross section, and Y a breaking load. Engineering requirements generally place certain tolerances on the variability in the resultant quality characteristic Y, which variability is in turn a function of the variabilities in each of the m different quality characteristics.

It follows theoretically that the quality characteristic Y will be controlled if the m independent characteristics are controlled. Knowing the distribution functions for each of the m different independent variables, it is possible to approximate very closely the per cent of the finished product which may be expected to have a quality characteristic Y within the specified tolerances. If, for example, it is desirable to minimize the variability in the resultant quality Y by proper choice of materials, and if standard distribution functions for the given quality characteristics are available for each of several materials, it is possible to choose that particular material which will minimize the variability of the resultant quality at a minimum of cost.

4. *Attainment of Uniform Quality even though Inspection Test is Destructive*

So often the quality of a material of the greatest importance to the individual is one which cannot be measured directly without destroying the material itself. So it is with the fuse that protects your home; with the steering rod on your car; with the rails that hold the locomotive in its course; with the propeller of an aeroplane, and so on indefinitely. How are we to know that a product which cannot be tested in respect to a given quality is satisfactory in respect to this same quality? How are we to know that the fuse will blow at a given current; that the steering rod of your car will not break under maximum load placed upon it? To answer such questions, we must rely upon previous experience. In such a case, causes of variation in quality are unknown and yet we are concerned in assuring ourselves that the quality is satisfactory.

Enough has been said to show that here is one of the very important applications of the theory of control. By weeding out assignable causes of variability, the manufacturer goes to the feasible limit in assuring uniform quality.

5. *Reduction in Tolerance Limits*

By securing control and by making use of modern statistical tools, the manufacturer not only is able to assure quality, even though it cannot be measured directly, but is also often able to reduce the tolerance limits in that quality as one very simple illustration will serve to indicate.

Let us again consider tensile strength of material. Here the measure of either hardness or density is often used to indicate tensile strength. In such cases, it is customary practice to use calibration curves based upon the concept of functional relationship between such characteristics. If instead of basing our use of these tests upon the concept of functional relationship, we base it upon the concept of statistical relationship, we can make use of planes and surfaces of regression as a means of calibration. In general, this procedure makes possible a reduction in the error of measurement of the tensile strength and hence the establishment of closer tolerances. This is true because, when quality can be measured directly and accurately, we can separate those samples of a material for which the quality lies within given tolerance limits from all others. Now, when the method of measurement is indirect and also subject to error, this separation can only be carried on in the probability sense assuming the errors of measurement are controlled by a constant system of chance causes.

not constant

independent w. respect to time. In our cases, independ

It is obvious that, corresponding to a given probability, the tolerance limits may be reduced as we reduce the error of measurement.

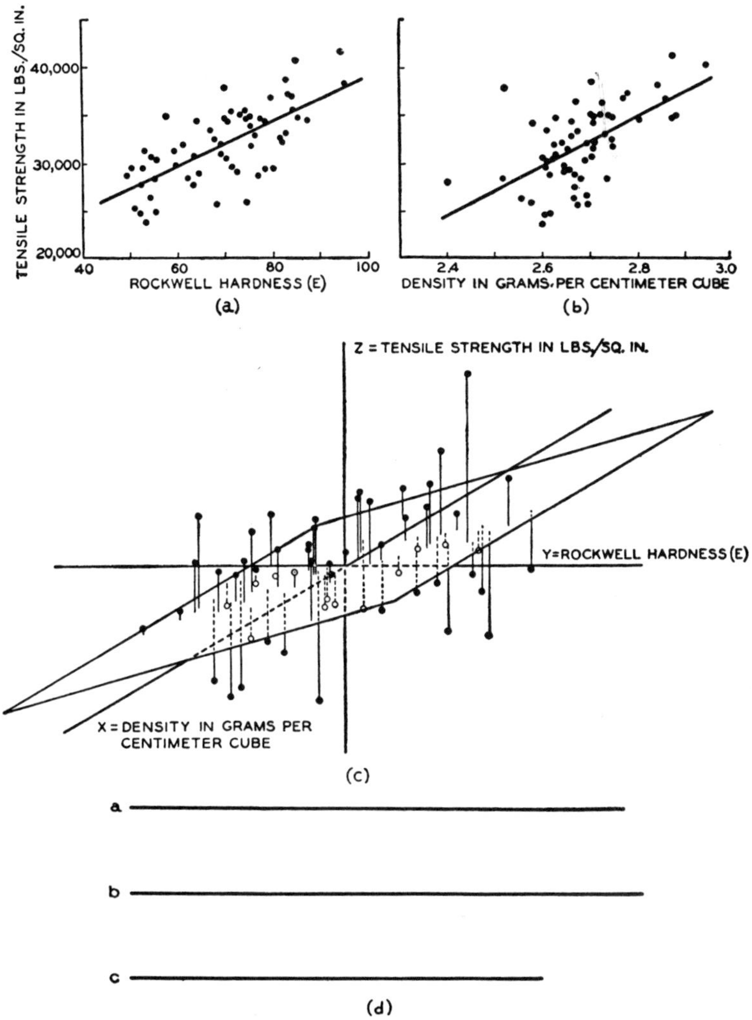

FIG. 14.—HOW CONTROL MAKES POSSIBLE IMPROVED QUALITY THROUGH REDUCTION IN TOLERANCE LIMITS.

Fig. 14 gives a simple illustration. Here the comparative magnitudes of the standard deviations of tensile strength about

w. respect to units e.g. dozens.

two lines of regression and the plane of regression are shown schematically by the lines in Fig. 14-*d*. The lengths of these are proportional to the allowable tolerance limits corresponding to a given probability. It is customary practice to use the line of regression between tensile strength and hardness. Note the improvement effected by using the plane of regression. By using the hardness and density together as a measure of tensile strength, the tolerance range on tensile strength corresponding to a given probability can be made less than it would be if either of these measures were used alone.

6. *Conclusion*

It seems reasonable to believe that there is an *objective state of control*, making possible the prediction of quality within limits even though the causes of variability are unknown. Evidence has been given to indicate that through the use of statistical machinery in the hands of an engineer artful in making the right kind of hypotheses, it appears possible to establish criteria which indicate when the state of control has been reached. It has been pointed out that by securing this state of control, we can secure the following advantages:

1. Reduction in the cost of inspection.
2. Reduction in the cost of rejection.
3. Attainment of maximum benefits from quantity production.
4. Attainment of uniform quality even though the inspection test is destructive.
5. Reduction in tolerance limits where quality measurement is indirect.

Part II

Ways of Expressing Quality of Product

A Review of the Methods for Reducing Large Numbers of Observations of Quality to a Few Simple Functions of These Data Which Contain the Essential Information

CHAPTER IV

Definition of Quality

1. *Introductory Note*

When we analyze our conception of quality, we find that the term is used in several different ways. Hence, it is essential that we decide, first of all, whether the discussion is to be limited to a particular concept of quality, or to be so framed as to include the essential element in each of the numerous conceptions. One purpose in considering the various definitions of quality is merely to show that in any case the measure of quality is a quantity which may take on different numerical values. In other words, the measure of quality, no matter what the definition of quality may be, is a variable. We shall usually represent this variable by the symbol X. In future chapters when we are discussing quality control, we shall treat of the control of the measurable part of quality as defined in any one of the different ways indicated below.

The more important purpose in considering the various definitions of quality is, however, to examine the basic requirements of effective specifications of quality.

2. *Popular Conception of Quality*

Dating at least from the time of Aristotle, there has been some tendency to conceive of quality as indicating the *goodness* of an object. The majority of advertisers appeal to the public upon the basis of the quality of product. In so doing, they implicitly assume that there is a measure of goodness which can be applied to all kinds of product whether it be vacuum tubes, sewing machines, automobiles, Grape Nuts, books, cypress flooring, Indiana limestone, or correspondence school courses. Such a concept, is, however, too indefinite for practical purposes.

3. *Conception of the Quality of a Thing as a Set of Characteristics*

Quality, in Latin *qualitas*, comes from *qualis*, meaning "how constituted" and signifies such as the thing really is. Suppose we consider a simple thing like water. What is it that makes water what it is? One might answer that it is the chemical combination of hydrogen and oxygen represented by the symbol H_2O. To do so is to evade the question, however, for to begin with we must know what we mean by the symbol H_2O. If we turn to a textbook on chemistry, we find that the quality of water is expressed in terms of its chemical and physical properties. For example, it is colorless in thin layers and blue in thick layers. It is odorless and tasteless, has a density of unity at 4 deg. C., a heat of vaporization of 540 calories at 100 deg. C., and remains a liquid within a certain temperature range. It dissociates at 1,000 deg. C. in accord with the formula

$$\underset{1.8\%}{H_2 + O} \rightleftarrows \underset{98.2\%}{H_2O},$$

and is an active catalyst. Even this description, however, is only an incomplete specification of water in terms of that which makes it what it is.

In general, the quality of a thing is that which is inherent in it so that we cannot alter the quality without altering the thing. It is that from which anything can be said to be such and such and may, for example, be a characteristic explainable by an adjective admitting degrees of comparison.

Going a little deeper we see that possibly without exception every conceptual "something" is really a group of conceptions more elementary in form. The minimum number of conceptions required to define an object may be called the qualities thereof. For example, Jevons says: "The mind learns to regard each object as an aggregate of qualities and acquires the power of dwelling at will upon one or other of those qualities to the exclusion of the rest."[1]

The same conception underlies the definition of quality of manufactured product as given by a prominent author on this subject. Thus he says: "The term 'quality', as applied to the products turned out by industry, means the characteristic or group or combination of characteristics which distinguishes one article from another, or the goods of one manufacturer from those of his competitors, or one grade of product from a certain factory from another grade turned out by the same factory." [2] In this sense a thing has qualities and not a quality. For example, a piece of material has weight density, dimensions, and so on indefinitely.

For our purpose we shall assume that, had we but the ability to see, we would find a very large number m' of different characteristics required to define what even the simplest thing really is. A thing is therefore formally defined in this sense, if the specific magnitudes of the m' characteristics are known.

Admittedly we do not know a single one of these—not even the number of possible ones in any given case. Those that we take as elementary we believe to be but a combination of several truly elementary ones, so that the nearest we can approach to the description of any physical thing is to say that it has a finite number of measurable characteristics, $X_1, X_2, \ldots, X_m$, where of course, m' is presumably greater than m.

Thus we might take the characteristics of capacity, inductance, and resistance as defining the quality of a relay. Geometrically speaking, the quality of a relay in this sense can be thought of as a point ($P \equiv X_{11}, X_{21}, X_{31}$) in three dimensional space with coordinate axes X_1, X_2, and X_3, see Fig. 15. Of course, to define the quality of the relay in terms of those characteristics which make it what it is would require a space of m' dimensions, where m' is the unknown number of inde-

[1] *The Principles of Science*, 2nd Edition, page 25.

[2] Radford, G. S., *The Control of Quality in Manufacturing*, published by Ronald Press Company, 1922, page 4.

pendent characteristics required to define a relay. For example, to characterize a monatomic gas molecule we need a space of six dimensions, since one dimension is required for each of three space coordinates and for each of three velocity components.

Quality then as we shall use it may be a quantity having known physical dimensions such as length, velocity, resistance; a quantity representing the magnitude of any entity in units of the same kind; or merely a number such as a rate, number defective, and so on.

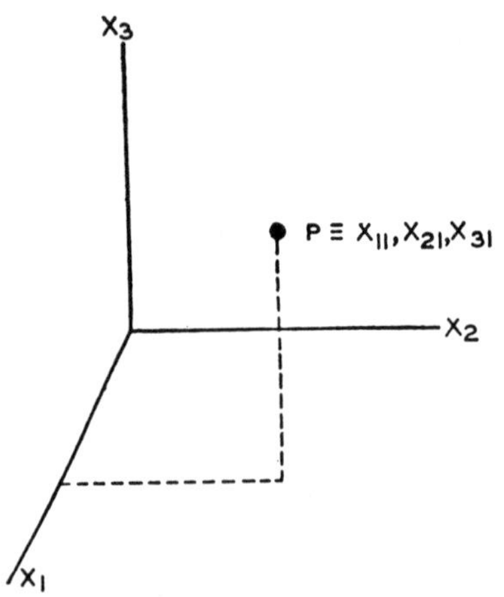

Fig. 15.—Quality as a Point in Space.

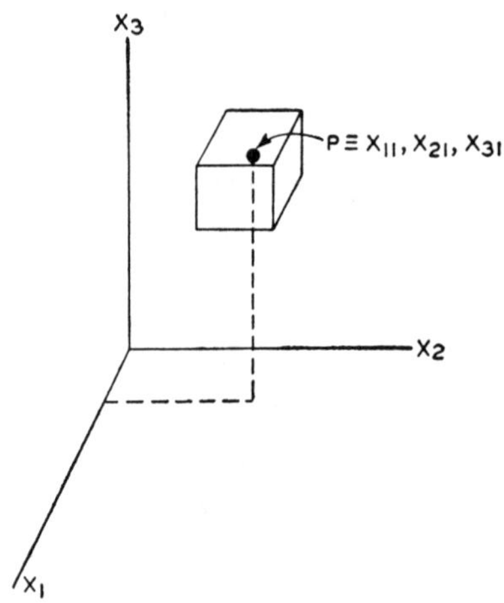

Fig. 16.—Quality Conforms if within Volume.

4. *Conception of the Quality of a Thing as an Attribute*

Customary engineering practice specifies the limits or tolerances within which the different quality characteristics are supposed to lie provided the single piece of apparatus or thing under study is to be considered as satisfactory or conforming to specifications. Geometrically this can be represented for the previous example involving three quality characteristics by Fig. 16. A piece of apparatus or thing having a quality falling within the rectangular element of volume is said to possess the *positive attribute* of conformance to specified standards. Obviously this element of volume may be large because often only a single lower or upper bound is given to some one or more of the quality characteristics. If the quality falls outside this volume, the piece of apparatus or thing is said to possess the *negative attribute* of non-conformance. The property of positive attribute is variously characterized as good, satisfactory, conforming, standard, and that of negative attribute is characterized as unsatisfactory, non-conforming, and so on.

5. *Quality of a Number of the Same Kind of Things*

To begin with, let us consider the information presented in Table 3 giving the measurements of tensile strength, hardness, and density on sixty specimens of a certain aluminum die-casting. This table gives three quality characteristics for each specimen.[1] To picture the quality of the group of sixty specimens, it is therefore necessary to consider the one hundred and eighty measures of the different quality characteristics given in this table. Now our graphical representation of quality becomes a real aid because we must have some method of visualizing the significance of a set of data such as that in Table 3.

First let us think only of the sixty values of tensile strength. How shall we arrive at a simple way of expressing the quality

FIG. 17.—QUALITY IN RESPECT TO TENSILE STRENGTH.

of the sixty specimens in respect to this characteristic? The answer is simple if we think of the sixty values of tensile strength plotted along a line such as indicated in Fig. 17. Here, of course, we have plotted only a few of the sixty points. This graphical presentation at once suggests that we seek some *distribution function* to represent the density of the points along the line. If we can find such a function and if this function can be integrated, it is obvious that the integral within

[1] The abbreviation psi is used here and elsewhere for pounds per square inch. All hardness measurements are given throughout this book in Rockwell's "E" even though the "E" may sometimes be omitted.

specified limits gives us the number of specimens having a value of tensile strength within these limits.

TABLE 3.—QUALITY EXPRESSED IN TABULAR FORM

Specimen	Tensile Strength in psi	Hardness in Rockwells "E"	Density in gm/cm³	Specimen	Tensile Strength in psi	Hardness in Rockwells "E"	Density in gm/cm³
1	29,314	53.0	2.666	31	29,250	71.3	2.648
2	34,860	70.2	2.708	32	27,992	52.7	2.400
3	36,818	84.3	2.865	33	31,852	76.5	2.692
4	30,120	55.3	2.627	34	27,646	63.7	2.669
5	34,020	78.5	2.581	35	31,698	69.2	2.628
6	30,824	63.5	2.633	36	30,844	69.2	2.696
7	35,396	71.4	2.671	37	31,988	61.4	2.648
8	31,260	53.4	2.650	38	36,640	83.7	2.775
9	32,184	82.5	2.717	39	41,578	94.7	2.874
10	33,424	67.3	2.614	40	30,496	70.2	2.700
11	37,694	69.5	2.524	41	29,668	80.4	2.583
12	34,876	73.0	2.741	42	32,622	76.7	2.668
13	24,660	55.7	2.619	43	32,822	82.9	2.679
14	34,760	85.8	2.755	44	30,380	55.0	2.609
15	38,020	95.4	2.846	45	38,580	83.2	2.721
16	25,680	51.1	2.575	46	28,202	62.6	2.678
17	25,810	74.4	2.561	47	29,190	78.0	2.610
18	26,460	54.1	2.593	48	35,636	84.6	2.728
19	28,070	77.8	2.639	49	34,332	64.0	2.709
20	24,640	52.4	2.611	50	34,750	75.3	2.880
21	25,770	69.1	2.696	51	40,578	84.8	2.949
22	23,690	53.5	2.606	52	28,900	49.4	2.669
23	28,650	64.3	2.616	53	34,648	74.2	2.624
24	32,380	82.7	2.748	54	31,244	59.8	2.705
25	28,210	55.7	2.518	55	33,802	75.2	2.736
26	34,002	70.5	2.726	56	34,850	57.7	2.701
27	34,470	87.5	2.875	57	36,690	79.3	2.776
28	29,248	50.7	2.585	58	32,344	67.6	2.754
29	28,710	72.3	2.547	59	34,440	77.0	2.660
30	29,830	59.5	2.606	60	34,650	74.8	2.819

In a similar way we may represent the sixty observed values of tensile strength and one other property, such as hardness, by sixty points in a plane. Again the graphical representation suggests the need for some distribution function which will give us the density of the points in this plane. In just the same way, the graphical representation of the values of tensile strength, hardness, and density in three dimensional space suggests the need for a distribution function indicating the density in space. The graphical representation of the sixty points in a plane and in space was given in Fig. 14.

In the inspection of product manufactured in quantities running into the thousands or even millions of pieces per year, it would be a very laborious task to measure and record as a

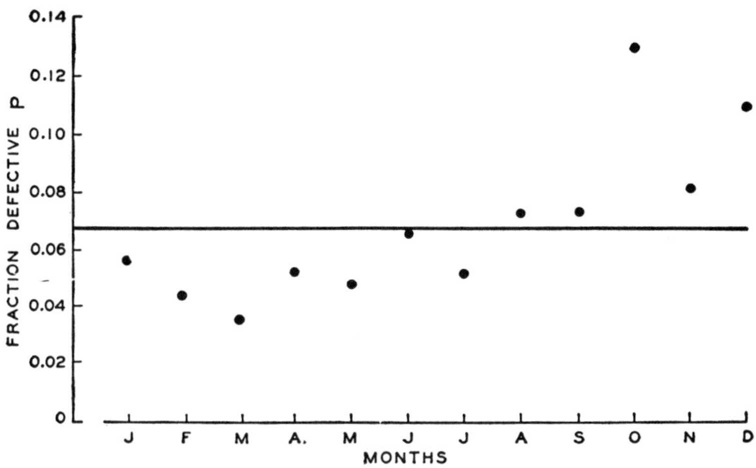

FIG. 18.—RECORD OF QUALITY IN TERMS OF FRACTION DEFECTIVE.

variable the quality characteristic for each piece of apparatus or piece-part. Instead, the practice is usually followed of recording only the fraction non-conforming or defective in each lot of size N. In the course of a year, then, we have a record such as shown graphically in Fig. 18 representing the quality of a given kind of apparatus measured in terms of fraction defective.

In the general case each piece of apparatus is supposed to possess several quality characteristics and the results of an inspection of a lot of size N on the basis of, say m, quality characteristics, $X_1, X_2, \ldots, X_m$, can be reported either as the fractions, $p_1, p_2, \ldots, p_m$, within limits for the respective characteristics or the fraction p within all the limits. Obviously, this fraction p does not give as much information about the product as the set of m fractions.

6. *Quality of Product*

Thus far we have considered the meaning of the quality of a number of the same kind of things such as the set of sixty specimens of a given kind of die-casting. Now we come to the problem of expressing the quality of a product for a given period of time where this product is composed of M different kinds of things, such as condensers, relays, vacuum tubes, telephone poles, and so on.

We must define quality of product in such a way that the numerical measure of this quality serves the following two purposes:

1. To make it possible for one to see whether or not the quality of product for a given period differs from that for some other period taken as a basis of comparison.
2. To make possible the comparison of qualities of product for two or more periods to determine whether or not the differences are greater than should be left to chance.

A. *Distribution of Quality Characteristics*

Let us assume that there are N_1 things of one kind such as condensers, N_2 things of another kind such as relays, and finally N_M things of the Mth kind. Let $m_1, m_2, \ldots, m_M$ represent the number of quality characteristics on the M different kinds of things. From what we have already seen, it is obvious that our picture of quality must be derived in some way from the $m_1 + m_2 + \ldots + m_M$ observed frequency distributions of the quality characteristics. The quality of product for two different periods consists of two such sets of frequency distributions. For example, Fig. 19 shows 12 observed frequency distributions for a single quality characteristic, efficiency, for a given kind of product over a period of twelve months. Since there were five quality characteristics for this particular kind of apparatus, the complete record of quality requires five sets of frequency distributions similar to

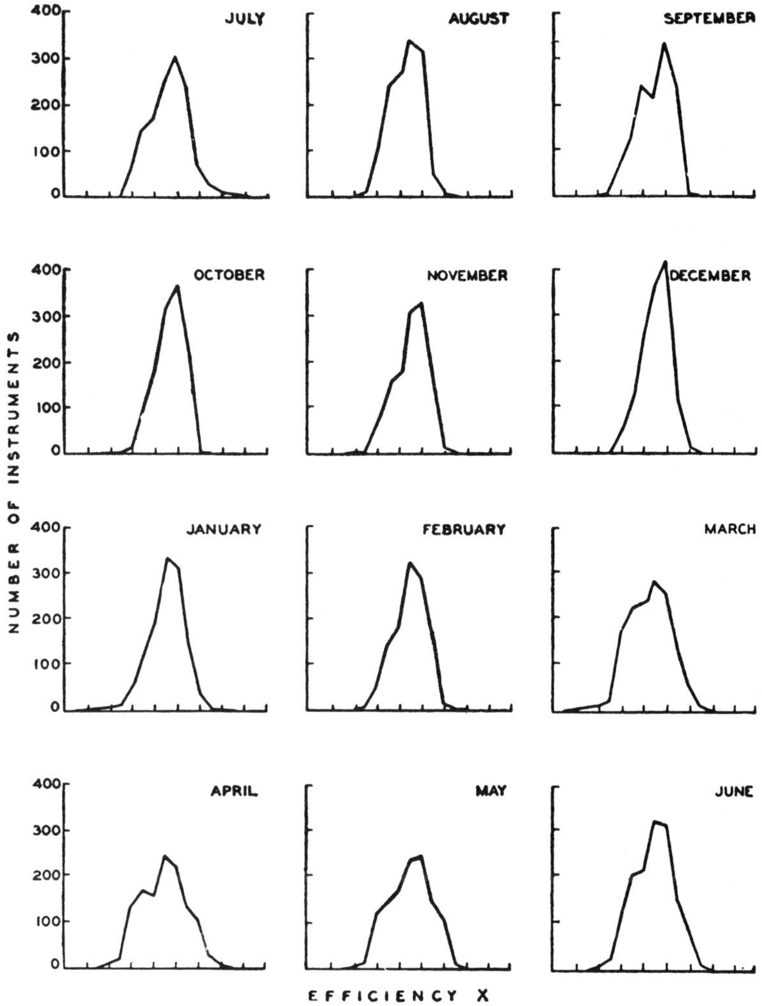

FIG. 19.—QUALITY RECORD IN TERMS OF OBSERVED FREQUENCY DISTRIBUTIONS.

those shown in Fig. 19. As already said, the corresponding picture of the quality of product consisting of *M* different kinds of apparatus or things would require as many sets of such distribution functions as there are quality characteristics. Such a picture contains the whole of the available information.

B. *Quality Statistics*

The information presented in the form of frequency distributions does not permit readily of quantitative comparison.

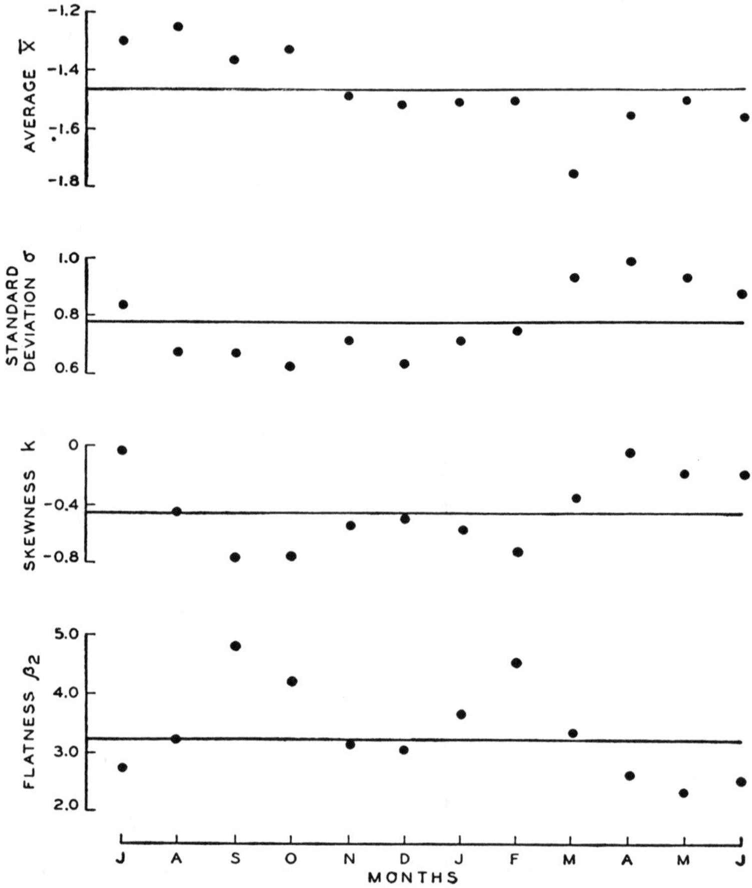

FIG. 20.—QUALITY RECORD IN TERMS OF STATISTICS.

To get around this difficulty, we may use instead of the frequency distribution itself some characteristic or *statistic* of this distribution, such as the fraction within a given range, the average, the dispersion, or the skewness. For example, the information given in Fig. 19 is presented in terms of certain of these statistics in Fig. 20. Whereas we have only one frequency distribution for each characteristic, we have one or more statistics for each distribution. These statistics, however, give us a quantitative picture of the variation in the given quality characteristic.

C. *Quality Rate*

The two measures of quality just considered are based upon the conception of quality as that which makes a thing what it is and, therefore, involve the use of as many quality characteristics as are required to define the product. In this sense, the quality of one thing cannot be added to that of another; for example, the quality of a condenser in terms of capacity, leakage, and so forth, cannot be added to the quality of a telephone pole in terms of its modulus of rupture and other physical properties.

If, however, we can find some measure of the goodness of a thing, no matter what it is, we can then get a single quantitative measure of quality of product. One way of doing this is to weight each quality characteristic. As an example, let us assume that for some one quality characteristic X_i of the product, we have the observed relative frequency distribution

$$\left.\begin{array}{l} X_{i1}, X_{i2}, \ldots, X_{ij}, \ldots, X_{in_i} \\ p_{i1}, p_{i2}, \ldots, p_{ij}, \ldots, p_{in_i} \end{array}\right\}, \qquad (4)$$

where the X's represent the n_i different observed values of the variable X_i, $p_{ij}N_i$ is the number of times that the characteristic X_{ij} was observed, and N_i is the total number of things having the quality characteristic X_i. By choosing a weighting factor $w_i(X_i)$ where w_i is a functional relationship different, in general, for each characteristic, we get a transformed frequency distribution

$$\left.\begin{array}{llll} w_i(X_{i1}), & w_i(X_{i2}), \ldots, & w_i(X_{ij}), \ldots, & w_i(X_{in_i}) \\ p_{i1}, & p_{i2}, \ldots, & p_{ij}, \ldots, & p_{in_i} \end{array}\right\}. \qquad (5)$$

It is assumed usually that the weights are additive so that the total weight W_i for the quality characteristic X_i on the N_i pieces of product having this characteristic is

$$W_i = N_i[p_{i1}w_i(X_{i1}) + p_{i2}w_i(X_{i2}) + \ldots + p_{ij}w_i(X_{ij}) + \ldots + p_{in_i}w_i(X_{in_i})]. \quad (6)$$

The corresponding total weight W for the whole product then becomes

$$W = W_1 + W_2 + \ldots + W_i + \ldots + W_{m_1 + m_2 + \cdots + m_M}, \tag{7}$$

where as above there are supposed to be $m_1 + m_2 + \ldots + m_M$ quality characteristics.

It is obvious that the total weight from month to month for any given product will vary because of the effects of unknown or chance causes which, as we have already seen, produce variations in the observed distributions of the respective quality characteristics. We also see that to be able to interpret the significance of variations in respect to this weight, we must be in a position to consider the significance of variations in the observed frequency functions from which this weight is calculated, assuming that for a given kind of product the number of pieces produced each month is approximately the same.

In general, an attempt is made to obtain a weighting factor which represents approximately the economic value of a quality characteristic having a given magnitude. Obviously, however, it is very difficult to attain such an ideal, and consequently the weights usually represent empirical factors.[1]

By dividing the weight W of product for a given period by the weight W_s of the same product over some previous period taken as a base, we get the customary form of index

$$I = \frac{W}{W_s}. \tag{8}$$

It should be noted that *the statement that the index of quality is such and such does not give any indication of what the quality is unless we take into account the details of the method underlying the formation of the index.* In fact a high or low index does not necessarily mean that the quality is good or bad in a given case unless it is known that for the particular index with which

[1] One very simple form of rate used extensively in the Bell System is described by Mr. H. F. Dodge in an article "A Method of Rating Manufactured Product," *Bell System Technical Journal,* Volume VII, pp. 350–368, April, 1928.

we are dealing, a high index means good and a low index means bad quality from the accepted viewpoint.

7. *Quality as a Relationship*

Often the quality of a thing, such as the quality of a manufacturing process, is of the nature of a relationship. As an example, we may consider the process of creosoting telephone poles. In general, the depth of penetration of the creosote appears to depend upon several factors, one of which is the depth of sapwood, as is evidenced by the data given in Table 4, showing the depth of sapwood and the corresponding depth of penetration for 1,370 telephone poles. In this case the relationship between these two factors is an important characteristic of the quality of the process.

To compare the quality of the creosoting process of one plant with that of each of several others, we must try to interpret the significance of observed differences in the results obtained by different plants, such as the seven records shown in Fig. 21. To facilitate comparisons of this character, we need to have available quantitative measures of the correlation or relationship between the quality characteristics corresponding to a given process.

The importance of the concept of relationship in specifying quality is more deeply seated than might be indicated by this simple problem. In trying to define the quality of a thing in terms of those characteristics which make it what it is, we called attention to the fact that we make use of what are perhaps secondary characteristics. For example, in expressing the quality of a thing in respect to strength we make use of measures of ductility, brittleness, and hardness—characteristics which are likely dependent to a certain degree upon some common factor more elemental in nature. Hence it follows that not only the magnitudes of the characteristics but also their interrelationships are significant in characterizing a thing. The representation of quality in m space as outlined in a previous paragraph lends itself to a quantitative expression of quality relationship.

TABLE 4.—QUALITY AS A RELATIONSHIP

X	Y	X	Y	X	Y	X	Y	X	Y	X	Y	X	Y	X	Y	X	Y	X	Y	X	Y	X	Y	X	Y	X	Y
4.60	1.90	3.00	1.20	3.20	1.50	3.70	2.00	2.20	2.15	3.00	1.80	3.25	2.20	2.60	1.50	2.20	1.10	1.35	0.70	4.40	1.60	4.50	2.40	3.90	1.40	3.10	2.15
2.15	1.30	2.90	1.80	2.30	1.75	2.70	0.80	1.90	1.50	1.60	1.00	3.20	1.85	2.10	1.20	2.20	1.20	3.30	1.05	5.40	2.40	2.80	1.30	2.70	1.50	4.10	3.40
3.70	1.60	3.55	1.50	4.10	2.00	4.40	1.90	4.10	2.90	4.20	1.05	2.75	2.20	3.50	2.15	2.70	1.10	3.10	1.40	2.05	1.60	2.10	1.70	2.05	1.00	1.30	0.80
2.70	2.20	3.30	2.00	3.50	1.45	2.50	1.20	2.80	2.45	2.90	2.30	3.50	1.60	3.60	1.70	3.15	0.80	3.80	1.20	2.90	1.10	1.15	0.90	3.30	1.00	4.00	1.80
3.20	1.50	3.40	1.85	1.60	0.90	3.60	2.05	2.15	1.90	3.00	0.95	2.35	1.10	3.60	1.45	2.25	0.90	2.70	0.80	3.30	2.20	3.30	1.60	2.80	1.60	2.40	1.20
2.40	1.70	3.80	2.40	3.70	1.90	3.70	1.80	1.90	1.30	2.85	0.85	2.50	1.20	3.20	0.85	2.40	1.10	1.55	1.00	2.80	1.20	1.75	0.95	1.15	0.80	2.60	1.35
2.15	1.15	1.70	1.00	1.75	1.10	1.50	0.85	1.80	1.15	1.95	0.80	2.70	2.50	2.90	2.10	1.60	1.45	2.30	1.00	3.60	2.30	2.10	1.50	1.85	1.40	2.60	1.10
1.90	1.50	3.10	1.80	2.50	1.50	2.60	1.60	3.60	2.20	2.90	1.40	2.00	1.05	2.35	1.00	3.05	1.40	2.60	1.90	3.40	1.70	3.20	2.00	2.80	1.50	2.55	1.40
3.50	1.50	2.50	1.90	2.30	1.55	2.00	1.20	1.75	0.90	2.60	1.10	2.45	1.35	3.30	1.15	3.65	2.00	3.35	1.85	1.65	1.15	3.70	1.00	2.00	1.35	2.10	1.00
3.50	2.70	2.95	1.35	3.40	1.50	3.60	2.15	3.90	2.55	1.90	1.50	3.05	1.25	3.20	2.65	1.95	1.80	2.65	1.20	2.60	2.05	2.25	1.65	1.95	1.15	3.55	2.05
2.10	1.05	3.00	2.00	2.85	1.25	1.90	1.20	1.90	1.60	2.85	1.25	3.00	2.30	2.35	1.80	4.40	0.90	2.65	1.10	2.45	1.15	3.20	1.45	3.70	1.80	3.40	1.35
2.45	1.60	2.75	1.20	2.60	1.50	3.65	2.00	2.25	1.60	2.80	1.40	2.05	1.50	3.70	1.50	2.40	1.40	3.05	0.70	3.55	1.65	4.00	3.60	1.45	1.10	3.50	1.50
3.30	1.45	2.65	1.65	3.50	1.40	3.00	1.10	2.30	0.90	2.20	0.90	2.60	1.00	2.60	1.15	2.50	0.75	1.50	0.80	1.40	0.75	1.90	1.30	2.70	2.40	3.40	1.10
2.90	1.65	2.25	1.35	3.70	1.35	3.05	1.50	2.10	0.95	3.10	1.50	1.90	0.90	1.60	1.05	3.40	1.20	1.60	1.45	3.05	1.20	3.60	1.65	3.70	1.80	3.00	2.20
3.10	2.10	3.90	3.30	3.90	1.30	4.00	2.85	2.30	1.75	2.60	0.80	4.20	2.10	3.85	1.85	3.75	1.95	2.10	1.15	3.80	2.75	3.00	1.05	4.00	2.65	3.30	2.50
3.50	1.60	1.70	1.55	2.05	1.60	2.70	2.00	3.35	2.85	3.70	1.10	3.25	1.95	1.95	1.50	2.65	1.00	3.25	2.75	1.85	1.05	1.75	1.10	3.40	1.60	2.90	1.40
1.50	0.85	2.70	1.25	3.15	1.75	3.10	1.50	3.25	2.30	2.90	0.90	3.25	1.25	2.45	1.55	2.20	1.40	2.85	1.60	1.55	0.85	2.30	1.70	2.70	1.40	2.45	1.25
2.95	1.55	3.10	1.35	3.35	1.90	3.20	1.75	3.30	1.65	2.80	2.55	2.80	0.90	2.45	1.00	2.90	1.45	3.20	2.00	3.50	2.40	2.75	1.30	3.25	2.20	2.35	1.35
2.90	0.90	4.10	1.10	4.05	1.30	2.40	1.50	2.15	1.20	3.05	1.90	2.60	0.90	2.25	1.60	2.70	1.00	2.70	2.40	4.30	1.30	4.20	1.05	3.30	1.70	2.50	1.50
1.70	0.85	2.55	1.40	2.10	1.40	2.80	1.40	2.30	1.50	2.40	1.45	3.40	0.95	1.95	1.35	2.20	1.10	3.40	1.90	2.85	1.90	2.80	1.90	2.70	1.35	2.85	2.00
1.10	1.00	2.40	1.30	3.05	1.05	3.40	2.10	1.65	0.95	3.20	1.70	3.00	2.50	2.50	1.80	2.50	1.00	2.90	1.35	2.70	1.20	2.60	1.70	2.50	0.75	2.70	1.60
2.70	1.20	2.80	1.60	2.20	0.90	1.65	0.75	3.05	1.30	1.85	1.60	2.50	1.80	2.90	1.40	1.95	1.20	3.00	2.00	3.70	2.10	2.10	1.20	3.00	0.65	4.40	1.55
3.10	0.85	4.70	1.50	2.40	0.90	4.50	1.90	3.90	0.70	5.00	2.60	4.90	1.70	4.00	2.50	3.10	0.85	3.40	2.90	2.70	2.10	3.05	1.95	3.15	1.60	3.10	1.50
3.30	1.80	4.15	3.00	4.25	2.65	3.40	1.40	3.60	1.95	2.70	1.55	3.05	1.35	4.20	3.10	2.25	1.10	3.00	0.70	2.40	0.40	4.00	1.60	4.30	2.55	3.50	1.30
2.80	1.15	2.75	0.80	3.20	2.10	1.30	0.60	2.85	0.90	4.00	2.40	2.85	1.30	3.60	1.20	3.20	2.20	2.30	1.65	2.25	0.85	3.50	2.30	2.55	1.55	3.00	1.15
3.20	2.55	2.80	1.90	2.65	1.15	2.10	1.10	2.05	1.50	2.15	1.65	2.65	1.20	3.65	2.40	2.05	1.25	2.90	2.60	2.70	1.80	3.10	0.80	1.90	1.25	5.20	4.70
3.50	1.80	3.70	1.70	4.80	2.70	4.80	2.90	4.00	1.80	3.70	1.70	2.70	2.05	3.20	2.05	2.60	0.95	2.70	1.75	1.15	0.55	1.75	1.60	1.40	1.05	3.60	2.65
1.70	1.00	1.90	1.50	1.95	1.00	3.75	3.35	2.85	2.30	3.20	1.25	3.00	1.60	2.70	2.00	1.90	1.00	3.00	2.85	2.05	1.30	2.40	0.90	2.70	2.60	2.55	1.40
2.50	0.80	3.45	2.90	2.15	1.50	2.05	1.10	2.20	1.40	2.40	1.40	3.45	2.20	1.20	0.80	2.00	1.05	3.45	0.85	1.60	0.80	3.10	2.15	4.00	2.70	4.40	1.50
4.10	2.60	3.10	1.50	3.30	0.80	3.05	2.00	4.55	3.15	4.05	2.50	3.10	1.00	3.75	2.50	3.30	0.80	2.35	1.05	2.00	1.60	1.25	0.75	2.40	1.10	4.15	1.75
2.70	1.05	3.90	1.25	4.00	1.25	3.90	3.20	3.70	1.80	3.40	2.30	3.40	2.40	2.50	1.10	2.30	1.40	2.90	1.70	1.30	1.00	2.00	1.70	2.50	1.10	3.90	3.30
2.70	1.20	1.60	0.90	3.60	0.90	2.50	1.00	1.60	0.90	2.70	1.50	3.10	1.20	1.90	0.70	3.30	1.40	2.00	1.20	1.80	1.00	2.30	1.30	3.30	1.10	1.70	1.40
2.60	1.90	4.70	1.20	3.50	1.70	1.60	0.90	2.80	2.10	2.10	0.70	2.10	0.90	2.80	1.00	1.90	0.80	4.00	1.20	4.30	2.10	4.20	1.50	2.60	1.40	3.90	1.80
3.40	1.80	2.60	1.50	4.10	2.70	3.10	1.50	2.40	0.70	1.95	0.70	1.90	1.25	2.20	1.25	2.50	1.30	2.35	1.25	2.00	0.75	3.20	1.80	2.15	1.10	4.15	2.80
4.50	3.55	5.00	4.15	3.35	1.05	2.20	1.25	2.50	0.60	2.55	1.00	1.60	0.60	2.40	1.20	1.70	1.15	3.15	1.40	2.60	1.10	4.10	2.60	3.80	1.00	3.85	2.60
2.95	1.20	2.95	2.40	2.40	1.50	3.40	1.40	3.30	1.55	3.80	1.90	3.80	2.30	3.40	0.90	4.00	2.65	3.40	1.45	3.80	1.05	4.20	3.50	2.05	1.35	2.50	2.35
3.15	1.25	4.20	2.10	4.20	2.20	3.40	1.25	2.15	0.70	2.95	2.10	3.00	2.10	3.50	1.80	3.25	1.15	4.30	2.00	2.30	0.95	3.60	2.10	3.30	1.20	4.60	2.75
2.30	0.80	2.30	1.80	3.50	1.35	3.30	1.25	2.30	1.20	1.60	1.05	3.50	1.80	2.90	1.90	2.85	1.55	3.60	2.60	1.65	1.30	1.25	0.90	2.95	1.40	3.10	1.50
1.80	1.20	2.35	1.35	1.65	0.75	1.40	0.80	1.55	0.75	3.15	2.90	3.25	1.35	2.70	1.10	1.65	1.05	3.25	1.10	2.85	1.50	2.35	1.15	2.15	1.25	2.65	0.90
1.80	0.95	3.00	1.80	1.70	0.70	3.25	2.30	2.80	1.95	3.45	1.60	2.00	1.00	2.75	2.20	1.75	1.25	2.85	1.00	2.25	1.00	2.15	1.30	2.25	1.60	3.00	1.10
1.70	1.05	2.80	2.00	3.50	1.70	2.90	1.50	3.70	2.00	3.60	1.00	3.60	1.60	2.45	1.50	3.60	2.20	3.95	2.15	2.90	1.50	1.95	1.60	3.25	1.35	2.90	1.35
1.55	1.40	3.50	1.85	2.50	1.45	4.10	2.15	2.80	1.85	3.50	1.30	3.20	1.30	2.85	2.10	2.75	2.25	3.10	1.20	4.00	2.40	3.60	1.10	3.80	1.60	3.70	2.60
2.05	0.80	3.40	1.60	2.55	0.90	2.55	1.60	2.90	1.85	3.80	2.80	1.75	1.35	2.10	1.00	2.35	1.05	3.65	2.25	3.95	0.85	2.05	1.20	2.50	1.25	2.40	1.50
2.80	1.15	2.35	1.70	3.10	1.40	4.00	2.10	2.10	1.30	2.20	1.30	4.10	2.30	2.00	0.90	4.40	1.20	3.20	1.60	3.20	0.80	3.75	3.40	2.40	1.95	4.10	1.50
4.20	2.65	3.50	2.90	3.50	1.50	2.25	0.90	3.30	1.65	2.50	1.70	3.60	1.75	2.55	2.20	3.80	1.30	3.40	2.80	3.14	2.95	2.70	1.30	2.30	1.70	2.60	1.70
2.05	0.85	2.50	2.05	2.90	1.10	3.05	1.55	3.20	1.05	3.20	1.50	2.05	1.30	1.75	1.10	2.85	1.40	2.00	0.90	1.80	1.05	2.65	2.35	3.70	1.50	2.50	0.80
3.20	1.20	1.70	0.60	1.70	0.50	3.10	1.60	2.10	0.80	3.70	1.65	3.10	2.60	3.60	2.00	2.60	1.05	2.00	1.15	3.30	2.30	3.70	2.10	2.00	0.75	2.65	1.90

2.90	1.50	2.50	1.10	3.70	2.05	3.30	1.10	3.00	1.60	3.00	1.20	4.00	1.20	3.90	1.50	3.50	2.20	2.35	0.70	3.80	1.40	3.90	2.40	4.60	1.50	3.90	1.60
2.30	1.25	3.85	1.80	3.90	1.60	2.80	1.00	3.30	1.50	3.10	1.80	3.00	1.30	2.85	1.20	2.90	1.40	2.90	1.60	2.70	1.50	1.80	1.20	1.65	1.00	2.20	1.70
4.50	1.50	2.30	1.50	1.90	1.05	2.30	1.10	3.80	1.00	3.60	3.00	2.80	1.10	2.90	1.60	2.70	1.55	4.00	0.80	2.30	1.40	2.60	1.30	2.00	1.30	3.05	1.80
3.05	2.30	2.25	1.45	3.30	2.20	2.70	1.60	2.00	0.85	1.95	0.90	2.90	0.75	1.20	0.30	2.55	1.20	4.80	1.50	4.70	1.40	2.45	1.15	1.95	1.00	1.90	1.00
2.15	1.30	3.10	1.15	2.80	1.65	2.90	1.25	1.85	1.05	2.20	0.80	2.35	1.15	2.25	1.20	2.10	0.70	2.45	1.20	2.70	0.90	1.55	1.10	2.05	0.70	2.90	1.30
2.50	1.75	2.80	1.85	3.00	0.80	2.70	1.30	1.70	1.20	3.60	1.60	3.80	1.40	3.90	2.90	3.70	2.20	4.60	2.90	3.80	2.20	2.50	0.70	2.50	1.10	2.45	1.50
2.05	1.65	2.65	0.95	2.60	1.75	3.00	1.20	2.45	0.90	4.50	2.15	2.55	2.45	3.30	1.90	2.60	0.95	2.85	1.50	3.10	2.00	4.00	2.10	3.30	1.90	1.40	1.15
2.20	1.45	3.00	1.70	1.50	0.85	1.60	1.35	2.75	1.85	2.50	1.30	3.70	2.10	2.30	1.90	2.35	1.20	1.90	1.35	1.95	0.95	2.00	1.10	3.50	3.20	5.00	1.70
3.50	1.10	1.80	1.05	3.00	1.60	3.70	1.70	3.50	1.40	3.40	1.75	2.00	1.30	2.00	0.60	3.10	1.50	1.80	1.50	2.60	1.20	2.65	1.70	1.60	1.10	1.25	0.80
2.50	1.25	1.80	1.20	3.30	1.30	2.30	1.70	2.95	1.40	2.70	2.40	3.10	1.30	1.65	0.75	1.20	0.95	4.35	2.50	2.50	1.00	3.35	1.75	3.65	1.05	1.80	1.00
1.85	1.05	1.50	0.80	4.35	3.00	2.00	1.15	2.35	1.00	3.80	1.40	3.60	2.80	2.85	2.65	2.90	2.70	3.30	1.30	3.70	1.30	3.60	1.20	1.45	1.00	2.55	1.35
2.15	1.00	2.40	1.10	2.80	1.00	3.50	1.00	5.00	3.70	2.80	1.80	2.30	1.10	2.40	2.20	3.20	2.00	3.40	2.10	3.10	1.00	2.10	1.30	3.70	2.10	2.60	1.30
2.00	0.80	4.00	1.15	2.30	1.70	2.10	1.50	3.90	2.30	2.70	1.30	2.55	1.10	2.60	1.70	1.55	0.95	5.20	4.00	2.65	1.00	1.75	0.95	5.10	3.00	3.60	2.45
2.00	1.25	2.75	1.80	3.20	1.55	2.20	0.80	3.95	3.25	2.60	2.05	2.95	0.70	2.85	1.45	3.60	3.10	3.05	1.50	2.85	2.00	3.65	2.30	3.80	2.55	2.95	1.70
2.75	0.80	3.15	2.15	3.15	1.90	2.55	1.70	3.20	1.90	2.90	1.00	2.35	1.25	2.00	0.95	1.95	0.90	2.85	1.40	2.60	0.90	2.25	1.60	2.45	1.10	2.80	1.15
3.40	1.00	3.60	1.20	2.90	1.05	3.70	1.55	4.10	2.00	3.70	2.20	3.40	3.25	2.50	0.80	3.80	1.65	2.90	0.95	1.50	0.85	3.70	2.00	3.10	1.65	3.00	1.80
4.65	3.90	3.90	2.85	4.40	2.60	3.60	2.50	4.60	4.00	4.25	3.30	4.20	3.00	3.10	1.10	3.40	1.80	2.50	1.05	2.05	1.20	4.40	2.00	1.60	0.50	2.40	1.00
4.85	3.80	2.00	1.30	3.20	2.10	3.15	1.70	4.40	2.40	2.50	1.80	3.05	1.20	3.20	1.50	2.70	2.60	2.80	0.80	2.35	1.10	2.60	1.35	2.60	1.20	3.85	2.20
3.20	1.80	3.50	2.25	4.40	3.50	3.70	3.10	3.75	3.50	1.90	1.60	3.70	2.30	2.40	1.20	3.15	1.60	2.25	1.80	4.80	2.40	2.65	1.50	4.30	2.10	3.95	1.50
2.55	1.05	4.15	1.60	2.85	1.20	2.80	1.10	3.20	2.10	2.40	1.15	3.70	2.20	2.10	1.00	4.10	1.15	3.15	0.90	2.15	0.90	3.00	1.40	2.20	1.30	1.90	0.80
2.30	0.90	1.45	0.90	2.35	1.20	1.40	0.80	4.00	1.50	2.00	1.05	1.95	1.25	2.55	1 20	4.10	2.10	4.30	3.60	3.50	2.20	3.00	1.50	3.00	1.30	4.00	2.70
2.60	1.90	1.90	1.80	2.50	1.05	2.70	1.30	1.70	0.90	2.50	1.60	3.35	1.25	2.15	1.10	1.80	1.60	2.30	2.20	2.65	1.10	3.15	1.00	3.50	1.80	3.60	1.85
3.90	2.10	3.70	2.05	3.65	1.80	3.00	0.95	3.30	1.55	2.80	1.50	3.40	2.35	2.80	1.60	3.00	1.45	3.10	1.20	3.50	1.60	3.05	1.80	2.85	1.10	3.00	1.45
3.05	1.80	3.60	1.40	1.85	1.15	2.50	1.30	1.50	1.30	3.25	2.45	2.10	0.50	1.90	1.30	1.85	0.90	3.60	3.25	3.20	1.20	2.50	1.60	3.30	0.90	2.50	1.25
4.40	1.90	2.50	1.20	3.30	1.30	2.70	0.95	1.95	1.35	1.95	1.30	2.50	1.00	2.90	1.00	4.30	1.10	2.00	1.00	3.50	2.80	2.55	1.30	3.15	1.40	2.75	1.45
2.75	1.35	4.50	1.90	3.60	1.75	3.20	1.10	3.05	0.95	4.80	1.90	2.65	1.15	2.35	1.55	3.95	2.30	3.60	1.60	2.00	1.20	3.50	2.55	1.45	1.10	3.90	2.90
1.35	0.60	2.20	1.70	2.30	1.35	1.95	0.60	3.95	2.20	3.00	2.10	2.85	1.05	3.50	1.40	3.30	1.75	2.90	1.50	2.95	2.70	3.20	1.90	3.30	1.40	2.50	2.20
3.30	1.40	4.00	2.35	2.05	0.85	2.20	1.30	3.60	1.85	2.30	1.30	2.00	0.85	1.70	0.90	2.50	1.15	2.70	1.80	3.05	0.65	2.10	1.15	2.50	0.80	1.30	1.10
2.10	0.85	2.95	2.30	2.65	1.60	2.25	1.50	1.70	0.85	2.65	0.90	3.20	2.10	1.40	0.75	2.55	1.10	2.75	1.00	3.35	1.50	4.20	1.95	2.10	1.10	3.75	1.20
2.60	0.80	2.20	0.95	1.90	1.10	3.00	2.00	2.00	1.00	2.90	2.30	2.00	0.75	3.95	2.95	2.50	0.90	3.30	2.30	2.70	1.00	1.35	0.85	2.55	2.00	2.80	1.00
2.30	1.20	2.60	1.00	2.30	1.40	2.45	0.90	3.10	1.00	1.95	1.00	2.40	1.20	2.90	2.60	3.50	3.10	3.65	1.50	4.10	1.70	3.65	2.80	3.60	1.50	3.00	0.70
4.05	2.15	4.70	0.80	2.55	1.80	2.35	1.30	4.20	2.10	3.50	2.10	3.70	0.85	3.70	2.40	4.70	3.00	4.90	3.15	2.60	1.25	4.40	3.00	4.50	3.25	4.40	2.40
4.10	1.70	4.40	2.00	4.00	1.35	4.50	2.65	2.55	0.85	1.65	1.20	4.35	1.20	4.00	2.00	3.50	2.45	3.30	2.20	2.00	0.55	4.60	1.15	4.60	2.30	2.40	1.30
4.30	1.40	4.50	3.00	2.40	0.80	2.80	1.70	3.05	1.90	3.60	2.30	2.60	2.15	2.75	1.50	2.40	2.00	2.20	1.30	2.70	1.40	3.50	1.70	3.45	1.40	4.05	2.80
2.05	1.10	2.40	1.40	2.15	1.20	2.15	1.10	3.40	2.50	3.90	2.50	2.50	1.30	3.00	1.40	3.40	1.90	2.65	1.35	2.50	1.20	3.00	1.90	1.25	0.90	3.50	1.40
2.20	0.65	3.10	0.85	1.80	1.15	1.55	1.25	3.15	1.70	2.00	1.25	3.00	2.00	3.15	2.20	3.15	2.10	4.55	1.65	1.85	1.35	1.75	1.00	4.15	1.70	3.15	1.25
3.40	1.70	2.20	1.50	1.60	1.00	2.55	0.70	3.10	1.60	2.55	1.55	3.80	1.20	3.45	2.45	3.35	1.05	3.15	2.15	3.20	1.90	2.15	0.95	2.70	0.90	2.65	1.70
2.70	1.30	4.35	2.80	3.00	1.40	2.15	1.40	2.30	0.70	3.60	1.85	4.25	2.50	4.00	3.30	1.20	1.00	3.20	2.50	1.65	1.50	4.50	2.20	1.70	1.45	3.10	1.50
4.10	2.70	2.10	2.00	2.70	1.60	3.00	1.50	4.30	2.35	1.85	1.40	2.40	1.70	2.30	1.40	1.15	0.80	2.50	1.50	2.50	1.55	3.90	2.25	3.80	2.45	4.80	2.25
2.80	2.20	3.80	2.15	4.50	3.50	2.70	1.40	2.90	1.30	1.20	0.95	2.45	1.85	2.55	1.95	2.25	1.35	3.30	2.80	3.50	2.90	3.15	2.80	2.60	1.30	2.80	2.10
3.50	3.25	2.70	2.00	3.80	3.00	2.60	1.10	2.60	0.90	2.70	1.55	2.15	1.50	3.00	0.95	2.80	1.45	2.95	2.05	2.65	1.20	3.90	2.20	3.20	2.10	2.85	1.50
3.40	2.00	2.95	1.60	2.05	1.70	2.25	1.45	2.90	1.65	2.80	2.55	3.30	2.20	3.05	1.90	2.40	1.35	2.75	1.30	3.35	2.10	3.05	2.00	3.00	1.95	2.35	1.10
5.10	3.80	3.35	1.60	2.05	1.60	2.45	1.30	3.70	1.90	3.60	2.00	3.40	2.75	0.90	0.65	2.65	1.20	3.30	1.25	3.60	0.80	3.90	2.90	4.00	2.15	2.30	1.00
1.95	0.90	3.40	2.45	3.50	2.10	3.00	2.40	1.40	1.00	2.35	1.00	2.15	1.10	3.00	1.50	3.10	1.15	3.15	1.90	3.80	2.40	5.20	1.00	3.00	1.60	3.40	2.05
2.45	2.00	2.05	1.60	3.80	1.70	3.30	1.30	2.10	1.40	5.00	0.85	4.65	1.45	4.35	1.60	1.65	0.80	2.80	1.20	2.70	1.35	3.80	2.70	1.65	1.05	2.80	2.20
4.00	2.65	1.70	1.00	2.40	1.70	3.45	2.20	2.20	1.50	2.45	1.50	2.45	1.30	3.80	2.65	3.50	0.70	2.05	1.20	2.30	1.35	3.60	1.75	3.00	2.25	3.90	1.80
3.00	1.05	2.05	0.85	2.95	1.80	3.60	1.95	2.70	1.65	3.00	1.30	2.25	1.10	1.35	0.90	2.50	1.75	2.25	1.30	3.90	2.60	3.15	1.15	1.75	0.75	2.20	1.80
3.05	1.20	3.00	2.00	3.05	1.10	2.50	1.40	2.50	1.40	4.00	1.50	3.40	2.10	3.10	1.60	3.80	2.10	2.70	1.20	2.85	1.05	2.05	1.00	3.30	1.30	1.80	1.10
1.30	0.75	2.50	0.90	2.50	0.85	2.40	1.10	3.05	2.70	2.25	1.90	1.70	1.35	3.00	2.20	3.00	2.65	2.20	1.60	2.30	1.70	2.90	1.50	2.95	1.30	3.50	2.85
3.70	2.30	2.35	1.40	3.40	2.00	2.70	2.30	2.35	1.50	3.00	1.50	3.00	1.50	2.30	1.70	2.65	1.50	3.50	2.30	2.75	2.10	3.70	2.30	3.50	2.40	2.15	1.50
2.00	1.30	2.20	1.15	2.55	1.90	3.50	2.10	2.80	1.50	2.70	1.70	3.60	2.10	2.10	1.40	2.30	1.80	2.90	1.30	2.90	2.30	3.65	2.20				

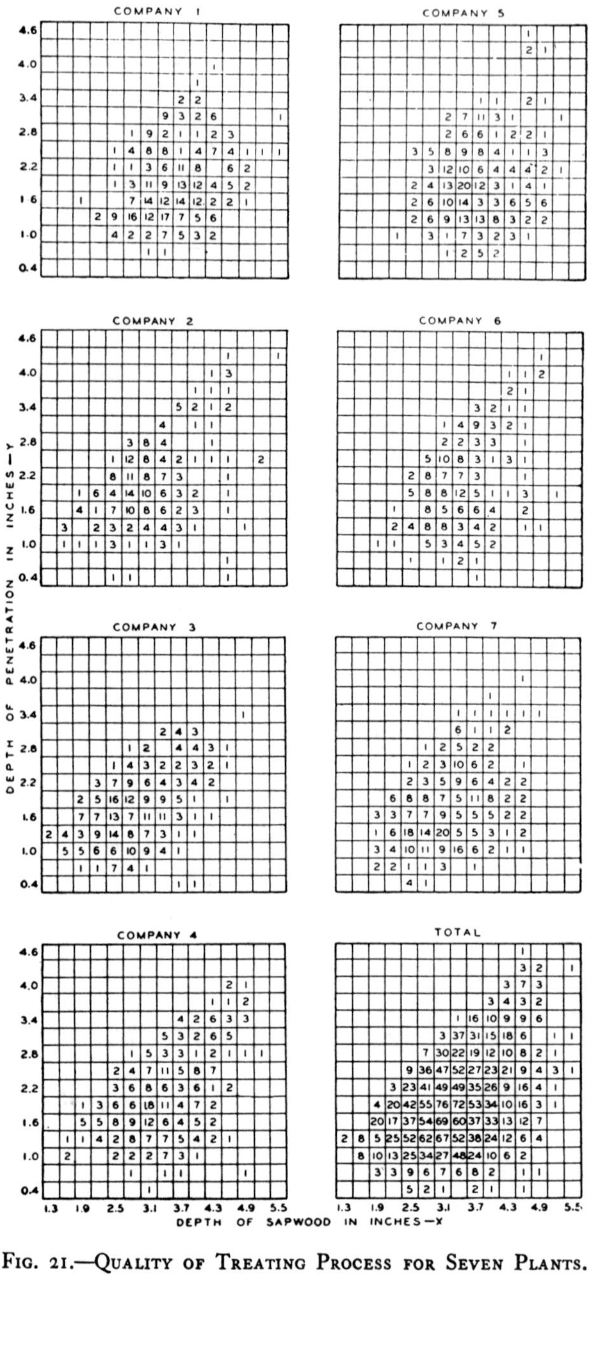

FIG. 21.—QUALITY OF TREATING PROCESS FOR SEVEN PLANTS.

8. *How Shall Quality be Defined?*

If we are to talk intelligently about the quality of a thing or the quality of a product, we must have in mind a clear picture of what we mean by quality. Enough has been said to indicate that there are two common aspects of quality. One of these has to do with the consideration of the quality of a thing as an *objective* reality independent of the existence of man. The other has to do with what we think, feel, or sense as a result of the objective reality. In other words, there is a *subjective* side of quality. For example, we are dealing with the subjective concept of quality when we attempt to measure the goodness of a thing, for it is impossible to think of a thing as having goodness independent of some human want. In fact, this subjective concept of quality is closely tied up with the utility or value of the objective physical properties of the thing itself.

For the most part we may think of the objective quality characteristics of a thing as being constant and measurable in the sense that physical laws are quantitatively expressible and independent of time. When we consider a quality from the subjective viewpoint, comparatively serious difficulties arise. To begin with, there are various aspects of the concept of value. We may differentiate between the following four[1] kinds of value:

1. Use
2. Cost
3. Esteem
4. Exchange

For example, although the air we breathe is useful, it does not have cost or exchange value, and until we are deprived of it we do not esteem it highly.

Although the use value remains comparatively fixed, we find that the significance of cost, esteem, and exchange values are relative and subject to wide variation. Furthermore, we do not have any universally accepted measures of such values. Our division of several different things of a given

[1] For a thorough discussion of this division of economic value see Walsh, C. M., *The Four Kinds of Economic Value*, Harvard University Press, Cambridge, 1926.

kind into two classes, good and bad, necessitates a quantitative, *fixed* measure which we do not have in the case of subjective value.

From the viewpoint of control of quality in manufacture, it is necessary to establish standards of quality in a quantitative manner. For this reason we are forced at the present time to express such standards, insofar as possible, in terms of quantitatively measurable physical properties. This does not mean, however, that the subjective measure of quality is not of interest. On the contrary, it is the subjective measure that is of commercial interest. It is this subjective side that we have in mind when we say that the standards of living have changed.

Looked at broadly there are at a given time certain human wants to be fulfilled through the fabrication of raw materials into finished products of different kinds. These wants are statistical in nature in that the quality of a finished product in terms of the physical characteristics wanted by one individual is not the same for all individuals. The first step of the engineer in trying to satisfy these wants is, therefore, that of translating as nearly as possible these wants into the physical characteristics of the thing manufactured to satisfy these wants. In taking this step intuition and judgment play an important rôle as well as the broad knowledge of the human element involved in the wants of individuals. The second step of the engineer is to set up ways and means of obtaining a product which will differ from the arbitrarily set standards for these quality characteristics by no more than may be left to chance.

The discussion of the economic control of quality of manufactured product in this book is limited to a consideration of this second step. The broader concept of economic control naturally includes the problem of continually shifting the standards expressed in terms of measurable physical properties to meet best the shifting economic value of these particular physical characteristics depending upon shifting human wants.

CHAPTER V

The Problem of Presentation of Data

1. *Why We Take Data*

You go to your tailor for a suit of clothes and the first thing that he does is to make some measurements; you go to your physician because you are ill and the first thing that he does is to make some measurements. The objects of making measurements in these two cases are different. They typify the two general objects of making measurements to be considered in our future discussion. They are:

(*a*) To obtain quantitative information.
(*b*) To obtain a causal explanation of observed phenomena.

Measurement to attain the first object enters into our everyday life because everything that we buy or sell is by the yard, pound, or some quantitative unit of measure. Such measurements also play an important rôle in scientific work. In fact, there was a time not so very long ago when it was felt that physical measurements were largely of this character; as, for example, those of the so-called physical constants, such as the charge on an electron, the coefficient of expansion of a material, and so on. Quite naturally, measurement to obtain quantitative information plays an important rôle in industry, particularly in the inspection of quality of product where it is necessary to have quantitative information to show just what the quality for a given period really is.

The second object of taking data is, however, of perhaps greater importance than the first in the field of research and development because here we are in search of physical principles to explain the observed phenomenon so that we may predict the future in terms of the past. In the control of quality of manufactured product, it is one thing to measure the quality to see whether or not it meets certain standards and it is quite another thing to make use of these measurements to predict and control the quality in the future.

We shall have occasion to lay stress on four kinds of causal interpretation, typical examples of which are:

A. We note differences between the qualities of a number of the same kind of things, such as apples on a tree, produced, insofar as we know, under the same essential conditions. The important question which we shall ask is: Should such differences be left to chance?

B. Having concluded in a given case that the differences in the qualities of a group of things are such as should be left to chance, we often want to discover the distribution of these qualities which we may expect to get in the long run. In terms of our simple illustration we want to discover the distribution of the size of apples to be expected under the same essential conditions over a long period of time. A study of this problem involves the use of some kind of mental picture of the way certain kinds of chance cause systems act in nature.

C. Two series of observations of some quality characteristic have been taken under what may or may not have been the same essential conditions. From an analysis of the data, we are called upon to determine whether or not the two conditions were essentially the same. Again using the apple tree illustration, we can picture two trees of the same kind treated with different fertilizers. The question to be considered is: Do the differences between the quality characteristics of the apples on one tree and those of the apples on another indicate that the fertilizers exerted a controlling influence?

D. We take sets of observations of m quality characteristics on a number of the same kind of thing, and from these try to determine whether or not there is any underlying causal relationship between the characteristics. For example, we might try to find out if the size of an apple is related to its acidity.

2. *The Problem of Presentation*

Starting with the raw data, the problem of presentation depends upon the way the data are to be used or, in other words, the kind of information that they are supposed to give. For example, the tailor's measurements for your suit of clothes must be presented practically in the detailed form in which they were taken.

In general, however, it is neither feasible nor desirable for one reason or another to present raw data in detail such as is done in Table 4 for the depth of sapwood and depth of penetration in telephone poles. Such a presentation usually requires too much space. Furthermore, data in this form do not furnish the quantitative information usually desired and are not readily interpretable in terms of causal relationships.

The problem of presentation involves the use of methods of analysis designed to extract from the raw data all of the essential information contained therein for the answer to questions which may be put in attaining the object for which the data were taken.

We shall consider briefly methods for presenting such data in both tabular and graphical forms which assist materially in helping one to obtain the information present in the original series of observations. We shall find, however, that the results thus obtained are for the most part qualitative, and for this reason do not effectively serve the purpose of comparing sets of data. To secure quantitative reduction of data, we must therefore introduce methods for summarizing a series of values of a given quality characteristic by means of a few simple functions which express quantitatively such things as the central tendency, dispersion, and skewness of the observed frequency distribution of the quality characteristic. In particular, we need quantitative measures of the relationship between quality characteristics.

We shall find that there are many ways of carrying out the details of such analyses and that there are many functions which measure such characteristics as central tendency, dispersion, and skewness, some of which are far more effective than others in giving the essential information.

3. *Essential Information Defined*

We take data to answer specific questions. We shall say that a set of statistics for a given set of data contains the *essential information* given by the data when, through the use of these statistics, we can answer the questions in such a way that further analysis of the data will not modify our answers to a practical extent.

4. *Statement of the General Problem*

The raw data with which we have to deal are usually given in one of the following ways. We may have a series of n observations of the quality of a single thing, such as n observations of the length of a rod, the resistance of a relay, or the capacity of a condenser; or we may have a series of n observations representing single observations of some quality characteristic on n different things, such as the 1,370 observations of the depth of sapwood previously given in Table 4.

In one case we have n values

$$X_1, X_2, \ldots, X_i, \ldots, X_n, \tag{9}$$

representing as many measurements of the same quality on one thing, and in the other case we have n values representing single measurements of the same quality on each of n things.

In a similar way, we may have a series of n successively observed values of a group of m quality characteristics on some one thing, or observed values of say m qualities on each of, let us say, n things. In either case we have a series of observations, such as

$$\left.\begin{array}{l} X_{11}, X_{12}, \ldots, X_{1i}, \ldots, X_{1n} \\ X_{21}, X_{22}, \ldots, X_{2i}, \ldots, X_{2n} \\ \cdot \quad \cdot \quad \cdot \quad \cdot \quad \cdot \quad \cdot \\ X_{j1}, X_{j2}, \ldots, X_{ji}, \ldots, X_{jn} \\ \cdot \quad \cdot \quad \cdot \quad \cdot \quad \cdot \quad \cdot \\ X_{m1}, X_{m2}, \ldots, X_{mi}, \ldots, X_{mn} \end{array}\right\} \tag{10}$$

Naturally, we always have a certain purpose in accumulating such a series of data, and the object of tabular and graphical presentation is to assist in the interpretation of the raw data in terms of the object for which they were taken. As already noted, the distributions of values of depth of sapwood and depth of penetration as given in Table 4 illustrate the first form (9) in which raw data may occur. Similarly, the two distributions taken together illustrate the second form (10).

Later we shall have occasion to make use of several simple geometrical conceptions in our study of the ways and means of presenting data. It will be helpful, therefore, for us to keep in mind some of the problems involved in the analysis of data, both from the viewpoint of presentation of facts and from that of causal interpretation stated in terms of these geometrical conceptions.

For example, the problem of presenting a series, such as (10), of m qualities on each of n things may be looked upon as that of locating a set of n points in a space of m dimensions in reference to certain lines, planes, or hypersurfaces. A simple illustration is that previously given in Fig. 14 where we may think of the points as being located in respect to the coordinate axes in one case and in respect to either the lines or planes of regression in the other case.

There are many ways in which we may set up this problem. For instance, in the case of two variables X and Y, we may seek some function $f(X, Y)$ such that $f(X, Y)dXdY$ tells us approximately how many of the observed values lie within the element of area X to $X + dX$ and Y to $Y + dY$. Such a function would give us approximately the density of the observed points in the plane. Sometimes, however, it is more convenient to have some measure of the clustering of the points about a curve $Y = f(X)$. It may be sufficient to know that approximately a certain per cent of the points lie within some band $f(X) \pm \varepsilon$ as shown in Fig. 22-*b*.

It may be of interest to note how some of the problems of causal interpretation mentioned at the beginning of this chapter can be expressed in terms of certain geometrical representations of the data. Thus, if we represent a series of *n* measurements of some quality characteristic by points along a straight line, we are often interested in knowing whether or

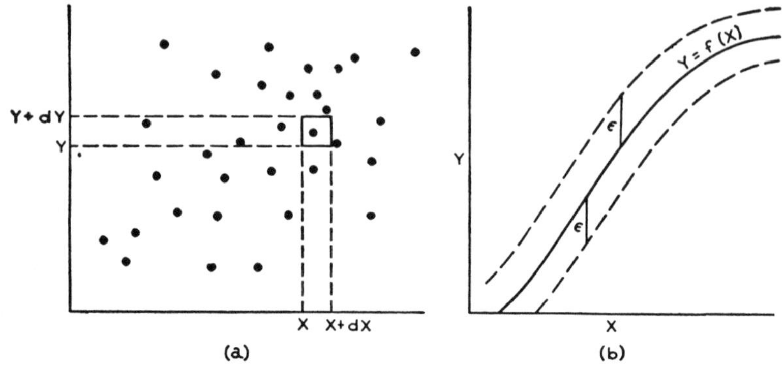

FIG. 22.—TWO METHODS OF REPRESENTING DATA.

not the particular spacing of the points indicates that the causes of variation between the observed values are such as should be left to chance, Fig. 23-*a*. Assuming that we have decided that the causes of variation should be left to chance,

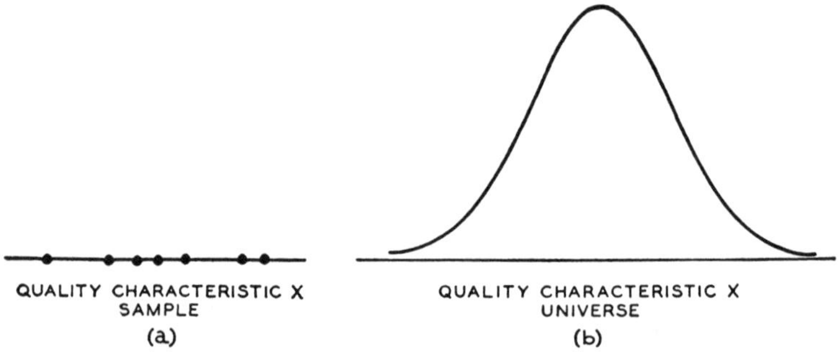

FIG. 23.—SCHEMATIC RELATION BETWEEN SAMPLE AND UNIVERSE.

we are usually interested in discovering the distribution of the variable to be expected if these same causes are allowed to operate for an indefinite period of time. In other words, we seek the universe of effects for a given cause system, Fig. 23-*b*.

It is obvious that the other problems of causal interpretation may also be given a geometric significance.

5. *True Versus Observed Quality*

Thus far we have purposely avoided the problem of trying to distinguish between true quality and the observed magnitudes of the quality characteristics. Obviously, it is necessary to try to do this since all measurements are subject to error. Hence, to obtain the essential information in respect to the distribution of true quality from a set of observed data such as either (9) or (10), we must have some means of correcting for errors of measurement existing in the original data.

To get a picture of what we mean by true quality, let us consider first a very simple illustration. What is the true length of the line *AB*? Strictly speaking, it does not have a

A————————————*B*

true length in the sense of an unchangeable value which is a constant of nature. On the contrary, we believe that the molecules at the ends of the line are jumping around in random fashion so that in the last analysis the line does not have a length except in the sense of some distribution of length or in the sense of some characteristic of a distribution function, such as an average.

Whereas, in the case of the length of the line (in fact the magnitudes of most physical quantities) the objective or true quality is a frequency distribution function, there are instances where we believe that the true quality is perhaps a fixed constant of nature. As an illustration, it appears that most physicists regard the charge on an electron as such an objective constant.

Even the most precise measurements of such a quantity, however, are subject to chance causes of variation or, as we say, errors of measurement. As evidence that there always remains a nucleus of chance causes of variation in even the best physical measurements, we may take the series of observed values of the charge on an electron originally given[1] by Millikan, Table 5. The problem of presenting the essential information contained in such a set of measurements of some quantity assumed to be a constant is that of finding the best estimate of this constant.

TABLE 5.—MILLIKAN'S OBSERVATIONS OF CHARGE ON AN ELECTRON

$e \times 10^{10}$

4.781	4.764	4.777	4.809	4.761	4.769
4.795	4.776	4.765	4.790	4.792	4.806
4.769	4.771	4.785	4.779	4.758	4.779
4.792	4.789	4.805	4.788	4.764	4.785
4.779	4.772	4.768	4.772	4.810	4.790
4.775	4.789	4.801	4.791	4.799	4.777
4.772	4.764	4.785	4.788	4.779	4.749
4.791	4.774	4.783	4.783	4.797	4.781
4.782	4.778	4.808	4.740	4.790	
4.767	4.791	4.771	4.775	4.747	

Now let us consider the meaning of true quality where we have one or more series of measurements (9) or (10) on a number of different things. It is obvious from what has been said that the true quality in such a case is a frequency distribution function. It is, however, not the objective frequency distribution function of the observed values, for these contain errors of measurement. It is rather this frequency distribution function corrected for errors of measurement. Since, in commercial work, the error of measurement is often large, it follows that the distribution of observed values may differ significantly from our best estimate of the true distribution function. Hence, in our discussion of the ways and means of presenting data, we must lay the basis for correcting, insofar as possible, the original data for errors of measurement.

[1] These data are those given in the first edition of Millikan's book *The Electron*, published by the University of Chicago Press. For our purpose, we shall neglect in all further discussions of these data the fact that certain corrections should be made as outlined by Millikan if we are concerned with the problem of giving the best estimate of the charge on an electron. To do this, it would also be necessary to weight the values as he has done. For the latest discussion of the use of these data in estimating the most probable value of the charge on an electron, see "Most Probable 1930 Values of the Electron and Related Constants," R. A. Millikan, published in the *Physical Review*, May 15, 1930, pp. 1231–1237.

CHAPTER VI

Presentation of Data by Tables and Graphs

1. *Presentation of Ungrouped Data*

Perhaps the most useful way of presenting an ungrouped distribution of raw data in tabular form is that in which the values of the variable are arranged or permuted in ascending order of magnitude. Such a permutation is termed a *frequency distribution.* Let us consider this form of presentation for the fifty-eight observed values of the charge on an electron given in Table 5.

Table 6.—Tabular Presentation of Permuted Series of Data

4.740, 4.747, 4.749, 4.758, 4.761, 4.764, 4.764, 4.764, 4.765, 4.767, 4.768, 4.769, 4.769, 4.771, 4.771, 4.772, 4.772, 4.772, 4.774, 4.775, 4.775, 4.776, 4.777, 4.777, 4.778, 4.779, 4.779, 4.779, 4.779, 4.781, 4.781, 4.782, 4.783, 4.783, 4.785, 4.785, 4.785, 4.788, 4.788, 4.789, 4.789, 4.790, 4.790, 4.790, 4.791, 4.791, 4.791, 4.792, 4.792, 4.795, 4.797, 4.799, 4.801, 4.805, 4.806, 4.808, 4.809, 4.810.

With this tabular arrangement we can easily obtain such characteristics of the observed distribution as *range, mode* or most frequently occurring value, and *median* or middlemost value, of the permuted variable.

Naturally we can present such a permuted series of magnitudes graphically in numerous ways, only one of which is given by way of illustration in Fig. 24.

In a similar way a set of observations representing measurements of several characteristics on each of several things may be arranged in tabular form by permuting one of the series of observations in ascending order of magnitude and then tabulating the corresponding values of the associated characteristics. Table 7 shows two such tabulations, there being in each case two quality characteristics.

Table 7-*a* gives the observed current I in amperes through a certain kind of carbon contact as the voltage E is changed. This is the everyday type of observed relationship presented in the customary tabular form in which one of the series of measurements, in this case voltage, is permuted in ascending order of magnitude.

TABLE 7.—TABULAR PRESENTATION OF RELATIONSHIP

Table 7-*a*		Table 7-*b*	
Voltage E in Volts	Current I in Amperes	Volume in Cu. Cm.	Area in Sq. Cm.
3	0.03	0.9	0.667
6	0.07	1.9	0.528
9	0.11	3.9	0.538
12	0.15	4.5	0.778
15	0.19	4.6	0.827
18	0.24	4.6	0.543
21	0.29	4.8	0.792
24	0.34	4.9	0.694
27	0.39	4.9	0.694
30	0.45	5.1	0.804
33	0.50	6.6	0.772
36	0.55	7.8	0.706
39	0.62	9.6	0.750
42	0.69	11.7	0.496
45	0.76	14.9	0.591
48	0.86	16.2	0.716
51	0.93	17.9	0.771
		18.2	0.489
		19.0	0.811
		19.2	0.792
		19.8	0.803
		26.8	0.664
		44.8	0.718

Table 7-*b* gives the measurements of two quality characteristics of each of twenty-three different kinds of granular carbon. In this case the series of observed values of the volume of the pores is permuted in ascending order of magnitude.

The corresponding customary graphical representations of such sets of data are presented in Fig. 25.

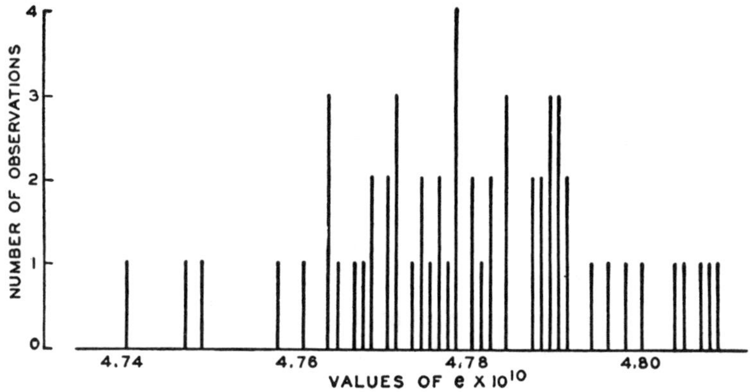

Fig. 24.—One Graphical Presentation of Permuted Series of Data.

In Fig. 25-*a*, there can be little doubt that the current is a function of the voltage *E*, although neither the tabular nor the graphical presentation gives the relationship quantitatively.

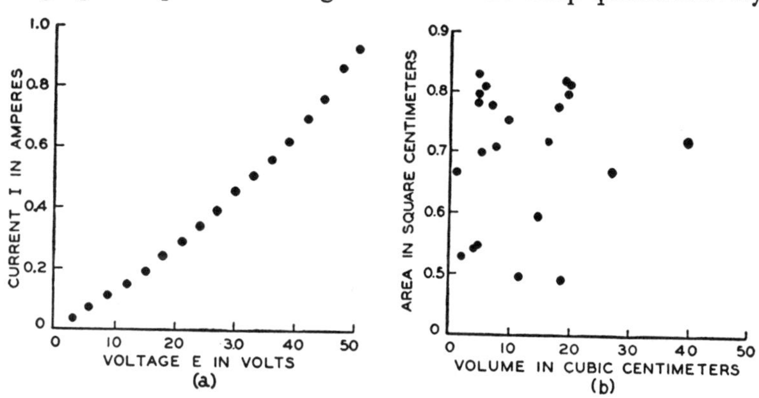

Fig. 25.—One Form of Graphical Presentation of Data of Table 7.

In Fig. 25-*b*, there is a definite question as to whether or not the two characteristics are related at all.

Now suppose we were to present in a similar way the

distribution of 1,370 observed values of depth of sapwood given in Table 4 and also the relationship between depth of sapwood and depth of penetration. To do this would require an excessive amount of space. To get around this difficulty of presentation when the number of observations is large, customary practice calls for the grouping of the original data.

2. *Presentation of Grouped Data*

We usually divide the range covered by a frequency distribution of observations into something like thirteen to twenty equal intervals or cells, the boundaries of which are so chosen that no observed value coincides therewith, thus avoiding uncertainty as to which cell a given value belongs. The number of things having a quality X lying within a cell is termed the *frequency* for that cell; in a similar way, the ratio of the frequency of a given value of X to the total number n of observations is termed a *relative frequency*. The series of

TABLE 8.—DISTRIBUTION OF DEPTH OF SAPWOOD

Cell Midpoints in Inches	Frequency	Cell Midpoints in Inches	Frequency
1.0	2	3.4	151
1.3	29	3.7	123
1.6	62	4.0	82
1.9	106	4.3	48
2.2	153	4.6	27
2.5	186	4.9	14
2.8	193	5.2	5
3.1	188	5.5	1

frequencies and of relative frequencies constitute *frequency and relative frequency distributions* respectively. The distribution of depth of sapwood can in this way be reduced to the form shown in Table 8. By thus grouping the original observations into cells, we secure a tabular presentation much simpler than that originally given in Table 4, but in the process we have slightly modified the original data.

By grouping, we get an improved picture of the clustering of the observed values about a central value somewhere near the cell whose midpoint is 2.8 inches, as is shown in Fig. 26. In the first diagram the black dots represent ordinates pro-

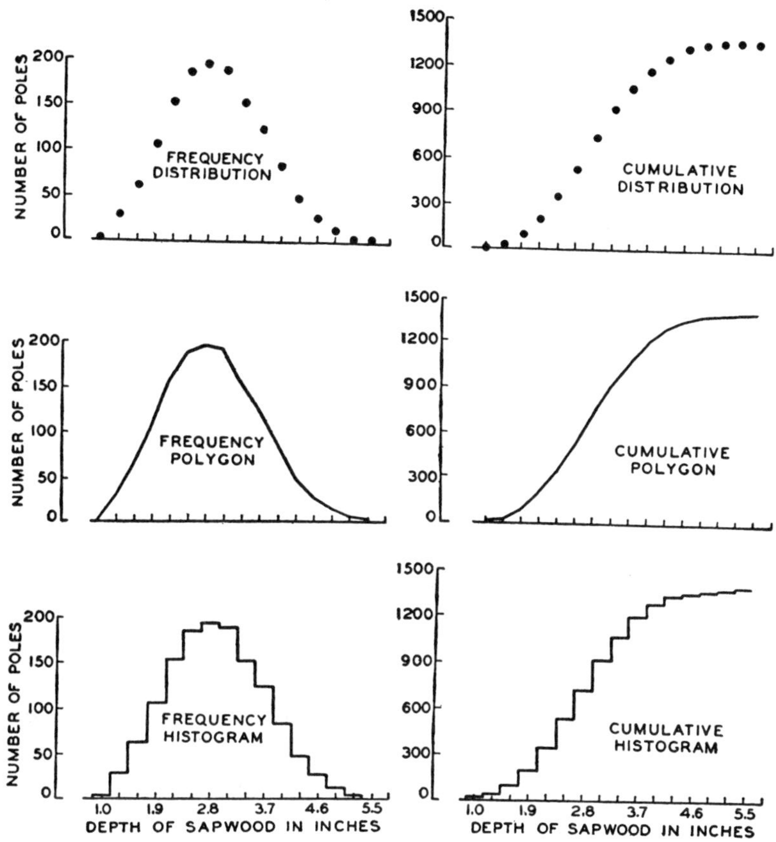

FIG 26.—GRAPHICAL PRESENTATION OF FREQUENCY DISTRIBUTION OF DEPTH OF SAPWOOD OF TELEPHONE POLES.

portional to the corresponding cell frequencies, the ordinate for a given cell being placed at the midpoint of that cell. If we join these ordinates by a broken line, we get the *frequency polygon*. The method of obtaining the *frequency histogram* is clearly indicated by the figure itself. An ordinate in such graphical presentations is termed a frequency, meaning thereby the frequency of occurrence in the associated cell.

We may plot as the ordinate at a given value of abscissa the total number of observations having a value equal to or less than that of the given value of abscissa. In this way we get the *cumulative distribution*, *cumulative polygon*, and *cumulative histogram* also shown in Fig. 26. These are often termed *ogives*. It is perhaps a matter of personal judgment depending upon the situation in hand as to whether the tabular or the graphical presentation of the frequency distribution of Table 8 is the more desirable.

Let us next try to present the data of Table 4 in such a way as to indicate whether or not there is any relationship between the two quality characteristics, depth of penetration Y and depth of sapwood X. In general, applying the same methods as those used above to obtain the reduced frequency distribution, we get the correlation table or scatter diagram of Fig. 27. The number of poles having values of depth of sapwood and depth of penetration lying within a given rectangle is printed in that rectangle.

If we were to erect a parallelepiped on each rectangle with a height proportional to the number in this rectangle, the resulting figure would be a *surface histogram*. We might also construct a *surface polygon* in a manner analogous to that used in constructing the frequency polygon.

What does the table or chart shown in Fig. 27 tell us about the relationship between the two variables therein considered? One thing is certain—the distribution of values of penetration in a given column corresponding to a given depth of sapwood depends upon the depth of sapwood. In other words, knowing the depth of sapwood, we have some information about the depth of penetration. We shall be content, therefore, to say for the present that these two qualities appear to be correlated and that, in general, the depth of penetration appears to be greater, the greater the depth of sapwood. Thus the table or chart of Fig. 27 does tell us something, but what it tells is qualitative and not quantitative. For example, it does not tell us how close a relationship exists between the two qualities.

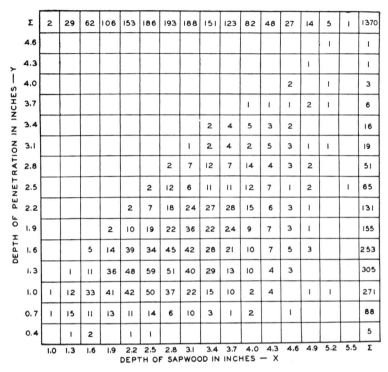

DEPTH OF PENETRATION IN INCHES — Y

Σ	2	29	62	106	153	186	193	188	151	123	82	48	27	14	5	1	1370
4.6															1		1
4.3														1			1
4.0													2		1		3
3.7											1	1	1	2	1		6
3.4									2	4	5	3	2				16
3.1								1	2	4	2	5	3	1	1		19
2.8							2	7	12	7	14	4	3	2			51
2.5						2	12	6	11	11	12	7	1	2		1	65
2.2					2	7	18	24	27	28	15	6	3	1			131
1.9				2	10	19	22	36	22	24	9	7	3	1			155
1.6			5	14	39	34	45	42	28	21	10	7	5	3			253
1.3		1	11	36	48	59	51	40	29	13	10	4	3				305
1.0	1	12	33	41	42	50	37	22	15	10	2	4		1	1		271
0.7	1	15	11	13	11	14	6	10	3	1	2		1				88
0.4		1	2		1	1											5
	1.0	1.3	1.6	1.9	2.2	2.5	2.8	3.1	3.4	3.7	4.0	4.3	4.6	4.9	5.2	5.5	Σ

DEPTH OF SAPWOOD IN INCHES — X

FIG. 27.—TABULAR PRESENTATION OF GROUPED DATA IN SCATTER DIAGRAM.

3. *Choice of Cell Boundaries*

The choice of from thirteen to twenty cells is to a large extent empirical. Experience has shown that, when the data are grouped in this way, it appears possible to retain most of the essential information in the ungrouped data. To take a larger number of cells often confuses the picture and, in particular, emphasizes sampling fluctuations, the significance of which will be considered later. In general, other things being equal, the outline of the frequency distribution is more regular the smaller the number of cells. This is illustrated by the two frequency distributions of the data of Table 4 shown in Fig. 28.

4. *Conclusion*

Both tabular and graphical presentations of original ungrouped data are cumbersome and often require a prohibitive amount of space, particularly when there are a large number of

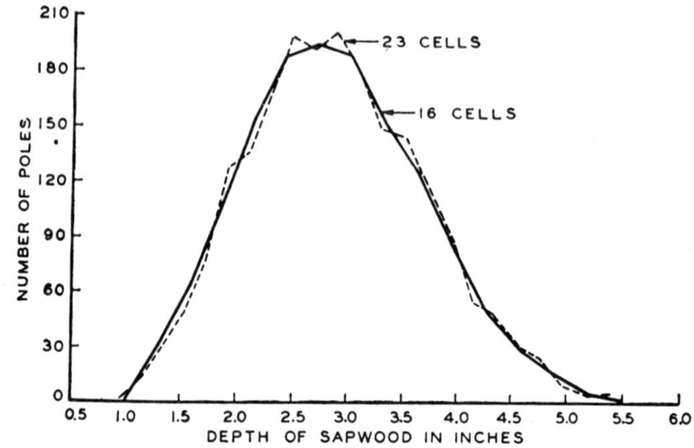

FIG. 28.—EFFECT OF CLASSIFICATION ON GRAPHICAL REPRESENTATION.

observed values. Grouping of raw data materially reduces the space required and makes possible a better picture of the observed distribution whether in one or more dimensions, although the data in this form are not readily susceptible of causal interpretation.

CHAPTER VII

PRESENTATION OF DATA BY MEANS OF SIMPLE FUNCTIONS OR STATISTICS

1. *Simple Statistics to Be Used*

Table 9 presents for ready reference a list of those functions or statistics which we shall consider, the ones marked by an asterisk being the most important in the theory of quality control.

TABLE 9.—COMMONLY USED FUNCTIONS OR STATISTICS

Fraction within Certain Limits	Measures of Central Tendency	Measures of Dispersion	Measures of Lopsidedness or Skewness	Measures of Flatness or Kurtosis	Measures of Relationship or Correlation
*Fraction defective p	*Arithmetic mean $\bar{X}$	*Standard deviation σ	*Skewness k	*Flatness β_2	*Correlation coefficient r
	$\frac{\text{Maximum}+\text{Minimum}}{2}$	Variance σ^2			Correlation ratio η
	Median	Mean deviation			
	Mode	Observed range			

2. *Fraction p Defective or Non-Conforming*

This simple measure of quality was described in Chapter IV of Part II as the fraction of the total number of observations lying within specified quality limits.

3. *Arithmetic Mean $\bar{X}$ as a Measure of Central Tendency*

By definition, the arithmetic mean $\bar{X}$ of n real numbers, $X_1, X_2, \ldots, X_i, \ldots, X_n$, is

$$\bar{X} = \frac{X_1 + X_2 + \ldots + X_i + \ldots + X_n}{n} = \frac{\sum_{i=1}^{n} X_i}{n}. \qquad (11)$$

An approximate value for the mean is often obtained from the grouped data as indicated in Table 10 which gives the 1,370 observed depths of sapwood grouped into 16 equal cells. The mean value obtained in this way will not, in general, be equal to that given by (11). For example, the mean value from the grouped data in Table 10 is 2.914 inches, whereas the mean obtained from (11) is 2.900 inches.

TABLE 10.—CALCULATION OF ARITHMETIC MEAN FROM GROUPED DATA

Mid-Cell Value in Inches	Deviation * in Cells from $\bar{o}$ X	Observed Frequency y	Xy
1.0	0	2	0
1.3	1	29	29
1.6	2	62	124
1.9	3	106	318
2.2	4	153	612
2.5	5	186	930
2.8	6	193	1,158
3.1	7	188	1,316
3.4	8	151	1,208
3.7	9	123	1,107
4.0	10	82	820
4.3	11	48	528
4.6	12	27	324
4.9	13	14	182
5.2	14	5	70
5.5	15	1	15
Σ	....	1,370	8,741

$$_1\mu_1 = \frac{\Sigma Xy}{\Sigma y} = \frac{8741}{1370} = 6.380292$$

$$m = \text{units per cell} = 0.3 \text{ inch}$$

$$\text{Arithmetic mean } \bar{X} = \bar{o} + m\,_1\mu_1 = 1.0 + 1.914088 = 2.914088 \text{ inches}$$

* The origin $\bar{o}$ is the mid-cell value of cell No. 0.

4. *The Standard Deviation σ as a Measure of Dispersion*

Given a set of n real numbers, $X_1, X_2, \ldots, X_i, \ldots, X_n$, the standard deviation σ of this set about its mean value $\overline{X}$ is, by definition,

$$\sigma = \sqrt{\frac{\sum_{i=1}^{n}(X_i - \overline{X})^2}{n}} = \sqrt{\frac{\sum_{i=1}^{n} X_i^2}{n} - 2\frac{\overline{X}\sum_{i=1}^{n} X_i}{n} + \overline{X}^2} = \sqrt{\frac{\sum_{i=1}^{n} X_i^2}{n} - \overline{X}^2}. \quad (12)$$

The exact value of σ can easily be obtained from (12) although this method of calculation introduces a prohibitive amount of work when the size n of the sample is large. For this reason as in the case of the average, we make use of the grouped data and calculate σ as indicated in Table 11.

TABLE 11.—CALCULATION OF THE STANDARD DEVIATION FROM THE GROUPED DATA

Mid-Cell Values in Inches	Deviation in Cells from $\bar{o}$ X	Observed Frequency y	Xy	X^2y
1.0	0	2	0	0
1.3	1	29	29	29
1.6	2	62	124	248
1.9	3	106	318	954
2.2	4	153	612	2,448
2.5	5	186	930	4,650
2.8	6	193	1,158	6,948
3.1	7	188	1,316	9,212
3.4	8	151	1,208	9,664
3.7	9	123	1,107	9,963
4.0	10	82	820	8,200
4.3	11	48	528	5,808
4.6	12	27	324	3,888
4.9	13	14	182	2,366
5.2	14	5	70	980
5.5	15	1	15	225
Σ	....	1,370	8,741	65,583

m = units per cell = 0.3 inch

$${}_1\mu_1 = \frac{\Sigma Xy}{\Sigma y} = \frac{8741}{1370} = 6.380292$$

$${}_1\mu_2 = \frac{\Sigma X^2y}{\Sigma y} = \frac{65583}{1370} = 47.870803$$

$$\mu_2 = {}_1\mu_2 - {}_1\mu_1^2 = 7.162677$$

$$\sigma = m\mu_2^{1/2} = 0.802895 \text{ inch}$$

Obviously, a small standard deviation usually indicates that the values in the observed set of data are closely clustered about the arithmetic mean; whereas, a large standard deviation indicates that these values are spread out widely about the arithmetic mean. For the time being it must suffice to picture the significance of this measure of dispersion somewhat after

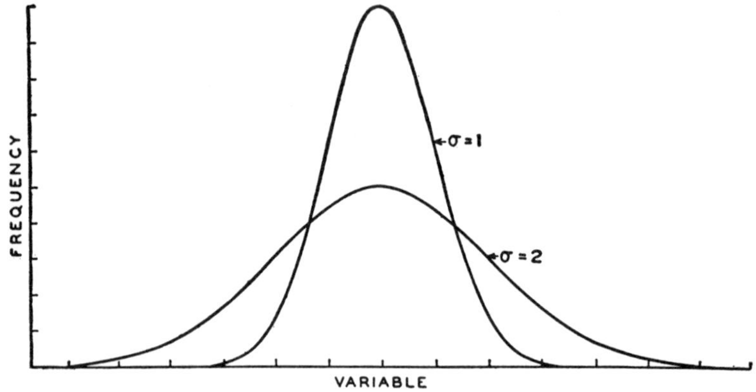

FIG. 29.—HOW THE STANDARD DEVIATION σ INDICATES DISPERSION. TWO DISTRIBUTIONS DIFFERING ONLY IN STANDARD DEVIATION.

the manner indicated in Fig. 29 which shows two continuous distributions of the same functional form, differing only in standard deviation.

5. *Skewness k*

The particular statistic which we shall use most extensively as a measure of the skewness of a distribution of n values of X is designated by the letter k and defined by the expression

$$k = \frac{\dfrac{\sum_{i=1}^{n}(X_i - \overline{X})^3}{n}}{\left[\dfrac{\sum_{i=1}^{n}(X_i - \overline{X})^2}{n}\right]^{3/2}} = \frac{\dfrac{\sum_{i=1}^{n} X_i^3}{n} - \dfrac{3\overline{X}\sum_{i=1}^{n} X_i^2}{n} + 2\overline{X}^3}{\sigma^3}, \qquad (13)$$

where $\overline{X}$ is the arithmetic mean and σ is the standard deviation of the n values of X. Of course, k may be either positive or negative. If the distribution is symmetrical, k is zero, but it should be noted that the condition $k = 0$ is not sufficient for

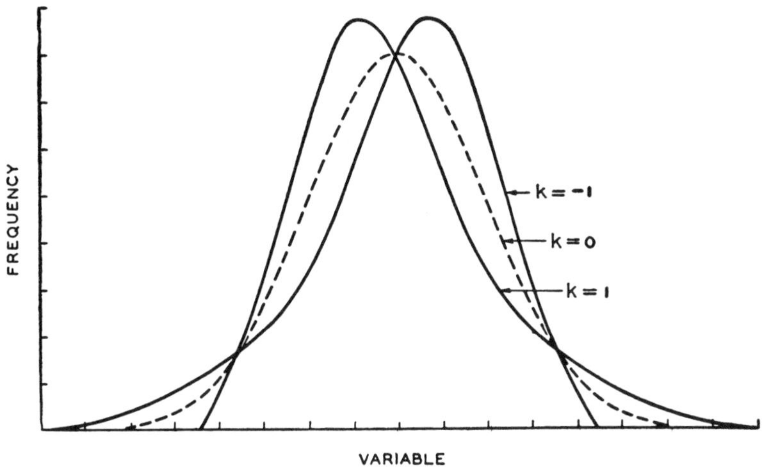

FIG. 30.—ILLUSTRATING USE OF k AS A MEASURE OF SKEWNESS

symmetry. Fig. 30 shows two continuous distributions of the same functional form, differing only in skewness.

6. *Flatness*[1] β_2

The statistic β_2 used as a measure of the flatness of the distribution is defined by the expression

$$\beta_2 = \frac{\sum_{i=1}^{n} (X_i - \bar{X})^4}{n} \left(\frac{n}{\sum_{i=1}^{n} (X_i - \bar{X})^2} \right)^2 = \frac{\frac{\sum_{i=1}^{n} X_i^4}{n} - 4\bar{X}\frac{\sum_{i=1}^{n} X_i^3}{n} + 6\bar{X}^2\frac{\sum_{i=1}^{n} X_i^2}{n} - 3\bar{X}^4}{\sigma^4}, \quad (14)$$

where the symbols used are those previously introduced. Fig. 31 pictures three symmetrical frequency distributions differing only in the degree of flatness.

[1] Also called kurtosis.

7. *Calculation of Statistics*

Let us see how simply the calculation of the four above-mentioned statistics may be carried out. For convenience we introduce a new term, the *moment* of a distribution. By definition, the jth moment, ${}_1\mu_j$, of a set of n values, X_1, X_2, $\ldots$, X_i, $\ldots$, X_n about the origin from which the values are measured is

$$ {}_1\mu_j = \frac{\sum_{i=1}^{n} X_i^j}{n}. \tag{15}$$

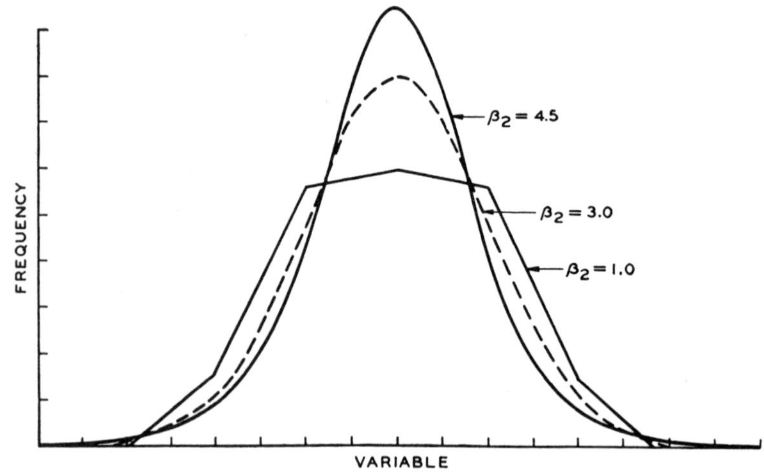

FIG. 31.—ILLUSTRATING USE OF β_2 AS A MEASURE OF FLATNESS OF DISTRIBUTION.

Similarly, the jth moment of this same set of numbers about the arithmetic mean $\overline{X}$ is

$$ \mu_j = \frac{\sum_{i=1}^{n} (X_i - \overline{X})^j}{n}. \tag{16}$$

It may readily be seen that the formulas for standard deviation, skewness, and flatness may be greatly simplified by expressing the results in terms of the moments of the distribution, as shown in the lower part of the data sheet of Table 12. The necessary computations for finding the four statistics for the distribution of depth of sapwood are also shown in this data sheet.

TABLE 12.—TYPICAL COMPUTATION SHEET

Subject	Date 2/21/30
Depth of Sapwood in inches	Calc. by MBC
	Checked MSH

Cell Mid-point	Cell Bound-ary	Deviation in Cells from ō, X	Observed Frequency y	yX	yX^2	yX^3	yX^4	Frequency in Per Cent
	0.850							
1.0		0	2	0	0	0	0	0.15
	1.150							
1.3		1	29	29	29	29	29	2.12
	1.450							
1.6		2	62	124	248	496	992	4.53
	1.750							
1.9		3	106	318	954	2,862	8,586	7.74
	2.050							
2.2		4	153	612	2,448	9,792	39,168	11.17
	2.350							
2.5		5	186	930	4,650	23,250	116,250	13.58
	2.650							
2.8		6	193	1,158	6,948	41,688	250,128	14.09
	2.950							
3.1		7	188	1,316	9,212	64,484	451,388	13.72
	3.250							
3.4		8	151	1,208	9,664	77,312	618,496	11.02
	3.550							
3.7		9	123	1,107	9,963	89,667	807,003	8.98
	3.850							
4.0		10	82	820	8,200	82,000	820,000	5.99
	4.150							
4.3		11	48	528	5,808	63,888	702,768	3.50
	4.450							
4.6		12	27	324	3,888	46,656	559,872	1.97
	4.750							
4.9		13	14	182	2,366	30,758	399,854	1.02
	5.050							
5.2		14	5	70	980	13,720	192,080	0.36
	5.350							
5.5		15	1	15	225	3,375	50,625	0.07
	5.650							
Σ			1,370	8,741	65,583	549,977	5,017,239	

m = units per cell = 0.3

$$_1\mu_1 = \frac{\Sigma yX}{\Sigma y} = \frac{8741}{1370} = \underline{6.380292}$$

$$_1\mu_2 = \frac{\Sigma yX^2}{\Sigma y} = \frac{65583}{1370} = \underline{47.870803}$$

$$_1\mu_3 = \frac{\Sigma yX^3}{\Sigma y} = \frac{549977}{1370} = \underline{401.443066}$$

$$_1\mu_4 = \frac{\Sigma yX^4}{\Sigma y} = \frac{5017239}{1370} = \underline{3662.218248}$$

$$\mu_2 = {_1\mu_2} - {_1\mu_1}^2 = \underline{47.870803 - 40.708126} = \underline{7.162677}$$

$$\mu_3 = {_1\mu_3} - 3{_1\mu_1}\,{_1\mu_2} + 2{_1\mu_1}^3$$

$$= \underline{401.443066 - 916.289104 + 519.459461} = \underline{4.613423}$$

$$\mu_4 = {_1\mu_4} - 4{_1\mu_1}\,{_1\mu_3} + 6{_1\mu_1}^2\,{_1\mu_2} - 3{_1\mu_1}^4$$

$$= \underline{3662.218248 - 10245.295930 + 11692.384081 - 4971.454567}$$

$$= \underline{137.851832}$$

$$\overline{X} = \bar{o} + m{_1\mu_1} = \underline{1.0 + .3(6.380292)} = \underline{2.914088}$$

$$\sigma = m\mu_2^{1/2} = \underline{0.3(2.070318)} = \underline{0.802895}$$

$$k = \frac{\mu_3}{\mu_2^{3/2}} = \frac{4.613423}{19.169601} = \underline{0.240663}$$

$$\beta_2 = \frac{\mu_4}{\mu_2^2} = \frac{137.851832}{51.303942} = \underline{2.686964}$$

A. *Errors of Grouping.*—It will be seen that all of the computations in the illustrative example make use of grouped data, thereby introducing a source of error. The question naturally arises as to whether or not an engineer should attempt to correct the moments thus obtained by some of the formulas, such as those of Sheppard, presented in almost every good text on statistical theory.

We shall consider three reasons why it seems likely that little is to be gained through the use of such corrections, at least in the class of problems considered in this book. These reasons are:

(*a*) The actual limitations imposed in the development of the formulas for correcting the moments necessitate sharp differentiation between those distributions to which their application is justified and other distributions; and yet it is not feasible to formulate rules which can be applied intelligently to differentiate between these two classes of distributions without a full knowledge of the somewhat involved theory underlying the corrections.

(*b*) The magnitudes of such corrections for the statistics are small, compared with the sampling errors of the statistics thus corrected, unless the sample size is very large, it being assumed that the interval of grouping is small compared with the maximum observed range of variation, as is the case when we use from 13 to 20 cells. Hence, in general, the corrections do not add much from the viewpoint of causal interpretation.

(*c*) The corrected moment may in some cases differ more from the moment obtained from the raw data than does the uncorrected moment. As a case in point, the standard deviation of the 1,370 observed values of depth of sapwood is 0.802555 inch as determined from the ungrouped data. The uncorrected moment obtained from the grouped data is 0.802895 inch; whereas the value of this moment corrected by Sheppard's formula is 0.798211 inch. Hence we see that in this example the correction factor does not correct. This situation may arise quite frequently, since the distribution of points within a given cell often does not satisfy the conditions tacitly assumed to exist in the applications of Sheppard's correction. Obviously, therefore, if one is to be sure that he has attained the correct moments for a given distribution, he must carry out the calculations of these moments from the ungrouped data.

Since it is difficult to determine when the corrections should apply, since the corrections are usually small compared with the sampling errors of the moments, and since the corrections may not correct, it seems that little can be gained by applying the customary correction factors.

B. *Number of Figures to be Retained.*—It will be noted that in the calculation of the statistics, the numerical work is carried out to more places than may often be used in the final form of presentation. The reason for doing this will become clear as we proceed, but one or two instances showing the necessity for such a procedure may not be out of place at this point.

In the problem just considered, suppose that we wish to determine the error of the average. In general, this will be expressed in terms of the observed standard deviation σ which in turn has its own error customarily taken to be $\frac{\sigma}{\sqrt{2n}}$, where n is the number of observations. Since the number of figures which we wish to retain in the average depends upon the error of the average, we must know this error before we can decide how many figures to retain. The calculation of this error, however, involves the use of the average itself. Hence we must carry enough figures in the average during the process of calculation of its error so that the final number of figures retained in the average will not be influenced by the number of figures retained in the calculation of the standard deviation.

It is obvious that the same line of reasoning applies in determining how many figures to retain in the standard deviation.

In the general case, starting with a series of observed values, our interpretation of the data involves the use of certain statistics expressed as symmetric functions of the data. Before we can tell definitely how many figures to retain at a given stage of the calculation, we must have completed all the calculations. Obviously we cannot carry an indefinitely large number of figures. The detailed calculations carried out in this book will serve to show what we have found to be satisfactory practice. It does not appear feasible, however, to lay down simple, practical, and infallible rules.

8. *Measures of Relationship*

As engineers, we are accustomed to think of two or more things as being related when we can express one of them as a mathematical function of the others. However, in the scatter diagram, Fig. 27, showing the observed values of depth of sapwood X and depth of penetration Y, we see that for a given value of X there are several values of Y so that these two quantities do not appear to be related in a functional way; although there does appear to be some kind of relationship between them. The knowledge of the depth of sapwood gives us some information about the depth of penetration. To measure this kind of relationship, we make use of the correlation coefficient.

By definition the *correlation coefficient* r between n pairs of values of X and Y is

$$r_{XY} = \frac{\dfrac{\sum_{i=1}^{n} X_i Y_i}{n} - \overline{X}\,\overline{Y}}{\sigma_X \sigma_Y}. \tag{17}$$

The method of calculating r is illustrated in Table 13.

We shall see later that the value of r must lie between $+1$ and -1. The significance of r must be developed as we proceed.

9. *Other Statistics*

Let us first consider measures of central tendency other than the arithmetic mean. By definition, an average of a series of n values of a variable is a number greater than the least and less than the greatest when all of the values of the

TABLE 13.—METHOD OF CALCULATING CORRELATION COEFFICIENT

X = Depth of Sapwood. Y = Depth of Penetration

(1) X	(2) Y	(3) n_1	(4) n_1XY
1.0	0.7	1	0.70
	1.0	1	1.00
1.3	0.4	1	.52
	0.7	15	13.65
	1.0	12	15.60
	1.3	1	1.69
1.6	0.4	2	1.28
	0.7	11	12.32
	1.0	33	52.80
	1.3	11	22.88
	1.6	5	12.80
1.9	0.7	13	17.29
	1.0	41	77.90
	1.3	36	88.92
	1.6	14	42.56
	1.9	2	7.22
2.2	0.4	1	0.88
	0.7	11	16.94
	1.0	42	92.40
	1.3	48	137.28
	1.6	39	137.28
	1.9	10	41.80
	2.2	2	9.68
2.5	0.4	1	1.00
	0.7	14	24.50
	1.0	50	125.00
	1.3	59	191.75
	1.6	34	136.00
	1.9	19	90.25
	2.2	7	38.50
	2.5	2	12.50
2.8	0.7	6	11.76
	1.0	37	103.60
	1.3	51	185.64
	1.6	45	201.60
	1.9	22	117.04
	2.2	18	110.88
	2.5	12	84.00
	2.8	2	15.68

(1) X	(2) Y	(3) n_1	(4) n_1XY
3.1	0.7	10	21.70
	1.0	22	68.20
	1.3	40	161.20
	1.6	42	208.32
	1.9	36	212.04
	2.2	24	163.68
	2.5	6	46.50
	2.8	7	60.76
	3.1	1	9.61
3.4	0.7	3	7.14
	1.0	15	51.00
	1.3	29	128.18
	1.6	28	152.32
	1.9	22	142.12
	2.2	27	201.96
	2.5	11	93.50
	2.8	12	114.24
	3.1	2	21.08
	3.4	2	23.12
3.7	0.7	1	2.59
	1.0	10	37.00
	1.3	13	62.53
	1.6	21	124.32
	1.9	24	168.72
	2.2	28	227.92
	2.5	11	101.75
	2.8	7	72.52
	3.1	4	45.88
	3.4	4	50.32
4.0	0.7	2	5.60
	1.0	2	8.00
	1.3	10	52.00
	1.6	10	64.00
	1.9	9	68.40
	2.2	15	132.00
	2.5	12	120.00
	2.8	14	156.80
	3.1	2	24.80

(1) X	(2) Y	(3) n_1	(4) n_1XY
4.0	3.4	5	68.00
	3.7	1	14.80
4.3	1.0	4	17.20
	1.3	4	22.36
	1.6	7	48.16
	1.9	7	57.19
	2.2	6	56.76
	2.5	7	75.25
	2.8	4	48.16
	3.1	5	66.65
	3.4	3	43.86
	3.7	1	15.91
4.6	0.7	1	3.22
	1.3	3	17.94
	1.6	5	36.80
	1.9	3	26.22
	2.2	3	30.36
	2.5	1	11.50
	2.8	3	38.64
	3.1	3	42.78
	3.4	2	31.28
	3.7	1	17.02
	4.0	2	36.80
4.9	1.0	1	4.90
	1.6	3	23.52
	1.9	1	9.31
	2.2	1	10.78
	2.5	2	24.50
	2.8	2	27.44
	3.1	1	15.19
	3.7	2	36.26
	4.3	1	21.07
5.2	1.0	1	5.20
	3.1	1	16.12
	3.7	1	19.24
	4.0	1	20.80
	4.6	1	23.92
5.5	2.5	1	13.75

$$n = 1{,}370$$

$$\Sigma n_1XY = 6{,}765.77 \qquad \overline{X}\,\overline{Y} = 4.637654$$

$$\frac{\Sigma n_1XY}{n} = 4.938518 \qquad \sigma_X\sigma_Y = 0.498779$$

$$r = \frac{\dfrac{\Sigma n_1XY}{n} - \overline{X}\,\overline{Y}}{\sigma_X\sigma_Y} = \frac{4.938518 - 4.637654}{0.498779} = 0.603201$$

variable are not equal and equal to the common value of the variable when all of the values of the variable are equal. Therefore, the arithmetic mean is only one of an infinite number of measures of central tendency. Typical means often used in characterizing data are the median, $\frac{\text{maximum } X + \text{minimum } X}{2}$, and mode. Naturally, we may expect the different kinds of averages of a series of numbers to differ among themselves. Just as an example, we give below four averages for the series of fifty-eight observed values of the charge on an electron.

$$\text{Median} = 4.785 \times 10^{-10} \text{ e.s.u.}$$

$$\frac{\text{Max.} + \text{Min.}}{2} = 4.775 \times 10^{-10} \text{ e.s.u.}$$

$$\text{Mode} = 4.779 \times 10^{-10} \text{ e.s.u.}$$

$$\text{Arithmetic mean} = 4.780 \times 10^{-10} \text{ e.s.u.}$$

Next, let us consider some measures of dispersion, skewness, and flatness other than those previously given. A measure of dispersion very commonly used in engineering work is the mean deviation μ defined for the case of n values of X by the expression

$$\mu = \frac{\sum_{i=1}^{n} |X_i - \bar{X}|}{n}, \tag{18}$$

where, as usual, the symbol $| \quad |$ represents the absolute value of a quantity. In the same way, any even moment of a distribution about its mean is a measure of dispersion, as is any odd moment of absolute values of the deviations from the mean. Hence, there is an indefinitely large number of possible measures of dispersion of this kind. Furthermore, if we turn to any standard text on statistical theory, we shall find other kinds of measures of dispersion, such as symmetric ranges, of which there is also an indefinitely large number.

In the same way, we may set up an unlimited number of different measures of skewness and flatness. Obviously, therefore, we need to have some general principle to guide us in choosing measures of such characteristics of a distribution of data as the central tendency, dispersion, skewness, and flatness.

One basis of choosing between two statistics as a measure of a characteristic of a distribution is the difference in the amount of labor involved in their calculation. As a case in point, such measures as the median, $\dfrac{\text{maximum } X + \text{minimum } X}{2}$, and mode, can readily be determined by observation of the observed frequency distribution; whereas, the calculation of the arithmetic mean involves considerable labor. It is believed, however, that the cost of the manual labor involved in the analysis of engineering data is for the most part a very small per cent of the cost of taking the data. If we can get more information out of one measure than we can out of another, the cost of analysis will not, in general, be a deciding factor.

Casting about for some more fundamental basis of choice, we take note of the fact that it is usually desirable to have a statistic which is an algebraic function of the data. It is obvious that these functions must be symmetric since they must be independent of the order in which the data were taken. It follows from algebraic theory that the chosen functions must be expressible in terms of what are generally known as *sum* functions, because all symmetric functions are so expressible. Now, the sum functions are defined as

$$\left.\begin{array}{l} S_1 = X_1 + X_2 + \ldots + X_i + \ldots + X_n \\ S_2 = X_1^2 + X_2^2 + \ldots + X_i^2 + \ldots + X_n^2 \\ \cdot \quad \cdot \quad \cdot \quad \cdot \quad \cdot \quad \cdot \quad \cdot \quad \cdot \\ S_j = X_1^j + X_2^j + \ldots + X_i^j + \ldots + X_n^j \\ \cdot \quad \cdot \quad \cdot \quad \cdot \quad \cdot \quad \cdot \quad \cdot \quad \cdot \end{array}\right\}. \tag{19}$$

Obviously, $\dfrac{S_j}{n}$ is the jth moment ${}_1\mu_j$ of the distribution about the origin.

The statistics $\overline{X}$, σ, k, β_2, and r satisfy the condition of being symmetric functions of the data, but still we must try to find out if they are the most useful symmetric functions. In the remaining chapters of Part II, we shall justify the use of these five statistics to the extent of showing that they go a long way towards expressing the total amount of information contained in a set of data.

CHAPTER VIII

Basis for Determining How to Present Data

1. *The Problem*

Let us consider again the distribution of the 1,370 observed values of depth of sapwood. So far as this or any similar set of data is concerned, we assume that one observation contributes just as much information as any other in the same set. The *total information* is given by the observed distribution. If, then, we are to present the total information, we must give the original frequency distribution. For reasons already considered, however, we find it desirable to condense the original data insofar as possible by calculating certain statistics. In the previous chapter we showed how to effect this reduction and illustrated the method by application to the distribution of depth of sapwood. The information contained in this distribution, reduced to the form of statistics, is given in Table 14.

Table 14.—Information in Form of Statistics

Average $\bar{X}$	$=$ 2.9141 inches
Standard Deviation σ	$=$ 0.8029 inch
Skewness k	$=$ 0.2407 inch
Flatness β_2	$=$ 2.6870 inches
Number of Observations n	$=$ 1,370

If the statistics of Table 14 actually contain the total information in the original series of observations, it should be possible to reproduce this distribution from these statistics. Obviously, it is not possible to do this, and therefore the statistics do not contain all of the information. However, they do contain a surprisingly large percentage, as we shall now see.

Table 15 gives the results of two attempts to reproduce the original distribution from the observed statistics. The second row is the distribution obtained from the average and standard deviation alone, while the third row is that obtained using, in addition, the skewness of the original distribution.

TABLE 15.—SHOWING HOW MUCH INFORMATION IS CONTAINED IN A FEW SIMPLE STATISTICS

Cell Midpoint	0.4	0.7	1.0	1.3	1.6	1.9	2.2	2.5	2.8	3.1	3.4	3.7	4.0	4.3	4.6	4.9	5.2	5.5
Observed Frequency	0	0	2	29	62	106	153	186	193	188	151	123	82	48	27	14	5	1
Normal Law Frequency	1	5	12	27	53	92	138	179	202	199	170	127	82	46	23	10	3	1
Second Approximation Frequency	0	0	9	25	55	99	149	189	207	193	159	116	77	46	25	13	6	2

That the approximate or theoretical distribution obtained through the use of the average $\bar{X}$, standard deviation σ, and skewness k is closer to the observed distribution than is that obtained through the use of only the first two of these statistics can be seen quite readily from Fig. 32.

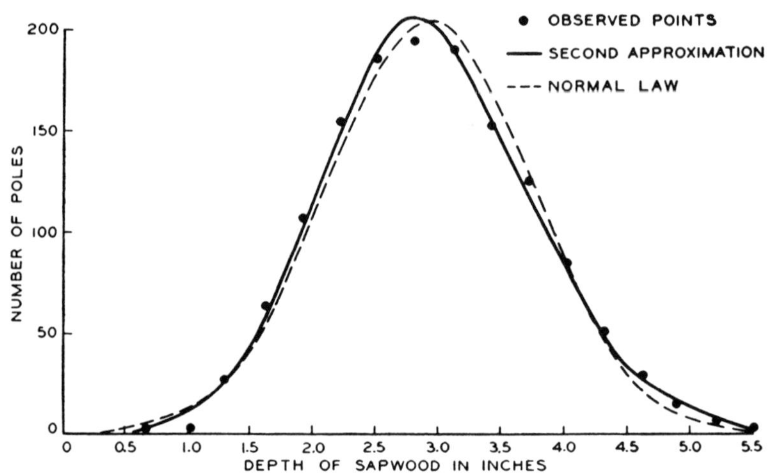

FIG. 32.—SIGNIFICANCE OF AVERAGE, STANDARD DEVIATION, AND SKEWNESS.

The surprising thing is that a knowledge of the average and standard deviation alone enables us to reproduce so closely the observed distribution in this case. Here, the approximation is so good that it is somewhat doubtful whether or not, from the viewpoint of presentation alone, we can attach any practical significance to the increase in the amount of information given by the introduction of the skewness over that given by the average and standard deviation alone. In fact, engineers are usually interested in knowing only the number of observations lying within certain relatively large ranges, such as the average $\overline{X}$ plus or minus two or three times the standard deviation σ. Table 16 presents the observed percentages of the 1,370 observations lying within these ranges together with those estimated from a knowledge of the average and standard deviation. A knowledge of k as here used adds nothing to the precision of our estimate of the number of observations lying within these or any other ranges symmetric in respect to the average.

TABLE 16.—PERCENTAGE OF OBSERVATIONS LYING WITHIN PARTICULAR RANGES

	Range $\overline{X} \pm 0.6745\sigma$	Range $\overline{X} \pm \sigma$	Range $\overline{X} \pm 2\sigma$	Range $\overline{X} \pm 3\sigma$
Estimated, Per Cent.......	50.00	68.27	95.45	99.73
Observed, Per Cent........	47.45	66.57	95.91	99.93
Difference, Per Cent.......	2.55	21.70	0.46	0.20

In the next few paragraphs we shall see how these simple statistics often enable us to approximate very closely the original distribution. In general, we shall find that the information contained in statistics calculated from moments higher than the second depends to a large extent upon the nature of the observed distribution; therefore, these statistics are somewhat limited in their usefulness. The really remarkable thing is that so much information is contained in the average and standard deviation of a distribution.

The specific problem to be considered is: Given a series of numbers, $X_1, X_2, \ldots, X_i, \ldots, X_n$, representing an observed distribution of some quality characteristic X such as any of those previously discussed, let us try to find some function $f(X, \bar{X}, \sigma, k, \beta_2)$ of X and the four statistics calculated from the observed distribution such that the integral

$$\int_a^b f(X, \bar{X}, \sigma, k, \beta_2)dX \qquad (20)$$

of this function from $X = a$ to $X = b$ gives approximately the total number of observed values lying within this same interval. When the approximation is good, we can say that the statistics contain practically all of the total information in the original distribution. In fact, as already noted, we can say that these statistics contain most of the information of practical engineering value when the approximation

$$\int_{\bar{X}-z\sigma}^{\bar{X}+z\sigma} f(X, \bar{X}, \sigma, k, \beta_2)dX \qquad (21)$$

is good, where, as before, the values of z with which we are usually most concerned are 0.6745, 1, 2 and 3.

Common sense tells us that the degree of approximation in a given case will depend upon the function f. Of course, it is desirable to be able to estimate the amount of information contained in the statistics independent of the function f. For reasons which will be considered later, we find that under the state of control of manufactured product the function f which is best in the majority of cases is the same for most quality characteristics. Hence, what we shall do is to show how much information is contained in these statistics for this limiting type of distribution function which is approached as we approach the state of control. We shall then review the work of the Russian mathematician, Tchebycheff, which makes it possible for us to see how much of the total information is contained in the average and standard deviation of a distribution independent of its functional form.

2. *Statistics to be Used when Quality is Controlled*

When the number n of measurements of some quality X have been made under the conditions of control, we find in general that the function f in (20) can be assumed to be one or the other of the following two forms without introducing practical difficulties:

$$f(x) = \frac{n}{\sigma\sqrt{2\pi}} e^{-\frac{x^2}{2\sigma^2}}, \tag{22}$$

or

$$f(x) = \frac{n}{\sigma\sqrt{2\pi}} e^{-\frac{x^2}{2\sigma^2}} \left[1 - \frac{k}{2}\left(\frac{x}{\sigma} - \frac{x^3}{3\sigma^3}\right)\right], \tag{23}$$

where $x = X - \bar{X}$.

Under the conditions of control, it may then be assumed that the integral of either one or the other of these two functions over a given range should give approximately the number of observed values within the corresponding range, particularly when the number n of observed values is comparatively large. We need, therefore, tables of values of the integrals of these functions for $n = 1$. The integral of (23) is

$$\int_0^x f(x)dx = \sigma \int_0^z \phi(z)dz = \int_0^z \frac{1}{\sqrt{2\pi}} e^{-\frac{z^2}{2}} dz - k\frac{1}{6\sqrt{2\pi}}\left[1-(1-z^2)e^{-\frac{z^2}{2}}\right] = F_1(z) - kF_2(z), \quad (24$$

where $F_1(z)$ is the integral of (22), and $z = \frac{x}{\sigma}$. Tables A and B give the functions $F_1(z)$ and $F_2(z)$ respectively.

Now we are in a place to see how the approximations given in Table 15 were obtained. The method is illustrated in detail in Tables 17 and 18 derived from approximations (22) and (23) respectively. Corrected moments were used in Tables 17 and 18 and Fig. 39.

We have already noted that k contains some information not contained in the average and standard deviation in the sense that the use of all three gives the closer of the two approximations to the observed frequency distribution of depth of sapwood. If, however, we are interested in the number of observed values within a symmetrical range about the observed

TABLE A.—VALUES OF $F_1(z) = \frac{1}{\sqrt{2\pi}}\int_0^z e^{-\frac{1}{2}z^2}dz$

z	$F_1(z)$	z	$F_1(z)$	z	$F_1(z)$	z	$F_1(z)$	z	$F_1(z)$	z	$F_1(z)$	z	$F_1(z)$
.00	.0000	.45	.1737	.90	.3160	1.35	.4115	1.80	.4641	2.25	.4878	2.70	.4966
.01	.0040	.46	.1773	.91	.3186	1.36	.4131	1.81	.4649	2.26	.4881	2.71	.4967
.02	.0080	.47	.1808	.92	.3212	1.37	.4147	1.82	.4656	2.27	.4884	2.72	.4968
.03	.0120	.48	.1844	.93	.3238	1.38	.4162	1.83	.4664	2.28	.4887	2.73	.4969
.04	.0160	.49	.1880	.94	.3264	1.39	.4178	1.84	.4671	2.29	.4890	2.74	.4970
.05	.0200	.50	.1915	.95	.3290	1.40	.4193	1.85	.4679	2.30	.4893	2.75	.4970
.06	.0239	.51	.1950	.96	.3315	1.41	.4208	1.86	.4686	2.31	.4896	2.76	.4971
.07	.0279	.52	.1985	.97	.3340	1.42	.4222	1.87	.4693	2.32	.4899	2.77	.4972
.08	.0319	.53	.2020	.98	.3365	1.43	.4237	1.88	.4700	2.33	.4901	2.78	.4973
.09	.0359	.54	.2054	.99	.3389	1.44	.4251	1.89	.4706	2.34	.4904	2.79	.4974
.10	.0399	.55	.2089	1.00	.3414	1.45	.4265	1.90	.4713	2.35	.4906	2.80	.4975
.11	.0438	.56	.2123	1.01	.3438	1.46	.4279	1.91	.4720	2.36	.4909	2.81	.4975
.12	.0478	.57	.2157	1.02	.3462	1.47	.4292	1.92	.4726	2.37	.4911	2.82	.4976
.13	.0517	.58	.2191	1.03	.3485	1.48	.4306	1.93	.4732	2.38	.4914	2.83	.4977
.14	.0557	.59	.2224	1.04	.3508	1.49	.4319	1.94	.4738	2.39	.4916	2.84	.4978
.15	.0596	.60	.2258	1.05	.3532	1.50	.4332	1.95	.4744	2.40	.4918	2.85	.4978
.16	.0636	.61	.2291	1.06	.3555	1.51	.4345	1.96	.4750	2.41	.4920	2.86	.4979
.17	.0675	.62	.2324	1.07	.3577	1.52	.4358	1.97	.4756	2.42	.4923	2.87	.4980
.18	.0714	.63	.2357	1.08	.3599	1.53	.4370	1.98	.4762	2.43	.4925	2.88	.4980
.19	.0754	.64	.2389	1.09	.3622	1.54	.4382	1.99	.4768	2.44	.4927	2.89	.4981
.20	.0793	.65	.2422	1.10	.3644	1.55	.4395	2.00	.4773	2.45	.4929	2.90	.4982
.21	.0832	.66	.2454	1.11	.3665	1.56	.4406	2.01	.4778	2.46	.4931	2.91	.4982
.22	.0871	.67	.2486	1.12	.3687	1.57	.4418	2.02	.4783	2.47	.4933	2.92	.4983
.23	.0910	.68	.2518	1.13	.3708	1.58	.4430	2.03	.4788	2.48	.4935	2.93	.4983
.24	.0949	.69	.2549	1.14	.3729	1.59	.4441	2.04	.4793	2.49	.4936	2.94	.4984
.25	.0987	.70	.2581	1.15	.3749	1.60	.4452	2.05	.4798	2.50	.4938	2.95	.4984
.26	.1026	.71	.2612	1.16	.3770	1.61	.4463	2.06	.4803	2.51	.4940	2.96	.4985
.27	.1064	.72	.2643	1.17	.3790	1.62	.4474	2.07	.4808	2.52	.4942	2.97	.4985
.28	.1103	.73	.2673	1.18	.3810	1.63	.4485	2.08	.4813	2.53	.4943	2.98	.4986
.29	.1141	.74	.2704	1.19	.3830	1.64	.4495	2.09	.4817	2.54	.4945	2.99	.4986
.30	.1179	.75	.2734	1.20	.3850	1.65	.4506	2.10	.4822	2.55	.4946	3.00	.4987
.31	.1217	.76	.2764	1.21	.3869	1.66	.4516	2.11	.4826	2.56	.4948	3.10	.4991
.32	.1255	.77	.2794	1.22	.3888	1.67	.4526	2.12	.4830	2.57	.4949	3.20	.4993
.33	.1293	.78	.2823	1.23	.3907	1.68	.4535	2.13	.4834	2.58	.4951	3.30	.4995
.34	.1331	.79	.2853	1.24	.3925	1.69	.4545	2.14	.4838	2.59	.4952	3.40	.4997
.35	.1369	.80	.2882	1.25	.3944	1.70	.4555	2.15	.4842	2.60	.4954	3.50	.4998
.36	.1406	.81	.2911	1.26	.3962	1.71	.4564	2.16	.4846	2.61	.4955	3.60	.4999
.37	.1443	.82	.2939	1.27	.3980	1.72	.4573	2.17	.4850	2.62	.4956	3.70	.4999
.38	.1481	.83	.2968	1.28	.3997	1.73	.4582	2.18	.4854	2.63	.4958	3.80	.5000
.39	.1518	.84	.2996	1.29	.4015	1.74	.4591	2.19	.4858	2.64	.4959	3.90	.5000
.40	.1554	.85	.3024	1.30	.4032	1.75	.4599	2.20	.4861	2.65	.4960	4.00	.5000
.41	.1591	.86	.3051	1.31	.4049	1.76	.4608	2.21	.4865	2.66	.4961		
.42	.1628	.87	.3079	1.32	.4066	1.77	.4617	2.22	.4868	2.67	.4962		
.43	.1664	.88	.3106	1.33	.4083	1.78	.4626	2.23	.4872	2.68	.4963		
.44	.1701	.89	.3133	1.34	.4099	1.79	.4633	2.24	.4875	2.69	.4965		

TABLE B.—VALUES OF $F_2(z) = \frac{1}{6\sqrt{2\pi}} [1 - (1 - z^2)e^{-\frac{1}{2}z^2}]$

z	$F_2(z)$	z	$F_2(z)$	z	$F_2(z)$	z	$F_2(z)$	z	$F_2(z)$	z	$F_2(z)$	z	$F_2(z)$
.00	.00000	.45	.01857	.90	.05806	1.35	.08848	1.80	.09597	2.25	.08798	2.70	.07742
.01	.00001	.46	.01933	.91	.05894	1.36	.08890	1.81	.09590	2.26	.08774	2.71	.07722
.02	.00004	.47	.02011	.92	.05980	1.37	.08930	1.82	.09584	2.27	.08749	2.72	.07702
.03	.00009	.48	.02089	.93	.06066	1.38	.08970	1.83	.09576	2.28	.08724	2.73	.07682
.04	.00016	.49	.02168	.94	.06152	1.39	.09008	1.84	.09568	2.29	.08699	2.74	.07663
.05	.00025	.50	.02248	.95	.06236	1.40	.09045	1.85	.09559	2.30	.08674	2.75	.07644
.06	.00036	.51	.02329	.96	.06320	1.41	.09080	1.86	.09549	2.31	.08650	2.76	.07625
.07	.00049	.52	.02411	.97	.06404	1.42	.09115	1.87	.09539	2.32	.08625	2.77	.07606
.08	.00064	.53	.02494	.98	.06486	1.43	.09148	1.88	.09527	2.33	.08600	2.78	.07588
.09	.00081	.54	.02578	.99	.06568	1.44	.09180	1.89	.09516	2.34	.08575	2.79	.07569
.10	.00099	.55	.02662	1.00	.06649	1.45	.09211	1.90	.09503	2.35	.08550	2.80	.07551
.11	.00120	.56	.02748	1.01	.06729	1.46	.09241	1.91	.09490	2.36	.08525	2.81	.07534
.12	.00143	.57	.02833	1.02	.06809	1.47	.09269	1.92	.09477	2.37	.08500	2.82	.07516
.13	.00167	.58	.02920	1.03	.06887	1.48	.09296	1.93	.09463	2.38	.08475	2.83	.07499
.14	.00194	.59	.03007	1.04	.06965	1.49	.09322	1.94	.09448	2.39	.08450	2.84	.07482
.15	.00222	.60	.03095	1.05	.07042	1.50	.09347	1.95	.09433	2.40	.08426	2.85	.07465
.16	.00253	.61	.03183	1.06	.07118	1.51	.09371	1.96	.09417	2.41	.08401	2.86	.07448
.17	.00285	.62	.03272	1.07	.07193	1.52	.09394	1.97	.09401	2.42	.08376	2.87	.07432
.18	.00319	.63	.03361	1.08	.07267	1.53	.09415	1.98	.09384	2.43	.08352	2.88	.07416
.19	.00355	.64	.03450	1.09	.07340	1.54	.09435	1.99	.09366	2.44	.08327	2.89	.07400
.20	.00392	.65	.03540	1.10	.07412	1.55	.09454	2.00	.09349	2.45	.08303	2.90	.07384
.21	.00432	.66	.03631	1.11	.07483	1.56	.09472	2.01	.09330	2.46	.08279	2.91	.07369
.22	.00473	.67	.03721	1.12	.07552	1.57	.09489	2.02	.09312	2.47	.08255	2.92	.07354
.23	.00516	.68	.03812	1.13	.07621	1.58	.09505	2.03	.09293	2.48	.08231	2.93	.07339
.24	.00561	.69	.03904	1.14	.07689	1.59	.09519	2.04	.09273	2.49	.08207	2.94	.07324
.25	.00607	.70	.03995	1.15	.07756	1.60	.09533	2.05	.09253	2.50	.08183	2.95	.07309
.26	.00656	.71	04086	1.16	.07822	1.61	.09546	2.06	.09233	2.51	.08159	2.96	.07295
.27	.00705	.72	.04178	1.17	.07886	1.62	.09557	2.07	.09213	2.52	.08136	2.97	.07281
.28	.00757	.73	.04270	1.18	.07950	1.63	.09567	2.08	.09192	2.53	.08112	2.98	.07267
.29	.00810	.74	.04362	1.19	.08012	1.64	.09577	2.09	.09170	2.54	.08089	2.99	.07254
.30	.00865	.75	.04453	1.20	.08073	1.65	.09585	2.10	.09149	2.55	.08066	3.00	.07240
.31	.00921	.76	.04545	1.21	.08133	1.66	.09592	2.11	.09127	2.56	.08043	3.10	.07118
.32	.00979	.77	.04637	1.22	.08192	1.67	.09599	2.12	.09105	2.57	.08020	3.20	.07016
.33	.01038	.78	.04728	1.23	.08250	1.68	.09604	2.13	.09082	2.58	.07998	3.30	.06933
.34	.01099	.79	.04820	1.24	.08306	1.69	.09608	2.14	.09060	2.59	.07975	3.40	.06866
.35	.01161	.80	.04911	1.25	.08361	1.70	.09612	2.15	.09037	2.60	.07953	3.50	.06813
.36	.01225	.81	.05002	1.26	.08416	1.71	.09614	2.16	.09014	2.61	.07931	3.60	.06771
.37	.01290	.82	.05093	1.27	.08468	1.72	.09616	2.17	.08991	2.62	.07909	3.70	.06739
.38	.01356	.83	.05183	1.28	.08520	1.73	.09616	2.18	.08967	2.63	.07888	3.80	.06714
.39	.01424	.84	.05274	1.29	.08571	1.74	.09616	2.19	.08943	2.64	.07866	3.90	.06696
.40	.01493	.85	.05363	1.30	.08620	1.75	.09615	2.20	.08919	2.65	.07845	4.00	.06683
.41	.01564	.86	.05453	1.31	.08668	1.76	.09613	2.21	.08895	2.66	.07824		
.42	.01635	.87	.05542	1.32	.08715	1.77	.09610	2.22	.08871	2.67	.07803		
.43	.01708	.88	.05631	1.33	.08760	1.78	.09606	2.23	.08847	2.68	.07782		
.44	.01782	.89	.05719	1.34	.08805	1.79	.09602	2.24	.08823	2.69	.07762		

Table 17.—Distribution of Depth of Sapwood Calculated from (22)

n = 1,370
$\overline{X}$ = 2.914088
σ = 0.798211

Subject	Date 2/21/30
Depth of Sapwood in inches	Calc. by MBC
	Checked MSH

Cell Mid-point	Cell Bound-ary	Devia-tion from $\overline{X}$ x	z (x/σ)	$F_1(z)$	Differ-ence	Fre-quency	Approxi-mate Frequency	Observed Fre-quency
	0.25	2.6641	3.3376	0.4995				
0.4					0.0010	1.4	1	
	0.55	2.3641	2.9618	0.4985				
0.7					0.0033	4.5	5	
	0.85	2.0641	2.5859	0.4952				
1.0					0.0087	11.9	12	2
	1.15	1.7641	2.2101	0.4865				
1.3					0.0198	27.1	27	29
	1.45	1.4641	1.8342	0.4667				
1.6					0.0390	53.4	53	62
	1.75	1.1641	1.4584	0.4277				
1.9					0.0672	92.1	92	106
	2.05	0.8641	1.0825	0.3605				
2.2					0.1004	137.5	138	153
	2.35	0.5641	0.7067	0.2601				
2.5					0.1305	178.8	179	186
	2.65	0.2641	−0.3309	0.1296				
2.8					0.1476	202.2	202	193
	2.95	0.0359	+0.0450	0.0180				
3.1					0.1451	198.8	199	188
	3.25	0.3359	0.4208	0.1631				
3.4					0.1240	169.9	170	151
	3.55	0.6359	0.7967	0.2871				
3.7					0.0924	126.6	127	123
	3.85	0.9359	1.1725	0.3795				
4.0					0.0597	81.8	82	82
	4.15	1.2359	1.5483	0.4392				
4.3					0.0337	46.2	46	48
	4.45	1.5359	1.9242	0.4729				
4.6					0.0164	22.5	23	27
	4.75	1.8359	2.3000	0.4893				
4.9					0.0070	9.6	10	14
	5.05	2.1359	2.6759	0.4963				
5.2					0.0025	3.4	3	5
	5.35	2.4359	3.0517	0.4988				
5.5					0.0009	1.2	1	1
	5.65	2.7359	3.4275	0.4997				
Σ					0.9992	1,368.9	1,370	1,370

TABLE 18.—DISTRIBUTION OF DEPTH OF SAPWOOD CALCULATED FROM (23)

$n = 1370$	
$\overline{X} = 2.914088$	
$\sigma = .798211$	
$k = .244925$	

Subject	Date 2/21/30
Depth of Sapwood in inches	Calc. by MBC
	Checked MSH

Cell Mid-point	Cell Boundary	Deviation from $\overline{X}$ x	$z(x/\sigma)$	$F_1(z)$	$F_2(z)$	$\pm kF_2(z)$	$F_1(z) \pm kF_2(z)$	Difference	Frequency	Observed Frequency
	0.85	2.0641	2.5859	0.4952	0.0799	0.0196	0.5148			
1.0								0.0065	9	2
	1.15	1.7641	2.2101	0.4865	0.0889	0.0218	0.5083			
1.3								0.0181	25	29
	1.45	1.4641	1.8342	0.4667	0.0958	0.0235	0.4902			
1.6								0.0399	55	62
	1.75	1.1641	1.4584	0.4277	0.0924	0.0226	0.4503			
1.9								0.0719	99	106
	2.05	0.8641	1.0825	0.3605	0.0729	0.0179	0.3784			
2.2								0.1084	149	153
	2.35	0.5641	0.7067	0.2601	0.0406	0.0099	0.2700			
2.5								0.1378	189	186
	2.65	0.2641	0.3309	0.1296	0.0105	0.0026	0.1322			
2.8								0.1501	207	193
	2.95	0.0359	0.0450	0.0180	0.0003	0.0001	0.0179			
3.1								0.1412	193	188
	3.25	0.3359	0.4258	0.1631	0.0164	0.0040	0.1591			
3.4								0.1160	159	151
	3.55	0.6359	0.7967	0.2871	0.0488	0.0120	0.2751			
3.7								0.0850	116	123
	3.85	0.9359	1.1725	0.3795	0.0791	0.0194	0.3601			
4.0								0.0560	77	82
	4.15	1.2359	1.5483	0.4392	0.0945	0.0231	0.4161			
4.3								0.0336	46	48
	4.45	1.5359	1.9242	0.4729	0.0947	0.0232	0.4497			
4.6								0.0184	25	27
	4.75	1.8359	2.3000	0.4893	0.0867	0.0212	0.4681			
4.9								0.0091	13	14
	5.05	2.1359	2.6759	0.4963	0.0779	0.0191	0.4772			
5.2								0.0040	6	5
	5.35	2.4359	3.0517	0.4988	0.0718	0.0176	0.4812			
5.5								0.0017	2	1
	5.65	2.7359	3.4275	0.4997	0.0684	0.0168	0.4829			
Σ								0.9977	1,370	1,370

average, it follows from (24) that the skewness k does not add to this information because the integral of (22) over a symmetrical range is identically the same as the integral of (23) over the same range.

In passing, we should note that the function (22) is the familiar bell-shaped *normal law* curve whose significant charac-

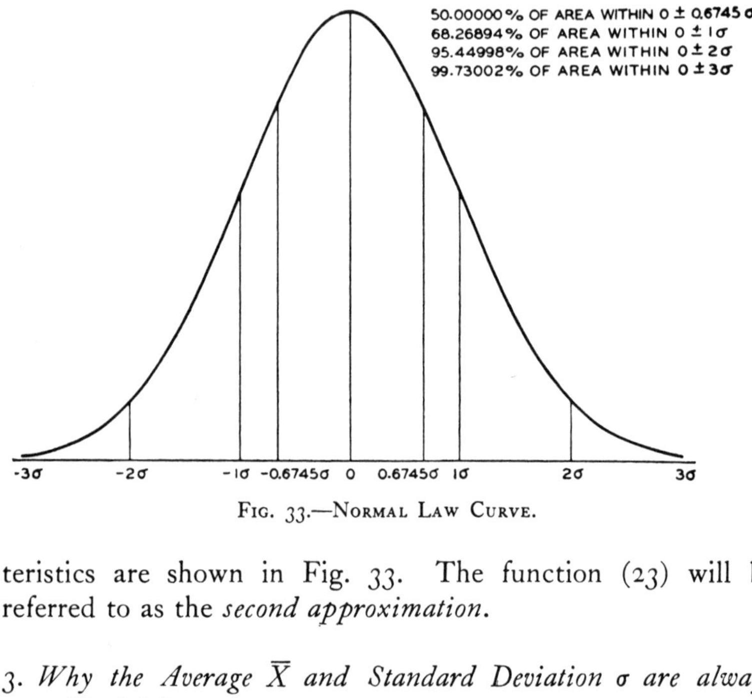

FIG. 33.—NORMAL LAW CURVE.

teristics are shown in Fig. 33. The function (23) will be referred to as the *second approximation*.

3. *Why the Average $\overline{X}$ and Standard Deviation σ are always Useful Statistics*

Let us consider the case where nothing is known about the distribution of observed values. To what extent are we justified in assuming that the average, standard deviation, skewness, and flatness contain significant information?

We have already seen that the amount of information given by these statistics of value in reproducing approximately the original distribution, depends upon the nature of the original distribution as reflected in the form of function f that would be required to satisfy the condition that its integral over a given range should be approximately equal to the number of observed values within this same range. However, even when nothing is known about the condition under which the distribution was observed, we find that the average and standard deviation enable us to estimate within limits which are quite satisfactory for most purposes, the number of observations lying within any symmetrical range $\bar{X} \pm z\sigma$, where z is greater than unity. In fact, the proportion of the total number of observed values within any such limits is always greater than $1 - \frac{1}{z^2}$. This follows from a general theorem, the proof of which can be framed in the simplest kind of elementary mathematics, as we shall now see.

Tchebycheff's Theorem.—Given any set of n observed values expressible by the frequency distribution of m different values,

$$X_1,\ X_2,\ \ldots,\ X_i,\ \ldots,\ X_m$$

$$p_1n, p_2n, \ldots, p_in, \ldots, p_mn$$

where p_in represents the number of values of X_i, then

$$\bar{X} = \frac{\sum_{i=1}^{m} p_in\, X_i}{\sum_{i=1}^{m} p_in} = \sum_{i=1}^{m} p_iX_i,$$

and

$$\sigma^2 = \frac{\sum_{i=1}^{m} p_in(X_i - \bar{X})^2}{\sum_{i=1}^{m} p_in}.$$

Let P_zn denote the number of values of X such that $x = (X - \bar{X})$ does not exceed numerically $z\sigma$ where $z > 1$, and $n - P_zn$ denote the number of values of x that do exceed $z\sigma$.

We may write

$$\sigma^2 = \Sigma_1 p_ix_i^2 + \Sigma_2 p_ix_i^2,$$

where Σ_1 denotes summation for all values of x_i which do not exceed $z\sigma$ and Σ_2 denotes summation for all values of x_i which do exceed $z\sigma$. Since all values of $p_i x_i^2$ are either positive or zero,

$$\sigma^2 \geq \Sigma_2 p_i x_i^2.$$

Obviously, therefore,

$$\sigma^2 > \Sigma_2 p_i z^2 \sigma^2$$

since all values of x_i included in the summation Σ_2 are greater than $z\sigma$. But

$$\Sigma_2 p_i = 1 - P_z.$$

Hence

$$\left.\begin{aligned} \sigma^2 &> (1 - P_z)z^2\sigma^2, \\ \text{or} \quad 1 &> (1 - P_z)z^2, \\ (1 - P_z) &< \frac{1}{z^2}, \end{aligned}\right\} \tag{25}$$

and

$$P_z > 1 - \frac{1}{z^2}. \tag{26}$$

We see that no matter what set of observed values we may have, the number of these values $P_z n$ lying within the closed range $\bar{X} \pm z\sigma$ is greater than $\left(1 - \frac{1}{z^2}\right)n$ whereas the number $(1 - P_z)n$ lying without this range is less than $\frac{1}{z^2}n$.

4. *Importance of Skewness k and Flatness* β_2

Given a set of any n real numbers $X_1, X_2, \ldots, X_i, \ldots, X_n$, what does a knowledge of the skewness k and flatness β_2 for this set of numbers really tell us independently of any assumption as to the nature of the distribution of the numbers as was made in deriving the theoretical distributions in Table 15? To get at this question, let us assume that the skewness k is equal to zero. Obviously, for a distribution to be symmetrical, it is a necessary condition that its skewness be zero. If this condition were also sufficient, it would be possible to say of the set of numbers given above that they were symmetrically distributed about the arithmetic mean value, and hence that there were just as many on one side of the mean as there were on the other. This would oftentimes be really worthwhile information.

It can readily be shown, however, that the condition $k = 0$ is not sufficient for symmetry. For example, the distribution

X:	2	-1	$\frac{1}{2}$	1
y:	1	16	16	6

satisfies the condition that its skewness is zero, although it is obviously not symmetrical about its mean value $X = 0$. In fact, it is far from being symmetrical as are many others which may be found by empirical methods. In this particular instance, instead of finding the set of numbers equally divided on either side of the average, we find sixteen on one side and twenty-three on the other. Hence we must conclude that a knowledge of k in itself does not present very much information.

In a similar way it can be shown that a knowledge of β_2 in itself does not present any very useful information about the distribution of a given set of n numbers.

These results are of considerable importance because they show that the tabulation of moments higher than the second for the purpose of summarizing the information contained in a set of data is likely to be of little value unless there is also given some function involving these statistics, the integral of which between any two limits gives an approximate value for the observed frequency corresponding to these two limits. In the general case, therefore, where one wishes to summarize an extensive series of observations which may not satisfy the condition of control, it is necessary to give a satisfactory function of this character to be used in interpreting the significance of the tabulated statistics from the viewpoint of presentation of the total information contained in the original set of data. Such functions are usually termed theoretical frequency distribution functions, and from the viewpoint of presentation of an observed set of data, it would appear that the one to be used is usually that one which satisfies best the condition described in Paragraph 1 of this chapter.

5. *Conclusion*

We may divide observed distributions into two classes—those that have and those that have not arisen under controlled conditions. For distributions of the first class, the three simple statistics, average $\overline{X}$, standard deviation σ, and skewness k contain almost all of the information in the original distribution. For those of the second class the most useful statistics are the average and standard deviation. These contain a large part of the total information in the original distribution, at least in respect to the number of observations lying within symmetrical ranges about the average.

CHAPTER IX

Presentation of Data to Indicate Relationship

1. *Two Kinds of Relationship*

Two kinds of relationship call for consideration: mathematical or functional, and statistical.

Functional Relationship.—If for each value of some variable X a given law assigns one or more values to Y, then we say that Y is a function of X and write

$$Y = f(X).$$

As a simple example, we may take

$$Y = c(X - a) + b.$$

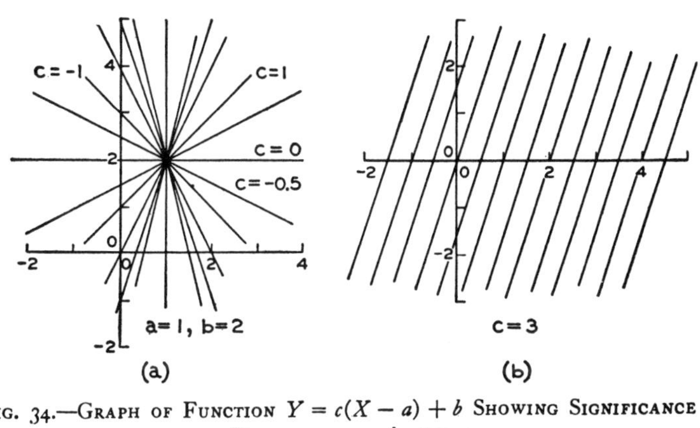

Fig. 34.—Graph of Function $Y = c(X - a) + b$ Showing Significance of Parameters a, b, and c.

Obviously, the graph of this function is a straight line passing through the point $X = a$, $Y = b$. The arbitrary constants a, b, and c in this function are called *parameters*. If we fix the values of a and b, and give to c all possible values, we get a pencil of lines through the point (a, b). Fig. 34-*a* shows such a pencil through the point (1, 2). In a similar way, if we fix the value of c and assign arbitrary values to a and b, we get a family of parallel lines. Fig. 34-b shows such a family for $c = 3$.

This simple example illustrates a general principle that should be kept in mind, viz., that the expression of a functional relationship involves two things:

1. The form of the functional relationship.
2. The specific values of the parameters in that relationship.

Thus, in the problem just considered, the form of the function is linear since Y varies directly as X. How it varies is fixed by the values of the parameters a, b, and c.

Statistical Relationship.—If for each value of some variable X a given law assigns a particular frequency distribution of values of Y not the same for all values of X, then we say that Y and X are statistically related. Two variables statistically related are said to be *correlated.*

If we let $z dX dY$ represent the frequency of occurrence of values of X within the interval X to $X + dX$ simultaneously with values of Y within the interval Y to $Y + dY$, the functional relationship

$$z = f(X, Y)$$

is said to characterize the statistical relationship between X and Y.

One important statistical relationship which will often be considered in further discussions is the so-called normal frequency function in two variables X and Y,

$$z = \frac{1}{2\pi\sigma_x\sigma_y\sqrt{1 - r^2}} e^{-\frac{1}{2(1-r^2)}\left(\frac{x^2}{\sigma_x^2} + \frac{y^2}{\sigma_y^2} - 2r\frac{xy}{\sigma_x\sigma_y}\right)}, \qquad (27)$$

where $x = X - \overline{X}$ and $y = Y - \overline{Y}$. This is the familiar bell-shaped frequency surface shown in Fig. 35. Obviously, five parameters $\overline{X}$, $\overline{Y}$, σ_x, σ_y, and r are involved in (27). Our interest at present is centered in the fact that the characterization of a statistical relationship involves two things—form and specific values of parameters—as did the characterization of functional relationship.

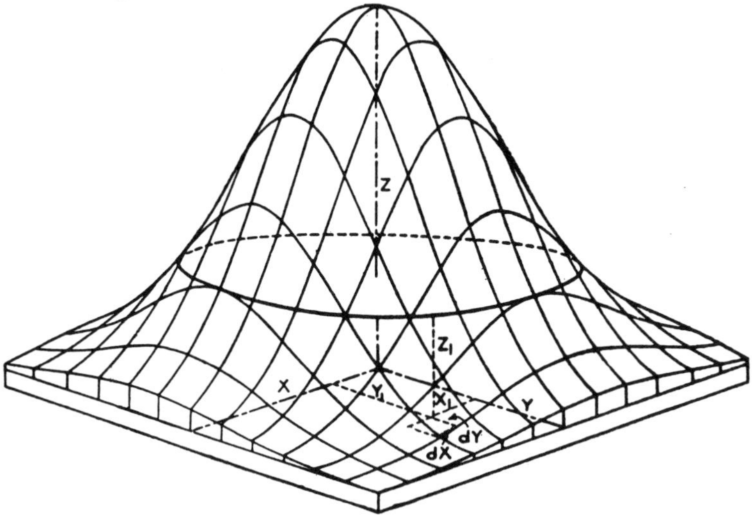

FIG. 35.—THE NORMAL SURFACE.

2. *Observed Relationship*

In our causal explanation or interpretation of data we assume that both functional and statistical relationships exist. In fact it is one of the fundamental objects of experimental investigation to determine these relationships or physical laws, as they are customarily called. This practical problem involves, in most instances, the formulation of the law from a study of the observed data, including both the functional form of the law and the estimate of the parameters in the law. Taking the simplest case of relationship between two quality characteristics X and Y, it is obvious that our formulation of the law and our estimate of the parameters must be based upon an observed set of, let us say, n pairs of simultaneously observed values of the two characteristics. In other words, the total information is tied up in these n pairs of values.

Suppose that we are studying the relationship between

two physical quantities, such as the length L of a rod and the temperature Θ at which this length is measured, or the distance s that a body falls starting from rest and the time t that it is falling. One object of such a study is the expression of the law of relationship. For example, we often assume that the empirical law relating the length and temperature of a rod of given material is linear, or, in other words, that the length varies directly with the temperature; i.e., $L = L_0(1 + \alpha\Theta)$, where L_0 is the original length of the rod, and α is the parameter indicating rate of increase with temperature. In a similar way, we say that the law relating s and t in the case of a freely falling body is $s = \frac{1}{2}at^2$, where a is a parameter. Having decided once and for all that the law in question is such and such, it remains for us to discover the best values of the parameters, as is illustrated by these two simple problems. A statement of the law and estimates of the parameters in that law is the common method of summarizing data indicating relationship.

However, even in the simple case where we believe that a functional relationship exists, it is a difficult matter to determine what this functional relationship likely is; and, having once decided what function to assume, we must choose one from among the many different possible ways of finding estimates of the required parameters. In other words, the problem of presenting data in this way is to a large extent indeterminate even when the assumed relationship is functional. It goes without saying that the indeterminateness becomes even greater when the relationship assumed to exist is statistical.

To emphasize what has just been said, let us try to find the relationship between the current through and the voltage across a carbon contact from the data given in Table 7. In this case there is no *a priori* basis for assuming the form of the law of relationship. If, however, we assume that it is functional and parabolic in form, or, in other words, if we assume that the current Y is related to the voltage X in the following way,

$$Y = a_0 + a_1X + a_2X^2,$$

we must find, from the data, estimates of the three parameters a_0, a_1, and a_2. If we had a universally accepted method of finding these parameters under these conditions, the problem of presenting relationship would be quite simple indeed. As we have already said, however, there are many different ways of estimating these parameters, four of which are:

1. Direct substitution of observed values.
2. Graphical method.
3. Method of least squares.
4. Method of moments.

The details of the methods of estimating the parameters in these different ways are given in standard treatises on curve fitting. It will serve our purpose here to consider merely the variability in some of the results obtained by these different methods. Two of the several possible sets of values for the parameters that can be obtained by direct substitution are those in the equations

$$Y = -0.01000 + 0.01333X + 0.00000X^2,$$

and

$$Y = 0.09000 - 0.00167X + 0.00056X^2.$$

Each of the following equations contains one of the infinite number of possible sets of values for the parameters obtainable by the particular method indicated.

1. Graphical Method

$$Y = -0.02446 + 0.01225X + 0.00012X^2,$$

2. Method of Least Squares [1]

$$Y = 0.00809 + 0.00967X + 0.00016X^2,$$

3. Method of Moments [2]

$$Y = 0.02649 + 0.00831X + 0.00018X^2.$$

[1] This equation was obtained by minimizing the vertical deviation of a point from the curve of fit. Obviously, this is only one of an infinite number of different ways in which the minimizing process could be carried out, by choosing different distances to minimize. We customarily minimize one of the three distances, vertical, horizontal, or perpendicular.

[2] We may use any three moments. The first three are usually chosen.

Obviously, any one of these equations is supposed to summarize the data of Table 7 in respect to relationship. It is apparent, however, that the details of this summary depend upon the choice of the method of calculating estimates of the parameters.

If in this case a different law of relationship is assumed to exist, the values of the parameters supposed to contain the information in the original set of data may be expected to be different from those given above. The difficulties of expressing relationship in this simple problem are multiplied many fold when the relationship is statistical instead of functional.

In the light of these considerations, it becomes apparent that the problem of presenting essential information in respect to relationship is a complicated one and that a complete discussion of the subject is beyond the scope of the present text. What we shall do in the remainder of this chapter is to consider the significance of the correlation coefficient as a measure of relationship, because we shall find it to be a satisfactory measure in most of the problems with which we have to deal.

3. *Information Given by the Correlation Coefficient* [1]

A. Let us assume that we have n simultaneously observed pairs of values of two quality characteristics X and Y. As a specific case, let us consider the observed set of sixty pairs of values of tensile strength and hardness previously given in Table 3 and shown graphically in Fig. 36. It may be shown that the line of best fit to such an array of points obtained by the method of least squares [2] through minimizing the squares of the vertical deviations of these points from this line is

$$y = r\frac{\sigma_y}{\sigma_x}x, \qquad (28)$$

where $x = X - \bar{X}$, and $y = Y - \bar{Y}$, the symbols $\bar{X}$, $\bar{Y}$, σ_x, σ_y, and r being expressed in terms of the n observed pairs of values

[1] It will be found helpful to read Chapter IV of *Mathematical Statistics* by H. L. Rietz in connection with the remainder of this chapter.

[2] Throughout the remainder of this chapter, a line of "best" fit is always to be taken in the least square sense.

of X and Y. In the same way, the equation of the line of best fit obtained by the method of least squares through minimizing the horizontal deviations of the points from this line is given by the equation

$$x = r\frac{\sigma x}{\sigma y}y. \qquad (29)$$

Similarly, the line of best fit obtained by minimizing the squares of the perpendicular deviations of the points from the line of fit is given by the equation

$$y = -\frac{1}{2r\sigma_x\sigma_y}\left[(\sigma_x^2 - \sigma_y^2) - \sqrt{(\sigma_x^2 - \sigma_y^2)^2 + 4r^2\sigma_x^2\sigma_y^2}\right]x. \qquad (30)$$

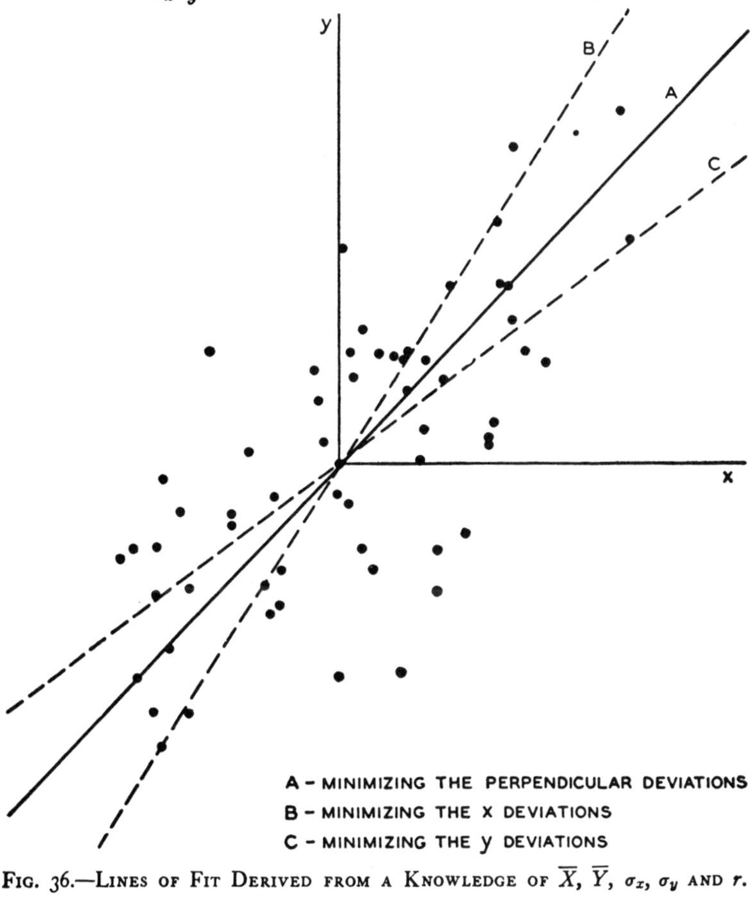

FIG. 36.—LINES OF FIT DERIVED FROM A KNOWLEDGE OF $\overline{X}$, $\overline{Y}$, σ_x, σ_y AND r.

Equation (30) with a positive sign before the radical gives the line of worst fit.

Having summarized the information in the sixty pairs of values of tensile strength and hardness in the form:

Average Tensile Strength $\overline{Y}$ in psi	$= 31869.4$
Average Hardness $\overline{X}$ in Rockwells	$= 69.825$
Standard Deviation σ_y of Tensile Strength in psi	$= 3962.9$
Standard Deviation σ_x of Hardness in Rockwells	$= 11.773$
Correlation Coefficient r	$= 0.683$

we may write down without further work the equations to the three lines of best fit just mentioned. They are

$$y = 229.904x,$$

$$x = 0.002029y,$$

$$y = 492.837x.$$

These are shown graphically in Fig. 36. In Figs. 36 and 40 the variables are expressed in terms of their respective standard deviations, and the units of the scales are made equal.

B. If, in a scatter diagram such as that showing the relationship between depth of sapwood and depth of penetration, we plot the averages of the column and row arrays, we get some such result as that indicated in Fig. 37. The line of best fit to the averages of the columns when each squared deviation is weighted by the number of points in the corresponding column is given except for errors of grouping by (28); similarly, except for errors of grouping, the line of best fit to the averages of the rows is given by (29). These two lines are called respectively the *lines of regression* of y on x and of x on y.

It is shown in elementary texts on statistics that, if all of the standard deviations in the column arrays are equal,[1] then for linear regression each is equal to the standard deviation s_y of the observed points in the scatter diagram about line (28), where

$$s_y = \sigma_y\sqrt{1 - r^2}. \tag{31}$$

[1] When this condition is satisfied, the distribution of y is said to be *homoscedastic*.

With this same restriction, if all of the standard deviations in the row arrays are equal, then it follows that each is equal to the standard deviation s_x of the points about line (29) and is given by the expression

$$s_x = \sigma_x\sqrt{1 - r^2}. \tag{32}$$

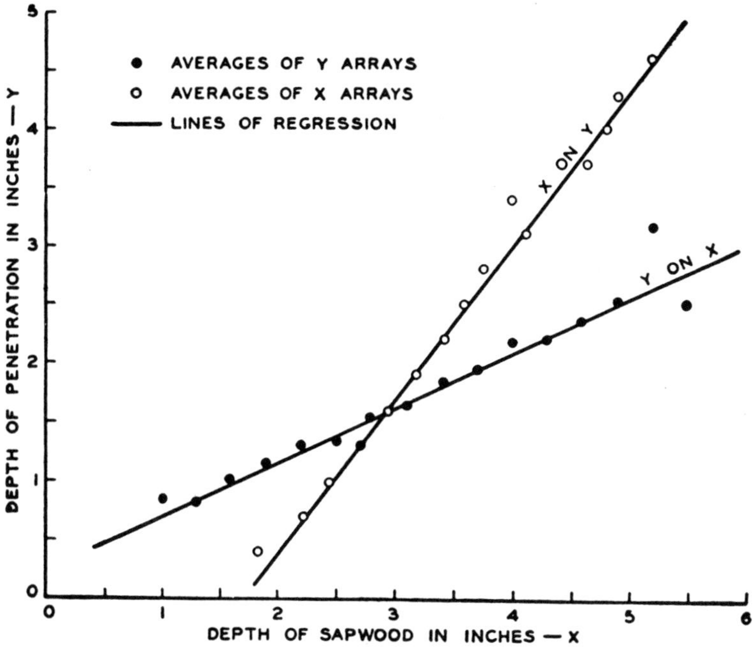

FIG. 37.—LINES OF REGRESSION.

Under these conditions, it follows from what has just been said and from Tchebycheff's theorem that the fraction of the total number of points in the scatter diagram within the band

$$y \pm zs_y \equiv r\frac{\sigma x}{\sigma y}x \pm zs_y \tag{33}$$

will be greater than $1 - \frac{1}{z^2}$.

If this scatter diagram has been obtained under conditions of control or, in other words, if the distributions in the row and column arrays are approximately normal, the number of points within such a band will be approximately that derived from the normal law integral. Fig. 38 shows such a band for the 1,370 pairs of values of depth of sapwood and depth of penetration for the case $z = 3$. Under controlled conditions, this band should include approximately 99.7 per cent of the

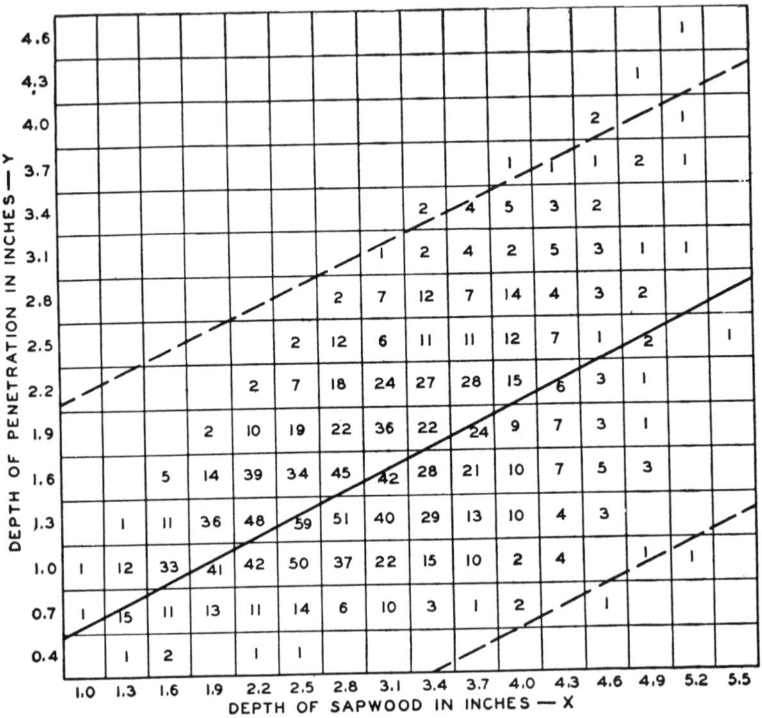

FIG. 38.—LINE OF REGRESSION AND 99.7 PER CENT LIMITS.

1,370 points. We find that it actually includes 99.1 per cent of the observed values, even though the data do not rigorously meet the condition of control.

What has just been said concerning the band about the line of regression of y on x holds good in a similar way for the corresponding band about the line of regression of x on y.

C. If we rewrite the equation (27) of the normal surface in the form

$$z = \frac{1}{2\pi\sigma_x\sigma_y\sqrt{1 - r^2}} e^{-\frac{\chi^2}{2}}, \tag{34}$$

we see that all values of x and y for a constant value χ_1 of χ lie on an ellipse defined by the equation

$$\frac{1}{1 - r^2}\left(\frac{x^2}{\sigma_x^2} + \frac{y^2}{\sigma_y^2} - \frac{2rxy}{\sigma_x\sigma_y}\right) = \chi_1^2. \tag{35}$$

By revolving the original axes through an angle α such that

$$\tan 2\alpha = \frac{2r\sigma_x\sigma_y}{\sigma_x^2 - \sigma_y^2}, \tag{36}$$

the equation of this ellipse for any value of χ becomes

$$ax_1^2 + by_1^2 = \chi^2, \tag{37}$$

where

$$a = \frac{1}{2(1 - r^2)}\left[\left(\frac{1}{\sigma_x^2} + \frac{1}{\sigma_y^2}\right) - \sqrt{\left(\frac{1}{\sigma_x^2} - \frac{1}{\sigma_y^2}\right)^2 + \frac{4r^2}{\sigma_x^2\sigma_y^2}}\right],$$

and

$$b = \frac{1}{2(1 - r^2)}\left[\left(\frac{1}{\sigma_x^2} + \frac{1}{\sigma_y^2}\right) + \sqrt{\left(\frac{1}{\sigma_x^2} - \frac{1}{\sigma_y^2}\right)^2 + \frac{4r^2}{\sigma_x^2\sigma_y^2}}\right].$$

Hence the semi-axes of any ellipse are

$$\frac{\chi}{\sqrt{a}} \quad \text{and} \quad \frac{\chi}{\sqrt{b}} \tag{38}$$

respectively.

When the observed frequency distribution in two dimensions has been obtained under controlled conditions and sometimes even when the conditions have not been controlled, the number n_χ within the ellipse χ is given approximately by the integral

$$\int_0^\chi e^{-\frac{\chi^2}{2}} \chi d\chi = 1 - e^{-\frac{1}{2}\chi^2}. \tag{39}$$

TABLE C

χ^2	Fraction Outside $e^{-\frac{1}{2}\chi^2}$	Fraction Inside $1-e^{-\frac{1}{2}\chi^2}$	Fraction Outside $e^{-\frac{1}{2}\chi^2}$	Fraction Inside $1-e^{-\frac{1}{2}\chi^2}$	χ^2
0.1	0.951229	0.048771	0.9000	0.1000	0.2107
0.2	0.904837	0.095163	0.8000	0.2000	0.4463
0.3	0.860708	0.139292	0.7500	0.2500	0.5754
0.4	0.818731	0.181269	0.7000	0.3000	0.7134
0.5	0.778801	0.221199	0.6000	0.4000	1.0217
0.6	0.740818	0.259182	0.5000	0.5000	1.3863
0.7	0.704688	0.295312	0.4000	0.6000	1.9326
0.8	0.670320	0.329680	0.3000	0.7000	2.4080
0.9	0.637628	0.362372	0.2500	0.7500	2.7726
1.0	0.606531	0.393469	0.2000	0.8000	3.2198
2.0	0.367879	0.632121	0.1000	0.9000	4.6052
3.0	0.223130	0.776870	0.0500	0.9500	5.9915
4.0	0.135335	0.864665	0.0100	0.9900	9.2104
5.0	0.082085	0.917915	0.0030	0.9970	11.8194
6.0	0.049787	0.950213	0.0027	0.9973	11.8290
7.0	0.030197	0.969803			
8.0	0.018316	0.981684			
9.0	0.011109	0.988891			
10.0	0.006738	0.993262			
11.0	0.004087	0.995913			
12.0	0.002479	0.997521			
13.0	0.001503	0.998497			
14.0	0.000912	0.999088			
15.0	0.000553	0.999447			
16.0	0.000335	0.999665			
17.0	0.000203	0.999797			
18.0	0.000123	0.999877			
19.0	0.000075	0.999925			
20.0	0.000045	0.999955			

From Table C we can read off the value of this integral for a large range of values of χ^2. Fig. 39 illustrates the method of constructing 50 per cent and 99.73 per cent ellipses for the distribution of 1,370 pairs of values of depth of sapwood and depth of penetration. Observation shows 49.9 per cent and 99.12 per cent within these ellipses.

X = Depth of Sapwood in inches

Y = Depth of Penetration in inches

$n = 1370$

$\bar{X} = 2.914088 \qquad \sigma_x = 0.798211$

$\bar{Y} = 1.591460 \qquad \sigma_y = 0.624872$

$r = 0.603201$

$$\tan 2\alpha = \frac{2r\sigma_x\sigma_y}{\sigma_x^2 - \sigma_y^2} = 2.439350$$

$$2\alpha = 67^\circ\ 42'\ 32''$$

$$\alpha = \underline{33^\circ\ 51'\ 16''}$$

$$a = \frac{1}{2(1-r^2)}\left[\frac{1}{\sigma_x^2} + \frac{1}{\sigma_y^2} - \sqrt{\left(\frac{1}{\sigma_x^2} - \frac{1}{\sigma_y^2}\right)^2 + \frac{4r^2}{\sigma_x^2\sigma_y^2}}\,\right] = 1.191941$$

$$b = \frac{1}{2(1-r^2)}\left[\frac{1}{\sigma_x^2} + \frac{1}{\sigma_y^2} + \sqrt{\left(\frac{1}{\sigma_x^2} - \frac{1}{\sigma_y^2}\right)^2 + \frac{4r^2}{\sigma_x^2\sigma_y^2}}\,\right] = 5.301130$$

$$\underline{ax_1^2 + by_1^2 = \chi^2}$$

Let $\chi^2 = 1.3863$ or $1 - e^{-\frac{1}{2}\chi^2} = 0.5000$

$\chi = 1.1774$

$\dfrac{\chi}{\sqrt{a}} = 1.0784 \qquad \dfrac{\chi}{\sqrt{b}} = 0.5114$

$1.191941x_1^2 + 5.301130y_1^2 = 1.3863$

Let $\chi^2 = 11.8290$ or $1 - e^{-\frac{1}{2}\chi^2} = 0.9973$

$\chi = 3.4393$

$\dfrac{\chi}{\sqrt{a}} = 3.1502 \qquad \dfrac{\chi}{\sqrt{b}} = 1.4938$

$1.191941x_1^2 + 5.301130y_1^2 = 11.8290$

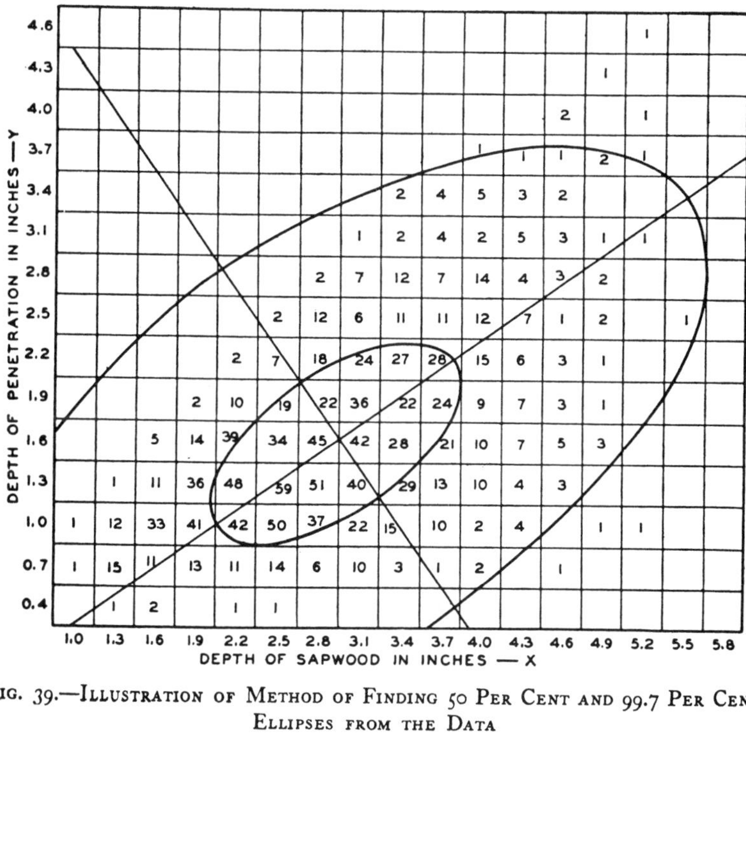

FIG. 39.—ILLUSTRATION OF METHOD OF FINDING 50 PER CENT AND 99.7 PER CENT ELLIPSES FROM THE DATA

Similar calculations of the correlation ellipses for the sixty pairs of simultaneously observed values of tensile strength and hardness previously discussed give the results shown graphically in Fig. 40. In this connection the line of best fit is that obtained by minimizing the perpendicular distances of the points from the line.

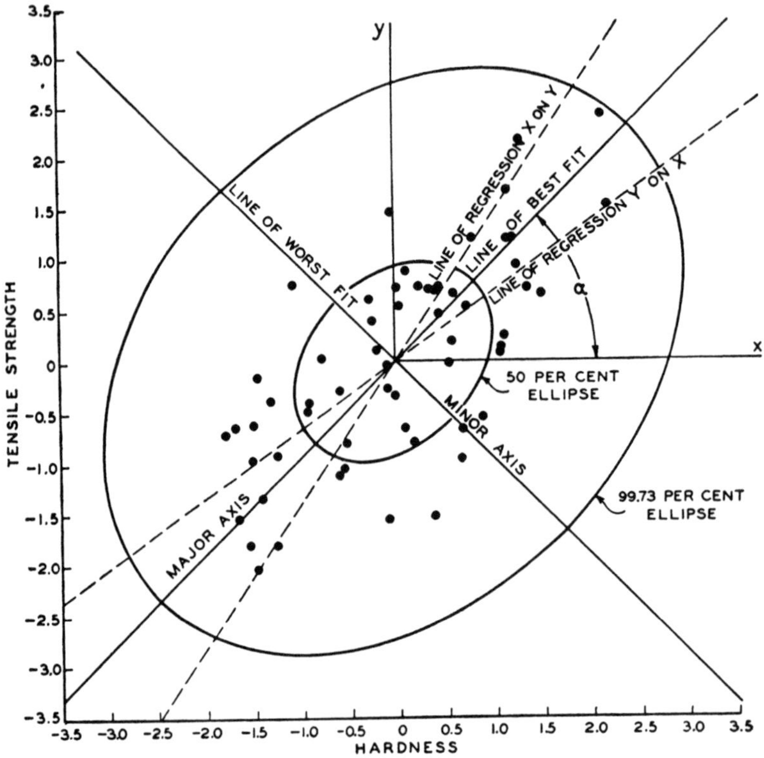

Fig. 40.—Information Given by Average, Standard Deviation, and Correlation Coefficient.

The striking thing about the illustrations considered in this paragraph is that, under certain conditions, a knowledge of the five statistics $\overline{X}$, $\overline{Y}$, σ_x, σ_y, and r gives us so much of the total information contained in the raw data.

If r be the correlation coefficient between any given set of n pairs of values X_1Y_1, X_2Y_2, . . . , X_iY_i, . . . , X_nY_n of any two variables X and Y, it is interesting to note that $r^2 = 1$ is both a necessary and sufficient condition that the set of points lie on the line (28), because $s_y = 0$ only when $r = \pm 1$. In this case s_x is also zero and the two lines of regression (28) and (29) coincide. In other words, $r^2 = 1$ is a necessary and sufficient condition that Y be a linear function of X. If r^2 is approximately equal to unity, it is not necessary that all of the points lie near the line of regression although a majority of them do. We must know something about the nature of the scatter before we can interpret r in this case.

4. *Relationship between Several Qualities*

What has been said about the relationship between two quality characteristics can easily be extended to the case of several. We shall consider here only the use of the correlation coefficient in determining the plane of best fit and the location of the observed points in a band about this plane for the case of three variables.

Let us assume that we have n sets of simultaneous values of three variables X, Y, and Z. Let $\bar{X}, \bar{Y}, \bar{Z}, \sigma_x, \sigma_y, \sigma_z, r_{xy}, r_{yz}$, and r_{zx} be the arithmetic means, standard deviations, and correlation coefficients respectively.

It may easily be shown that the plane of regression of z on x and y, when $x = X - \bar{X}$, $y = Y - \bar{Y}$, and $z = Z - \bar{Z}$, is given, except for errors of grouping, by the following expression

$$z = a + bx + cy, \tag{40}$$

where

$$a = 0,$$

$$b = \frac{\sigma_z(r_{xz} - r_{yz}r_{xy})}{\sigma_x(1 - r_{xy}^2)}, \tag{41}$$

$$c = \frac{\sigma_z(r_{yz} - r_{xy}r_{xz})}{\sigma_y(1 - r_{xy}^2)}. \tag{42}$$

These equations show that a knowledge of averages, standard deviations, and correlation coefficients [1] gives us the

[1] Obviously $r_{xy} = r_{yx}$, etc.

information required to construct such a plane. As an illustration, Table 19 gives these statistics for the sixty sets of values of tensile strength, hardness, and density previously given in Table 3.

TABLE 19.—INFORMATION OF TABLE 3 GIVEN IN TERMS OF SIMPLE STATISTICS

	Density X in gm/cm.^{3}	Hardness Y in Rockwells	Tensile Strength Z in psi
Arithmetic Mean....	2.6785	69.825	31,869.4
Standard Deviation..	0.0986	11.773	3,962.9

$r_{xy} = 0.616 \qquad r_{yz} = 0.683 \qquad r_{xz} = 0.657$

Substituting these values in (40) we get

$$z = 15310.35x + 150.988y.$$

The standard deviation $\sigma_{z \cdot yx}$ of the points from this plane is given approximately [1] by

$$\sigma_{z \cdot yx} = \sigma_z \frac{\begin{vmatrix} 1 & r_{yz} & r_{xz} \\ r_{yz} & 1 & r_{xy} \\ r_{xz} & r_{xy} & 1 \end{vmatrix}^{1/2}}{(1 - r_{xy}^2)^{1/2}} = 2,638.5 \text{ psi.} \qquad (43)$$

The graphical representation of the plane was given in Fig. 14.

Under conditions of control the number of points within the band formed by the two parallel planes spaced at a distance $z\sigma_{z \cdot yx}$ on either side of the plane of regression should be approximately given by the normal law integral, Table A.

Naturally we can duplicate the above discussion for the planes of regression of y on z and x and of x on y and z.

Equation (43) enables us to measure the scatter of the observed points in Fig. 14 from the plane of regression shown therein. It is of interest to compare the standard deviation $\sigma_{z \cdot yx}$ with the corresponding standard deviations s_{zy} and s_{zx}

[1] The numerical result given in (43) is obtained by using more decimal places than shown in Table 19. Cf. Paragraph 7, Chapter 7, Part II.

measuring respectively the standard deviation of the points from the line of regression of z on y and z on x. It is easily verifiable that the equations of these two lines of regression are

$$z = r_{yz}\frac{\sigma z}{\sigma y}y = 229.964y,$$

and

$$z = r_{xz}\frac{\sigma z}{\sigma x}x = 26{,}418.993x.$$

It also follows that

$$s_{zy} = \sigma_z\sqrt{1 - r_{yz}^2} = 2{,}893.98 \text{ psi}$$

and

$$s_{zx} = \sigma_z\sqrt{1 - r_{xz}^2} = 2{,}987.028 \text{ psi.}$$

Both of these standard deviations are larger than $\sigma_{z \cdot xy}$ given by (43), the relative magnitudes being represented by the lengths of the lines in Fig. 14-*d*.

5. *Measure of Relationship—Correlation Ratio*

Given any set of n pairs of values $X_1Y_1, X_2Y_2, \ldots, X_iY_i, \ldots, X_nY_n$, another useful measure of relationship is the correlation ratio η_{yx} of Y on X. By definition

$$\eta_{yx}^2 = 1 - \frac{s_{1y}^2}{\sigma_y^2}$$

where s_{1y}^2 is the mean square of deviations from the means of the arrays of y's.

The correlation ratio η_{xy} of X on Y may be defined in a similar manner.

It is shown in elementary texts[1] that the square of the correlation ratio must lie between 0 and 1 and satisfies the expression

$$1 \geq \eta_{yx}^2 \geq r^2.$$

The condition that $\eta_{yx}^2 = 1$ is sufficient to prove that the variable Y can be expressed as a single-valued functional rela-

[1] Cf. Rietz, loc. cit.

tionship of X, and that the condition $\eta_{yx}^2 - r^2 = 0$ is satisfied if and only if the regression of y on x is linear. Since the square of the correlation ratio can never be less than the square of the correlation coefficient, it follows that r is zero if η_{yx}^2 is zero. However, the condition that $r = 0$, does not necessarily mean that $\eta_{yx} = 0$.

Furthermore, it should be noted that the correlation coefficient r may be zero even though Y is a function of X. Rietz [1] has shown that this is true, for example, when

$$Y = \cos \lambda X.$$

6. *Measure of Relationship—General Comments*

From the viewpoint of presentation of information to show statistical relationship, it is necessary to do more than simply tabulate statistical measures such as the correlation coefficient and correlation ratio.[2] It will be recalled that a similar statement had to be made in respect to the interpretation of moments of a frequency distribution higher than the second. In contrast with this situation, however, we have seen that the average and standard deviation of the distribution contain a large amount of the total information given by that distribution independent of its nature. Of course, the knowledge of these

[1] "On Functional Relations for which the Coefficient of Correlation is Zero," *Quarterly Publications of the American Statistical Association*, Vol. XVI, September, 1919, pp. 472–476.

[2] Incidentally, it should be noted that both the correlation coefficient and the correlation ratio are only measures of certain characteristics of correlation defined in the first paragraph of the present chapter. In other words, the frequency distribution functions of the x arrays of y's need not all be alike and hence there may be definite correlation although $r = 0$ and $\eta_{yx} = 0$. A case in point is the scatter diagram of numbers shown below and typical of an indefinitely large number which might be constructed.

			1			
		1	2	1		
	1	2	4	2	1	
1	2	4	8	4	2	1
	1	2	4	2	1	
		1	2	1		
			1			

two statistics gives us perfectly definite information about an observed set of n pairs of values of any two variables X and Y. Thus we can say:

(*A*) If $r^2 = 1$, then y is related to x by a linear function.
(*B*) If $\eta_{yx}^2 = 1$, it follows that Y is a function of X or that $Y = f(X)$.
(*C*) The regression of y on x is linear if and only if $\eta_{yx}^2 - r^2 = 0$.

However, other values of r and η do not give us such positive information. For example, if $r^2 = 0$, it does not necessarily follow, as we have already seen, that there is no correlation between Y and X. Similarly, if $\eta_{yx}^2 = 0$, then $r = 0$, but if $r = 0$, it does not necessarily follow that $\eta_{yx}^2 = 0$. Moreover the conditions

$$r^2 \doteq 1$$

$$\eta_{yx}^2 \doteq 1$$

$$\eta_{yx}^2 - r^2 \doteq 0$$

do not necessarily tell us much about the correlation between Y and X.

We have seen what a useful tool the correlation coefficient r is under certain conditions. We must have been struck, however, with the interesting fact that neither r nor any other measure of relationship gives a fraction of the total information definable within certain limits irrespective of the nature of the relationship, a condition that is satisfied by the average $\bar{X}$ and standard deviation σ of an observed distribution. In other words, no matter whether we express the relationship as functional or statistical, the significance of a given parameter is in the present state of our knowledge dependent upon the form of the relationship, whereas certain information is given by the average $\bar{X}$ and standard deviation σ of a frequency distribution independent of the form of the distribution, and this is made useful through the Tchebycheff theorem.

Part III

Basis for Specification of Quality Control

A Statement of the Necessary and Sufficient Conditions for the Specification of a Controlled Quality

CHAPTER X

Laws Basic to Control

1. *Control*

We like to believe that there is law and order in the world. We seek causal explanations of phenomena so that we may predict the nature of the these same phenomena at any future time. As stated in Part I, a phenomenon that can be predicted, at least within limits associated with a given probability, is said to be *controlled*. Prediction only becomes possible through the acquisition of knowledge of principles or laws.

2. *Exact Law*

By an exact[1] law we shall mean a rule whereby we can predict with a high degree of precision the future course of some phenomenon.

An illustration will serve to clarify this definition. If we impose an electromotive force $E \sin \omega t$ upon the simple circuit, Fig. 41, with inductance L, capacity C, and resistance R, the current i at any time t is given by the solution of the differential equation

$$E \sin \omega t = L\frac{di}{dt} + Ri + \frac{\int i dt}{C}.$$

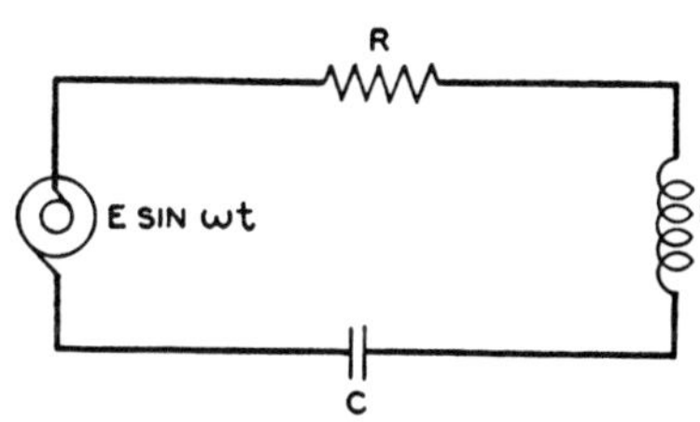

Fig. 41.—Example of Controlled Phenomenon Obeying an Exact Law.

The current through this circuit is, therefore, a simple example of a controlled phenomenon obeying an exact law, in this case a differential equation.

[1] Of course no physical law is exact in the rigorous mathematical sense. The significance of this term as here used will become clear as we proceed.

Of this same character are the numerous laws of physics and chemistry, such as Newton's laws, Fermat's principle, Maxwell's equations, the principle of least action, and so on. Naturally, the control of quality of manufactured product involves the use of all known exact laws of this character. These laws alone, however, are not enough to insure control because, as we have already noted in Part I, the variability in quality often is unexplainable upon the basis of known exact laws. We say that such variations are produced by unknown or chance causes.

If then we are to secure control of quality of product, we must make use not only of exact laws but also of laws of chance, sometimes termed statistical laws. Perhaps the basic law of this character is the law of large numbers.

3. *Law of Large Numbers*

If we flip a coin, either the head or the tail must come up. If we repeat the experiment again and again, we find that there is a certain constancy in the nature of the results obtained and that this constancy appears to be independent of whether you flip the coin or whether I flip it; whether the coin is flipped in some far-off country or at home. From every corner of the world, we get evidence of a certain constancy in the experimental results; i.e., it appears that the observed ratio of the number of times that a head comes up to the total number of throws approaches in a certain sense a constant value for a given coin. This kind of experience is, however, not limited to coin throwing; and, as a result, the following general principle is accepted as a law of nature:

Whenever an event may happen in only one of two ways, and the event is observed to happen under the same essential conditions for a large number of times, the ratio p of the number of times that it happens in one way to the total number of trials appears to approach a definite limit, let us say **p**, *as the number of trials increases indefinitely.*

Symbolically we may state this law in the form

$$\underset{n \to \infty}{L_S}\ p = \mathbf{p}, \tag{44}$$

where L_s stands for what we shall term a statistical limit,[1] which differs from a mathematical limit in that we do not reach a number n_0 of trials such that, for all values of n greater than n_0, the ratio of the number of times an event happens to the number of trials differs from some fixed value by less than some previously assigned small quantity ε.

We shall call this limiting value **p** an *objective probability*, and we shall assume that this objective probability of an event happening under the same essential conditions may be used in the same mathematical sense as we use measures of *a priori* probability in the mathematical theory of probability.

Mathematical or *a priori* probability is usually defined in some such way as the following: If an event can happen in a definite number n of mutually exclusive ways, all ways being equally alike, and if m of these ways be called favorable, then the ratio $\frac{m}{n}$ is the *a priori* probability of the favorable event. For example, in the tossing of a coin the number n of ways in which the event may happen is considered to be two—head or tail. If the turning up of a head is taken as favorable and if the two ways the event may happen are equally likely, the *a priori* probability of a head is $\frac{1}{2}$. In a practical case, we never *know* whether or not the ways an event may happen are equally likely; often we do not even know the number n of ways. Hence we cannot calculate the *a priori* probability of an event. Assuming the existence of an *a priori* probability **p** of an event, the best we can ever hope to do is to adopt some estimate p of this probability which may not and, in general, will not be the true objective value **p**.

Obviously, the concept of *a priori* probability is not the same as that of a statistical limit. Furthermore, even though an *a priori* probability of an event does exist in an objective sense, it is not necessary that even an infinite sequence of trials will lead to the establishment of this *a priori* probability that can be accepted in a rigorous logical sense. On the other hand, if we *knew* in a given case that an objective *a priori*

[1] See Fig. 1 of Appendix II as an illustration of the way p approaches a statistical limit.

probability did exist, it appears that we would most likely have faith that the more observations we took in determining an empirical measure of this objective probability, the better our estimate would become. In general it appears that we must believe that estimates of probabilities derived from large samples are, in the long run, better than those derived from small samples. In other words, it is perhaps reasonable to believe that our best estimates of *a priori* objective probabilities are those values which we determine through large samples. So far as the present book is concerned, *a priori* probabilities and probability distributions will be characterized by a bold-faced notation wherever necessary for the sake of clearness. Whether we think of these as statistical limits or simply as mathematical entities should not influence to a marked extent their practical significance in that in any case the important thing to note is the way in which estimates of these probabilities represented by the regular symbols are actually derived from the data.[1]

A slightly more extended form of this law of large numbers is as follows: If we make a series of n measurements

$$X_1, X_2, \ldots, X_i, \ldots, X_n$$

of some quality characteristic X in such a way that each measurement is made under the same essential conditions, the ratio p of the number of times that an observed value X will be found to lie within any specified range X_r to X_s to the total number n will approach a statistical limit $\mathbf{p}$ as the number n is increased indefinitely.

A still more general statement of this law is: If we take a series of m samples of n measurements,

$$\left.\begin{matrix} X_{11}, & X_{12}, & \ldots, & X_{1i}, & \ldots, & X_{1n} \\ X_{21}, & X_{22}, & \ldots, & X_{2i}, & \ldots, & X_{2n} \\ \cdot & \cdot & \cdot & \cdot & \cdot & \cdot \\ \cdot & \cdot & \cdot & \cdot & \cdot & \cdot \\ X_{m1}, & X_{m2}, & \ldots, & X_{mi}, & \ldots, & X_{mn} \end{matrix}\right\}, \qquad (45)$$

[1] It will be found helpful to read, in this connection, the discussions of the definitions of statistical limit and probability found in such books as Fry's *Probability and Its Engineering Uses*, Coolidge's *Probability*, and Rietz's *Mathematical Statistics*.

in such a way that each one of the m samples is drawn under the same essential conditions, and if we let Θ be a symmetric function or statistic of the n values of X in a sample of size n, the ratio p of the number of times that the observed value of Θ will be found to lie within the range Θ_1 to Θ_2 to the total number m of samples will approach a definite statistical limit $\mathbf{p}$ as the number m of samples is increased indefinitely. Functions of this type are termed statistical laws.

To control quality we must make use of both exact and statistical laws.

4. *Point Binomial in Relation to Control*

If p is the mathematical or *a priori* probability of the occurrence of an event or success and q is the mathematical or *a priori* probability of the non-occurrence of the event, it readily follows [1] that the probabilities of 0, 1, 2, 3, . . . , i, . . . , n occurrences of the event in n trials are given by the successive terms of the point binomial

$$(q + p)^n.$$

It also follows that:

$$\text{Average number of successes} = pn. \tag{46}$$

$$\text{Standard deviation of number of successes} = \sqrt{pqn}. \tag{47}$$

We are now in a position to consider evidence in justification of our assumption of the existence of the law of large numbers.

5. *Evidence of the Existence of the Law of Large Numbers*

A. *Tossing a Coin or Throwing Dice.*—Experience shows that, if we throw what appears to be a symmetrical coin or die a very large number of times, the statistical limit of the ratio of the number of heads to the total number of throws of the coin is $\frac{1}{2}$. Similarly, if the occurrence of 1, 2, or 3 on a symmetrical die be termed a success, the statistical limit of the ratio of the number of successes to the total number of throws of the die is $\frac{1}{2}$. If then our previous assumptions are

[1] See any elementary textbook on probability.

justified, we should expect[1] to find the relative frequencies of occurrence of 0, 1, 2, 3, . . . , n successes in a large number of throws of n dice to be given by the successive terms of the point binomial $(\frac{1}{2} + \frac{1}{2})^n$.

We may make use of some of the experimental results obtained by throwing n dice a large number of times to see how closely the observed frequency distribution of successes checks that of the point binomial. The second column of Table 20 gives the observed relative frequencies of 0, 1, 2, 3, . . . , twelve successes in 4,096 throws of twelve dice.[2] The third column of this table gives the mathematical probabilities, or, in other words, the successive terms of the point binomial $(\frac{1}{2} + \frac{1}{2})^{12}$.

A little observation shows that the second and third columns reveal a striking agreement. In other words, it appears that

Table 20.—Relation between Mathematical Probabilities and Experimental Results

Number of Successes	Observed Relative Frequency p	Mathematical Probability $(\frac{1}{2} + \frac{1}{2})^{12}$	Number of Successes	Observed Relative Frequency p	Mathematical Probability $(\frac{1}{2} + \frac{1}{2})^{12}$
0	0.0000	0.0002	7	0.2068	0.1934
1	0.0017	0.0029	8	0.1309	0.1208
2	0.0146	0.0161	9	0.0627	0.0537
3	0.0483	0.0537	10	0.0173	0.0161
4	0.1050	0.1208	11	0.0027	0.0029
5	0.1785	0.1934	12	0.0000	0.0002
6	0.2314	0.2256			

the rule of procedure followed in calculating the mathematical probabilities in this particular case leads to a close prediction of the experimental results. We return in Part VI to consider more critically the closeness of check between the mathematical probabilities and the observed relative frequencies.

[1] Strictly speaking, we know that the conditions of symmetry are not satisfied by actual coins and dice, hence the statement here made is only approximately true.

[2] These data are given in *An Introduction to the Theory of Statistics*, by G. Udny Yule (8th ed.), p. 258.

B. *Sampling Experiment.*—If we were to draw a series of n chips with replacement from a bowl containing a large number of similar chips each marked with a given number, common experience leads us to believe that the observed relative frequency of the occurrence of a given number would approach as a statistical limit the relative frequency of this number in the bowl as the number of trials increased indefinitely. It follows that, if we were to draw a series of n chips with replacement and then a series of say $2n$ chips, the observed frequency distribution of numbers in the sample of $2n$ chips should approach closer to the actual frequency distribution of numbers in the bowl than should the observed frequency distribution of say only n chips; or, in general, the larger the number in the sample, the closer, in the statistical sense, should be the approach of the observed frequency distribution of the sample to the true distribution in the bowl. The results of the following experiment give evidence that such a prediction, made upon the assumption of the existence of the law of large numbers, appears to be justified.

Successive samples of 5, 10, 20, 100, and 1,000 chips were drawn with replacement from a bowl in which the frequency distribution of the numbers on the chips in the bowl was that indicated in the upper left-hand corner of Fig. 42. The observed relative frequency distributions of numbers for the samples of different size are also shown in this figure. We witness the smoothing out of the distribution with increase in the size of sample as is predicted upon the assumption of the law of large numbers.

C. *Distribution of Number of Alpha Particles.*—In 1910, Rutherford and Geiger [1] observed the distribution of frequencies with which 0, 1, 2, . . . , n alpha particles struck a screen of constant dimensions in successive equal intervals of time. The objective probability of a particle striking the screen as estimated from this experiment is 0.046; and, assuming that this can be used as a mathematical probability in a point

[1] "The Probability Variations in the Distribution of α Particles," *Philosophical Magazine*, Series 6, Vol. XX, 1910, p. 698.

binomial $(q+p)^n$ where $q + p = 1$, we get the smooth frequency distribution shown in Fig. 43. The agreement between the observed relative frequencies and those calculated from the point binomial is further justification for our belief in the law of large numbers.

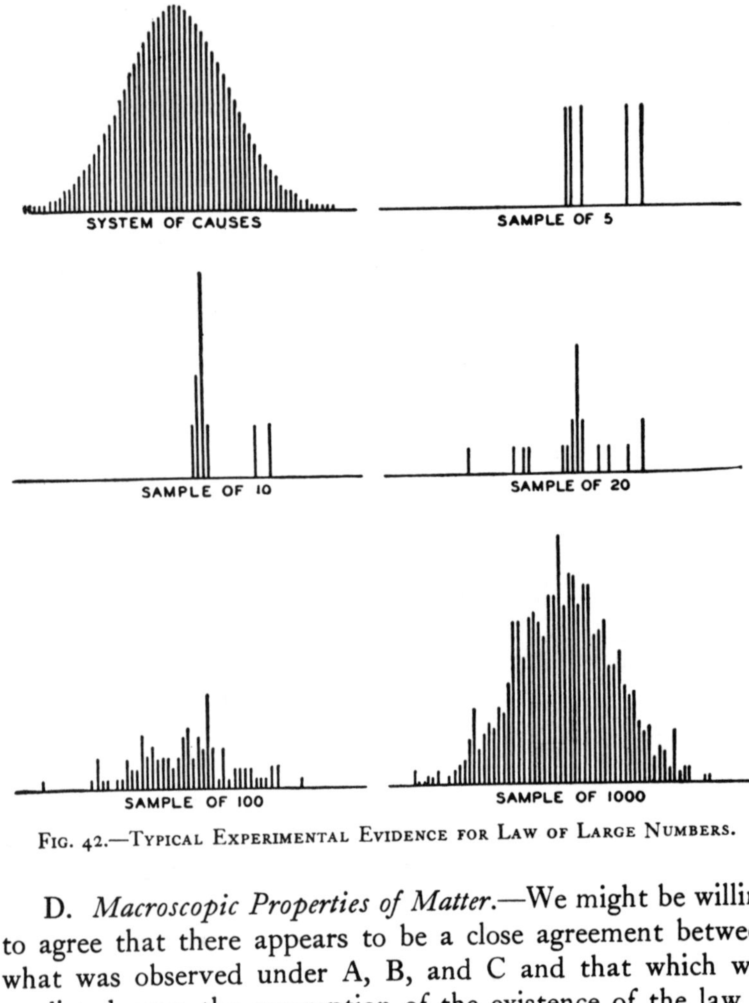

Fig. 42.—Typical Experimental Evidence for Law of Large Numbers.

D. *Macroscopic Properties of Matter.*—We might be willing to agree that there appears to be a close agreement between what was observed under A, B, and C and that which was predicted upon the assumption of the existence of the law of large numbers, and yet we might not appreciate the full extent to which this law is basic to our modern conceptions of physical and chemical laws. Perhaps our best justification for belief in this law comes from study of the macroscopic properties of matter expressed in terms of its microscopic properties.

For example, we believe that a gas is made up of a large number of molecules dancing about in a way characterized

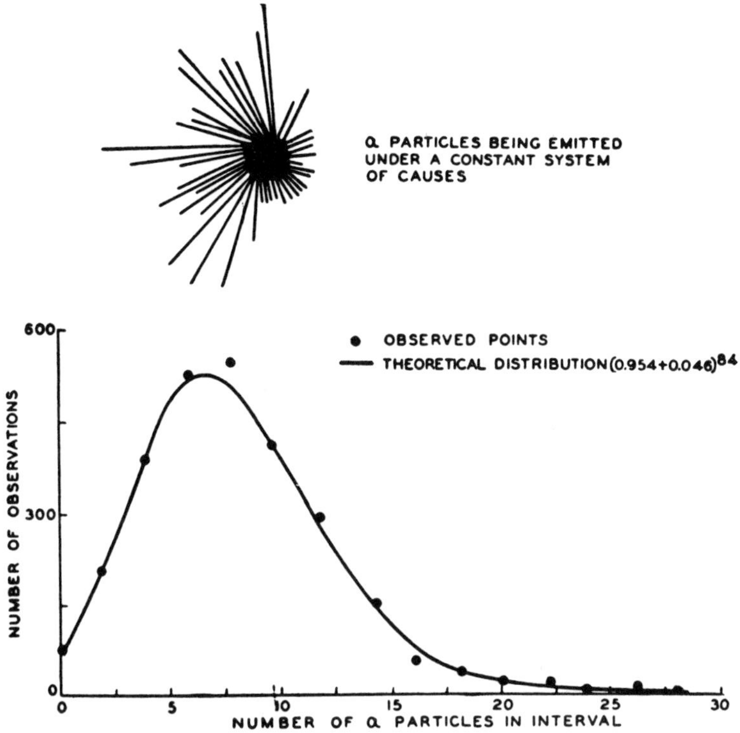

Fig. 43.—Frequency Distribution of Alpha Particles.

by the Brownian motion previously considered. For a single molecule the properties of greatest importance are perhaps those of position, velocity, and mass. In most practical applications, however, we do not interest ourselves so much in these as we do in the properties of a group of molecules, such as pressure, viscosity, temperature, and entropy. Now, it is shown in elementary texts on kinetic theory that these four properties are statistical in nature and result from a state in which the law of large numbers applies with great precision.

For example, it is shown in discussions of kinetic theory that the pressure p of a gas containing ν molecules, each of mass m, is given in terms of the root mean square velocity $\sqrt{\overline{v^2}}$ by the expression

$$p = \tfrac{1}{2}m\nu\overline{v^2}. \tag{48}$$

Thus we see that the pressure of a gas is a statistical average dependent upon the law of large numbers for its constancy and yet under constant temperature conditions we know that the pressure remains constant within the precision of our measurements.

In a similar way, we find the law of large numbers playing an important rôle in the discussion of Brownian motion, the fluctuation in density of a fluid, the distribution of velocities of electrons emitted from a hot filament, the distribution of thermal-radiation among its different frequencies, rates of diffusion and evaporation, rates of thermal and electrical conduction, rate of momentum transfer, rates of thermal and photo-chemical reactions, and so on indefinitely.

Upon the basis of results such as indicated under A, B, C, and D, we make the following assumption:

There exist in nature systems of chance causes which operate in a way such that the effects of these causes can be predicted after the manner just indicated, by making use of customary probability theory in which objective probabilities in the limiting statistical sense are substituted for the mathematical probabilities.

Stated in another way, we assume that there are discoverable constant systems of chance causes which produce effects in a way that may be predicted.

6. *Controlled or Constant System of Chance Causes*

The unknown causes producing an event in accordance with the law of large numbers will be called a *constant system of chance causes* because we assume that the objective probability that such a cause system will produce a given event is independent of time.

In other words, a cause system is constant if the phenomenon produced thereby satisfies the conditions characterized by either (44) or (45).

7. *Meaning of Cause* [1]

As human beings, we want a cause for everything but nothing is more elusive than this thing we call a cause. Every cause has its cause and so on *ad infinitum.* We never get quite to the *infinitum.* In this sense there must always exist a certain amount of topsy-turviness about the world as we perceive it. All that we can do is to find certain practical rules or relationships among the things which we observe. In doing this, we introduce a lot of terms which we cannot explain in the fundamental sense, but which we use to great advantage as, for example, mass, energy, electron, and so on. Under these conditions we go ahead undaunted and introduce theories as to how these things are related, even though we do not know what these things are that we talk about.

As an example, we have theories of light, but we do not know what light is. In some ways it acts like a wave, in others like a corpuscle. From our viewpoint, the justification of the use of either the wave theory or the corpuscular theory of light is that it helps one to attain the desired end. So, in the simple theory of control, we talk about causes even though we do not know what a cause really is any more than we know what light or electricity is. Nevertheless, when we apply control theory, as we do in this book, it is just as easy to get a "feeling" for what we mean by cause in a specific case as it is to get a feeling for what we mean by light when we talk about it.

8. *Variable System of Chance Causes*

All systems of chance causes are not constant as two simple examples will serve to show. Fig. 44 shows the fluc-

[1] An interesting discussion of *cause* and *effect* will be found in W. E. Johnson's *Logic*, Vol. III, treating of the logical foundations of science, and published by the Cambridge University Press, 1924.

tuations [1] in general business conditions over the period from 1919 to 1928. Similar curves could be given for the fluctuations in market prices of individual commodities or stocks. It is well recognized that the causes of such fluctuations are, for the most part, unknown. The general belief is, however, that variations of this character show distinct trends and possibly cyclic movements—the existence of either rules out the constancy of the cause system.

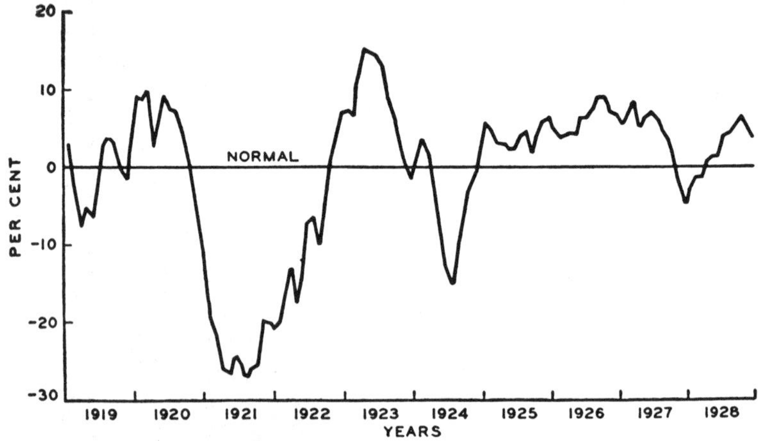

FIG. 44.—GENERAL BUSINESS COMPARED WITH NORMAL.

Fig. 45 shows the growth in the number of Bell-owned telephones in the United States from 1876 to 1928. Similar curves of growth could be given for sales of almost all commodities, such as radio sets, electric washing machines, perfumes, automobiles, and so on indefinitely. Always in such curves there are certain irregularities introduced by chance causes. In fact, the causes of such growth in a particular case are usually unknown, although they certainly do not exhibit the characteristics of a constant system.

[1] Weber, P. J., "An Index of General Business Activity," *Bell Telephone Quarterly*, April, 1929, pp. 124–131.

9. *Statistical Laws*

Constant systems of chance causes give rise to frequency distributions, often called statistical laws.[1] One such is the law of mortality, and another is the law of distribution of dis-

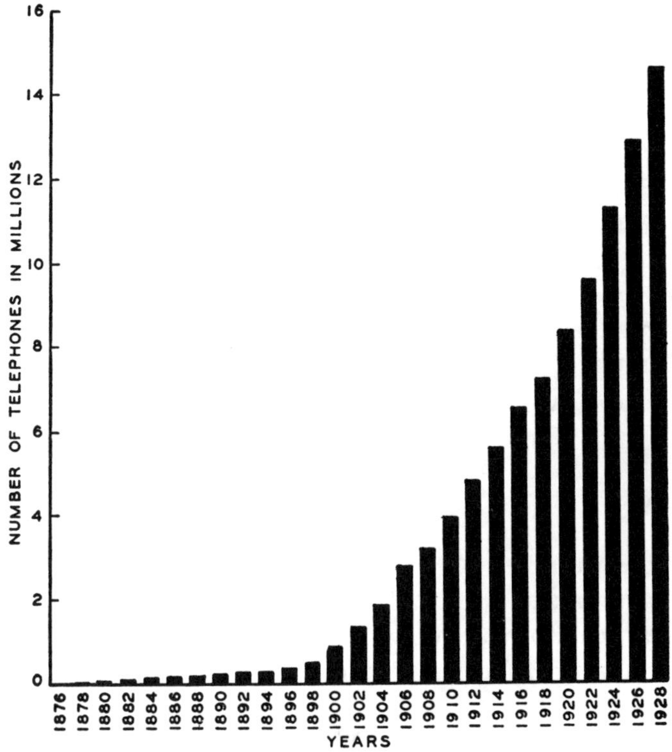

FIG. 45.—NUMBER OF TELEPHONES IN THE BELL SYSTEM.

placements of a particle under Brownian motion, both of which were mentioned in Part I.

Another well-known example is Maxwell's law of distribution of molecular velocities,

$$dy = Ae^{-\frac{cv^2}{2}} dv_x\, dv_y\, dv_z, \tag{49}$$

[1] It will be noted that a frequency distribution as here used is in the sense of an objective *law* of distribution whereas, in Part II, it was simply introduced as a function such that its integral over a given range is a fair approximation to the observed number of observations falling within that range.

where dy is the probability of a molecule having a velocity v with components lying within the respective ranges v_x to $v_x + dv_x$, v_y to $v_y + dv_y$, and v_z to $v_z + dv_z$; and where A and c are constants for a particular kind of molecule in a given state. We may transform this law into one which gives us the probability dy that a molecule will have a speed between v and $v + dv$. By so doing we get

$$dy = Be^{-\frac{cv^2}{2}}v^2dv, \tag{50}$$

where B is a constant different from A. The constants A, B, and c in these equations can be determined experimentally for a gas under given conditions and these laws may then be used to predict either the number of molecules having an x, y, or z component within given limits or a speed v within a given range.

Equation (50) may be stated in terms of the root mean square speed $\sqrt{\overline{v^2}}$ in the following way

$$dy = 4\pi\left(\frac{3}{2\pi\overline{v^2}}\right)^{3/2} e^{-\frac{3v^2}{2\overline{v^2}}}v^2dv. \tag{50-a}$$

Using the value 461.2 meters per second at zero degrees centigrade determined from (48) for the root mean square speed of an oxygen molecule, we get the distribution of speeds of one thousand oxygen molecules given [1] in Table 21.

TABLE 21.—DISTRIBUTION OF SPEEDS

Meters per Second	Number of Molecules	Meters per Second	Number of Molecules
0–100	13– 14	400–500	202–203
100–200	81– 82	500–600	151–152
200–300	166–167	600–700	91– 92
300–400	214–215	700	76– 77

Fig. 46 shows schematically the shape of this distribution

[1] Data taken from Meyer's *Kinetic Theory of Gases.*

curve and the relationship between the mean speed $\bar{v}$, root mean square speed $\sqrt{\overline{v^2}}$, and modal speed $\check{v}$.

$$\text{The mean speed } \bar{v} = 424.9 \text{ meters per second}$$

$$\text{Root mean square speed } \sqrt{\overline{v^2}} = 461.2 \text{ meters per second}$$

$$\text{Most probable speed } \check{v} = 376.6 \text{ meters per second}$$

Obviously, if the quality of a product is controlled in the sense that the fluctuations therein obey the law of large numbers and hence some statistical distribution law, we must know

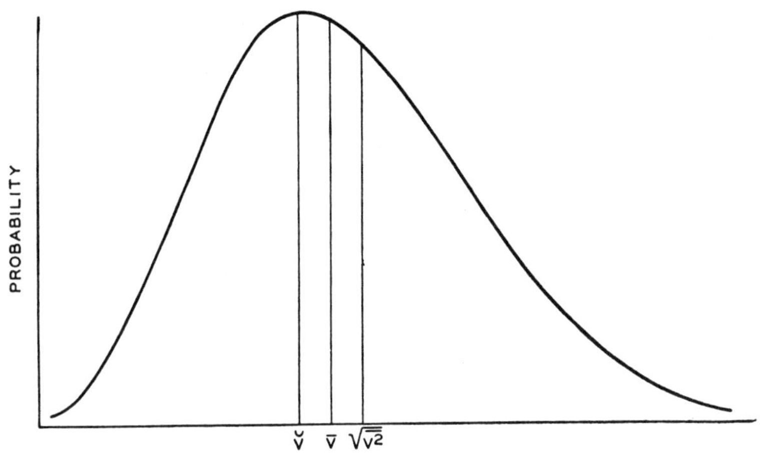

FIG. 46.—A STATISTICAL LAW—ONE FORM OF MAXWELL'S LAW FOR OXYGEN MOLECULES.

this law in order to predict how many pieces of product will have qualities lying within given limits. To be of use in this as in any other problem, statistical theory must provide us with statistical distribution laws.

It is but natural, therefore, that attempts should have been made to discover and tabulate all such laws. As early as 1756 a law of error was proposed, and in quite rapid succession other simple laws of error were suggested. Some of these, including the normal law of Laplace and Gauss, are shown in the first five rows of the table in Fig. 47.

DATE	NAMES	GENERAL CHARACTERIZATION OF CHANCE	PARTICULAR CHARACTERIZATION OF CHANCE	NATURE OF DISTRIBUTIONS OF CHANCE EFFECTS	EXPRESSION OF THE LAW OF CHANCE		REFERENCES
					Analytical Form	Graphical Form	
1756 1773	SIMPSON AND LAGRANGE	FLUCTUATIONS AROUND THE ARITHMETIC MEAN.	1. POSITIVE AND NEGATIVE DEVIATIONS CAUSED BY CHANCE AND EQUALLY LIKELY. 2. THE MEAN VALUE IS NEARER TO THE TRUTH THAN ANY OTHER SINGLE OBSERVATION.	SYMMETRY IN DISTRIBUTION. LIMITED RANGE OF VARIATION.	$y = \pm mx + c$	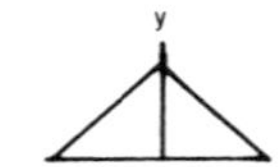	E. WHITTAKER A. ROBINSON J. KEYNES I. TODHUNTER
1774	LAPLACE	DITTO	DITTO	SYMMETRY IN DISTRIBUTION. UNLIMITED RANGE OF VARIATION.	$y = \frac{m}{2} e^{-mx}$	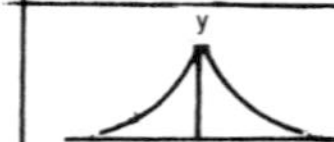	H.L. RIETZ I. TODHUNTER
1778	DANIEL BERNOULL	DITTO	DITTO	SYMMETRY IN DISTRIBUTION. LIMITED RANGE OF VARIATION.	$y = \sqrt{r^2 - x^2}$	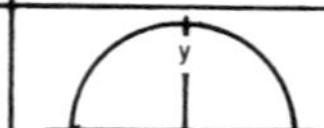	ARNE FISHER I. TODHUNTER
1809	GAUSS	DITTO	1. PROBABILITY OF A DEVIATION FROM THE AVERAGE IS A FUNCTION ONLY OF THE MAGNITUDE OF DEVIATION. 2. THE MEAN VALUE IS MOST PROBABLE VALUE 3. DEVIATIONS ARE SMALL (THEIR CUBES ARE NEGLIGEABLE). 4. THE NUMBER OF OBSERVATIONS IS LARGE.	1. SYMMETRY IN DISTRIBUTION. 2. UNLIMITED RANGE IN VARIATION. 3. OBSERVED CHANCE EFFECTS DISTRIBUTIONS IN ALL EXPERIMENTAL DATA ARE GOVERNED BY THE LAW OF CHANCE EXPRESSED IN GAUSSIAN NORMAL LAW OF ERRORS.	$y = \frac{h}{\sqrt{\pi}} e^{-h^2 x^2}$	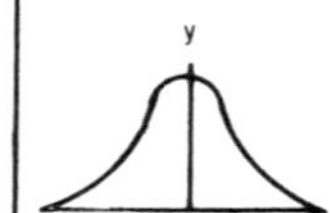	E. WHITTAKER A. ROBINSON J. BERTRAND ARNE FISHER
1812	LAPLACE	DITTO AND: CHANCE DISTRIBUTIONS OF ELEMENTS OBSERVABLE IN NATURE AND IDENTICAL WITH APRIORI DISTRIBUTIONS OF SUCCESSES IN REPEATED CONSTRUED SCHEMES (URNS, COINS, DICE ETC.)	1. THE NUMBER OF ELEMENTS CONSTITUTING THE CHANCE EFFECT IS LARGE. 2. VARIATIONS IN CONSTITUENTS ARE INDEPENDENT AND OBEY THE SAME LAWS OF FREQUENCY. 3. CHANCE EFFECTS ARE AGGREGATED BY SIMPLE SUMMATION.	1. SYMMETRY IN DISTRIBUTION. 2. UNLIMITED RANGE IN VARIATION. 3. OBSERVED CHANCE EFFECTS DISTRIBUTIONS REPRESENT AN APPROXIMATION TO THE LAW OF CHANCE.	$y = \frac{1}{\sqrt{2\pi p_2}} e^{-\frac{x^2}{2p_2}}$	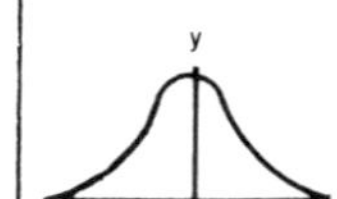	E. WHITTAKER A. ROBINSON F. EDGEWORTH J. BERTRAND I. TODHUNTER
1837 1832- 1849	POISSON AND QUETELET	CHANCE EFFECTS INFLUENCE ALL VARIATIONS AND CONSTANCIES IN THE UNIVERSE.	1. STABILITY OF CHANCE EFFECTS IS MANIFESTED ONLY THOUGH A LARGE NUMBER OF OBSERVATIONS. 2. SERIES OF OBSERVATIONS ARE INDEPENDENT. 3. AN ARITHMETIC MEAN IS AN ESTIMATE OF TRUE VALUE. 4. EMPIRICAL FREQUENCY IS AN ESTIMATE OF APRIORI PROBABILITY. 5. THE LARGER IS A NUMBER OF OBSERVATIONS THE BETTER ARE THESE ESTIMATES.	1. AN APPARENT CASUAL IRREGULARITY IN OBSERVED EVENTS IS GOVERNED BY THE UNIVERSAL LAW OF LARGE NUMBERS. 2. SYMMETRICAL AS WELL AS ASSYMETRICAL DISTRIBUTIONS OF FINAL EFFECTS OF CHANCE.	$y = \frac{1}{\sqrt{2\pi p_2}} e^{-\frac{x^2}{2p_2}} = \varphi(x)$ $y = \frac{e^{-m} m^x}{x!} = \psi(x)$	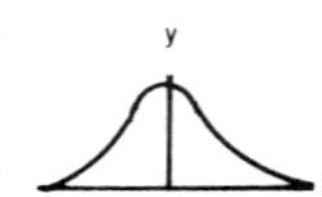	ARNE FISHER J. KEYNES A. TSCHUPROW E. SLUTSKY

1879	GRAM	THE LAWS OF CHANCE EFFECTS DISTRIBUTIONS MAY BE IDENTIFIED WITH CONTINUOUS FUNCTIONS REPRESENTABLE BY SERIES OF TERMS GENERATED FROM CERTAIN ASSUMED PRIMARY FUNCTIONS (GENERATING FUNCTIONS)	GENERATING FUNCTION IS NORMAL LAPLACIAN FUNCTION.	1. SYMMETRICAL 2. ASSYMETRICAL — DISTRIBUTIONS	$y = a_0\varphi^0(x) + a_1\varphi^1(x) + a_2\varphi^2(x) + \dots$ $\varphi^0 = \frac{1}{\sigma\sqrt{2\pi}} e^{-\frac{(x-M)^2}{2\sigma^2}}, \varphi^n = \frac{d^n}{dx^n}[\varphi^0]$	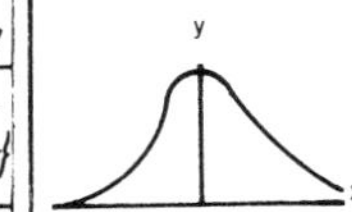	ARNE FISHER
1889	THIELE		DITTO		$y = \frac{S_0}{\sqrt{2\pi\lambda_2}} e^{-\frac{(x-\lambda_1)^2}{2\lambda_2}} \left\{1 + \frac{\lambda_3}{6\lambda_2^3}\left[(x-\lambda_1)^3 - 3\lambda_2(x-\lambda_1)\right] + \frac{\lambda_4}{24\lambda_2^4}\left[(x-\lambda_1)^4 - 6\lambda_2(x-\lambda_1)^2 + 3\lambda_2^2\right] + \dots\right\}$		THIELE ARNE FISHER
1905	CHARLIER		GENERATING FUNCTIONS ARE NORMAL LAPLACIAN FUNCTION OR POISSON'S EXPONENTIAL.	1. LIMITED 2. UNLIMITED — RANGES OF VARIATIONS	$y = c_0\psi(x) + c_1\Delta^1\psi(x) + c_2\Delta^2\psi(x) + \dots$ $\Delta\psi(x) = \psi(x) - \psi(x-1)$ $\Delta^2\psi(x) = \Delta\psi(x) - \Delta\psi(x-1)$		CHARLIER, ARNE FISHER
1895 1916	K. PEARSON	"CHANCE EFFECTS ARE REPRESENTABLE BY FREQUENCY FUNCTIONS AND DO NOT FOLLOW IN THEIR MODE OF OPERATIONS THE ARTIFICIAL SCHEMES ASSOCIATED WITH EXPERIMENTS WITH COINS, DICE, OR URNS".	1. POSITIVE AND NEGATIVE CHANCE EFFECTS ARE NOT EQUALLY PROBABLE. 2. THE NUMBER OF ELEMENTARY CAUSE GROUPS IS NOT INFINITE. 3. ELEMENTARY CAUSE GROUPS DO NOT CONTRIBUTE INDEPENDENT ELEMENTS BUT CORRELATED ONES.	1. ASSYMETRY IN DISTRIBUTION. 2. FINITE RANGE OF VARIATION. 3. NON EXISTANCE OF ONE UNIVERSAL LAW OF CHANCE.	$\frac{1}{y}\frac{dy}{dx} = \frac{a_0 + x}{c_0 + c_1x + c_2x^2 + \dots}$	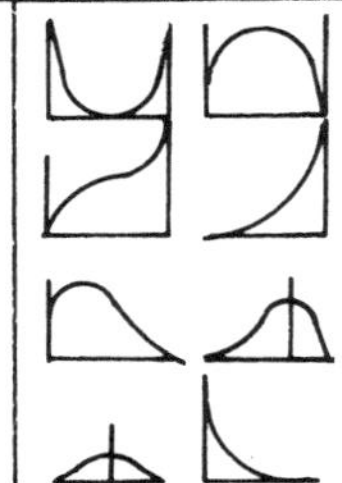	K. PEARSON
1904- 1905	EDGEWORTH	CHANCE EFFECTS IN A MAGNITUDE ARE PRODUCED IN FORM OF FREQUENCY WITH WHICH DIFFERENT VALUES ARE ASSUMED BY THIS MAGNITUDE DEPENDING ON A NUMBER OF VARYING ELEMENTS.	1. THE LARGER IS A NUMBER OF ELEMENTS THE MORE FREELY THEIR FREQUENCY LAWS MAY DIFFER FROM NORMAL LAW. 2. AGGREGATION OF ELEMENTS IS REPRESENTABLE BY A LINEAR FUNCTION OF THEIR VALUES. 3. VARIATIONS IN VALUES OF ELEMENTS MAY BE INDEPENDENT AS WELL AS CORRELATED.	DITTO	$y = e^{-k_1\frac{1}{3!}\left(\frac{d}{dx}\right)^3 + k_2\frac{1}{4!}\left(\frac{d}{dx}\right)^4 - \dots (-1)^n k_n\left(\frac{d}{dx}\right)^{n+2}} \frac{1}{\sqrt{2\pi k}} e^{-\frac{x^2}{2k}}$	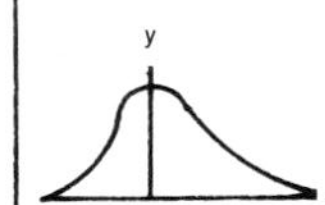	EDGEWORTH
1903- 1916	J. KAPTEYN	CHANCE CAUSES MUST BE CONSIDERED IN CONNECTION WITH THE MAGNITUDE OF ELEMENT AFFECTED BY CAUSES.	THE NUMBER OF CHANCE CAUSES IS FINITE. CHANCE CAUSES ARE NOT INDEPENDENT.	1. FREQUENCY CURVE REPRESENTS EVIDENCE AS TO THE CHARACTER OF CAUSES WORKING IN A GIVEN CASE. 2. IN ASSYMETRICAL FREQUENCY DISTRIBUTION ALWAYS IS GENERATED BY CERTAIN SYMMETRICAL FUNCTION.	$y = \frac{F'(x)}{\varepsilon\sqrt{2\pi}} e^{-\frac{1}{2\varepsilon^2}\left[F(x) - F(x_0) - M\right]^2}$	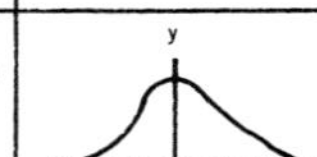	J. KAPTEYN
1910- 1916	TSCHUPROW	CHANCE EFFECTS ARE TREATED AS CHANCE VARIABLES DETERMINED BY THEIR LAWS OF DISTRIBUTIONS AND LAWS OF STOCHASTIC CONSTRAINTS.	A FUNCTION OF CHANCE EMPIRICAL DATA APPROACHES (STOCHASTICALLY) THE LIMIT SET BY A CORRESPONDING FUNCTION OF A APRIOR CHARACTERISTICS OF A GIVEN SET OF DATA.	STATISTICAL METHOD GIVES A BEST ESTIMATE OF THE COMPLEX ULTIMATE EFFECTS OF CHANCE CAUSES IN FORM OF APRIORI VALUES OF PARAMETERS DETERMINED FROM EMPIRICAL RESULTS.	$y = F(x, \lambda_1', \lambda_2', \dots \lambda_m')$		TSCHUPROW

FIG. 47—HOW CHANCE EFFECTS HAVE BEEN PORTRAYED.

An attempt was made to apply the normal law to many observed distributions, but it was soon found to be unsatisfactory in a majority of problems. This situation gave rise to an active search for more general laws, some of which are indicated in the last six rows of the table in Fig. 47.

Two of these general laws should be briefly considered here as we shall have occasion to refer to them in one way or another. One is that of Pearson represented by the differential equation

$$-\frac{1}{y}\frac{dy}{dx}=\frac{x+\dfrac{\sigma\sqrt{\beta_1}(\beta_2+3)}{10\beta_2-12\beta_1-18}}{\dfrac{\sigma^2(4\beta_2-3\beta_1)}{10\beta_2-12\beta_1-18}+\dfrac{\sigma\sqrt{\beta_1}(\beta_2+3)}{10\beta_2-12\beta_1-18}x+\dfrac{2\beta_2-3\beta_1-6}{10\beta_2-12\beta_1-18}x^2}, \quad (51)$$

where y is the relative frequency function of the deviation x from the arithmetic mean, β_1 is the square of the skewness k, σ is the standard deviation, and β_2 is the measure of flatness. This general law obviously gives rise to several special laws depending upon the functional form of the solution of (51). In turn the form of the law depends upon the values of β_1 and β_2, as illustrated in Fig. 48. The upper part of this figure shows some of Pearson's laws fitted to observed data, the corresponding values of β_1 and β_2 being given at the bottom of the figure.

It is shown in elementary treatises on frequency curves that some of the laws [solutions of (51)] are valid for whole areas in the $\beta_1\beta_2$ plane; whereas others are valid only for points lying on a certain curve; still others only for one point as is the normal law which corresponds to the point $\beta_1 = 0$, $\beta_2 = 3$, as is readily seen by substitution of these values in (51). Pearson and his followers claim that these laws have been found to cover practically all cases coming to their attention.

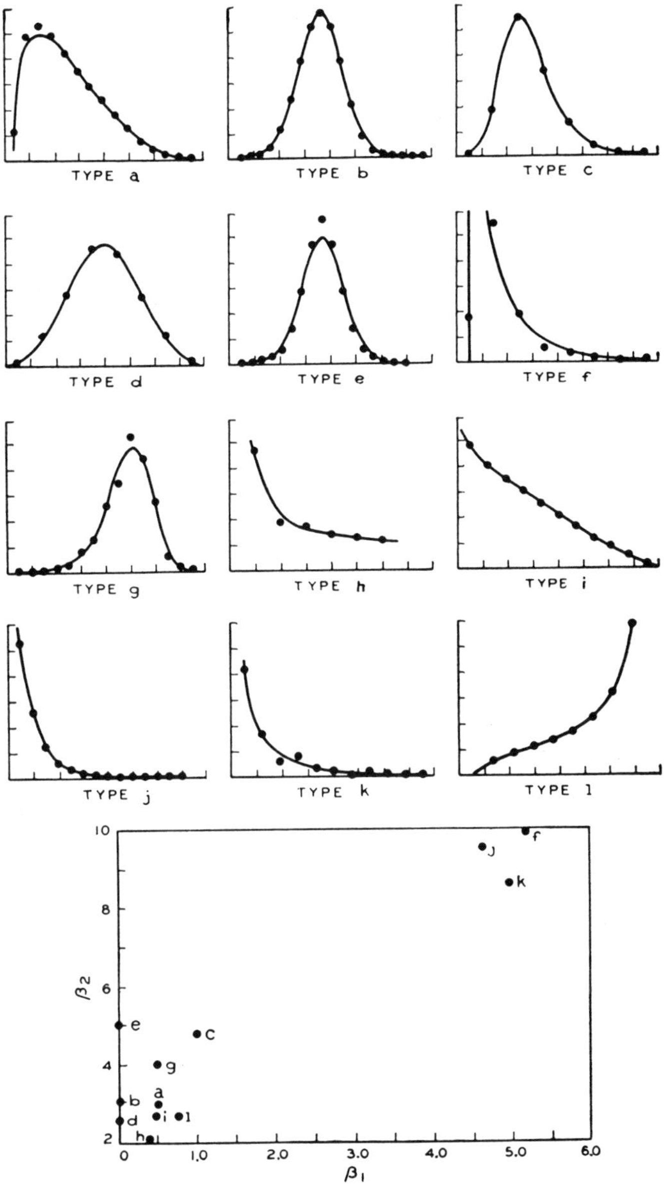

FIG. 48.—RELATIONSHIP BETWEEN PEARSON TYPES AND β_1 AND β_2.

The other important general law is the Gram-Charlier series

$$f(z) = \frac{1}{\sigma}\phi_0(z)\left[1 - \frac{k}{3!}(3z - z^3) + \frac{1}{4!}(\beta_2 - 3)(3 - 6z^2 + z^4)\right.$$

$$+ \frac{1}{5!}\left(10k - \frac{\mu_5}{\sigma^5}\right)(-15z + 10z^3 - z^5)$$

$$\left. + \frac{1}{6!}\left(30 - 15\frac{\mu_4}{\sigma^4} + \frac{\mu_6}{\sigma^6}\right)(-15 + 45z^2 - 15z^4 + z^6) + \ldots\right], \quad (52)$$

where $\phi_0(z) = \frac{1}{\sqrt{2\pi}}e^{-\frac{z^2}{2}}$, and $z = \frac{x}{\sigma}$. By taking enough terms and using the proper parameters, this law may be made to fit almost any frequency distribution.

10. *Exact and Statistical Laws—A Comparison*

Perhaps the most important characteristic difference between an exact and a statistical law is that the former states something that is true for a single thing or event, whereas the latter states something that is true on the average or in the long run. The exact law applies to the individual thing, whereas the statistical law applies to a group of the same kind of things.

In general we like to think that exact laws apply under conditions where the physical phenomena are quite well understood, as is true for the current through a simple circuit discussed at the beginning of this chapter. In a similar way, we think of statistical laws as applying where the details of the phenomena are not so thoroughly understood. Between these two apparent extremes lies that great body of facts or data which have not been explained in terms of either of the two kinds of laws just considered; yet even here we find rules or laws which make possible a kind of prediction. Two illustrations will serve to clarify this statement.

We have already called attention to the problem of the economists in forecasting business conditions. There are companies devoting all their time to forecasting. In general, they claim to have discovered a way of breaking down a time series, such as that shown in Fig. 44, into four parts:

(*a*) Trends, (*c*) Seasonals,
(*b*) Cycles, (*d*) Erratic Fluctuations.

An outline of the technique involved in such a study is given in most of the elementary books on business statistics. A rule for forecasting developed in this way is sometimes called a law although most people would, to say the least, probably insist on calling it an empirical law. To refer to it as an empirical law, however, is somewhat misleading, because any law, insofar as it is derived from experience, is empirical. This point we shall have occasion to emphasize again and again as we proceed. Perhaps the best that we can say is that the degree of empiricism is greater in this case than it is in the case of the so-called exact or statistical laws already considered.

Such rules as are used in business forecasting have to do in general with data, the causal explanation or interpretation of which is not thoroughly understood. In other words, here, as in the case of statistical laws, the phenomena themselves are to a large extent attributable to chance or unknown causes. It should be noted, however, that here probability theory does not apply directly because the conditions for the law of large numbers do not hold. This point has been emphasized by Persons.[1] In other words, probability theory does not apply simply because a phenomenon is attributable to chance causes.

Let us next consider the phenomenon of growth which comes nearer to being reduced to an exact law than does that of customary economic time series. The literature on this subject is very extensive. Fig. 49 shows the forecast of the population growth of the United States.[2] It is interesting indeed to see

[1] Persons, Foster, and Hettinger, *The Problem of Business Forecasting*, Houghton Mifflin & Co., New York, 1924.

[2] Raymond Pearl, *The Biology of Population Growth*, Alfred Knopf, New York, 1925. This book includes an appendix with 165 references.

how closely the observed points fall on this logistic curve, the equation for which is

$$y = \frac{197.27}{1 + 67.32e^{-0.0313x}}. \tag{53}$$

By means of this law, Pearl predicts the future course of population growth to the year 2100, at which time the population is to be approximately 197,000,000.

The general law of growth

$$y = d + \frac{k}{1 + e^{a_1x + a_2x^2 + a_3x^3 + \dots + a_nx^n}} \tag{54}$$

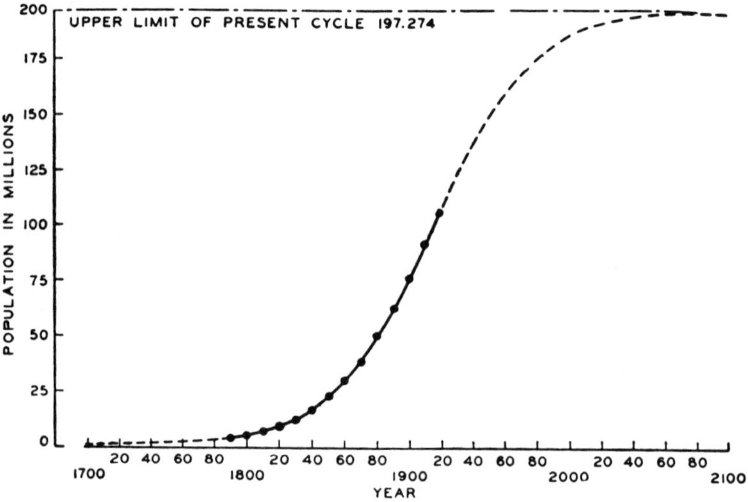

FIG. 49.—FORECAST OF POPULATION GROWTH OF THE UNITED STATES.

is shown by Pearl to be applicable to a large number of different kinds of populations, and for this reason it may be claimed that the law is less empirical than the laws used in forecasting business conditions. It would perhaps be generally agreed, however, that this law of growth is more empirical than Newton's laws of motion.

If we were to observe the growths in population for a large number of pairs of fruit flies, we could expect upon the basis of the work of Pearl and others, that these growths would vary about the law of growth. It seems reasonable to believe that we would find a statistical distribution at any point along the line as indicated in Fig. 50. Such a phenomenon is of interest because it suggests the possibility of the use of probability theory in predicting the deviation from this line—something that economists in general feel cannot be done in connection with economic forecasts.

The causal basis for this frequency distribution might be set up after the manner in which hereditary influences are explained by Whittaker and Robinson.[1] They assume that

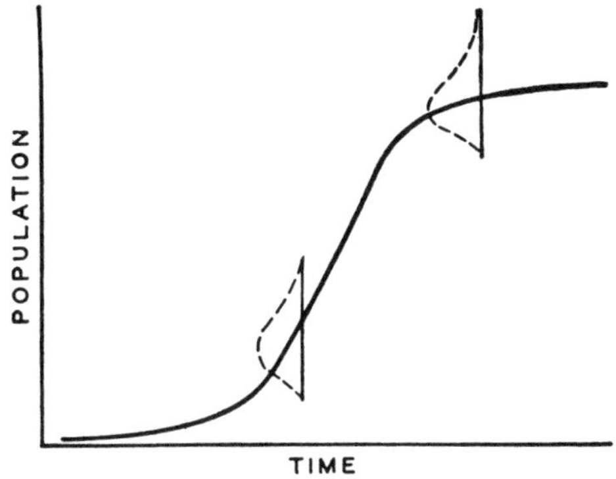

Fig. 50.—Statistical Distribution at Any Point in a Law of Growth.

the chest measure of an individual, for instance, is the result of a very great number of chance causes present in the heredity and environment of the individual. This suggests a type of law derivable upon a causal basis similar to that involved in the study of chemical kinetics. The growth curve under these conditions may be thought of as an exact law, and the distribution about this curve at any point may be thought of as a statistical law. In other words, the general law of growth may be a combination of exact and statistical laws. This suggests another viewpoint in respect to the so-called exact law which is worth considering briefly.

As an illustration of an exact law, we have used the dif-

[1] *The Calculus of Observations*, Blackie & Son, Ltd., London, p. 167.

ferential equation relating the current in a circuit to the inductance, capacity, and resistance of that circuit. The current, even though it appears to be continuous, is really a flow of a number of discrete units of charge or electrons. Thus, if we could see what is actually taking place when the current appears constant, we would likely find that the number of electrons per second passing a given point is not constant. The apparent constancy is, as in the case of the pressure of the gas, the result of the law of large numbers. Hence we see that our exact law is, in the last analysis, statistical in the sense that the current is a phenomenon obeying the law of large numbers. It should also be noted that all exact laws are subject to statistical laws of error about which we shall hear more as we proceed.

11. *Summary*

From what has been said in this chapter, it seems reasonable to draw the following conclusions:

A. It is not feasible to make pieces of product identical one with another. Hence a controlled product must be one of variable quality.

B. To be able to say that a product is controlled, we must be able to predict, at least within limits, the future variations in the quality.

C. To be able to make such predictions, it is necessary that we know certain laws.

D. These laws may be exact, empirical, or statistical. Exact laws are generally stated in terms of the differential equations of physics and chemistry. Statistical laws are the frequency distributions arising from the very general law of large numbers. All other laws are empirical. The technique of finding and using exact and statistical laws is better established than that of finding and using what we term empirical laws.

CHAPTER XI

Statistical Control

1. *Conditions for Control*

If there is a causal orderliness in events and phenomena as we postulate, then it follows that, to one with perfect knowledge, everything is predictable and therefore controlled. However, for practical purposes the quality of product is controlled only to the extent that we know the laws that make prediction possible. For one to be able to say that a phenomenon is controlled, it is necessary and sufficient that he know the laws which make prediction possible.

In practice, however, we must start with an observed set of data representing the fluctuations in some phenomenon and try to determine from these whether or not the product is controlled. Such a procedure involves, as do all scientific attempts to discover natural laws, logical induction in that we must employ some such argument as this: Since the observed fluctuations are such as might have occurred provided the phenomenon obeyed such and such laws, then it follows that these laws do control this phenomenon; whereas all that we are rigorously justified in saying is that these laws *may* control this phenomenon. For this reason we perhaps never can say that the behavior of a phenomenon in the past is sufficient to prove that the phenomenon is controlled by a given set of known laws. All that we can ever say is that experience has shown that such behavior appears to be sufficient.

Furthermore it is a significant fact, as we have seen in the previous chapter, that empirical laws do not make possible the prediction of erratic fluctuations upon the basis of probability theory. If product is controlled only in this empirical sense, it follows that we cannot obtain the economic advantages discussed in Part I. For this reason it is desirable to attain the state of statistical control in which the natural law of large numbers makes prediction possible.

2. *Necessary and Sufficient Conditions for Statistical Control*

We shall assume that the necessary and sufficient condition for statistical control is that the causes of an event satisfy the law of large numbers as do those of a constant system of chance causes. If a cause system is not constant, we shall say that an *assignable cause of Type 1* is present. Assignable causes of this type in an economic series are such things as trends, cycles, and seasonals; and in a production process, they are such things as differences in machines and in sources of raw material.

Stated in terms of effects of a cause system, it is necessary that differences in the qualities of a number of pieces of a product *appear* to be consistent with the assumption that they arose from a constant system of chance causes. We say appear because, as is always the case in trying to find a law controlling a phenomenon, we can never be sure that we have discovered the law. Obviously such appearance is not sufficient in the logical sense although it must be in the practical sense.

3. *Necessary and Sufficient Conditions—Continued*

Let us see how the law of large numbers gives a basis for determining from the observed fluctuations in a phenomenon whether or not it is statistically controlled. For this purpose let us consider the practical problem presented in Part I, Chapter II, Paragraph 2.

If this product is statistically controlled, there is an objective probability **p** that a piece of this product will be defective. It follows, as we have seen in our previous discussion of experimental evidence for the existence of the law of large numbers, that the observed fractions defective in successive samples of size n should be clustered or distributed about the value $p = \mathbf{p}$ in accord with the terms of the point binomial $(\mathbf{q} + \mathbf{p})^n$.

Graphically this means that, if we take the observed values of the fraction defective p as ordinates and a series of numbers corresponding to a sequence of samples of size n as abscissae, the observed fractions should be distributed about the ordinate $\mathbf{p}$ after the manner indicated schematically in Fig. 51.

The frequency distribution of values of p observed in an infinite sequence of samples of size n should be some curve

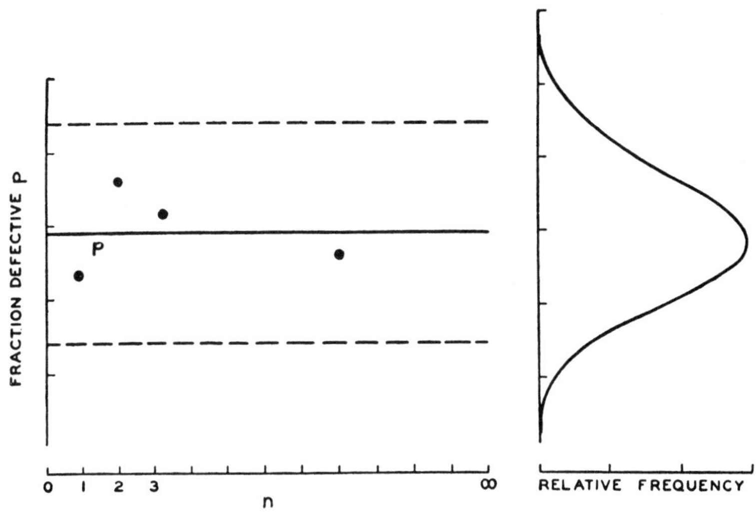

Fig. 51.—Schematic of Objective Condition.

such as that indicated at the right of the figure. This is the picture of what happens in this very simple case deduced from the postulated law of large numbers.

The practical problem involves induction instead of deduction. We start with a sequence of observed values of the fraction defective, and from this we try to determine whether or not the quality as measured by fraction defective is statistically controlled. As indicated in Part I, the method of attack is to establish limits of variability of p, represented by the dotted lines parallel to the line $p = \mathbf{p}$ in Fig. 51, such that,

"consistent with" does not mean stop

when a fraction defective is found outside these limits, looking for an assignable cause is worth while.

How to establish these limits is the question of utmost importance, because it must be satisfactorily answered if statistical control of a production process is to be a practical objective. Experience like that presented in Part I leads us to believe that it is feasible to establish workable rules for setting these limits. These rules will be presented in Part VI. For the present we shall confine our attention to a consideration of some of the fundamental problems which must be considered in the establishment of a scientific basis for setting such limits.

A. Obviously, it is not possible to observe an infinite sequence in order to discover the objective probability **p** even though it exists and is discoverable in this way. In practice, therefore, we must substitute some experimentally determined value for the objective value **p**.

B. Assuming for the sake of argument that in some manner we have found the true objective value **p**, it follows from what has previously been said that, no matter how we set the limits about the line $p = \mathbf{p}$ (so long as they are not outside the limits of the frequency distribution at the right of Fig. 51), some of the observed fractions will fall outside these limits. Therefore, if we look for trouble in the form of assignable causes of Type I every time an observed fraction falls outside these limits, we shall look a certain number of times even though none exists. Hence we must use limits such that through their use we will not waste too much time looking unnecessarily for trouble.

C. The fact that an observed set of values of fraction defective indicates the product to have been controlled up to the present does not prove that we can predict the future course of this phenomenon. We always have to say that this can be done provided the same essential conditions are maintained, and, of course, we never know whether or not they are maintained unless we continue to experiment. If experience were not available to show that a state of statistical equilibrium once reached is usually maintained, we could not attain most of the economic advantages of Part I. Evidence of the type given in Figs. 6 and 11 seems to justify our belief in the constancy of the condition of statistical equilibrium when it is once attained, subject to the limitation that there is no *a priori* reason for believing that an assignable cause has entered the production process.

CHAPTER XII

Maximum Control

1. *Maximum Control Defined*

The object of industrial research is to establish ways and means of making better use of past experience. To do this it is essential that research reveal natural laws. The ideal goal sometimes pictured for research is complete knowledge of all the laws of nature so that one could predict the future course of all phenomena. The belief in the existence of such a goal rests upon the assumption of a causal orderliness of the universe.

If a manufacturer could tell what the quality of each piece of product is going to be, or, more generally, if we could predict exactly the future course of a phenomenon, then we could say that this quality or phenomenon exhibited maximum control. This amounts to assuming that, with perfect knowledge of the universe, it would be possible to obtain exact control of quality of product because the element of chance fluctuation in quality could be removed.

It is important to note, however, that such a goal is neither feasible nor economic. To emphasize this point, let us take a very simple illustration. All of us are perhaps willing to admit that it is not feasible to find the causes which control the course of a single molecule of a gas. It is also reasonable to believe that there is a state reached in the control of quality beyond which it is just as foolish to try to go as it is to try to find the causes of the motion of a given molecule.

Suppose, however, that we did have knowledge which would enable us to set down the differential equations of motion of a system of molecules. Assuming that one could solve these, a little calculation shows that he would have to live something like 10^{12} years to set down his results for only a thimbleful of molecules at room temperature even though he worked 12 hours per day. Obviously the results of such perfect knowledge would not be usable in an economic sense.

In other words, it is believed that there is a limit beyond which it is not economically feasible to go in trying to eliminate chance fluctuations.

Common sense guides us in setting conditions to be satisfied by a cause system in a state of maximum control. If one were ill and were told by his physician that there were likely a very large number of causes of his illness, he would feel more discouraged about his condition than he would if he were told that there was only one cause. This follows because it is customarily found to be difficult to ferret out and assign a single cause of illness when there are several unknown causes. What has just been said is true subject to the limitation that each cause produces practically the same effect as any other. Naturally, if one of the causes is known to produce a predominating effect, a person will feel that there is greater likelihood of his being able to find this cause than if each of the causes produces the same component effect. This kind of experience leads us to postulate that it is not feasible to explain in terms of specific causes those phenomena which are attributable to a very large number of causes such as the throw of a head on a coin, the motion of molecules, the daily fluctuations in the price of a stock, hereditary influences, and so on.

Therefore *maximum control* for our purpose will be defined as the condition reached when the chance fluctuations in a phenomenon are produced by a constant system of a large number of chance causes in which no cause produces a predominating effect.

However, in order that these conditions for maximum control may be of practical use, they must be expressed in terms of the effects of the causes. This is obviously necessary because we cannot find out anything about the causes except through their effects. We shall soon discover that serious difficulties are involved in trying to set up necessary conditions for maximum control in terms of the distribution of effects of a constant cause system.

2. *Characteristics of Maximum Control—Molecular Phenomena*

At first thought one might expect to find that the distribution of displacements of a particle undergoing Brownian motion should be characteristic of maximum control. Since, as previously noted, this distribution is normal and corresponds to the point (0, 3) in the $\beta_1\beta_2$ plane (Fig. 52), one might be led to ask if there is an objective point of maximum control.

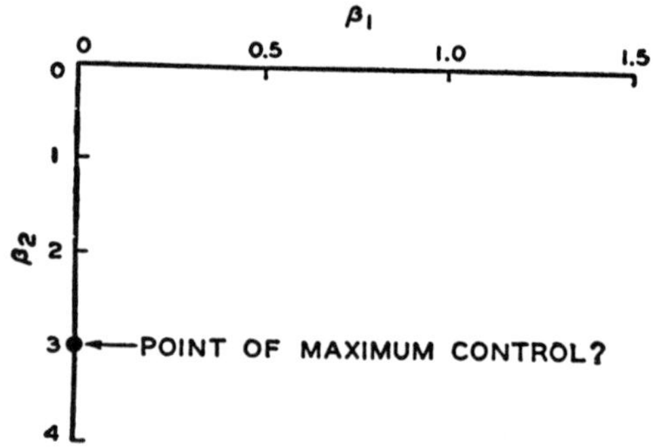

FIG. 52.—IS THERE AN OBJECTIVE POINT OF MAXIMUM CONTROL?

As we have already seen, however, the distribution of molecular velocities is not normal even though this distribution obviously arises under a condition of maximum control to the same extent as does the distribution of displacements. This fact alone is sufficient to show that there is not an objective point of maximum control.

3. *Necessary Conditions for Maximum Control—Simple Cause System*

Let us assume that there are a finite number m of independent causes,

$$C_1, C_2, \ldots, C_i, \ldots, C_m,$$

and that the resultant effect of these causes is the sum of their individual effects.

In one case let us assume that these m causes produce effects

$$x_1, x_2, \ldots, x_i, \ldots, x_m$$

respectively, with probabilities

$$p_1, p_2, \ldots, p_i, \ldots, p_m.$$

In the other case let us assume that the probability of the ith cause ($i = 1, 2, \ldots, m$) producing a contribution x in the interval x to $x + dx$ is

$$f_i(x)\, dx.$$

A little consideration shows that such systems may be said to exhibit maximum control when:

$$\begin{bmatrix} p_i = p_j \\ x_i = x_j \\ m \text{ large,} \end{bmatrix} \quad \text{and} \quad \begin{bmatrix} f_i(x) = f_j(x) \\ m \text{ large.} \end{bmatrix} \tag{55}$$

Obviously the first set of conditions gives rise to a discontinuous distribution, the ordinates of which are the terms of the point binomial $(q + p)^m$ where the effect of each cause is assumed to be unity. As we know, such a distribution is smooth and unimodal. Hence smoothness and unimodality are necessary conditions for maximum control in terms of effects for this simple discontinuous cause system.

It is readily shown for the point binomial that

$$\beta_1 = \frac{(q-p)^2}{pqm} \quad \text{and} \quad \beta_2 = 3 + \frac{1 - 6pq}{pqm}. \tag{56}$$

From these equations we see that no matter what the values of p and q are, the values of β_1 and β_2 approach the normal law values 0 and 3 respectively as m becomes large. This state of affairs is shown graphically in Fig. 53. Hence we see under what conditions the distribution of effects for such a simple cause system approaches normality, characterized by $\beta_1 = 0$ and $\beta_2 = 3$. Of course, the condition that $\beta_1 = 0$ and $\beta_2 = 3$, although necessary for normality, is not sufficient.

To one not accustomed to think of distribution functions

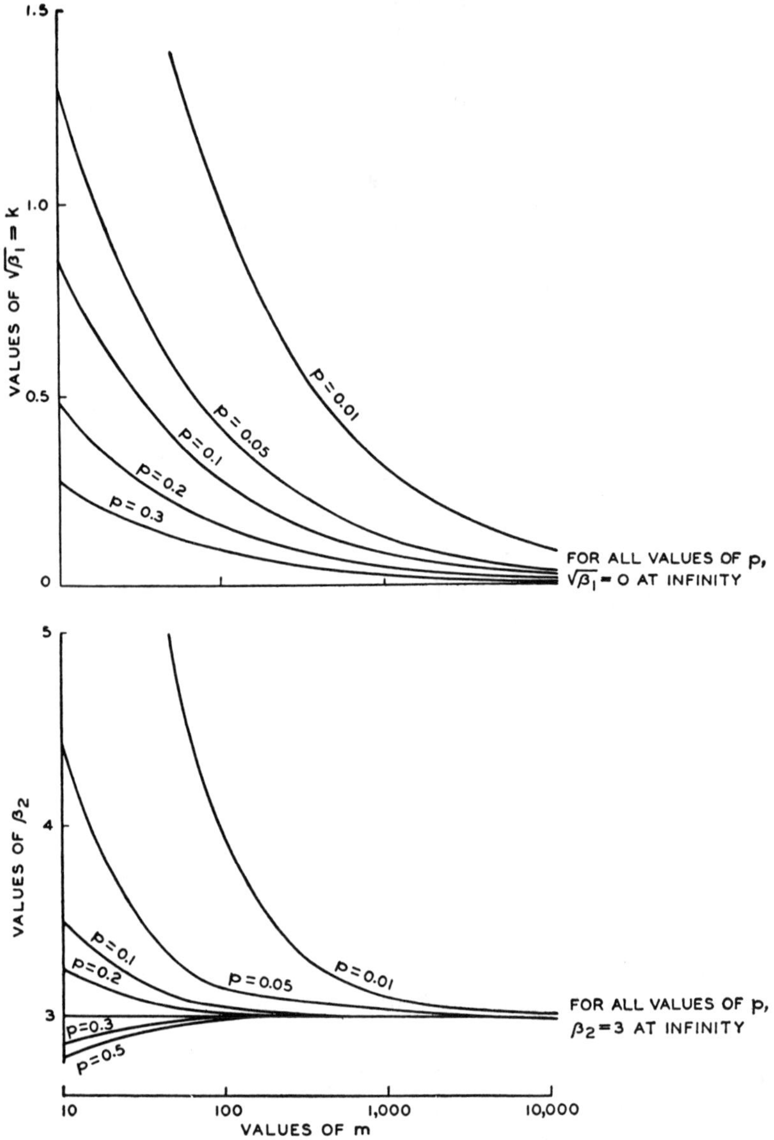

FIG. 53.—CONDITIONS UNDER WHICH DISTRIBUTION OF EFFECTS APPROACHES NORMALITY.

in terms of β_1 and β_2, Fig. 54 is of interest because it gives two binomial distributions fitted by theoretical curves. In the one case $p = q = \frac{1}{2}$ and the number m of causes is 16. In the other case $p = 0.1$, $q = 0.9$, and $m = 100$. This figure illustrates

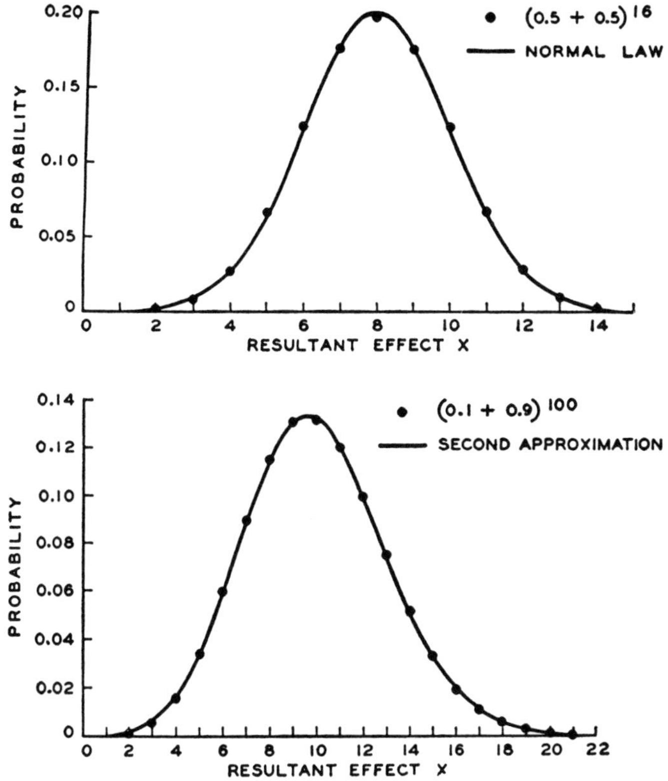

FIG. 54.—APPROACH TO NORMALITY WITH INCREASE IN NUMBER OF CAUSES.

the rapid approach to normality with increase in the number of causes irrespective of the value of p.

For the continuous cause system, it may be shown[1] that

$$\beta_1 = \frac{B_1}{m} \quad \text{and} \quad \beta_2 = \frac{B_2 - 3}{m} + 3, \tag{57}$$

[1] Subject only to limitations not met in practice. See for example, Romanovsky, V., "On the Distribution of an Arithmetic Mean in a Series of Independent Trials," *Bulletin of the Russian Academy of Science*, 1926.

where β_1 and β_2 represent the distribution of the resultant effect of the operation of m continuous causes and B_1 and B_2 represent the cause function $f(x)$. From (57) we see that no matter what the distribution function of a cause is, the distribution function of the resultant effect will approach normality as the number m of causes increases indefinitely.

The rate of approach to normality, however, is much more rapid than we might at first expect, as we shall see in Part IV in our discussion of the distribution function of the arithmetic mean.

4. *Necessary Conditions—Some Criticisms*

That chance causes produce equal component effects is obviously not a necessary condition for maximum control, although the discussion of the previous paragraph is thus limited through (55). Thus, in our previous reference to the difficulty of ferreting out a cause of illness from among many causes, it was not necessary to impose the restriction that the causes should produce equal effects. On the other hand, some restrictions must be placed on the relative magnitudes of the effects as well as upon the number of effects in order that it appear reasonable that one cause may be separated from the others. For example, few of us, strictly speaking, are ever ill from a single cause, and yet we know that causes of illness are findable. It is perhaps enough to insure feasibility of discovery of a cause that the effect of this cause be large compared with the resultant effect of all others. It is not possible, however, to say how large the effect of one cause must be in respect to the resultant effect in order that it be discoverable. Hence we cannot write down explicit requirements to be fulfilled by a cause system in order that it represent the state of maximum control.

However, so long as one cause does not produce an effect greater than the resultant effect of all the others, it seems reasonable to believe that considerable trouble will be experienced in discovering this cause when there are a large number of other causes. With this restriction on the relative magnitudes of component effects, the distribution of resultant effects may be shown to approach normality as the number of causes is increased indefinitely subject to limitations of no practical interest. Perhaps this fact gives credence to a somewhat widespread popular belief that normality is a limiting condition approached whenever the number of causes is large.

Before too much significance is attached to this fact we must recall that, as shown in the second paragraph of this chapter, normality cannot be, rigorously speaking, a necessary condition for maximum control.

From a practical viewpoint we are most concerned with the need for sufficient conditions for maximum control. We want to be able to say that, since the distribution of observed effects of a chance cause system is of such and such nature, therefore the cause system is in the state of maximum control. Neglecting for the present the limitations of all inductive inferences of this type, let us see if approximate normality is a sufficient condition for maximum control.

That this condition is in itself not sufficient can easily be seen by looking at Fig. 55. Here we have two identical normal curves (broken curves) with their averages separated by one and one-half times the standard deviation of either. The result of compounding these two distributions is shown by the black dots. The smooth solid curve is a normal one fitted to the resultant distribution. Suppose now that product comes from two sources, the corresponding qualities being distributed normally as shown by the broken curves. Obviously we could not readily detect the existence of the difference between the two sources by an examination of the resultant curve assuming normality to indicate maximum control. The possibility of such a situation arising in practice, however, is precluded, if we apply the test for maximum control only in those cases where we have first assured ourselves that the data exhibit statistical control.

For these reasons it is believed that *approximate normality of an observed distribution arising under controlled conditions* may be taken as indicating that the cause system is in a state of maximum control. On the other hand, the fact that an observed distribution is not approximately normal is not sufficient evidence that the phenomenon is not in the state of maximum control.

Some may argue that there exists a general law characteristic of the state of maximum control. Suppose then that we make such an assumption. In practice we would always try to fit the observed distribution with this general law; and, having successfully done this, we would argue that the phenomenon exhibited maximum control. Since one can fit almost

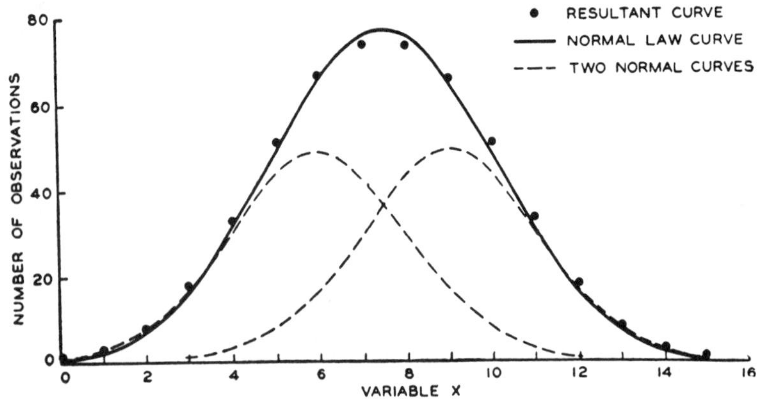

FIG. 55.—EVIDENCE THAT NORMALITY ALONE IS NOT SUFFICIENT CONDITION FOR CONTROL.

any distribution by taking enough terms in a general law such as the Gram-Charlier series, the conclusion that the phenomenon exhibits maximum control is foreordained. For this reason it does not appear that much is to be gained by such a test.

5. *Some Practical Conclusions*

It appears that there is no characteristic of an observed distribution which in itself is sufficient to indicate a state of maximum control. If, however, the effects appear to have arisen under controlled conditions and at the same time exhibit normality, there is good reason to believe that a state of maximum control of the cause system has been reached. The occasions when these two conditions are satisfied, however, are so rare that the test is of little utility. We have also seen that normality of a distribution is not a necessary condition for maximum control.

When a phenomenon has been shown to exhibit control, we have likely gone about as far as we can in detecting the existence of assignable or discoverable causes by standard tests. Our experience shows that after assignable causes of Type I have been found and eliminated, the observed distribution is usually smooth and unimodal. Furthermore, most distributions exhibiting control have been found to be sufficiently near normal to be fitted by the first two terms of the Gram-Charlier series previously referred to as the second approximation (23).

Part IV

Sampling Fluctuations in Quality

A Discussion of the Sampling Fluctuations in the Simple Statistics Used in the Control of Quality

CHAPTER XIII

Sampling Fluctuations

1. *Sample*

One dictionary definition of sample is: "A part of anything presented as evidence of the whole." Thus, the people living in New York City constitute a sample of those living in the United States. The top layer in a barrel of apples is a sample of those in the barrel. The fish taken from a lake are a sample of those in the lake. The instruments inspected from the product of a given day constitute a sample of that day's product. In each of these instances, the whole of the thing sampled is finite in the sense that there is a finite number of people in the United States, apples in a barrel, and so on.

We may, however, think of any one of these samples as a sample of the whole of the possible number of things which the same cause system could produce if it continued to function indefinitely. In this sense the product for a given period is a sample of that which can be produced by the same manufacturing process. Millikan's measurements of the charge on an electron are a sample of the indefinitely large number of measurements that can be made by this method.

On the one hand, we are interested in what the sample tells us about a finite lot or number of things. On the other hand, we are interested in what the sample tells us about the cause system producing the sample—in this sense all our experience is a sample. Thus the data used in establishing natural laws is a sample from the possible infinite set of data that these laws could give.

2. *Sampling Fluctuations*

Even though produced under essentially the same conditions, no two things are identical in the sense that no two apples on the same tree are identical. The differences, as we have said, are attributed to the effects of chance or unknown causes. If we look at one thing after another produced under presumably the same conditions, we find that the quality varies from piece to piece. Such variations are called *sampling variations* or *fluctuations*.

These sampling variations may be produced by either variable or constant systems of chance causes. As seen in Part III, there is reason to believe that we may find and eliminate variable chance causes, but not those of a constant system in which there is no predominating cause. Hence we must always have sampling fluctuations in the quality of product. However, if produced by a constant system, they are controlled sampling fluctuations in that they can be predicted by well-established probability theory.

3. *Simple Illustration of Sampling Fluctuations*

Let us start our study of sampling with an experiment in which 4,000 drawings of a chip from a bowl were made with replacement; that is, after drawing a chip, it was replaced and thoroughly mixed with the others before another was drawn.

In the bowl there were 998 circular chips on each of which there was a number. Forty chips were marked 0, 40 were marked − 0.1, 40 were marked + 0.1, and so on as shown in Table 22. Before replacing a chip in the bowl, the number was recorded. The 4,000 observed values are given in Table A, Appendix II.

In this experiment we have as near an approach as is likely feasible to the condition in which the law of large numbers applies[1] since, to the best of our knowledge, the same essential conditions can be maintained. The differences between successive numbers drawn are beyond our control.

Dividing the observed values into four sets of 1,000 each, we get the four grouped frequency distributions of columns 3, 4, 5, and 6 in Table 23. Column 2 gives the corresponding distribution in the bowl.

[1] Cf. Paragraph 3, Chapter X, Part III.

TABLE 22.—MARKING ON 998 CHIPS FOR SAMPLING EXPERIMENT

Marking on Chip X	Number of Chips	Marking on Chip X	Number of Chips	Marking on Chip X	Number of Chips	Marking on Chip X	Number of Chips
−3.0	1	−1.5	13	0.0	40	1.5	13
−2.9	1	−1.4	15	0.1	40	1.6	11
−2.8	1	−1.3	17	0.2	39	1.7	9
−2.7	1	−1.2	19	0.3	38	1.8	8
−2.6	1	−1.1	22	0.4	37	1.9	7
−2.5	2	−1.0	24	0.5	35	2.0	5
−2.4	2	−0.9	27	0.6	33	2.1	4
−2.3	3	−0.8	29	0.7	31	2.2	4
−2.2	4	−0.7	31	0.8	29	2.3	3
−2.1	4	−0.6	33	0.9	27	2.4	2
−2.0	5	−0.5	35	1.0	24	2.5	2
−1.9	7	−0.4	37	1.1	22	2.6	1
−1.8	8	−0.3	38	1.2	19	2.7	1
−1.7	9	−0.2	39	1.3	17	2.8	1
−1.6	11	−0.1	40	1.4	15	2.9	1
						3.0	1

TABLE 23.—GROUPED FREQUENCY DISTRIBUTIONS IN SAMPLING EXPERIMENT

Cell Midpoint	Distribution in Bowl	Observed Distributions			
		Sample No. 1	Sample No. 2	Sample No. 3	Sample No. 4
−3.0	3	5	1	2	2
−2.5	9	9	14	10	9
−2.0	28	36	24	29	25
−1.5	65	55	51	72	49
−1.0	121	123	113	124	112
−0.5	174	165	187	181	191
0	198	203	195	180	204
0.5	174	172	176	169	182
1.0	121	123	125	120	123
1.5	65	68	71	67	64
2.0	28	31	31	32	25
2.5	9	8	8	11	12
3.0	3	2	4	3	2

As is to be expected, no two of the observed distributions are the same, and no one of them is the same as that in the bowl. In fact the differences between these five distributions are quite marked as is evident from their graphical presentations in Fig. 56. The differences look much like those previ-

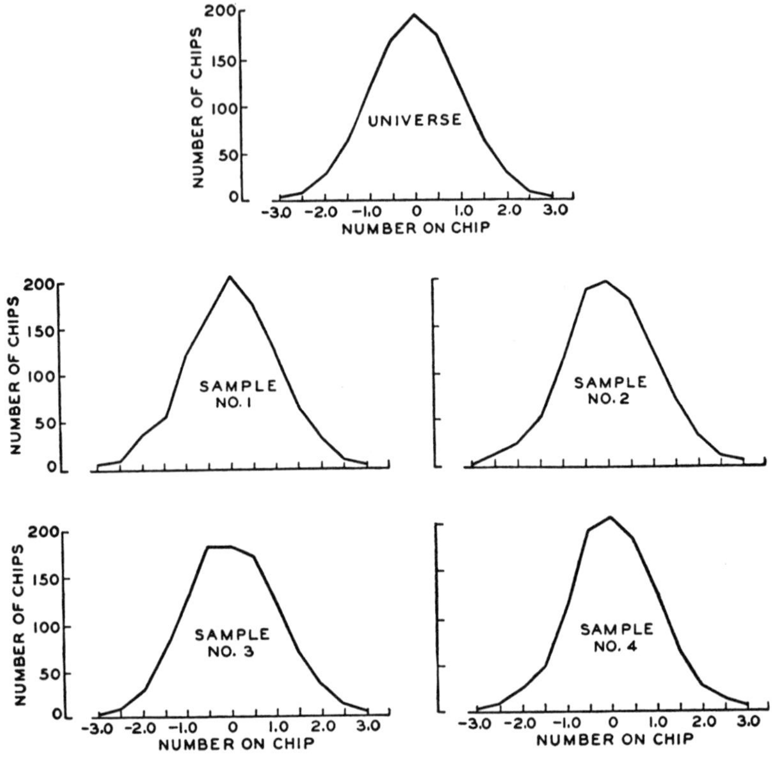

Fig. 56.—Sampling Fluctuations under Controlled Conditions.

ously shown in Fig. 19—so much so, in fact, that one might hesitate to say that the distributions in Fig. 19 reveal any evidence of lack of statistical control, although, as we shall soon see, an assignable cause was present in that case. Hence we see that we may be misled if we depend upon the qualitative appearance of deviations to indicate the presence of an assignable cause. What we need in such a case is some quantitative measure of the deviation of the distribution in a sample from that in the bowl to be used as a basis for detecting lack of control.

4. *Sampling Fluctuations in Simple Statistics*

We shall use simple statistics such as the average $\bar{X}$, standard deviation σ, skewness $k = \sqrt{\beta_1}$, and flatness β_2 for expressing quantitatively the differences between the observed distributions. For example, columns 2 to 5 of Table 24 give the observed values of these statistics for the four observed distributions of Table 23. We see how the observed distributions differ quantitatively in respect to these simple statistics. Column 6 of Table 24 gives, for comparison purposes, the values of these same statistics for the distribution in the bowl.

TABLE 24.—OBSERVED VALUES OF STATISTICS FOR DISTRIBUTIONS GIVEN IN TABLE 23

	Observed Distributions				Distribution in Bowl
	Sample No. 1	Sample No. 2	Sample No. 3	Sample No. 4	
Average	0.0015	0.0445	−0.0060	0.0365	0
Standard Deviation	1.0219	1.0019	1.0317	0.9739	1.0070
Skewness	−0.0903	−0.0126	0.0631	0.0038	0
Flatness	2.9257	2.9904	2.7996	3.0757	2.9302

Instead of performing such an experiment to determine how samples differ, we try to predict such variability in the probability sense. To do this, we must find the distribution functions of averages, standard deviations, and other statistics in samples of size n drawn from the distribution in the bowl. Usually this is a complicated mathematical procedure, as we shall soon see. Therefore, to begin with, we shall take a simple example in which the distribution functions can be derived by elementary arithmetic.

5. *Simple Problem in Prediction of Sampling Fluctuation—Problem of Distribution*

Suppose that there are just four similar chips in a bowl, and that these are marked 1, 2, 3, and 4 respectively. Suppose that samples of 4 are to be drawn with replacement. The problem to be considered is the prediction of sampling fluctuations in the simple statistics.

Since the number of ways of choosing r things from n things where each of the r things may be any one of the n things is n^r, it follows that a sample of four may be chosen in $4^4 = 256$ different ways. Obviously not all of the 256 samples will be different. A little study will show that the different possible samples are those given in Column 1 of Table 25, and that the number of ways in which these may be drawn are as given in Column 2. The corresponding distributions of statistics $\overline{X}$, σ, k, and β_2 can now be set down as in the last four columns of this same table. The frequency distributions of these and certain other statistics are shown graphically in Fig. 57.

It is of interest to note that the method of finding the distributions in Fig. 57 is purely an analytical one involving simple arithmetic. One sets down all of the possible samples of size four that can be drawn from the bowl, and then finds the averages, standard deviations, and other statistics for this set of possible samples.

If we assume that the sampling fluctuations in the statistics of samples drawn from such a bowl satisfy the law of large numbers, it follows from evidence given in Part III that the observed distributions of statistics in samples of size four may be expected to approach[1] as statistical limits the respective

[1] This involves the assumption that *similar* in the phrase "similar chips" has the significance of the phrase "equally likely" so often used in probability theory. It seems reasonable to believe, however, that "equally likely" is a concept which has significance for the external world rather than for mathematics. On this point it will be of interest to read "Probability as Expressed by Asympototic Limits of Pencils of Sequences," by E. L. Dodd, published in the *Bulletin of the American Mathematical Society*, Vol. 36 (1930), pp. 299–305. For example, he says: "In pure mathematics, the word *probability* may be taken to signify simply the ratio of the number of objects in a subset to the number in the set, so long as discrete or arithmetic probability is being considered. It is, indeed, as far outside the field of mathematics to determine whether two events are equally likely as to determine whether two bodies have the same mass. Even in the applications, the rôle of pure mathematics is merely to count expeditiously the elements of sets and subsets, or, more generally, to determine certain measures of sets, which are believed by competent judges to depict adequately situations in the external world."

TABLE 25.—SIMPLE PROBLEM IN DISTRIBUTION THEORY

Sample	Number of Times Sample Occurs	$\bar{X}$	σ	k	β_2
1111	1	1.00	0	0	Indeterminate
2222	1	2.00	0	0	
3333	1	3.00	0	0	
4444	1	4.00	0	0	
1112	4	1.25	0.4330	1.1547	2.3333
1113	4	1.50	0.8660	1.1547	2.3333
1114	4	1.75	1.2990	1.1547	2.3333
2221	4	1.75	0.4330	−1.1547	2.3333
2223	4	2.25	0.4330	1.1547	2.3333
2224	4	2.50	0.8660	1.1547	2.3333
3331	4	2.50	0.8660	−1.1547	2.3333
3332	4	2.75	0.4330	−1.1547	2.3333
3334	4	3.25	0.4330	1.1547	2.3333
4441	4	3.25	1.2990	−1.1547	2.3333
4442	4	3.50	0.8660	−1.1547	2.3333
4443	4	3.75	0.4330	−1.1547	2.3333
1122	6	1.50	0.5000	0	1.0000
1133	6	2.00	1.0000	0	1.0000
1144	6	2.50	1.5000	0	1.0000
2233	6	2.50	0.5000	0	1.0000
2244	6	3.00	1.0000	0	1.0000
3344	6	3.50	0.5000	0	1.0000
1123	12	1.75	0.8292	0.4934	1.6281
1124	12	2.00	1.2247	0.8165	2.0000
1134	12	2.25	1.2990	0.2138	1.2798
2213	12	2.00	0.7071	0	2.0000
2214	12	2.25	1.0897	0.6520	2.0970
2234	12	2.75	0.8292	0.4934	1.6281
3312	12	2.25	0.8292	−0.4934	1.6281
3314	12	2.75	1.0897	−0.6520	2.0970
3324	12	3.00	0.7071	0	2.0000
4412	12	2.75	1.2990	−0.2138	1.2798
4413	12	3.00	1.2247	−0.8165	2.0000
4423	12	3.25	0.8292	−0.4934	1.6281
1234	24	2.50	1.1180	0	1.6400

distributions of these same statistics shown in Fig. 57. In general, the prediction of sampling fluctuations in statistics of samples of size n drawn from a distribution such as that in the bowl requires the knowledge of the distribution functions of these same statistics. Observed fluctuations may or may not have in them component effects of variable chance causes.

6. *Relation of Sample to Universe*

Let us now examine the relationship between some of the simple statistics for the universe (Fig. 57-*a*) and the averages or expected values of the distributions of these same statistics. For example, Column 1 of Table 26 gives the values of some of the simple statistics of the universe, and Columns 2 and 3 give the corresponding expected values for samples of size four and ∞ respectively.

TABLE 26.—RELATION OF SAMPLE TO UNIVERSE

	Universe	Sample $n = 4$	Sample $n = \infty$	Correction Factor	Standard Deviation
Average	2.5000	2.5000	2.5000		
Median	2.5000	2.5000	2.5000		
Root Mean Square Deviation	1.1180	0.9178	1.1180	1.2181	0.3755
Mean Deviation	1.0000	0.8086	1.0000	1.3826	0.4052
Skewness k	0	0	0		
Flatness β_2	1.6400	1.7562	1.6400		

The important thing to note is that *the expected value of a given statistic in samples of size n is not necessarily equal to the value of this statistic for the universe so long as the sample size n is a finite number.* Suppose now that the statistics of the universe are unknown although the functional form is known. We see that, if we wish to estimate a given statistic for the universe from that for a sample of size n, a correction factor is required. Two such factors are given in Table 26 for the case in hand.

Another interesting point is that a statistic of the universe may be estimated from the same or other statistics of a sample.

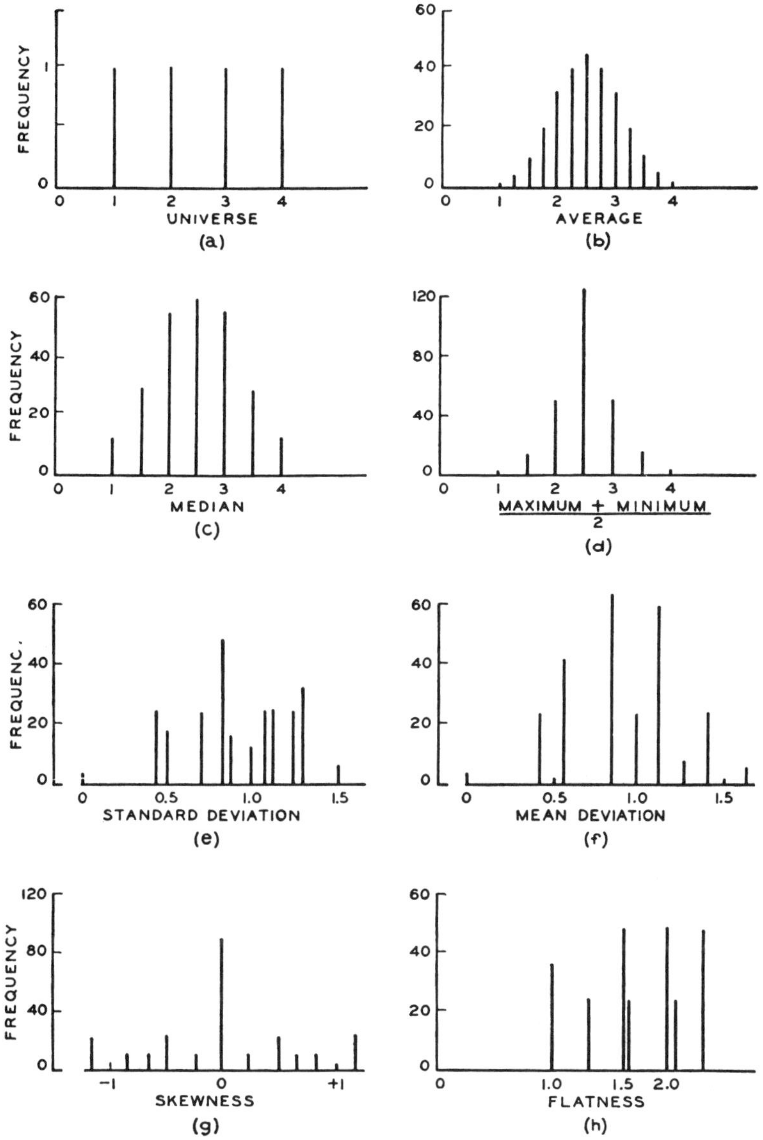

FIG. 57.—DISTRIBUTION OF STATISTICS FOR SAMPLES SHOWN IN TABLE 25.

Thus either 1.2181 times the standard deviation of a sample of four or 1.3826 times the mean deviation of a sample of four may be used as estimates of the standard deviation of the universe (57-*a*). The standard deviations of these estimates, however, are not equal. We say that one is more efficient than the other. As a measure of this *efficiency*[1] we take the ratio of the squares of the respective standard deviations. For the simple case under consideration the efficiency of the root mean square estimate is $\frac{(0.4052)^2}{(0.3755)^2} = 1.1644$.

It is suggested that the reader start with some simple universe other than the one used in this chapter and find for this chosen universe the distributions of the four simple statistics for some sample size. By such a procedure, one easily discovers that the distribution function of a given statistic involves a sample size n and depends upon the functional form of the universe. It is also discovered that, in general, the correction factors required to go from the expected value of a statistic in a sample of size n to the same statistic of the universe depend upon the nature of the universe and upon the size of the sample.

In other words, we come in this way to see that the problem of interpreting a sample involves the *specification* of the universe and the *determination of the distribution function* of a given statistic in samples of a given size drawn from this universe.

[1] This measure of efficiency is defined as follows: The standard deviation of the mean of m_1 corrected *root mean square deviations* (in samples of four) is $0.3755/\sqrt{m_1}$ while the standard deviation of the mean of m_2 corrected *mean deviations* in samples of four is $0.4052/\sqrt{m_2}$. If these two standard deviations are to be equal, we must have

$$\frac{0.3755}{\sqrt{m_1}} = \frac{0.4052}{\sqrt{m_2}}.$$

Hence the efficiency of the *root mean square deviation* is

$$E = \frac{m_2}{m_1} = \frac{(0.4052)^2}{(0.3755)^2}.$$

7. *The Problem of Determining the Allowable Variability in Quality from a Statistical Viewpoint*

If the quality X of a product is statistically controlled, the probability dy that a unit of this kind of product will have a quality X lying within the range X to $X + dX$ is expressible as a function f of the quality X and m' parameters, or formally

$$dy = \mathbf{f}(X, \lambda_1, \lambda_2, \ldots, \lambda_i, \ldots, \lambda_{m'})dX. \tag{58}$$

We have seen that samples of size n drawn from such a product exhibit sampling fluctuations. These fluctuations may be measured quantitatively in terms of some statistic Θ of the samples, such as average, standard deviation, etc. For each such statistic there is some relative frequency distribution function

$$\mathbf{f}_\Theta(\Theta, n),$$

representing the distribution of possible values of the statistic Θ in samples of size n drawn from the universe (58). It follows that the probability dy_Θ of an observed value of the statistic Θ falling within the range Θ to $\Theta + d\Theta$ is given by the relationship

$$dy_\Theta = \mathbf{f}_\Theta(\Theta, n)d\Theta. \tag{59}$$

In general, the distribution functions of the universe and of the statistics may be either continuous or discontinuous. Thus, in Paragraph 5 of this chapter we considered in detail the distribution functions of several statistics for samples of four drawn from a discontinuous universe. Later we shall consider distribution functions for continuous universes.

An allowable variability in quality will be defined as one that may reasonably be classed as a sampling fluctuation, or, in other words, one that may reasonably be attributed to the effects of a constant system of chance causes.

In the next two chapters we shall consider in some detail the nature of the frequency distribution functions characterizing sampling fluctuations in some of the simple statistics previously introduced.

CHAPTER XIV

Sampling Fluctuations in Simple Statistics under Statistical Control

1. *Method of Attack*

In this chapter we shall assume that the universe of possible effects of the cause system is known, and that the sampling fluctuations obey the law of large numbers. Distribution functions of statistics basic in the theory of control and in the establishment of quality standards are discussed in sufficient detail to make clear their use throughout the remaining chapters of the book.

Only those points are discussed which have been found helpful in answering practical problems of the following type:

A. How shall we determine when quality is statistically controlled?
B. How shall we establish standards of quality?
C. How shall we establish allowable limits in design?
D. How shall we establish allowable limits of variation from standard quality?
E. How shall we select a representative sample of product?
F. How large a sample shall we take?

The reader primarily interested in such questions may wish to turn immediately to those sections outlining the answers which have been found satisfactory in practice. He will find, however, that these questions, like many of those confronting us every day, do not permit of answers which can be considered as final. One common question will suffice as an illustration of what is meant: What should a child learn in school? No one knows *the* answer to this question, and yet we must adopt an answer in the form of an established curriculum. For the most part, we have faith that students of education having a knowledge of the fundamental difficulties involved in getting *the* answer will be able to make progress in that direction. Similarly, one interested in *the* answers to the several questions stated in the previous paragraph will find that some parts of the following discussion which at first appear abstract and impractical may actually prove to be the most helpful in the establishment of fundamental principles upon which to base production methods.

Starting with the assumption that the universe of possible effects of the controlled system of chance causes is of the form

$$y = \mathbf{f}(X, \lambda_1, \lambda_2, \ldots, \lambda_i, \ldots, \lambda_{m'}),$$

we shall need to know the probability **P** that a statistic of a sample of size n produced by this constant system of causes will fall within the range Θ_1 to Θ_2 given formally by the integral

$$\mathbf{P} = \int_{\Theta_1}^{\Theta_2} \mathbf{f}_{\Theta}(\Theta, n)d\Theta.$$

We shall find that the distribution function of the statistic depends upon the function **f** of the universe of effects of the cause system, and that the distribution functions of even the simple statistics are unknown except for a very limited number of forms of the function **f**. In fact, we shall find that for the most part the distribution functions of the simple statistics are known only when the distribution function **f** of the possible effects of the cause system is normal.

Since, however, the normal function involves the assumption that the variable X may extend from $-\infty$ to $+\infty$, and since we do not know of any quality X which rigorously satisfies this condition, we see that the theoretical frequency distribution functions which we are to use never can represent practical conditions rigorously. In this same connection, much of the theory is based upon the assumption of continuity of the observable values of the quality X; although this can never be attained in practice because of inherent limitations in our measuring instruments. Experimental results obtained by sampling under controlled conditions are introduced to indicate, in a more or less practical way, the significance of the two limitations just stated.

Even when the distribution function $\mathbf{f}_{\Theta}(\Theta, n)$ of a statistic Θ is not known so that we cannot calculate the probability $\mathbf{P}$ that Θ will lie within a given range, the results of comparatively recent theoretical work enable us to obtain quite satisfactory estimates of the probability $\mathbf{P}$, provided we know the expected value $\bar{\Theta}$ of Θ in samples of size n and the standard deviation σ_{Θ} of Θ measured about the expected value $\bar{\Theta}$. Oftentimes we know the moments of a distribution function, although we do not know the functional form. The work of Tchebycheff referred to in Part II makes it possible for us to say that the probability $\mathbf{P}_{t\sigma_{\Theta}}$ that an observed value of Θ will fall within the limits $\bar{\Theta} \pm t\sigma_{\Theta}$ satisfies the inequality

$$\mathbf{P}_{t\sigma_{\Theta}} > 1 - \frac{1}{t^2},$$

where t is not less than unity. We may also use Tchebycheff's theorem to advantage when the indefinite integral of the distribution function is unknown even though the function is known.

Comparatively recent work has given us the expected values and standard deviations of most of the statistics which now appear to be useful in quality control work. Furthermore, these expected values and standard deviations are known for discrete and finite universes of the type which we have to deal with in practice. Hence, we have available for use a certain amount of theoretical work which is immediately applicable to commercial conditions, and which enables us to state at least a lower bound to the probability associated with a symmetric range about the expected value of a statistic.

Recently Camp[1] and Meidell[2] have shown that the probability $\mathbf{P}_{t\sigma_\Theta}$ satisfies the inequality

$$\mathbf{P}_{t\sigma_\Theta} > 1 - \frac{1}{2.25t^2},$$

provided:

(*a*) The distribution function $\mathbf{f}_\Theta(\Theta, n)$ of the statistic Θ is unimodal with a modal value $\breve{\Theta}$ coinciding with the expected value $\bar{\Theta}$.

(*b*) The distribution function $\mathbf{f}_\Theta(\Theta, n)$ of the statistic Θ is monotonic on either side of the modal value.

Hence it follows that if we can show that the distribution function of the statistic satisfies the Camp-Meidell conditions, we can estimate the probability associated with a symmetric range about the expected value within closer limits than we can if we know nothing whatsoever about the form of the distribution function of the statistic. In certain instances it is sufficient for practical purposes to be able to show that the modal value is approximately equal to the expected value, and that the distribution function is monotonic about the mode. In this connection, it might be noted that the Camp-Meidell relation applies strictly to a continuous function, although it may easily be shown that this limitation is of no practical significance in the cases where we make use of this theory.

Experimental results are introduced wherever necessary to bridge over gaps in available theory. These same experimental results will be used extensively in the remaining chapters of the book wherever we consider the problem of interpretation of a sample.

In our discussion we shall use bold-faced type to indicate the parameters and functional form of the universe of effects of the cause system and also the expected values, standard deviations, and other functions derived from known distribution functions of statistics. The regular italic notation

[1] Camp, B. H., "A new Generalization of Tchebycheff's Statistical Inequality," *Bulletin of the American Mathematical Society*, Vol. 28, 1922, pp. 427–432.

[2] Meidell, M. B., "Sur un problème du calcul des probabilités et les statistiques mathématiques," *Comptes Rendus*, Vol. 175, 1922, pp. 806–808.

will be used for the corresponding observed characteristics of a sample as indicated in Table 27.

TABLE 27.—NOTATIONS FOR UNIVERSE AND SAMPLE

	Universe	Sample
Distribution	$f(X, \boldsymbol{\lambda}_1, \boldsymbol{\lambda}_2, \ldots, \boldsymbol{\lambda}_{m'})$	$f(X, \lambda_1, \lambda_2, \ldots, \lambda_m)$
Fraction Defective or Fraction within Given Limits	$\mathbf{p}$	p
Average	$\bar{\mathbf{X}}$	$\bar{X}$
Standard Deviation	$\boldsymbol{\sigma}$	σ
Skewness	$\mathbf{k} = \sqrt{\boldsymbol{\beta}_1}$	$k = \sqrt{\beta_1}$
Flatness	$\boldsymbol{\beta}_2$	β_2

2. *Fraction Defective* [1]

That the fraction defective should play an important rôle in modern production is at once apparent when one considers that so many quality measurements are made with a go-no-go gauge. It is but natural, therefore, to consider first the nature of the sampling fluctuations in this fraction under controlled conditions.

The distribution function for the observed fraction defective p or fraction found between any two specified limits X_1 and X_2 in samples of size n drawn from a controlled product of any functional form whatsoever is given by the terms of the point binomial

$$(\mathbf{q} + \mathbf{p})^n. \tag{60}$$

The expected value $\bar{\mathbf{p}}$, modal value $\breve{\mathbf{p}}$, and standard deviation $\boldsymbol{\sigma}_p$ of this distribution function are given by the following relationships: [2]

$$\breve{\mathbf{p}} = \bar{\mathbf{p}} = \mathbf{p} \tag{61}$$

$$\boldsymbol{\sigma}_p = \sqrt{\frac{\mathbf{pq}}{n}}. \tag{62}$$

[1] The derivation of the formulas cited in this paragraph are given in almost any elementary text on statistical theory.

[2] Of course the modal and expected values of p are not always equal. However, the difference is too small to be of any practical importance in most applications.

In these relationships **p** is the probability that a constant cause system will produce a defective piece of product.

We see at once that the first distribution function (60) that we have chosen is not normal. In fact, it is not even continuous. As pointed out in Part III, however, the point binomial theoretically can be approximated quite closely by the ordinates (or appropriate areas) of a normal curve of the same mean value and standard deviation as the point binomial, provided **p** is approximately equal to $(1 - \mathbf{p})$ and n is very large. We saw in this same connection, however, that the approximation is quite good when $\mathbf{p} = 1 - \mathbf{p}$ even if n is no greater than 16; similarly when $\mathbf{p} = 0.1$ and n is no greater than 100. This gives us, therefore, some idea of the degree of precision which we can expect to attain by assuming that the distribution of the observed fraction defective p is normal.

Since the modal and expected values of p may be considered equal, and since the discrete distribution can be quite accurately fitted by a function satisfying the Camp-Meidell requirements, it follows that the Camp-Meidell inequality may be assumed to give a close approximation to the lower bound of the probability associated with any symmetrical range about the expected value **p**. Knowing the standard deviation of **p**, we may make use of the normal law integral to calculate the probability that an observed fraction p will fall within any two limits p_1 and p_2, provided the values of **p** and n are such that the normal law is a satisfactory approximation. If the conditions are such that we cannot use the normal law, we may always make use of this value of **p** and its standard deviation in establishing limits with probability bounds in accord with the Tchebycheff inequality.

3. *Average—Normal Universe*

Perhaps the arithmetic mean is used in engineering work more often than any other statistic to express the central tendency of a group of data. We shall therefore consider next the fluctuation of this statistic in samples of size n drawn from a normal universe. It is a simple matter to show that under these conditions the distribution of the average $\bar{X}$ is normal with a standard deviation $\frac{\sigma}{\sqrt{n}}$, where σ is the standard deviation of the universe. So long, therefore, as we are dealing with samples from a known normal universe, it is a very simple matter to obtain from Table A the value of the probability that an observed average will fall within any two arbitrarily chosen limits. Hence, from a theoretical viewpoint, we need give no further consideration to the distribution of the average of a sample from a normal universe. It is of interest, however, to see how closely experimental results may be expected to check the theoretical ones, even though we cannot, for reasons previously cited, experiment with samples drawn from a strictly normal universe.

Perhaps we cannot duplicate the conditions under which we should expect to find agreement between theory and practice more closely than by drawing chips from a bowl in the manner described in the previous chapter. Obviously, the distribution in the bowl is discontinuous and does not extend to either side of the average beyond three times the standard deviation; whereas a normal distribution is continuous and extends to infinity in both directions. It is of interest, therefore, to note how closely the observed distribution of 1,000 averages of four, Fig. 58, approaches normality. The data of Table A, Appendix II, were divided as indicated into 1,000 groups of four each.

4. *Average—Non-Normal Universe*

Even for so simple a statistic as an average, we do not know the distribution function when the universe is not normal.[1] We do, however, know the moments of this distribution function in terms of the moments of the universe.

[1] For exceptions see "On the Means and Squared Standard Deviations of Small Samples from any Population" by A. E. R. Church, *Biometrika*, Vol. XVIII, pp. 321–394, 1926, and "On the Frequency Distribution of the Means of Samples from Populations of Certain of Pearson's Types," by J. O. Irwin, *Metron*, Vol. VIII, pp. 51–106.

As in the case of averages from a normal universe, the expected value of averages is the average $\bar{\mathbf{X}}$ of the universe. Similarly, the standard deviation $\sigma_{\bar{X}}$ of this distribution is equal to $\dfrac{\sigma}{\sqrt{n}}$ where σ is the standard deviation of the universe. With this information we are in a position to apply Tchebycheff's theorem.

We may do better than this, however, because it is known that the skewness $\mathbf{k}_{\bar{X}}$ and the flatness $\beta_{2\bar{X}}$ of the distribution

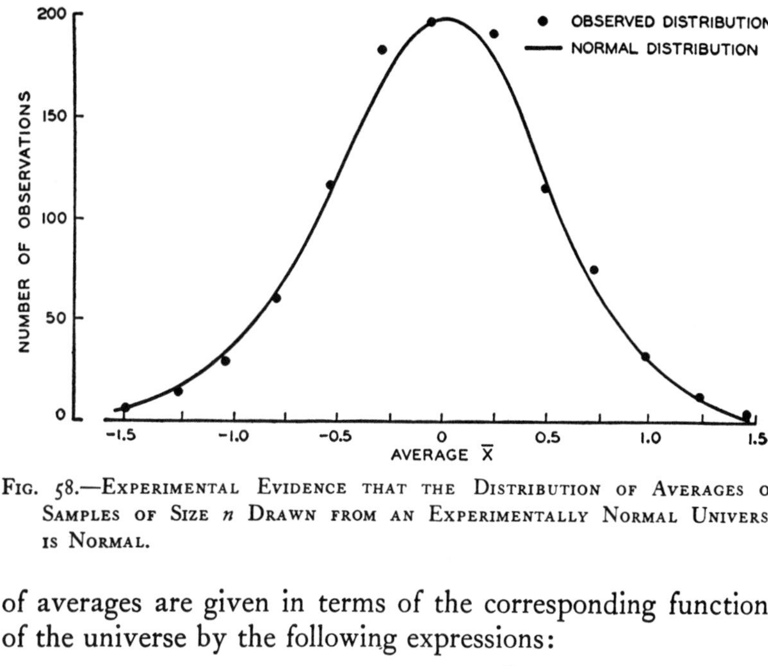

FIG. 58.—EXPERIMENTAL EVIDENCE THAT THE DISTRIBUTION OF AVERAGES OF SAMPLES OF SIZE n DRAWN FROM AN EXPERIMENTALLY NORMAL UNIVERSE IS NORMAL.

of averages are given in terms of the corresponding functions of the universe by the following expressions:

$$\left.\begin{aligned} \mathbf{k}_{\bar{X}} &= \frac{\mathbf{k}}{\sqrt{n}}, \\ \beta_{2\bar{X}} &= \frac{\beta_2 - 3}{n} + 3. \end{aligned}\right\} \qquad (63)$$

From (63), we see that, if the sample size n is made large enough, no matter what the skewness and flatness of the universe are, the skewness and flatness of the distribution of averages of samples of size n approach normality as characterized by the values 0 and 3 respectively. It remains for us to show that, even for comparatively small values of n, the distribution of averages may be considered to be normal to a high degree of approximation, thus making possible the use of the normal integral, Table A, in establishing sampling limits.

Again we shall appeal to the use of experimental data. Tables B and C of Appendix II give the results of 4,000 draw-

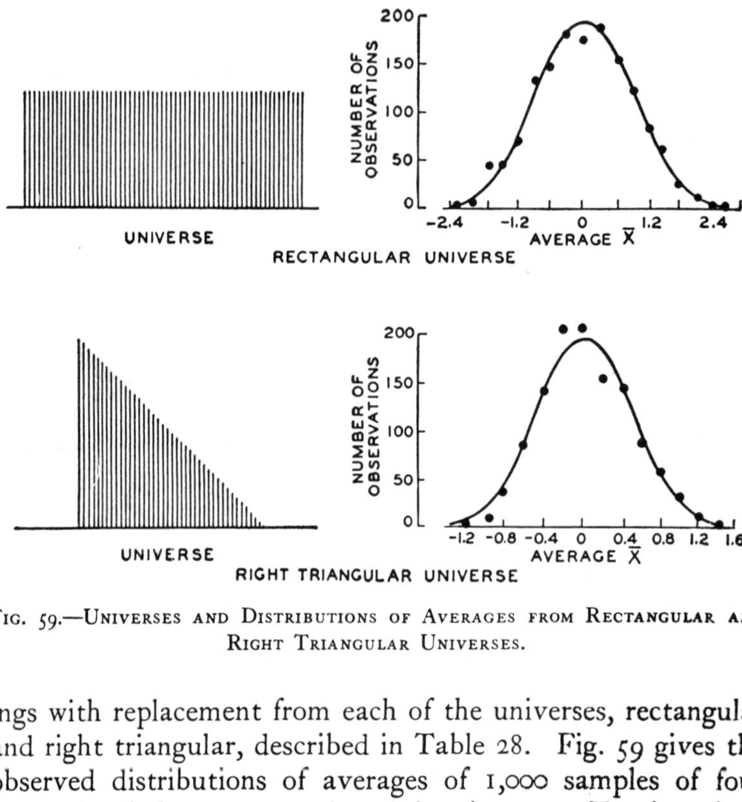

FIG. 59.—UNIVERSES AND DISTRIBUTIONS OF AVERAGES FROM RECTANGULAR AND RIGHT TRIANGULAR UNIVERSES.

ings with replacement from each of the universes, rectangular and right triangular, described in Table 28. Fig. 59 gives the observed distributions of averages of 1,000 samples of four for each of the two experimental universes. To show how closely these observed distributions actually approach normality, we have drawn smooth normal curves having expected values and standard deviations determined from theory upon the basis of our knowledge of the universes. The closeness of fit is striking and illustrates the rapid approach of the distribution to normality as the sample size is increased. Such evidence, supported by more rigorous analytical methods beyond the scope of our present discussion, leads us to believe that in almost all cases in practice we may establish sampling

TABLE 28.—MARKING ON CHIPS FOR EXPERIMENTAL UNIVERSES

Rectangular Universe				Right Triangular Universe			
Marking on Chip X	Number of Chips	Marking on Chip X	Number of Chips	Marking on Chip X	Number of Chips	Marking on Chip X	Number of Chips
−3.0	2	0.0	2	−1.3	40	0.7	20
−2.9	2	0.1	2	−1.2	39	0.8	19
−2.8	2	0.2	2	−1.1	38	0.9	18
−2.7	2	0.3	2	−1.0	37	1.0	17
−2.6	2	0.4	2	−0.9	36	1.1	16
−2.5	2	0.5	2	−0.8	35	1.2	15
−2.4	2	0.6	2	−0.7	34	1.3	14
−2.3	2	0.7	2	−0.6	33	1.4	13
−2.2	2	0.8	2	−0.5	32	1.5	12
−2.1	2	0.9	2	−0.4	31	1.6	11
−2.0	2	1.0	2	−0.3	30	1.7	10
−1.9	2	1.1	2	−0.2	29	1.8	9
−1.8	2	1.2	2	−0.1	28	1.9	8
−1.7	2	1.3	2	0.0	27	2.0	7
−1.6	2	1.4	2	0.1	26	2.1	6
−1.5	2	1.5	2	0.2	25	2.2	5
−1.4	2	1.6	2	0.3	24	2.3	4
−1.3	2	1.7	2	0.4	23	2.4	3
−1.2	2	1.8	2	0.5	22	2.5	2
−1.1	2	1.9	2	0.6	21	2.6	1
−1.0	2	2.0	2				
−0.9	2	2.1	2				
−0.8	2	2.2	2				
−0.7	2	2.3	2				
−0.6	2	2.4	2				
−0.5	2	2.5	2				
−0.4	2	2.6	2				
−0.3	2	2.7	2				
−0.2	2	2.8	2				
−0.1	2	2.9	2				
		3.0	2				

limits for averages of samples of four or more upon the basis of normal law theory.

5. *Standard Deviation—Normal Universe*

The distribution function of the standard deviation has been studied by "Student,"[1] Pearson,[2] and Fisher.[3] They have shown that the distribution function of the observed standard deviation σ for samples of size n may be expressed in terms of the standard deviation σ' of the universe in the following way:

$$dy = \frac{n^{\frac{n-1}{2}}}{2^{\frac{n-3}{2}}\left(\frac{n-3}{2}\right)!}\frac{\sigma^{n-2}}{\sigma'^{n-1}}e^{-\frac{n\sigma^2}{2\sigma'^2}}d\sigma. \qquad (64)$$

We note at once that the distribution of σ is asymmetric, although it approaches symmetry as the size n of the sample increases. Although we have the distribution function in this case, we do not have a table of its integral as we have for the normal law. Obviously, however, (64) is unimodal; and it may be easily shown that the modal value $\breve{\sigma}$ and the expected value $\bar{\sigma}$ are given respectively by

$$\breve{\sigma} = \sqrt{\frac{n-2}{n}}\,\sigma' = c_1\sigma', \qquad (65)$$

and

$$\bar{\sigma} = \sqrt{\frac{2}{n}}\frac{\left(\frac{n-2}{2}\right)!}{\left(\frac{n-3}{2}\right)!}\,\sigma' = c_2\sigma'. \qquad (66)$$

We shall have many occasions to make use of the factors c_1 and c_2 occurring in these two equations. Hence they are

[1] *Biometrika*, Vol. VI, 1908, pp. 1–25; Vol. XI, 1917, pp. 416–417; *Metron*, Vol. V, No. 3, 1925, pp. 18–21.

[2] *Biometrika*, Vol. X, 1915, pp. 522–529.

[3] *Ibid.*, pp. 507–521; *Proc. Cambridge Phil. Soc.*, Vol. XXI, 1923, pp. 655–658; *Metron*, Vol. V, No. 3, 1925, pp. 3–17 and 22–32.

tabulated in Table 29 for sample sizes most likely to be of interest.

TABLE 29.—CORRECTION FACTORS c_1 AND c_2

n	c_1	c_2	n	c_1	c_2
3	0.57735	0.72360	22	0.95346	0.96545
4	0.70711	0.79788	23	0.95553	0.96697
5	0.77460	0.84069	24	0.95743	0.96837
6	0.81650	0.86863	25	0.95917	0.96965
7	0.84515	0.88820	30	0.96609	0.97475
8	0.86603	0.90270	35	0.97101	0.97839
9	0.88192	0.91388	40	0.97468	0.98111
10	0.89443	0.92275	45	0.97753	0.98322
11	0.90453	0.92996	50	0.97980	0.98491
12	0.91287	0.93594	55	0.98165	0.98629
13	0.91987	0.94098	60	0.98319	0.98744
14	0.92582	0.94529	65	0.98450	0.98841
15	0.93094	0.94901	70	0.98561	0.98924
16	0.93541	0.95225	75	0.98658	0.98996
17	0.93934	0.95511	80	0.98742	0.99059
18	0.94281	0.95765	85	0.98817	0.99115
19	0.94591	0.95991	90	0.98883	0.99164
20	0.94868	0.96194	95	0.98942	0.99208
21	0.95119	0.96378	100	0.98995	0.99248

For sample sizes greater than five, the difference between modal and expected values of standard deviation is so small that in most practical problems we may assume that the Camp-Meidell inequality applies, where the standard deviation of the distribution of σ is taken to be $\frac{\sigma}{\sqrt{2n}}$.

Here again it is not feasible to duplicate theoretical conditions in practice. It is therefore interesting to see how closely the 1,000 standard deviations in samples of four drawn from the experimentally normal distribution previously described can be approximated by (64). The results of such a comparison are shown in Fig. 60. The closeness of fit between the observed and theoretical distributions certainly appears to warrant our acceptance of the theory as a guide to practice in such a case. It is also of interest to note how closely the

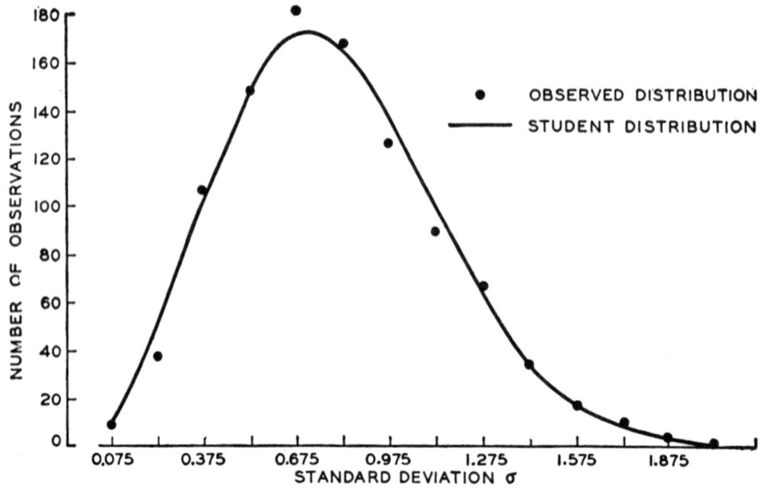

FIG. 60.—DISTRIBUTION OF STANDARD DEVIATIONS IN SAMPLES OF FOUR DRAWN FROM NORMAL UNIVERSE

theoretical and observed values of modal and average standard deviation agree as indicated in Table 30.

TABLE 30.—AGREEMENT OF THEORETICAL AND OBSERVED VALUES OF MODAL AND AVERAGE VALUES OF STANDARD DEVIATION

	Theoretical	Observed in 1,000 Samples of Four
Modal Standard Deviation in Samples of Four.....	0.7071	0.7168
Expected or Average Standard Deviation in Samples of Four....................................	0.7979	0.8007

6. *Standard Deviation—Non-Normal Universe*

Theoretically, we know nothing about the distribution function of the standard deviation of samples from a non-normal universe—not even the values of the moments. If, then, we are to be able to establish ranges of variability within which the observed values of standard deviation may be expected to fall for samples drawn from other than a normal universe, we must rely at the present time upon empirically determined results.

To indicate the nature of the results to be expected, it is of interest therefore to consider the observed distributions of standard deviations of samples of four drawn from rectangular and right triangular universes. These are shown in Fig. 61.

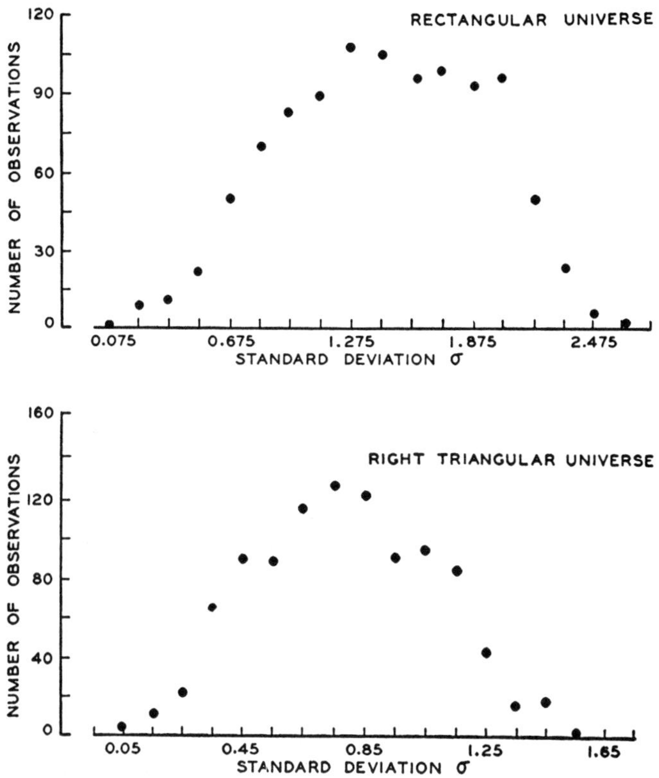

FIG. 61.—DISTRIBUTIONS OF STANDARD DEVIATIONS OF SAMPLES OF FOUR DRAWN FROM RECTANGULAR AND RIGHT TRIANGULAR UNIVERSES.

As is to be expected, the modal and average values of the observed distributions are less than the standard deviations of the respective universes, Table 31. These results show that since the modal and expected values are approximately equal, it would be possible to apply the Camp-Meidell inequality except for the fact that the standard deviation is not known. In other words, we are not in a place to set sampling limits on the standard deviation of samples drawn

TABLE 31.—EXPECTED AND MODAL VALUES OF STANDARD DEVIATION

	Rectangular Universe	Right Triangular Universe
Modal Standard Deviation in Samples of Four.	1.4639	0.7761
Average Standard Deviation in Samples of Four.	1.4325	0.7865
Standard Deviation of Universe..............	1.7607	0.9539

from other than a normal universe, unless the divergence from normality is so small as to warrant our belief that the distribution function (64) is a reasonable approximation. In cases where this assumption is not justified, we may make use of the square of the standard deviation or the *variance* as it is termed.

7. *Variance*

For variance, as for standard deviation, we know the distribution function when sampling from a normal universe. It is

$$dy = C(\sigma^2)^{\frac{n-3}{2}} e^{-\frac{n\sigma^2}{2\sigma'^2}} d(\sigma^2), \tag{67}$$

where C is a constant. In fact, "Student"[1] first found this distribution function empirically, and from it derived the distribution of σ.

When the sampled universe is not normal, we know merely the moments of σ^2 expressed in terms of those of the universe.[2] The expected variance and the standard deviation of variance are

$$\left.\begin{aligned} \overline{\sigma^2} &= \frac{n-1}{n}\sigma'^2 \\ \text{and} \qquad \sigma_{\sigma^2} &= \frac{\sigma'^2}{n}\sqrt{\frac{n-1}{n}[(n-1)\beta_2' - n + 3)]} \end{aligned}\right\} \tag{68}$$

[1] Loc. cit. The distribution was later found rigorously by R. A. Fisher, loc. cit.

[2] See, for example, A. E. R. Church, "On the Means and Squared Standard Deviations of Small Samples from any Population," *Biometrika*, Vol. XVIII, Nov., 1926, pp. 321–394.

in terms of the standard deviation σ and the flatness β_2 of the universe. Obviously, without further investigation based upon the use of higher moments of the distribution function of variance than those given in (68), we cannot establish sampling limits in general with an assurance much greater than that afforded by the application of the Tchebycheff relationship.

8. *Ratio* $z = \dfrac{\bar{X} - \bar{\mathbf{X}}}{\sigma}$ — *Normal Universe*

Thus far we have considered the distribution functions of some of the simple statistics taken one at a time. We shall find that another very helpful way of looking at this problem is to consider the ratio z of the deviation in the average to the standard deviation of the sample. "Student"[1] was the first to derive the distribution of z for samples drawn from a normal universe. His results are given by (69):

$$dy = \frac{\left(\frac{n-2}{2}\right)!}{\sqrt{\pi}\left(\frac{n-3}{2}\right)!}(1 + z^2)^{-\frac{n}{2}}dz. \qquad (69)$$

It is useful to know that the standard deviation σ_z is always equal to $\dfrac{1}{\sqrt{n-3}}$. The distribution of z is symmetrical about the expected value $\bar{\mathbf{z}} = 0$, and the table of the integral of this function originally given by "Student" has now been extended by "Student"[1] and Fisher.[1]

Fig. 62 shows how the distribution function of z differs from the normal law for the case $n = 4$. The broken curve is the normal law with the same standard deviation as the observed distribution of z derived from the thousand samples of four drawn from a normal universe. Two things should be noted. First, although the two distribution functions are symmetrical, they differ widely for small sample sizes. Second, we should

[1] Loc. cit.

note how closely "Student's" theoretical distribution fits the observed points in Fig. 62.

If the samples are drawn from other than a normal universe, very little of importance in the theory of control is known about the distribution of z other than that derived from an

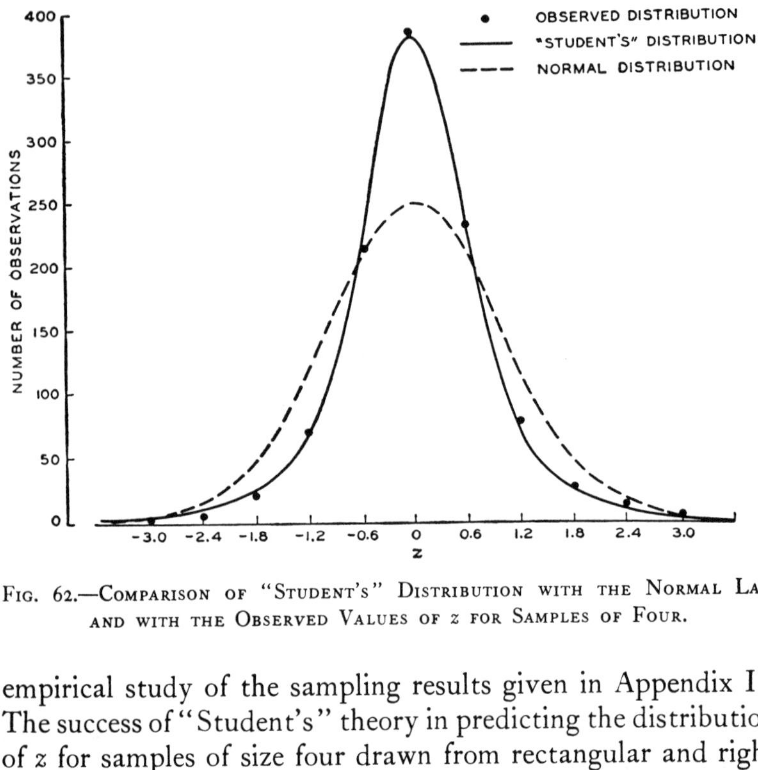

FIG. 62.—COMPARISON OF "STUDENT'S" DISTRIBUTION WITH THE NORMAL LAW AND WITH THE OBSERVED VALUES OF z FOR SAMPLES OF FOUR.

empirical study of the sampling results given in Appendix II. The success of "Student's" theory in predicting the distribution of z for samples of size four drawn from rectangular and right triangular universes is indicated in Fig. 63. There can be little doubt that "Student's" distribution is a closer approximation to the observed distribution than is the normal law. Analysis of these results indicates that for most ranges $-z$ to $+z$ (when $z \leq 3$) the associated probability given by "Student's" distribution must be considered as an upper bound[1]

[1] See for example, "Small Samples—New Experimental Results," by W. A. Shewhart and F. W. Winters, *Journal of American Statistical Association*, Vol. 23, pp. 144–153, 1928.

when sampling from a universe with values of $\boldsymbol{\beta}_1$ and $\boldsymbol{\beta}_2$ lying in the $\beta_1\beta_2$ plane above the line

$$\beta_2 - \beta_1 - 3 = 0.$$

9. *Distribution of Average and Standard Deviation*

We shall now briefly outline another way in which sampling limits may be set on statistics. Instead of considering the distribution of each statistic separately, we may consider the distribution of pairs of simultaneously observed values of two statistics. As an example, Fig. 64 shows such distributions for averages and standard deviations of the samples from the

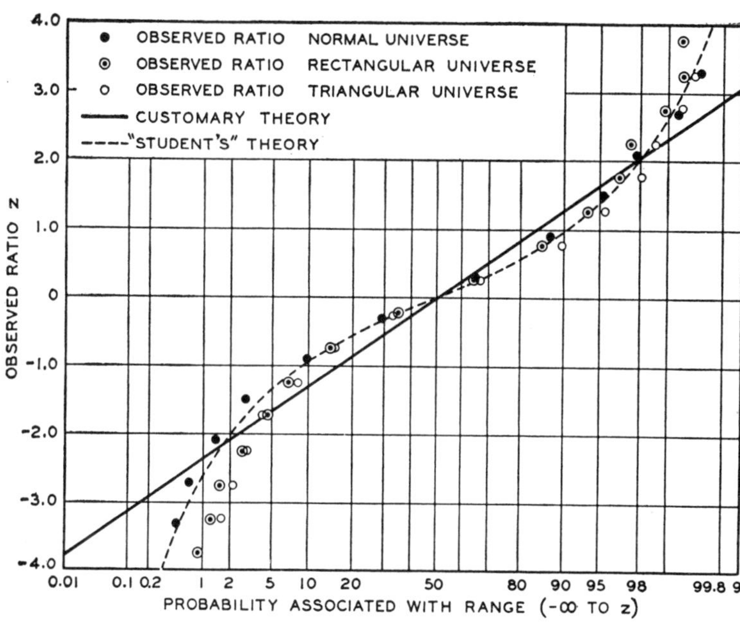

FIG. 63.—PROBABILITY ASSOCIATED WITH RANGE ($-\infty$ TO z).

normal, rectangular, and right triangular universes. It is apparent that the distributions for the rectangular and right triangular universes differ materially from that of the thousand samples drawn from the normal universe. For control purposes

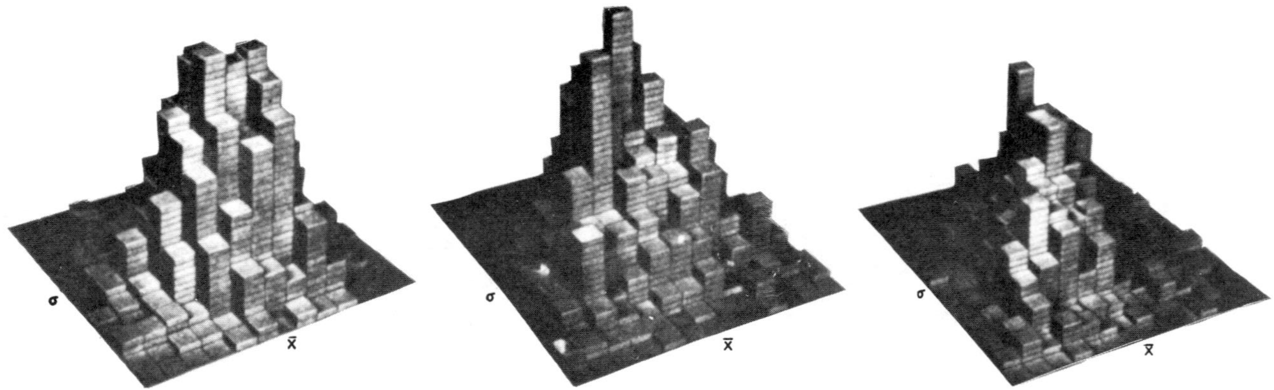

NORMAL UNIVERSE (a) | RECTANGULAR UNIVERSE (b) | RIGHT TRIANGULAR UNIVERSE (c)

FIG. 64.—OBSERVED FREQUENCY SURFACE HISTOGRAMS SHOWING CORRELATION BETWEEN THE AVERAGE AND STANDARD DEVIATION IN SAMPLES OF SIZE $n = 4$.

we may make use of the form of presentation given in Fig. 65 showing the curves of regression of average on standard deviation. For the samples drawn from a normal universe, we see that the regression curve is a horizontal line. In the other cases, however, the regression is non-linear. For the rectangular universe the curve of regression is a parabola symmetrical about the ordinate through the mean of the distribution; for the right triangular universe the curve of regression cannot be so simply described.

Recent work of Neyman [1] gives the equation of the curve of regression of the average on variance in terms of the moments of the universe. Neyman also gives the standard deviation of the distribution from this curve of regression.

These results of Neyman were used in constructing the theoretical curve of regression and the dotted limits corresponding to three times the standard deviation of the distribution about the line of regression for the data presented in Fig. 65. Of course we are not justified in using Neyman's work in this particular way, except to get an approximation. Therefore, it is interesting to note that the results so established include approximately 99 per cent of the observed values as they should if the distribution about the curve of regression were normal and the theoretical value of the standard deviation used in constructing the limits were not subject to computational error.

So far as we are concerned at the present moment, emphasis is to be laid upon the importance of these results as indicating the wide variety of possible ways in which we may establish limits within which observed statistics may be expected to fall. In such a case the theoretical determination of the regression curve together with the standard deviation of an array about such a curve gives us a basis for establishing limits which we may interpret at least upon the basis of Tchebycheff's relationship. A review of the theoretical work that has already been done in this connection, however, indicates certain

[1] "On the Correlation of the Mean and the Variance in Samples Drawn from an 'Infinite' Population," *Biometrika*, Vol. XVIII, pp. 401–413, 1926.

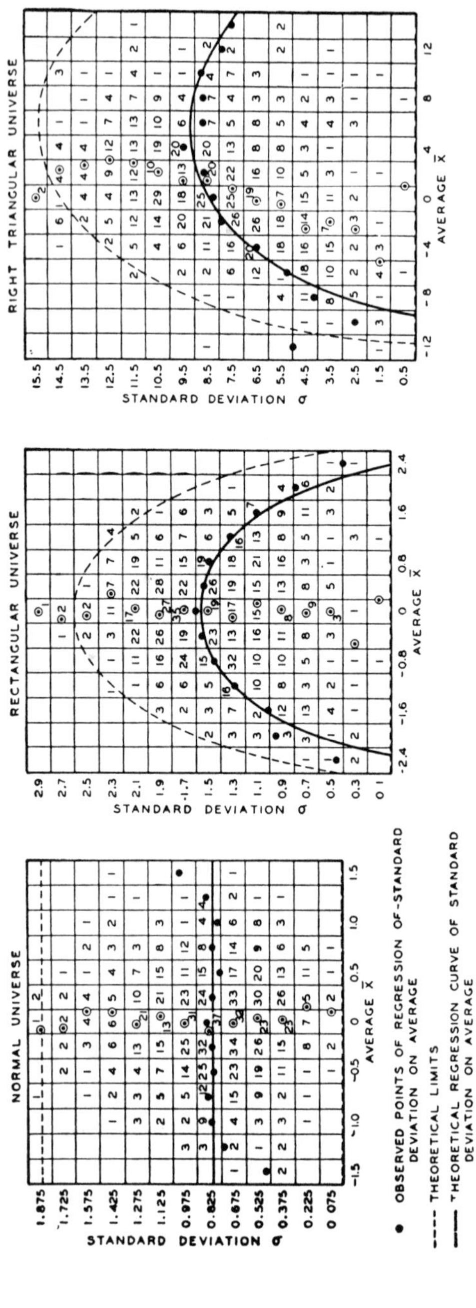

Fig. 65.—Control Charts Taking into Account the Correlation between Standard Deviation and Average for Samples of 4.

inherent difficulties in attaining a high degree of precision in the derivation of the necessary regression curve and the standard deviation from such a curve.

10. *A Word of Caution*

Before passing on to a consideration of the distribution functions of other statistics, it is well to sound a further word of caution about accepting theoretical results in the form of distribution functions of statistics derived upon assumptions of continuity of universe where for one reason or another the measurements cannot be made under the ideal conditions assumed. As an illustration, it is interesting to examine the effect of grouping in any universe, such for example as the rectangular one, upon the regression of the variance on the average in small samples. We find that the apparent closeness of fit of a second order parabola to the means of variances depends upon the number of cells. The approximation in many cases is not very good as is illustrated by Fig. 66 corresponding to the scatter diagram of the 256 pairs of values of variance and standard deviation based upon the data of Table 25. Obviously the mean values of variance corresponding to a given average and represented by the solid dots do not lie on a second order parabola. It follows that the precision of the estimate of the number of points to be expected outside the limits derived after the manner of those shown in Fig. 65 is quite uncertain. In fact, we cannot use Tchebycheff's theorem in connection with the parabola of regression to estimate even the upper bound to this number.

The reader may appreciate now the significance of the experimental results previously cited to show that the effect of grouping into a finite number of cells and the effect of the finite range of the experimental universe were not sufficient to invalidate the application of the distribution functions for averages, standard deviations, and ratios of deviations in averages to observed standard deviations derived upon the assumption of a continuous universe of infinite range. As a result of these considerations, we see that in the derivation of a distribution function for a given statistic in a sample of size n drawn from a given universe, we must realize that in practice we can never attain the condition of continuous universe.

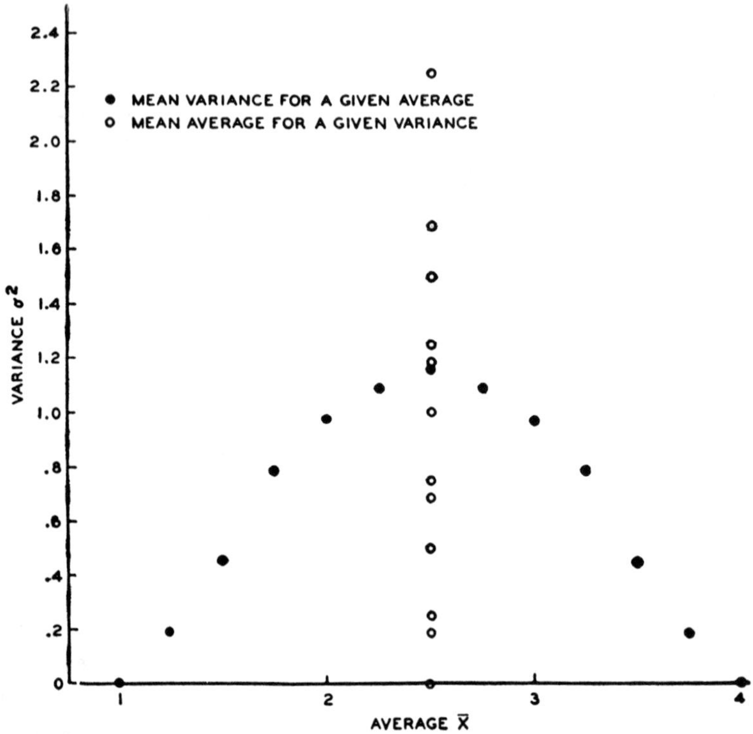

FIG. 66.—SCATTER DIAGRAM FOR AVERAGES AND VARIANCES OF ALL POSSIBLE SAMPLES OF FOUR FROM UNIVERSE 1, 2, 3, 4.

Of course, it must be kept in mind that so far as theory is concerned, it is quite possible that the curve of regression even for a continuous universe is not rigorously a second order parabola. In other words, the theory involved above rests upon the assumption that a second order parabola is simply a good first approximation to the actual curve. This fact, however, does not invalidate the argument of the previous paragraphs to the effect that the form of the best fitted curve of regression depends to a certain extent at least upon the number of cells into which the universe is divided.

11. *Skewness k and Flatness β_2*

Very little is known about the characteristics of the distribution function of either k or β_2 except for large samples drawn from a normal universe under which conditions these distribution functions approach normality. It has long been known, however, that the standard deviations of these two statistics in samples of n drawn from a normal universe are

$$\sigma_k = \sqrt{\frac{6}{n}}, \tag{70}$$

and

$$\sigma_{\beta_2} = \sqrt{\frac{24}{n}}. \tag{71}$$

If the sample size n is of the order of magnitude of 500 or more, we may assume that the distribution functions of these statistics about $\mathbf{k}$ and $\boldsymbol{\beta}_2$ respectively of the universe are such that the normal law integral may be assumed to give approximate values for the probabilities associated with symmetrical ranges about the expected values.[1]

12. *Other Measures of Central Tendency*

In our discussion of quality control methods, we shall have occasion to use two measures of central tendency other than the arithmetic mean. These are the median and the $\frac{\text{Max.} + \text{Min.}}{2}$. The distribution function for the median of samples of n drawn from a normal universe is known to approach normality as the sample size becomes indefinitely large. Little is known, however, about the distribution of medians in samples drawn from other than a normal universe or in small samples drawn from any universe. Also the dis-

[1] Isserlis, L., "On the Conditions under which the 'Probable Errors' of Frequency Distributions have a Real Significance," *Proceedings of the Royal Society*, Series A, Vol. XCII, 1915, pp. 23–41.

tribution function of the $\frac{\text{Max.} + \text{Min.}}{2}$ is apparently not known except for samples of n drawn from a rectangular universe.[1]

For both these measures of central tendency, we can say that their distribution functions for symmetrical universes are symmetrical so that the expected value for both distribution functions is the average $\bar{X}$ of the universe. Although, in general, we do not know the standard deviation of either measurement for small samples from even a normal universe, we do know that the standard deviation of the median in large samples from a normal universe is $\frac{1.253\sigma}{\sqrt{n}}$, where σ is the standard deviation of the universe.

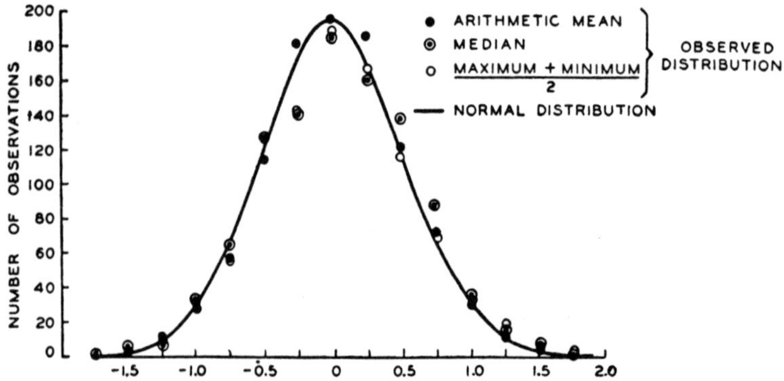

FIG. 67.—DISTRIBUTIONS OF THREE MEASURES OF CENTRAL TENDENCY IN SAMPLES OF SIZE FOUR DRAWN FROM A NORMAL UNIVERSE.

Wherever it has been found necessary to make use of the distribution functions of these two measures for small samples, they have been determined empirically. For example, Fig. 67 shows the experimentally determined distributions of these two measures for the 1,000 samples of four from the normal universe previously mentioned. For purposes of comparison we have included the theoretical and observed distributions of

[1] Rider, P. R., "On the Distribution of the Ratio of Mean to Standard Deviation in Small Samples from Non-Normal Universes," *Biometrika*, Vol. XXI, pp. 124–141, 1929.

arithmetic means of these samples. We see that all of these are approximately normal. Obviously they would be identical one with another for samples of size two. The observed standard deviations shown in Table 32 are, however, significantly different one from another, indicating that the measures differ in efficiency as defined in Paragraph 6 of the previous chapter.[1]

TABLE 32.—CHARACTERISTICS OF DISTRIBUTIONS OF THREE MEASURES OF CENTRAL TENDENCY

Measure of Central Tendency	Average $\bar{\Theta}$	Standard Deviation σ_Θ	Skewness k_Θ	Flatness $\beta_{2\Theta}$	Efficiency as Compared to that of Mean as 100 Per Cent: Observed for Samples of 4	Efficiency as Compared to that of Mean as 100 Per Cent: Theoretical for Large Samples
Arithmetic Mean	0.014	0.502	−0.038	2.985	100.0	100.0
Median	0.026	0.559	−0.028	2.921	80.6	63.8
$\frac{\text{Max.} + \text{Min.}}{2}$	0.036	0.547	−0.015	2.986	84.2	

The theoretical efficiency for the measure $\frac{\text{Max.} + \text{Min.}}{2}$ even for large samples is not known, although it is known that it will be less than that of the median. The interesting thing to note is that the efficiency of a measure depends upon the sample size. For example, that of the median starts with 100 per cent for sample size $n = 2$ and drops off to 63.8 per cent for large samples.

13. *Other Measures of Dispersion*

One of the competing measures of dispersion, particularly in engineering work, is the mean deviation. In general our state of knowledge in respect to the theoretical distribution

[1] See discussion in Chapter XIX of Part VI for special interpretation of efficiency for the case of small samples. Just as in Paragraph 6 of the previous chapter, efficiency here applies to the estimate of the mean $\bar{X}$ of the universe obtained from the mean of m medians or values of $\frac{\text{Max.} + \text{Min.}}{2}$ in samples of four.

of the mean deviation even for samples from the normal universe is in a far less satisfactory state than is that of the standard deviation under similar conditions. For large samples it is true that the distribution function of the mean deviation is sufficiently near normal for us to use the normal integral in establishing sampling limits in control theory. Under these conditions, however, the efficiency of the mean deviation is only about 88 per cent.

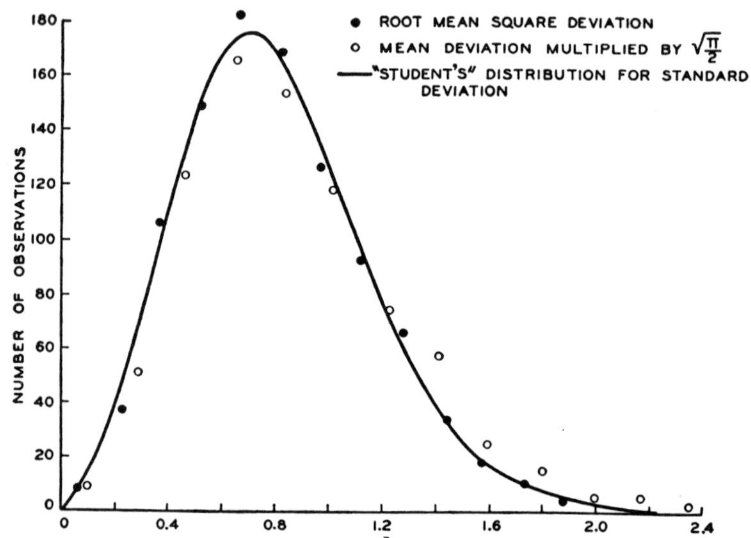

FIG. 68.—EMPIRICALLY DETERMINED DISTRIBUTION OF ROOT MEAN SQUARE AND MEAN DEVIATIONS IN SAMPLES OF FOUR.

The empirically determined distribution of the thousand mean deviations (multiplied by $\sqrt{\pi/2}$) in samples of four is presented in Fig. 68. We see that it is distinctly different in functional form from that of either the theoretical or the observed distribution of standard deviations of this same group of 1,000 samples of four. We also see from Fig. 68 and Table 33 that the mean and modal values of the distribution of mean deviations differ from those of the corresponding distribution of standard deviations. Hence, until further theoretical work has been done, the use of the mean deviation for small samples offers comparatively serious limitations as compared with the use of the standard deviation. Furthermore, we shall see that under these conditions the standard deviation is the more efficient measure.[1] Hence we should not expect to find many cases in quality control work where the mean deviation is to be preferred to the standard deviation as a measure of dispersion.

TABLE 33.—CHARACTERISTICS OF DISTRIBUTION OF THREE MEASURES OF DISPERSION

Basis of Estimate of Standard Deviation	Average $\bar{\Theta}$	Mode $\breve{\Theta}$	Standard Deviation σ_Θ	Skewness k_Θ	Flatness $\beta_{2\Theta}$
Root Mean Square Deviation...	0.8007	0.7161	0.340	0.486	2.952
$\sqrt{\frac{\pi}{2}}$ (Mean Deviation)........	0.8612	0.7353	0.379	0.622	3.261
$X_4 - X_1$....................	2.0030	1.7564	0.875	0.548	3.030

Sometimes we need to use a measure of dispersion which can be readily obtained on the job. For this purpose we may make use of the absolute value of the range between the maximum and minimum observed values in samples of size n.

The observed distribution of ranges in samples of four drawn from a normal universe is given in Fig. 69. The average of the thousand observed ranges is 2.003σ where σ is the standard deviation of the universe. Upon the basis of these experimental results, we could take $\frac{1}{2.003}$ times the range as an approximate value of the standard deviation of the universe; or looked at in another way, knowing the standard deviation of the normal universe, we may set limits within which the observed range in the sample size n may be expected to fall with a given probability **P** if, as in the previous examples, we can find the distribution function of this range.

[1] Chapter XIX of Part VI.

Considerable theoretical work has been done within recent years in an attempt to find this distribution function. For example, Tippett[1] gives the expected value and standard deviation of the distribution of ranges in samples of size n drawn from a normal universe. From his results we get Fig. 70. He also gives the theoretical values β_1 and β_2 of the distribution of the range. In this way, he shows that the distribution of this statistic diverges more and more from normality as the size n of the sample is increased. Obviously, therefore, the

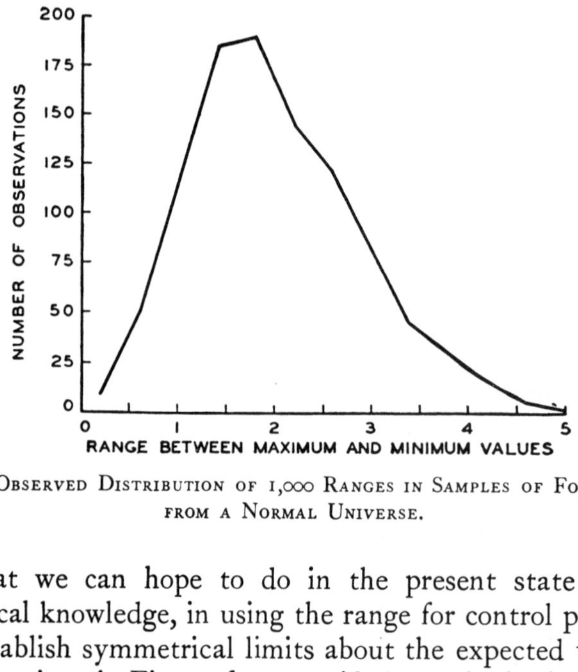

FIG. 69.—OBSERVED DISTRIBUTION OF 1,000 RANGES IN SAMPLES OF FOUR DRAWN FROM A NORMAL UNIVERSE.

best that we can hope to do in the present state of our theoretical knowledge, in using the range for control purposes, is to establish symmetrical limits about the expected value of the range given in Fig. 70 for a specified sample size by making use of theoretical standard deviations also given in this figure. Since we do not know the distribution function, all that we can say is that Tchebycheff's theorem applies to the limits thus established.

In this same connection, it is interesting to compare the

[1] "On the Extreme Individuals and the Range of Samples taken from a Normal Population," *Biometrika*, Vol. XVII, pp. 364–387, December, 1925.

observed distribution functions of estimates of the standard deviation σ of the universe derived from the root mean square deviations, mean deviations, and ranges for the thousand samples of size four drawn from the normal universe. These distributions are shown in Fig. 71. The root mean square and mean deviation estimates of the standard deviation σ are those usually employed in error theory although they are not consistent as we shall see in Part VI. We shall have occasion later, in discussing the efficiency of measurements,

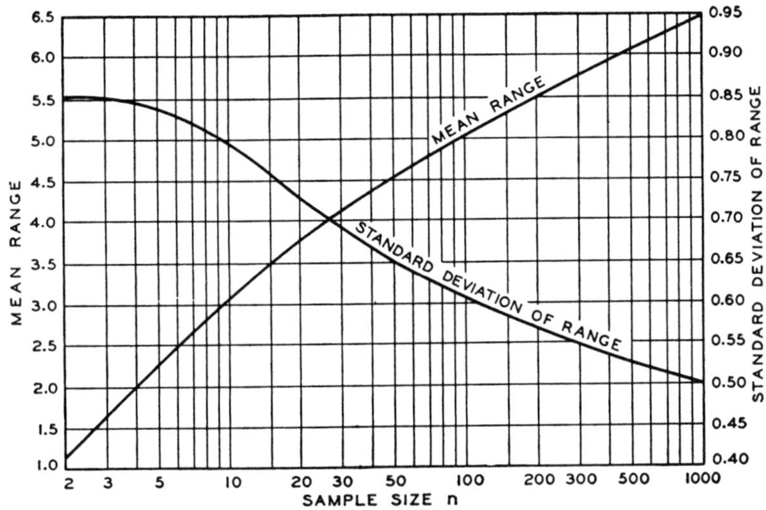

Fig. 70.—Theoretical Values of Mean Range and Standard Deviation of Range for Samples of Size *n*.

to emphasize the significance of the differences in these three distributions.

Sometimes in commercial work we may have occasion to use a range other than the extreme range because often the available data represent the quality of product after a previous inspection has excluded the extremes. We shall enter into this discussion only far enough to indicate the nature of the problems involved.

At the present time we must rely almost entirely upon the results of empirical studies to indicate the nature of the distribution functions that we may expect to get under such conditions, and also to determine how these functions depend upon the functional form of the universe from which samples are drawn. Fig. 72-*a* shows the observed distributions of four ranges in samples of four drawn from a normal universe. To obtain these distributions, the four values in each of the thousand samples of four were arranged in ascending order of magnitude. Thus, if we let X_1, X_2, X_3, X_4, represent the

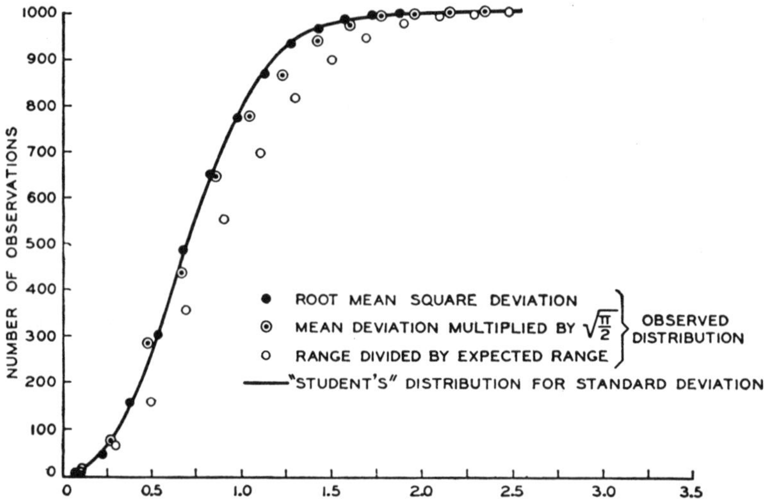

FIG. 71.—DISTRIBUTIONS OF THREE ESTIMATES OF STANDARD DEVIATION OF UNIVERSE.

values in a sample thus arranged, the four ranges are: the extreme range $X_4 - X_1$, the range between the first and second $X_2 - X_1$, the range between the second and third $X_3 - X_2$, and the range between the third and fourth $X_4 - X_3$.

The striking thing to be observed is that the distribution functions of the last three ranges are less symmetrical than that of the extreme range. Furthermore, the standard deviation of the extreme range is larger than that of any one of the other three distributions in absolute magnitude, although when expressed as a coefficient of variation, the variation in the extreme range is less than that in any other. For purposes of comparison, the distribution function of observed differences between successive pairs of observed values is also reproduced in this figure. Table 34 shows the observed expected value, standard deviation, skewness, and flatness for these five distributions.

TABLE 34.—CHARACTERISTIC OF DISTRIBUTION OF RANGES

Range	Average $\bar{\Theta}$	Standard Deviation σ_Θ	Skewness k_Θ	Flatness $\beta_{2\Theta}$
$X_2 - X_1$	0.7863	0.6087	1.2133	4.5604
$X_3 - X_2$	0.6338	0.4941	1.2451	4.5974
$X_4 - X_3$	0.7752	0.5953	1.1672	4.3608
$X_4 - X_1$	2.0044	0.8759	0.5627	3.0312
Successive Drawings	1.2136	0.8661	0.9140	3.5884

Turning our attention to Figs. 72-*b* and 72-*c*, we see the marked influence of the functional form of the universe upon the distribution functions of the ranges. This is significant in connection with our present study in that it shows that the interpretation of control limits set upon some statistic such as a range depends much more upon the nature of the functional form of the universe than does the interpretation of similar limits placed upon standard deviations and, particularly, limits placed upon arithmetic means.

14. *Chi Square*

The statistic χ^2 is a measure of the resultant effect of sampling fluctuations in the cell frequencies. Thus, if the universe of possible effects be divided into m cells such that in a sample of size n the expected frequencies in these cells are respectively $y_1, y_2, \ldots, y_i, \ldots, y_m$; and if the observed frequencies for a given sample in these same cells are $y_1, y_2, \ldots, y_i, \ldots, y_m$, χ^2 is defined by the relationship

$$\chi^2 = \sum_{i=1}^{m} \frac{(y_i - \mathbf{y}_i)^2}{\mathbf{y}_i}.$$

In 1900, Pearson [1] gave the distribution function of the statistic χ^2, which may be written

$$\mathbf{f}_{\chi^2}(\chi^2, m) = Ce^{-\frac{\chi^2}{2}}(\chi^2)^{\frac{m-3}{2}} d(\chi^2), \tag{72}$$

where C is a constant.

Similarly it may be shown that the expected value $\overline{\chi^2}$, the

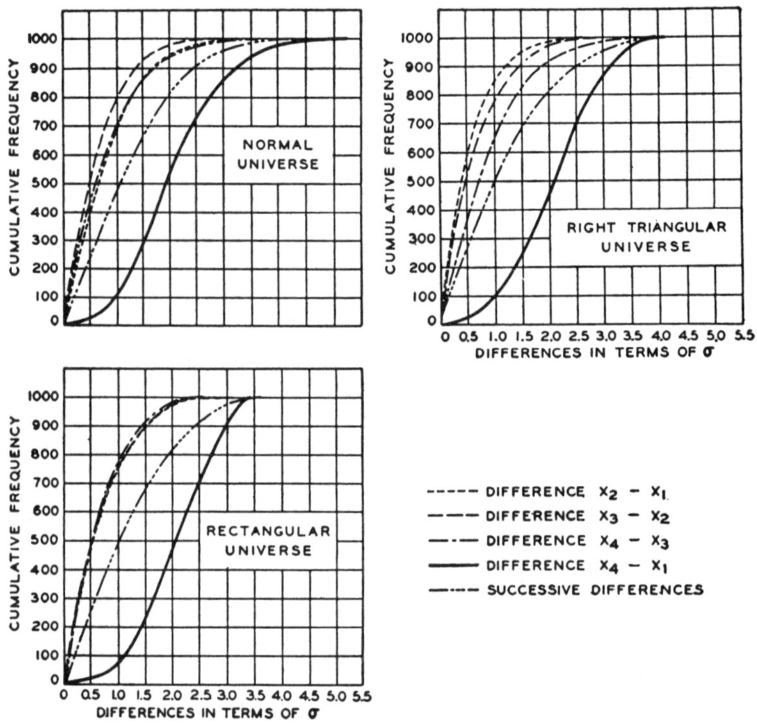

FIG. 72.—HOW DISTRIBUTIONS OF ORDERED DIFFERENCES DEPEND UPON THE UNIVERSE.

[1] Karl Pearson "On the Criterion that a Given System of Deviations from the Probable in the Case of a Correlated System of Variables is such that it can be Reasonably Supposed to have Arisen from Random Sampling," *Philosophical Magazine*, 5th Series, Vol. L, 1900, page 157.

modal value $\breve{\chi}^2$, and the standard deviation σ_{χ^2} of χ^2 are given by

$$\left.\begin{aligned}\overline{\chi^2} &= m - 1\\ \breve{\chi}^2 &= m - 3\end{aligned}\right\}. \tag{73}$$

$$\sigma_{\chi^2} = \sqrt{2(m-1)}. \tag{74}$$

Tables of values of the integral of the χ^2 function for the range of values of number m of cells of most importance were

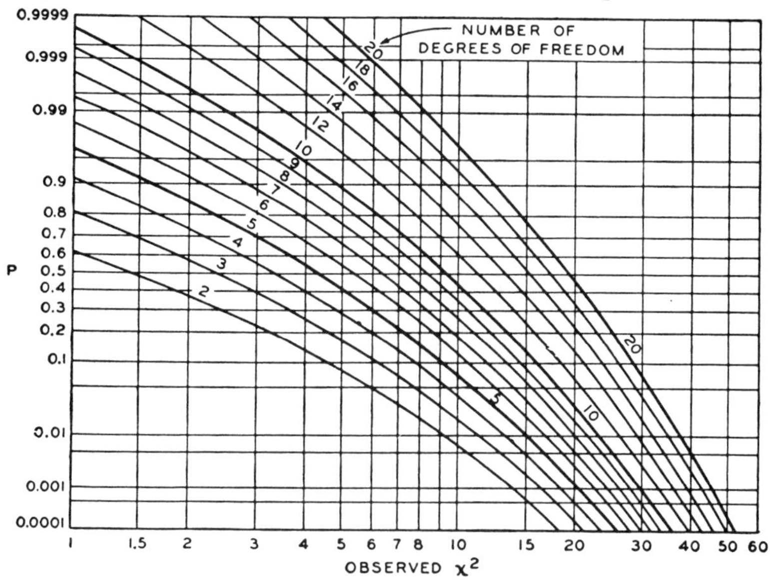

FIG. 73.—PROBABILITY ASSOCIATED WITH A GIVEN VALUE OF χ^2.

originally given by Elderton and are reproduced in useful form in Pearson's Tables.[1]

Tables in slightly different form are given by Fisher.[2] Making use of these tables, we can read off the probability **P** associated with almost any pair of limits in which we may happen to be interested. Fig. 73 indicates the way in which the probability associated with a given value of χ^2 varies with the number of degrees of freedom.[3]

[1] *Tables for Statisticians and Biometricians*, Table XII.

[2] *Statistical Methods for Research Workers.*

[3] The number of degrees of freedom is equal to one less than the number of cells if, as we have assumed above, the universe frequencies are known *a priori*.

The distribution function of χ^2 is unimodal; and since the mean and the mode differ by only two, the Camp-Meidell inequality applies quite accurately to symmetrical ranges about the expected value. Furthermore, it is of interest to note that, for a comparatively large number m of cells, the

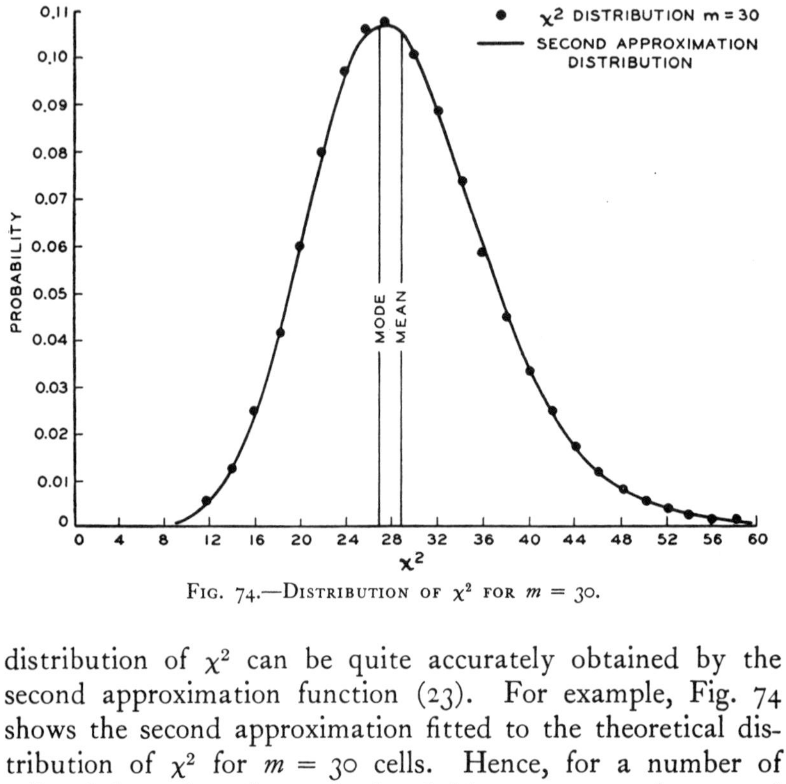

FIG. 74.—DISTRIBUTION OF χ^2 FOR $m = 30$.

distribution of χ^2 can be quite accurately obtained by the second approximation function (23). For example, Fig. 74 shows the second approximation fitted to the theoretical distribution of χ^2 for $m = 30$ cells. Hence, for a number of cells of the order of magnitude of thirty or more, the normal probability function can be used to give a close approximation to the probability associated with a symmetric range about the expected value.

It is of interest to note that the distribution of χ^2 is not explicitly limited by the functional form **f** of the universe or by the number n in a sample. A limitation, however, does enter in that the functional form of the distribution depends upon the assumption that the variable x_i is distributed normally, where $x_i = y_i - \mathbf{y}_i$. From our study of the point binomial distribution function, we see that this assumption requires that the probability $\mathbf{p}_i$ associated with the ith cell must be such that the probability distribution $(\mathbf{q}_i + \mathbf{p}_i)^n$ is approximately normal. This condition cannot be rigorously fulfilled, nor do we have any available analytical method for determining its significance. We may, however, again make use of the experimental results presented in Appendix II, this time to give information of an empirical nature which indicates the magnitude of the effect of grouping upon the distribution of χ^2. We shall make use here of only the four samples of one thousand drawings each from the normal universe.

TABLE 35.—CALCULATIONS INVOLVED IN DETERMINING χ^2.

True Distribution $\mathbf{y}$	Observed Distribution y	$y - \mathbf{y}$	$(y - \mathbf{y})^2$	$\frac{(y - \mathbf{y})^2}{\mathbf{y}}$
3	5	2	4	1.333
9	9	0	0	0.000
28	36	8	64	2.286
65	55	10	100	1.538
121	123	2	4	0.033
174	165	9	81	0.466
198	203	5	25	0.126
174	172	2	4	0.023
121	123	2	4	0.033
65	68	3	9	0.138
28	31	3	9	0.321
9	8	1	1	0.111
3	2	1	1	0.333
				$\chi^2 = 6.741$ $P = 0.873$

For purposes of reference, Table 35 shows the calculations involved in determining the value of χ^2 for the first sample of one thousand, grouped into thirteen cells. We see that the probability $\mathbf{p}$ associated with the end cells is only $\frac{3}{998}$, which is exceedingly small. We may, therefore, consider the

TABLE 36.—EFFECT OF GROUPING ON χ^2

True Distribution y	Observed Distributions															
	Sample No. 1				Sample No. 2				Sample No. 3				Sample No. 4			
	13 Cells	11 Cells	9 Cells	7 Cells	13 Cells	11 Cells	9 Cells	7 Cells	13 Cells	11 Cells	9 Cells	7 Cells	13 Cells	11 Cells	9 Cells	7 Cells
3	5				1				2				2			
9	9	14			14	15			10	12			9	11		
28	36	36	50		24	24	39		29	29	41		25	25	36	
65	55	55	55	105	51	51	51	90	72	72	72	113	49	49	49	85
121	123	123	123	123	113	113	113	113	124	124	124	124	112	112	112	112
174	165	165	165	165	187	187	187	187	181	181	181	181	191	191	191	191
198	203	203	203	203	195	195	195	195	180	180	180	180	204	204	204	204
174	172	172	172	172	176	176	176	176	169	169	169	169	182	182	182	182
121	123	123	123	123	125	125	125	125	120	120	120	120	123	123	123	123
65	68	68	68	109	71	71	71	114	67	67	67	113	64	64	64	103
28	31	31	41		31	31	43		32	32	46		25	25	39	
9	8	10			8	12			11	14			12	14		
3	2				4				3				2			
χ^2	6.741	5.630	4.882	0.833	10.710	6.911	5.519	4.614	4.455	3.900	3.885	3.364	9.174	7.924	7.291	6.761
$\overline{\chi^2}$	12	10	8	6	12	10	8	6	12	10	8	6	12	10	8	6

advisability of grouping the tails of the distribution after the manner often suggested in the literature. Table 36 shows the effect of grouping the tails of each of the four experimental distributions. In all but one case the observed value of χ^2 is less than the theoretical expected value, although the average difference between the two decreases as we increase the probability associated with the last cell by decreasing the number m of cells. These experimental results indicate that the effect of the limitation as to the normality of the distribution of the variable x_i may be much more serious from an experimental viewpoint than one might be led to believe by reading the literature on the subject. In any case the use of χ^2 in control work must be subjected to careful scrutiny to eliminate the obvious effects of grouping even under conditions where, as in the present case, we should expect the χ^2 test to be applicable.

15. *Summary*

Broadly speaking, distribution functions of statistics are basic tools with which the engineer interested in quality control must work. In this chapter we have sketched briefly the present state of our knowledge of the distribution functions of some of the more important statistics. A summary of these results is given in Table 37. From this we see how little is really known about the distribution functions of even the simple statistics, particularly when the universe is not normal, with the two exceptions, viz., the fraction defective p and the average $\bar{X}$.

Subject to limitations set forth in this chapter, we can make use of the average and standard deviation of a statistic, even when the distribution function is not known. When theoretical information about the distribution of a statistic is not available either in the form of the function or certain moments of the function, and we have reason to believe that the universe is not normal, we may make use of the empirical laws presented herein to indicate the extent to which the normal law theory may be applied. We see that there is much

TABLE 37.—SUMMARY OF AVAILABLE INFORMATION IN RESPECT TO SOME OF THE MORE IMPORTANT STATISTICS

Statistic Θ	Distribution Function $f_\Theta(\Theta, n)$		Expected Value $\bar{\Theta}$ in Samples of Size n		Standard Deviation σ_Θ		Modal Value $\breve{\Theta}$	
	f Normal	f not Normal	f Normal	f not Normal	f Normal	f not Normal	f Normal	f not Normal
p	$(q + p)^n$	$(q + p)^n$	p	p	$\sqrt{\frac{pq}{n}}$	$\sqrt{\frac{pq}{n}}$	p	p
$\bar{X}$	Normal	Approximately normal	$\bar{X}$	$\bar{X}$	$\frac{\sigma}{\sqrt{n}}$	$\frac{\sigma}{\sqrt{n}}$	$\bar{X}$	$\bar{X}$‡
σ	(64)		Table 29 (66)		$\frac{\sigma}{\sqrt{2n}}$*		Table 29 (65)	
σ^2	(67)		$\frac{n-1}{n}\sigma^2$	$\frac{n-1}{n}\sigma^2$	(68)	(68)	$\frac{n-3}{n}\sigma^2$	
z	(69)		0		$\frac{1}{\sqrt{n-3}}$		0	
k			0†		$\sqrt{\frac{6}{n}}$			
β_2			3†		$\sqrt{\frac{24}{n}}$			
χ^2	(72)	(72)	(73)	(73)	(74)	(74)	(73)	(73)
Median			$\bar{X}$		$\frac{1.253\sigma}{\sqrt{n}}$†		$\bar{X}$	
Range			Fig. 70		Fig. 70			
$\frac{\text{Max.} + \text{Min.}}{2}$			$\bar{X}$				$\bar{X}$	

* Correction for sample size of little commercial significance. † If n is large. ‡ Subject to limitations stated in the text.

room for future development in distribution theory, all of which will have a direct bearing on the theory of control. However, we shall soon see that in many cases the gain in precision through possible developments of this nature may not be of so great practical importance as might at first be expected.

CHAPTER XV

Sampling Fluctuations in Simple Statistics—Correlation Coefficient

1. *Correlation Coefficient*

Having considered in the previous chapter the distribution functions for statistics of a single variable, we now turn our attention to the distribution function of simultaneously observed quality characteristics correlated one with another. Since, as is to be expected, the problem of deriving the distribution functions for correlation statistics is in general much more difficult than those previously considered, we shall confine our attention to the use of the correlation coefficient as a measure of relationship. In Part II we saw how this simple function may be used to present the information contained in a single set of n data. There, however, we did not consider how much an observed value of r tells us about what we may expect to get in the future under the same essential conditions or, in other words, under the same constant system of chance causes. What was said there about the correlation coefficient as an expression of observed relationship is true for a given sample. Naturally, however, even under controlled conditions this statistic is subject, as are those previously studied, to sampling fluctuations.

As an illustration Fig. 75 shows the observed scatter diagrams and corresponding values of correlation coefficient for eight samples of five simultaneous pairs of values produced by the same constant system of causes wherein there was no correlation or commonness of causation between the two variables. In other words, the correlation $\mathbf{r}$ in the universe was zero; yet we find in one sample an observed correlation of -0.82.

The method of obtaining these eight samples was as follows: Eighty consecutive values were taken from Table A, Appendix II, and these were grouped into forty pairs by taking the first and second, the third and fourth, and so on. The first five pairs were taken as the first sample, the second five pairs as the second sample; and in this way eight samples of five pairs each were obtained from a non-correlated universe. The result of this experiment is sufficient to show the importance of knowing the distribution function of the correlation

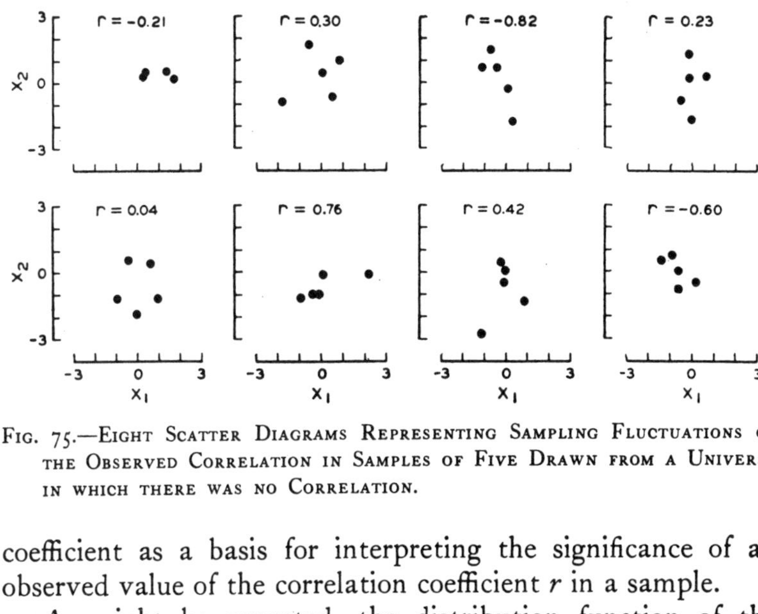

FIG. 75.—EIGHT SCATTER DIAGRAMS REPRESENTING SAMPLING FLUCTUATIONS OF THE OBSERVED CORRELATION IN SAMPLES OF FIVE DRAWN FROM A UNIVERSE IN WHICH THERE WAS NO CORRELATION.

coefficient as a basis for interpreting the significance of an observed value of the correlation coefficient r in a sample.

As might be expected, the distribution function of the observed correlation r in samples of n drawn from a universe in which the correlation is $\mathbf{r}$ involves both $\mathbf{r}$ and the sample size n. Table 38 presents experimental evidence. Thus Column 2 of this table shows the observed distribution of correlation coefficient r in one hundred samples of four drawn from a universe in which the correlation $\mathbf{r}$ was 0. It will be seen that the mean value $\bar{r}$ is 0.0300 and that the standard deviation σ_r is 0.5620. The distribution itself is approximately rectangular. In a similar way, Column 4 shows the observed

TABLE 38.—OBSERVED DISTRIBUTIONS OF CORRELATION COEFFICIENTS

$n = 4$						$n = 25$							
$\mathbf{r} = 0$		$\mathbf{r} = 0.5$		$\mathbf{r} = 0.895$		$\mathbf{r} = 0$		$\mathbf{r} = 0.5$		$\mathbf{r} = 0.9$		$\mathbf{r} = 0.98$	
Cell Mid-point	Fre-quency	Cell Mid-point	Fre-quency	Cell Mid-point	Fre-quency	Cell Mid-point	Fre-quency	Cell Mid-point	Fre-quency	Cell Mid-point	Fre-quency	Cell Mid-point	Fre-quency
−0.90	12	−0.90	4	0.15	1	−0.60	1	−0.12	1	0.800	3	0.950	1
−0.60	11	−0.60	3	0.30	0	−0.45	2	0.0	0	0.825	3	0.956	1
−0.30	16	−0.30	7	0.45	2	−0.30	6	0.12	1	0.850	6	0.962	4
0.0	16	0.0	12	0.60	7	−0.15	18	0.24	6	0.875	22	0.968	5
0.30	17	0.30	16	0.75	11	0.0	25	0.36	14	0.900	22	0.974	17
0.60	17	0.60	37	0.90	57	0.15	23	0.48	25	0.925	18	0.980	30
0.90	11	0.90	46	1.05	22	0.30	11	0.60	29	0.950	10	0.986	19
								0.72	10	0.975	2	0.992	9
$m =$	100	$m =$	125	$m =$	100	$m =$	86	$m =$	86	$m =$	86	$m =$	86
$\bar{r} =$	0.0300	$\bar{r} =$	0.4872	$\bar{r} =$	0.8790	$\bar{r} =$	0.0087	$\bar{r} =$	0.5009	$\bar{r} =$	0.8968	$\bar{r} =$	0.9792
$\sigma_r =$	0.5620	$\sigma_r =$	0.4673	$\sigma_r =$	0.1515	$\sigma_r =$	0.1932	$\sigma_r =$	0.1522	$\sigma_r =$	0.0377	$\sigma_r =$	0.0116

distribution of r for one hundred and twenty-five samples drawn from a universe in which $\mathbf{r}$ was 0.5. The differences between columns 2, 4, and 6 are attributable to the fact that $\mathbf{r}$ is not the same in the three cases. Columns 8, 10, 12, and 14 give the distributions of observed values of the correlation coefficient in samples of twenty-five for different values of $\mathbf{r}$. A comparison of these results with those in the other part of the table indicates the influence of the size of sample.

2. *Distribution Function of Correlation Coefficient*

From experimental results, "Student"[1] derived in 1908 an empirical distribution function of correlation coefficient r in samples of n drawn from a normal universe in which $\mathbf{r} = 0$. In 1913 Soper[2] obtained the mean and the standard deviation of the distribution of correlation coefficient to second approximations for samples of n drawn from a normal universe with correlation coefficient $\mathbf{r}$. In 1915 R. A. Fisher[3] showed that the distribution function of r is

$$y = \frac{(1 - \mathbf{r}^2)^{\frac{n-1}{2}}}{\pi\,(n - 3)!}(1 - \mathbf{r}^2)^{\frac{n-4}{2}} \frac{d^{n-2}}{d(r\mathbf{r})^{n-2}} \left(\frac{\cos^{-1}(-\mathbf{r}r)}{\sqrt{1 - \mathbf{r}^2 r^2}}\right). \qquad (75)$$

This function is so complicated as to require a table of values giving the distributions for different values of universe correlation $\mathbf{r}$ and sample size n. Such tables were provided in 1917 by Soper[4] and others, and the reader is referred to these for a comprehensive and detailed picture of the distribution of the correlation coefficient. It will be of interest, however, to note the way it varies with the size of sample and the correlation in the universe as shown in Fig. 76.

[1] "On the Probable Error of a Correlation Coefficient," *Biometrika*, Vol. VI, p. 302 et seq.

[2] "On the Probable Error of the Correlation Coefficient to a Second Approximation," *Biometrika*, Vol. IX, 1913, page 91, et seq.

[3] "Frequency Distribution of the Values of the Correlation Coefficient in Samples from an Indefinitely Large Population," *Biometrika*, Vol. X, 1915, page 507, et seq.

[4] H. E. Soper, A. W. Young, B. M. Cave, A. Lee, K. Pearson, "On the Distribution of the Correlation Coefficient in Small Samples," *Biometrika*, Vol. XI, 1917, pp. 328–413

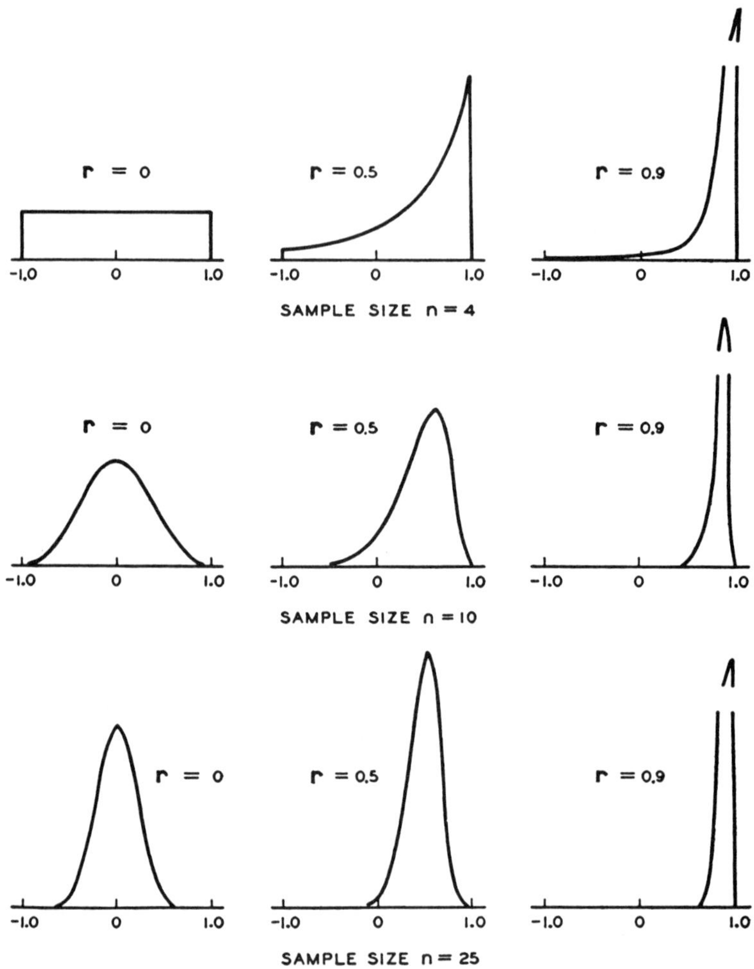

FIG. 76.—TYPICAL DISTRIBUTIONS OF CORRELATION COEFFICIENT.

3. *Standard Deviation σ_r of Correlation Coefficient*

The article by Soper and others shows that the standard deviation σ_r of the correlation coefficient in samples of n is given approximately by the simple formula

$$\sigma_r = \frac{1 - \mathbf{r}^2}{\sqrt{n - 1}}. \qquad (76)$$

The degree of approximation is indicated by the curves in Fig. 77.

In general, it will be seen that, except when the sample size n is small and the universe correlation $\mathbf{r}$ is large, formula (76) gives a two-place accuracy. For greater precision the reader must refer to the tables.

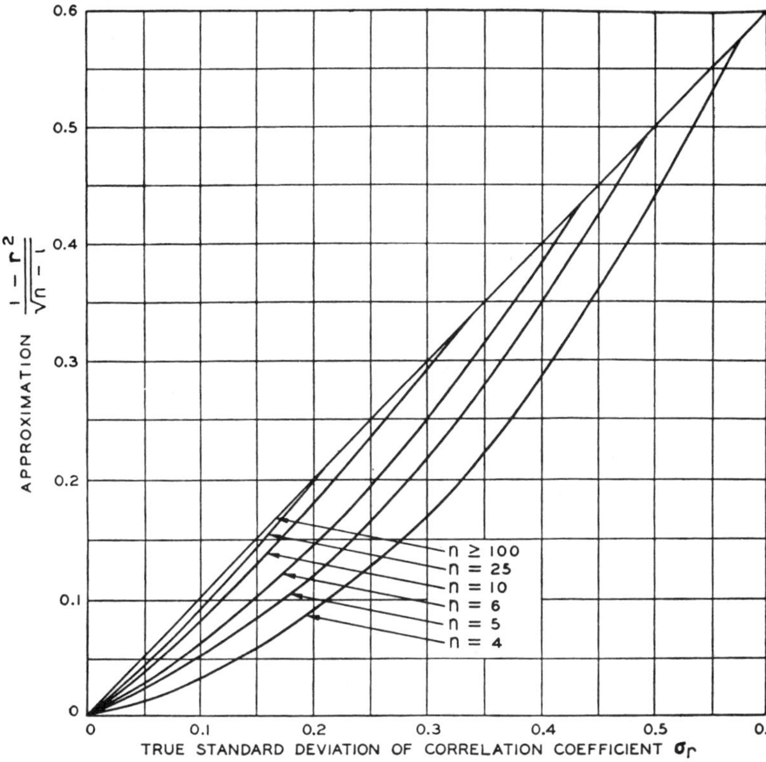

FIG. 77.—STANDARD DEVIATION OF CORRELATION COEFFICIENT IN RELATION TO THE SIMPLE APPROXIMATION (76).

4. *Modal and Expected Values of Correlation Coefficient*

Except for the case of samples from a normal universe with correlation coefficient $\mathbf{r} = 0$, the modal value $\breve{\mathbf{r}}$ and the expected or mean value $\bar{\mathbf{r}}$ of correlation coefficient do not coincide with the universe value $\mathbf{r}$. Fig. 78 shows the relationship between these three values for several sample sizes.

We see that for samples of less than twenty-five the absolute differences $|\mathbf{r} - \breve{\mathbf{r}}|$ and $|\mathbf{r} - \bar{\mathbf{r}}|$ are quite large. Even for $n \geq 25$, we often have occasion to make corrections for the fact that these two differences are not zero.

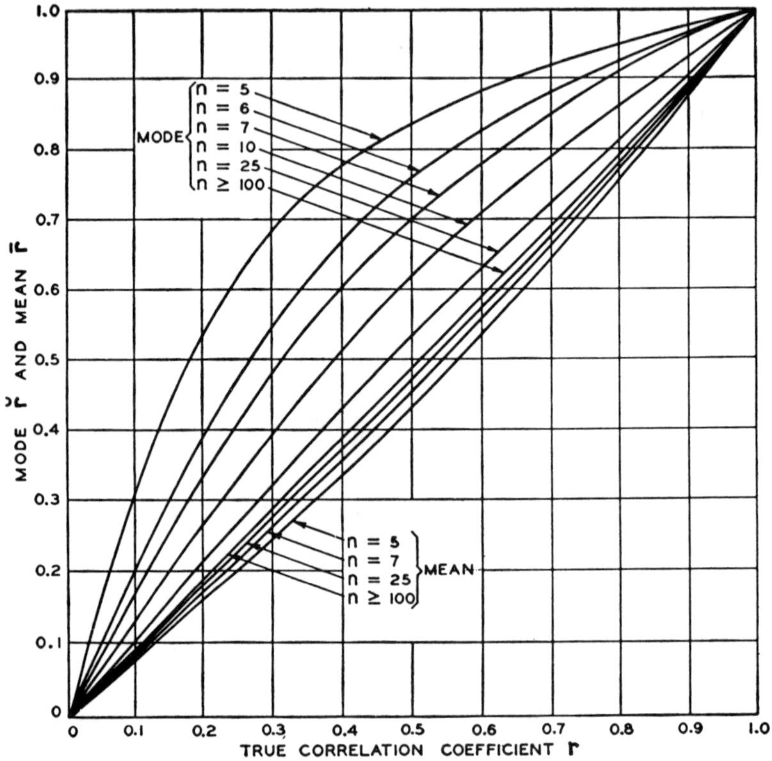

FIG. 78.—RELATIONSHIP OF MODAL VALUE $\breve{\mathbf{r}}$ AND EXPECTED VALUE $\bar{\mathbf{r}}$ IN SAMPLES OF SIZE n FROM A NORMAL UNIVERSE WITH CORRELATION COEFFICIENT $\mathbf{r}$.

5. *Transformed Distribution of Correlation Coefficient*

Let us consider the problem of establishing sampling limits on the observed value of correlation coefficient in samples of n drawn from a normally correlated universe for which the correlation coefficient is $\mathbf{r}$. The tables of $\bar{\mathbf{r}}$ and σ_r previously referred to, make it possible to write down limits

$$\bar{\mathbf{r}} \pm t\sigma_r,$$

and applying Tchebycheff's inequality, we can say that the probability of observing a value of r within these limits is greater than $1 - \frac{1}{t^2}$. Since, as is illustrated in Fig. 76, the shape of the distribution function changes so much with size of sample and the correlation of the universe, the actual probability associated with such a pair of limits will vary materially for different sample sizes and different values of $\mathbf{r}$.

Under these conditions, some of the recent work of Fisher[1] can be used to good advantage. He has shown that the distribution of z where

$$z = \tfrac{1}{2}[\log_e (1 + r) - \log_e (1 - r)] \qquad (77)$$

is approximately normal independent of the sample size and the correlation coefficient $\mathbf{r}$ in the normally correlated universe. Furthermore, he has shown that

$$\sigma_z = \frac{1}{\sqrt{n - 3}}, \qquad (78)$$

where σ_z is the standard deviation of the distribution of the transformed variable z.

Fisher has also shown that the expected value $\bar{\mathbf{z}}$ is greater numerically than $\mathbf{z}$ by an amount $\frac{\mathbf{r}}{2(n - 1)}$ where $\mathbf{z}$ is the value of z given by (77) for $r = \mathbf{r}$.

Making use of these results we can establish sampling limits $\bar{\mathbf{z}} \pm t\sigma_z$ such that to a high degree of approximation the probability that an observed value of z in samples of size n drawn from a normally correlated universe with correlation coefficient $\mathbf{r}$ will fall within the range fixed by these limits is given by the normal law integral.

6. *Conditions under which Distribution of r has Significance*

What has been said about the sampling fluctuations of r has significance only when all samples are drawn from the

[1] *Statistical Methods for Research Workers*, Second Edition, 1928.

same constant system of chance causes, so that the probability **p** that the point (X, Y), corresponding to an observed pair of values of X and Y, will fall within a given area X to $X + dX$ and Y to $Y + dY$ is constant for each observed pair of values.

Correlation between variables coming from non-constant cause systems is termed *spurious* correlation. A correlation coefficient calculated from n observed pairs of values arising from a non-constant system of chance causes is a spurious correlation coefficient for which the sampling distribution function (75) does not apply. Such a coefficient is not subject to the usual interpretation as a measure of relationship discussed more in detail in the following section. If then we do not take great care to eliminate lack of constancy in the cause system giving rise to a set of n pairs of values of two variables, we may obtain a false conception of the relationship between these variables. This is very important as we shall now show by a simple illustration.

Let us assume that we are using Rockwell hardness Y as a measure of tensile strength X for nickel silver sheet and that for this kind of material of given thickness the relationship is statistical in that the probability of an observed pair of values (X, Y) falling within the rectangle X to $X + dX$ and Y to $Y + dY$ is constant. It can easily be shown under these conditions that the correlation coefficient **R** between X and Y for two universes considered as one, or for the total number of observations is

$$\mathbf{R} = \frac{\mathbf{r}\sigma_x\sigma_y + \frac{ab}{4}}{\sqrt{\left(\sigma_x^2 + \frac{a^2}{4}\right)\left(\sigma_y^2 + \frac{b^2}{4}\right)}}, \tag{79}$$

where the difference between expected values of tensile strength and that between expected values of Rockwell hardness are a and b respectively.

This equation shows that, under these assumptions, the spurious correlation **R** may be either greater or less than **r**. Fig. 79 gives a simple illustration. The two sets of dots represent two sets of 12 observed pairs of values of tensile strength and hardness for nickel silver sheets of two thicknesses. The observed correlations of the two groups taken separately are $r_1 = 0.59$ and $r_2 = 0.54$; considered together the correlation R is 0.90. Lines of regression (1, 2, and 3) of hardness on tensile strength are shown for correlations r_1, r_2, and R respectively. Obviously R is a spurious coefficient. To use it as an indication of the statistical relationship between hardness and tensile

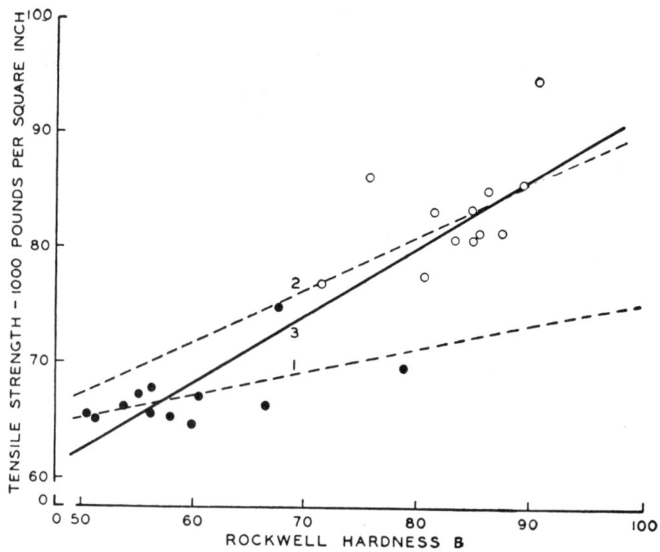

FIG. 79.—EFFECT OF SPURIOUS CORRELATION.

strength would obviously be misleading. Furthermore, as already stated, the distribution function (75) does not apply to this case.

7. *Commonness of Causation Measured by r*

Let us assume that we have any two physical quantities X_1 and X_2, and that variations in the first are produced by $(l + s)$ independent causes, which we shall designate by

$$U_1, U_2, \ldots, U_l, V_1, V_2, \ldots, V_s,$$

whereas variations in the second are produced by $(l + m)$ independent causes

$$U_1, U_2, \ldots, U_l, W_1, W_2, \ldots, W_m,$$

so that l of the causes are common to the two variables.

Let us consider first the following simple hypotheses concerning the causes:

(1) Each cause produces a single effect, and this effect is unity for all of the causes.
(2) The probability that any one of the causes produces its effect is constant and equal to $\mathbf{p}$.
(3) The resultant effect X_1 or X_2 is made up of the sum of the effects of the individual causes.

These conditions, of course, lead to a binomial distribution of effects for each of the variables X_1 and X_2.

Denote by z the contribution to X_1 and X_2 of the l common causes, by x the contribution of the V's, and by y that of the W's. Then, for any particular operation of the cause systems,

$$X_1 = x + z,$$

and

$$X_2 = y + z.$$

It may easily be shown that under these conditions

$$\mathbf{r}_{X_1X_2} = \frac{l}{\sqrt{(l+s)(l+m)}}. \tag{80}$$

If $s = m$ so that there are the same number $(l + m)$ of causes for each of the variables X_1 and X_2, then

$$\mathbf{r} = \frac{l}{l+m}, \tag{81}$$

or the ratio of the number of common causes to the total number of causes in either variable.

Let us consider now the more general case in which X_1 and

X_2 are related to their respective causes by some unknown functional relationship. Thus

$$X_1 = F_1(U_1, U_2, \ldots, U_l, V_1, V_2, \ldots, V_s),$$

and

$$X_2 = F_2(U_1, U_2, \ldots, U_l, W_1, W_2, \ldots, W_m).$$

Now we shall think of the U's, V's, and W's as symbols for groups of causes, each group producing a discontinuous distribution of effects.

Assuming that X_1 and X_2 can each be expanded in a Taylor's series, that terms beyond the first powers in the expansions can be neglected, that equal deviations in the U's, V's, and W's produce deviations in X_1 and X_2 proportional to the corresponding number of causes, and that the standard deviation of effects of one of the $l + s + m$ causes is the same as that of any other, it may be shown that $\mathbf{r}_{X_1X_2}$ is again given by (80).

8. *Simple Example Showing How Correlation Coefficient Measures Commonness of Causation*

Let us take eight chips experimentally identical—three red, three green, and two white. On each chip let us mark one side with zero and the other with unity. Now let these chips be tossed; let z be the sum of the numbers turned up on the two white ones, and x and y be the corresponding sums on the green and red ones, see Fig. 80.

We may think of the turning up of a chip as a cause and the number on a chip as the effect of the cause. If we let X_1 be the sum of the numbers on the three green and two white ones, and similarly let X_2 be the corresponding sum on the three red and the same two white ones, then X_1 and X_2 may be thought of as two variables having two out of a total of five causes of variation common to both.

In general, the resultant effect of the first system is

$$X_1 = x + z,$$

and that of the second system is

$$X_2 = y + z.$$

Inasmuch as each observed value of X_1 and X_2 has a common component, i.e., the effect of the two common causes, we would naturally expect a certain relationship between the values of X_1 and X_2 in successive operations of the two systems.

Now the correlation coefficient $\mathbf{r}_{X_1X_2}$ between X_1 and X_2 is a measure of this relationship; and since these two systems of causes obey all the laws laid down for the general case in Paragraph 7, we have merely to set $l = 2$, $m = 3$, and we have

$$\mathbf{r}_{X_1X_2} = \frac{2}{2+3} = 0.400.$$

The observed correlation coefficient between X_1 and X_2 in one observed set of 500 pairs of values was 0.422, giving a rather close check on the expected value 0.400.

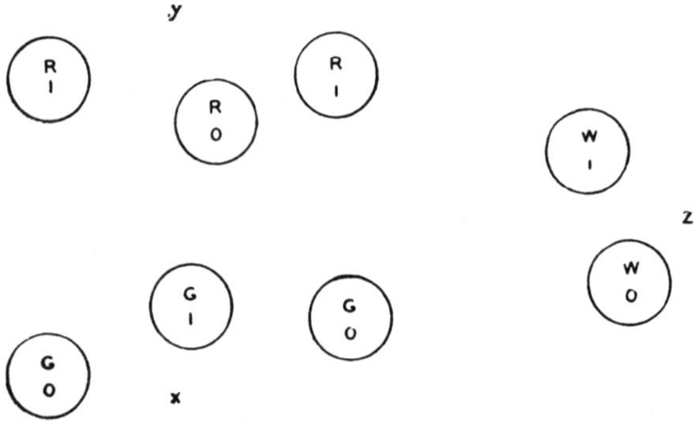

Fig. 80.—Two Systems Having Two Causes in Common.

Fig. 81 gives the scatter diagram and lines of regression for these 500 observed values of X_1 and X_2.

Practical Significance.—In Chapter IV attention was directed to the fact that the quality of material must be expressed in terms of physical characteristics which are, in general, not independent one of another because we do not know the independent ultimate quality characteristics or properties of a thing which make it what it is. In this connection the importance of considering not only the quality characteristics that are used in expressing quality but also the relationships between these was emphasized. We are now in a position to see more clearly the reason for so doing.

Let us consider first the simplest kind of a case in which we have a product with two quality characteristics, X_1 and X_2. It is apparent that simply to specify that the two quality characteristics should be controlled about the averages $\bar{X}_1$ and $\bar{X}_2$ with standard deviations σ_1 and σ_2 does not place the

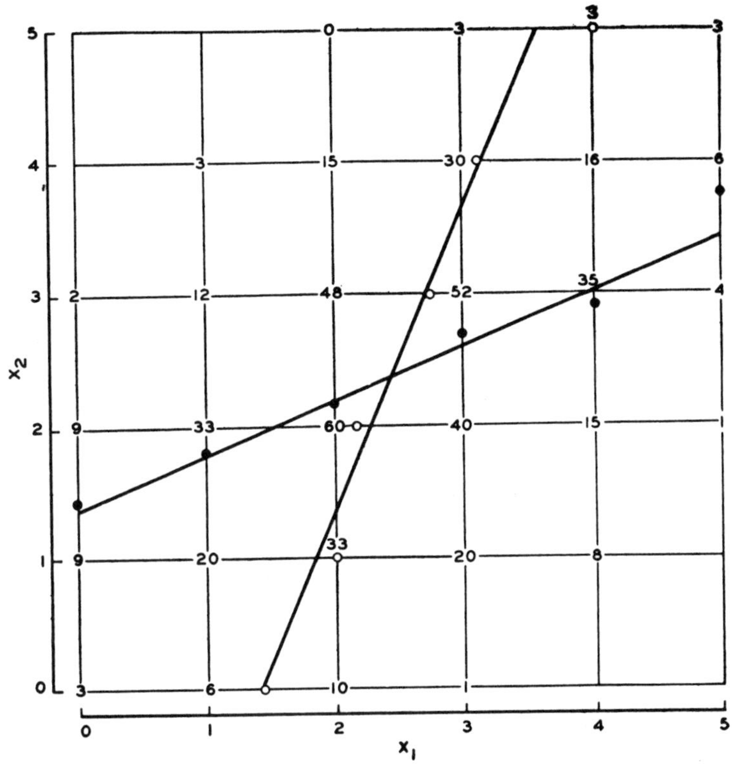

Fig. 81.—Scatter Diagram and Lines of Regression for 500 Observed Values.

same requirement on the constancy of the inherent quality of the material as to state that these two properties shall be controlled in the way just indicated and in addition that the correlation between them shall be, let us say, homoscedastic and linear with a coefficient of correlation **r**. In the second form of specification in which the nature of the correlation between the two characteristics is specified, we have introduced certain restrictions on the quality of the material in that the two characteristics must have a common causal source of an amount consistent with the causal interpretation of **r** outlined above.

Passing to the more complicated case where the quality of the material is specified in terms of *m* quality characteristics $X_1, X_2, \ldots, X_i, \ldots, X_m$, there is a corresponding interpretation of the correlations which becomes of importance in the consideration of ways and means of specifying the quality of materials. It is beyond the scope of our present discussion to do more than call attention to some of the recent developments in statistical theory indicating possible causal interpretations of certain inter-relations between all the pairs of the *m* variables measured in terms of the correlation coefficients. For example, it has been known for several years that four variables may be thought of as due to one general causal factor plus four specific non-correlated factors when

$$\mathbf{r}_{12}\mathbf{r}_{34} = \mathbf{r}_{13}\mathbf{r}_{24} = \mathbf{r}_{14}\mathbf{r}_{23}.$$

T. L. Kelley[1] has recently given an interesting discussion of the causal significance of inter-relationships of this character. Such work suggests an avenue of approach to the difficult problem of specifying quality in terms of those attributes which make it what it is.

9. *Interpretation of r in General*

The correlation coefficient is often used as a measure of relationship when the condition of constancy of cause system is not satisfied. This is particularly true of time series. We shall consider one simple example in sufficient detail to show that the sampling distribution for such a coefficient of correlation is not necessarily the same as that discussed above, and that the above interpretation of *r* as a measure of commonness of causation does not apply.

[1] *Crossroads in the Mind of Man*, Chapter III, Stanford University Press, 1928.

For this purpose we shall use an example given by Yule [1] in his presidential address before the Royal Statistical Society in November, 1925. The data are given in Fig. 82 and show the apparent relationship between the number of marriages in the Church of England and the decrease in the standard mortality rate over the same period. In this case the observed value of r is 0.95.

Needless to say this value of r may be thought of, as in Part II, as a summary presentation of the observed pairs of

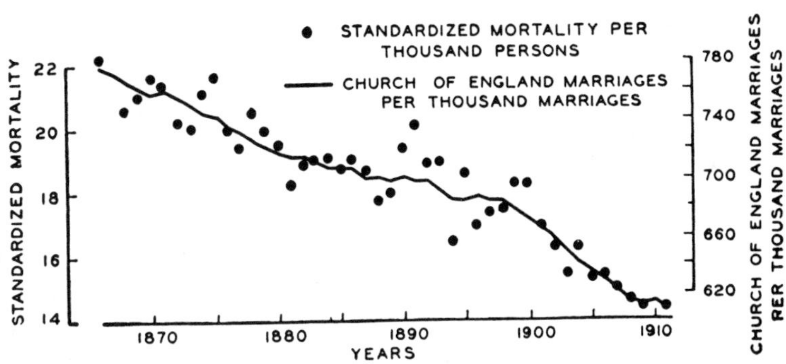

FIG. 82.—EXAMPLE OF A NONSENSE CORRELATION.

values. For example, an assumed line of regression would involve the statistic r. However, one is led to agree with Yule that there is no causal relationship between the two quantities shown in Fig. 82. Even if there were, the interpretation of r as a measure of commonness of causation in the sense of the previous two paragraphs would not hold.

[1] "Nonsense Correlations between Time Series," *Journal of Royal Statistical Society*, Vol. LXXXIX, pp. 1–64.

CHAPTER XVI

Sampling Fluctuations in Simple Statistics—General Remarks

1. *Two Phases of Distribution Theory*

Starting with the simple problem discussed in detail in Chapter XIII of Part IV, we have noted that there are two phases to the theory of distribution.

A. *Mathematical Distribution.*—Given a discrete universe, it is theoretically possible to set down all of the ways in which one may draw therefrom a sample of size n just as we did in the case of the simple example discussed in Paragraph 5 of Chapter XIII. It is then possible to calculate any given statistic for any one of the N possible samples. The fundamental nature of the problem of determining the mathematical distribution of a given statistic may then be represented schematically as in Table 39. The first column of this table is supposed to stand for the N possible different samples. Obviously, θ_{ij} stands for the value of the ith statistic for the jth sample, the permuted column of values corresponding to any statistic θ_i representing the distribution of possible values of that statistic.

The problem of determining the mathematical distribution of a given statistic θ_i is that of finding the distribution corresponding to the N possible different samples. This part of the work, it should be noted, is purely *formal* or *mathematical.* From a logical viewpoint, this table has nothing to do with the universe in which we live until we have connected it up in some way or other with reality. This we shall now do.

B. *Objective Distribution.*—We may think of the equation of control (58) as defining the universe of possible values of X from which we may select all possible different sets of samples of size n just as we have done above. Strictly speaking this is true only when (58) is discrete. If it is continuous we can, of course, calculate the relative frequency of occurrence of a statistic within a given interval.

TABLE 39.—SCHEMATIC OF DISTRIBUTION OF STATISTICS

Sample	Statistic Θ_1	Statistic Θ_2	. .	Statistic Θ_i	. .	Statistic Θ_s
1	Θ_{11}	Θ_{21}	. .	Θ_{i1}	. .	Θ_{s1}
2	Θ_{12}	Θ_{22}	. .	Θ_{i2}	. .	Θ_{s2}
.	.	.	. .	.	. .	.
.	.	.	. .	.	. .	.
.	.	.	. .	.	. .	.
.	.	.	. .	.	. .	.
.	.	.	. .	.	. .	.
.	.	.	. .	.	. .	.
j	Θ_{1j}	Θ_{2j}	. .	Θ_{ij}	. .	Θ_{sj}
.	.	.	. .	.	. .	.
.	.	.	. .	.	. .	.
.	.	.	. .	.	. .	.
.	.	.	. .	.	. .	.
.	.	.	. .	.	. .	.
.	.	.	. .	.	. .	.
N	Θ_{1N}	Θ_{2N}	. .	Θ_{iN}	. .	Θ_{sN}

In a similar way, it should be possible to calculate mathematically the distribution of any statistic for a sample of given size drawn from such a universe of possible effects. Up to this stage, the procedure is, as before, purely mathematical. At this point we make use of the postulate of control previously discussed in which we assume that there exist constant systems of chance causes such that the observed distribution of effects approaches in the statistical sense the mathematical distribution function. It does not appear feasible to justify this assumption other than in an empirical way as we have tried to do in Parts I and III. The comments of Dodd [1] again become relevant. Whether one chooses to call a mathematical distribution a probability distribution or not would seem to be a matter of choice. The mathematical distribution itself, as any mathematical formula, merely becomes a tool in the hands of an experimentalist.

It is essential therefore that in all that follows we carefully keep in mind the difference between the mathematical theory of distribution and the physical theory of distribution which it would appear must rest upon the assumption that the law of large numbers is a law of nature.

2. *Importance of Distribution Theory*

Again let us return to the simple problem discussed in Chapter XIII of Part IV. I think that most people would agree that if they were to draw samples of four from an experimental universe such as described in that chapter, they would get as statistical limits the distributions shown in Fig. 57. I doubt, however, that many of us would have much of an idea how the distributions of standard deviation, mean deviation, skewness, and flatness, would look in such a case until we had gone through the mathematics of distribution as was done there. This is just the kind of situation that the engineer of control faces when he considers the problem of predicting what he may expect to get in the future based upon an assumed equation of control of the type (58).

It is obvious that the reasonable way of predicting under such conditions, assuming the existence of the law of large numbers, is to make use of mathematical distribution theory such as that briefly discussed in the previous chapters. Our excursion into the field of mathematical distribution theory, however, has been a sort of pleasure trip in which we stopped to look at a few things which in the present state of our knowledge appear to be of immediate practical interest. It is well, therefore, that we take another look at this field for the purpose

[1] Loc. cit.

of getting a little better picture of the theory of mathematical distribution as a useful tool.

3. *Mathematical Distribution Theory—Method of Attack*

Given the problem of determining the distribution function of a given statistic Θ for samples of size n drawn from a given universe, there are, in general, two methods of attack depending to a certain extent upon whether the universe is discrete or continuous. One of these methods consists in finding the exact mathematical distribution function through the use of integral calculus. The other, already illustrated in the previous chapters, consists in finding merely certain moments of the distribution function.

As a simple example of the exact method, let us consider the problem of determining the distribution function of x where $x = x_1 + x_2$. Furthermore, let us assume that values of x_1 and x_2 are normally distributed about zero.

One method of finding the distribution of x is to fix on a definite range, say x to $x + dx$, and then to find the total probability of the occurrence of all possible combinations of x_1 and x_2 which will yield a value of x within the prescribed interval. The distribution function of x thus obtained will be the one desired.

The probability that x_1 lies within the interval x_1 to $x_1 + dx_1$ at the same time that x_2 lies within the interval x_2 to $x_2 + dx_2$ is given by the expression

$$p = \frac{1}{\sigma_1\sqrt{2\pi}} e^{-\frac{x_1^2}{2\sigma_1^2}} dx_1 \frac{1}{\sigma_2\sqrt{2\pi}} e^{-\frac{x_2^2}{2\sigma_2^2}} dx_2.$$

Having fixed on a value of x_1, and x being initially fixed, the value of x_2 is of necessity $x - x_1$. Hence we may write

$$p = \frac{1}{\sigma_1\sqrt{2\pi}} e^{-\frac{x_1^2}{2\sigma_1^2}} dx_1 \frac{1}{\sigma_2\sqrt{2\pi}} e^{-\frac{(x-x_1)^2}{2\sigma_2^2}} dx_2,$$

which for a proper choice of dx_1 and dx_2 is the probability, to within infinitesimals of higher order, of pairs x_1 and x_2 which yield a value of x within the interval x to $x + dx$. When x_1

is allowed to take all values between $-\infty$ and $+\infty$ and dx_1 is made to approach zero, we see that the sum of terms like **p** approaches the total probability that $x_1 + x_2$ lies within the prescribed interval.

Hence the total probability $\mathbf{P}(x)dx$ that the sum $x_1 + x_2$ lies within the interval x to $x + dx$ is by definition

$$\mathrm{P}(x)dx = \frac{1}{\sigma_1\sigma_2 2\pi}\int_{x_1=-\infty}^{x_1=+\infty} e^{-\frac{1}{2}\left(\frac{x_1^2}{\sigma_1^2}+\frac{(x-x_1)^2}{\sigma_2^2}\right)}dx_1 dx = \frac{1}{\sqrt{(\sigma_1^2+\sigma_2^2)2\pi}}e^{-\frac{x^2}{2(\sigma_1^2+\sigma_2^2)}}\,dx,$$

since $dx_2 \rightarrow dx$ as $dx_1 \rightarrow 0$.

Thus we are led to the well-known result that the distribution of a sum of two variables, each of which is normally distributed, is normal with a variance equal to the sum of the variances of the given normal distributions. This method may be extended to a linear sum of any number of variables. Whittaker and Robinson[1] show how through the use of Fourier's Integral Theorem it is possible to obtain the distribution function of a linear function of deviations in a more elegant manner.

If one can obtain in some such way an exact distribution function, it is theoretically possible to obtain the integral of this function over any given range, either exactly or by quadrature methods.

As an illustration of the modern mathematical tools available for finding the moments of the distribution of a statistic, let us consider one[2] method of finding the moments of the mean of a sample of n drawn from any discrete universe.

Assume that the universe is defined by s different values

$$X_1, X_2, \ldots, X_i, \ldots, X_s,$$

the relative frequencies of which are

$$\mathrm{p}_1, \mathrm{p}_2, \ldots, \mathrm{p}_i, \ldots, \mathrm{p}_s$$

respectively.

[1] Loc. cit., p. 168. See also the very interesting papers, "Application of Thiele's Semi-Invariants to the Sampling Problem," C. C. Craig, *Metron*, Vol. 7, No. 4, Dec. 31, 1928, pp. 51–107, and "Sampling When the Parent Population is of Pearson's Type III," C. C. Craig, *Biometrika*, Vol. XXI, Parts 1 to 4, Dec. 1929, pp. 287–293.

[2] V. Romanovsky, loc. cit.

Let the frequency of

$$X_1, X_2, \ldots, X_s$$

in a sample of n independent trials be

$$f_1, f_2, \ldots, f_s,$$

where, of course, some of the f's may be zero.

Then our problem is to investigate the distribution of

$$\overline{X} = \frac{\sum_{i=1}^{s} f_i X_i}{n}$$

in possible sets of n trials.

Denote the average and higher moments of the distribution of the universe by

$$\overline{\mathbf{X}}, \mu_2, \mu_3, \ldots, \mu_i, \ldots,$$

and of the distribution of the mean by

$$\overline{\mathbf{X}}_{\overline{X}}, \mu_{2\overline{X}}, \mu_{3\overline{X}}, \ldots, \mu_{i\overline{X}}, \ldots,$$

where, in each case, the moments are measured about the mean.

What we shall do is to express the $\mu_{\overline{X}}$'s in terms of the μ's, which for a given universe are known constants. Since the mean value of $\overline{X}$ in an indefinitely large number of samples is $\overline{\mathbf{X}}$, we may replace $\overline{\mathbf{X}}_{\overline{X}}$ by $\overline{\mathbf{X}}$ in finding expressions for the higher moments of $\overline{X}$.

Romanovsky has developed an elegant and simple way of obtaining these moments as follows: Consider the function of t defined by

$$U = \left[\sum_{i=1}^{s} \mathbf{p}_i e^{\frac{t}{n}(X_i - \overline{\mathbf{X}})}\right]^n$$

$$= \left[\mathbf{p}_1 e^{\frac{t}{n}(X_1 - \overline{\mathbf{X}})} + \mathbf{p}_2 e^{\frac{t}{n}(X_2 - \overline{\mathbf{X}})} + \ldots + \mathbf{p}_s e^{\frac{t}{n}(X_s - \overline{\mathbf{X}})}\right]^n.$$

By the multinomial theorem we have

$$U = \sum \frac{n!}{f_1!\, f_2! \ldots f_s!}\left[\mathbf{p}_1 e^{\frac{t}{n}(X_1 - \overline{\mathbf{X}})}\right]^{f_1}\left[\mathbf{p}_2 e^{\frac{t}{n}(X_2 - \overline{\mathbf{X}})}\right]^{f_2} \ldots \left[\mathbf{p}_s e^{\frac{t}{n}(X_s - \overline{\mathbf{X}})}\right]^{f_s}$$

$$= \sum \frac{n!}{f_1!\, f_2! \ldots f_s!} \mathbf{p}_1^{f_1} \mathbf{p}_2^{f_2} \ldots \mathbf{p}_s^{f_s} e^{-\frac{t}{n}\sum_{i=1}^{s} f_i (X_i - \overline{\mathbf{X}})}, \qquad (a)$$

the summation being extended to all f's whose sum is n.

Now the factor

$$\frac{n!}{f_1!\,f_2!\,\ldots\,f_s!}\mathrm{p}_1^{f_1}\,\mathrm{p}_2^{f_2}\ldots\mathrm{p}_s^{f_s}$$

is the probability of getting in n trials $f_1\,X_1$'s, $f_2\,X_2$'s, . . . , $f_s\,X_s$'s. Or, in other words, this factor is the probability of getting an $\overline{X}$ constructed in a particular way. Also for a particular construction of $\overline{X}$, the exponent of e is

$$\frac{t}{n}\sum_{i=1}^{s} f_i(X_i - \overline{\mathbf{X}}) = t(\overline{X} - \overline{\mathbf{X}}).$$

Making use of this fact, we have, on differentiating U r times with respect to t and then setting $t = 0$,

$$\left(\frac{d^r U}{dt^r}\right)_{t=0} = \sum \frac{n!}{f_1!\,f_2!\,\ldots\,f_s!}\mathrm{p}_1^{f_1}\,\mathrm{p}_2^{f_2}\ldots\mathrm{p}_s^{f_s}(\overline{X} - \overline{\mathbf{X}})^r. \qquad (b)$$

This is true since each differentiation of a particular term in the sum (a) merely multiplies this term by $(\overline{X} - \overline{\mathbf{X}})$.

By virtue of the way in which the right-hand side of (b) has been built up, it is clear that this sum is precisely the rth moment $\mu_{r\overline{X}}$ of the mean about its mean value. The method of obtaining any moment of $\overline{X}$ is then a very simple one. To facilitate the work, set

$$w = \sum_{i=1}^{s} \mathrm{p}_i e^{\frac{t}{n}(X_i - \overline{\mathbf{X}})}.$$

Then

$$U = w^n.$$

Then the zeroth moment of $\overline{X}$ is

$$(U)_{t=0} = (\mathrm{p}_1 + \mathrm{p}_2 + \ldots + \mathrm{p}_s)^n = 1.$$

$$\mu_{1\overline{\mathbf{X}}} = \left(\frac{dU}{dt}\right)_{t=0} = \left[nw^{n-1}\frac{1}{n}\sum_{i=1}^{s}\mathrm{p}_i e^{\frac{t}{n}(X_i - \overline{\mathbf{X}})}(X_i - \overline{\mathbf{X}})\right]_{t=0}$$

$$= \sum_{i=1}^{s} \mathrm{p}_i(X_i - \overline{\mathbf{X}}) = 0.$$

$$\mu_{2\bar{X}} = \left(\frac{d^2U}{dt^2}\right)_{t=0}$$

$$= \left[\frac{w^{n-1}}{n}\sum_{i=1}^{s} p_i e^{\frac{t}{n}(X_i-\bar{X})}(X_i-\bar{X})^2 + \frac{n-1}{n}w^{n-2}\left(\sum_{i=1}^{s} p_i e^{\frac{t}{n}(X_i-\bar{X})}(X_i-\bar{X})\right)^2\right]_{t=0}$$

$$= \frac{1}{n}\sum_{i=1}^{s} p_i(X_i - \bar{X})^2 = \frac{\mu_2}{n}.$$

In an exactly similar way, it can be shown that

$$\mu_{3\bar{X}} = \frac{\mu_3}{n^2} \quad \text{and} \quad \mu_{4\bar{X}} = \frac{3(n-1)}{n^3}\mu_2^2 + \frac{\mu_4}{n^3}.$$

Denoting by $\beta_{1\bar{X}}$ and $\beta_{2\bar{X}}$ the skewness and flatness respectively of the distribution of the averages, we have by definition

$$\beta_{1\bar{X}} = \frac{\mu_{3\bar{X}}^2}{\mu_{2\bar{X}}^3} = \frac{\mu_3^2}{n^4}\frac{n^3}{\mu_2^3} = \frac{\beta_1}{n}$$

$$\beta_{2\bar{X}} = \frac{\mu_{4\bar{X}}}{\mu_{2\bar{X}}^2} = \left(\frac{3(n-1)}{n^3}\mu_2^2 + \frac{\mu_4}{n^3}\right)\frac{n^2}{\mu_2^2} = \frac{\beta_2 - 3}{n} + 3,$$

where β_1 and β_2 are the skewness and flatness respectively of the universe. Of course it is possible, by the above method, to go much further than this and to find expressions for $\beta_{i\bar{X}}$ of any desired order i. However, our present purpose is merely to illustrate one of the modern methods of finding the moments of the distribution of a statistic.

A. *Some Numerical Results.*—To fix in our minds the significance of the above results, let us use them to calculate the statistics of the universe of averages, column 3, Table 25. We get

$$\bar{X}_{\bar{X}} = \bar{X} = 2.500000000$$

$$\sigma_{\bar{X}} = \frac{\sigma}{\sqrt{n}} = \frac{1.11803398 87}{2} = 0.55901699435$$

$$\beta_{1\bar{X}} = \frac{\beta_1}{n} = \frac{0}{4} = 0$$

$$\beta_{2\bar{X}} = \frac{\beta_2 - 3}{n} + 3 = \frac{1.64 - 3}{4} + 3 = 2.660000000.$$

These results obtainable through the use of the first four moments of the universe without going through the details of getting the distribution in column 3, Table 25, are the same to the number of places shown as the results obtained directly from the distribution in column 3.

In this same connection, it will be interesting to compare the values of mean variance $\overline{\sigma^2}$ and σ_{σ^2} obtained from (68) for the distribution of variance in samples of four drawn from the experimental universe of Chapter XIII with that calculated directly from column 4 of Table 25.

From (68) we get

$$\overline{\sigma^2} = \frac{n-1}{n}\sigma^2 = \tfrac{3}{4}(1.25) = 0.9375$$

$$\sigma_{\sigma^2} = \frac{\sigma^2}{n}\sqrt{\frac{n-1}{n}[(n-1)\beta_2 - n + 3]}$$

$$= \frac{1.25}{4}\sqrt{\tfrac{3}{4}[3(1.64) - 4 + 3]} = 0.3125\sqrt{0.75(3.92)}$$

$$= (0.3125)(1.714642820) = 0.535825881 2.$$

These results check to the number of places shown those obtained directly.

B. *Comparison of the Two Methods.*—Whenever the exact distribution of a statistic can be found by integration, we have more information than can be provided by the knowledge of any number of moments of the distribution of the same statistic. In other words, when the distribution of a statistic Θ_i is known as a function of Θ_i, the probability that the statistic will take on values lying between any given limits can be found either by direct integration or by quadrature methods.

On the other hand, if only the moments of the distribution of Θ_i are known, we can never be quite sure what the form of the distribution is. For example, $\beta_{1\overline{X}} \rightarrow 0$ and $\beta_{2\overline{X}} \rightarrow 3$ as n becomes large but even if we actually had $\beta_{1\overline{X}} = 0$ and

$\beta_{2\bar{X}} = 3$, we could not infer that the distribution of $\bar{X}$ was normal; for obviously the distribution defined by

X:	-1	0	$+1$
f:	1	4	1

has[1] $\beta_1 = 0$, $\beta_2 = 3$, $\beta_3 = 0$, which are identical with the first three betas for a normal universe, although this distribution is far from normal. As a matter of fact, it would be necessary in this instance to go as far as the sixth moment before we would discover any difference between it and the normal law function, so far as moments are concerned.

Suppose then, that the universe we started with had a form such that the distribution of means actually was identical with the simple one given above, but we had calculated merely the moments of this distribution by the above method. We would find that the first five moments were identical with those of the normal law, and we might perhaps be tempted to infer that the distribution of means was normal, although, as we have seen, such an inference would in fact be far from the truth.

4. *Mathematical Distribution Theory—Important Results*

Looking back over the work in the previous chapters, we see that distribution theory provides us, in certain instances, with distribution functions of a given statistic θ of the form $f_\theta(\theta, n)$ such that the integral of this function for a given range gives us the probability of occurrence of a value of θ within that range. Illustrations of this type are the distribution functions of average, standard deviation, and correlation coefficient.

Similarly, we may have distribution functions of a ratio z between two statistics θ_i and θ_j such that $f_z(z, n)dz$ represents the probability of occurrence of a value of z within the interval z to $z + dz$. This kind of function has been illustrated by the distribution of the ratio of the error of the average to the observed standard deviation.

[1] Of course, uncorrected moments are used here.

The other important form of distribution to be noted is that of the distribution of two statistics Θ_i and Θ_j, such that $f_{\Theta_i, \Theta_j}(\Theta_i, \Theta_j, n)d\Theta_i d\Theta_j$ represents the probability of the occurrence of values of Θ_i and Θ_j within the rectangle Θ_i to $\Theta_i + d\Theta_i$ and Θ_j to $\Theta_j + d\Theta_j$.

It is important to note also that the distribution function of a given statistic depends upon the functional form of the universe from which the sample is drawn, and that, in general, the average or expected value $\bar{\Theta}$ in samples of size n is not the same as the value of this same statistic for the universe.

5. *Mathematical Distribution Theory—Present Status*

Any summary of the status of distribution theory today will likely be out of date before the ink is dry. Here, as in the field of modern physics, progress is so rapid and along so many different lines that even those actively engaged in extending the theory find it difficult to keep abreast of all that is being done. A few brief remarks, however, may be of service to the engineer who cares to become acquainted with some of the important recent contributions.

The exact distribution of means of samples from normal populations dates back at least to the time of Gauss, whereas the exact distribution of variance and standard deviation were found in 1915 by R. A. Fisher.[1] In the same article, Fisher gives the exact distribution of the correlation coefficient in samples from an indefinitely large normal population. The same author has since given the exact distributions of the regression coefficient,[2] partial correlation coefficient,[3] and multiple correlation coefficient,[4] assuming a normal universe.

[1] Loc. cit.

[2] "The Goodness of Fit of Regression Formulae and the Distribution of Regression Coefficients," *Journal of the Royal Statistical Society*, Vol. LXXXV, Part IV, 1922, pp. 597–612.

[3] "The Distribution of the Partial Correlation Coefficient," *Metron*, Vol. III, No. 3–4, 1924, pp. 329–332.

[4] "The General Sampling Distribution of the Multiple Correlation Coefficient," *Proceedings of the Royal Society*, A, Vol. 121, 1928, pp. 654–673.

Pearson,[1] Romanovsky,[2] and Wishart [3] have also studied these same distributions.

In 1925, Hotelling [4] gave the distribution of the square of the correlation ratio subject to the conditions that the variates are not correlated, that the population is indefinitely large, and that the variates are normally distributed.

Exact distributions of means for certain of the Pearson type curves other than the normal have been given by Church,[5] Irwin,[6] and Craig.[7]

Important contributions to the theory of distribution through the use of moments have been made by Pearson,[8] Tchouproff,[9] Church,[10] Fisher,[11] and Wishart.[12]

The list of references given in the last few paragraphs is by no means complete. Instead, it is selective and is intended to indicate the rapid development[13] that is going on in this field.

1 "Researches on the Mode of Distribution of the Constants of Samples Taken at Random from a Bivariate Normal Population," *Proceedings of the Royal Society*, A, Vol. 112, 1926, pp. 1–14.

2 "On the Distribution of the Regression Coefficient in Samples from a Normal Population," *Bulletin de l'Academie des Sciences de l'U. S. S. R.*, 1926, pp. 645–648.

3 "The Generalized Product Moment Distribution in Samples from a Normal Multivariate Population," *Biometrika*, Vol. XXA, 1928, pp. 32–52.

4 "The Distribution of Correlation Ratios Calculated from Random Data," *Proceedings of the National Academy of Science*, Vol. 11, No. 10, 1925, pp. 657–662. Tables of the integral of the function given by Hotelling have recently been given by T. L. Woo, *Biometrika*, Vol. XXI, 1929, pp. 1–66.

5 Loc. cit.

6 Loc. cit.

7 Loc. cit.

8 "On the Probable Errors of Frequency Constants," *Biometrika*, Vol. II, 1903, pp. 273–281 and Vol. IX, 1913, pp. 1–10. "Further Contributions to the Theory of Small Samples," *Biometrika*, Vol. XVII, 1925, pp. 176–179.

9 "On the Mathematical Expectation of the Moments of Frequency Distributions," *Biometrika*, Vol. XII, pp. 185–210.

10 Loc. cit.

11 "Moments and Product Moments of Sampling Distributions," *Proceedings of London Mathematical Society*, Vol. 30, 1929, pp. 199–238.

12 "A Problem in Combinatorial Analysis Giving the Distribution of Certain Moment Statistics," *Proceedings of London Mathematical Society*, Vol. 28, 1929, pp. 309–321; *Proceedings of Royal Society of Edinburgh*, Vol. XLIX, 1929, pp. 78–90.

13 Rider, P. R., "A Survey of the Theory of Small Samples," *Annals of Mathematics*, Vol. 31, No. 4, pp. 577–628, October, 1930. An excellent bibliography is appended to this article.

6. *Importance of Distribution Theory—Further Comments*

We are now in a position to consider a little more critically than has been done the significance of some of the recent work on the mathematical theory of distribution as it bears upon the theory of control.

Assuming that an engineer is going to make use of statistical theory in helping him to do what he wants to do, it is but natural that he must sooner or later express what he wants to do in terms of some distribution function of a given quality X which he is to take as standard; that is to say, he must specify as a standard of what he wants to do some distribution function typified by the equation (58) of control

$$dy = \mathbf{f}(X, \boldsymbol{\lambda}_1, \boldsymbol{\lambda}_2, \ldots, \boldsymbol{\lambda}_i, \ldots, \boldsymbol{\lambda}_{m'})dX. \tag{58}$$

Assuming the existence of a constant system of causes having as its objective statistical limit this equation of control, it is necessary to set up limits on one or more different statistics of samples of size n. In many cases the control engineer may also desire to set up limits upon the allowable variation in X itself and in the fraction of the observed values of X which lie beyond some particular pre-assigned value.

Let us consider first the problem so often met in practice of setting a limit $\bar{\mathbf{X}} + t\boldsymbol{\sigma}$ on the variable X such that the objective probability that an observed value of X will fall between this limit[1] and $+\infty$ is $\mathbf{p}$, where $\bar{\mathbf{X}}$ and $\boldsymbol{\sigma}$ are the average and standard deviation of the universe (58) of control. To do this it is necessary to find the value of t from the equation

$$\mathbf{p} = \int_{\bar{\mathbf{X}}+t\boldsymbol{\sigma}}^{\infty} \mathbf{f}(X, \boldsymbol{\lambda}_1, \boldsymbol{\lambda}_2, \ldots, \boldsymbol{\lambda}_i, \ldots, \boldsymbol{\lambda}_{m'})dX.$$

Expressed in this general way, the formal problem of establishing the value of t for a given value $\mathbf{p}$ appears to be quite simple. When, however, we consider the theory of frequency distributions, we find that this problem is not so simple as it appears when the value t corresponding to the

[1] The same discussion obviously applies to the negative tail.

chosen value of **p** is greater than three, at least for most of the standard functions involving not more than four parameters. In fact, certain of these frequency functions may be found to have negative frequencies for values of X outside of a symmetrical range something[1] like $\bar{\mathbf{X}} \pm 3\sigma$. This is true of the second approximation (23) for certain values of **k**.

This fact is significant because it shows that when an engineer attempts to set some particular limit $\bar{\mathbf{X}} + t\sigma$ such that the objective probability of an observed value falling beyond this limit shall be **p** (where **p** is perhaps of the order of 0.001 or less), even the solution of the formal problem may be difficult. Of course, he might appeal to experience, observe the value of X a large number of times under what he assumes to be a controlled condition, and in this way try to approach as a statistical limit the exact objective frequency distribution to which any of the customary theoretical distributions would simply be an approximation. One does not need to go far to see, however, that such a procedure is not, in general, feasible if for no other reason than because it would require a large number of trials in order to justify the establishment of such a limit in anything like a satisfactory manner—it being true, of course, that one could never be sure of results obtained in this way.

Passing to the more general problem of establishing sampling limits on any statistic θ in samples of n drawn from the universe (58), it is of practical importance to note that with but few exceptions the exact frequency distribution function of such a statistic is unknown even when the universe (58) is continuous. When the universe is not continuous—it never is in practice—we must be satisfied with a knowledge of the moments of the distribution function of the statistic expressed in terms of the moments of the universe (58). For example, in the previous paragraph we have spoken briefly of a method of expressing any moment of the average of a sample of n in terms of the

[1] This point is emphasized in the writings of Edgeworth and is touched upon in various places in Bowley's summary of "Edgeworth's Contributions to Mathematical Statistics," published by the Royal Statistical Society, 1928.

moments of the universe. We have seen that to be able to specify the moments of the distribution of averages in samples of size n beyond the fourth moment requires a knowledge of moments of the universe higher than the fourth.

This is significant from an engineering viewpoint because it shows that if we are going to try to establish sampling limits even on such a simple statistic as the arithmetic mean with a comparatively high degree of precision in respect to the objective probability associated with the tail of this distribution, we must certainly be in a position to specify the moments of the accepted standard (58) of control beyond the fourth—something that it is obviously very difficult to do.

What we have said in respect to the establishment of sampling limits on the average is all the more true when we attempt to establish limits on other statistics such, for example, as the variance. This follows from the work of Tchouproff and Church [1] showing that the equation relating the fourth moment of the distribution of variance in samples of n to the moments of the universe involves the *eighth* moment of the universe—to obtain which is certainly not feasible.

There is another reason why it is difficult to attain great precision in the estimate of the probability associated with an asymmetrical range as we shall now see. Several times in the previous section we pointed out the significance of the fact that sampling from a discrete universe may give results radically different from those obtained when sampling in a similar way from a continuous universe. This is particularly important because we seldom see fit to classify measurements into more than ten to twenty cells, and it does not appear feasible to introduce moment corrections which allow us to go from the discrete to the continuous case with a known degree of precision.

We have considered at some length the approach of the distribution of the average to normality with increase in sample size irrespective of the parent population (58) as characterized by the first two β's of this distribution. The comparatively

[1] Loc. cit.

recent work of Holzinger and Church [1] shows that the distribution function of averages from a U-shaped universe is not even unimodal for small samples and appears to approach unimodality and symmetry only for samples of the order of fifty or more. In fact, they conclude that the distribution function of averages of less than fifty cannot be satisfactorily represented by a continuous curve. In such a case we must rely upon the application of the Tchebycheff inequality as we have done.

This kind of evidence indicates the nature of the difficulites involved in trying to establish asymmetrical limits on the sampling fluctuations of any statistic and it helps us appreciate the significance of the powerful Tchebycheff inequality in the establishment of symmetrical limits with at least a known upper bound to the error that we may make in the estimate of the probability associated with these limits provided only that we know the two simple statistics $\overline{\mathbf{X}}$ and σ of the universe.

The fact that we do not, in general, know the exact distribution function of measures of correlation other than the correlation coefficient in terms of the specified correlation in the universe precludes the use of these statistics in that we cannot establish their control limits. For this reason, we have not discussed the mathematical distribution theory for these statistics.

[1] "On the Means of Samples from a U-shaped Population," *Biometrika*, Vol. XX-A, pp. 361–388.

PART V

Statistical Basis for Specification of Standard Quality

The Establishment of Economic Tolerances and Standards of Quality Involves the Use of Three Simple Statistics

CHAPTER XVII

Design limits on Variability

1. *Tolerances*

Since all pieces of a given kind of product cannot be made identical, it is customary practice to establish allowable or *tolerance* ranges of variability for each of the measured quality characteristics. For example, if a shaft is to work in a bearing, we must allow for a certain clearance. In such a case the specifications usually require that a shaft have a diameter not less than some minimum nor more than some maximum value, and that the diameter of the bearing must not be less than some minimum nor more than some maximum value. An illustration taken from practice is:

Diameter of Shaft	Maximum limit 0.7500 inch
	Minimum limit 0.7496 inch
Diameter of Bearing	Maximum limit 0.7507 inch
	Minimum limit 0.7502 inch

Assuming that the diameters can be measured accurately to the fourth decimal place, we see that the minimum and maximum clearances are 0.0002 inch and 0.0011 inch respectively.

The tolerance range for a given quality X is defined as the range between the maximum and minimum tolerance limits specified for this quality, Fig. 83. Sometimes these limits are called tolerances. Perhaps more often, however, these limits are given in the form $X_1 = X - \Delta X$ and $X_2 = X + \Delta X$, and in this case ΔX is called a tolerance. To avoid any misunderstanding that might arise because of the apparent lack of uniformity in the definition of tolerance we shall use the terms *tolerance range* and *tolerance limits* wherever necessary to make the meaning clear.

2. *Tolerances Where 100 Per Cent Inspection Cannot Be Made*

Where the quality X can be inspected on every piece of apparatus by some go-no-go gauge, it is easy to separate product into two classes—that which does and that which does not fall within the tolerance range. If, however, we are testing for

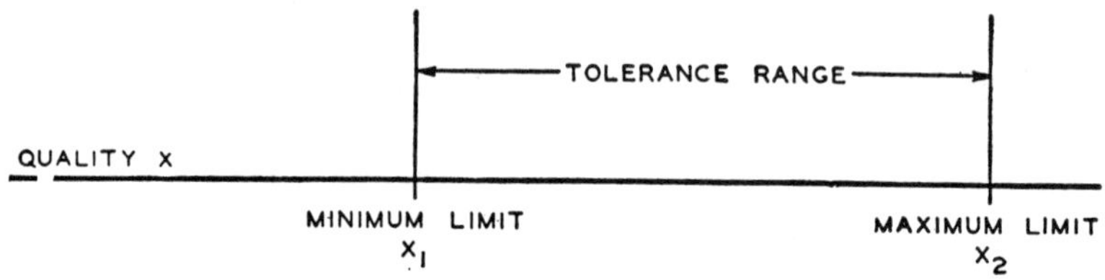

FIG. 83.—RELATIONSHIP BETWEEN TOLERANCE RANGE AND TOLERANCE LIMITS.

some quality such as tensile strength, it is obviously not possible to make 100 per cent inspection to see that the tolerance is met.

In this case our information about a lot of N pieces of product must be obtained from tests made on a sample of n pieces. The usual practice is to establish tolerance limits for the quality X and also tolerance limits for the fraction defective in the lot, or, in other words, the fraction of the total number of pieces of product in the lot having a quality X lying outside the tolerance limits for this quality, Fig. 84. Usually zero is taken as the lower limit for the fraction defective in the lot. Since our information must depend upon a sample, it is also necessary to establish tolerance limits on the fraction defective found in the sample, the lower limit being zero. These two kinds may be thought of as lot and sample tolerances, and they are related one to the other through a risk associated with the given sampling plan as will be indicated in Part VII, thus making it necessary for the sample tolerance to depend upon the number n in the sample.

3. *Importance of Control in Setting Economic Tolerance*

In general, a tolerance range on a quality X should be as small as possible. If it is too small, however, the rejections will be excessive. In other words, the design engineer tries to balance the rate of increase in value of reducing a tolerance range against the rate of increase of cost of such a procedure because of increased reiections.

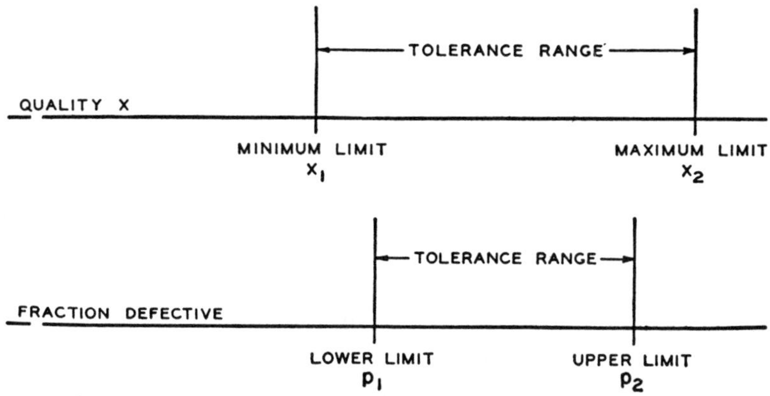

FIG. 84.—TWO SETS OF TOLERANCE LIMITS NECESSARY WHEN 100 PER CENT INSPECTION CANNOT BE MADE.

From what has previously been said, it is obvious that, if a design engineer knows that the quality X of a material or

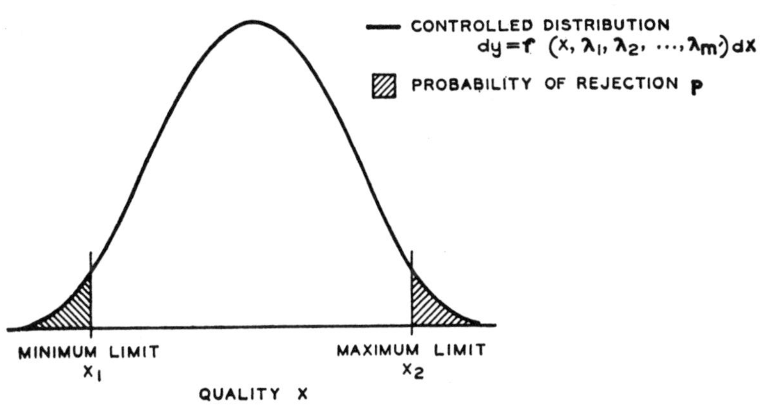

FIG. 85.—TOLERANCE ON FRACTION DEFECTIVE FOR CONTROLLED QUALITY.

piece-part entering into his design is statistically controlled in accord with some probability distribution such as illustrated by the smooth curve, Fig. 85, then he knows the expected number pN of rejections that will occur in the production of a number N of these piece-parts for a given set of limits. Only under these conditions of control is it a comparatively simple process to find an economic tolerance range.

Hence, to set an economic tolerance range it is necessary that the qualities of materials and piece-parts be controlled.

4. *Tolerances where 100 Per Cent Inspection Cannot be Made—Importance of Control*

When 100 per cent inspection cannot be made, we never *know* that the tolerance on a quality X is being met, even though it is met in the sample. Later we shall show that any inference about what exists in the remainder of the lot from what was found in the sample depends entirely upon what we *assume* about the lot before the sample was taken, and that the significance of such an assumption depends upon whether or not we assume that the product is controlled. If, however, instead of trying to use the double tolerance described in Paragraph 2 above, the design engineer makes use of raw materials and piece-parts previously shown to be statistically controlled with accepted expected values and standard deviations, he need only specify that the qualities of all materials and piece-parts going into his design be controlled with accepted average values and standard deviations.

Hence we see that it is very desirable to know that the quality of a product is controlled when it cannot be given 100 per cent inspection.

5. *Tolerances for Quality of Finished Product in Terms of Tolerances of Piece-parts*

Let us consider a very simple problem. Assume that an engineer wishes to design a circuit containing m different pieces of standard apparatus, such as relays, transformers, and so on. Suppose that he wishes to set a tolerance range on the overall resistance in the circuit and that the tolerance limits on the resistances of these m different pieces of apparatus are respectively R_{11} and R_{12}; R_{21} and R_{22}; . . . ; R_{i1} and R_{i2};

. . . ; R_{m1} and R_{m2}. What shall the engineer use as the tolerance range for the overall resistance?

The answer to the question is obviously

$$R_{12}+R_{22}+\ldots+R_{i2}+\ldots+R_{m2}-R_{11}-R_{21}-\ldots-R_{i1}-\ldots-R_{m1},$$

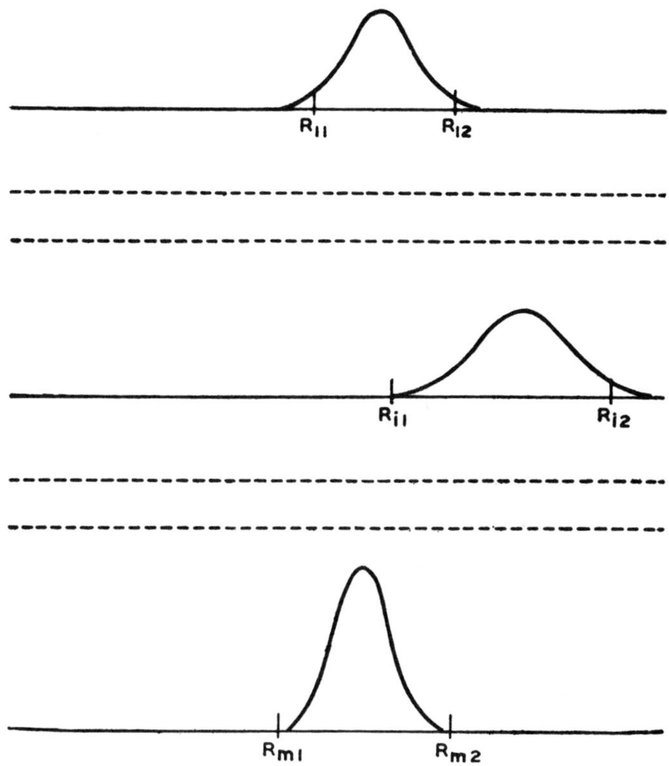

FIG. 86.—TOLERANCE RANGES ON OBSERVED DISTRIBUTIONS.

if we hold to the definition of a tolerance as the range between the maximum and minimum possible values of the quality. Before accepting this answer, however, let us consider the problem further.

Oftentimes we find that the previously observed distributions in the m different resistances are somewhat as indicated by the smooth distribution curves in Fig. 86. We see that in some instances the tolerances are such as to cause rejections in both the upper and lower ranges of the resistance as in the case of the quality R_1. At other times the condition may be such as indicated for the resistances R_i and R_m.

When the number m of different resistances is large, it is obvious that the number of times that we may expect to get a combination of m resistances chosen at random (one each from the m different kinds of resistances) that will add up to either the maximum or minimum limit is very small indeed. The question arises, therefore, as to whether or not it is economical to allow in design for an over-all tolerance range equal to the range between the possible maximum and minimum resistances that may occur.

Let us consider this problem upon the basis of the assumption that each of the m kinds of apparatus is manufactured under conditions such that the resistances are controlled about average values

$$\bar{\mathbf{R}}_1, \bar{\mathbf{R}}_2, \ldots, \bar{\mathbf{R}}_i, \ldots, \bar{\mathbf{R}}_m,$$

with standard deviations

$$\sigma_1, \sigma_2, \ldots, \sigma_i, \ldots, \sigma_m.$$

For the sake of simplicity, let us assume that the resistances are normally controlled, or, in other words, that the distribution function for each resistance is normal. From what has previously been said, it would be quite reasonable to adopt the tolerance limits

$$\bar{\mathbf{R}}_i \pm 3\sigma_i$$

on the ith resistance. If we adopted such a set of m tolerance limits, and followed the practice previously described of taking the difference between the sums of the maximum and minimum possible resistance as the tolerance for the sum of the resistances, we would have a tolerance range such as that schematically indicated in Fig. 87-*a*. Let us now consider why such a tolerance range may not be economical.

As may be shown, the expected distribution of the sum of m resistances chosen from the m different kinds of resistances as indicated above would be normal with an expected or mean value equal to $\Sigma\bar{\mathbf{R}}_i$ and a standard deviation

$$\sigma = \sqrt{\sigma_1^2 + \sigma_2^2 + \ldots + \sigma_i^2 + \ldots + \sigma_m^2}.$$

Suppose that we assume, as a simple case, that each of the m standard deviations is equal to, let us say, σ_1. It is obvious that the standard deviation of the sum is

$$\sigma = \sqrt{m}\sigma_1.$$

Starting with these simple assumptions, we may easily draw the frequency distribution function of the resultant resistance

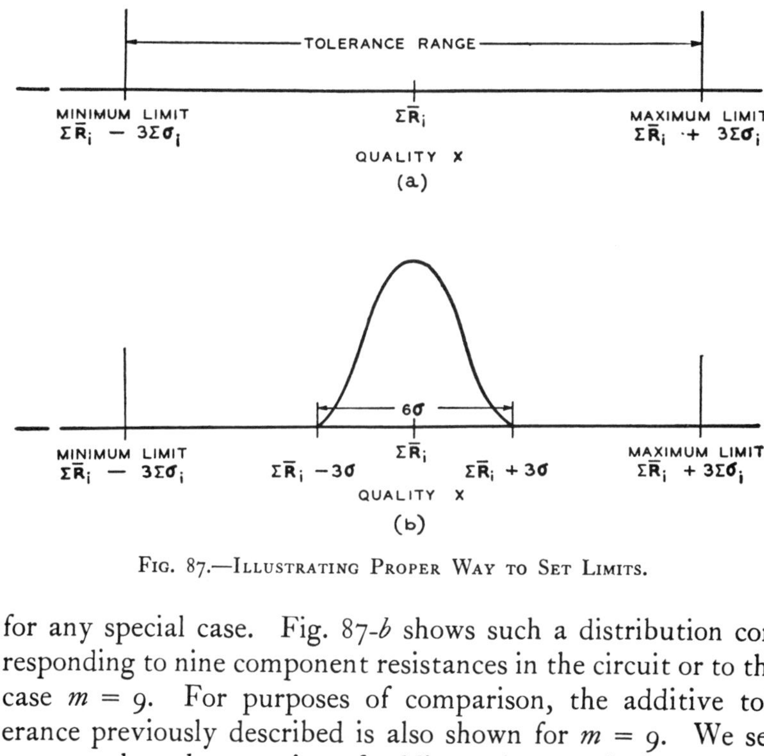

FIG. 87.—ILLUSTRATING PROPER WAY TO SET LIMITS.

for any special case. Fig. 87-*b* shows such a distribution corresponding to nine component resistances in the circuit or to the case $m = 9$. For purposes of comparison, the additive tolerance previously described is also shown for $m = 9$. We see at once that the practice of adding tolerance limits may be uneconomical because the chance is relatively very small that a resultant resistance would ever lie outside the limits $\Sigma\bar{\mathbf{R}}_i \pm 3\sigma$.

Having considered this simple illustration, we are in a

position to discuss the general problem of setting overall tolerance limits in terms of tolerance limits of piece-parts.

6. *The General Problem of Setting Tolerances on Controlled Product*

As a perfectly general case, let us assume that the quality X upon which we wish to set tolerance limits depends upon the qualities $X_1, X_2, \ldots, X_i, \ldots, X_m$ of m different piece-parts or kinds of raw material. Interpreted from the viewpoint of control, this means that we wish to set two limits on X which will include a certain fraction $\mathbf{P}$ of the product in the long run. We shall show how this can be done upon the basis of the assumption that each of the m component qualities are controlled about expected values

$$\overline{\mathbf{X}}_1, \overline{\mathbf{X}}_2, \ldots, \overline{\mathbf{X}}_i, \ldots, \overline{\mathbf{X}}_m,$$

with standard deviations

$$\sigma_1, \sigma_2, \ldots, \sigma_i, \ldots, \sigma_m,$$

subject to certain limitations.

Let us assume that we may write

$$X = F(X_1, X_2, \ldots, X_i, \ldots, X_m).$$

Furthermore, let us assume that the quality X may be expanded in a Taylor's series so that to a first order of approximation we may write

$$X = F(\overline{\mathbf{X}}_1, \overline{\mathbf{X}}_2, \ldots, \overline{\mathbf{X}}_i, \ldots, \overline{\mathbf{X}}_m) + a_1 x_1 + a_2 x_2 + \ldots + a_i x_i + \ldots + a_m x_m,$$

where

$$x_i = X_{ij} - \overline{\mathbf{X}}_i$$

and

$$a_i = \left(\frac{\partial F}{\partial X_i}\right)_{\overline{\mathbf{X}}_i},$$

it being understood that X_{ij} in this case is any one of the possible values of the quality X_i.

It may easily be shown under these conditions that the expected value $\bar{\mathbf{X}}$ and the standard deviation σ_X of the distribution of quality X of product assembled at random are given by the following equations:

$$\left.\begin{aligned}\bar{\mathbf{X}} &= F(\bar{\mathbf{X}}_1, \bar{\mathbf{X}}_2, \ldots, \bar{\mathbf{X}}_i, \ldots, \bar{\mathbf{X}}_m)\\ \sigma_X &= \sqrt{a_1^2\,\sigma_1^2 + c_2^2\,\sigma_2^2 + \ldots + a_i^2\,\sigma_i^2 + \ldots + a_m^2\,\sigma_m^2}\end{aligned}\right\}. \quad (82)$$

No matter what the nature of the distribution functions $f_1(X_1), f_2(X_2), \ldots, f_i(X_i), \ldots, f_m(X_m)$, Equations (82) enable us to write down the expected resultant quality $\bar{\mathbf{X}}$ and the standard deviation σ_X of this quality about the expected value subject to the limitations already considered. Making application of Tchebycheff's theorem, we can say that the probability $\mathbf{P}_{t\sigma}$ that the resultant quality will lie within the interval

$$\bar{\mathbf{X}} \pm t\sigma_X$$

satisfies the inequality

$$\mathbf{P}_{t\sigma_X} > 1 - \frac{1}{t^2}.$$

For example, one can say with certainty that in the long run more than $(1 - \frac{1}{9})$ of the product will have a quality X lying within the limits $\bar{\mathbf{X}} \pm 3\sigma_X$. In the simple case considered in the previous paragraph, where it is assumed that the distribution function for each of the m quality characteristics is normal, we see that the probability $\mathbf{P}_{3\sigma_X}$ is equal to 0.9973. It is exceedingly important from our present viewpoint to note that so long as we know nothing about the distribution function of each of the m quality characteristics, we can only make use of (82) in connection with Tchebycheff's theorem. The more we know about these functions, the more accurately we can establish the probability $\mathbf{P}_{t\sigma_X}$.

If the distribution functions of the m quality characteristics are alike in respect to their second, third and fourth moments, it may easily be shown that the skewness $\mathbf{k}_X$ and the flatness

β_{2_X} of the distribution of quality X are given[1] by the following equations:

$$\left.\begin{aligned} \mathbf{k}_X &= \frac{\mathbf{k}}{\sqrt{m}} \\ \beta_{2_X} &= \frac{\beta_2 - 3}{m} + 3 \end{aligned}\right\}, \tag{83}$$

where $\mathbf{k}$ and β_2 are the skewness and flatness of the distribution of any one of the m quality characteristics. Thus we see that under these conditions the skewness and flatness of the resultant distribution will be approximately normal, even though the individual qualities are distributed in a way such that their skewness and flatness are appreciably different from zero and three respectively.

In the more general case, where the distribution functions for the m different quality characteristics are not all alike, it may also be shown that the distribution of the resultant effect X will approach normality[2] as $m \to \infty$.

These results are of great importance as indicating the magnitude of the advantages that accrue from specifying the distribution of any one of the m qualities other than by saying that they shall be controlled about known average values with known standard deviations. Even though the distribution function of X approaches normality as m increases, it is usually true in a specific case that it would be very difficult to characterize the functions of the m component qualities with such precision as to enable the determination of the probability $\mathbf{P}_{t\sigma_X}$ to within, let us say, 1 per cent. In other words, it appears that, from a design viewpoint, there are many advantages to be gained by specifying that the quality of raw materials and piece-parts shall be controlled about known averages and with known standard deviations, although it appears that the advantages to be gained by trying to specify the functional forms of the controlled distributions and more than these two parameters of the distributions are offset by certain disadvantages.

[1] Compare with (63).

[2] See Appendix I.

Hence from a design viewpoint we conclude that the specification of control should include the specification of expected value $\bar{\mathbf{X}}_i$ *and standard deviation* σ_i *of any quality characteristic* X_i.

We are now in a place to consider the more general problem of designing a complicated piece of apparatus so that the quality of the product will have minimum variability.

7. *Design for Minimum Variability*

Again let us assume that the resultant quality X is a function F of the qualities $X_1, X_2, \ldots, X_i, \ldots, X_m$, or that

$$X = F(X_1, X_2, \ldots, X_i, \ldots, X_m),$$

and that we wish to make a product having an expected quality $\bar{\mathbf{X}}$ with minimum standard deviation σ_X.

We shall assume that the m quality characteristics are controlled about expected values $\bar{\mathbf{X}}_1, \bar{\mathbf{X}}_2, \ldots, \bar{\mathbf{X}}_i, \ldots, \bar{\mathbf{X}}_m$ with standard deviations $\sigma_1, \sigma_2, \ldots, \sigma_i, \ldots, \sigma_m$.

Making the same kind of assumptions as in Paragraph 6 about the expansibility of the quality X by means of Taylor's theorem, we may write

$$\sigma_X = \sqrt{a_1^2\sigma_1^2 + a_2^2\sigma_2^2 + \ldots + a_i^2\sigma_i^2 + \ldots + a_m^2\sigma_m^2},$$

$$\bar{\mathbf{X}} = F(\bar{\mathbf{X}}_1, \bar{\mathbf{X}}_2, \ldots, \bar{\mathbf{X}}_i, \ldots, \bar{\mathbf{X}}_m),$$

where, as in the preceding paragraph, a_i is a function of the m mean values. Our problem now is one of minimizing σ_X subject to the restriction imposed by the last equation. This will be recognized as a problem in the theory of maxima and minima. Expressed in terms of the Lagrange indeterminate multiplier λ it involves the solution of the following $m + 1$ equations:

$$\left.\begin{aligned} \frac{\partial(\sigma_X^2)}{\partial\bar{\mathbf{X}}_i} - 2\lambda\frac{\partial F}{\partial\bar{\mathbf{X}}_i} = 0 \\ \bar{\mathbf{X}} = F(\bar{\mathbf{X}}_1, \bar{\mathbf{X}}_2, \ldots, \bar{\mathbf{X}}_i, \ldots, \bar{\mathbf{X}}_m) \end{aligned}\right\}. \qquad (84)$$

It may not be feasible to solve this set of $m + 1$ equations for the unknowns $\overline{\mathbf{X}}_1, \overline{\mathbf{X}}_2, \ldots, \overline{\mathbf{X}}_m$ and λ because of their com-

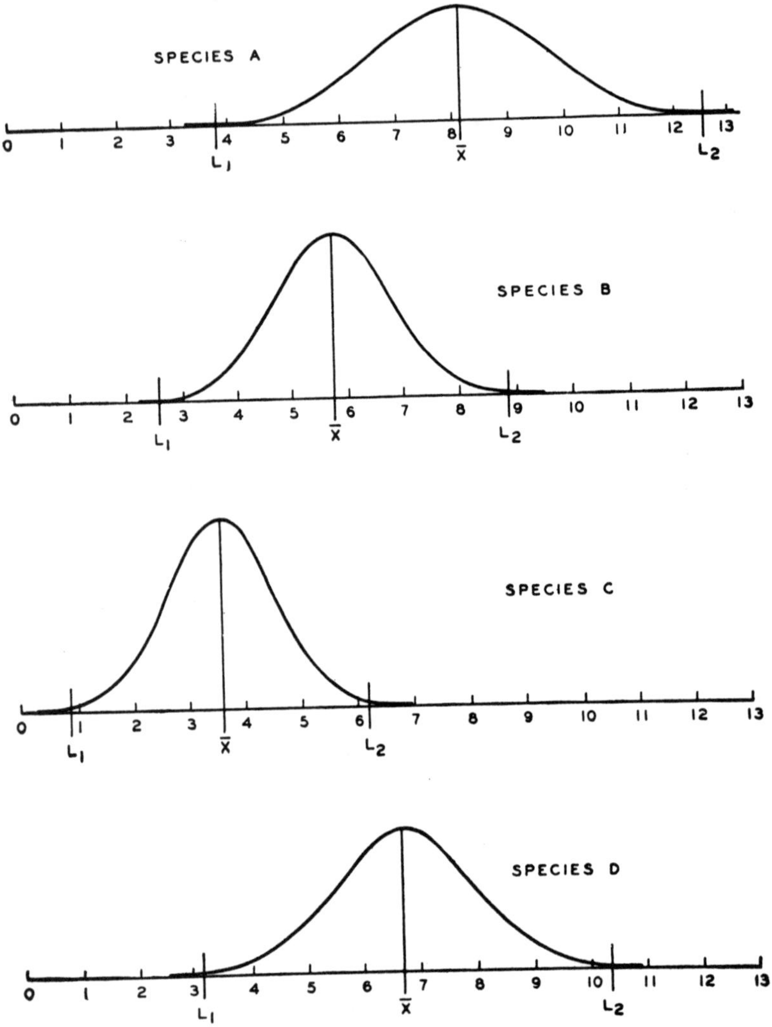

FIG. 88.—TYPICAL RELATION BETWEEN EXPECTED VALUES AND STANDARD DEVIATIONS.

plexity. Again it is possible that the solution may contain zero, infinite, or imaginary values of the $\overline{\mathbf{X}}$'s. Such solutions are obviously of no practical significance. We see that, in addition to knowing that the qualities of piece-parts and raw materials are controlled, *it is essential only to know the averages and standard deviations of the distribution functions of the component qualities.*

In practice limitations are often imposed upon the possible magnitudes of the expected values of the *m* quality characteristics other than those already considered. For example, one or more of these quality characteristics may be properties of material such as density, tensile strength, resistance, coefficient of expansion, and so on. Obviously, in choosing the expected values in such a case, we are limited to the expected values of the available raw materials, unless we develop some alloy having the desired expected value.

Also, in practice, the choice of an expected value of a quality cannot usually be made independent of the choice of its standard deviation. Thus in the case of a physical property of a material there is, in general, some relationship between the expected value of the property or quality and its standard deviation. This fact is illustrated in Fig. 88 showing the relative expected values and standard deviations of modulus of rupture of four kinds of telephone poles. We see that, broadly speaking, the standard deviation increases with increase in expected modulus of rupture.

CHAPTER XVIII

SPECIFICATION OF STANDARD QUALITY

1. *Standard Quality*

We often think of a standard of quality as being either a specified value X_s or a value X lying within some specified tolerance limits X_1 and X_2. If, however, we try to produce all units of a given kind of product with a standard quality X_s, the best we can hope to do, as we have seen in Parts I and III,

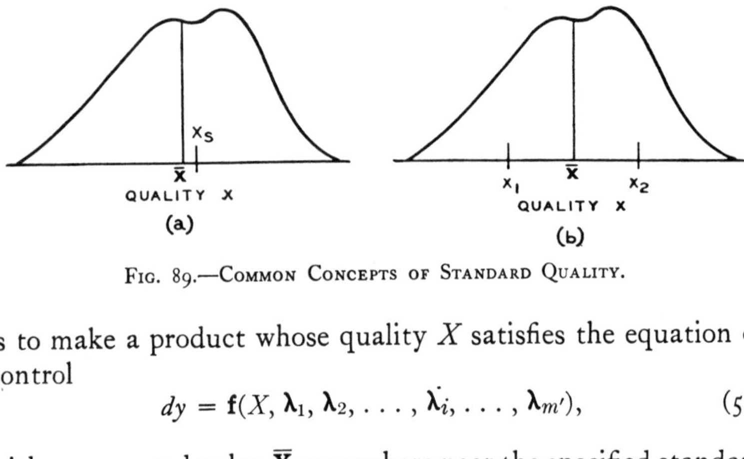

FIG. 89.—COMMON CONCEPTS OF STANDARD QUALITY.

is to make a product whose quality X satisfies the equation of control

$$dy = \mathbf{f}(X, \boldsymbol{\lambda}_1, \boldsymbol{\lambda}_2, \ldots, \boldsymbol{\lambda}_i, \ldots, \boldsymbol{\lambda}_{m'}), \tag{58}$$

with an expected value $\bar{\mathbf{X}}$ somewhere near the specified standard or ideal value X_s as indicated schematically in Fig. 89-*a*. Similarly, if one attempts to make a product all units of which will have a quality within the tolerance range X_1 to X_2, he will usually end up, after having done everything feasible to attain constancy, by making a product whose quality will be distributed as indicated schematically in Fig. 89-*b*. It is possible that the tolerance limits X_1 and X_2 will lie outside the limits of the curve (58) although this is seldom the case.

These standards are, as it were, ideals. We may, however, gain certain advantages by looking upon standard quality in a slightly different way as being the distribution function representing what we can hope to do in our attempt to attain an ideal standard quality. This objective standard quality distribution represents what we may expect to get when we have done everything feasible to eliminate assignable causes of variability in the quality. Hence, if we are to be able to interpret the significance of observed variability in quality, it is necessary to adopt or specify some such distribution function to be accepted as a standard for each quality characteristic. Then, so long as the observed variability in quality of n pieces of product may be interpreted as a sampling fluctuation in the effects of the constant system of chance causes characterized by the accepted standard distribution function for this quality characteristic, there is no need to worry over the observed variation because it is likely that there is nothing that we can do about it.

The question now to be considered is: What are the factors that determine how far we should try to go in specifying distribution functions to be used as standards? In the previous chapter we have shown that, from a design viewpoint, it is usually satisfactory to specify only the average $\bar{\mathbf{X}}$ and the standard deviation σ of the distribution, whereas complete specification would require the functional form $\mathbf{f}$ and the numerical value of each of the m' parameters. Furthermore, it is obvious that the specification must be such as to provide a satisfactory basis for detecting lack of control in the two important design characteristics $\bar{\mathbf{X}}$ and σ of the distribution of effects of the chance cause system.

It is necessary that we consider at this time the character of the specification to be required, because upon the choice of specification depends much of the treatment to follow in the discussion of the two problems:

(*a*) Establishment of sampling limits to detect lack of control to be treated in Part VI.

(*b*) Statistical estimation involved in establishing quality standards to be treated in Part VI.

2. *Types of Specification*

Type I: The probability of the production of a defective piece of product shall be **p**.

This type of specification corresponds to making the tolerance limits either $-\infty$ and some value X_2, or some value X_1

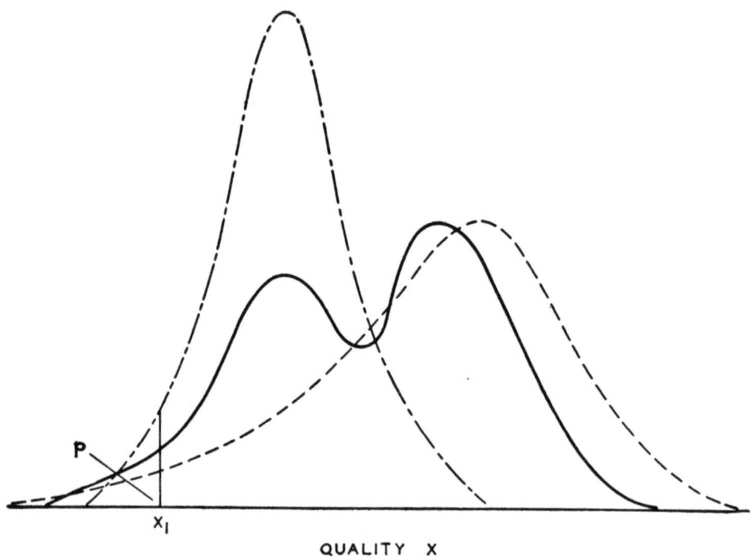

FIG. 90.—THREE UNIVERSES OF EFFECTS SATISFYING THE SPECIFICATION THAT THE PROBABILITY **p** SHALL BE CONSTANT.

and $+\infty$, and to specifying that the probability of X lying outside such a tolerance shall be **p**. It is obvious that this form of specification does not fix the form of the distribution function (58). For example, Fig. 90 shows three distribution functions which satisfy the specification Type I, although they are distinctly different. Hence the necessary design information, viz., the average and standard deviation of the distribution function, is not fixed by this type of specification.

It follows from what was said in Part IV that we may establish sampling limits within which the observed fraction p

defective in a sample of n may be expected to fall with a specified probability **P**. Hence this form of specification provides a basis for detection of lack of control although it fails to give requisite design information.

Type II: The expected or average quality shall be $\overline{\mathbf{X}}$.

This form of specification is sometimes considered when we would like to specify that the quality should be some ideal standard value X_s. It is apparent that there is an indefinitely large number of frequency functions satisfying this specification, but differing in respect to dispersion, skewness, and other characteristics as is illustrated schematically in Fig. 91.

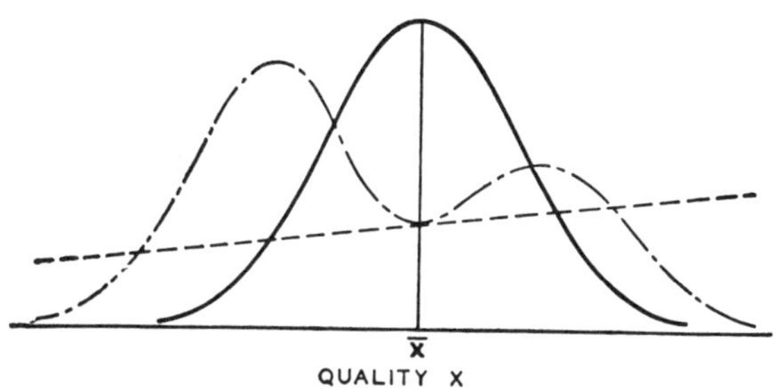

Fig. 91.—Three Universes of Effects Satisfying the Specification that the Expected Value Shall Be $\overline{\mathbf{X}}$.

It follows that specification Type II fails to give the information which makes possible the establishment of design limits on the variability of quality. Neither does it give information basic to the establishment of limits within which the observed quality may be expected to vary without indicating lack of control. Hence this form of specification is of comparatively little value from the viewpoint either of design or control.

Type III: The average or expected quality shall be $\overline{\mathbf{X}}$ *and the standard deviation shall be* σ.

This specification gives the requisite design information, and so long as quality of product satisfies this specification, we know from Tchebycheff's theorem that the probability $\mathbf{P}_{t\sigma}$ that a piece of product will have a quality X lying within the range between the two limits $\overline{\mathbf{X}} \pm t\sigma$ is greater than $1 - \frac{1}{t^2}$. This statement is true independent of whether the function **f** in the objective equation of control is or is not continuous.[1]

To emphasize the importance of the use of Tchebycheff's theorem in this connection, we show in Fig. 92 four distributions having approximately the same average $\bar{\mathbf{X}}$ and standard deviation σ. The dotted limits are drawn at $\bar{\mathbf{X}} \pm 3\sigma$. Hence we should expect to find more than 89 per cent of the total area for each distribution within the limits. In fact, no matter what distribution we might construct with average $\bar{\mathbf{X}}$ and standard deviation σ, we would find that more than 89 per cent of the area would fall within the dotted limits.

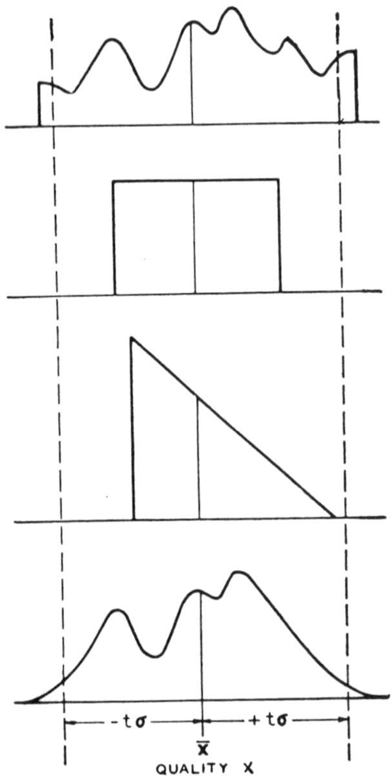

FIG. 92.—FOUR UNIVERSES OF EFFECTS SATISFYING THE SPECIFICATION THAT THE EXPECTED VALUE SHALL BE $\bar{\mathbf{X}}$ AND STANDARD DEVIATION SHALL BE σ.

From the viewpoint of control, we have seen in Part IV that sampling limits may be set on averages of size n if we know σ and that the probability associated with any limits X_1 to X_2 for the average $\bar{X}$ of a sample of n is given quite accurately by the normal law integral, at least when n is large. Furthermore, sampling limits can be established for observed standard deviation or variance in samples of n, and the probability associated with a given range σ_1 to σ_2 can be quite accurately estimated if we can assure ourselves that the function **f** is approximately normal.

[1] This is true at least for objective distributions of the type possible in practice.

From this discussion we conclude that the specification Type III is far superior to either of the two types previously mentioned.

Type IV: The average, standard deviation, skewness, and flatness of the distribution of quality X shall be $\overline{\mathbf{X}}$, σ, **k**, *and* $\boldsymbol{\beta}_2$.

Let us see what the specification of **k** and $\boldsymbol{\beta}_2$ adds in the way of valuable information. In the first place, the knowledge of these two statistics of the distribution function adds nothing to our knowledge of the integral of the function over any range X_1 to X_2 over and above that given by $\overline{\mathbf{X}}$ and σ and the use of Tchebycheff's theorem. This statement rests upon the assumption that we know nothing about the function **f**.

Under the same conditions the knowledge of **k** and $\boldsymbol{\beta}_2$ is of little practical value from a control viewpoint, since, as we have seen in Part IV, not even the expected values and standard deviations of k and β_2 for samples of size n are known for other than normal universes, so that we cannot establish sampling limits on these two statistics.

Hence we come to the important conclusion that the specification of standard quality in terms of $\overline{\mathbf{X}}$ and σ gives us the maximum amount of usable information, unless we specify **f**.

3. *Importance of Specifying the Function* **f**.

From the discussion of Chapter XII, Part III, we see that there is some justification for the belief that the distribution of a controlled quality is approximately normal or at least is approximately representable by the first two terms of a Gram–Charlier series, which has previously been referred to as the second approximation (23). If then we specify that the function **f** shall be normal with $\overline{\mathbf{X}}$ and σ as the two parameters, the specification becomes complete from the viewpoint of both design and control in that we know for such a product the probability associated with any interval X_1 to X_2, and we can set sampling limits on almost all of the common statistics, Table 37. Similarly, if we specify that **f** shall be the first two terms of a Gram–Charlier series, we can make use of most of the distribution functions of the simple statistics for a normal universe as first approximations, and the normal law integral gives the probability associated with any symmetrical interval $\bar{\mathbf{X}} \pm t\sigma$. In these two cases we find $\bar{\mathbf{X}}$ and σ playing an important rôle.

Formally, of course, the specification of **f** and each of the m' parameters makes possible the determination[1] of the probability associated with any interval X_1 to X_2. We have seen, however, that little is known about sampling fluctuations in statistics of samples of n drawn from such universes with the exception of average, variance, and χ^2. Hence, from a control viewpoint, having specified $\bar{\mathbf{X}}$ and σ, the specification of **f** or of any number of parameters does not add as much as one might at first expect. However, we shall soon see that we must specify **f** in order to make possible the most accurate estimates of such statistics, as **p**, **k**, and $\boldsymbol{\beta}_2$.

4. *Specification—Further Discussion.*

Thus far we have considered the problem of specification as though we could make the function **f** and parameters $\boldsymbol{\lambda}_1$, $\boldsymbol{\lambda}_2, \ldots, \boldsymbol{\lambda}_i, \ldots, \boldsymbol{\lambda}_{m'}$, whatsoever we chose to make them. Obviously we do not have such freedom of choice. We assume that there is one and only one objective distribution function representing the state of control for each quality X, although we do not assume that these functions are necessarily even of the same form **f** for all qualities. This means that the distribution function for any quality X must be *found* before it can be specified. Our previous discussion is of interest therefore in indicating the relative importance of different forms of specification, thus indicating the extent to which we should try to go in finding the distribution function of control in a specific case.

In any case we need to estimate the expected value $\bar{\mathbf{X}}$ and standard deviation σ of the objective distribution representing the state of control. Whether we try to go further and specify **p**, **k**, $\boldsymbol{\beta}_2$, and **f** depends upon whether or not the kind of information given by such a specification justifies the added expense of estimating these characteristics of the objective distribution

[1] The use of complicated quadrature methods is often necessary.

and the expense of the extensive inspection required to assure the producer that the quality of product does not vary beyond reasonable sampling limits in respect to these characteristics.

It is of interest to point out at this stage of our discussion that the specification of **p**, **k**, and $\boldsymbol{\beta}_2$ introduces a problem in estimation, the solution of which requires the assumption of a particular functional form **f**. To illustrate this point, let us assume that we have a comparatively small sample, say five observations, in which we are to estimate **p**. Assuming that the objective **p** is of the order of 0.01 as is often the case in practice, it is obvious that we cannot use the observed fraction p in a small sample as a basis of estimating **p**. The best we can do perhaps is to make use of our estimates of $\overline{\mathbf{X}}$ and $\boldsymbol{\sigma}$ derived from the sample as a basis for the estimate of **p**. On the other hand, the estimate of **p** derived in this way involves an assumption as to the functional form **f**. We may, by making use of Tchebycheff's relationship, state certain bounds within which it is likely that **p** lies.

Of course, when we have a large sample representing what we assume to be the condition of control, it is possible to use the observed fraction p as a basis for an estimate of **p**, although even then it is reasonable to believe that we should consider the general functional form of the distribution in arriving at an estimate. For example, Column 2 of Table 40 gives a distribution of observed values [1] of a variable X. Column 3 of this table gives a theoretical distribution based upon the assumption that the distribution function is

$$y = y_0\left(1 + \frac{x^2}{a^2}\right)^{-m} e^{-v \tan^{-1} \frac{x}{a}}.$$

The theoretical and observed distributions, shown in Fig. 93, indicate close agreement between theory and observation. When there is such close agreement it seems reasonable to assume that the integral of the assumed theoretical distribution between any two limits X_1 and X_2 should be taken into con-

[1] Elderton, W. P., *Frequency Curves and Correlation.*

sideration along with the observed fraction p within the same limits in estimating the objective fraction **p**. In other words, we see that the estimate of **p** required in a specification involves the assumption of a particular functional form **f** which in turn must be justified upon the grounds that it appears to be the objective frequency function representing the condition of control in this specific case.

TABLE 40.—IMPORTANCE OF DISTRIBUTION FUNCTIONS IN ESTIMATING FRACTION IN TAIL OF DISTRIBUTION

Cell Midpoint	Observed Distribution of Variable X	Type IV Distribution of Variable X
5	10	6
10	13	16
15	41	49
20	115	135
25	326	321
30	675	653
35	1,113	1,108
40	1,528	1,535
45	1,692	1,712
50	1,530	1,522
55	1,122	1,074
60	610	604
65	255	274
70	86	102
75	26	32
80	8	8
85	2	2
90	1	1
95	1	0
Σ	9154	9154

We have seen in the previous paragraphs that if we are to make use of information given by $\mathbf{k}$ and $\boldsymbol{\beta}_2$, we must also have a specification of **f**. Thus, in the example just quoted from Elderton, the observed values of k and β_2 are 0.073 and 3.170 respectively. The fact that the use of these two observed values of k and β_2 in the assumed functional form **f** gives an apparently close fit to the observed data, provides us with a certain amount of assurance that the objective values of skewness **k** and flatness β_2 are, for example, different from 0 and 3 respectively corresponding to the normal law, or that they are somewhere in the neighborhood of the values derived from the observed data.

Enough has been said to show that the problem of estimation involved in the specification of characteristics other than $\bar{X}$ and

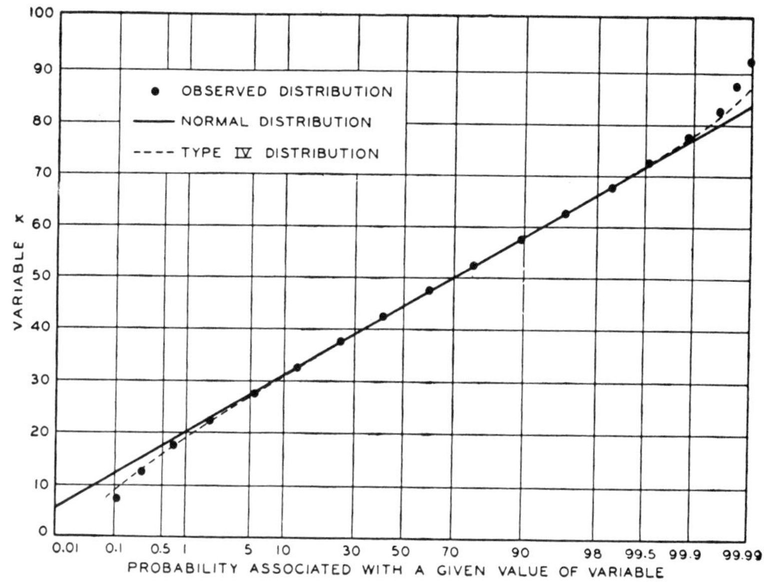

FIG. 93.—GRAPHICAL PRESENTATION OF DATA IN TABLE 40.

σ and the objective fraction **p** of the distribution of control involves the assumption of specific forms for **f**.

5. *Conclusion*

The specification of quality from the viewpoint of both design and control should provide $\bar{X}$ and σ. In certain cases it is desirable that we specify **p** so as to provide a basis for catching erratic troubles which, as we shall see later, may not be detected through sampling limits established on statistics used to detect lack of control in $\bar{X}$ and σ. The accurate estimate of p, however, involves the introduction of some assumption as to the functional form f of the distribution (58) of control. The specification of k and β_2 is, in general, of less importance than that of p, $\bar{X}$, and σ.

Part VI

Allowable Variability in Quality

Five Criteria for Determining
When Variations in Quality
Should Not Be Left to Chance

CHAPTER XIX

Detection of Lack of Control in Respect to Standard Quality

1. *The Problem*

In Part V we saw that standard quality is characterized by the equation of control

$$dy = \mathbf{f}(X, \lambda_1, \lambda_2, \ldots, \lambda_i, \ldots, \lambda_{m'})dX. \qquad (58)$$

In particular, we saw that it is desirable to maintain constancy of this distribution at least in respect to the average $\bar{\mathbf{X}}$ and standard deviation σ. Of course the qualities of samples of n pieces of product of standard quality may be expected to show sampling fluctuations.

The problem to be considered in this chapter is that of establishing an efficient method for detecting the presence of a cause of variability other than one of the chance causes belonging to the group which gives the accepted standard distribution (58), or of determining when an observed sample is such that it is unlikely that it came from a constant cause system characterized by this distribution.

2. *The Basis for Establishing Control Limits*

Knowing the distribution function (58), we saw in Part IV that it is possible, in general, to find a distribution function $\mathbf{f}_\Theta(\Theta, n)$ for a given statistic Θ calculated for samples of size n such that the integral

$$\mathbf{P} = \int_{\Theta_1}^{\Theta_2} \mathbf{f}_\Theta(\Theta, n)d\Theta \qquad (85)$$

gives the probability that the statistic Θ will have a value lying within the limits Θ_1 to Θ_2. Of course, if the function $\mathbf{f}_\Theta(\Theta, n)$

is limited in both directions, we may choose Θ_1 and Θ_2 such that $\mathbf{P} = 1$; and, in this case, any observed value of Θ falling outside the limits is a positive indication that standard quality is not being maintained. If the function $\mathbf{f}_\Theta(\Theta, n)$ in (85) is discontinuous we must replace the integral sign by the symbol of summation Σ for discrete ordinates and change our discussion accordingly. The conclusions, however, remain unchanged.

For the most part, however, we never know $\mathbf{f}_\Theta(\Theta, n)$ in sufficient detail to set up such limits. More important yet is the fact that, even if we knew the function well enough to set up limits within which a statistic Θ must fall provided the cause system has not varied from the accepted standard, we could not say that the occurrence of an observed value of Θ within this range is sufficient to prove that the sample came from a constant system characterized by the accepted standard distribution function (58).

How then shall we establish allowable limits on the variability of samples? Obviously, the basis for such limits must be, in the last analysis, empirical. Under such conditions it seems reasonable to choose limits Θ_1 and Θ_2 on some statistic such that the associated probability $\mathbf{P}$ is *economic* in the sense now to be explained. If more than one statistic is used, then the limits on all the statistics should be chosen so that the probability of looking for trouble when any one of the chosen statistics falls outside its own limits is economic.

Even when no trouble exists, we shall look for trouble $(1 - \mathbf{P})N$ times on the average after inspecting N samples of size n. On the other hand, the smaller the probability $\mathbf{P}$ the more often in the long run may we expect to catch trouble if it exists. We must try to strike a balance between the advantages to be gained by increasing the value $\mathbf{P}$ through reduction in the cost of looking for trouble when it does not exist and the disadvantages occasioned by overlooking troubles that do exist. It is conceivable, therefore, that there is some economic value $\mathbf{P}$ or pair of limits Θ_1 and Θ_2 for each quality characteristic. It is perhaps unnecessary to say that the determination of the economic value $\mathbf{P}$ and the associated limits must be an approximation in any case. Furthermore, it is obviously necessary to adopt some value which will be acceptable for practically all quality characteristics, although the economic value **P** for one quality may not be the same as that for another.

With these points in mind we shall consider a few principles to guide our choice of Θ_1 and Θ_2. In general, it is reasonable to believe that the objective economic values of Θ_1 and Θ_2 are not symmetrically spaced in respect to the expected value $\bar{\Theta}$ of the statistic. It is perhaps more reasonable to assume that they are so spaced as to cut off equal tails of the function $\mathbf{f}_\Theta(\Theta, n)$. Under these conditions it is reasonable to try to set limits Θ_1 and Θ_2 that will satisfy this condition. From the discussion in Part IV we see, however, that even when the distribution (58) is known, the distribution function $\mathbf{f}_\Theta(\Theta, n)$ for a given statistic Θ is seldom known in sufficient detail to make it possible to choose Θ_1 and Θ_2 to cut off equal tails. Even more important is the fact that we seldom care to specify **f** accurately enough to make possible the setting of such limits.

For these reasons we usually choose a symmetrical range characterized by limits

$$\bar{\Theta} \pm t\sigma_\Theta \tag{86}$$

symmetrically spaced in reference to $\bar{\Theta}$. Tchebycheff's theorem tells us that the probability **P** that an observed value of Θ will lie within these limits so long as the quality standard is maintained satisfies the inequality

$$\mathbf{P} > 1 - \frac{1}{t^2}.$$

We are still faced with the choice of t. Experience indicates that $t = 3$ seems to be an acceptable economic value.

Hence the method for establishing allowable limits of variation in a statistic Θ depends upon theory to furnish the expected value $\bar{\Theta}$ and the standard deviation σ_Θ of the statistic Θ and upon empirical evidence to justify the choice of limits $\bar{\Theta} \pm t\sigma_\Theta$.

3. *Choice of Statistic to Detect Change in Average Quality*

Suppose, for example, that

$$dy = \mathbf{f}(X, \lambda_1, \lambda_2, \ldots, \lambda_i, \ldots, \lambda_{m'})dX, \tag{58}$$

with an expected value $\bar{\mathbf{X}}$, is the standard of quality and that we are to detect a change in quality in which only the expected value changes from $\bar{\mathbf{X}}$ to $\bar{\mathbf{X}} + \Delta\bar{\mathbf{X}}$. What statistic of the sample should we use to detect this change in order to minimize the number of observations required?

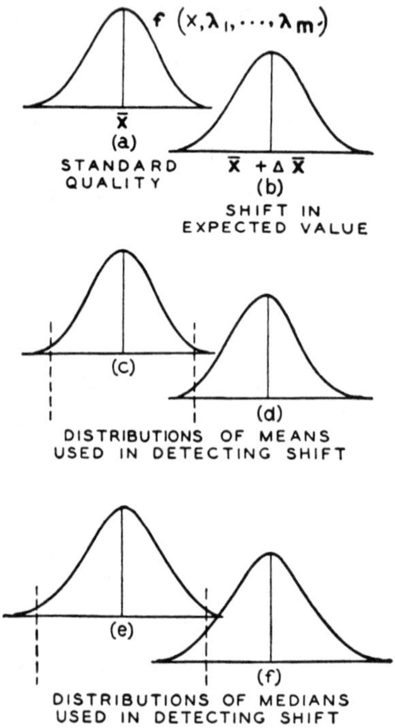

FIG. 94.—ILLUSTRATING IMPORTANCE OF PROPER CHOICE OF STATISTICS.

To start with, let us assume that (58) is a normal distribution. Obviously then, we might use either the median or arithmetic mean of a sample to detect a change $\Delta\bar{\mathbf{X}}$ in the expected value $\bar{\mathbf{X}}$. To illustrate, let us assume that the standard quality is distributed as in Fig. 94-*a* and that the shift $\Delta\bar{\mathbf{X}}$ in expected value is represented by Fig. 94-*b*. Let us assume also that the distribution of arithmetic means and that of medians are normal as indicated in Figs. 94-*c* and 94-*e* respectively. This situation is practically met when the sample size is large, in which case the standard deviation of the distribution of medians is $1.253 \dfrac{\sigma}{\sqrt{n}}$ and that of means is $\dfrac{\sigma}{\sqrt{n}}$. These values of standard deviation were used in drawing Figs. 94-*c* and 94-*e*. Limits including equal areas of Figs. 94-*c* and 94-*e* are shown. The curves of Figs. 94-*d* and 94-*f* represent the distributions of averages and medians about the expected value $\overline{\mathbf{X}} + \Delta\overline{\mathbf{X}}$. Obviously, the area of Fig. 94-*d* outside the dotted limits for means is greater than the area of Fig. 94-*f* outside the limits for medians. Hence, for a given increase $\Delta\overline{\mathbf{X}}$, we may expect to have an indication of trouble more often by limits set on arithmetic means than by those set on medians.

In general, if Θ_1 and Θ_2 are two statistics (such as median and arithmetic mean) used to detect a change in some characteristic $\boldsymbol{\Theta}$ of the universe; if the functions $\mathbf{f}_{\Theta_1}(\Theta_1, n)$ and $\mathbf{f}_{\Theta_2}(\Theta_2, n)$ are symmetric, monotonic, and unimodal; if the standard deviations of Θ_1 and Θ_2 fall off in the same way with increase in sample size n; and if $\bar{\boldsymbol{\Theta}}_1 = \bar{\boldsymbol{\Theta}}_2 = \boldsymbol{\Theta}$, then we may say that that statistic having the smaller standard deviation should be used in detecting the change $\Delta\overline{\mathbf{X}}$.

Now, if there exists a statistic Θ such that the use of any other statistic Θ_1 does not throw any further light upon the value of the parameter to be estimated, then Θ is said to be a *sufficient statistic*, and is, of all statistics of this class, the one to use, provided it can be shown that it is also the most efficient.

In this connection, some very useful theory has been contributed by R. A. Fisher.[1] He shows that if $\boldsymbol{\sigma}$ and $\boldsymbol{\sigma}_1$, the standard deviations of Θ and Θ_1 respectively, fall off as $\frac{1}{\sqrt{n}}$, and if Θ and Θ_1 are normally correlated with correlation coefficient $\mathbf{r}$, then the above criterion of sufficiency leads to the relationship

$$\boldsymbol{\sigma} = \mathbf{r}\boldsymbol{\sigma}_1,$$

showing that Θ is more efficient than Θ_1 and that under the given conditions

$$\mathbf{r} = \sqrt{E}, \tag{87}$$

where E is the efficiency of Θ_1 as compared to Θ. If, in practice, we find that the correlation surface for two statistics, such as the median and arithmetic mean, is normal and satisfies (87), then it is reasonable to assume that the more efficient of the

[1] "On the Mathematical Foundations of Theoretical Statistics," *Philosophical Transactions*, Series A, Vol. 222, pp. 309–368, 1922.

two is a sufficient statistic and perhaps also the most efficient statistic that can be used. It should be noted that under the given conditions the more efficient of the two statistics has the smaller standard deviation and hence is the better one to use in detecting a change of parameter.

We have already seen that the distribution of medians for samples of size $n = 4$ from a normal universe is symmetrical and not so very different from normal, whereas the distribution of arithmetic means is normal in this case. It is interesting to see, therefore, whether or not the arithmetic mean is not only better than the median for detecting a shift $\Delta\overline{\mathbf{X}}$ but really the best statistic that can be used.

Fig. 95 shows the observed scatter diagram of correlation between medians and means for samples of four. In this case the observed efficiency E and correlation coefficient r are

$$E = 0.80$$

$$r = 0.899,$$

and (87) is practically satisfied. Since we know of no statistic whose standard deviation falls off more rapidly than $\frac{1}{\sqrt{n}}$, we may conclude that the arithmetic mean is the best statistic to be used for detecting a shift $\Delta\overline{\mathbf{X}}$, subject to the conditions stated above.

We are not in a place to prove that the average is the best statistic when the distribution function (58) is not normal. However, since we do not know of a better statistic than the arithmetic mean to detect a shift of $\Delta\overline{\mathbf{X}}$ when the universe differs from normality by no more than it usually does in practice, we shall always make use of the arithmetic mean for this purpose.

It is of interest to note that the efficiency E of the median in respect to the arithmetic mean for samples of n drawn from a normal universe decreases asymptotically with increase in sample size from 100 per cent for $n = 2$ to 63 per cent when n is large, as indicated in Fig. 96. The point for $n = 4$ is that observed for the 1,000 samples of four. This curve shows that for large samples the efficiency of the median is such that it contains only about 63 per cent of the information in respect to the change $\Delta\overline{\mathbf{X}}$; in other words, that the average of a sample

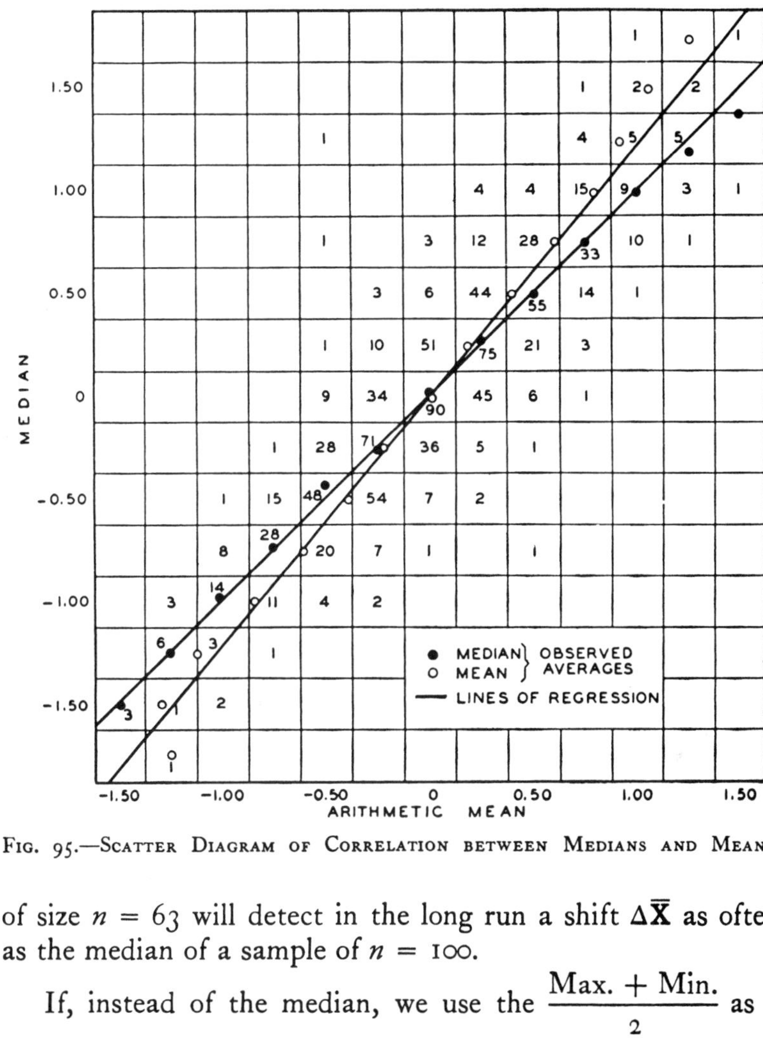

FIG. 95.—SCATTER DIAGRAM OF CORRELATION BETWEEN MEDIANS AND MEANS.

of size $n = 63$ will detect in the long run a shift $\Delta\overline{\mathbf{X}}$ as often as the median of a sample of $n = 100$.

If, instead of the median, we use the $\frac{\text{Max.} + \text{Min.}}{2}$ as a statistic, we have seen that the efficiency is 100 per cent for samples of two and about 88 per cent for samples of four.

By making use of some of the recent work of Tippett,[1] E. S. Pearson, and N. K. Adyanthāya,[2] we may show that the efficiency of the $\frac{\text{Max.} + \text{Min.}}{2}$ falls off as indicated in Fig. 96. This curve is in striking contrast to that for medians.

The concept of efficiency here used is different from that introduced in Part IV, and is perhaps the more usual one. It is simply the ratio of the sample sizes of two different

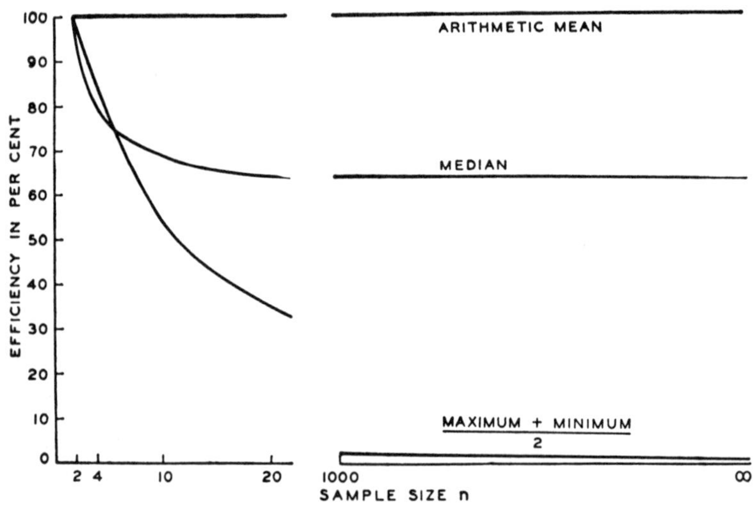

Fig. 96.—Efficiency of the Median and $\frac{\text{Max.} + \text{Min.}}{2}$ as a Function of Sample Size n.

consistent statistics required to give the same standard deviation.

Consider for example the arithmetic mean $\bar{X}$ and median M of a sample of n. The standard deviation of $\bar{X}$ in samples of n drawn from a normal universe with standard deviation σ is $\sigma/\sqrt{n}$ and for medians M, the standard deviation is $c(n)\sigma$,

[1] "On the Extreme Individuals and the Range of Samples Taken from a Normal Population," *Biometrika*, Vol. XVII, December, 1925.

[2] Egon S. Pearson and N. K. Adyanthāya, "The Distribution of Frequency Constants in Small Samples from Symmetrical Populations," *Biometrika*, Vol. XX-A, pp. 356–360.

where $c(n)$ is some function of n which approaches $1.253/\sqrt{n}$ as n becomes large.

Choose a particular sample size n_M for the median and find the sample size $n_{\bar{X}}$ for the arithmetic mean required to give the same standard deviation as that of the median for the chosen sample size. This requires merely the solution of the equation

$$\frac{\sigma}{\sqrt{n_{\bar{X}}}} = c(n_M)\sigma$$

for $n_{\bar{X}}$. In fact

$$n_{\bar{X}} = \frac{1}{c^2(n_M)},$$

and therefore by definition the efficiency of the median for the chosen value of n_M is

$$E = \frac{n_{\bar{X}}}{n_M} = \frac{1}{n_M c^2(n_M)}.$$

The trouble with this value of efficiency for small values of n is that it depends upon the fact that the value of n_M was chosen first. Thus if we assign to $n_{\bar{X}}$ the same value n_M, and solve for the new value n'_M we should come out with the same value of E, if the efficiency for small samples is to have the same interpretation as for large samples. However, if we solve for n'_M from the equation

$$\frac{\sigma}{\sqrt{n_M}} = c(n'_M)\sigma,$$

and then take the ratio $E = \dfrac{n_M}{n'_M}$, it will be found to be different, in general, from the value of E computed above.

In other words, this means that for small samples we get one curve of efficiency by assigning to n_M an increasing sequence $n_1, n_2, \ldots$ and a different curve of efficiency when $n_{\bar{X}}$ is assigned the same series of values.

For this reason the curves of Fig. 96 should not be considered as exact but as merely indicating, in a general way, how the efficiency of the median or $\frac{\text{Max.} + \text{Min.}}{2}$ falls off with increasing sample size.

4. *Choice of Statistic to Detect Change in Standard Deviation*

Suppose now that we consider the problem of determining the statistic which will detect a change only in the standard deviation of the effects of the cause system. Let us start, as in the previous paragraph, with the case where the universe of effects (58) is normal. Naturally, we may use any one of several infinite sets of estimates of σ as a means for detecting a change $\Delta\sigma$. Thus, for example,

$$\mathbf{m}_i = \frac{2}{\sigma\sqrt{2\pi}}\int_0^{\infty} x^i e^{-\frac{x^2}{2\sigma^2}} dx = \frac{\sigma^i 2^{\frac{i}{2}}}{\sqrt{\pi}}\Gamma\left(\frac{i+1}{2}\right), \tag{88}$$

where $x = X - \overline{\mathbf{X}}$, and $i = (1, 2, 3, \ldots)$. For a given value of i, we can write

$$\sigma^i = b\mathbf{m}_i,$$

where b is a constant for a particular i. Obviously, the ith moment m_i of the absolute values of the deviations in a sample from the observed average $\overline{X}$ of a sample can be used as an estimate of σ in samples of size $n = \infty$. In other words, the statistic

$$\Theta = (bm_i)^{\frac{1}{i}}$$

may be used as an estimate of σ if the sample size is sufficiently large.

In general, the distribution function $\mathbf{f}_\Theta(\Theta, n)$ of any statistic Θ is not symmetrical; hence the expected value $\bar{\Theta}$ is not σ. This situation is represented schematically in Fig. 97. For samples of a given size n, there is some constant c by which to divide Θ so that the expected value of $\frac{\Theta}{c}$ becomes equal to $\mathbf{\Theta}$.

Hence $\frac{\Theta}{c}$ may be used as an estimate of $\mathbf{\Theta}$ or in this case of σ; it is called a *consistent* estimate.

In a similar way we may make use of either a symmetrical or an asymmetrical range as an estimate of σ. For example, we have already considered the distribution of 1,000 observed ranges in samples of four drawn from a normal universe. The statistics for these distributions were given in Table 34. Since these ranges are measured in terms of the standard deviation of the universe, the empirical factors for estimating σ are those

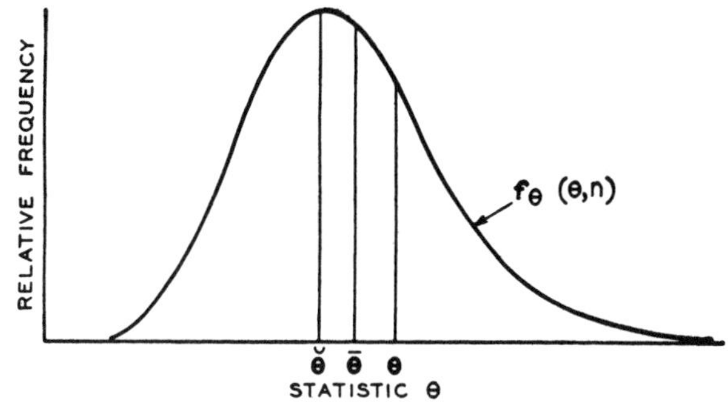

FIG. 97.—SCHEMATIC ASYMMETRICAL DISTRIBUTION OF A STATISTIC.

given in Table 41. Now, as in the discussion of Fig. 97, if $\bar{\Theta}$ represents the expected value of the distribution of any range θ, the expected value of the distribution of $\frac{\theta}{c}$ is Θ or the statistic θ of an infinite sample or of the universe. Of course,

TABLE 41.—EMPIRICAL FACTORS FOR ESTIMATING σ

Range	$X_4 - X_1$	$X_2 - X_1$	$X_3 - X_2$	$X_4 - X_3$
Empirical Factor for Estimation	2.0044	0.7863	0.6338	0.7752

this statement rests on the assumption that θ is measured in units of Θ as in Table 41. The second row of this table gives the empirically determined factors with which to transform the observed ranges into consistent estimates of σ. It will be noted that we use Θ as a statistic of an infinite universe. If Θ is also a parameter in the equation of control (58), as it usually is, then there is some parameter λ numerically equal to Θ.

Enough has been said to show that there is an indefinitely large number of ways in which to estimate σ. Which one shall we choose as being the most likely to detect a change $\Delta\sigma$?

Let us start with a comparison of the standard and the mean deviation as a basis for estimating σ. In Part IV we saw that the expected value for small samples is not equal to σ for either of these statistics, the situation being that characterized by Fig. 97. Hence, before we can use either statistic as an estimate of σ, we must know the correction factor for transforming the statistic into one for which the expected value will be σ. Such correction factors are given in Table 29 for the standard deviation σ of the sample and a similar table could be given for the mean deviation.

Of course these factors approach unity as the sample size becomes large. If we also assume that the distributions of these two statistics approach normality as the sample size n becomes large, we can make use of the same reasoning as that given in Paragraph 3 to show that σ is the better estimate since the mean deviation estimate is only 88 per cent efficient.

When the sample size is small, these two estimates have more nearly the same efficiency. This situation is shown in Fig. 98. The question arises as to whether or not the standard deviation σ is the most efficient statistic for estimating σ from a small sample, assuming that it is the most efficient for a large sample. The only available method for doing this is to apply the test of (87) which is strictly applicable only when the correlation between the two estimates is normal, which condition is, as we know, not fulfilled in this case. The experimental results for the 1,000 samples of four are shown in Fig. 99. The correlation coefficient r in this case is 0.895, whereas the efficiency of the estimate $1.1547\ m_1$ as compared with the estimate 1.2533σ is practically 100 per cent. We are, therefore, uncertain from this test whether or not the standard deviation is the most efficient estimate although we see from Fig. 98 that even for small samples it is more efficient than the mean deviation. The difference is negligible, of course, for comparatively small samples.

It will be of interest now to consider the efficiency of the range between the maximum and minimum values of a sample as an estimate of σ. Again making use of the work of Tippett,[1] E. S. Pearson, and N. K. Adyanthāya,[2] we get the range efficiency curve shown also in Fig. 98. The very rapid decrease in efficiency of the estimate derived from the range is striking. The same concept of efficiency is used here as was used in Paragraph 3. We have here an added difficulty in that the

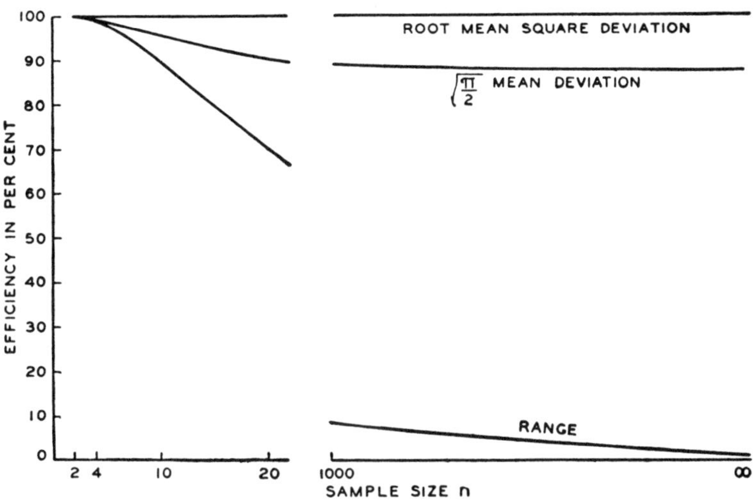

FIG. 98.—EFFICIENCY OF $\sqrt{\frac{\pi}{2}}$ TIMES MEAN DEVIATION AND RANGE AS ESTIMATES OF σ COMPARED WITH THAT OF THE STANDARD DEVIATION.

root mean square deviation, $\sqrt{\pi/2}$ mean deviation, and the range are not even consistent estimates of σ. For this reason the curves of Fig. 98 are supposed merely to indicate, in a general way, how the efficiencies of the above two statistics fall off with increasing n.

It should be noted that, in our discussion of the importance of choosing the most efficient statistic for detecting a change $\Delta\bar{X}$ or $\Delta\sigma$, we tacitly assumed that the distribution functions of the statistics compared were symmetrical and of the

[1] Loc. cit.
[2] Loc. cit.

same functional form. This is a very important requirement for, in general, the most efficient statistic in the sense of being the one with the smallest standard deviation need not be the statistic most likely to catch a given change in $\overline{\mathbf{X}}$ or σ. For

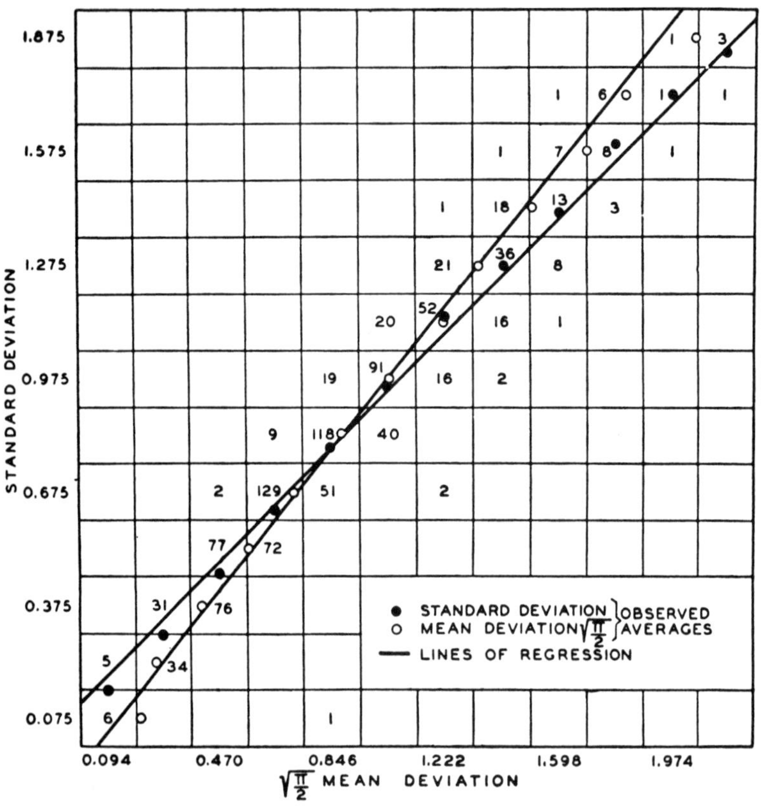

FIG. 99.—CORRELATION BETWEEN STANDARD DEVIATION AND $\sqrt{\frac{\pi}{2}}$ TIMES MEAN DEVIATION FOR SAMPLES OF FOUR FROM A NORMAL UNIVERSE.

example, the comparison of the four ranges of Table 41 for detecting a given change $\Delta\sigma$ involves the algebraic magnitude of $\Delta\sigma$, and the knowledge of the functional forms of the distribution of the different ranges. The same could be said of the comparison of the statistics based upon the moments m_i of the absolute values of the deviation. To make such a comparison is certainly not practicable at the present time.

It appears, therefore, that there is good reason to choose the standard deviation σ of the sample as a basis for the estimate of the standard deviation $\boldsymbol{\sigma}$ of the universe to detect a change $\Delta\boldsymbol{\sigma}$.

5. *Additional Reason for Choosing the Average $\bar{X}$ and Standard Deviation σ*

We are now in a place to consider an additional and very important reason for choosing the average $\bar{X}$ of a sample to detect a change $\Delta\bar{\mathbf{X}}$ and the standard deviation σ to detect a change $\Delta\boldsymbol{\sigma}$. The previous discussion has been limited to the assumption that the universe or distribution (58) of standard quality is normal.

In Part IV, however, we saw that, no matter what the nature of the distribution function (58) of the quality is, the distribution function of the arithmetic mean approaches normality rapidly with increase in n, and in all cases the expected value of means of samples of n is the same as the expected value $\bar{\mathbf{X}}$ of the universe. Hence the arithmetic mean is usable for detecting a change $\Delta\bar{\mathbf{X}}$ almost equally well for any universe of effects which we are likely to meet in practice. It appears that the same cannot be said of any other known statistic.

We also saw in Part IV that, although the distribution function $\mathbf{f}_\sigma(\sigma, n)$ of the standard deviation σ of samples of n is not known for other than the normal universe, nevertheless the moments of the distribution of variance σ^2 are known in terms of the moments of the universe. Hence we can always establish limits

$$\overline{\boldsymbol{\sigma}^2} \pm t\boldsymbol{\sigma}_{\sigma^2}$$

within which the observed variance in samples of size n should fall more than $100\left(1 - \frac{1}{t^2}\right)$ per cent of the total number of times a sample of n is chosen, so long as the quality of product is controlled in accord with the accepted standard.

This generality of usefulness is not shared by any other known estimate of σ or, more specifically, of σ^2.

6. *Choice of Statistic to Detect Change* $\Delta \mathbf{r}$ *in the Correlation Coefficient* $\mathbf{r}$

In the present state of our knowledge of the distribution of product moments, the only available basis for detecting a change $\Delta \mathbf{r}$ is the distribution function (75) of the correlation coefficient in samples of size n.

7. *Choice of Method of Using Statistics*

Having chosen statistics with which to detect variability from standard quality, it remains for us to choose the way of

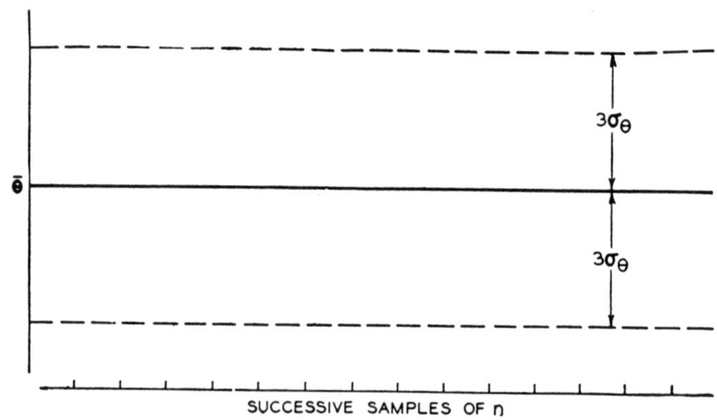

FIG. 100.—SIMPLE FORM OF CONTROL CHART.

using them. We shall illustrate this point by a discussion of the ways of using the average $\bar{X}$ and standard deviation σ of samples of size n.

Making use of the control limits

$$\bar{\Theta} \pm 3\sigma_{\Theta},$$

we may construct a *control chart* such as shown in Fig. 100. The occurrence of a value of Θ outside these limits is taken as an indication of a significant variation from standard quality or as an indication of trouble.

Instead of using this simple form of chart for each of several statistics, we may use a chart based upon the probability of the simultaneous occurrence of the different statistics. Two possible forms of such charts for two statistics Θ_1 and Θ_2 are shown in Fig. 101. In Fig. 101-*a* the occurrence of a sample for which the point (Θ_1, Θ_2) falls outside the shaded area is taken as an indication of trouble, the boundary of this area having been chosen so that the probability **P** of falling within the boundary is economic. Similarly, in Fig. 101-*b*, the probability **P** of falling inside the dotted limits on either side of the

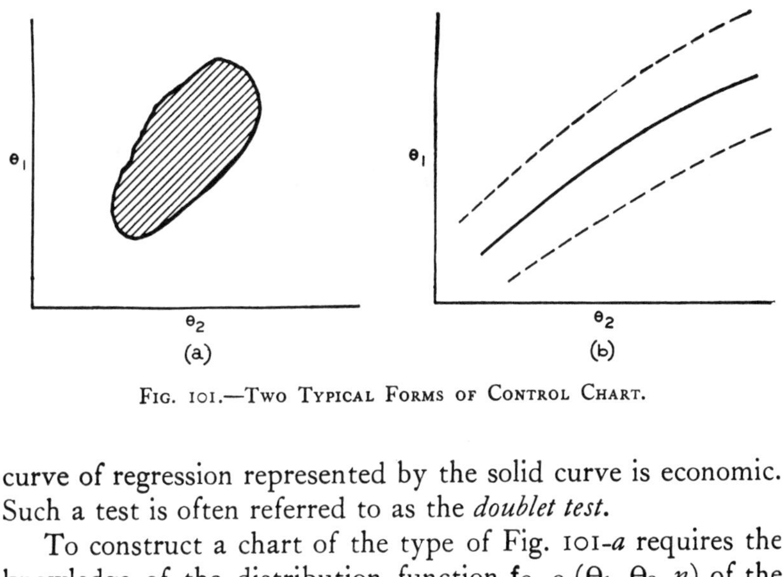

Fig. 101.—Two Typical Forms of Control Chart.

curve of regression represented by the solid curve is economic. Such a test is often referred to as the *doublet test.*

To construct a chart of the type of Fig. 101-*a* requires the knowledge of the distribution function $f_{\Theta_1, \Theta_2}(\Theta_1, \Theta_2, n)$ of the two statistics Θ_1 and Θ_2. For the averages and standard deviations of samples from a normal universe this function rapidly approaches normality as we see from a study of the distribution functions of $\overline{X}$ and σ of Part IV. Hence we can set up correlation ellipses corresponding to a desired probability **P**. In general, however, little is known about the distribution function of pairs of statistics, even for the arithmetic mean and standard deviation, for samples from other than a normal universe.

The work of Neyman already referred to in Chapter XIV of Part IV makes possible the construction of a chart of the form of Fig. 101-*b* for averages and variances of samples from any known universe. This theory also makes it possible to establish approximate limits for pairs of averages and standard devia-

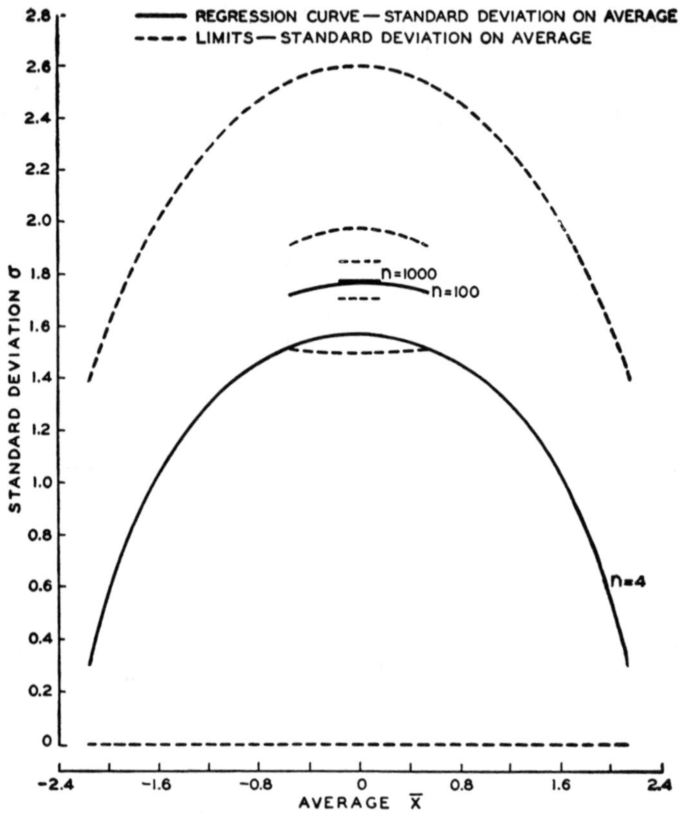

FIG. 102.—EFFECT OF SAMPLE SIZE ON LIMITS.

tions. Fig. 102, for example, shows such sets of limits for samples of $n = 4$, $n = 100$, and $n = 1000$. This figure is of particular interest in that it indicates that such a test may be more sensitive to a change in the functional form **f** of the universe when the sample is small than when it is large. In other words, such a chart can be made sensitive to changes in the function representing standard quality, even though the average $\bar{X}$ and standard deviation σ of the universe remain constant.

8. *Choice of Method of Using Statistics—Simple Example*

Table 42 gives forty observed values of tensile strength of steel strand in pounds per square inch (psi). Let us assume

TABLE 42.—TENSILE STRENGTH OF STEEL STRAND

Company No. 1		Company No. 2	
12,600	13,800	14,300	14,550
13,750	14,250	13,900	14,250
13,440	13,370	14,460	13,390
13,960	13,510	14,480	14,130
13,570	13,110	14,170	13,910
13,550	13,400	13,610	13,180
13,570	13,860	13,990	13,790
13,430	13,440	14,140	13,810
13,250	13,900	13,400	13,260
13,320	13,910	14,290	14,550

that the accepted standard quality for the tensile strength of this particular product is normally distributed with

$$\bar{X} = 13{,}540 \text{ psi,}$$

and

$$\sigma = 440 \text{ psi.}$$

Is there any indication that the quality of product of either supplier is significantly different from standard quality in the sense that the observed samples may not be considered as random samples from standard quality? In what follows, we shall describe three different ways of using the statistics $\bar{X}$ and σ to answer this question.

A. One way is to construct control charts for averages and standard deviations of samples of twenty with the following limits. Of course, $\bar{\sigma}$ is $440c_2$ where the value of c_2 is that given in Table 29 for $n = 20$:

$$\bar{\bar{X}} \pm 3\frac{\sigma}{\sqrt{n}} = 13{,}540 \pm 3\frac{440}{\sqrt{20}} = \begin{cases} 13{,}245 \\ 13{,}835, \end{cases}$$

and

$$\bar{\sigma} \pm 3\frac{\sigma}{\sqrt{2n}} = 423 \pm 3\frac{440}{\sqrt{40}} = \begin{cases} 214 \\ 632. \end{cases}$$

This is done in Fig. 103. Using this method, we assume that there is an indication of the existence of significant deviations

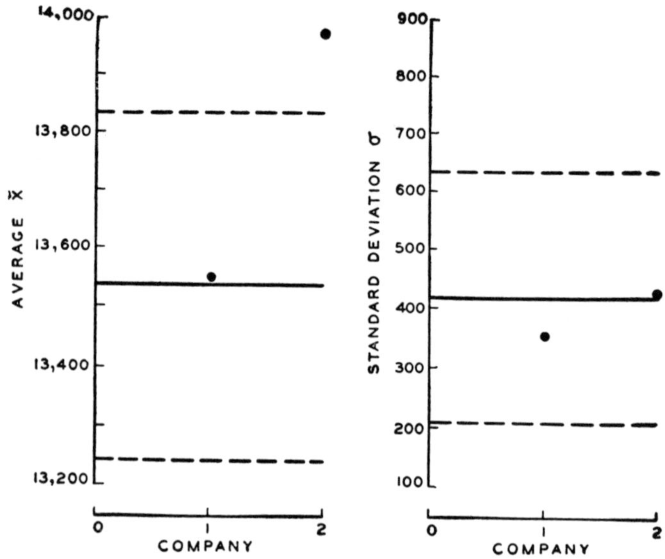

FIG. 103.—ONE FORM OF CONTROL CHART TEST.

from standard if the observed values of either average or standard deviation or both for a given sample fall outside of the control chart limits.

The observed values of average and standard deviation for the two samples of twenty are represented by the black dots. We take the fact that one of the averages falls outside its limits as an indication of lack of control in respect to standard quality.

B. Another way of testing whether or not the two samples of twenty came from standard quality is to construct a control chart of the type shown in Fig. 101-*a*. Since for samples of twenty from a normal universe [1] the correlation surface of $\overline{X}$ and σ is approximately normal, we may construct the ellipse which should include, let us say, $\mathbf{P} = 99.73$ per cent of the observed pairs of values of $\overline{X}$ and σ. Doing this for the case in hand, we get the results shown schematically in Fig. 104.

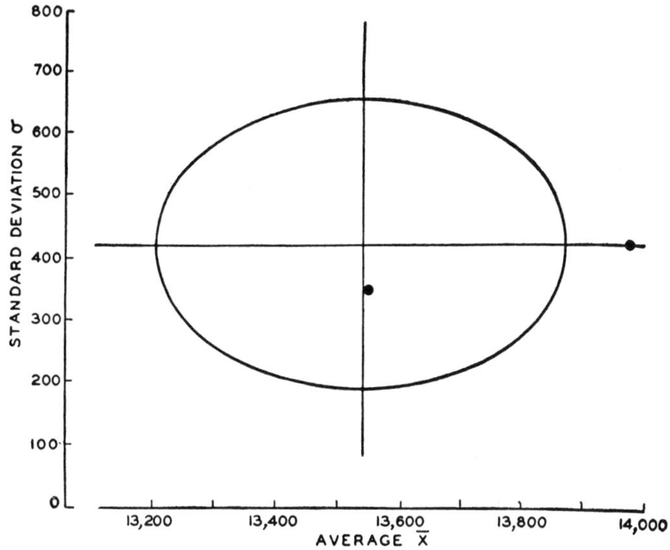

FIG. 104.—ANOTHER CONTROL CHART TEST.

The fact that one point is outside this ellipse is taken as an indication of trouble.

C. A third way of testing whether or not the two samples came from standard quality is to test whether or not the differences

$$|\overline{X}_1 - \overline{X}_2| = 428.50,$$

and

$$|\sigma_1 - \sigma_2| = 71.28$$

are likely to have occurred if both samples came from standard

[1] Cf. Chapter XV, Part IV.

quality. Obviously a test of this nature comparable with the previous two is to consider the occurrence of an absolute difference in averages greater than

$$3\frac{\sigma}{\sqrt{\frac{n}{2}}} = 3\frac{440}{\sqrt{10}} = 417.42,$$

or in standard deviations greater than

$$3\frac{\sigma}{\sqrt{n}} = 3\frac{440}{\sqrt{20}} = 295.16$$

as indicative of trouble. Again we get a positive indication.

9. *Choice of Method of Using Statistics—Continued*

Let us look at the results obtained by the three different tests just described. It will be seen that the first test indicates

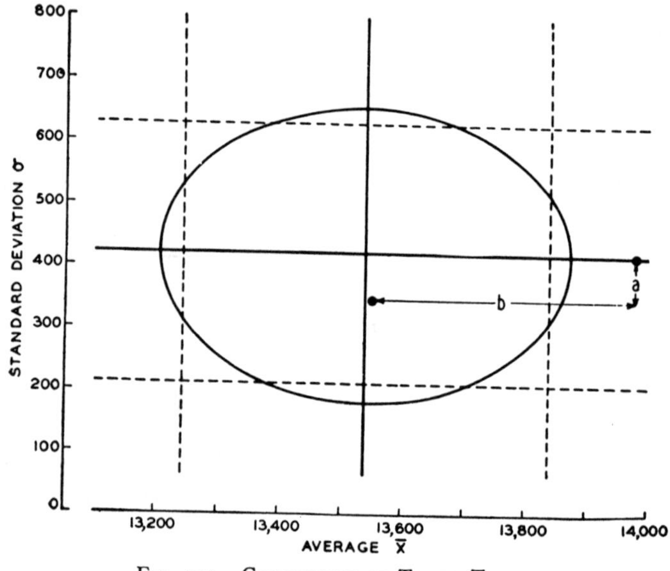

Fig. 105.—Comparison of Three Tests.

trouble when a point $(\bar{X}, \sigma)$ falls outside the dotted rectangle in Fig. 105, whereas the second test indicates trouble when a point falls outside the ellipse. It is easy to see that the two tests are inherently different. In the first place the probabilities associated with the areas of the rectangle and ellipse are 0.9946 and 0.9973 respectively. More important, however, is the fact that the two tests could not be made to exclude the same region even if the areas were equal.

Now the third test is basically different from the other two in that it indicates trouble when either the distance *a* or *b* exceeds certain limits.

Since, as in the simple illustration of the previous paragraph, experience indicates that the three tests so often give consistent results, since the third test is obviously very difficult to apply when we have many samples of size n, and since the second test is more difficult to apply than the first although it gives approximately the same results, the first test appears to be the practical choice.

10. *Choice of Statistic for Detecting Change in Universe of Effects*

Let us consider next the problem of detecting a variation from standard quality represented by a change of cause system from one which gives standard quality, say

$$dy = \mathbf{f}(X, \lambda_1, \lambda_2, \ldots, \lambda_i, \ldots, \lambda_{m'})dX, \tag{58}$$

to one which gives something different from standard and represented by some unknown distribution of the form

$$dy = \mathbf{f}_1(X, \lambda'_1, \lambda'_2, \ldots, \lambda'_i, \ldots, \lambda'_{m''})dX.$$

Perhaps the single statistic most sensitive to a change of this type is the χ^2 function. Subject to the limitations set forth in Part IV, we may divide the original distribution into any number of cells and calculate χ^2 for samples of size n grouped into the chosen cells. A control chart for χ^2 may then be constructed by making use of the known values of $\overline{\chi^2}$ and σ_{χ^2}. In general, it is desirable to use a grouping which gives as nearly as possible equal probabilities for all cells. One difficulty is that the χ^2 control chart can only be used for comparatively large samples.

11. *Detection of Failure to Maintain Standard Quality*

Thus far we have considered the comparatively simple problem of detecting a change of a given kind and amount in the effects of a constant cause system, such as a change $\Delta\overline{\mathbf{X}}$ in expected value or a change $\Delta\sigma$ in the standard deviation of the effects of the cause system, *everything else remaining fixed*. In practice, however, we never know that the quality has changed from standard in a specific way. What we do is to take a sample of n to determine whether or not the product has changed. It may or may not have changed one or many times within the period in which the sample of n is being taken. Our success in detecting trouble in such a case depends among other things upon the way in which the sample is taken, or, more specifically, upon whether or not the sample of n comes from one or more constant systems of causes.

For example, in testing whether or not the tensile strength of strand, Table 42, had been controlled in accord with standard quality, we divided the data into two groups of twenty observations, one group from each of the two suppliers. Of course we could have tested in a similar way the hypothesis that the forty observations came from a standard production process. Thus, the control limits in pounds per square inch (psi) on average $\overline{X}$ and standard deviation σ of samples of forty from product of standard quality are respectively:

$$13{,}540 \pm 3\frac{440}{\sqrt{40}} = \begin{cases} 13{,}331 \\ 13{,}749 \end{cases}$$

$$432 \pm 3\frac{440}{\sqrt{80}} = \begin{cases} 284 \\ 580 \end{cases}$$

The fact that the observed average of the forty values of tensile strength falls outside the control limits would be taken as evidence of lack of control. Hence, no matter which test had been applied in this case, the result would have been the same. It may easily be shown, however, that the results of two such tests may not be the same. That is to say, if trouble does exist in that the product as tested by a sample of n comes from two constant systems of causes in the sense that n_1 pieces come from a cause system with constants

$$\bar{X}_1 \quad \text{and} \quad \sigma_1,$$

and n_2 pieces come from another system with constants

$$\bar{X}_2 \quad \text{and} \quad \sigma_2,$$

it is possible that a test for trouble using the total sample n may or may not give an indication of trouble. The same is true of the test based upon the use of the samples n_1 and n_2. Furthermore, one test may be positive and the other negative.

Therefore it might appear that it makes little difference how a set of n data representing lack of standard control is grouped before applying the test for detecting trouble of this kind. In other words, this would mean that an inspector trying to detect variation from standard quality would be able to do so equally well irrespective of whether or not he was able to divide the data in a sample of size n into subgroups corresponding to different constant systems of causes. To draw such a conclusion would be utterly misleading and against what is perhaps the most generally accepted step in the scientific method, that is, classification. Assuming for the moment, however, that in the long run a test using the whole group of n data as a unit is just as likely to detect trouble as one using the subgroups of data obtained by accurate classification, there still would be a definite advantage in classifying the data before applying the test. Obviously, the ultimate object is not only to detect trouble but also to find it, and such discovery naturally involves classification. The engineer who is successful in dividing his data initially into *rational* subgroups based upon rational hypotheses is therefore inherently better off in the long run than the one who is not thus successful.

For such an engineer the statistical tests described in this chapter constitute a powerful tool in testing his hypotheses and in determining the extent to which an investigation must be carried in order to check beyond reasonable doubt whether or not a given hypothesis is justified.

Suppose, for example, that an engineer wishes to determine how large a sample is required to detect variation from standard quality by an amount $\Delta\bar{\mathbf{X}}$ in the expected value, where it is assumed that the functional form **f** and all other parameters remain the same. It is a simple matter to show that the required sample size n is given by the solution of the equation

$$\Delta\bar{\mathbf{X}} = 2t\frac{\sigma}{\sqrt{n}}, \qquad (89\text{-}a)$$

where t is generally taken as three for reasons already set forth.

In a similar way one finds that the number required to detect a change only in standard deviation and of an amount $\Delta\sigma$ is given by the solution of

$$\Delta\sigma = 2t\frac{\sigma}{\sqrt{2n}}. \qquad (89\text{-}b)$$

For example, the size of sample determined from (89-*a*) is such that the probability of detecting trouble of the nature of a change only in $\bar{\mathbf{X}}$ and of an amount $\Delta\bar{\mathbf{X}}$ is approximately 0.99 if $t = 3$. We can go even further and say that with this sample size the probability of detecting trouble in the form of a change only in $\bar{\mathbf{X}}$ is greater than 0.99 if the shift is greater than $\Delta\bar{\mathbf{X}}$ used in (89-*a*).

A similar interpretation may be given to the value of n derived from (89-*b*).

Thus we see how statistical theory becomes a useful tool after we have taken the scientific step of classification of data into rational subgroups. Moreover we see that, even though classification is not as it should be, statistical tests often indicate the presence of trouble. Of course, these advantages are attained with a knowledge that we shall not look for trouble when it does not exist more than a certain known fraction $(1 - \mathbf{P})$ of the total number of times that a sample of size n is observed.

CHAPTER XX

Detection of Lack of Control

1. *The Problem*

In the previous chapter we considered the comparatively simple problem of detecting lack of control in respect to an accepted standard distribution. Now we shall consider the problem of detecting lack of control in the sense of lack of constancy in the unknown cause system. To make clear the inherent difference in these two problems, let us consider once more the data on tensile strength of strand as given in Table 42. The three tests of the previous chapter merely served to indicate whether or not it is likely that the data came from a *specified* constant cause system. The corresponding question to be considered now is whether or not they come from *some* constant cause system of unknown functional form $\mathbf{f}$, unknown average $\overline{\mathbf{X}}$, and unknown standard deviation $\boldsymbol{\sigma}$.

The tests of the previous chapter made use of assumed known values of $\overline{\mathbf{X}}$ and $\boldsymbol{\sigma}$. The corresponding tests which we can use in this chapter must involve estimates $\overline{X}$ and σ, say, of the unknown average $\overline{\mathbf{X}}$ and standard deviation $\boldsymbol{\sigma}$ of the objective but unknown distribution representing the condition of control, if it be controlled.

Two criteria to guide us in making the estimates $\overline{X}$ and σ are:

A. The estimates $\overline{X}$ and σ used as a basis for detecting lack of control must be such that, if the quality from which the sample of size n is drawn is controlled with an average $\overline{\mathbf{X}}$ and a standard deviation $\boldsymbol{\sigma}$, then the following two statistical limits should be fulfilled:

$$\left.\begin{array}{r} \underset{n \to \infty}{L_S}\ \overline{X} = \overline{\mathbf{X}} \\ \underset{n \to \infty}{L_S}\ \sigma = \boldsymbol{\sigma} \end{array}\right\}. \tag{90}$$

B. Insofar as possible, the estimates should be chosen so that, if the quality is not controlled, the estimates $\overline{X}$ and σ actually used shall be those which will be most likely to indicate the presence of trouble or, in this case, lack of constancy in the cause system.

2. *Choice of Method of Estimating* $\overline{\mathbf{X}}$ *and* σ

Let us start by considering estimates $\overline{X}$ and σ in psi derived from the data of Table 42 in two different ways as follows:

(*a*) Let

$$\overline{X} = \frac{\sum_{i=1}^{40} X_i}{40} = 13{,}763.75,$$

and

$$\sigma = \left(\frac{\sum_{i=1}^{40} (X_i - \overline{X})^2}{40}\right)^{1/2} = 442.20.$$

(*b*) Let

$$\overline{X} = \frac{\sum_{i=1}^{40} X_i}{40} = 13{,}763.75,$$

and

$$\sigma = \frac{1}{c_2}\,\frac{\sigma_1 + \sigma_2}{2} = 400.45,$$

where σ_1 and σ_2 are the standard deviations of the first and second groups of twenty observed values and where c_2 is the factor given in Column 3 of Table 29.

Obviously the condition (90) is satisfied by the estimates (*a*) and (*b*). It may easily be shown, however, that if the subgroups are rational, then the estimate σ of type (*b*) is on the average less than the corresponding estimate of type (*a*).

Therefore, under these conditions criteria involving the use of estimates (*b*) will in the long run detect trouble more often than similar criteria involving estimates (*a*). Hence it is reasonable to choose method (*b*) for estimating $\overline{X}$ and σ.

3. *Choice of Test Criterion for Detecting Lack of Control*

Having chosen a pair of estimates $\bar{X}$ and σ, we may use them in any criterion in which we may use $\mathbf{\bar{X}}$ and $\boldsymbol{\sigma}$. As an illustration let us apply the three criteria of the previous chapter, making use of $\bar{X}$ and σ calculated as in (*b*). The results of the application of the first two criteria are shown graphically in Fig. 106. Obviously both of these criteria give a negative indication of lack of control. Comparing Fig. 105 with Fig. 106

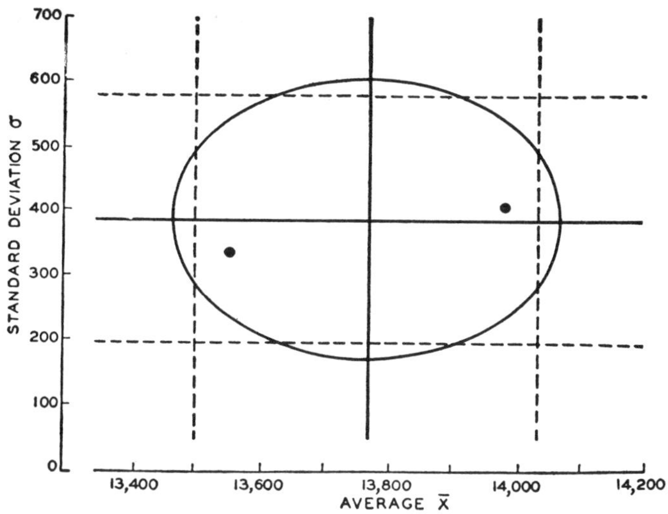

FIG. 106.—TESTS FOR CONTROL.

we see that, whereas one point is out of limits in Fig. 105, neither point is out in Fig. 106. This is interpreted as meaning that, although the observed data are consistent with the assumption of the existence of a controlled state upon the basis of the criteria used, the equation of control is likely not the accepted standard used in the previous chapter.

Now since the difference 428.50 psi in averages exceeds $3\frac{\sigma}{\sqrt{n/2}} = 379.9$ psi, the third test criterion gives indication of lack of control.

As previously explained, this is the kind of situation which often arises in which the indications of two criteria are not the same. Our decision in such a case involves the use of judgment. In this particular instance and for reasons outlined in the previous chapter, we choose the first type of control chart test corresponding to the rectangular limits of Fig. 106.

With the above discussion as an introduction, we shall now describe criteria which have been found to work successfully in the detection of lack of control.

CONTEXT Dependent

4. *Criterion I—General*

Given a set of n data to determine whether or not they came from a constant system of causes, we take the following steps:

A. Divide the n data into m rational subgroups[1] of $n_1, n_2, \ldots, n_i, \ldots, n_m$ values each.

B. For each statistic to be used, use estimates $\bar{\Theta}$ and σ_Θ satisfying as nearly as possible conditions *A* and *B* of Paragraph 1.

C. Construct control charts with limits

$$\bar{\Theta} \pm 3\sigma_\Theta$$

for each statistic.

D. If an observed point falls outside the limits of this chart, take this fact as an indication of trouble or lack of control.

5. *Criterion I—Attributes*

In this case we make use of a control chart with limits

$$\bar{p} \pm 3\sigma_p$$

where $\bar{p}$ is the fraction defective in the total set of n observations and

$$\sigma_p = \sqrt{\frac{\bar{p}\,\bar{q}}{\bar{n}}},$$

where $\bar{n}$ is the average sample size. The lower limit is taken as zero if $\bar{p} - 3\sigma_p \leq 0$.

[1] Note in Fig. 55 the difficulties encountered if the data are not divided into rational subgroups.

Example: Carrying out these computations for the Type A data of Table 1, we get the following results:

Month	$p = \frac{n_1}{n}$	Month	$p = \frac{n_1}{n}$	Month	$p = \frac{n_1}{n}$
January........	0.0076	May.........	0.0301	September....	0.0048
February......	0.0082	June.........	0.0060	October......	0.0280
March........	0.0117	July.........	0.0076	November....	0.0112
April..........	0.0050	August.......	0.0051	December....	0.0059

$$\bar{p} = \frac{\Sigma n_1}{\Sigma n} = 0.0109,$$

$$\sigma_p = \sqrt{\frac{\bar{p}\,\bar{q}}{\bar{n}}} = 0.0047,$$

$$\bar{p} + 3\sigma_p = 0.0250,$$

$$\bar{p} - 3\sigma_p = -\ 0.0032 \text{ (hence taken to be 0.0000).}$$

With this information we get the control chart of Fig. 4-*a*. The fact that points fall outside the limits was taken as indicating the presence of assignable causes of variability, at least some of which were later discovered, thus justifying the indication of trouble given by the test.

6. *Criterion I—Variables—Large Samples*

Given a series of n observed values $X_1, X_2, \ldots, X_i, \ldots, X_n$ divisible into m rational subgroups of $n_1, n_2, \ldots, n_i, \ldots, n_m$ values each, we make use of control charts with limits

$$\bar{X} \pm 3\sigma_{\bar{X}} \quad \text{and} \quad \sigma \pm 3\sigma_\sigma,$$

where $\bar{X}$ is the average of the n observed values and

$$\sigma = \sqrt{\frac{n_1\sigma_1^2 + n_2\sigma_2^2 + \ldots + n_i\sigma_i^2 + \ldots + n_m\sigma_m^2}{n_1 + n_2 + \ldots + n_i + \ldots + n_m}}, \qquad (91)$$

TABLE 43.—TYPICAL APPLICATION OF CRITERION I

Cell Midpoints	Frequency											
	July	Aug.	Sept.	Oct.	Nov.	Dec.	Jan.	Feb.	Mar.	Apr.	May	June
−5.5		1	2	1	1		1	2	4	1		
−5.0			1			1	1	1	3	2	1	
−4.5								1	7			
−4.0				1	2			5	12	7	5	9
−3.5			3	1	1		5	10	24	19	15	24
−3.0	55	10	1	12	59	49	48	52	167	130	116	116
−2.5	141	90	119	99	157	152	137	125	221	168	146	206
−2.0	168	238	238	171	179	249	177	195	239	157	171	215
−1.5	249	265	213	312	302	359	320	330	281	241	237	322
−1.0	305	335	332	366	327	414	285	309	254	215	243	318
−0.5	231	313	238	234	161	117	162	140	134	132	150	153
0.0	64	46	3	3	11	9	13	27	49	100	106	79
0.5	26	2					1	2	4	24	10	8
1.0	9							1	1	4		
1.5	2											
Σ	1,250	1,300	1,150	1,200	1,200	1,350	1,150	1,200	1,400	1,200	1,200	1,450

Frequency Distributions for Data of Twelve Polygons of Fig. 19

	July	Aug.	Sept.	Oct.	Nov.	Dec.	Jan.	Feb.	Mar.	Apr.	May	June	Total
Average $\overline{X}$	−1.298	−1.250	−1.368	−1.325	−1.504	−1.512	−1.490	−1.505	−1.765	−1.550	−1.501	−1.577	−1.475
Std. Dev. σ	0.829	0.672	0.673	0.623	0.713	0.638	0.710	0.754	0.923	0.985	0.921	0.862	0.786
Skewness k	−0.009	−0.439	−0.785	−0.770	−0.541	−0.490	−0.573	−0.717	−0.353	−0.093	−0.191	−0.192	−0.424
Flatness β_2	2.729	3.287	4.854	4.208	3.143	3.025	3.673	4.566	3.331	2.637	2.390	2.519	3.401
Sample Size n	1,250	1,300	1,150	1,200	1,200	1,350	1,150	1,200	1,400	1,200	1,200	1,450	

Statistics for above Frequency Distributions

$$^*\sigma_{\overline{X}} = \frac{\sigma}{\sqrt{\bar{n}}} = 0.022204 \qquad \overline{X} \text{ control limits } \begin{cases} \overline{X} + 3\sigma_{\overline{X}} = -1.408 \\ \overline{X} - 3\sigma_{\overline{X}} = -1.541 \end{cases}$$

$$\sigma_\sigma = \frac{\sigma}{\sqrt{2\bar{n}}} = 0.01569 \qquad \sigma \text{ control limits } \begin{cases} \sigma + 3\sigma_\sigma = 0.833 \\ \sigma - 3\sigma_\sigma = 0.739 \end{cases}$$

$$\sigma_k = \sqrt{\frac{6}{\bar{n}}} = 0.069171 \qquad k \text{ control limits } \begin{cases} k + 3\sigma_k = -0.217 \\ k - 3\sigma_k = -0.632 \end{cases}$$

$$\sigma_{\beta_2} = \sqrt{\frac{24}{\bar{n}}} = 0.138343 \qquad \beta_2 \text{ control limits } \begin{cases} \beta_2 + 3\sigma_{\beta_2} = 3.816 \\ \beta_2 - 3\sigma_{\beta_2} = 2.986 \end{cases}$$

* $\bar{n}$ = 1,254 or average sample size for 12 months.

σ_i being the standard deviation of the ith rational subgroup. If the sizes of the subgroups are practically equal, we have

$$\sigma_{\bar{X}} = \frac{\sigma}{\sqrt{n}} \quad \text{and} \quad \sigma_\sigma = \frac{\sigma}{\sqrt{2n}}.$$

If the sizes of the subgroups are not equal, the limits for a given subgroup i must be made to depend upon the sample size n_i for that group.

Obviously, the condition that the statistical limit

$$\underset{n \to \infty}{L_s} \; \sigma = \boldsymbol{\sigma}$$

is not satisfied when n_i is small. It seems reasonable to believe in the light of our previous discussion of the distribution function of the standard deviation that, so long as the minimum size of a subgroup does not fall below, let us say, twenty-five, the estimate σ given by (91) approximately satisfies this limit condition.

If the rational subgroups contain a large number of observations, we may also make use of control charts for the skewness k and flatness β_2.

Example 1: Table 43 gives the observed frequency distributions and the control limits for the twelve monthly records of quality shown previously in Fig. 19. Fig. 107 shows the results in graphical form. The fact that some of the points fell outside control limits was taken as an indication of lack of control for which the assignable causes were later discovered.

Example 2: Let us apply Criterion I to the data of Fig. 21 to determine whether or not there is any indication that the depth of penetration for the seven treating plants is controlled. The requisite computations are given in Table 44.

In this case the sample sizes are too small to justify the use of k and β_2 and the sizes differ so much among themselves that it is necessary to use variable limits as shown in Fig. 108. Lack of control, the causes of which were later discovered, is indicated by both the averages and correlation coefficients.

TABLE 44.—TYPICAL APPLICATION OF CRITERION I TO CORRELATION COEFFICIENT

X = Depth of Sapwood in inches
Y = Depth of Penetration in inches

Company	Number of Poles	Number of Borings	$\bar{X}$	σ_X	$\bar{Y}$	σ_Y	r_{XY}
1	48	350	3.5611	0.6060	1.8966	0.6326	0.2597
2	50	239	3.1552	0.6922	2.0795	0.7091	0.4403
3	50	316	2.8959	0.6667	1.7016	0.5925	0.4913
4	47	323	3.3963	0.7093	2.0653	0.7153	0.1584
5	48	346	3.6107	0.5935	1.9642	0.6865	−0.1815
6	50	241	3.4012	0.5987	2.0320	0.7546	0.4181
7	50	346	3.1850	0.6385	1.6832	0.6563	0.3855
Total	343	2161	3.3242	0.6863	1.9053	0.6911	0.3926
				$\bar{\sigma}_X = 0.6436$ $^*\bar{\sigma}_X = 0.6422$		$\bar{\sigma}_Y = 0.6781$ $^*\bar{\sigma}_Y = 0.6736$	$\bar{r}_X = 0.2817$ $^*\bar{r}_{XY} = 0.2656$

Statistics for Data of Fig. 21

Calculation of Correlation Control Chart—Company 1†:

$$\sigma_r = \frac{1 - r_1^2}{\sqrt{n_1 - 1}} = \frac{1 - (0.2597)^2}{\sqrt{349}} = 0.050$$

$$\text{Control limits}\begin{cases} r + 3\sigma_r = 0.415 \\ r - 3\sigma_r = 0.117 \end{cases}$$

* Weighted Average. † Limits for other six companies calculated as for Company 1.

Example 3: As a third example, let us apply Criterion I to a set of data which may reasonably be assumed to be controlled and see if the result of the test is consistent. For this purpose, we may make use of the four observed distributions of 1,000 given in Table 23. Since these data were obtained under conditions as nearly controlled as we may reasonably hope to attain, all observed points should fall within the limits. Fig. 109

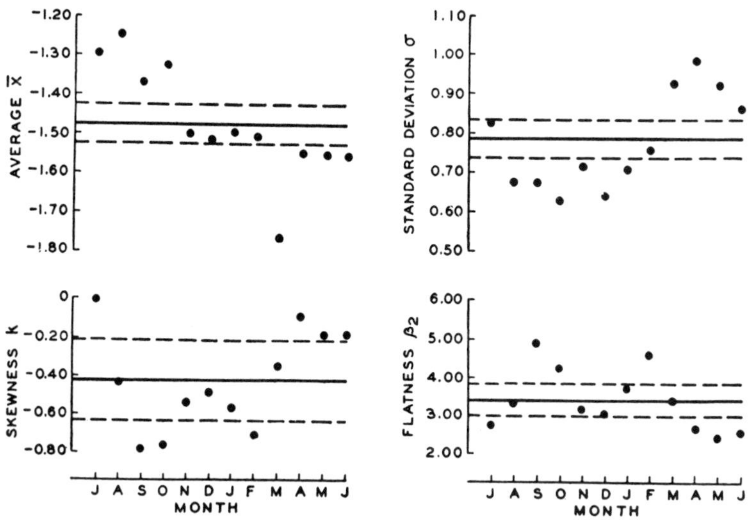

FIG. 107.—CONTROL CHARTS FOR DATA OF FIG. 19 AND TABLE 43, INDICATING LACK OF CONTROL.

shows that they do. The positive indication of control is consistent with the facts as we believe them to be. Of course, as previously noted, a few points should fall outside control limits in the long run even though there is no lack of control.

7. *Criterion I—Variables—Small Samples*

Given a series $X_1, X_2, \ldots, X_i, \ldots, X_n$ of n observed values of X that may be divided into m rational subgroups of equal size, control charts with limits

$$\bar{X} \pm 3\sigma_{\bar{X}} \quad \text{and} \quad \bar{\sigma} \pm 3\sigma_{\sigma}$$

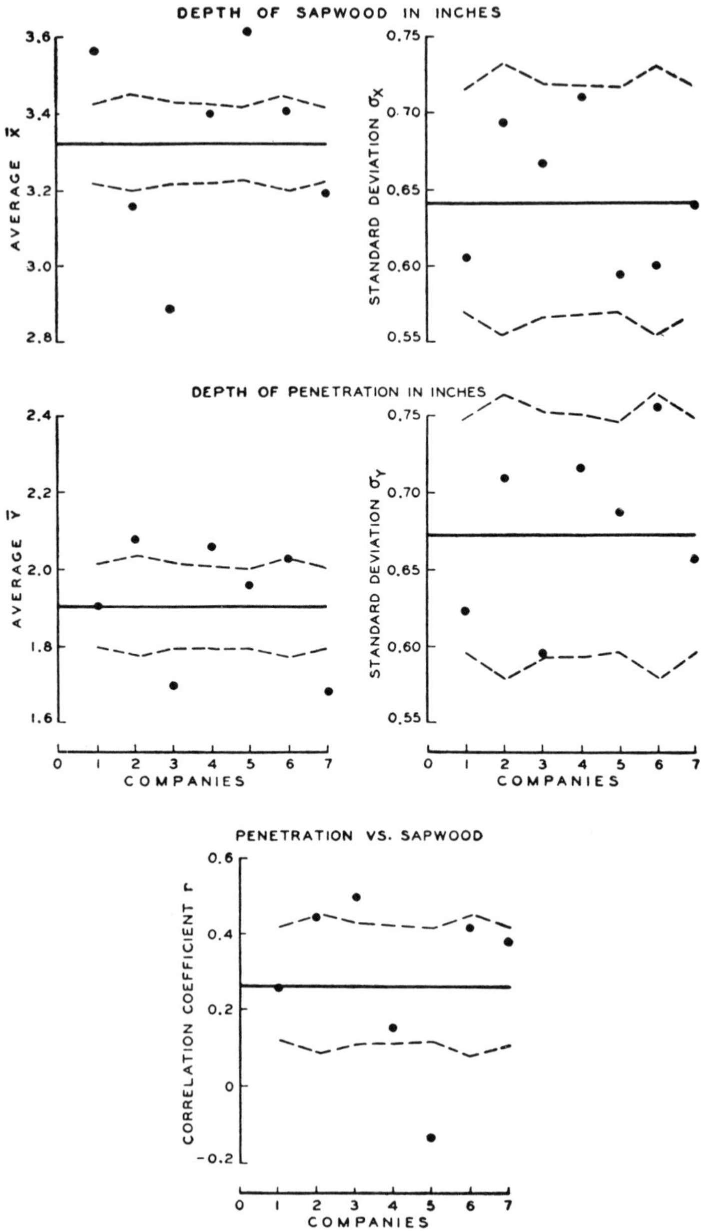

Fig. 108.—Control Charts for Data of Table 44 and Fig. 21.

constitute what we shall term the Criterion I test for small samples, where

$$\bar{X} = \frac{\bar{X}_1 + \bar{X}_2 + \ldots + \bar{X}_i + \ldots + \bar{X}_m}{m}$$

$$\bar{\sigma} = \frac{\sigma_1 + \sigma_2 + \ldots + \sigma_i + \ldots + \sigma_m}{m}$$

$$\sigma = \frac{\bar{\sigma}}{c_2}.$$

In these expressions c_2 is the factor given in Table 29, $\bar{X}_i$ is the average, and σ_i the standard deviation of the ith subgroup.

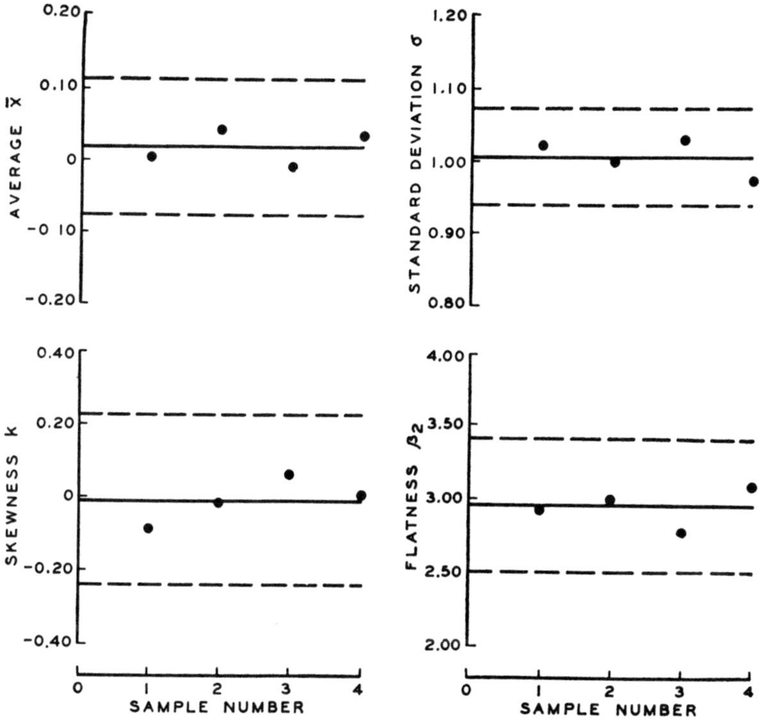

Fig. 109.—Control Chart Test Applied to Controlled Data Gives Consistent Results.

Example 1: The problem to be considered first is one previously reported in the literature.[1] It is to determine whether

[1] Appendix to report of Committee B2XV of the American Society for Testing Materials, published in the *Proceedings* of that Society for 1929.

or not the tensile strength in psi of a given alloy as produced by five different companies is controlled where five tests on as many pieces of product from each of five companies gave the following results in pounds per square inch:

	Companies				
	C	*D*	*G*	*W*	*S*
Average $\overline{X}$	29,314	24,660	28,210	31,988	34,332
Standard Deviation σ	1,198	2,434	528	1,243	1,006

The details of the method of calculating the control limits are shown below:

$$\overline{X} = \frac{29{,}314 + 24{,}660 + 28{,}210 + 31{,}988 + 34{,}332}{5} = 29{,}701$$

$$\bar{\sigma} = \frac{1{,}198 + 2{,}434 + 528 + 1{,}243 + 1{,}006}{5} = 1{,}281.8$$

$$\sigma_{\overline{X}} = \frac{\bar{\sigma}}{c_2\sqrt{n}} = \frac{1{,}281.8}{0.8407\sqrt{5}} = 682$$

$$\overline{X} + 3\sigma_{\overline{X}} = 31{,}747$$

$$\overline{X} - 3\sigma_{\overline{X}} = 27{,}655$$

$$\sigma_{\sigma} = \frac{\bar{\sigma}}{c_2\sqrt{2n}} = \frac{1{,}281.8}{0.8407\sqrt{10}} = 482$$

$$\bar{\sigma} + 3\sigma_{\sigma} = 2{,}728$$

$$\bar{\sigma} - 3\sigma_{\sigma} = -\ 164 \text{ (taken as zero)}$$

The corresponding control charts, Fig. 110, indicate lack of control or significant differences between the tensile strengths of this alloy manufactured by the different suppliers.

Example 2: Let us next consider the set of two hundred and four measurements of insulation resistance previously given in Table 2 of Part I. In this case there was no basis for dividing the data into rational subgroups other than that it is reasonable to believe that the cause system may have changed in the course of taking the measurements. Accordingly we divided the data into groups of four, starting with the first four and continuing in the order in which they were taken. The control chart for

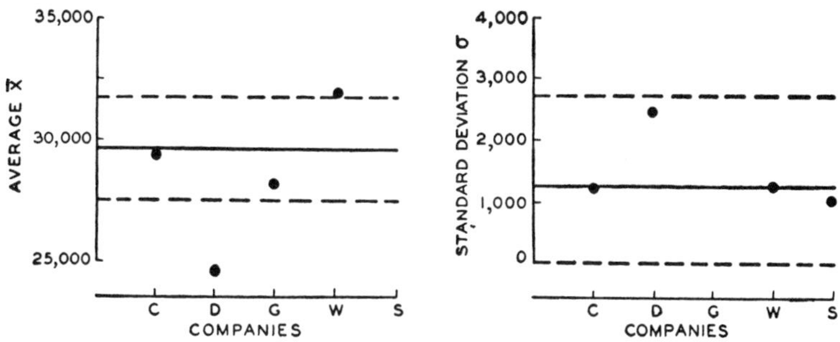

FIG. 110.—CONTROL CHART FOR SMALL SAMPLES SHOWING LACK OF CONTROL.

averages shown in Fig. 7-*a* and that for standard deviations shown in Fig. 111 indicate lack of control. As was pointed out in Part I the causes for lack of control were found and removed.

The reader may question why the original data were grouped into subsamples of four instead of some other number. A little

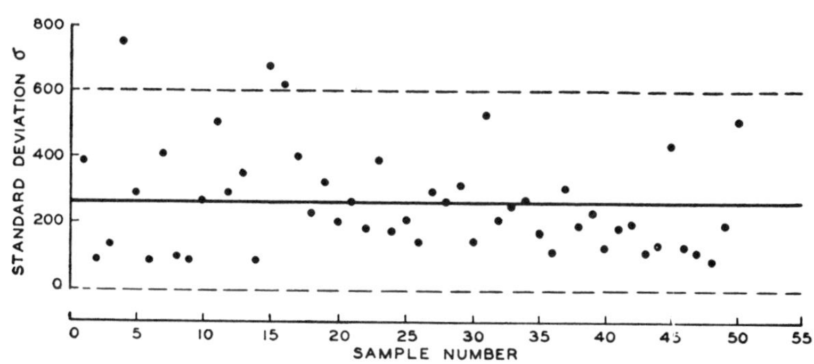

FIG. 111.—CONTROL CHART FOR STANDARD DEVIATIONS OF SAMPLES OF FOUR—DATA OF TABLE 2.

consideration will show that there is nothing sacred about the number four although there are several reasons why it may be the most satisfactory when there is no *a priori* knowledge to justify any other sample size.

Obviously, if the cause system is changing, the sample size should be as small as possible so that the averages of samples do not mask the changes. In fact single observations would be the most sensitive to such changes. Why then do we not use a sample size of unity? The answer is that if we do, we are faced with the difficulty of choosing the standard deviation to be used in the control charts. Of course, we might use the standard deviation σ of the entire group of observations but, in doing so, we would find that $\sigma = 465.21$, a value distinctly larger than that of $\frac{\bar{\sigma}}{c_2} = 328.26$. A little consideration will show that, in general, this condition will occur in the long run whenever the cause system is not constant in respect to the expected value $\bar{\mathbf{X}}$, although the expected values of σ and $\frac{\bar{\bar{\sigma}}}{c_2}$ are equal when there is no change in the cause system. Thus the test in which we would use the standard deviation σ of the whole group of n observations is not so sensitive, in general, as the one proposed in which we divide the data into small subgroups in the order in which they were taken. In fact, the sensitivity of the test will increase, in general, with decrease in subsample size until the size of the sample is such that the data in any given subgroup come from a constant system of chance causes. In the absence of any *a priori* information making it possible to divide the data into rational subgroups, there would be some advantage therefore in reducing the subsample size to unity. To do so, however, would obviously defeat our purpose since we could not then obtain an estimate σ to use in the control charts. Hence we must choose some subsample size greater than unity. Sizes 2 and 3 offer some difficulties in the way of computation of σ and so we go to a sample of four.

Now we are in a position to see how important it is to record the data in the order in which they were taken when we have no *a priori* basis for dividing the data into rational subgroups. If this is not done, there would obviously be no sense in trying to apply Criterion I.

8. *Use of Criterion I—Some Comments*

In the practical application of Criterion I, particularly in the case of small samples, certain questions arise. One of these is: How many subgroups of four must we have before we are justified in using Criterion I? That this question is important is at once apparent because the expected probability of a statistic falling within the ranges established by Criterion I approaches the economic limiting value only as the total number n of observations approaches infinity. This difference in expected probability, however, even for two subsamples of four is likely less than 0.02 and certainly less than 0.05. Hence, the effect in the long run of using Criterion I when the total number of observations is small is to indicate lack of control falsely on an average of perhaps five times in 100 trials instead of three times in, let us say, 1,000 trials which it would do when the total number n is large. In almost every instance we can well afford to take this added precaution against overlooking trouble when the total number of observations is small. It appears reasonable, therefore, that the criterion may be used even when we have only two subsamples of size not less than four. In this case, of course, we may wish to apply additional tests although, as we have already seen in the earlier part of this chapter, such tests will perhaps in the majority of cases give consistent results.[1] The principal thing to be kept in mind is, however, that the main purpose of such a criterion is to detect lack of control in a continuous production process where we have a whole series of samples so that the question as to the minimum number of subsamples becomes of minor importance.

We may also ask how the indications of Criterion I depend

[1] In work not yet published, F. W. Winters has investigated the efficiency of this criterion for the case of small samples from two normal subgroups, assuming that the data have been divided objectively. In other words, he has determined the probability that the use of Criterion I with a given sample size will detect a difference of a given amount in the averages of two objective subgroups. For example, he has shown that the efficiency varies all the way from 4 per cent for a sample of four and an objective difference of σ (the common standard deviation of the objective subgroups) to 97 per cent for a sample of twenty and an objective difference of 2σ. On the other hand the probability that this Criterion will lead us to look for trouble needlessly is, under the first condition, .0085, and under the second, .00014.

upon the universe from which the sample is drawn, especially in the case of small samples. It will have been observed that the factor c_2 used in setting limits for standard deviation is based upon the assumption that the samples are drawn from a normal universe whereas, in general, we know that this condition is not rigorously fulfilled. Furthermore, we have seen that the distribution function of both the average $\bar{X}$ and standard deviation σ of samples of a given size depends upon the nature of the universe. Hence, the probability associated with the limits in the control charts for the average $\bar{X}$ and standard deviation σ depends upon the universes from which the samples were drawn.

Of course, the distribution of averages, even for samples of four, is approximately normal independent of the universe so that the probabilities associated with control charts for averages are closely comparable irrespective of the nature of the universes. This is not true, however, in respect to the distribution of standard deviations.

We may get around this difficulty partly by using the control chart for the expected variance of the universe since, as we have seen, the expected value is related to the variance of the universe in a known manner. This makes it possible to establish the base line of the control chart for variance—something which cannot be done for the standard deviation unless the functional form of the universe is known. On the other hand, the standard deviation of the variance involves the flatness β_2 of the universe and hence cannot be estimated with great accuracy in most practical cases.

Under these conditions, it seems reasonable to believe that comparatively little can be gained in most cases by making use of the variance instead of the standard deviation. In this connection, it is of interest to cite a typical instance of the way in which the control chart method, making use of averages and standard deviations for small samples, gives indications consistent with facts when we apply the test to samples of four drawn from either of the three types of universes previously described. For example, Fig. 112 shows the results of the test

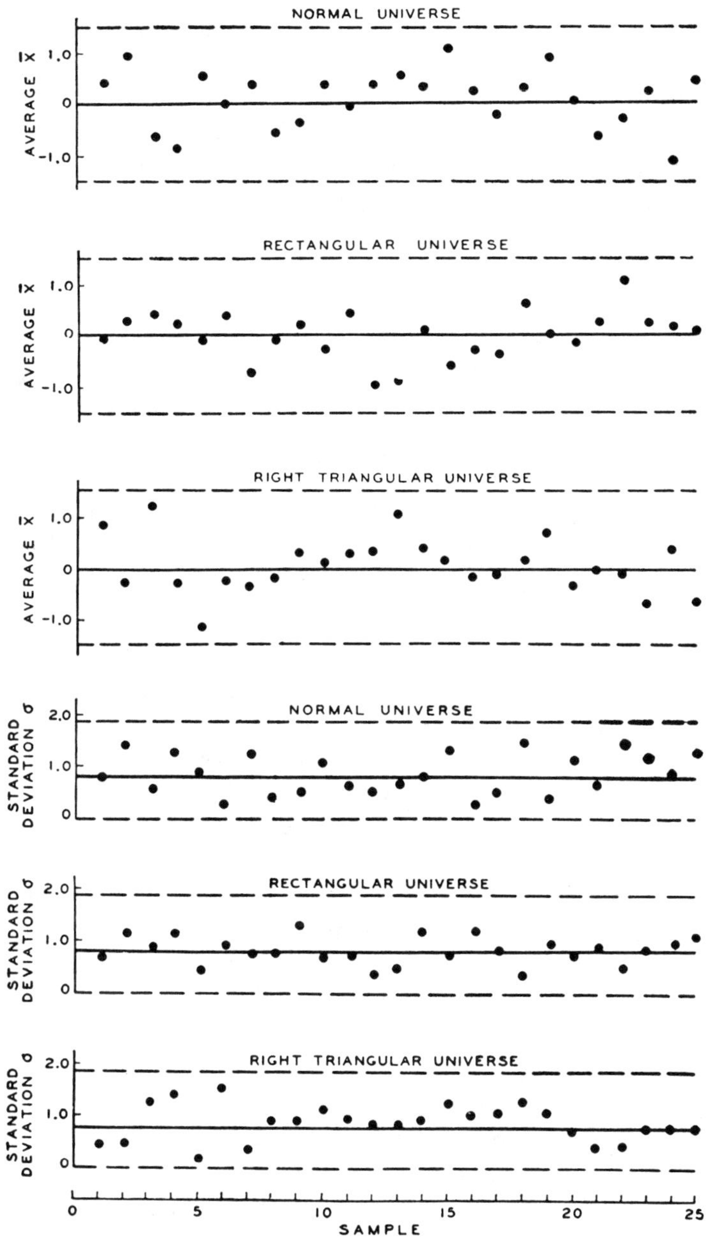

Fig. 112.—Criterion I Applied to 25 Samples of 4 from Each of 3 Universes—Values in Terms of σ of their Respective Universe.

applied to twenty-five samples of four from each of the three experimental universes. In each case all of the points are within the limits as we should expect them to be under the controlled conditions supposed to exist in drawing these samples. The results of the test are obviously consistent with the facts assumed *a priori* to be true in this particular instance.

9. *Criterion II*

We shall close this chapter with a description of another criterion and illustrate its use by application to the 204 data of Table 2. Having the data divided into m subgroups of size n, we calculate the ratio $\frac{|d|}{\sigma_d}$ as indicated in the data sheet of Table 45. If the ratio is greater than three, this fact is taken to indicate lack of control. We shall call this test Criterion II.

This test provides a means of judging the nature of the conditions under which the sampling has been done. Thus, if all samples are produced by the same constant system of causes, or, in other words, if the sampling has been done in what we term Bernoulli fashion, then the expected value of d is zero. If, however, conditions change between each observation of a subgroup but the same set of changes occur in the process of obtaining each subgroup of observations, then the expected value of d is greater than zero, and in such cases the sampling is said to be done in Poisson fashion. Or again, if conditions remain constant for any subgroup of observations but change in any one of a finite number of ways from subgroup to subgroup, then the expected value of d is less than zero and the sampling is said to be done in Lexian fashion.

However, even though the sampling is actually done in Bernoulli fashion, the observed value of d may be positive, zero, or negative due to sampling fluctuations. Hence, we must have some way of judging when the deviations of d from zero are sufficiently great to indicate either a Poisson or a Lexian selection of samples.

The standard deviation of d based upon Bernoulli sampling

TABLE 45.—DATA SHEET FOR CRITERION II—DATA OF TABLE 2

Calculation of $\frac{|d|}{\sigma_d}$

Number of observations $N = 204$
Size of subgroup $n = 4$
Number of subgroups $m = 51$

Sample Number	Average $\bar{X}_i$ of Sample	$\bar{X}_i^2$	Variance σ_i^2 of Sample
1	4,430.0000	19,624,900.0000	149,512.5000
2	4,372.5000	19,118,756.2500	7,606.2500
3	3,827.5000	14,649,756.2500	17,656.2500
. . . . .	. . . .	. . . .	. . . .
51	5,100.0000	26,010,000.0000	11,250.0000
Σ	229,407.0000	1,038,119,072.0700	4,832,876.1050
Av.	4,498.1765	20,355,275.9229	94,762.2766

$$\sigma_{\bar{X}}^2 = \frac{\sum_{i=1}^{m} \bar{X}_i^2}{m} - \bar{\bar{X}}^2 = 20{,}355{,}275.9229 - (4{,}498.1765)^2$$

$$\sigma_{\bar{X}}^2 = \underline{121{,}684.3586}$$

$$\overline{\sigma^2} = \frac{\sum_{i=1}^{m} \sigma_i^2}{m} = \underline{94{,}762.2766}$$

$$d = \frac{n}{n-1}\overline{\sigma^2} - \frac{m}{m-1} n\sigma_{\bar{X}}^2 = -\underline{370{,}122.4810}$$

$$\sigma_d = \left[\sqrt{\frac{2(mn-1)}{m(m-1)(n-1)}}\left(\frac{n}{n-1}\overline{\sigma^2}\right)\right] = \underline{29{,}107.6083}$$

$$\frac{|d|}{\sigma_d} = \frac{370{,}122.4810}{29{,}107.6083} = \underline{12.7157}$$

provides such a measure of significance. The formula for σ_d was obtained upon the assumption that the samples had been drawn from a normal universe, in which case $\overline{\sigma^2}$ and $\sigma_{\bar{X}}^2$ are uncorrelated. If the universe is not normal, this formula for σ_d will not necessarily give the correct result, although from the viewpoint of detecting lack of control this simply means that the probability that $\frac{|d|}{\sigma_d}$ will exceed 3 differs somewhat from 99 per cent, or, in other words, we may on the average look for trouble a little more often or a little less often than one time in a hundred when it actually does not exist.

CHAPTER XXI

Detection of Lack of Control—Continued

1. *Introductory Statement*

In the previous chapter we considered the problem of detecting lack of constancy of a cause system or the presence of an assignable cause of Type I. In this chapter we shall consider the problem of detecting the presence of a predominating cause or group of causes forming a part of a constant system. Such a cause will be referred to as an assignable cause of Type II. In the latter part of this chapter we shall consider what is perhaps the only available method for detecting the presence of assignable causes when the data are such that they cannot be grouped into rational subgroups and when no information is available other than the observed distribution.

Assuming that the variable X satisfies the equation (58) of control, how can we detect the presence of a predominating cause or group of causes? As a basis for our consideration of this question, let us return to the picture of a constant system of chance causes presented in Part III. There we assume that such a system is composed of, let us say, m ultimate independent causes

$$C_1, C_2, \ldots, C_i, \ldots, C_m,$$

producing effects which compound linearly. It will be recalled that we do not presume to be able to describe any one of these m causes. The most that we can usually hope to do is to put our fingers on some secondary cause made up of several of the independent contributing causes.

To make this point clear, let us think of the unknown group

of m causes of error in some physical measurement such as that of the coefficient of expansion of a steel rod. Some of the secondary or macroscopic causes of error would be temperature fluctuations, non-homogenous heating of the rod, etc. Such a cause obviously includes a group of the elementary causes. We may represent this situation schematically as follows:

$$C_1, C_2, \ldots, \underbrace{\boxed{C_i, C_{i+1}, C_{i+2}, \ldots, C_{i+j}}}_{\text{Macroscopic Cause } Y}, \ldots, C_m.$$

With this picture in mind, two methods of detecting the presence of an assignable group of causes suggest themselves. They are the well-known Method of Concomitant Variation and the Method of Differences of elementary logic. The first method is to vary the cause Y and see if we get an accompanying change in the resultant effect of the cause system. The other method is to remove the cause Y and observe whether or not the resultant effect is modified.

In the general case where X is a chance or statistical variable subject to sampling fluctuation, the effect either of varying the cause Y or of removing this cause must be shown to be significant in the sense of being greater than can reasonably be attributed to sampling fluctuations in the variable X.

It should be noted that both of these methods require that the analyst be successful in choosing the macroscopic cause which is findable in the objective sense. Hence, in the application of such a test, one must make full use of his powers of imagination, supposition, idealization, comparison and analogy in the utilization of all available data.

2. *Criterion III*

Let us assume that we are to discover whether or not there is an assignable or predominating cause of variability in a variable X satisfying the equation of control, namely,

$$dy = \mathbf{f}(X, \lambda_1, \lambda_2, \ldots, \lambda_i, \ldots, \lambda_{m'})dX. \tag{58}$$

The application of Criterion III involves three steps:

(*A*) Pick out some controlled variable Y which may or may not be an assignable cause of Type II.

(*B*) Obtain n simultaneously observed pairs of values X_1Y_1, $X_2Y_2, \ldots, X_iY_i, \ldots, X_nY_n$ and determine the correlation coefficient r.

(*C*) If r lies outside the limits

$$0 \pm \frac{3}{\sqrt{n-1}},$$

take this fact as an indication that Y is an assignable cause.

If the correlation between Y and X is normal, we see that Criterion III indicates that there is a significant degree of commonness of causation or, in other words, that the observed correlation coefficient r is greater than can reasonably be attributed to sampling fluctuations where, as before, we choose sampling limits corresponding to three times the standard deviation of the statistic used in measuring the fluctuations. Since, as we have seen in Part III, there is reason to believe that the correlation between two controlled variables is at least approximately normal, we may assume that the positive indication of Criterion III is indicative of a significant degree of commonness of causation between the two variables, and to this extent Y may be considered to be in most cases an assignable cause.

From what has been said about the sampling fluctuations of the correlation coefficient, it is obvious that, if small samples are to be used, it is preferable to state the test in terms of the variable z given by (77). If z, as given by this equation, lies outside the range

$$0 \pm \frac{3}{\sqrt{n-3}},$$

the criterion is said to give a positive indication that Y is an assignable cause in the sense of our present discussion. So long as the sample size n does not exceed twenty-five, it is perhaps better to use the z transformation.

Example 1: We shall consider a case in which it is very desirable to control the hardness of a particular kind of apparatus. In this instance, each piece of apparatus consisted of two parts welded together, the materials for the two parts coming from different sources. Table 46 gives the hardness measurements on each of the two parts for fifty-nine pieces of this apparatus. Is there any evidence of the existence of an assignable group of causes of variability in hardness?

TABLE 46.—HARDNESS MEASUREMENTS ON WELDED PARTS

Sample Number	Hardness		Sample Number	Hardness		Sample Number	Hardness	
	Part 1	Part 2		Part 1	Part 2		Part 1	Part 2
1	50.9	44.3	21	48.7	36.8	41	47.9	36.7
2	44.8	25.7	22	44.9	36.7	42	45.8	35.3
3	51.6	39.5	23	46.8	37.1	43	47.9	35.5
4	43.8	19.3	24	49.6	37.8	44	45.8	35.1
5	49.0	43.2	25	51.4	33.5	45	49.1	33.2
6	45.4	26.9	26	45.8	37.5	46	50.0	36.1
7	44.9	34.5	27	48.5	38.3	47	47.3	35.9
8	49.0	37.4	28	46.2	30.7	48	46.9	35.2
9	53.4	38.1	29	49.5	33.9	49	49.1	38.1
10	48.5	33.0	30	50.9	39.6	50	48.2	35.9
11	46.0	32.6	31	47.5	36.9	51	46.9	33.8
12	49.0	35.4	32	45.0	37.5	52	49.0	37.6
13.	43.4	36.2	33	46.6	32.4	53	44.7	35.5
14	44.4	32.5	34	48.0	39.8	54	51.7	36.2
15	46.6	31.5	35	44.5	35.3	55	45.2	34.4
16	50.4	38.1	36	48.5	38.3	56	44.8	27.5
17	45.9	35.2	37	46.0	38.1	57	42.4	31.1
18	47.3	33.4	38	48.9	35.0	58	48.5	36.8
19	46.6	30.7	39	46.3	34.9	59	50.1	34.4
20	47.3	36.8	40	46.1	32.9			

Now the only common source of causation was the heat treatment given the apparatus after the two parts were welded together. Hence the variability in the heat treatment might be an assignable cause. If it is, we should expect to find that the correlation coefficient r between the hardness measurements in Table 46 is significant in terms of Criterion III.

Applying the test we find that the observed correlation $r = 0.513$ lies outside the limits

$$0 \pm \frac{3}{\sqrt{59 - 1}}.$$

Hence we conclude that the heat treatment constitutes an assignable cause of variability in the hardness of the finished product. This conclusion has since been justified by further studies.

3. *Criterion IV*

Let us assume, as before, that the variable X satisfies the equation (58) of control. The application of Criterion IV involves the following steps:

(*A*) Obtain n observations $X_1, X_2, \ldots, X_i, \ldots, X_n$ of the variable X and calculate some statistic Θ_{i1} for this set of n observed values.

(*B*) Choose some variable Y which may or may not be an assignable cause and obtain n values of the variable X under a condition where it is known that the variable Y can in no way influence the variability in X. Making use of this new series of n observed values, determine the value of the statistic Θ_i and let us call this value Θ_{i2}.

(*C*) If

$$|\Theta_{i1} - \Theta_{i2}| > 3\sigma_{\Theta_{i1} - \Theta_{i2}},$$

we take this fact as an indication that Y was an assignable cause.

For reasons which we have already considered, it is usually sufficient to make use of the two statistics, average and standard deviation, in terms of which we say that Y is an assignable cause if either of the following inequalities is satisfied:

$$|\bar{X}_1 - \bar{X}_2| > 3\sqrt{\frac{1}{n}(\sigma_1^2 + \sigma_2^2)}$$

$$|\sigma_1 - \sigma_2| > 3\sqrt{\frac{1}{2n}(\sigma_1^2 + \sigma_2^2)}.$$

Example: Fig. 113 shows the cross-sectional view of a common type carbon transmitter. It is but natural to expect that the physical properties, such as resistance, efficiency, etc., of

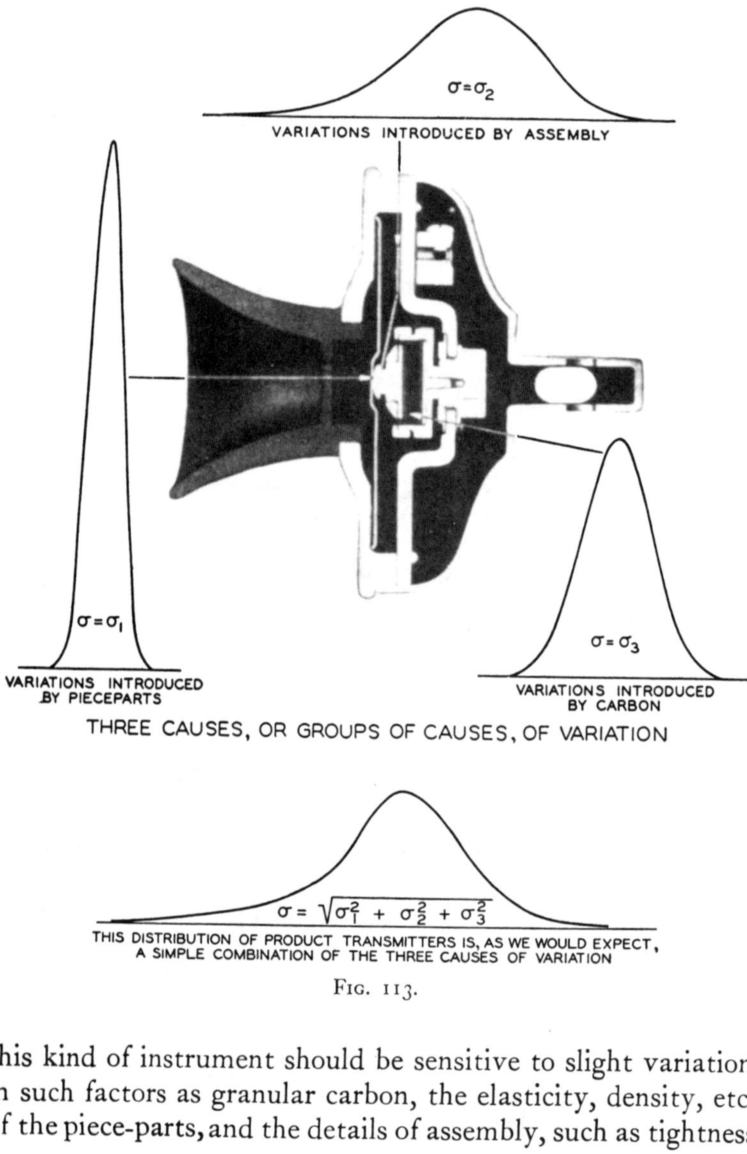

FIG. 113.

this kind of instrument should be sensitive to slight variations in such factors as granular carbon, the elasticity, density, etc., of the piece-parts, and the details of assembly, such as tightness, with which the screws are set and the care with which the respective parts are centered.

It is of interest to see how much influence each one of these three factors exerts upon the general variability of the qualities of the completed instrument. The method for investigating the influence of each factor immediately suggests itself—it is the use of Criterion IV.

To apply this method we must eliminate the influence of all but one of the factors and study the resulting distribution of quality attributable to the remaining factor or constant system of chance causes. The results of such a study on one quality characteristic gave the three distributions shown in Fig. 113, the standard deviations of which were σ_1 for piece-parts, σ_2 for assembly, and σ_3 for carbon.

If σ represents the standard deviation in quality of the completed instrument in a sample of n and

$\sigma_{1.23}$ = standard deviation in samples of n when piece-part variations are eliminated,

$\sigma_{2.13}$ = standard deviation in samples of n when assembly variations are eliminated, and

$\sigma_{3.12}$ = standard deviation in samples of n when carbon variations are eliminated,

then the application of Criterion IV to standard deviations states that piece-parts, assembly and carbon represent assignable groups of causes if

$$|\sigma - \sigma_{1.23}| > 3\sqrt{\frac{1}{2n}(\sigma^2 + \sigma^2_{1.23})},$$

$$|\sigma - \sigma_{2.13}| > 3\sqrt{\frac{1}{2n}(\sigma^2 + \sigma^2_{2.13})},$$

and

$$|\sigma - \sigma_{3.12}| > 3\sqrt{\frac{1}{2n}(\sigma^2 + \sigma^2_{3.12})}.$$

In this case it was found that each of these three inequalities was satisfied and hence we conclude that all three factors actually represent assignable cause groups of variation.

Furthermore, since the value of σ is approximately given by

$$\sqrt{\sigma_1^2 + \sigma_2^2 + \sigma_3^2},$$

we conclude that these three groups operate independently and contribute practically the entire amount of variability observed in the completed instrument.

4. *Criterion V*

Oftentimes the observed data are given in a form such that no one of the four previously described criteria can be used.

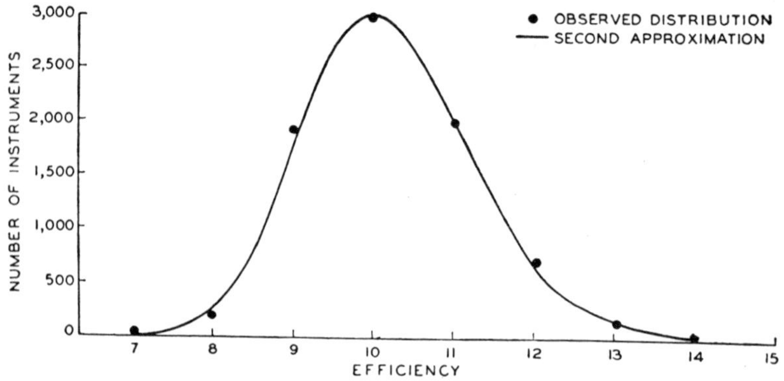

FIG. 114.—IS THERE ANY INDICATION OF LACK OF CONTROL? CRITERION V ANSWERS: "YES."

As a specific illustration we may consider the observed frequency distribution of efficiency of 7,686 pieces of one kind of apparatus represented by the black dots in Fig. 114. Is there any indication of lack of control?

The instruments in this group had come to the central testing laboratory from eight different shops. The measurements when submitted for analysis, however, had been grouped together, giving the frequency distribution of Fig. 114 and the fourth column of the upper half of Table 47.

The method of detecting lack of control in this case is as follows:

A. Calculate the average $\overline{X}$, the standard deviation σ, and the skewness k from the n observations and use these in the expression [1]

$$\int_{x_1}^{x_2} \frac{1}{\sigma\sqrt{2\pi}}\left[1 - \frac{k}{2}\left(\frac{x}{\sigma} - \frac{1}{3}\frac{x^3}{\sigma^3}\right)\right] e^{-\frac{x^2}{2\sigma^2}} dx$$

to calculate the theoretical frequencies $y_{\Theta 1}, y_{\Theta 2}, \ldots, y_{\Theta m}$ for the m cell intervals into which the original data have been grouped, it being understood that $x = X - \overline{X}$.

B. Calculate

$$\chi^2 = \sum_{i=1}^{m} \frac{(y_i - y_{\Theta i})^2}{y_{\Theta i}}.$$

C. Read from the curves [2] of Fig. 73 the probability P of obtaining a value of χ^2 as large as or larger than that observed, where the number of degrees of freedom is taken as four less than the number m of cells.

D. If the probability P is less than 0.001, take this fact as an indication of lack of control.

Example 1: The details of the application of this criterion to the data of Fig. 114 are shown above in the data sheet of Table 47. It will be noted that Sheppard's corrections are used in this case. The smooth solid curve of Fig. 114 appears to fit the observed points very well indeed. However, Criterion V detects what the eye does not see. In accordance with the conditions of Criterion V, we conclude upon the basis of its application that the quality of this product was not controlled.

Although the observations originally presented were grouped together without reference to the shops from which they came, it later became possible to subdivide the data upon this basis. Definite evidence of lack of constancy of the cause system was thus revealed by the control chart of Fig. 115, and the assignable causes of variability were found. In other words, the indication of Criterion V was correct.

[1] This is the second approximation already referred to in Parts II and III. The theoretical frequencies may be calculated with the aid of Tables A and B.

[2] More extensive tables of $P(\chi^2)$ are given by K. Pearson in his *Tables for Statisticians and Biometricians.*

TABLE 47.—DATA SHEET FOR CRITERION V.

Subject: Apparatus Type A	INSPECTION ENGINEERING ANALYSIS SHEET	Date 1-14-26 / Calc. by MBC / Checked MSH

	1	2	3	4	5	6	7	8	9	10	11	12
0	6.0	5.5	0	6	0	0	0	0	0	6	484	242.000
1	7.0	6.5	1	18	18	18	18	18	2	16		
2	8.0	7.5	2	164	328	656	1312	2624	289	−125	15625	54.066
3	9.0	8.5	3	1904	5712	17136	51408	154224	1716	188	35344	20.597
4	10.0	9.5	4	2904	11616	46464	185856	743424	2984	−80	6400	2.145
5	11.0	10.5	5	1916	9580	47900	239500	1197500	1952	−36	1296	.664
6	12.0	11.5	6	662	3972	23832	142992	857952	625	37	1369	2.190
7	13.0	12.5	7	101	707	4949	34643	242501	110	−9	81	.736
8	14.0	13.5	8	11	88	704	5632	45056	10	1	1	.100
9		14.5										
10												
11												
12												
13												
	Σ			7686	32021	141659	661361	3243299	7688			$X^2 = 322.498$
						m = units per cell = 1			Number of cells = 8			P = .000

Moments about origin $\bar{o}$ (The origin $\bar{o}$ is the mid-point value of cell no. o)

$$1\mu_1 = \frac{\Sigma yX}{\Sigma y} = \frac{32021}{7686} = 4.166146 \qquad \bar{X} = \bar{o} + m_1\mu_1 = 6.0 + 4.166146 = 10.166146$$

$$1\mu_2 = \frac{\Sigma yx^2}{\Sigma y} = \frac{141659}{7686} = 18.430783$$

$$1\mu_3 = \frac{\Sigma yX^3}{\Sigma y} = \frac{661361}{7686} = 86.047489$$

$$1\mu_4 = \frac{\Sigma yX^4}{\Sigma y} = \frac{3243299}{7686} = 421.974889$$

Cor. Moments:

$$\sigma = m\mu_2^{1/2} = (.990678)^{1/2} = .995328$$

$$k = \frac{\mu_3}{\mu 2^{3/2}} = \frac{.313182}{.986050} = .317613$$

$$\beta_2 = \frac{\mu_4}{\mu_2^2} = \frac{3.142229}{.981443} = 3.201642$$

Uncorrected moments about arithmetic mean $\bar{X}$

$$\mu_2 = 1\mu_2 - 1\mu_1^2 = 18.430783 - 17.356772 - 1.074011$$

$$\mu_3 = 1\mu_3 - 3_1\mu_1\, 1\mu_2 + 2_1\mu_1^3 = 86.047489 - 230.355999 + 144.621692 = .313182$$

$$\mu_4 = 1\mu_4 - 4_1\mu_1\, 1\mu_3 = 6_1\mu_1^2\, 1\mu_2 - 3_1\mu_1^4 = 421.974889 - 1433.945608 + 1919.393390 = -903.772603 = 3.650068$$

Corrected moments about $\bar{X}$ (Sheppard's Corrections)

$$\mu_2\,(\text{cor.}) = \mu 2 - 0.083333 = 1.074011 - .083333 = .990678$$

$$\mu_4\,(\text{cor.})\ \mu_4 - 0.5\,\mu_2 + 0.029167 = 3.650068 - 537006 + .029167 = 3.142229$$

	1	2	3	4	5	6	7	8	9	10	11
	Mid-cell value	Cell Bound.	Dev. from $\bar{X}$ x	(x/δ) z	F(z)	f(z)	kf(z)	F(x) ± kf(z)	Diff.	Freq.	Approx. Freq.
0	6.0	5.5	4.6661	4.6880	.5000	.0665	.0211	.5211	−.0001	−.7686	−1
1	7.0	6.5	3.6661	3.6834	.4998	.0674	.0214	.5212	.0002	1.5372	2
2	8.0	7.5	2.6661	2.6787	.4963	.0778	.0247	.5210	.0376	288.9936	289
3	9.0	8.5	1.6661	1.6740	.4529	.0960	.0305	.4834	.2232	1715.5152	1716
4	10.0	9.5	.6661	.6693	.2484	.0371	.0118	.2602	.3882	2983.7052	2984
5	11.0	10.5	.3339	.3354	.1314	.0107	.0034	.1280	.2540	1952.2440	1952
6	12.0	11.5	1.3339	1.3401	.4099	.0880	.0279	.3820	.0813	624.8718	625
7	13.0	12.5	2.3339	2.3448	.4905	.0856	.0272	.4633	.0143	109.9098	110
8	14.0	13.5	3.3339	3.3495	.4995	.0691	.0219	.4776	.0013	9.9918	10
9		14.5	4.3339	4.3342	.5000	.0665	.0211	.4789			
10											
11											
12											
13											
14											
15											

Example 2: In the development of methods of preserving telephone poles, it is of interest to know the distribution of thickness of sapwood to be expected for poles of a given kind and to know whether or not this quality of poles is controlled. Early in this study a set of 1,528 measurements of depth of sapwood on as many chestnut poles became available, although at that time it was not possible to divide this set of data into rational subgroups.

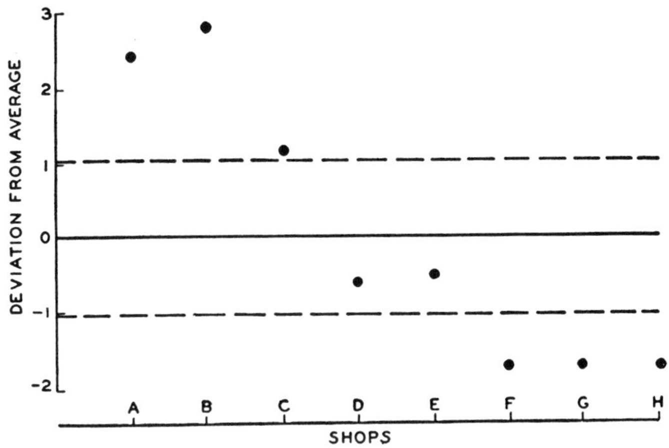

FIG. 115.—FURTHER EVIDENCE OF LACK OF CONTROL FOR DATA OF FIG. 114.

The observed and theoretical distributions of depth of sapwood are shown by the black dots and the smooth curve of Fig. 116. The probability P of obtaining a value of χ^2 as large as or larger than that observed is much less than 0.001. Hence a search for assignable causes was begun and the following three were found:

(*a*) The men who made the measurements favored even numbers.

(*b*) The thickness of sapwood was determined from borings, and no allowance was made for shrinkage of these during the time that the measurements were being taken.

(*c*) The expected thickness of sapwood was found to depend upon whether the poles had come from one or the other of the slopes of a mountain range. In the sample of 1,528 poles some had come from one slope and some from another.

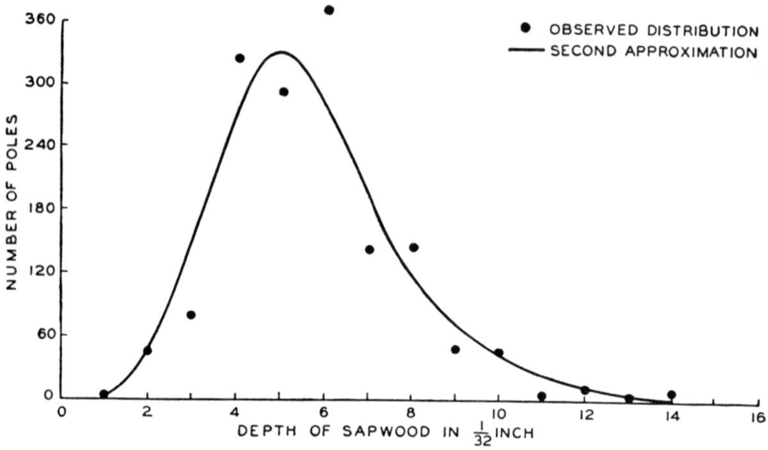

Fig. 116.—Criterion V Indicates the Presence of Assignable Causes.

Example 3: In the initial stages of the production of a kind of equipment for which electrical resistance was an important quality characteristic, the observed frequency distribution was that given by the dots in Fig. 117. The application of Cri-

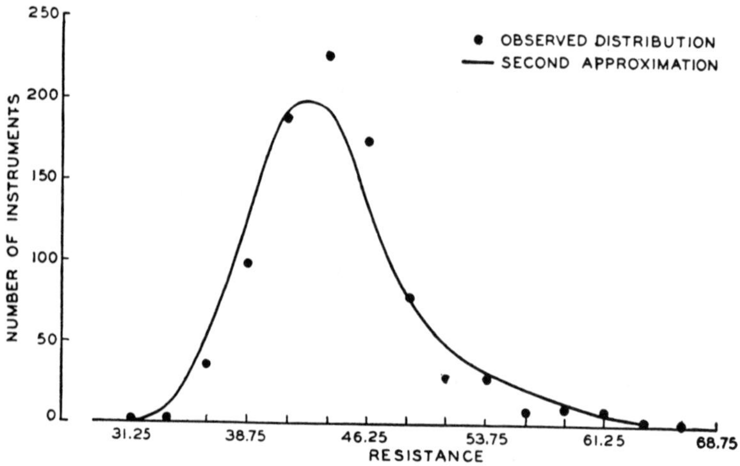

Fig. 117.—Criterion V Gives Positive Test, Indicating Trouble.

terion V indicated the presence of assignable causes in that the probability of occurrence of a value of χ^2 as large as or larger than that observed was much less than 0.001.

Further investigation revealed that assignable causes had entered the production process and affected the resistance of a small group of the instruments in the original lot. After the measurements for this small group had been separated from the others, the resultant distribution was found to be that given in Fig. 118. Criterion V applied to this resultant dis-

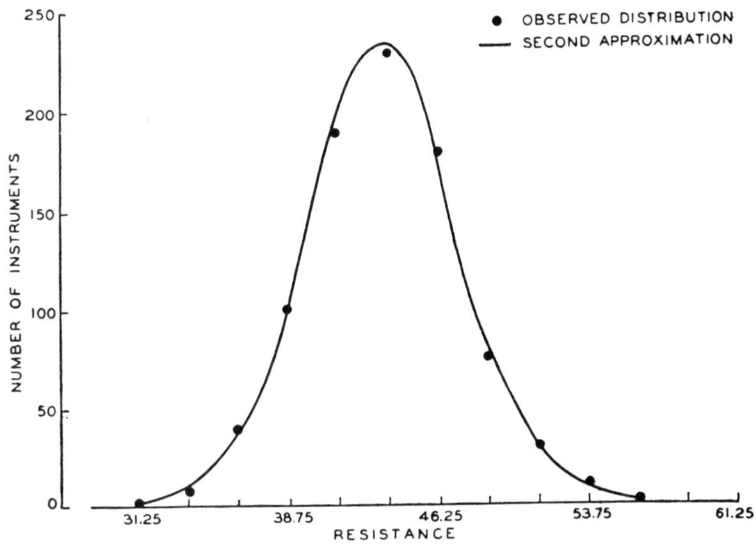

FIG. 118.—TROUBLE REMOVED—CRITERION V GIVES NEGATIVE TEST.

tribution gave a negative test, indicating that the trouble had been removed.

5. *Criticism of Criterion V*

In the first place the test is based upon the use of a particular frequency function, viz., the second approximation. Are we justified in assuming that quality free from assignable causes is always distributed in accord with this statistical law or frequency distribution? Is it necessary and sufficient to show that the quality of a product differs no more from a second

TABLE 48.—CHI SQUARE FOR EACH OF THE FOUR DISTRIBUTIONS OF SAMPLES OF 1,000 EACH FROM THE NORMAL UNIVERSE USING OBSERVED ESTIMATES FOR PARAMETERS

Sample No. 1			Sample No. 2			Sample No. 3			Sample No. 4		
Theoretical y_Θ	Observed y	$\frac{(y-y_\Theta)^2}{y_\Theta}$	Theoretical y_Θ	Observed y	$\frac{(y-y_\Theta)^2}{y_\Theta}$	Theoretical y_Θ	Observed y	$\frac{(y-y_\Theta)^2}{y_\Theta}$	Theoretical y_Θ	Observed y	$\frac{(y-y_\Theta)^2}{y_\Theta}$
3	5	1.333	2	1	0.500	4	2	1.000	2	2	0.000
10	9	0.100	8	14	4.500	10	10	0.000	7	9	0.571
29	36	1.690	25	24	0.040	30	29	0.033	23	25	0.174
66	55	1.833	61	51	1.639	68	72	0.235	59	49	1.695
121	123	0.033	116	113	0.078	122	124	0.033	116	112	0.138
173	165	0.370	172	187	1.308	172	181	0.471	176	191	1.278
195	203	0.328	199	195	0.080	193	180	0.876	205	204	0.005
173	172	0.006	179	176	0.050	172	169	0.052	183	182	0.005
121	123	0.033	126	125	0.008	120	120	0.000	126	123	0.071
67	68	0.015	69	71	0.058	67	67	0.000	66	64	0.061
29	31	0.138	30	31	0.033	29	32	0.310	27	25	0.148
10	8	0.400	10	8	0.400	10	11	0.100	8	12	2.000
3	2	0.333	4	4	0.000	4	3	0.250	2	2	0.000
	χ^2	6.612			8.694			3.360			6.146

approximation curve than may be attributed to sampling fluctuations?

In Part III it was shown that there is no such known necessary and sufficient condition for control. However, it was shown that, for a very wide range of constant systems of chance causes, the second approximation is approached as we approach the theoretical conditions of maximum control although no frequency function is a sufficient, even though it be a necessary, condition for maximum control unless it be known *a priori* that the chance cause system is constant.

Now let us consider the use made of the Chi Square test in this criterion. Let us assume for the sake of argument that it is necessary and sufficient to show that the distribution function is the second approximation in order to show that the cause system is free from assignable causes. In this case can we rely upon the Chi Square test to detect the presence of assignable causes when the theoretical distribution is calculated from the second approximation using estimates of the three parameters derived from the observed data?

We have seen how the Chi Square test works when the distribution function is known *a priori*, both as to functional form and the values of the parameters. The question now to be considered is: How will it work, if we know *a priori* the functional form but not the parameters?

To make the problem specific, let us consider the four distributions of 1,000 observations each from the normal universe previously used to illustrate the use of the Chi Square test when the true distribution $y_1, y_2, \ldots, y_i, \ldots, y_m$ into m cells is known *a priori*. Now, however, let us calculate theoretical distributions for each of the four samples of 1,000 by using the observed values of the averages and standard deviations in the normal function. Table 48 gives the four distributions derived in this way together with the calculated values of χ^2, using a thirteen-cell grouping.

It is of interest to compare the observed values of χ^2 in Table 48 with those previously calculated for the same four samples of 1,000 making use of the *a priori* known distribution,

Table 36. These two sets of values are shown in columns 2 and 3 of Table 49. The average χ^2 in the third column is

TABLE 49.—OBSERVED VALUES OF χ^2

Sample Number	Chi Square		Probability		
				Theoretical Distribution	
	A Priori Known Distribution	Theoretical Distribution	*A Priori* Known Distribution	12 Degrees of Freedom	10 Degrees of Freedom
1	6.741	6.612	0.873	0.880	0.760
2	10.716	8.694	0.554	0.728	0.562
3	4.455	3.360	0.972	0.991	0.969
4	9.174	6.146	0.688	0.908	0.802
Average.....	7.772	6.203	0.772	0.877	0.773

definitely less than that in the second, and the average probability calculated for the values of χ^2 from the theoretical frequencies is 0.877 as compared with the average of 0.772 corresponding to the chi squares computed from the known *a priori* frequencies.

A little consideration shows that in the calculation of χ^2 from theoretical frequencies, we must make allowance for the fact that estimates of parameters are used instead of true values. We see that, when the *a priori* cell frequencies $\mathbf{y}_1, \mathbf{y}_2, \ldots, \mathbf{y}_i, \ldots, \mathbf{y}_m$ are known, the only restriction on the observable cell frequencies $y_1, y_2, \ldots, y_i, \ldots, y_m$ is that

$$y_1 + y_2 + \ldots + y_i + \ldots + y_m = n.$$

In other words, the set of m variables $(y_i - \mathbf{y}_i)$, $(i = 1, 2, \ldots, m)$, has $m - 1$ degrees of freedom. Obviously, however, the set of m variables $(y_i - y_{\Theta i})$ has $m - 3$ degrees of freedom because we have three conditions imposed upon the possible cell frequencies, viz.,

$$\Sigma y_i = n,$$

$$\Sigma y_i X_i = n\bar{X},$$

$$\Sigma y_i (X_i - \bar{X})^2 = n\sigma^2.$$

When we make allowance for the loss of three degrees of freedom instead of one, we get the probabilities in the sixth column of Table 49, the average of which is 0.773 as compared with the corresponding average 0.772 for the values of χ^2 calculated from the *a priori* known cell frequencies. This close check should strengthen our faith in the usefulness of the χ^2 test when the functional form is known *a priori* and the parameters are estimated from the data.

We must consider briefly certain other characteristics of the Chi Square test. Obviously the total number of observations must be large before we can apply the test, particularly when the parameters in the frequency function must be estimated from the observed data. In quality control work we seldom try to use Criterion V unless the sample size n is at least 1,000. When the sample size is very large, it becomes important that the method of estimating the parameters in the theoretical frequency distribution is such that the statistical limit

$$\underset{n \to \infty}{L_S} \frac{1}{n}(y_i - y_{\Theta i}) = 0$$

is satisfied. Otherwise the observed value of χ^2 as n is increased indefinitely will always approach infinity even though the quality is controlled in accord with the assumed functional distribution. Enough has been said to indicate the nature of some of the limitations to be placed upon the use of the Chi Square test involved in Criterion V.

Thus we see that Criterion V is a far less satisfactory test than Criterion I where the latter can be applied. We see that Criterion V in practice will usually give indication of the presence of assignable causes even though the product is controlled, unless the objective distribution is rigorously given by the second approximation. The criterion likely errs on the side of indicating trouble when it does not exist, although this is not a serious handicap in most industries until the state of control has been practically reached. By such time a producer will generally have set up his inspection practices so that his data are divided into rational subgroups and Criterion I may be applied.

6. *Rôle of Judgment in Choice of Criteria*

Even though, in general, an engineer need not go beyond the use of the five criteria previously described, certain exceptions may arise. Such a case is shown in Fig. 119 in which we have a control chart for averages of samples of four supposed to have been drawn from a normal universe in the order plotted. Would you conclude that the cause system is constant because Criterion I is satisfied? Almost anyone will answer this question in the negative. The probability of getting from a controlled system twenty-five samples with averages decreasing from sample to sample is so exceedingly small compared with the probability of getting twenty-five samples not so ordered

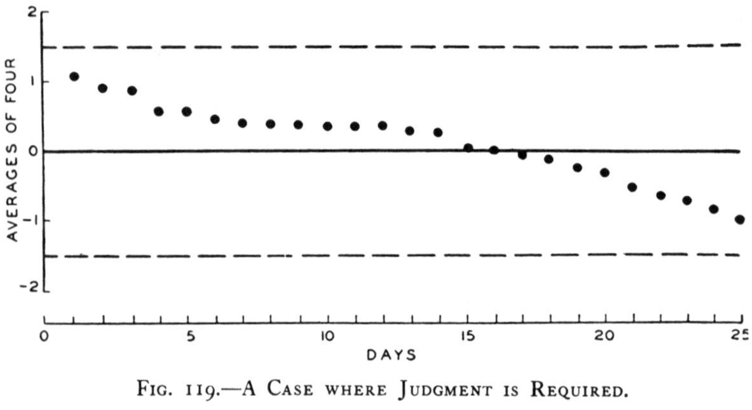

Fig. 119.—A Case where Judgment is Required.

as to suggest the presence of an assignable cause or trend. Here is a case then where common sense suggests the use of a criterion other than one of the five.

As another example of a situation requiring judgment in the use of criteria, let us consider again the distribution of successes in 4,096 throws of twelve dice where the throw of a 1, 2, or 3 is to be considered a success. A manufacturer of these dice might reasonably have wished to produce dice which are not biased. In such a case the distribution of successes, Column 2 of Table 50, should not differ from that given by the successive terms of the point binomial, 4,096 $(\frac{1}{2} + \frac{1}{2})^{12}$ by more than may be attributed to sampling fluctuations. Would he conclude that the discrepancy between the theoretical and observed distributions indicates bias? To answer this question he might

TABLE 50.—DOES THE DISCREPANCY BETWEEN THEORETICAL AND OBSERVED DISTRIBUTION INDICATE BIAS?

Number of Successes	Observed Frequency	Theoretical Frequency $4096(\frac{1}{2}+\frac{1}{2})^{12}$	Number of Successes	Observed Frequency	Theoretical Frequency $4096(\frac{1}{2}+\frac{1}{2})^{12}$
0	0	1	7	847	792
1	7	12	8	536	495
2	60	66	9	257	220
3	198	220	10	71	66
4	430	495	11	11	12
5	731	792	12	0	1
6	948	924			

apply Criterion V. Doing so, he would get a probability of fit of 0.0015. Since this probability exceeds the value 0.001 set as a limit in the statement of Criterion V, he would be supposed to conclude that the product was controlled in the sense that it did not show a significant bias from the *a priori* standard.

If, however, we compare the graph of the smooth curve through the frequencies determined from the binomial expansion, Fig. 120, with the observed values, we see that the smooth curve appears to be shifted to the left.

Instead of using Criterion V, we might have compared the observed fraction $p = 0.512$ of success with the expected value 0.500 upon the basis of the assumption of no bias. We might take the occurrence of a value of p outside the range $0.500 \pm 3\sigma_p$, where σ_p is the standard deviation of p in samples of size n, as being significant. In this case

$$\sigma_p = \sqrt{\frac{\frac{1}{2}\,\frac{1}{2}}{1{,}000}} = 0.0158.$$

Hence this test indicates control as did Criterion V, because the observed value $p = 0.512$ is well within the limits of $0.500 \pm 3(0.0158)$. Thus both tests indicate control.

It is left as an exercise for the reader to calculate the theoretical distribution upon the assumption that the dice were biased so that the probability of success is the observed value 0.512. He will find that the probability of fit is thus remarkably

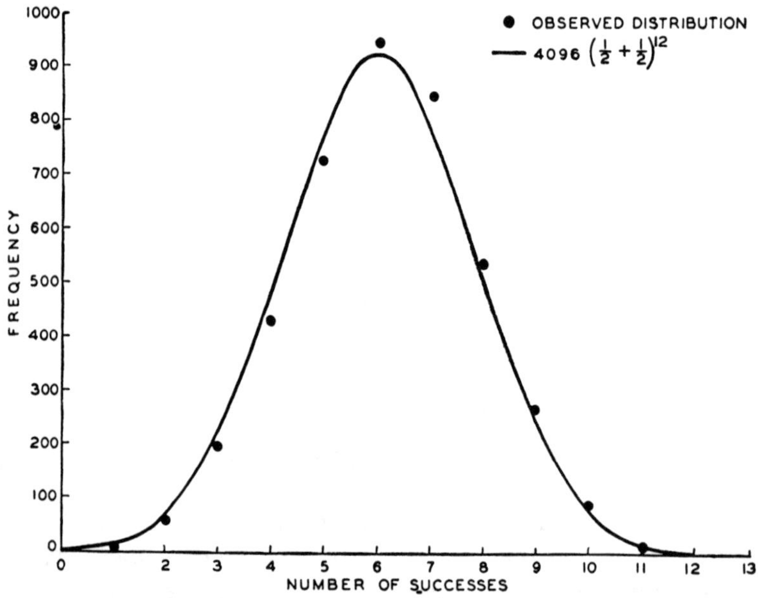

FIG. 120.—THE FACT THAT THE SMOOTH THEORETICAL CURVE APPEARS TO BE SHIFTED TO THE LEFT SUGGESTS LACK OF CONTROL EVEN THOUGH CRITERION V GIVES NEGATIVE TEST.

improved, and that the differences between observed and corresponding theoretical cell frequencies show a mixture of signs as they should. In this case he will find that the observed results are more likely on the assumption of bias than on that of no bias. Most likely his judgment will lead him to accept the hypothesis that the dice are biased.

7. *Sampling Inspection in Relation to Control—Attributes*

We are now in a position to consider the significance of control in relation to sampling inspection designed to give the consumer certain assurance in respect to the quality of product which he receives.

The consumer, in general ignorant of the production process, naturally wants some protection against accepting a bad lot of product. Of course, the ideal situation would be to inspect the entire lot and thus make absolutely certain of its quality. This, however, is often a too costly procedure. Hence the consumer is willing to compromise and use sampling inspection provided it is not likely that the quality of the sample will indicate that the lot is good when, in reality, it contains more defects than he is willing to tolerate. Two such sampling methods for protecting the consumer will now be discussed.

A. *A Priori Method:* The essential element in this method is that, if a lot containing the tolerance number of defective pieces is submitted for inspection, the chance that it will be accepted on the basis of a *random* sample is a given value P, whereas if the lot contains more than the tolerance number of defective pieces, the probability that it will be accepted on the same basis is less than P.

For example, let us assume that a lot of N pieces of product is to be inspected and that the number c of defective pieces found in a sample of n is to be made the basis of acceptance or rejection of the lot. The consumer is perhaps willing to accept a certain amount of defective material provided the number of such pieces thus accepted does not exceed some fixed percentage of the lot, commonly known as the tolerance p_t. In fact we shall assume that, if a tolerance lot,—one containing p_tN defective pieces—is submitted for inspection the consumer wishes to have some assurance that he will accept only a fraction P of such lots in the long run. This fraction P has been called the consumer's risk and it is merely the probability that a tolerance lot will be accepted upon the basis of the sample.[1]

[1] This risk is discussed in an article by H. F. Dodge and H. G. Romig, "A Method of Sampling Inspection," *Bell System Technical Journal*, October, 1929.

It remains merely to specify the sample size n and acceptance number c in such a way that the probability of finding this number or less of defective pieces in the sample taken from a tolerance lot is a given value P.

Mathematically these factors are related by the following equation:

$$P = \frac{1}{C_n^N}\left[C_n^{q_tN} + C_{n-1}^{q_tN}\,C_1^{p_tN} + C_{n-2}^{q_tN}\,C_2^{p_tN} + \ldots + C_{n-c}^{q_tN}\,C_c^{p_tN}\right], \quad (92)$$

where C_j^i means the number of combinations of i things taken j at a time and $q_t = 1 - p_t$. Having assigned P a definite value,

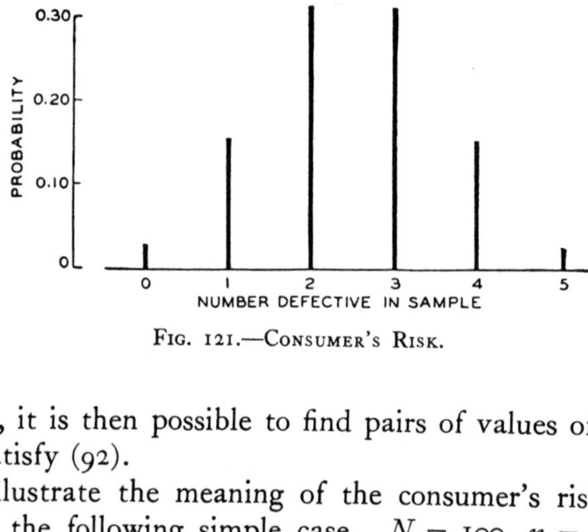

FIG. 121.—CONSUMER'S RISK.

say 0.10, it is then possible to find pairs of values of n and c which satisfy (92).

To illustrate the meaning of the consumer's risk, let us consider the following simple case. $N = 100$, $n = 50$, $p_t =$ 5 per cent, $c = 1$, $q_t = 95$ per cent. The consumer's risk is then the probability of finding 1 or 0 defective pieces in the sample of fifty taken from the lot of one hundred containing five defective pieces. Substituting the necessary values in (92), we find $P = 0.1811$, which is equal to the sum of the first two ordinates of Fig. 121.

B. *A Posteriori Method:* This method also offers the consumer a certain protection against accepting bad lots, i.e., those containing the tolerance number or more of defective pieces.

The essential point of difference between this and the method just described is that the present method[1] attempts to find the probability that a lot contains more than X defective pieces if c defective pieces are found in a random sample of n. A little consideration will show that this kind of risk is quite different from the consumer's risk previously described and that the nature of the assumption that must be made before this risk can be given is quite different from that made in the *a priori* method.

Specifically, it is necessary to assume the *a priori* existence probability distribution of lots of a given size N in respect to the number of defective pieces contained therein. Having made this assumption, it is then possible to calculate the probability that each of the possible lots would have given the sample. The *a posteriori* probability that the lot contains just M defective pieces is then the ratio of the probability that a lot of size N containing M defective pieces existed and caused the sample to the sum of the probabilities that lots containing 0, 1, 2, . . . , N defective pieces existed and caused the sample. It follows from this that the *a posteriori* probability that the lot contains more than M defective pieces is the sum of a series of the above ratios found by allowing the number of defective pieces in the lot to vary from $M + 1$ to N inclusive.

To illustrate this method, consider again the above example and let us find the *a posteriori* probability that the lot of one hundred pieces contains more than the tolerance number of defective pieces, assuming that the sample shows only one defective piece. As a very simple *a priori* assumption we shall assume that all possible constitutions of lots are equally probable, i.e., the probabilities of the existence of lots containing 0, 1, 2, . . . , 100 defective pieces are all equal to $\frac{1}{101}$. Then the existence probability distribution of possible lots is that shown graphically in Fig. 122-*a* and given in Column 2 of Table 51 as existence probabilities $\alpha_0, \alpha_1, \ldots, \alpha_i, \ldots, \alpha_N$.

[1] This method of sampling is discussed in an article by Paul P. Coggins "Some General Results of Elementary Sampling Theory," *Bell System Technical Journal*, January, 1928.

The next step is to calculate the probability that each of the possible lots could have given the observed sample. These are the productive probabilities $\beta_0, \beta_1, \ldots, \beta_i, \ldots, \beta_N$ shown in Fig. 122-*b* and Column 3 of Table 51. At this stage we should

TABLE 51.—CALCULATION OF *a posteriori* PROBABILITY

(1) Number Defective in Lot M_i	(2) *A priori* Existence Probability α_i	(3) *A priori* Productive Probability β_i	(4) *A posteriori* Probability $\frac{\alpha_i\beta_i}{\Sigma\alpha_i\beta_i}$
0	1/101	0	0
1	1/101	0.500000	0.252475
2	1/101	0.505051	0.255026
3	1/101	0.378788	0.191269
4	1/101	0.249922	0.126198
5	1/101	0.152947	0.077231
6	1/101	0.088870	0.044875
7	1/101	0.049635	0.025063
8	1/101	0.026838	0.013553
9	1/101	0.014112	0.007126
10	1/101	0.007237	0.003654
11	1/101	0.003627	0.001831
12	1/101	0.001778	0.000898
13	1/101	0.000854	0.000431
14	1/101	0.000402	0.000203
15	1/101	0.000185	0.000093
16	1/101	0.000084	0.000042
17	1/101	0.000037	0.000019
18	1/101	0.000016	0.000008
19	1/101	0.000008	0.000004
20	1/101	0.000003	0.000002
21	1/101	0.000001	0.000001
*22	1/101	0.000000	0.000000

* Probabilities in columns (3) and (4) for $M \geq 22$ do not affect the sixth place of decimals.

note that certain of the β's are necessarily zero,—lots of one hundred containing less than one defective piece or more than fifty-one defective pieces could not have produced the sample. For β's corresponding to number of defects lying between these limits, the probability $\alpha_i\beta_i$ that a lot containing just i defective pieces existed and caused the sample is

$$\alpha_i\beta_i = \frac{1}{101} C_{49}^{100-i} C_1^i.$$

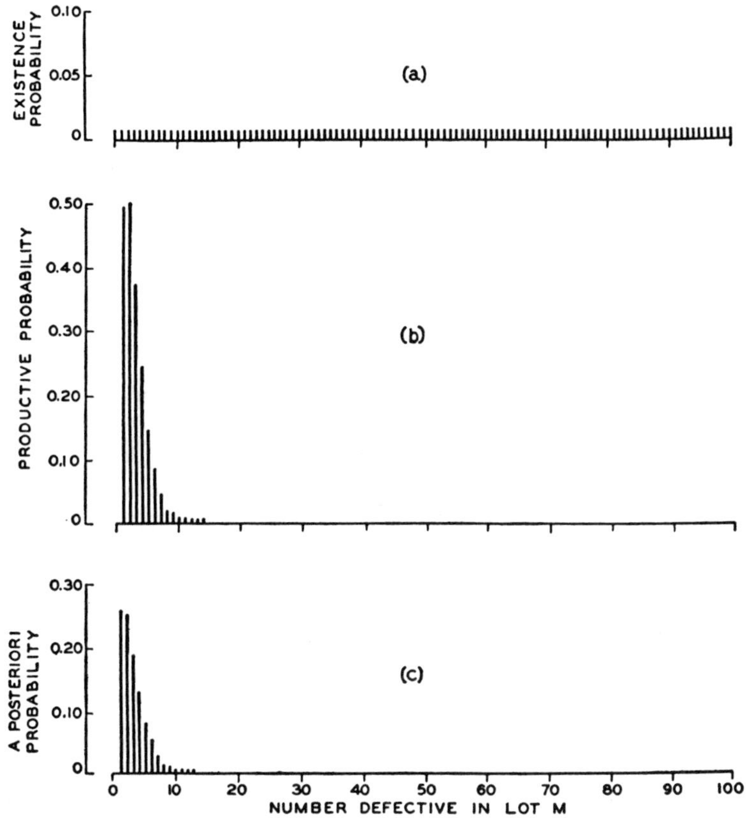

FIG. 122.—RELATION BETWEEN PROBABILITIES.

The *a posteriori* probability that the lot contains just i defective pieces is

$$\frac{\alpha_i\beta_i}{\sum_{i=0}^{N} \alpha_i\beta_i}.$$

These probabilities are shown in Column 4 of Table 51. Hence, for the given special case, the *a posteriori* probability P_1 that the lot contains more than the tolerance number (five) of defective pieces is found by summing the probabilities in Column 4 corresponding to $M = 6, 7, \ldots, 100$. Thus

$$P_1 = \frac{\sum_{i=6}^{100} \alpha_i \beta_i}{\sum_{i=0}^{100} \alpha_i \beta_i} = 0.0978.$$

Hence P_1 is the consumer's assurance that the lot is bad upon the basis of the given assumption and is represented graphically by the sum of the ordinates of Fig. 122-*c* from $M = 6$ to $M = 100$.

It is perhaps worthwhile to point out that, if the manufacturing process is controlled, the probability that a lot of N pieces contains the tolerance or more of defective pieces is known as soon as the equation (58) of control is known. The *a priori* consumer's risk, however, even under these conditions, has an additional protective feature in that even among the proportion of lots which contain the tolerance number of defective pieces the consumer will accept only a certain fraction P of them. Among those lots containing more than the tolerance number defective, less than the fraction P of them will be accepted.

If the quality is controlled in the sense that the probability of the production process producing a defective piece of apparatus is $\mathbf{p}$, it can be shown that the *a posteriori* method of determining the constitution of a lot of product tells us nothing other than would have been inferred *a priori*. In fact, if the condition just stated is satisfied, it can be shown that the *a posteriori* probability that the lot N contains say $c + X$ defective pieces, having found c defective pieces in a sample of n, is precisely

$$C_X^{N-n} \mathbf{q}^{N-n-X} \mathbf{p}^X.$$

This expression, however, is nothing more than the *a priori* probability that the balance $(N - n)$ of the lot contains just

X defective pieces and is known as soon as the condition of control is met.

It is of importance to note that, in order to be able to state the probability that a lot of N pieces of a product contains not more than X defectives *after* examining a sample of n in which c defective are found, we must assume something about the constitution of the lot *before* the sample of n was taken. Now, as we have seen, we approach the condition where we can say something about a lot of size N before the sample of size n is taken as we approach the condition of control.

Hence we see that even from the viewpoint of consumer protection, it is an advantage to have attained as nearly as possible the condition of control.

Part VII

Quality Control in Practice

A Summary of the Fundamental Principles Underlying the Theory of Control and an Outline of the Method of Attaining Control of Quality from Raw Material to Finished Product

CHAPTER XXII

Summary of Fundamental Principles

1. *Introductory Statement*

The subject of quality control as considered in the previous chapters is comparatively new. The theory is based upon certain statistical concepts—physical properties and physical laws are both assumed to be statistical in nature.[1] With the introduction of statistical theories and statistical laws comes a need for a new concept of causation.[2] Our understanding of the theory of quality control requires that our fundamental concepts of such things as physical properties, physical laws, and causal explanations undergo certain changes, since industrial development rests upon the application of the laws relating the physical properties of materials.

The object of industrial research is to establish ways and means of making better and better use of past experience. Insofar as research continues to reveal certain rules or laws which exist in the production of the finished product whose quality characteristics satisfy some human need, we may expect industry to be interested in research. That industries do have

[1] This development is in accord with modern physics in that statistical theory is basic to a causal explanation of atomic phenomena. For example, Louis De Broglie, recipient of the Nobel Prize for Physics in 1929, says "Consequently there are no longer any rigorous laws but only laws of probability."—*Wave Mechanics*, page 9, Metheun & Co., Ltd., 1930.

[2] This is true also in the field of pure physics. See for example Arthur Haas, *Wave Mechanics and the New Quantum Theory*, published by Constable & Co., London, 1928, He says, "In contrast to the sharply defined causality which is evident in macroscopic physics, the latest theories have emphasized the indeterminate nature of atomic processes; they assume that the only determinate magnitudes are the statistical magnitudes which result from the elementary processes of physics."

such an interest in this form of human endeavor seems to be a well-established fact. It is estimated that during the year 1927 upwards of $200,000,000 was spent in industrial research in approximately 1,000 laboratories in the United States.[1] This gives the order of magnitude of the sum of money that is being spent annually in the effort to find out how to do something tomorrow that we do not know how to do today. All effort, however, in this direction is obviously not included in formal research programs. Who, for example, in some way or other has not made use of past experience?

It is rather startling to see how much progress was made by that part of the human race which *never* had any knowledge of applied science as such. Long before any one worried over the physical principles which govern the use of the lever and of the wedge, use had been made of both of these mechanical devices. Long before any one had arrived at the generalization known as the Law of the Conservation of Energy, our forefathers had transformed mechanical energy into heat energy to start their fires. These two illustrations are sufficient to indicate that progress in the use of past experience does not depend upon the knowledge of scientific laws as we know them today. The *rate* of progress on the other hand does depend upon this knowledge. In a similar way, we do not have to know the theory of control to make progress in the improvement of quality of product. But, as the physical sciences have led to useful generalizations which increase the rate of progress, so also does the knowledge of the principles of control.

To indicate the relationship which the theory of control bears to exact science, it is interesting to consider six stages in the development of better ways and means of making use of past experience. They are:

1. Belief that the future cannot be predicted in terms of the past.

2. Belief that the future is pre-ordained.

[1] Grondahl, L. O., "The Rôle of Physics in Modern Industry," *Science*, August 23, 1929, pp. 175–183.

3. Inefficient use of past experience in the sense that experiences are not systematized into laws.
4. Control within limits.
5. Maximum control.
6. Knowledge of all laws of nature—exact science.

It is conceivable that some time man will have a knowledge of all the laws of nature so that he can predict the future quality of product with absolute certainty. This might be considered a goal for applied science, but indications today are that it is not a practical one. At least we are a long way from such a goal; for years to come the engineer must be content with the knowledge of only comparatively few of the many conceivable laws of nature where we think of the term law in the sense of Newton's Laws of Motion. Furthermore, the engineer is fully aware of the fact that, whereas it is conceivably possible with the knowledge of these laws to predict the future quality of product with absolute certainty, it is not in general feasible to do so any more than it is feasible to write down the equations of motion (were it possible to do so) for a thimble full of molecules of air under normal conditions. The engineer is fully aware that, whereas in the laboratory one may often be able to hold conditions sufficiently constant that the action of a single law may be observed with high precision, this same degree of constancy cannot in general be maintained under what appear today to be necessary conditions of commercial production. In fact, if we are to believe, as do many of the leaders of scientific thought today, that possibly the only kind of objective constancy in this world is of a statistical nature, then it follows that the complete realization of the sixth stage is not merely a long way off but impossible.[1]

We have seen that the principle of control plays an important rôle in laboratory research in what is ordinarily termed pure science. We have seen that it is necessary, in general, in all such work to attain as nearly as possible to certainty in the

[1] Bridgman, P. W., loc. cit.

assurance that the observations supposed to have been taken under the same essential conditions have actually been taken in this way. As an efficient tool in testing whether or not this condition has been satisfied, we have the criteria of Part VI. We have seen that the criteria for maximum control (Part III) give a test which indicates the limit to which it is reasonable that research may go in revealing causes of variability in a set of observations presumably taken under a constant system of chance causes. We have also seen that many of the quantities with which we actually deal in the so-called exact sciences are but averages of statistical distributions assumed to be given by what we have chosen to term a constant system of chance causes.

Let us now consider the need for control as an integral part of any industrial program. In most cases we can distinguish five more or less distinct steps in such a program. They are:

1. A study of the results of research to provide principles and numerical data upon which to base a design.

2. The application of such information in the construction of an ideal piece of apparatus designed to satisfy some human want, where no attention is given to the cost.

3. Production of tool-made samples under supposedly commercial conditions.

4. Test of tool-made samples and specification of quality requirements that can presumably be met under commercial conditions.

5. Development of production methods.

From this viewpoint the results of design, development, and production are grounded on the initial results of research. What is more important in our present study is the fact that often causes of variability enter in the last four steps which by the very nature of the problem are not experienced in the research laboratory. For example, we have the possibility of assignable causes entering through different sources of material, the human element, and variable conditions which affect the production process.

One possible method of obtaining satisfactory quality under such conditions is to make wherever possible 100 per cent inspection of the product at the time it is ready for delivery. In many cases, however, this cannot be done because of the destructive nature of the tests; in any case the cost of inspection must be considered. Furthermore, if indications of the presence of assignable causes of variability are discovered in the quality of final product, it is not easy to locate the causes because the data of final tests may have been taken long after the causes have ceased to function. Even more important, as we have seen in previous chapters, is the fact that the quality may appear controlled in the end and yet there may be assignable causes of variability at one or more steps in production. For these reasons, it seems highly desirable that the measurements made in *each* of the last four of the steps mentioned above be tested to determine whether or not there is any indication of lack of control. If there is, it may be necessary that a further study be made in the laboratory to assist in finding the assignable causes of variability.

We must emphasize the importance of control in setting standards for the raw materials that enter into the production process. Most physical properties are subject to the influence of presumably large numbers of chance causes. Therefore, if we are to make efficient use of data representing these properties, the data must have been taken under controlled conditions. Before we can use experimental results with any assurance of their giving a controlled product, it is highly desirable that we make use of tests to determine whether or not the data have been secured under controlled conditions.

Furthermore, in the development of processes of production, it should be of advantage to apply tests to detect lack of control and then to weed out the assignable causes of variability as they occur, with the assurance of the kind already indicated in previous chapters, that after this process of weeding out has once led to a product which appears to be controlled, future product will remain in the same state unless obvious assignable causes of variability enter.

Thus the theory of control plays an important part in the various stages of applied science. It is desirable that the departments of design, development, and production keep the laboratory research department informed as to evidence of the existence of assignable causes wherever they arise up to the time that product goes to the consumer.

The theory is also of value in the study of the life history of product. Obviously, when equipment goes into the field it meets many and varied conditions, the influence of which on the quality of product is not in general known. Such an example would be the varied conditions under which telephone poles are placed throughout the United States. *A priori*, it is reasonable to believe that the life of the pole depends in a large way upon the service conditions. Among the exceedingly large number of variables which may influence the life of the pole, little information is available to indicate the importance of any one. The value of laboratory research in improving the quality of a pole through life must take into account ways and means of preservation suited to each of the various conditions. Naturally, therefore, it is of interest to know when the variability in the quality of the material at any stage in life is such as to indicate the existence of an assignable cause so that further research may be instituted to find ways and means of effectively removing this cause. Field engineers, therefore, find need for analytical methods of detecting evidence of lack of control in the quality of product at any time as revealed by life data so that they can call this fact to the attention of the laboratory staff.

In this chapter we shall discuss briefly such fundamental concepts as physical property, physical law, and cause, basic to every step in control.

2. *Object of Control*

As already stated, the object of control is to enable us *to do what we want to do within economic limits.*

As we have seen in Part I, it is necessary to postulate that when we have done everything that we can do to eliminate variability in a quality X, we arrive at a state of statistical control in which we can say that the probability dy of an observed value X falling within the range X to $X + dX$ is given by the equation of control

$$dy = \mathbf{f}(X, \boldsymbol{\lambda}_1, \boldsymbol{\lambda}_2, \ldots, \boldsymbol{\lambda}_i, \ldots, \boldsymbol{\lambda}_{m'})dX. \qquad (58)$$

3. *Physical Properties*

In the previous chapters we have seen that perhaps the closest that a physical quality attains to constancy is in the sense that objectively it may be represented by a distribution function (58) characterizing a state of control. It follows that the complete specification of any quality requires the establishment of an equation of control of the form (58) both in respect to functional form $\mathbf{f}$ and the values of the m' parameters contained therein. It has been shown in Part V that for most practical purposes it is sufficient to attempt to specify simply two characteristics of this distribution, namely, the average or expected value $\bar{\mathbf{X}}$ and the standard deviation $\boldsymbol{\sigma}$.

Examples: To emphasize the statistical nature of materials still often treated as constants, let us look through a microscope at a cross section of a piece of ordinary steel,[1] Fig. 123. What we see is anything but a homogeneous isotropic body. Why this heterogeneous structure? The answer is—It is produced by chance or unknown causes.

What is the effect of such irregularities upon the physical properties of steel when produced in some useful form as, for example, supporting strand, a piece of which is shown in Fig. 124? The answer is that a physical property, say the breaking load of such strand will, if we are able to eliminate assignable causes of variation, be some distribution function as indicated in Fig. 125. The smooth curve in this figure

[1] Lucas, F. F., "Structure and Nature of Troostite," *Bell System Technical Journal*, January, 1930.

represents the objective distribution of control (58) for this particular case, as inferred from the study of observed data.

Fig. 123.—Microscopic Cross Section of Steel.

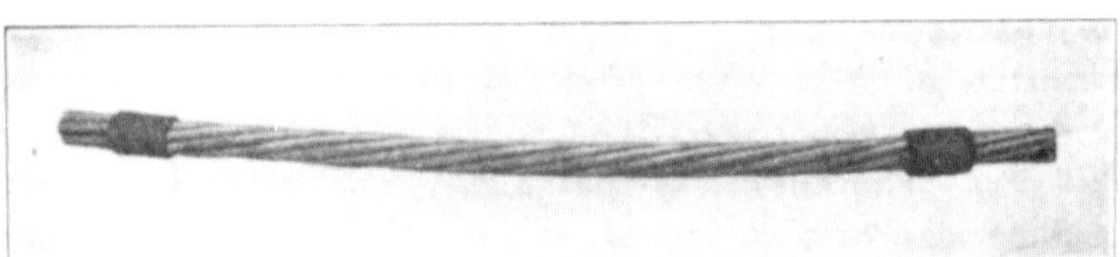

Fig. 124.—Piece of Supporting Strand.

As we have said above, it is usually sufficient to specify merely the average $\overline{X}$ and standard deviation σ of such a distribution.

Now let us look at a cross section of another important structural material,—wood, Fig. 126. This time we do not need a microscope to see the effects of chance causes upon the structure of the material.

Fig. 88 in Part V shows roughly what such irregularities do to the modulus of rupture of four kinds of telephone poles.

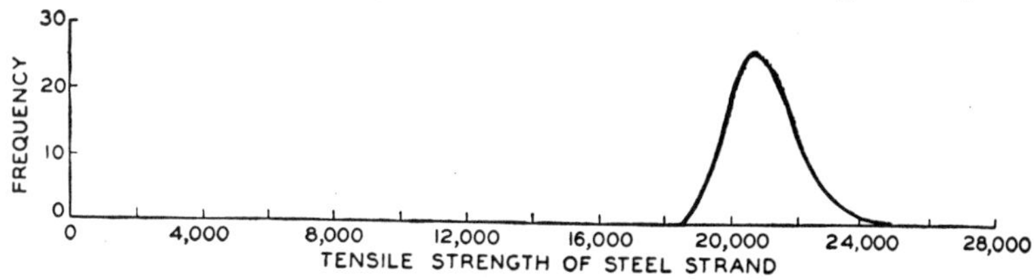

Fig. 125.—Tensile Strength Distribution for Strand Shown in Fig. 124.

Note the wide spreads of these distributions as compared with their means.

These two illustrations are sufficient to show that the variation introduced by constant systems of chance causes into

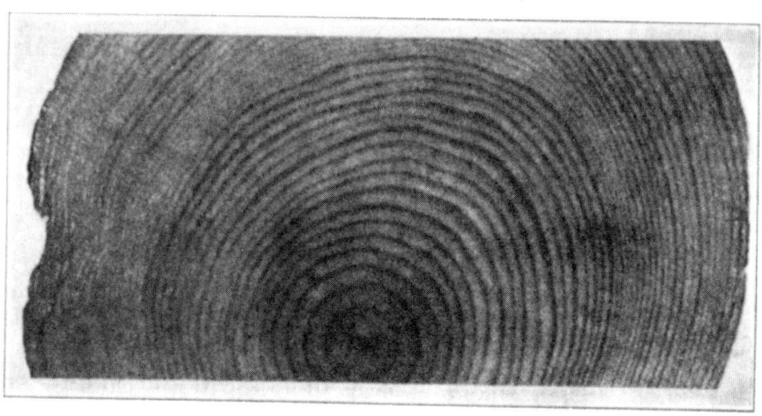

Fig. 126.—Cross Section of Pole.

the physical properties of materials are so large that they need to be taken into account in the use of these materials.

Shortly we shall see what methods are available in the literature for establishing objective distributions for standards of physical properties.

4. *Physical Laws*

In Part III we discussed briefly three different kinds of laws, viz., exact, statistical, and empirical. In this section we shall contrast the first two kinds in the hope that by so doing we may take over the part of the concept of exact law that is common with that of statistical law, and that we may see clearly wherein the concepts of the two laws differ, insofar as this bears upon the theory of quality control.

Let us consider first the harmonic oscillation of a vibrating system characterized by the equation

$$m\frac{d^2X}{dt^2} + k\frac{dX}{dt} + sX = 0$$

where X is a linear displacement, t is the time, m is the mass, k is the frictional force proportional to velocity and sX is the restoring force. The solution of this differential equation

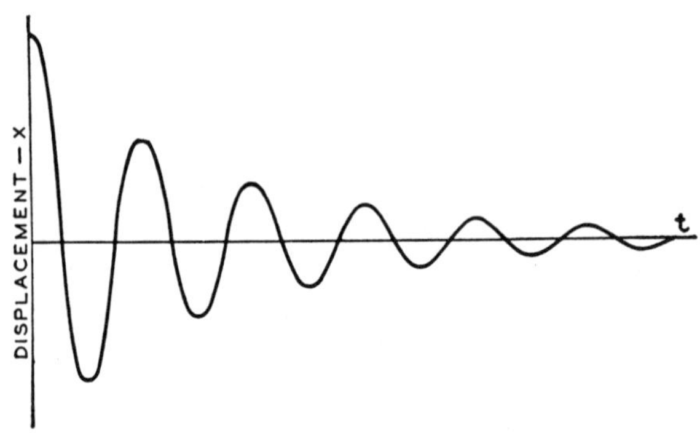

FIG. 127-*a*.—BASIS FOR EXACT PREDICTION.

gives us the displacement X as a function of the time t. In other words, starting with a knowledge of m, k, s, and X at $t = 0$, we can predict with great precision the displacement at any future time t. Fig. 127-*a* typifies such a prediction.

Let us now consider what is involved in prediction in a statistical sense. Let us contrast with this simple problem that of predicting the number of times that a head will be turned up in n throws of a penny. As was pointed out in

Part III, the practical method of making prediction in this case is to assume that there is some point binomial

$$(\mathbf{q} + \mathbf{p})^n$$

where $\mathbf{q} + \mathbf{p} = 1$ such that the successive terms of this expansion represent the probabilities of occurrence of 0, 1, 2, 3, . . . n heads in n throws. It follows that the standard deviation

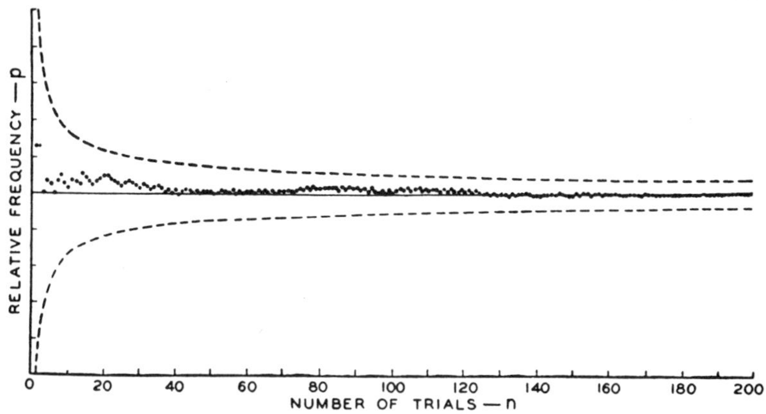

FIG. 127-*b*.—BASIC INFORMATION FOR STATISTICAL PREDICTION.

σ_p of the relative frequency p of heads in n trials is given by the relationship

$$\sigma_p = \sqrt{\frac{\mathbf{pq}}{n}}.$$

If $\mathbf{p} = \frac{1}{2}$ it follows from what has already been said that approximately all of the observed values of p in future trials should lie within the dotted limits,

$$\mathbf{p} \pm 3\sqrt{\frac{\mathbf{pq}}{n}},$$

shown in Fig. 127-*b*. The dots in this figure indicate the experimental results of throwing a penny two hundred times.

Now let us compare the results in these two cases. Prediction in the first case involves the assumption that the dynamical system behaves in a way such that when we substitute measurable values of m, k, and s in the differential equation the solution of this equation gives a satisfactory prediction of the future displacement of the mass. In an analogous way, as indicated in previous chapters, it appears that we may expect to find (in the objective sense) a value of **p** for a given penny such that when used as indicated above, we may establish limits such as those given in Fig. 127-*b*.

The two methods of prediction are alike in that they require the experimental establishment of certain parameters. They differ in that one makes use of these parameters in a differential equation, the other in a binomial expansion. They are alike in that we do not know *a priori* that the mathematics used in either case is the mathematics that should be used.

Now suppose that we were to try to make N dynamical systems to have as nearly as possible the same values for m, k, and s. In the same way let us suppose that we take N pennies that appear to be alike so far as we can determine. If we were to start oscillation in each of the N dynamical systems with the same displacement and observe the resultant displacement, we would expect that each of the systems would follow the curve in Fig. 127-*a* quite accurately. Similarly, if we were to throw each of the N coins a large number of times, we would expect to get something like the three records shown below, Fig. 128, representing the results of two hundred throws of each of three different pennies.

The systems are alike in that the smooth curve in Fig. 127-*a* represents what we may expect to get on the average when we try to duplicate the dynamical systems as nearly as possible and the straight line $\mathbf{p} = \frac{1}{2}$ in Fig. 127-*b* represents the expected value for a symmetrical coin. In the statistical case, however, there is a certain *indeterminateness* as compared with the so-called exact case. Although we can say in the statistical case with considerable assurance that the observed values of p will lie within certain limits and that these limits will decrease proportionately to the square root of n, we cannot say anything determinate about the way the observed values will approach the value **p**.

In the dynamical case, if t is made indefinitely large, we

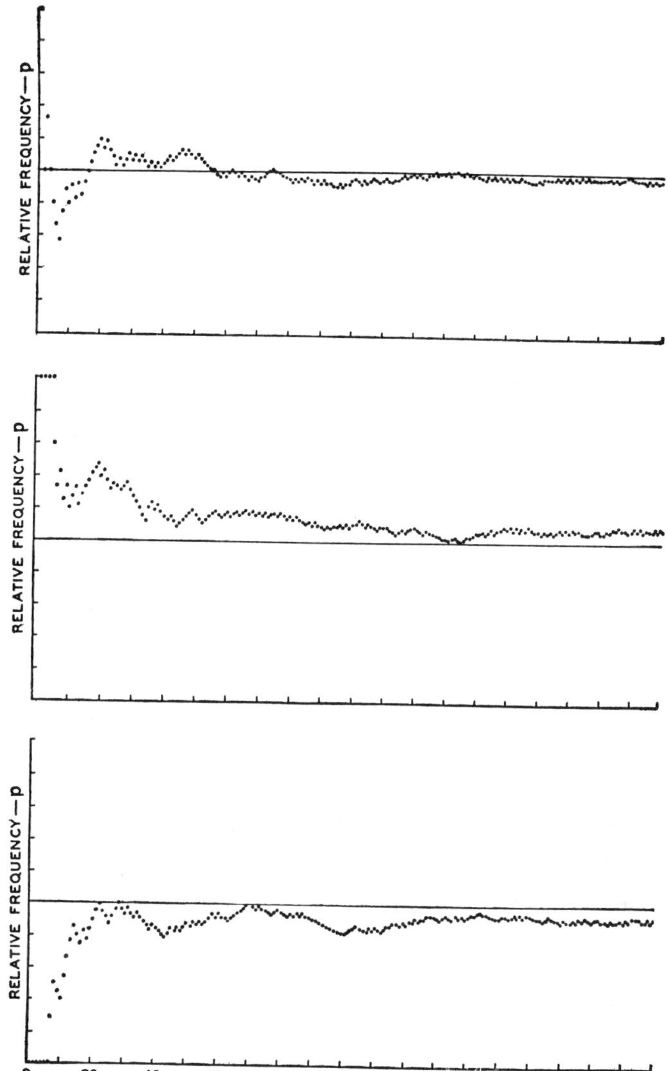

FIG. 128.—BASIC INFORMATION FOR STATISTICAL PREDICTION.

can say that the corresponding value of X will approach the value zero as a mathematical limit. On the other hand, we can say in the statistical case that for each of the N pennies, the observed fraction p in n throws will approach as a statistical limit the value **p**. In the first case we can say very definitely how the displacement will approach the value zero. In the second case we can say scarcely anything about the way the value p will approach **p**.

This fundamental limitation of indefiniteness, however, is not solely limited to the statistical case when we come to think of the determination of the parameters which must be found in either case. In Part III we pointed out that our success in being able to predict a phenomenon by means of statistical theory rests ultimately upon the assumption that we can find the parameters in certain functions through use of a statistical limit. In a similar way, the values of m, k, and s can only be obtained in practice through averaging observed values of these factors taken under presumably the same essential conditions. In other words the objective values of m, k, and s are in themselves statistical limits.

Strictly speaking, all that we can say in the exact case is that the probability of the displacement at a given time t lying within a given range is a certain constant value. Similarly, we can say in the case of throwing a coin under the same essential conditions that the probability of observing a given number of heads in a given number of throws is a constant. In other words in both instances what we really assume to be constant is a certain statistical distribution. In both cases there is the same kind of indeterminateness although it appears in a slightly different way.

5. *Causal Explanation*

We have made much use of the concept of a constant system of chance causes. It is essential that we consider a little more carefully the significant difference between causal explanation as it is usually accepted and causal explanation in the statistical sense.

It is customary to think of a cause as being an antecedent event which is always followed by one or more definite events or consequents. The antecedent event in such a case is the cause and the consequents are the effects of the cause. For example, the presence of a tubercle bacillus in the lungs of a human individual may produce many different effects, such as a high temperature, change in composition of blood, loss of appetite, and so on. Some of these effects, however, may be produced by other causes. The situation in such a case is indicated schematically in Fig. 129, in which *A* and *B* are ante-

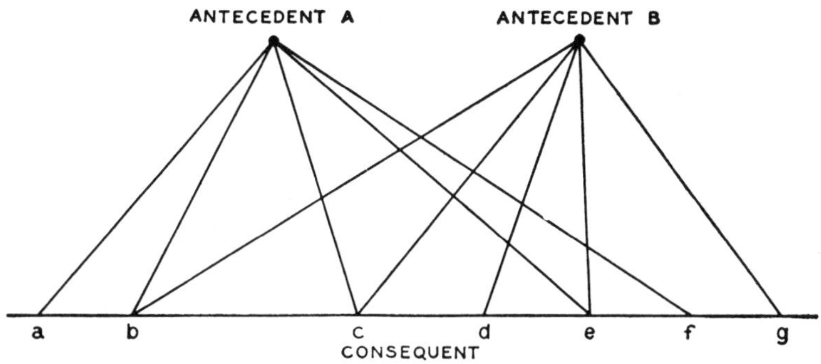

FIG. 129.—SCHEMATIC OF CAUSAL RELATIONSHIP.

cedents with corresponding consequents indicated by small letters.

If we can state in a given case all of the consequents belonging to a given antecedent event, it is generally agreed that we may go with certainty from effect to cause. Of course in the practical case we meet with the serious difficulty of not being able to state all of the consequents corresponding to a given antecedent. This point, however, we do not care to consider at present.

The point that we do wish to make is this. Causal explanation in this accepted sense assumes that whenever we have an antecedent *A* such as indicated above, it is always followed by effects (consequents) *a*, *b*, *c*, *e*, and *f*. With this picture of cause let us now contrast the concept of chance cause already illustrated in some detail in Part III and Appendix I. Immediately we note a characteristic difference between the concept of a chance cause and the older concept of cause. For example, in our discussion of Appendix I we treat of very simple systems composed of m different causes. It is assumed that each cause may be followed by one or the other of two events, that is one or the other of two different values of X. In other words, it appears that we can never hope to tie up a chance cause with a given event because for each chance cause more than one event is always possible.

Let us go a little further in the amplification of this point. Let us suppose that we have n observed values

$$X_1, X_2, \ldots, X_i, \ldots, X_n$$

of some variable quality X taken under controlled conditions represented by the equation of control (58). We may think of the cause of this sample as being the particular equation of control representing the conditions under which the samples were drawn. It is apparent, however, that in general any series of n observed values such as indicated above may have come from any one of let us say N different universes which we may characterize as follows:

$$\left.\begin{aligned}
dy_1 &= \mathbf{f}_1\,(X, \boldsymbol{\lambda}_{11}, \boldsymbol{\lambda}_{12}, \ldots, \boldsymbol{\lambda}_{1i}, \ldots, \boldsymbol{\lambda}_{1m'_1})\; dX, \\
dy_2 &= \mathbf{f}_2\,(X, \boldsymbol{\lambda}_{21}, \boldsymbol{\lambda}_{22}, \ldots, \boldsymbol{\lambda}_{2i}, \ldots, \boldsymbol{\lambda}_{2m'_2})\; dX, \\
&\ldots\ldots\ldots\ldots\ldots\ldots\ldots\ldots, \\
dy_j &= \mathbf{f}_j\,(X, \boldsymbol{\lambda}_{j1}, \boldsymbol{\lambda}_{j2}, \ldots, \boldsymbol{\lambda}_{ji}, \ldots, \boldsymbol{\lambda}_{jm'_j})\; dX, \\
&\ldots\ldots\ldots\ldots\ldots\ldots\ldots\ldots, \\
dy_N &= \mathbf{f}_N(X, \boldsymbol{\lambda}_{N1}, \boldsymbol{\lambda}_{N2}, \ldots, \boldsymbol{\lambda}_{Ni}, \ldots, \boldsymbol{\lambda}_{Nm'_N})\, dX.
\end{aligned}\right\} \qquad (93)$$

Under the above condition we may never state with certainty what one of the N universes the observed sample came from. Each of the N universes is a possible cause but our interpretation of a sample must always be *indefinite* in that under the above conditions we can never be certain as to the origin of that sample. Cause in the older scientific sense, therefore, has a certain determinateness about it which must of necessity be absent in the statistical case.

The two kinds of cause, however, do have this much in common that is very important from the viewpoint of the theory of control—the choice of a cause in a given case largely depends upon the intuitive faculty of the human mind. In other words, we cannot in general write down rules for the correct selection of a cause. It is, however, one of the objects of logic to lay down ways and means of testing postulated causal explanations.

An interesting illustration may be drawn from the field of investigation as to the origin of the planets. Two fundamental rival hypotheses are described in a popular way in a comparatively recent article by F. R. Moulton.[1] The first of these he describes as follows:

> Laplace started with a heated gaseous mass rotating as a solid. With loss of heat by radiation, it contracted and rotated more rapidly. At various stages of the contraction the centrifugal acceleration at the equator of the rotating mass equaled the gravitational acceleration toward its center. At these places the contracting mass left behind gaseous rings which were concentrated into planets by the mutual gravitation of their parts. In six cases, after the contracting rings had assumed approximately spherical forms they similarly contracted and left behind smaller rings, which became satellites. This theory is delightfully simple and can be stated in a few sentences. It makes few demands upon the imagination to conceive of its various steps and it requires no sustained mental effort to organize them into a unified whole. It raises no unanswered questions and arouses no doubts. The account of the creation and the origin of the earth in Genesis is not simpler.

He then summarizes the second in the following words:

> In striking contrast with the foregoing, consider the planetesimal hypothesis. The fundamental point of view adopted in it is that the stars of our galaxy constitute a group of mutually related objects, the evolution of each depending in part upon its relationships to the others. They mix and mingle with one another, in the course of time, somewhat like molecules in a gas. At the time of the dynamic

[1] The Planetesimal Hypothesis—*Science*, December 7, 1928, Volume LXVIII, Number 1771, pp. 549–559.

adventure of a suitable near approach of one star to another, planets are born from the parent suns. These planets grow up around nuclei by the accretion of countless little planets (planetesimals) born at the same time. Not only in the broad sweep of events leading to the birth of the planets as independent objects does this theory differ completely from the Laplacian, but also all the dynamical considerations involved in the growth and evolution of the planets are wholly different. More than one commentator on the planetesimal hypothesis has regarded with favor the origin of the planets by dynamic approach as being likely, and has then utterly failed to realize that the growth and evolution of the planets could not have been along the lines that are consonant with the Laplacian theory. The new hypothesis gives an entirely new earth and lays down a new basis for the development of dynamic geology.

In other words, these two hypotheses may be thought of as A and B in Fig. 129. The effects in this case to be explained are the characteristics of the solar family.

Now let us see how the process of checking an hypothesis or cause in the older sense corresponds with that of checking an hypothesis or cause in the statistical sense. The essential difference is this. In the first case we may be able to find that some of the observable phenomena cannot be effects of the postulated cause. In such a case it is customary to reject or modify the hypothesis. For example, this is true in respect to the Laplacian hypothesis as to the origin of the earth referred to above. In the statistical case, however, it is not so easy to reject an hypothesis, as we shall now see.

Suppose, for example, that we attempt to test the hypothesis that a sample of n observed values of a quantity X came from let us say the first universe of (93). We have already touched upon this problem in Part VI in the discussion of the choice of statistic to be used in a given case and of the choice of method of using this statistic. Let us look at this problem in a more general way. We may represent a sample of size n as a point in n dimensional space. In a similar way we may represent all of the possible different samples of size n that may be drawn from an assumed universe as points in this same space. To get a test of whether or not the observed sample came from the assumed universe, it appears to be necessary to establish certain contours in this n dimensional space within which the points corresponding to an observed sample must fall if we are to accept the hypothesis that it came from the assumed universe. Naturally there are an indefinite number of ways of setting up such contours and the choice of any one is quite arbitrary on the part of the individual scientist as was the corresponding choice of statistic in Part VI.

In any given case there are in general an indefinitely large number of possible hypotheses. Hence, in addition to the problem of establishing arbitrary contours upon which to test a given hypothesis, we must consider the problem of judging between alternative hypotheses. Here again we come upon the indeterminateness of the statistical method. It appears that there is no ultimate ground upon which to base our final choice.[1]

6. *Measurement of Average* $\bar{\mathbf{X}}$ *and Standard Deviation* σ

The concept of physical properties and phenomena as frequency distributions introduces the concept of measurement of such distributions. Since for most engineering purposes it is sufficient to know the average $\bar{\mathbf{X}}$ and standard deviation σ of such a distribution, we shall consider the problem of measuring these two characteristics.

Assuming that the set of n observed values,

$$X_1, X_2, \ldots, X_i, \ldots, X_n,$$

of a quality characteristic X satisfy the equation (58) of control, it follows from the law of large numbers that the observed average $\bar{X}$ and standard deviation σ can be made to approach, in the statistical sense, as close as we please to $\bar{\mathbf{X}}$ and σ respectively by making the sample size n sufficiently large. In

[1] See in this connection the especially interesting and valuable article by J. Neyman and E. S. Pearson entitled "On the Use and Interpretation of Certain Test Criteria for Purposes of Statistical Inference," Part I, *Biometrika*, Volume XX-A, July, 1928, pp. 175-240, Part VII, *Biometrika*, Volume XX-A, pp. 263-294, December, 1928.

Also see pp. 303-314 of A. N. Whitehead's *Process and Reality*, Macmillan Company, 1929.

other words, it follows from the law of large numbers and Tchebycheff's theorem that, by making n sufficiently large, we can bring as close to unity as we please the objective probability **P** that the inequality

$$|\bar{X} - \bar{\mathbf{X}}| \leq \varepsilon$$

will be satisfied, ε being any previously assigned positive quantity.

In practice, however, it is not feasible to take an indefinitely large number of observations. In fact, we must often be satisfied with estimates of $\bar{\mathbf{X}}$ and σ derived from comparatively small samples. For example, we may wish to determine an approximate standard for a quality X of a given kind of apparatus from measurements of this quality on from five to twenty-five tool-made samples. Or again, we may wish to adopt a standard for the physical property of some new material or alloy from measurements made on comparatively few pieces. We shall now consider various ways of doing this.

A. *A Posteriori Probability Method.*—This method has been discussed in a very interesting and novel manner by Molina and Wilkinson.[1] Assuming that the set of n observed values of the variable X have come from a normal universe

$$f(X) = \frac{1}{\sigma\sqrt{2\pi}} e^{-\frac{(X-\bar{\mathbf{X}})^2}{2\sigma^2}},$$

in which $\bar{\mathbf{X}}$ and σ are unknown, the *a posteriori* probability $P(\bar{\mathbf{X}})d\bar{\mathbf{X}}$ that the true mean lies within the interval $\bar{\mathbf{X}}$ to $\bar{\mathbf{X}} + d\bar{\mathbf{X}}$ is given by

$$P(\bar{\mathbf{X}})d\bar{\mathbf{X}} = Ad\bar{\mathbf{X}} \int_0^{\infty} \frac{W(\bar{\mathbf{X}}, \sigma) e^{-\frac{\sum_{i=1}^{n}(X_i - \bar{\mathbf{X}})^2}{2\sigma^2}}}{\sigma^n} d\sigma, \qquad (94)$$

where A is a constant and $W(\bar{\mathbf{X}}, \sigma)d\bar{\mathbf{X}}d\sigma$ is the *a priori* probability, before the observations were made, that the true mean and standard deviation were within the intervals $\bar{\mathbf{X}}$ to $\bar{\mathbf{X}} + d\bar{\mathbf{X}}$ and σ to $\sigma + d\sigma$ respectively.

[1] "The Frequency Distribution of the Unknown Mean of a Sampled Universe," *Bell System Technical Journal*, Vol. VIII, October, 1929, pp. 632–645.

To get a definite answer in a given case, certain assumptions must be made in order to give the parameters in (94) specific values in terms of the statistics of the set of n observed values of the quality X, and in every case one must assume some particular form for the function $W(\bar{\mathbf{X}}, \sigma)$. In other words, before any measurements are made, one must choose some one function $W(\bar{\mathbf{X}},\sigma)$ out of the indefinitely large number of possible functions.

Assuming that $\bar{\mathbf{X}}$ and σ are independent, we may write

$$W(\bar{\mathbf{X}}, \sigma) = W_1(\bar{\mathbf{X}})W_2(\sigma).$$

Making these various general assumptions and certain others of a more detailed nature, the authors then assign to the parameters in the functions W_1 and W_2 twenty-one sets of values out of a possible infinite number of such sets, and find as many probable and 99.73 per cent errors for a single example. Their results are shown graphically in Fig. 130.[1] The startling and very important thing to note is the great significance that must be attached to the choice of the *a priori* existence probability functions $W_1(\bar{\mathbf{X}})$ and $W_2(\sigma)$ *before* any measurements are taken.

Of course, any one of the twenty-one or, in fact, of the indefinitely large number of probability distributions $P(\bar{\mathbf{X}})d\bar{\mathbf{X}}$ of (94) gives us only the *a posteriori* probability that the true mean lies within a specified range, whereas we wish to get usable estimates of $\bar{\mathbf{X}}$ and σ. Hence, even though one goes through the *a posteriori* solution under the conditions stated above, it is likely that he will take the observed average $\bar{X}$ as his best estimate of $\bar{\mathbf{X}}$. As for an estimate of σ, it will be expressible as a multiple of the observed standard deviation, let us say $c\sigma$, the value of c depending upon the particular assumptions made in applying (94).

B. *Maximum Likelihood Method.*—In the particular case just considered the probability P of the simultaneous occurrence of the set of observed values $X_1, X_2, \ldots, X_i, \ldots, X_n$ within

[1] The authors used the precision constant h instead of σ in this paper. However, they have also shown the distribution of σ (the dotted lines) for the first seven sets of assumptions.

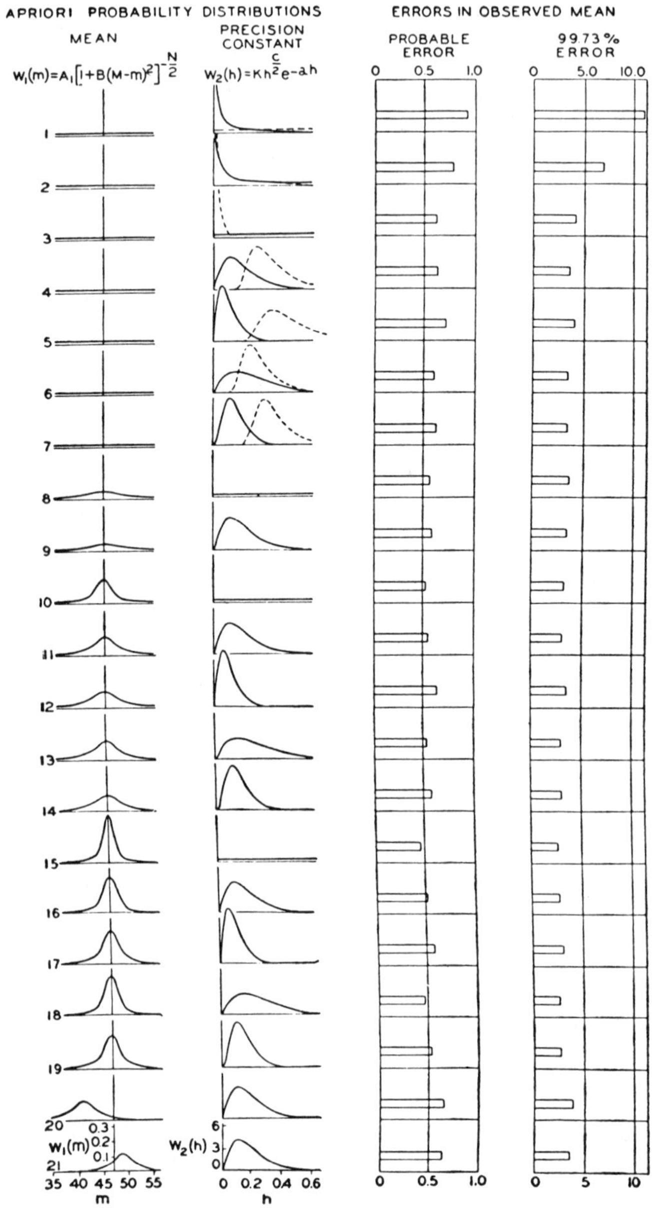

FIG. 130.—SIGNIFICANCE OF *a priori* EXISTENCE PROBABILITY FUNCTIONS.

the respective intervals X_1 to $X_1 + dX_1$, X_2 to $X_2 + dX_2, \ldots,$ X_i to $X_i + dX_i, \ldots, X_n$ to $X_n + dX_n$ is

$$P = \prod_{i=1}^{n} \frac{1}{s\sqrt{2\pi}} e^{-\frac{(X_i - m)^2}{2\sigma^2}} dX_i,$$

where m and s are universe parameters. That value of m which will make P a maximum is given by the solution of the equation

$$\frac{\partial(\log P)}{\partial m} = 0,$$

since P is a maximum when $\log P$ is a maximum. This gives the observed average $\bar{X}$ as an estimate of $\bar{\mathbf{X}}$.

Similarly the condition

$$\frac{\partial(\log P)}{\partial s} = 0$$

gives the observed standard deviation σ as the estimate of $\boldsymbol{\sigma}$.

Since the expected value $\bar{\sigma}$ of the observed standard deviation in samples of size n drawn from a normal universe is less than the standard deviation $\boldsymbol{\sigma}$ of the universe, it is obvious that the estimates of $\boldsymbol{\sigma}$ derived by the likelihood method are too small in the long run, particularly if the sample size n is small.

C. *Empirical Method.*—Assuming, as before, that we are sampling from a normal universe free from assignable causes, there is perhaps no better estimate of $\bar{\mathbf{X}}$ than the average $\bar{X}$ of the sample. If, however, there is any reason to believe that a few of the observed values were influenced by assignable causes, this fact should be taken into consideration.

If we assume that we are sampling from other than a symmetrical universe, it becomes all the more important that we make use of the average $\bar{X}$ of the sample of size n as an estimate of the average $\bar{\mathbf{X}}$ of the universe of possible effects.

Coming to the estimate of the standard deviation $\boldsymbol{\sigma}$ of the normal universe, we have seen that *a posteriori* probability theory does not provide a direct method of establishing a specific value as the best estimate and that the likelihood method leads to an estimate which is too small in the long run. Referring to Fig. 97 indicating the important characteristics of the distribution of an observed statistic Θ, say standard deviation, we might be led to base our estimate of σ on the assumption that the observed σ is the modal σ of the distribution of this statistic. In other words, we might take as an estimate

$$\sqrt{\frac{n}{n-2}}\,\sigma = \frac{\sigma}{c_1},$$

where c_1 is given in column 2 of Table 29. To do so, however, means that in the long run estimates made in this way are too large. An estimate that will be consistent in the long run is $\frac{\sigma}{c_2}$ where c_2 is also given in Table 29.

There is thus some justification under these conditions for adopting $\frac{\sigma}{c_2}$ as an estimate of σ. In any case the observed standard deviation σ becomes the basis of an estimate. Hence it seems reasonable that it should be tabulated together with any correction thereof adopted as an estimate in a given case.

The estimate of σ of a non-normal universe presents additional difficulties since, in general, we do not know the distribution function of observed standard deviations in samples of n. Here again the observed standard deviations in the long run are too small, in the sense that the expected value in samples of size n from a given universe is less than the standard deviation σ of that universe.

7. *Measurement of Average* $\overline{X}$ *and Standard Deviation* σ—*Practical Example*

Let us consider the significance of previous results in a simple practical case. Four pieces of shoulder leather from a given source were found to have the following tensile strengths expressed in pounds per square inch:

5,290	2,950
4,850	5,960

Upon the basis of this information, what shall we choose as estimates of the average $\bar{\mathbf{X}}$ and standard deviation $\boldsymbol{\sigma}$ of the tensile strength of leather from this source assuming that this quality is controlled.

From what has been said in the previous section it is apparent that the answer to this question depends upon many factors. It depends upon more or less arbitrary assumptions as do the answers to many practical questions. In each case, however, it is likely that the average $\bar{X} = 4{,}762.5$ and the observed standard deviation $\sigma = 1{,}118.6$ will be made the basis of the estimate. Furthermore, it is obvious that the interpretation of these depends upon the size n of the sample, in this case four. For these reasons it appears that in the tabulation of results of this character the experimentalist should always record the observed average $\bar{X}$, standard deviation σ, and sample size n.

In general it is perhaps reasonable to believe that the experimentalist who is in charge of taking the data is in the best position to make a reasonable assumption upon which to base an estimate. For this reason it is desirable that he record what he considers to be the best values to take as estimates of the average $\bar{\mathbf{X}}$ and the standard deviation $\boldsymbol{\sigma}$ of quality X assumed to be controlled. It is likely in this case that the average $\bar{X}$ will be taken as the estimate of $\bar{\mathbf{X}}$. In the same way it is likely that $\boldsymbol{\sigma}$ will be taken as a quantity larger than σ. As we have said in the previous section, the estimate $\frac{\sigma}{c_2}$ is a consistent estimate in that in the long run the average of an indefinitely large number of such estimates would give the true value $\boldsymbol{\sigma}$ assuming that the universe of control is normal.

Anyone who wishes to make use of these results may use the observed average and standard deviation and the sample size as a basis for his own estimates of $\bar{\mathbf{X}}$ and $\boldsymbol{\sigma}$, or he may choose to use those selected by the experimentalist himself. In this way he is free to make his own postulates basic to estimating $\bar{\mathbf{X}}$ and $\boldsymbol{\sigma}$.

CHAPTER XXIII

Sampling—Measurement

1. *Place of Measurement in Control*

In any program of control we must start with observed data; yet data may be either good, bad, or indifferent. Of what value is the theory of control if the observed data going into that theory are bad? This is the question raised again and again by the practical man.

Even though it is necessary, as a starting point in the theory of control, to tabulate the results of n measurements of some physical quality X in terms of the average $\bar{X}$ and the standard deviation σ, the engineer often reacts in something like the following way. He will likely admit that this method is an excellent one to follow if, as he says, the data are known to be good, but he will often argue in a given case that the data are not good enough to make it worth while to record more than perhaps the average and the range. He may go so far as to throw out one or more of the observed values before taking even the average and the range. In fact I have heard industrial research men say that they can get more out of a set of data just by looking at it than anyone without their *experience* can get by the most refined analysis.

In discussing this point at a recent round-table conference [1] on presentation of data, one prominent engineer had this to say:

> Most frequently we are confronted with expressing results that have been obtained by empirical methods in the hands of fallible

[1] Conference held in New York, December 5, 1929, under the auspices of the American Society of Mechanical Engineers and the American Society for Testing Materials.

operators on more or less representative samples of generally very heterogeneous materials. When we go to discuss the precision of our methods, we always have three factors which have not been controlled. We have the question of the authenticity of the sample; we have the question of the operator; and we have the question of the method itself. Hence it becomes a very complicated problem to apply the mathematical methods of analysis to these data.

A number of years ago I read somewhere an expression which has always struck me. It said something about mathematics being a mill that grinds with exceeding fineness and yet a mill that is no better than the grain that is put in it. So it always seemed that in our work the first thing we had to do was to attempt to develop the limit of precision of our methods after we had at least something to start with; then we could determine the effect of the presence of the operator. From that point we could determine the authenticity of our samples and we would be in a better position to analyze our crop of results.

Not only in the fields of industrial research and engineering do we get such a reaction. We find it also in the field of so-called exact science—for example, physics. Thus in a recent paper by Millikan discussing the value of electronic charge,[1] emphasis is laid upon the importance of the human judgment of the experimentalist, as is typified by the following paragraph:

This value of the electron is also that at which Birge finally arrives as a result of his survey of the whole field of fundamental constants. It is true that he reanalyzes for himself my individual oil-drop readings and weights them so that he gets from them the value 4.768 ± 0.005 in place of my value 4.770 ± 0.005, a result that is so much nearer mine than my experimental uncertainty that I am quite content—indeed gratified—but I may perhaps be pardoned for still preferring my own graphical weightings, since I thought at the time, and still think, that I got the best obtainable results in that way from my data. The person who makes the measurements certainly has a slight advantage in weighting over the person who does not, and the graphical method by which I got at my final estimated uncertainty is, I think, in the hands of the experimenter himself more dependable than least squares.

In this way we get into the following dilemma: The engineer questions the usefulness of refined methods of analysis

[1] Loc. cit., Part II.

because his data are not good; the research man questions their use because he does not need them. The sooner an engineer appreciates this situation, the sooner will he become an influence in getting good data such that he can use in the theory of control to effect certain economies previously discussed.

Everyone will admit that in the literature there are numerous sets of bad data. As an illustrative case we find the following statement [1] in a recent paper on thermionic emission:

> Most of the observations on emission made up to 1914, and a considerable number of those made since then, are almost worthless because of the poor vacuum conditions under which they were made.

2. *All Measurement a Sampling Process*

An element of chance enters into every measurement; hence every set of measurements is inherently a sample of certain more or less unknown conditions. Even in the few instances where we believe that the objective reality under measurement is a constant, the measurements of this constant are influenced by chance or unknown causes. Hence, the set of measurements of any quantity, even though the quantity itself be a constant, is a sample of a possible infinite set of measurements which we might make of this same quantity under essentially the same conditions.

From this viewpoint, measurement is a sampling process designed to tell us something about the universe in which we live that will enable us to predict the future in terms of the past through the establishment of principles or natural laws. In fact, we may think of the process of examining a subgroup n of a larger group of N things along this same line in the sense that we look at the n things and try to predict what we would find if we were to look at the remaining $N - n$ things.

In the measurement of anything four kinds of errors may arise:

A. Constant { Theoretical
Instrumental
Personal

[1] Saul Dushman, *Reviews of Modern Physics*, Volume II, pp. 381–476, 1930.

B. Mistakes $\begin{cases} \text{Manipulative} \\ \text{Observational} \\ \text{Numerical} \end{cases}$

C. Effect of Assignable Causes, Type I

D. Effect of Constant Chance Systems $\begin{cases} \text{Methodological} \\ \text{Instrumental} \\ \text{Physiological} \end{cases}$

3. *Good Data*

Three prerequisites of good data are:

A. They shall come from a constant system of chance causes—in other words, they must satisfy the criteria of Part VI if they are sufficiently numerous that such tests can be applied. If this condition is not fulfilled, we must rely upon the experimentalist's ability to eliminate all causes of lack of constancy in the chance cause system.

B. They shall be free from constant errors of measurement and mistakes.

C. They shall provide a basis for estimating the error of measurement.

4. *Correction of Data for Constant Errors*

Let us consider the simplest kind of measurement, viz., that of a so-called physical constant such as one of those in the equation of electron emission as a function of temperature of the form

$$I = aT^{1/2}e^{-\frac{b}{T}}$$

where

$$I = \text{emission per unit area,}$$
$$T = \text{absolute temperature,}$$

and *a* and *b* are constants characteristic of the emitting surface.

Dushman [1] considers in some detail the constant errors that

[1] Loc. cit.

must be taken into account in making such measurements. Some of the most important sources of theoretical instrumental error are:

A. Error in measurement of surface area at maximum temperature.
B. Temperature gradients along emitting surface.
C. Presence of adsorbed and occluded gases in emitter.
D. Presence of gases in tube.
E. Cooling effect of leads.
F. Effect of anode voltage.
G. Error in measurement of temperature.

Errors (*A*) and (*E*) are largely eliminated through design; (*B*), (*F*), and (*G*) are such that the observed data can be corrected with the aid of available but complicated theory. Errors from sources (*C*) and (*D*) are eliminated by proper baking of bulb, flashing of the filament, and evacuation of the system.

Thus we get a picture of the technique required either to correct for or remove two of the sources of constant error in one very important physical measurement. A more detailed study of this problem of correcting data for constant errors will emphasize the fact that the degree of success will depend among other things upon the intuition, reason, theoretical knowledge, experience and technique of the experimentalist. Is it any wonder that engineering and even research data often fail to satisfy the prerequisite of being free from constant errors of the instrumental and theoretical kinds?

It is also true that to correct for personal errors often presents a real problem. Often one finds a set of data revealing the psychological tendency on the part of the observer to favor certain numbers, a case of which was noted in Part VI. One of the most troublesome characteristics of such errors is the fact that many of the psychological errors from their very nature are such that we do not readily detect them in ourselves. Witness for example the tendency for us to *feel* that the two lines *a* and *b* in Fig. 131 are not of equal length although we know better.

The method of detecting and eliminating assignable causes has been discussed in sufficient detail in Part VI and hence need not be considered here. It would perhaps be of interest

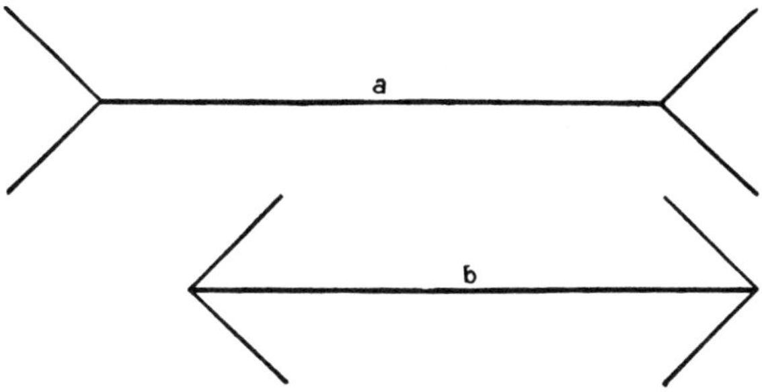

FIG. 131.—HOW MUCH LONGER IS *a* THAN *b*?

to show how mistakes can often be singled out even by analytical methods. To do so, however, is out of place here because the best method of correcting for these is to take care not to make them, or to provide two independent observers.

5. *Errors Introduced by Constant Systems of Chance Causes*

After the state of constancy in the chance cause system has been reached, the problem of correcting data for errors of

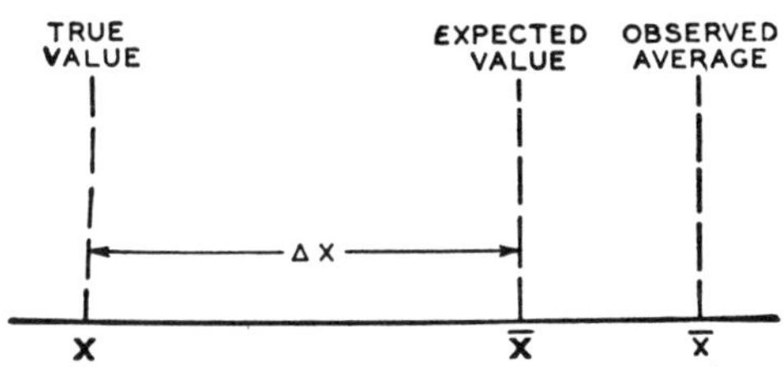

FIG. 132.—PROBLEM OF ELIMINATING ERRORS OF MEASUREMENT.

measurement may be schematically indicated as in Fig. 132. In this the true value is represented by **X**, the expected observed value by $\bar{\mathbf{X}}$ and the average of a sample of size n by $\bar{X}$. The distance ΔX represents the resultant constant error which must be taken care of as indicated in the previous section.

Under the assumption of constancy of the cause system, it follows that

$$\underset{n \longrightarrow \infty}{L_S} \bar{X} = \bar{\mathbf{X}}$$

where the limit L_S is statistical.

In practice we usually take the observed average $\bar{X}$ as our best estimate of $\bar{\mathbf{X}}$ and hence make our constant error correction with $\bar{X}$ as a base. Our problem is not solved, however, until we form some reasonable estimate of the probability that the inequality $|\bar{X} - \bar{\mathbf{X}}| \leq \varepsilon$ is satisfied where ε is some preassigned positive quantity. To do this it is necessary to obtain some estimate of the true standard deviation σ of the objective distribution of observed values. Except in the case of small samples we usually take the observed value of standard deviation as the best estimate of σ. If we let

$$z = \frac{\varepsilon}{\sigma/\sqrt{n}}$$

then we may, subject to the usual assumption of normality of the distribution of error, use the normal law probability table to estimate the probability that the absolute difference exceeds $z\sigma/\sqrt{n}$.

Thus we see that the complete discussion of the measurement of the simplest kind does involve the use of statistical as well as physical theory.

An interesting illustration of such a system of errors attributable to a physiological source is that shown in Fig. 133 representing the distribution of minimum audible sound intensity.[1] It is particularly interesting to note how closely the observed distribution is approximated by the normal law.

6. *Correction for Constant Chance Errors of Measurement*

Let us next consider the case where the thing measured is itself a constant chance variable with average $\bar{\mathbf{X}}_T$ and standard deviation σ_T. Furthermore, let us assume that the error of

[1] For a discussion of these results see "Some Applications of Statistical Methods," by W. A. Shewhart, *Bell System Technical Journal*, Vol. III, No. 1, January, 1924.

measurement is such that the expected value of the measurement coincides with $\overline{\mathbf{X}}_T$ and that the standard deviation of the error of measurement is σ_E.

Assuming that the error of measurement compounds linearly with the true value and that there is no correlation between them, it follows [1] that

$$\sigma_0 = \sqrt{\sigma_T^2 + \sigma_E^2}, \tag{95}$$

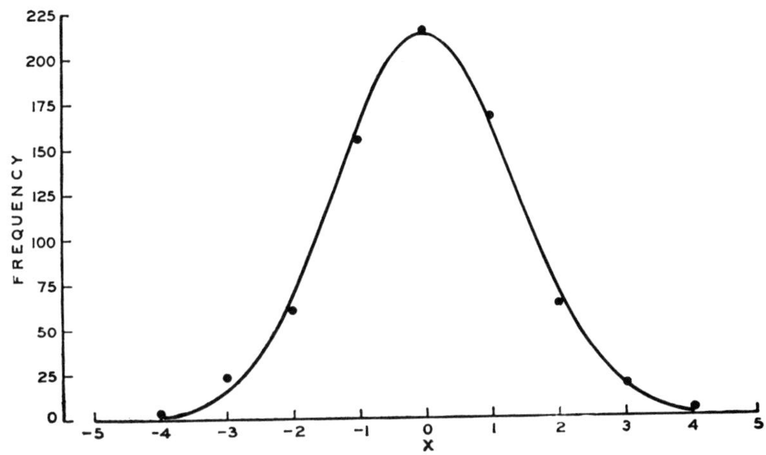

FIG. 133.—DISTRIBUTION OF MINIMUM SOUND INTENSITY.

where σ_0 is the standard deviation of the objective distribution of observed values. Fig. 134 shows schematically the relationship between the objective true distribution $\mathbf{f}_T(X)$ and the objective observed distribution $\mathbf{f}_0(X)$.

Example: Table 52 gives two observed distributions—one is the distribution of single measurements of efficiencies of 15,050 pieces of a given kind of equipment; the other is the distribution of five hundred measurements on a single instrument. It had previously been shown experimentally that there

[1] If there is no correlation between the thing measured and the error of measurement, we may think of an observed value X as being the sum of a true value X_T and an error E. Hence from section 3 of Chapter XVI, Part IV, we get (95). Another way of arriving at this result is given by W. A. Shewhart in an article "Correction of Data for Errors of Measurement," *Bell System Technical Journal*, Vol. V, pp. 11–26, 1926.

TABLE 52.—TYPICAL CALCULATION INVOLVED IN ELIMINATING ERRORS OF MEASUREMENT

Measurements on a Single Instrument		Single Measurement on Each of a Number of Instruments	
Cell Midpoint	Frequency	Cell Midpoint	Frequency
2.8	2	0.0	13
3.1	16	0.5	10
3.4	46	1.0	8
3.7	88	1.5	43
4.0	138	2.0	100
4.3	113	2.5	815
4.6	71	3.0	1,761
4.9	22	3.5	2,397
5.2	4	4.0	3,431
		4.5	3,703
		5.0	2,165
		5.5	510
		6.0	77
		6.5	15
		7.0	2
$n = 500$ $\bar{X}_E = 4.0606$ $\sigma_E = 0.4423$		$n = 15{,}050$ $\bar{X}_0 = 4.0251$ $\sigma_0 = 0.8116$	

was no correlation between efficiency and error of measurement. Since the numbers of measurements are large, we may assume that $\boldsymbol{\sigma}_0 = \sigma_0$ and $\boldsymbol{\sigma}_E = \sigma_E$ where σ_0 and σ_E are the observed standard deviations given in Table 52. With this assumption we get

$$\sigma_T = \sqrt{\sigma_0^2 - \sigma_E^2} = \sqrt{(0.8116)^2 - (0.4423)^2} = 0.6805.$$

7. *Analysis of Bad Data*

We are now in a better position to consider the practical problem of the engineer in trying to determine how far he shall go in analyzing his results. Again take as a simple illustration measurements of some so-called physical constant such as those considered earlier in this chapter.

There is no known method for estimating the true value **X** of the constant and the true standard deviation σ of the error of measurement from a set of n bad data—data that do not satisfy any one of the three prerequisites of good data. We cannot say, however, that the man who took these data cannot intuitively arrive at good (or at least practical) estimates of both **X** and σ. Men of genius such as Poincaré claim often to advance intuitively first and logically afterwards.[1]

We have seen how intuition, hypothesis, imagination, and the like are basic to the process of finding and correcting for constant and assignable errors of measurement. If we turn to the history [2] of science and scientific method, we do not

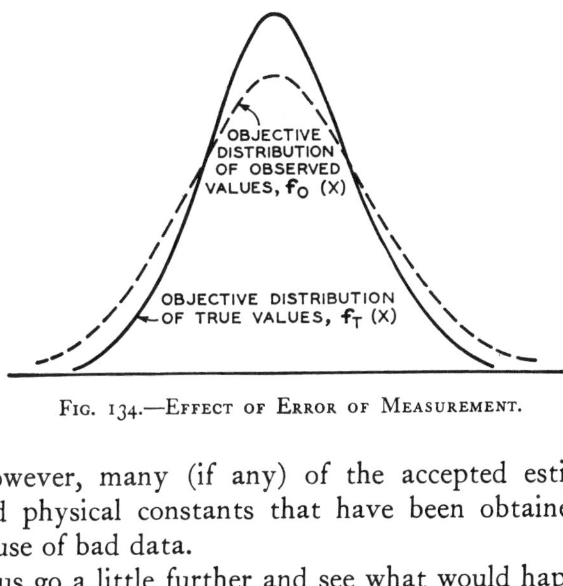

FIG. 134.—EFFECT OF ERROR OF MEASUREMENT.

find, however, many (if any) of the accepted estimates of so-called physical constants that have been obtained by intuitive use of bad data.

Let us go a little further and see what would happen if we were to accept results obtained from bad data through the

[1] See Dubs, *Rational Induction*, Chicago University Press, 1930, on this point. Such questions lead us into the fields of logic, psychology, and philosophy in an attempt to reduce to a rational basis the rôle played by each of these in measurement. Other references along this line are given in Appendix III.

[2] References in Appendix III.

intuition of the experimentalist. Immediately the analysis of data would be removed from the field of logic and we would have to accept a result simply on the basis of the *authority* of the experimentalist. Then we would face the difficult task of determining the *ultimate* authority. Such a method is certainly not scientific, nor does history reveal much ground for belief that it is a method which can be relied upon to give satisfactory results.

In the light of this situation it seems reasonable to believe that we are not justified in basing industrial development on intuitive analyses of data. This does not mean that experimental science has not profited by hunches that have come to those in the process of collecting data later found to be bad. The very fact that an experimentalist feels that his data are bad is usually an incentive to get good data. A research man is usually concerned with the fact that he may unknowingly get bad data. Here it is that the mathematical theory of detecting the presence of assignable causes (Part VI) comes to his aid.[1] To get the best results through the use of these criteria requires that the data be divided into rational subgroups and that at least the averages and standard deviations of these subgroups be known.

8. *Analysis of Good Data*

Good data in general are expensive. In the process of getting them many measurements are usually taken, from which a few are finally chosen as being good.

Furthermore, even though the cost of getting good data is large, experience shows that the cost of making the most efficient analytical study of such data is relatively small.

In Part VI the problem of choosing statistics to be used and of choosing the best way of using them was considered.

[1] In this connection the following quotation from *Mathematics of Life and Thought* by A. R. Forsyth is of interest. "Briefly, the science of mathematics cannot be a substitute for essential experiment; but it can show how experiments and observations, duly systematized, can be elucidated so as to discriminate between what is principle and what is detailed consequence of principle." The criteria described in Part VI help to discriminate between what should be and what should not be left to chance.

The fact that one statistic is often much more efficient than another is of considerable economic importance. For example, in general, the standard deviation of n good observations is just as good as the mean deviation of 1.14 n such data. To take on the average one hundred and fourteen observations where one hundred would do is an unnecessary waste of money which becomes significantly large in extensive industrial research programs.

To use the range in such a case instead of the standard deviation effectively results in throwing away a very large fraction of the information in respect to dispersion contained in the observed data. For example, if the sample size n is approximately sixty, the efficiency of the range is only about 50 per cent when compared with the standard deviation. As n increases beyond this value, the efficiency of the range rapidly decreases. In the face of this fact we sometimes find the range instead of the standard deviation tabulated in the literature.[1]

Table 53 is taken from an engineering report, and gives the modulus of rupture for three species of telephone poles. To

TABLE 53.—ILLUSTRATING INEFFICIENT METHOD OF TABULATING DATA

Species	Number n of Poles in Sample	Modulus of Rupture in psi			Efficiency of Max.—Min.
		Average	Maximum	Minimum	
A	4	3,985	5,690	2,980	100
B	16	5,978	7,090	4,460	75
C	100	5,787	7,790	3,490	35

have tabulated only the ranges in Cases B and C amounted to throwing away approximately 25 per cent and 65 per cent of the information available in the original data. This statement is based upon the assumption that the original data were good and that they came from an approximately normal universe. Of course, the range in bad data may give the experi-

[1] Examples of this kind are Tables 4 and 12 in the first edition of the very interesting book, *Timber, Its Strength, Seasoning, and Grading* by Harold S. Betts, McGraw-Hill Book Company, pp. 34 and 91, 1919.

mentalist some indication of the effects introduced by assignable causes of Type I. As indicated in the previous section, however, the interpretation of the range or any other statistic derived from bad data should be made by the experimentalist and can be accepted by another only upon the authority of the experimentalist.

For a sample of four, practically all of the information contained in the data is retained by using the range.

It is for such reasons that efficiency in analysis and presentation of data has been considered so often in the previous chapters. Graphical methods of analysis have not been given any attention simply because experience has shown them to be inferior to and less efficient than analytical ones.[1]

9. *Minimizing Cost of Measurement—Simple Example*

Let us consider the following simple problem: What is the most economical way of measuring a quality X controlled by a constant system of causes to insure with a given probability $\mathbf{P}$ that the average of the measurements will not deviate in absolute magnitude from the average $\overline{\mathbf{X}}_T$ by more than a preassigned quantity ε. Let us assume that:

a_1 = cost of selecting each unit and making it available for measurement,

a_2 = cost of making each measurement,

n_1 = number of units selected,

n_2 = number of measurements made on each unit,

σ_E = objective standard deviation of errors of measurement,

and

σ_T = objective standard deviation of true magnitudes of the measured characteristic.

[1] Whittaker and Robinson make the following statement in the preface of their classic, *The Calculus of Observations*: "When the Edinburgh Laboratory was established in 1913, a trial was made, as far as possible, of every method which had been proposed for the solution of problems under consideration, and many of these were graphical. During the ten years which have elapsed since then, graphical methods have almost all been abandoned, as their inferiority has become evident, and at the present time the work of the Laboratory is almost exclusively arithmetical."

Let us take $P = 0.9973$, then the range $\bar{\mathbf{X}}_T \pm 3\sigma_{\bar{X}_0}$ includes 99.73 per cent of the observed averages $\bar{X}_0$, and hence $\varepsilon = 3\sigma_{\bar{X}_0}$.

The average of n_2 measurements made on one unit is to be taken as the observed value X_0 of the true magnitude $\bar{\mathbf{X}}_T$ for that unit. This average has the standard deviation $\sigma_E/\sqrt{n_2}$. Hence, from (95), the objective standard deviation of the observed values is given by

$$\sigma_0^2 = \sigma_T^2 + \sigma_{E_{\bar{X}}}^2 = \sigma_T^2 + \frac{\sigma_E^2}{n_2},$$

where $\sigma_{E\bar{X}^2}$ is the objective standard deviation of errors of averages of n_2. Thus the objective standard deviation $\sigma_{\bar{X}_0}$ of the average of n_1 observed values is

$$\sigma_{\bar{X}_0} = \frac{\sigma_0}{\sqrt{n_1}} = \sqrt{\frac{\sigma_T^2 + \dfrac{\sigma_E^2}{n_2}}{n_1}}, \qquad (96)$$

which gives the relationship

$$n_1 = \frac{\sigma_T^2 + \dfrac{\sigma_E^2}{n_2}}{\sigma_{\bar{X}_0}^2}$$

between n_1 and n_2.

Taking the cost of inspection as

$$C = a_1 n_1 + a_2 n_1 n_2,$$

and using customary methods this can be shown to be a minimum when

$$n_2 = \frac{\sigma_E}{\sigma_T}\sqrt{\frac{a_1}{a_2}}.$$

The following values correspond to one practical case:

$\varepsilon = 0.3$ unit	$a_1 = \$0.50$
$\sigma_E = 0.3$ unit	$a_2 = \$0.02$
$\sigma_T = 0.9$ unit	$P = 0.9973$

With the aid of this theory we find that the most economical method of measurement in this case requires two observations on each of eighty-six units. Here, as in general, we take observed values of σ_E and σ_T in large samples as estimates of $\boldsymbol{\sigma}_E$ and $\boldsymbol{\sigma}_T$ respectively.

10. *How Many Measurements?*

Perhaps the question most frequently raised by those interested in the control of quality is: How many measurements shall be taken? Of course, for such a question to be answerable, it must be understood to mean something like this: How many measurements shall be taken in order that one may have a given assurance that such and such is true subject to certain specific assumptions? When so stated the question usually has an objective answer.

Sometimes the question is put briefly as follows: How large a sample shall be taken? When so stated, however, care must be exercised to differentiate between the size of sample, meaning thereby the number of things measured, and the size of sample, meaning thereby the number of measurements, where one thing may be measured more than once. The significance of these remarks will be apparent as we proceed.

To introduce the subject, let us ask a very simple question: Assuming that we know that a quality X is normally controlled with standard deviation $\boldsymbol{\sigma}$, how many measurements of this quality must we make in order that the probability will be, let us say, 0.9973 that the deviation of the average of n observed values from the true but unknown arithmetic mean $\overline{\mathbf{X}}$ be not greater in absolute magnitude than some given value $\Delta\overline{X}$.

From what has previously been said we see that the size n of the sample required in this case is rigorously given by the relation

$$\Delta\overline{X} = 3\frac{\boldsymbol{\sigma}}{\sqrt{n}}.$$

In practice, however, we do not know $\boldsymbol{\sigma}$. In fact, this factor is only obtainable as a statistical limit when the sample size n is made indefinitely large. What we can do under such conditions is to estimate $\boldsymbol{\sigma}$ from available data. Calling this estimate σ, we may solve for n in the equation

$$\Delta\bar{X} = 3\frac{\sigma}{\sqrt{n}}.$$

We can then say that the size n of the sample thus obtained is the one required, assuming that $\sigma = \boldsymbol{\sigma}$.

Perhaps the most important thing to note in this connection is that the standard deviation of the average decreases inversely as the square root of the number of observations, because this indicates the order of increase in the precision of the average with increase in the number of observations under the assumed conditions.

In general, if we know that we are sampling from a constant system of chance causes, we can say that the standard deviation of an estimate of any one of the objective statistics, fraction defective $\mathbf{p}$, average $\bar{\mathbf{X}}$, standard deviation $\boldsymbol{\sigma}$, and correlation coefficient $\mathbf{r}$, decreases inversely as the square root of the size of the sample, even though we do not know the magnitudes of the respective standard deviations in a given case. Furthermore, given the standard deviation as a function of sample size, for any statistic derived from a sample from a specified universe, we have, as indicated, a means of determining the significance of increasing the sample size.

It is very important to note that *the answer given to the question of how many measurements is in each case limited by the assumption that the variable X is controlled.* If we ask a similar question in a case where we are not willing to assume to begin with that the data are controlled, it is first necessary to try to determine by criteria already described whether or not the variable under consideration satisfies this condition.

Example: Recent investigations [1] have been made by the American Rolling Mill Company to determine the life of ferrous materials under different corrosion conditions. Data obtained

[1] R. F. Passano and Anson Hayes, "A Method of Treating Data on the Lives of Ferrous Materials," *Proceedings of the American Society for Testing Materials*, Vol. 29, Part II, 1929.

from a certain kind of sheet material immersed in Washington tap water showed that the average time of failure of such samples was $\bar{X} = 874.89$ days and the standard deviation of the time of failure was $\sigma = 85.31$ days. One kind of practical question of interest to the research engineer of this company is: What sample size n must be used in order that for similar test conditions, the probability shall be 0.90 that the average time for failure determined from the n tests will be in error by not more than 5 per cent of the average of the universe?

Assuming that the observed values of average and standard deviation are the true values for the universe, and that averages of samples of n are distributed normally, we may answer this question as follows: The allowable error is 5 per cent of 874.89 days or 43.74 days, and this must correspond to a probability of 0.90 or to an error of $1.645\ \sigma/\sqrt{n}$ as found from Table A of Part II. Hence n is found by solving the equation

$$1.645\sigma/\sqrt{n} = 43.74$$

having assumed that $\sigma = 85.31$. In this way, we get $n = 10$.

11. *Law of Propagation of Error—Practical Significance*

Most measurements are indirect in that the quality Y to be measured is derived from measures of let us say m other qualities

$$X_1, X_2, \ldots, X_i, \ldots, X_m$$

to which it is either functionally or statistically related. In this section we shall consider the functional case, examples of which are met in everyday work.

A simple illustration is the measurement of the density D of a solid by the formula

$$D = \frac{w_1}{w_1 - w_2}$$

where w_1 and w_2 are the weights of the solid in air and water respectively.

If the solid is such that we can measure its volume V in a more direct way than by determining the difference $w_1 - w_2$ we may use the formula

$$D = \frac{w_1}{V}$$

to obtain the density.

The choice of method of measurement involves at least two things:

A. Determination of effect of errors of measurement in each of the m qualities upon the standard deviation of the calculated values of Y.

B. Choice of most efficient method of measuring Y.

Let

$$Y = F(X_1, X_2, \ldots, X_i, \ldots, X_m)$$

be the functional relationship between the quality Y to be measured and the m other qualities upon whose measurements the calculated (measured) value of Y depends, as the calculated value of D depends upon the observed values of w_1 and w_2 above.

Assuming that F can be expanded in a Taylor's series and that terms containing higher powers in the x's than the first may be neglected, we have

$$Y = F(\overline{\mathbf{X}}_1, \overline{\mathbf{X}}_2, \ldots, \overline{\mathbf{X}}_m) + x_1\left(\frac{\partial F}{\partial X_1}\right)_{\overline{\mathbf{X}}_i} + x_2\left(\frac{\partial F}{\partial X_2}\right)_{\overline{\mathbf{X}}_i} + \cdots + x_m\left(\frac{\partial F}{\partial X_m}\right)_{\overline{\mathbf{X}}_i},$$

where $x_i = X_i - \overline{\mathbf{X}}_i$, and the derivatives are formed for the mean values of the X's. Under these conditions we have as in Part V

$$\overline{\mathbf{Y}} = F(\overline{\mathbf{X}}_1, \overline{\mathbf{X}}_2, \ldots, \overline{\mathbf{X}}_m),$$

and

$$\sigma_y = \sqrt{a_1^2\sigma_1^2 + a_2^2\sigma_2^2 + \cdots + a_i^2\sigma_i^2 + \cdots + a_m^2\sigma_m^2}, \quad (97)$$

where

$$a_i = \left(\frac{\partial F}{\partial X_i}\right)_{\overline{\mathbf{X}}_i},$$

σ_i is the standard deviation of the measurement of X_i, and σ_y is the standard deviation of the indirect measurements of Y.

Equation (97) is the law of propagation of error, and gives us the information called for under (*A*).

If for the simple problem of measuring density we let

$\overline{w}_1$ = expected weight in air,

$\overline{w}_2$ = expected weight in water,

σ_1 = standard deviation of measurement of w_1,

σ_2 = standard deviation of measurement of w_2,

and σ_D = standard deviation of error of measurement of D,

we have on applying (97)

$$\sigma_D = \frac{1}{\overline{w}_1 - \overline{w}_2}\sqrt{\overline{w}_2{}^2\sigma_1{}^2 + \overline{w}_1{}^2\sigma_2{}^2}.$$

By a process exactly similar to that used in Paragraph 7, Chapter XVII of Part V, we can determine the mean values

$$\overline{X}_1, \overline{X}_2, \ldots, \overline{X}_i, \ldots, \overline{X}_m$$

(if they exist) which will minimize σ_y. By comparing the minimum values of σ_y obtainable by different methods we can arrive at the most efficient method of measuring Y.

12. *Measurement through Statistical Relationship*

Let us consider the problem of measuring some physical quality such as tensile strength which cannot be measured except through the use of some statistical relationship unless we resort to a destructive test.

Let us start with a simple question. How can we be sure as to whether or not the tensile strength of the bar in Fig. 135 lies within specified limits Y_1 and Y_2? The answer is: Break it and find out. However, since we cannot break it and use it too, we must be satisfied with the answer to a slightly different question: How shall we test the bar indirectly through statistically correlated variables? Let us start with the illustration introduced in Part I, Fig. 14. Let us consider first the correlation between tensile strength Y and hardness X. We can never expect to be sure that the tensile strength of tested material will lie within two specified limits Y_1 and Y_2 by making sure that the hardness lies within some two limits X_1 and X_2. The situation is shown[1] schematically in Fig. 136, for the

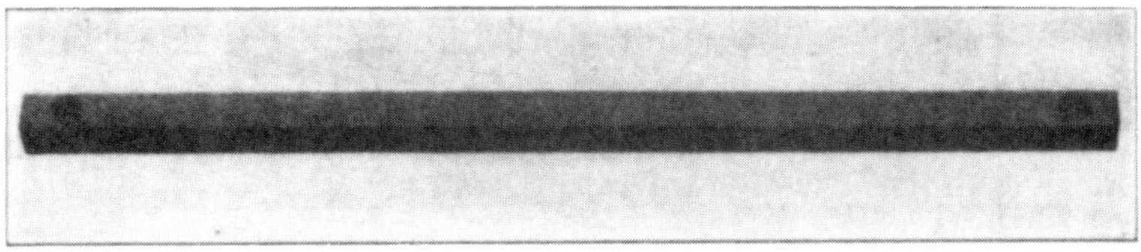

FIG. 135.—TEST BAR.

data of Fig. 14-*a*. In such a case values of tensile strength may be expected to be found in the shaded area of the figure between the limits X_1 and X_2 and outside the limits Y_1 and Y_2.

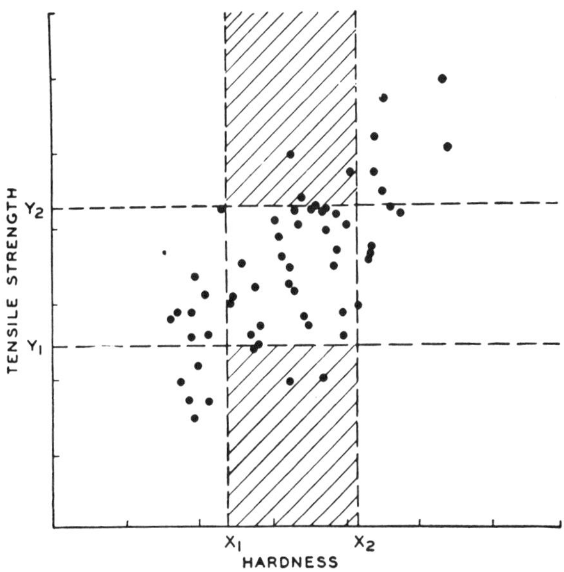

FIG. 136.—WHY ONE CANNOT BE SURE THAT STRENGTH LIES WITHIN SPECIFIED LIMITS.

If, and only if, the product is controlled in respect to the two correlated variables Y and X, can we predict how many pieces

[1] Mathematical details considered in Part II.

of material having quality X within the range X_1 to X_2 will have quality Y within the range Y_1 to Y_2. In other words, the use of indirect statistical measures must be based upon the assumption that the probability **P** that the point corresponding to an observed pair of values X and Y will fall within a given rectangle is constant.

A. *Calibration.*—Suppose one has a lot of N pieces like the one shown in Fig. 135, and wants to mark each of them with a

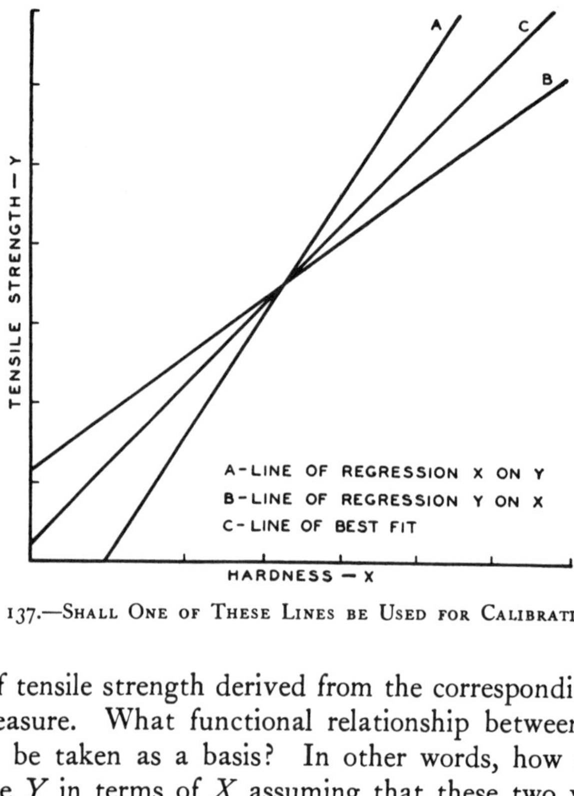

FIG. 137.—SHALL ONE OF THESE LINES BE USED FOR CALIBRATION?

value of tensile strength derived from the corresponding hardness measure. What functional relationship between Y and X shall be taken as a basis? In other words, how shall we calibrate Y in terms of X assuming that these two variables are normally correlated? Shall we take one of the three lines illustrated in Fig. 137?

Let σ_y = standard deviation of objective distribution of tensile strength Y,

σ_x = standard deviation of objective distribution of hardness X,

$\mathbf{r}$ = correlation coefficient between X and Y in objective distribution of X and Y.

It follows from the discussion of lines of regression in Part II that the line of regression of tensile strength on hardness

$$y = \mathbf{r}\frac{\sigma_y}{\sigma_x}x,$$

where $y = Y - \overline{\mathbf{Y}}$ and $x = X - \overline{\mathbf{X}}$, gives the expected or average value of y to be associated with a given value of x. In other words, if we were to mark with $\frac{\mathbf{r}\sigma_y}{\sigma_x}x$ each of a very large number n test pieces that gave a hardness value $\overline{\mathbf{X}} + x$, and then we were to break these to determine their tensile strength, we should expect to find that the average tensile strength of the n pieces would be $\frac{\mathbf{r}\sigma_y}{\sigma_x}x$, although the observed tensile strengths would be distributed about this value.

Furthermore we should expect 99.73 per cent of the n pieces to have tensile strengths measured in terms of deviations, within the limits

$$\frac{\mathbf{r}\sigma_y}{\sigma_x}x \pm 3\sigma_y\sqrt{1 - \mathbf{r}^2},$$

since as we have seen in Part II, the standard deviation of any y array about its mean in this simple case is

$$\mathbf{s}_y = \sigma_y\sqrt{1 - \mathbf{r}^2}. \qquad (98)$$

In fact, if the regression of y on x is linear and the scatter of points is homoscedastic, then the standard deviation of each array of y's about the mean $\mathbf{r}\frac{\sigma_y}{\sigma_x}x$ is given by (98) and we can say by virtue of Tchebycheff's inequality that more than

$100\left(1 - \frac{1}{t^2}\right)$ per cent of the y values may be expected to lie within the band

$$r\frac{\sigma_y}{\sigma_x}x \pm ts_y. \qquad (99)$$

Where the correlation surface is normal, the number of points lying within such a band is given by the normal law integral. Under the same conditions, similar statements hold with respect to the regression of x on y. It is sometimes argued that some line other than the line of regression should be used as a measure of y in terms of x. One such suggestion is that line for which the sum of the squares of the perpendicular distances of the points in the xy plane to this line is a minimum. The reason for choosing the line of regression instead of this or any other line is that this is the only line about which we can make the general statements previously made in connection with the range (99).

In the discussion of Fig. 14 it was pointed out that the use of the plane of regression of tensile strength Z on hardness Y and density X is a better measure of tensile strength than either the line of regression of Z on X or Z on Y. This follows because the standard deviation,

$$\sigma_{z \cdot xy} = \sigma_z\left[\frac{1 - r_{xy}^2 - r_{xy}^2 - r_{xz}^2 + 2r_{xy}r_{yz}r_{xz}}{1 - r_{xy}^2}\right]^{1/2}$$

of the values of tensile strength from the plane of regression is less than either

$$s_{zx} = \sigma_z\sqrt{1 - r_{xz}^2},$$

or

$$s_{zy} = \sigma_z\sqrt{1 - r_{yz}^2},$$

where s_{zx} and s_{zy} are the standard deviations of tensile strength from the lines of regression of z on x and z on y respectively.

B. *Effect of Error of Measurement.*—Thus far we have considered the problem of measuring some quantity such as tensile strength Y through its statistical relationship with some other quantity, let us say hardness X. In general, the observed values of both tensile strength and hardness are in themselves subject to error. Let us assume for example that

σ_{x_0} = The standard deviation of the objective distribution of the observed values of hardness,

σ_{y_0} = The standard deviation of the objective distribution of the observed values of tensile strength,

σ_{x_T} = The standard deviation of the objective distribution of true values of hardness,

σ_{y_T} = The standard deviation of the objective distribution of true values of tensile strength,

$\mathbf{r}_0$ = The true correlation between the observed values of hardness and tensile strength,

and $\mathbf{r}$ = The true correlation between the true values of hardness and tensile strength.

It can easily be shown that under these conditions

$$\mathbf{r}_0 = \frac{\sigma_{x_T}\sigma_{y_T}}{\sigma_{x_0}\sigma_{y_0}}\mathbf{r}. \qquad (100)$$

From this relationship we see that the correlation between the observed values of two correlated variables is always less than the correlation between the true values, unless the error of measurement of each of the variables is zero. In other words, the smaller the error of measurement for each of the variables, the more precise will be the regression method of measuring one in terms of the other.

C. *Conclusion.*—To be able to measure through the use of statistical relationship, *it is necessary that the variables be controlled.* In the simple case of normally correlated variables the line or plane of regression has certain advantages as a calibration line or plane over any other.

It should be noted, however, that the use of a statistical calibration curve involves the introduction of a concept quite different from that underlying the use of a calibration curve based upon a functional relationship. The use of statistical relationship introduces a certain indeterminateness not present in the use of the functional relationship. To make this point clear let us suppose that we had, say one hundred bars, such as shown in Fig. 135, and let us suppose that we wished to test these for tensile strength indirectly through the use of the Rockwell hardness measure.

If we assume that tensile strength Y is functionally related to X, as

$$Y = f(X), \tag{101}$$

where f is a single valued function, then for every X there is one and only one value of Y. If we use such a calibration curve, we can mark each of the one hundred bars with a value Y which will be the tensile strength of that bar except for errors of measurement.

If, however, the two quantities Y and X are related statistically and we use a line of regression

$$y = \mathbf{r}\frac{\sigma_y}{\sigma_x}x, \tag{102}$$

where $y = Y - \overline{\mathbf{Y}}$ and $x = X - \overline{\mathbf{X}}$, then we cannot say that for a given value of X there is only one value as given by the line of regression of y on x. Instead for every X there is an array of Y's, the mean of which under controlled conditions will be the value of Y given by (102). Here we run into the kind of indeterminateness discussed in the last chapter.

Equation (80) expressing $\mathbf{r}$ as a measure of the commonness of causation under simplified and controlled conditions may help one to form a better picture of the significance of the line of regression (102) as a calibration curve. Unless $\mathbf{r}$ is unity there are always causes of variation in Y that are not present in X. Even under these simple conditions if we could be sure that the correlation coefficient r and the variable X were controlled, we could not be sure that Y was controlled and we could not be sure of the interpretation of y as given by (102) except in the sense that the mean value of y for a given X would be given by (102). *A priori*, however, it seems unlikely that Y will be uncontrolled if both r and X are controlled. At least it appears that the best we can hope to do in trying to control Y through the measure X is to try to control r and X.

D. *Example:* Since the use of statistical relationship plays such an important rôle in measurement, it may be of interest to consider another simple problem. Many machine measures of quality depend upon the use of statistical relationship. A very important type of machine in the telephone plant is that introduced to supplant measures depending upon the human

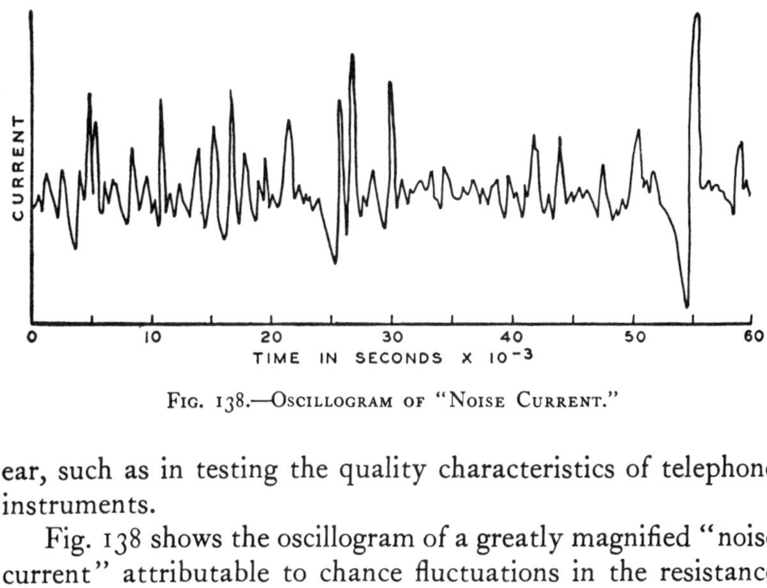

FIG. 138.—OSCILLOGRAM OF "NOISE CURRENT."

ear, such as in testing the quality characteristics of telephone instruments.

Fig. 138 shows the oscillogram of a greatly magnified "noise current" attributable to chance fluctuations in the resistance of a certain kind of telephone instrument. It is obviously desirable to go as far as one can in reducing such noise to a minimum and in controlling the effect of this kind of distortion as measured by the human ear. Consequently, all instruments of this type are tested to make sure that they meet specification requirements in respect to this kind of distortion. Of course, the cost of doing this by ear would be prohibitive; therefore it is desirable to secure the economic advantages of a machine measure.

A little consideration will show, however, that it is almost hopeless to expect to be able to find a machine measure of such fluctuations in current that will be functionally related to the measures of the human ear. The best we can hope to do is to find some machine measure X which is statistically related to the ear measure Y.

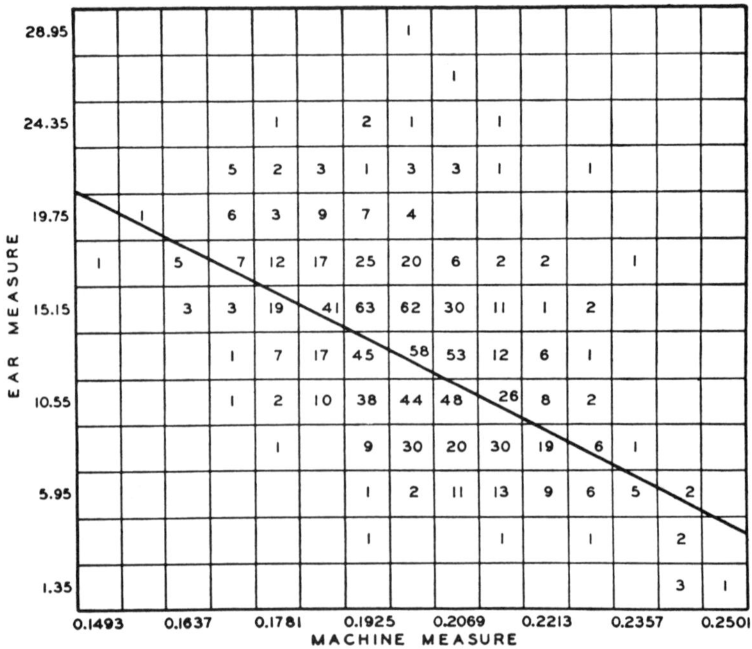

FIG. 139.—HOW SHALL WE CALIBRATE MACHINE MEASURE IN TERMS OF EAR MEASURE?

Fig. 139 shows the calibration scatter diagram of a machine measure X and ear measure Y on 942 instruments. These data were obtained under conditions of control as determined by the criteria described in Part VI. The solid line in this figure represents the line of regression of the ear measure Y on the machine measure X. The fact that the difference $\eta_{yx}{}^2 - r^2$ is approximately zero indicates that we are justified in assuming linear regression. This incidentally is what we should expect to get for reasons outlined in Part III.

For reasons given previously in this section, it appears that there is good ground for the belief that we may control the quality Y determined by the ear by controlling the quality X determined by the machine in respect to both the average $\bar{X}$ and the standard deviation σ_x in samples of size n. To check the calibration of such a machine, it is necessary that the correlation r between the ear measure Y and the machine measure X for a sample of n instruments be controlled in the sense of the criteria of Part VI.

CHAPTER XXIV

Sampling

1. *Fundamental Considerations*

Table 54 gives the results of measurements of modulus of rupture on twenty-four telephone poles of species D. Based upon these data, what can we say as to the strength of this species?

Assuming that no assignable causes of variation of Type I are present, or in other words, assuming that these poles came from a constant system of chance causes, it follows from the discussion of the previous chapter that reasonable estimates of the average $\bar{X}$ and standard deviation σ of the distribution of

Table 54.—Modulus of Rupture of Twenty-Four Type D Telephone Poles

Pole Number	Modulus of Rupture	Pole Number	Modulus of Rupture
1	3,643	13	5,385
2	5,195	14	5,843
3	3,925	15	6,905
4	4,595	16	5,696
5	4,482	17	7,392
6	6,248	18	6,184
7	6,012	19	4,885
8	6,697	20	6,182
9	7,117	21	6,201
10	5,340	22	7,334
11	8,712	23	5,497
12	5,819	24	4,621

Average = 5,829 psi
σ = 1,159 psi

modulus of rupture given by the assumed constant system of causes are

$$\bar{X} = \bar{\mathbf{X}} = 5{,}829 \text{ psi}$$

$$\frac{\sigma}{c_2} = \boldsymbol{\sigma} = 1{,}197 \text{ psi.}$$

So far as the distribution of the twenty-four observed values is concerned, there is no definite evidence of lack of constancy in the chance cause system. Under these conditions one would be led to the conclusion that the average strength and standard deviation of this species of telephone pole are 5,829 psi and 1,197 psi respectively.

Any one who knows anything about the strength characteristics of timber would likely and justly challenge such a conclusion. For example, such a one would likely ask what effect moisture content has on the strength of poles of this species, knowing as they would that moisture is at least for most species an assignable cause of variation in strength.

Dividing the poles in respect to moisture content in this case leads to the results shown in Fig. 140. There can be little doubt that moisture content is an assignable cause in this case. How then, does this effect the validity of our conclusion arrived at upon the assumption of constancy?

From Fig. 140 it appears that there is a difference of the order of magnitude of 1,000 psi between the strength when the pole is dry and that when it is wet. What strength one may expect to find in the future then may be something nearer 5,000 psi than the predicted 5,829 psi if the poles to be tested are wet. It appears that prediction based upon a sample coming from a non-constant system or non-controlled system of chance causes may differ widely from what the future will reveal. What reliance then, asks the engineer, can be placed on sampling results? The answer is that prediction based upon a sample from a non-controlled universe in which the causes of lack of control are unknown is likely always to be in error just as a measurement uncorrected for constant errors always in the long run is in error. *Sampling theory applies to samples arising under controlled conditions.* Too much emphasis cannot be laid upon this fact. *To be able to make accurate predictions from samples, we must secure control first just as to make accurate physical measurements, we must eliminate constant errors.*

In this section we have approached the problem of interpreting a sample from a practical angle, and in so doing, have been led to see the importance of control. Having read Parts III, IV, and VI, one sees that the only theoretical basis of

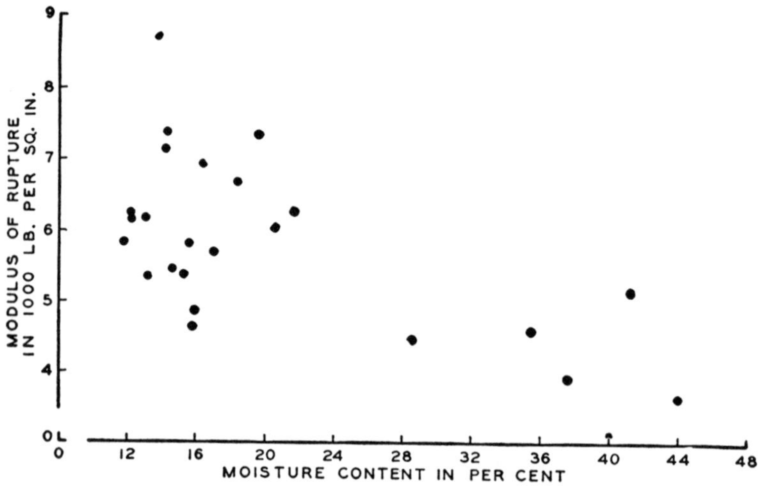

FIG. 140.—WHY CONSTANCY OF CAUSE SYSTEM IS ESSENTIAL FOR PREDICTION.

interpreting a sample is the assumption that it arose under controlled conditions characterized by (45) in the most general case, or in other words, by the fact that the sample was taken under the same essential conditions that will maintain throughout the future so that the universal physical law of large numbers applies.

2. *Random Sample*

A sample taken under conditions where the law of large numbers (45) applies will be termed a random sample. This concept of random is of fundamental importance in the theory of control. By simple illustrations we shall now try to make clear how this concept differs from that of some of the prevalent definitions of random in order that no confusion may arise in the use of the term in this book.

Yule in that treasure house for statisticians, *An Introduction to the Theory of Statistics*, indicates that the usual concept of random sample is one drawn with replacement, though he criticizes the use of the term random because it is so often taken to be synonomous with haphazard. Caradog Jones [1] apparently would also have us believe that a random sample is one drawn with replacement. For example, he says in effect: To select 99 sheep from 999, number each sheep and place in a box 999 tickets numbered 1 to 999, one to correspond to each sheep, then pick out 99 tickets in succession being careful to replace each and shake up the box before picking out the next; if there were absolutely no difference between the tickets such as would cause one to be picked more easily than another, the selection made in this way would be random.

Now, if a random sample were only that kind of a sample and if the theory of sampling had to start with that kind of a sample, one can well imagine how enthusiastic a purchaser of 999 sheep would be about the theory. To such a man that method of sampling would be foolish.

Not only is it foolish from a practical viewpoint in certain cases to try to take this kind of a sample—very often indeed, it is *impossible* to take a sample with replacement. As an illustration: How would you take a sample tensile strength test with replacement from the coil of wire in Fig. 141?

The kind of sample described by Yule and Jones is random, of course, but so are other kinds of samples as will be apparent from a study of the generalized law of large numbers (45). Thus either a sample without replacement or a Poisson sample may be random in this general sense.

[1] *A First Course in Statistics*, G. Bell & Sons, Ltd., London, 1924.

3. *Sampling for Protection*

Various methods of setting up sampling schemes to give definite consumer's risks were outlined in the last chapter of Part VI. A study of the subject matter of the references there given shows that the conclusions drawn rest upon the assumption that samples are selected at random. In other words, assuming that there are N items in the lot to be inspected, it is necessary that the sample of n required by one of these sampling

FIG. 141.—HOW SHOULD WE CHOOSE A RANDOM SAMPLE OF THE TENSILE STRENGTH OF THIS COIL OF WIRE?

schemes, for a certain consumer's risk, be drawn at random. The risks calculated in this way apply so long as the samples are random. If, however, the samples are not random, the risks do not necessarily hold.[1]

The kind of random sample required by the risk theory can be obtained by sampling without replacement from a bowl containing N identical chips marked 1 to N where it is assumed that the chips have been thoroughly stirred before the sample of n is drawn. We can see, therefore, the nature of the difficulties involved in getting a random sample of the poles from the pole yard of Fig. 142.

As another illustration let us consider the problem involved in drawing a random sample of soldered terminals from fifty panels such as the one shown in Fig. 143 where there are 4,500 terminals on each panel.

[1] Cf. Sec. 1 of this chapter.

We need not go further to see that it is very seldom feasible to draw a sample in which the experimental conditions requisite for randomness have been secured. Therefore we must rely upon the engineering ability of the inspector to divide as in Part VI the total lot N to be sampled into, let us say, m subgroups which *a priori* may be expected to differ assignably. A sample may then be drawn from each subgroup of the right size to insure that the chosen risk is met by the sampling test for each particular group. These remarks are sufficient to emphasize the importance of *a priori* information about the lot prior to the taking of a sample.

Now let us consider the problem of selecting a sample from a shipment of ten carloads of boxed material, there being twelve items in a box and roughly 1,000 boxes in a car. Obviously it is not feasible to arrange experimentally for a random sample to be drawn. The next best thing is to try to divide the total of $N = 120{,}000$ items into m rational subgroups. If, however, we know nothing about the manufacturing process or the conditions under which the lot was produced, we are faced with the necessity of doing something that we cannot do; yet we know that unless the sampling is done as it should be, sampling theory does not apply.

FIG. 142.—HOW SHOULD WE CHOOSE A SAMPLE OF THE POLES IN THIS YARD?

Thus we see how important it is that the consumer know assignable causes of variation if he is to devise a sampling plan to insure that the product accepted is of satisfactory quality. If the product is controlled, one can easily set up a satisfactory sampling plan, but if it is controlled, the plan is often not needed. If the product is not controlled, the consumer needs to know the assignable causes of variation so as to establish an adequate sampling scheme.

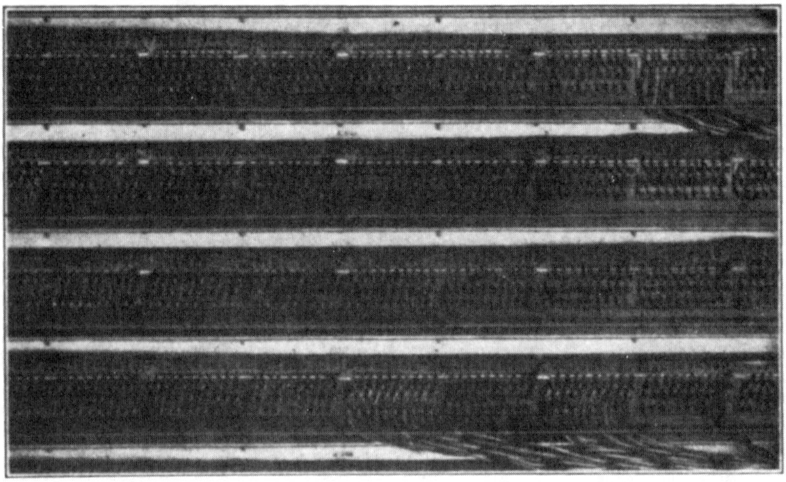

FIG. 143.—HOW SHOULD WE CHOOSE A SAMPLE OF THE SOLDERED TERMINALS IN THIS PANEL?

In this way we come to see the advantage of control to both consumer and producer. Just as each of these now secure advantages through cooperating in laying down specifications [1] for quality, it is reasonable to believe that each will soon try to obtain the mutual benefits of control.

4. *Representative Sample*

A sample that is representative of what we may expect to get if we take additional samples, is one satisfying the general

[1] On this point see H. F. Moore's *Text-Book of the Materials of Engineering*, 4th Edition, Chapter XVII, McGraw-Hill Book Company, 1930.

condition (45) of the law of large numbers. In other words, if we let N be the total universe, finite or infinite, to be sampled, we should try to divide the universe on an *a priori* basis into m objective rational subgroups as represented schematically in Fig. 144. The total sample of n should then be divided between these m subgroups in such a way as to give some indication of what we may expect to get from each group.

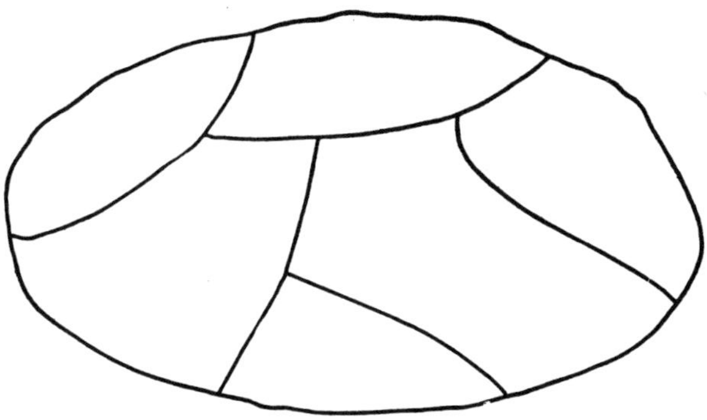

FIG. 144.—SCHEMATIC OF DIVISION INTO RATIONAL SUBGROUPS.

5. *Size of Sample*

We have seen in the previous chapter and in the last chapter of Part VI that the size of sample always depends upon what we assume *a priori* to be the conditions under which we are sampling. In any case the interpretation of the sample rests upon the assumption of control, or upon the assumption that the law of large numbers holds in the particular case. Thus we need to know if the quality of the product gives evidence of control, and in this way we are forced to come back to the problem discussed in Part VI.

A very simple case will illustrate this point. Several years ago an engineer reported trouble on the job because the width of saw-slots in the screw heads was under minimum requirements so that the available screw-drivers could not be used. The question was raised as to how large a sample n should be inspected in each lot of size N to protect against the recurrence of this trouble. Investigation revealed that a sampling plan was already in use in which a certain fraction was taken from each lot of *N*. Just a little engineering investigation showed that the only assignable cause of the kind of trouble reported was wearing of the saw blade that made the slot. The obvious thing to do was to inspect the blade and not the screws. The important question was not "how many," but rather "how." A few measurements of the saw blade to control the product were worth far more than many measurements made blindly, as it were, on the screws to find trouble that should have been, and could easily have been, eliminated.

6. *Size of Sample—Continued*

To summarize, we may say that the answer to the question as to size of sample depends first of all upon whether or not we can assume that the product is controlled. However, to determine whether or not the product is controlled, it is necessary to use the sampling process after the manner discussed in detail in Part VI. The answer to the question—How large a sample? depends upon the following five important things considered in that chapter:

A. Ability of engineer to divide data into objective rational subgroups.
B. Choice of statistics.
C. Choice of limits for statistics.
D. Choice of method of using statistics.
E. The way control is specified.

Illustrative examples showing the importance of each of these five factors have already been considered in Part VI. It may be of interest, however, to give one more illustration here to show the importance of choosing the right statistic in detecting lack of control.

Fig. 145-*a* shows the observed fraction defective in a certain kind of apparatus over a period of ten months. Beginning about April, the rejections for this kind of apparatus became excessive. It is of interest, therefore, to see how this trouble could have been detected through the use of a control chart on fraction defective. Such a chart (Criterion I, Part VI) is shown

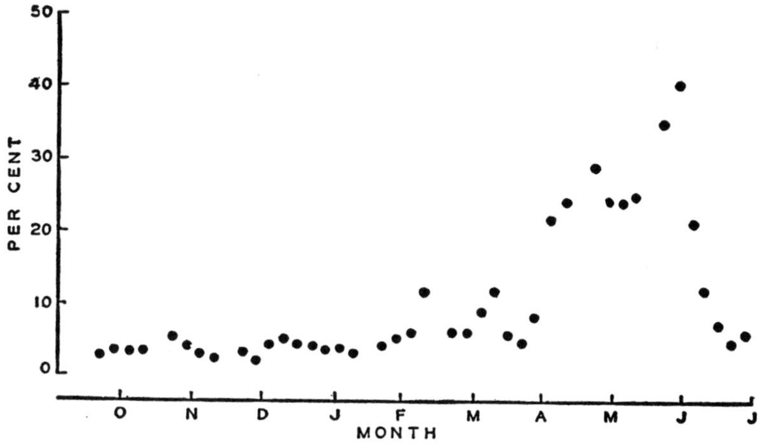

FIG. 145-*a*.—WHEN DID TROUBLE ENTER?

in Fig. 145-*b*. An indication of the presence of assignable causes of variation is given by this chart eight weeks in advance. Investigation revealed that it was very likely that the assignable cause at this particular time was the same as that found to have

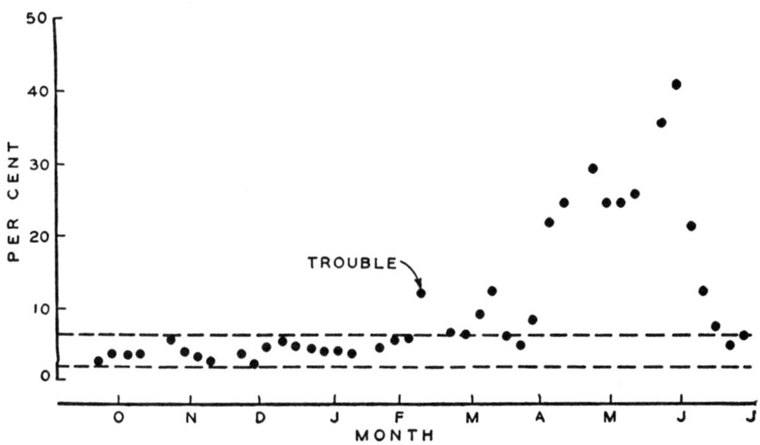

FIG. 145-*b*.—EVEN AN INEFFICIENT CONTROL CHART CAUGHT TROUBLE EIGHT WEEKS IN ADVANCE.

caused the trouble beginning about the second week in April.

As shown in Parts V and VI, the average is usually a much more sensitive detector of assignable causes than is the fraction defective. It so happened that the quality of a few instruments of this particular kind had been measured as a variable each week over this same period. Applying Criterion I to these data, we get the results shown in Fig. 145-*c*. Evidence

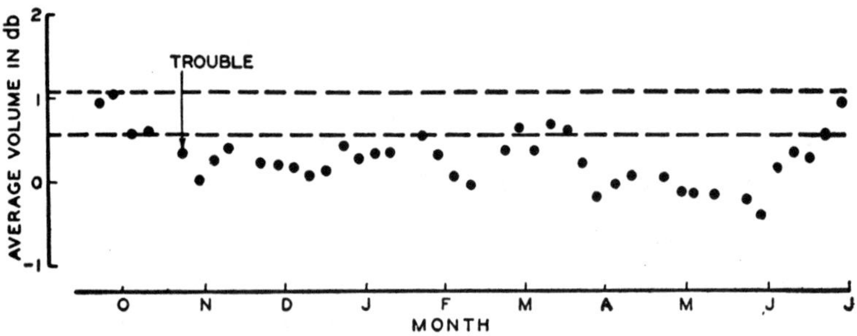

FIG. 145-*c*.—EFFICIENT CONTROL CHART CAUGHT THE TROUBLE SIXTEEN WEEKS IN ADVANCE.

of lack of control is given by this chart sixteen weeks prior to that given by Fig. 145-*b*.

Such results are typical of those experienced every day in the analysis of inspection data to detect lack of control.

Having assured ourselves that the product is controlled about a certain level of quality, it may be desirable in some instances to set up sampling limits to give a certain assurance that the quality in a given lot meets certain limits. From what has been said in previous sections, it appears, however, that the size of sample required to give the desired assurance depends upon the following factors:

a. Kind of risk.
b. Magnitude of risk.
c. Kind of sampling scheme.
d. Kind of specification.
e. Previous information as to the quality of product.

Obviously, therefore, the answer to the question—How large a sample?—even when product is controlled—depends upon several factors. Of course, the need for protective sampling schemes is very much reduced when we have the assurance that quality is being controlled.

7. *Size of Sample—Continued*

To emphasize the importance of the conclusions stated in the previous section, let us consider very briefly four typical problems.

A. Quite recently, the head of a large organization interested in the production of linseed oil raised the following question. Three shiploads of flaxseed constituting a lot of approximately 65,000 bushels had been received. A test sample for chemical analysis had been taken from each shipload, the manner of taking being unknown. An order had been accepted for several thousand dollars' worth of oil at a price based upon the results found in the sample. When sufficient oil to fill the order was extracted from a portion of the flaxseed, it was found that the average oil content was so much less than that of the sample that the producer suffered considerable loss. The question asked was: How many samples should be taken under similar circumstances in the future in order to prevent the recurrence of such loss?

If we turn to almost any book on the specification of properties of materials for design purposes, we shall find problems of which the following three are typical.

B. Given the observed distribution, Table 55, of resistance of a sample of 904 pieces of a given kind of apparatus, what is the tolerance limit X_2 that will not be exceeded more than, let us say, 0.5 per cent of the time?

C. The tensile strength of Code A wire shall not be less than 21,000 pounds per square inch. How many samples shall be taken in order to insure that the specification is being met on a carload lot?

D. Fig. 146 shows a typical cross section of a coating material. One of the specification requirements is that this coating shall have an average weight between twenty-five and fifty milligrams per square inch. The question is: How shall we sample this product to insure that this quality specification is being met?

TABLE 55.—HOW SHOULD WE CALCULATE TOLERANCE LIMITS?

Resistance in Ohms	Number of Pieces	Resistance in Ohms	Number of Pieces
31.25	2	51.25	30
33.75	3	53.75	30
36.25	37	56.25	10
38.75	99	58.75	11
41.25	189	61.25	9
43.75	228	63.75	3
46.25	175	66.25	1
48.75	76	76.25	1

It follows from what was said in the previous section that we cannot give definite answers to these questions in their present form. It will be noted that in no case are we justified in assuming that the material is controlled upon the basis of

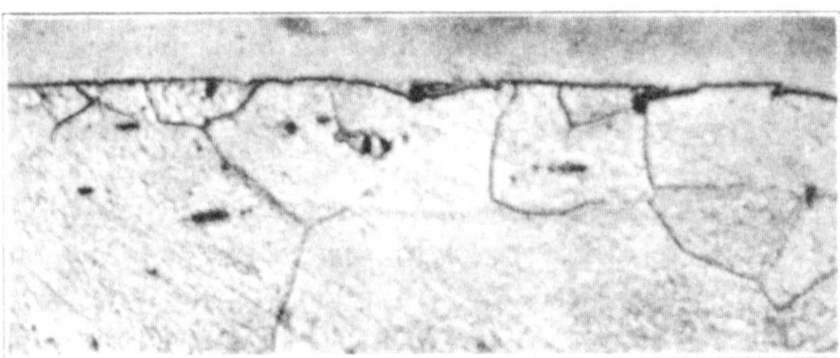

FIG. 146.—TYPICAL CROSS SECTION OF A PROTECTIVE COATING—NOTE IRREGULAR LINE OF DEMARKATION BETWEEN COATING AND METAL.

the information given. On the contrary, questioning revealed in each of these typical cases that *a priori* there were good grounds for the belief that the quality was not controlled. In not one of the four cases did the engineer proposing the problem know what assignable causes were likely to influence the particular set of data giving rise to the question.

Without this kind of information, any answer to the question —How large a sample?—is likely to be greatly in error because, as we have seen, the presence of unknown assignable causes may play havoc with the conclusions derived upon the basis of any sampling scheme which tacitly assumes, as it must, that the sample is random or, in other words, that it has come from a controlled system of chance causes. Before any one of the four questions previously proposed can be given a reasonable answer, it is therefore necessary to know whether or not we are justified in assuming control, and if control cannot be assumed, it is necessary that we employ the sampling scheme that will make the best use of *a priori* knowledge of assignable causes.

8. *Sampling in Relation to Specification of Quality*

In Part V the advantages of specifying control of quality were considered in some detail. It was pointed out that wherever possible we should specify the average $\bar{X}$ and standard deviation σ of the objective distribution of control. It is of interest to note that we are led to this same conclusion from the viewpoint of sampling theory because, strictly speaking, it is only under the condition of control that we have a basis for interpreting samples.

CHAPTER XXV

The Control Program

1. *Résumé*

Five important economic reasons for controlling the quality of manufactured product were considered in Part I. In Chapter XXI of Part VI, we saw that, from the viewpoint of consumer protection, it is also advantageous to have attained the state of control. If only to assure the satisfactory nature of quality of product which cannot be given 100 per cent inspection, the need for control would doubtless be admitted.

In a very general sense, we have seen that the scientific interpretation and use of data depend to a large extent upon whether or not the data satisfy the condition of control (58). The statistical nature of things and of relationships or natural laws puts in the foreground this concept of distribution of effects of a constant system of chance causes. For this reason, it is important to divide all data into rational subgroups in the sense that the data belonging to a group are supposed to have come from a constant system of chance causes.

We have considered briefly the application of five important criteria to check our judgment in such cases. We have seen, however, that such tests do not take the place of, but rather supplement, the inherent ability of the individual engineer to divide the data into rational subgroups. Thus we see clearly how statistical theory serves the engineer as a tool.

2. *Control in Research*

Since observed physical quantities are, in the last analysis, statistical in nature, it is desirable that the results of research be presented in a form easily interpreted in terms of frequency distributions. As a specific instance, the design engineer must depend upon the results of research to give him a basis for establishing the requisite standard of quality characterized, as we have seen in Part V, by the arithmetic mean $\bar{\mathbf{X}}$ and the standard deviation σ of a controlled quality X.

Naturally the research engineer is always interested in detecting and eliminating causes of variability which need not be left to chance. Hence the criteria previously discussed often become of great assistance as is shown in Part VI. The data of research are good or bad, depending upon whether or not assignable causes of variability have been eliminated. In most instances the data which have been divided into rational subgroups can best be summarized by recording the average, standard deviation, and sample size for each subgroup.

3. *Control in Design*

Our discussion of this phase of the subject in Part V indicated the advantages to be derived through specification of the condition of control in terms of the arithmetic mean $\bar{\mathbf{X}}$ and standard deviation σ of any prescribed quality characteristic X.

4. *Control in Development*

From the results of measurements of quality on tool-made samples supposedly produced under essentially the same conditions, we may attain tentative standards of quality expressible in terms of averages and standard deviations. These tentative standards may then be used as a basis for the construction of control charts in accord with Criterion I for the purpose of detecting and eliminating assignable differences of quality between tool-made samples and those produced under shop conditions.

5. *Control in Commercial Production*

It is obviously desirable that a method of detecting lack of control be such that it indicates the presence of assignable causes of variability before these causes have had time to affect a large per cent of the product. For this reason, the method to be used on the job should involve a minimum number of computations. Here again Criterion I usually proves satisfactory.

6. *Control in the Purchase of Raw Material*

As is to be expected, a prevalent source of lack of control is selection of raw material. It is not necessary that the different sources of material come from what could be considered to be the same constant cause system, but it is desirable that each source of a given material be controlled within itself. As an example, a physical property such as the tensile strength of a given species of timber may be assignably different for different sections of the country although within one section

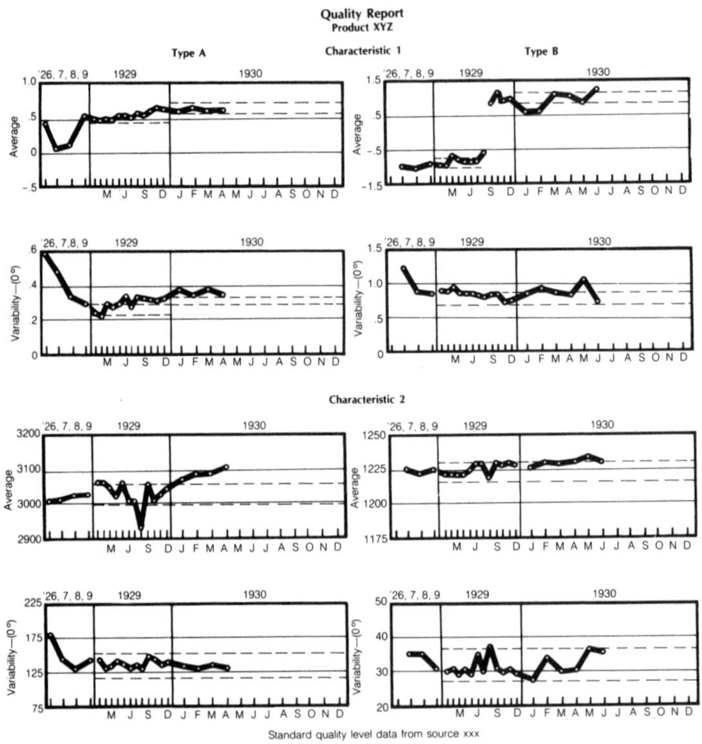

Fig. 147.

TABLE 56.—SCHEMATIC FORM OF SUMMARY QUALITY CONTROL REPORT

Quality	Quality Indication		Nature of Cause	Action Taken or Called for
	Controlled	Not Controlled		
X_1	√			
X_2		√	New source of raw material.	No other source of raw material available. Nothing can be done unless we change the kind of raw material called for in the design specification.
X_3		√	Raw material comes from sources assignably different.	Should secure material only from sources A, B, and C.
X_4		√	Poor assembly occasioned by new operators.	Source of trouble eliminated.
X_5		√	Unknown.	Further investigation under way.
X_6		√	Low insulation caused by improper washing of insulation material before assembly.	Source of trouble eliminated.
.....	.....	......	....	....
.....	.....	......	....	....
X_m	.....	......	....	....

this variability may be such as to be attributable to a constant system of causes. In the same way, we may have sources of supply of piece-parts produced by different units of an organization or different manufacturers wherein there are assignable differences between the product coming from different sources even though each source represents a controlled product in itself. Such a condition can easily be taken care of in the use of the material, since the object of securing control from a design viewpoint is, as we have seen, the prediction of variability in the finished product.

7. *Quality Control Report*

The quality report should, in general, do two things:

a. Indicate the presence of assignable causes of variation in each of the quality characteristics,

b. Indicate the seriousness of the trouble and the steps that have been taken to eliminate it.

Fig. 147 is a page from a typical quality report which fulfills the first requirement. Information similar to that shown schematically in Table 56 meets the second requirement.

Appendices

APPENDIX I

Resultant Effects of Constant Cause Systems

1. *Introductory Remarks*

Our discussion of the problem of establishing the necessary and sufficient conditions for maximum control was based upon the following three assumptions:

A. The resultant effect X of the operation of the m causes is the sum of the effects of the separate causes.

B. The number m of causes is large.

C. The effect of any one cause is finite and is not greater than the resultant effect of all the others.

It was stated that under these conditions the distribution of resultant effects of a cause system approached normality as the number m of causes was increased indefinitely, at least in the sense that the skewness $\sqrt{\beta_{1\Sigma X}}$ and the flatness $\beta_{2\Sigma X}$ of this distribution approach 0 and 3 respectively. We shall now consider the basis for this statement in more detail.

To start with it will be found helpful in trying to get an appreciation of the significance of the three limitations to carry through the details of finding the distribution of resultant effects of a few simple systems. For this purpose we shall consider eight such systems characterized as follows:

$$\text{(a)}\begin{cases} m = 5 \\ x: \quad 0\ 1;\quad 0\ 1;\quad 0\ 1;\quad 0\ 1;\quad 0\ 1. \\ \mathbf{p}: \quad \frac{5}{6}\ \frac{1}{6};\quad \frac{5}{6}\ \frac{1}{6};\quad \frac{5}{6}\ \frac{1}{6};\quad \frac{5}{6}\ \frac{1}{6};\quad \frac{5}{6}\ \frac{1}{6}. \end{cases}$$

$$\text{(b)}\begin{cases} m = 5 \\ x: \quad 0\ 1;\quad 0\ 2;\quad 0\ 3;\quad 0\ 4;\quad 0\ 5. \\ \mathbf{p}: \quad \frac{1}{6}\ \frac{5}{6};\quad \frac{2}{6}\ \frac{4}{6};\quad \frac{3}{6}\ \frac{3}{6};\quad \frac{4}{6}\ \frac{2}{6};\quad \frac{5}{6}\ \frac{1}{6}. \end{cases}$$

(c) $\begin{cases} m = 5 \\ x: \quad 0\ 1;\ \ 0\ 2;\ \ 0\ 3;\ \ 0\ 4;\ \ 0\ 5. \\ p: \quad \frac{5}{6}\ \frac{1}{6};\ \frac{5}{6}\ \frac{1}{6};\ \frac{5}{6}\ \frac{1}{6};\ \frac{5}{6}\ \frac{1}{6};\ \frac{5}{6}\ \frac{1}{6}. \end{cases}$

(d) $\begin{cases} m = 7 \\ x: \quad 0\ 1;\ \ 0\ 2;\ \ 0\ 3;\ \ 0\ 4;\ \ 0\ 5;\ \ 0\ 6;\ \ 0\ 7. \\ p: \quad \frac{5}{6}\ \frac{1}{6};\ \frac{5}{6}\ \frac{1}{6};\ \frac{5}{6}\ \frac{1}{6};\ \frac{5}{6}\ \frac{1}{6};\ \frac{5}{6}\ \frac{1}{6};\ \frac{5}{6}\ \frac{1}{6};\ \frac{5}{6}\ \frac{1}{6}. \end{cases}$

(e) $\begin{cases} m = 10 \\ x: \quad 0\ 1;\ \ 0\ 2;\ \ 0\ 3;\ \ 0\ 4;\ \ 0\ 5;\ \ 0\ 6;\ \ 0\ 7;\ \ 0\ 8;\ \ 0\ 9;\ \ 0\ 10. \\ p: \quad \frac{5}{6}\ \frac{1}{6};\ \frac{5}{6}\ \frac{1}{6};\ \frac{5}{6}\ \frac{1}{6};\ \frac{5}{6}\ \frac{1}{6};\ \frac{5}{6}\ \frac{1}{6};\ \frac{5}{6}\ \frac{1}{6};\ \frac{5}{6}\ \frac{1}{6};\ \frac{5}{6}\ \frac{1}{6};\ \frac{5}{6}\ \frac{1}{6};\ \frac{5}{6}\ \frac{1}{6}. \end{cases}$

(f) $\begin{cases} m = 5 \\ x: \quad 0\ 1;\ \ 0\ 1;\ \ 0\ 1;\ \ 0\ 1;\ \ 0\ 1. \\ p: \quad \frac{5}{6}\ \frac{1}{6};\ \frac{4}{6}\ \frac{2}{6};\ \frac{3}{6}\ \frac{3}{6};\ \frac{2}{6}\ \frac{4}{6};\ \frac{1}{6}\ \frac{5}{6}. \end{cases}$

(g) $\begin{cases} m = 6 \\ x: \quad 0\ 1;\ \ 0\ 2;\ \ 0\ 4;\ \ 0\ 4;\ \ 0\ 2;\ \ 0\ 1. \\ p: \quad \frac{1}{2}\ \frac{1}{2};\ \frac{1}{2}\ \frac{1}{2};\ \frac{1}{2}\ \frac{1}{2};\ \frac{1}{2}\ \frac{1}{2};\ \frac{1}{2}\ \frac{1}{2};\ \frac{1}{2}\ \frac{1}{2}. \end{cases}$

(h) $\begin{cases} m = 5 \\ x: \quad 0\ 1;\ \ 0\ 2;\ \ 0\ 4;\ \ 0\ 8;\ \ 0\ 16. \\ p: \quad \frac{1}{2}\ \frac{1}{2};\ \frac{1}{2}\ \frac{1}{2};\ \frac{1}{2}\ \frac{1}{2};\ \frac{1}{2}\ \frac{1}{2};\ \frac{1}{2}\ \frac{1}{2}. \end{cases}$

The notation used in describing the cause systems can be made clear by considering only the first one. Here we have a system of $m = 5$ causes. Each of these five causes may produce an effect of either 0 or 1. For each cause the probability of zero effect is $\frac{5}{6}$ and that of unit effect is $\frac{1}{6}$.

Using this cause system we may illustrate the method of finding the distribution of resultant effects. Obviously the magnitude of this effect may take on values 0, 1, 2, 3, 4, 5. The probability that the resultant effect will be zero is the compound probability of each component cause producing zero effect or $(\frac{5}{6})^5$. In a similar way the probabilities of getting a resultant effect equal to 1, 2, 3, 4, or 5 are respectively $5(\frac{1}{6})(\frac{5}{6})^4$, $10(\frac{1}{6})^2(\frac{5}{6})^3$, $10(\frac{1}{6})^3(\frac{5}{6})^2$, $5(\frac{1}{6})^4(\frac{5}{6})^1$, and $(\frac{1}{6})^5$. In this way we get the following distribution:

Resultant Effect X	0	1	2	3	4	5
Probability	0.401878	0.401878	0.160751	0.032150	0.003215	0.000129

This is shown graphically in Fig. 1-*a*. The distributions of the resultant effects of the seven other systems are also shown in Fig. 1. What significance do these results have?

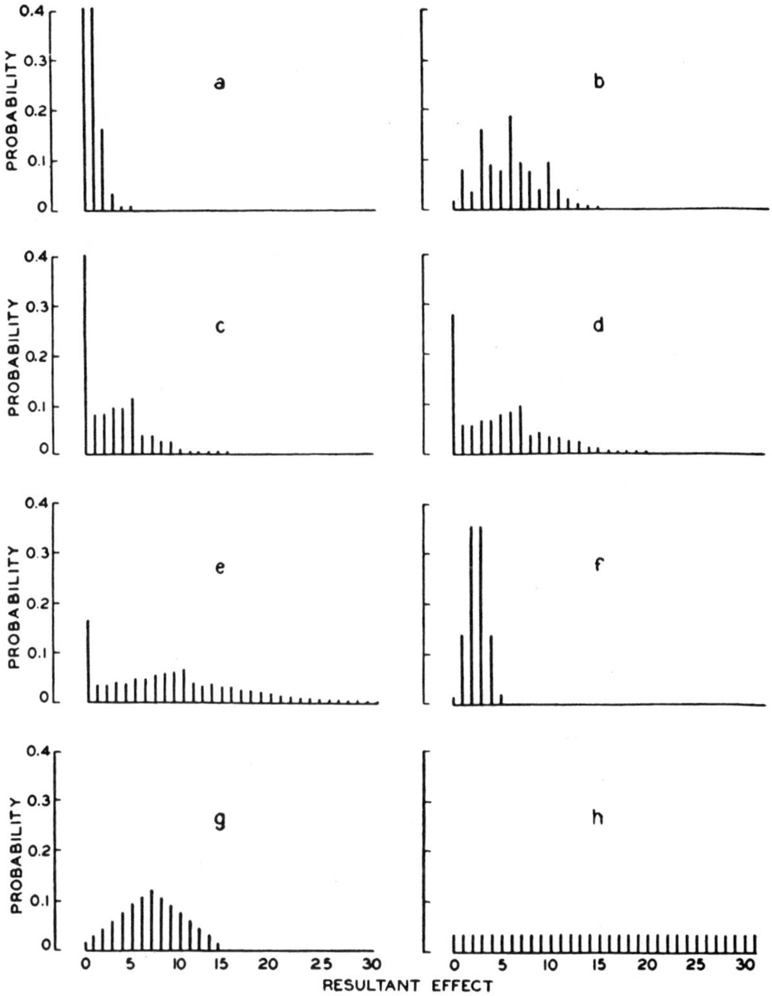

FIG. 1.—DISTRIBUTION OF RESULTANT EFFECTS OF SIMPLE CAUSE SYSTEMS.

In the first case we see that the distribution of resultant effects will always be characterized by the point binomial. Hence it will always monotonically decrease on either side of the mode—in other words, it is a *smooth* distribution. Distributions *b*, *c*, *d*, and *e* indicate the effect of lack of uniformity among the component causes. From this viewpoint smoothness is a necessary condition. That it is not, however, a sufficient condition is evidenced by systems *f*, *g*, and *h*.

As long as the component causes are the same, we have already seen (Fig. 53) that the distribution of resultant effects approaches normality as the number of causes is increased. The condition that there shall be an indefinitely large number of causes is, however, certainly not sufficient as is shown by systems *g* and *h*, for in these cases the shapes of the distributions will always be those shown in Fig. 1-*g* and *h*. Of course, if we admit that the effect of any cause must be finite, systems such as *g* and *h* with an indefinitely large number *m* of causes are ruled out.

2. *Practical Significance of Results*

In practice one is confronted with an observed distribution and from its nature must often decide whether or not it is worth while looking for assignable causes of either Type I or Type II. We shall concern ourselves here only with the problem of deciding whether or not an observed distribution

TABLE 1.—THERMAL UNITS PER CU. FT. OF GAS

1,391	1,318	1,203	1,291
1,416	1,268	1,380	1,273
1,367	1,294	1,349	1,242
1,258	1,368	1,360	1,231
1,289	1,330	1,313	1,320
1,199	1,254	1,351	1,340
1,275	1,226	1,289	1,420

gives evidence of the presence of a predominating cause, that is, an assignable cause of Type II.

Let us consider a typical problem. The operation data for a certain gas plant for one month expressed in terms of arbitrary thermal units per cubic foot of gas produced from oil by cracking are those given below in Table 1. The data are tabulated in the order in which they were taken. Ideal operation calls for as high and as nearly constant value as can economically be attained.

The following question was raised by the Director of Research of the large organization interested in these results:

> If I understand the methods of statistics correctly, it should be possible to determine from these data whether or not there is a predominating cause of variation, and hence to determine whether or not it should be reasonable to expect that a marked improvement in product can be made by controlling one or at least a few causes of variation. Am I right in this interpretation of the possibilities of statistical methods?

In answer to such a question we can at least say something like the following. If we divide the data into subgroups of four in the order in which they were taken and apply Criterion I of Part VI, we get no evidence of lack of control, as may easily be verified by the reader. Assuming that the quality is controlled, we may now consider the evidence for the presence of a predominating effect. An examination of these data shows that they are more or less uniformly distributed over the range of variation as one might expect with a cause system such as (*h*). In other words, the observed results are consistent with the hypothesis that a predominating cause was present. Needless to say such evidence is not conclusive: it is suggestive.

3. *Analytical Results*

Let us now find expressions for the skewness $\sqrt{\beta_{1\Sigma X}}$ and flatness $\beta_{2\Sigma X}$ of the distribution of resultant effects under simplifying assumptions.

If we let μ_{i_j} represent the *i*th moment of the effects of the *j*th cause about their expected value, it may be shown [1] that

$$\sigma^2 = \mu_2 = \sigma_1^2 + \sigma_2^2 + \ldots + \sigma_j^2 + \ldots + \sigma_m^2,$$

$$\mu_3 = \mu_{3_1} + \mu_{3_2} + \ldots + \mu_{3_j} + \ldots + \mu_{3_m},$$

and

$$\mu_4 = \sum_{j=1}^{m} (\mu_{4_j} - 3\sigma_j^4) + 3\mu_2^2,$$

[1] See for example *Elements of Statistics*, by A. L. Bowley, published by P. S. King & Son, Ltd., 1920, pp. 291–292.

where μ_i is the ith moment of the resultant effect of the m causes about the expected value of the resultant effect.

From these results we get

$$\beta_{1_{\Sigma X}} = \frac{\mu_3^2}{\mu_2^3} = \frac{\left(\sum_{j=1}^{m} \mu_{3j}\right)^2}{\mu_2^3} \tag{1}$$

and

$$\beta_{2_{\Sigma X}} = \frac{\mu_4}{\mu_2^2} = \frac{\sum_{j=1}^{m} (\mu_{4j} - 3\sigma_j^4) + 3\mu_2^2}{\mu_2^2} = \frac{\sum_{j=1}^{m} (\mu_{4j} - 3\sigma_j^4)}{\mu_2^2} + 3. \tag{2}$$

As a simple case let us assume that the distribution of effects of $(m - 1)$ of the component causes are the same, at least in respect to their second, third and fourth moments, all of which are assumed to be finite, which we shall denote by $\mathbf{M}_2$, $\mathbf{M}_3$, and $\mathbf{M}_4$. Let us assume that the remaining cause is predominating in the sense that the corresponding three moments of its effects are $b_2\mathbf{M}_2$, $b_3\mathbf{M}_3$, and $b_4\mathbf{M}_4$, where b_2, b_3, and b_4 are all positive and greater than unity. Under these conditions, we get

$$\beta_{1_{\Sigma X}} = \frac{(m - 1 + b_3)^2}{(m - 1 + b_2)^3} \frac{\mathbf{M}_3^2}{\mathbf{M}_2^3}$$

and

$$\beta_{2_{\Sigma X}} = \frac{(m - 1 + b_4)\mathbf{M}_4 - 3(m - 1 + b_2^2)\mathbf{M}_2^2}{(m - 1 + b_2)^2\mathbf{M}_2^2} + 3.$$

Evidently these two expressions approach 0 and 3 respectively as the number m of causes becomes indefinitely large, assuming that b_2, b_3, and b_4 are finite. In this way we come to see that the skewness and flatness of a distribution of resultant effects will, in general, be approximately 0 and 3 if the number m of causes is *very* large.

4. *Economic Significance of Control from a Design Viewpoint*

In Chapter III of Part I we called attention to the fact that as a result of control we attain maximum benefits from quantity production. Only general statements as to obtaining these benefits were given at that time. In Part III, however, we developed the theoretical basis for control, making it now possible to show specifically how control enables us to attain these benefits. We shall consider here only the simplest kind of examples.

A. *Example 1.*—Suppose that an assembly is to be made in which two washers are to be used, one brass and the other mica. Assume that it is desirable to maintain as closely as possible a uniform overall thickness of these two washers. This could be done, of course, by selecting the pairs of brass and mica washers to give the desired thickness. Such a process, however, would tend to counterbalance the benefits of quantity production, since the economies rising from assembly processes result from interchangeability of piece-parts.

Table 2 gives the results of measurements of thickness on one hundred tool-made samples each of mica and brass washers to be used in the manner previously indicated in the assembly of an important piece of telephone equipment. The reader may easily satisfy himself that both of these distributions are sufficiently near normal to indicate that each of the piece-parts was controlled, and we shall therefore assume this to be the case. For this size of sample we are perhaps justified in assuming that the observed standard deviations of these two distributions may reasonably be taken as the standard deviations σ_1 and σ_2 of the objective controlled distributions of mica and brass washers respectively. The theory of the previous section shows that under these conditions the standard deviation of a random assembly of two washers, one of each kind, is

$$\sigma = \sqrt{\sigma_1{}^2 + \sigma_2{}^2}.$$

Furthermore, it follows that the distribution of the sum of the thickness in such a random assembly will be normally distributed about a mean value which is the sum of the mean values of the two objective distributions.

Upon this basis, therefore, the design engineer is justified

TABLE 2.—TYPICAL DISTRIBUTION REQUISITE FOR EFFICIENT DESIGN

Thickness of Mica in Inches	Number of Washers	Thickness of Brass in Inches	Number of Washers
0.0088	1	0.0182	1
0.0089	1	0.0185	1
0.0092	1	0.0186	2
0.0093	1	0.0187	2
0.0094	1	0.0188	2
0.0095	1	0.0190	2
0.0098	2	0.0191	3
0.0099	1	0.0192	3
0.0100	2	0.0193	3
0.0101	5	0.0195	5
0.0102	2	0.0196	6
0.0103	3	0.0197	5
0.0104	7	0.0198	4
0.0105	5	0.0199	1
0.0106	8	0.0200	3
0.0107	10	0.0201	8
0.0108	10	0.0202	4
0.0109	7	0.0203	5
0.0110	5	0.0204	7
0.0111	3	0.0205	4
0.0112	5	0.0206	3
0.0113	6	0.0207	3
0.0114	6	0.0208	6
0.0115	3	0.0210	3
0.0116	3	0.0211	1
0.0119	1	0.0212	1
		0.0213	3
		0.0214	2
		0.0215	3
		0.0216	2
		0.0220	1
		0.0222	1

in predicting that the overall thickness of random assemblies of mica and brass washers will be distributed as shown in Fig. 2. The dots in this figure show how closely the first one hundred assemblies made from manufactured product check the prediction. Furthermore, if the observed average thickness of each distribution is taken as the expected value of the distribution, the design engineer can easily calculate the percentage of assemblies that will be defective in respect to overall thickness subject to the assumptions that have been made.

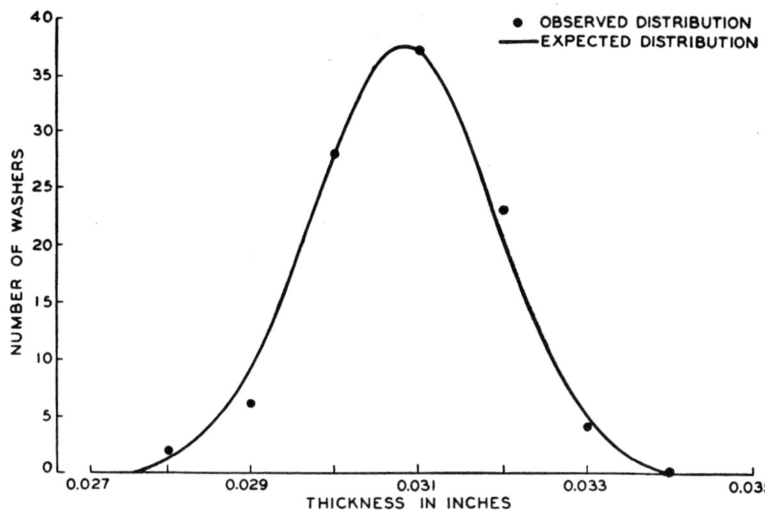

FIG. 2.—STATISTICAL METHOD MAKES PREDICTION IN DESIGN POSSIBLE.

B. *Example 2.*—For a shaft to operate in a bearing it is, of course, necessary to have a certain clearance. Thus, if ρ_1 and ρ_2 represent the radii of the bearing and shaft respectively, then the specification will, in general, state that the difference $\rho_1 - \rho_2$ must satisfy the inequality

$$d_1 \leq \rho_1 - \rho_2 \leq d_2,$$

where d_1 and d_2 are both positive. This situation is represented schematically in Fig. 3.

In most instances the shaft and bearing are fitted. Sometimes, however, it is of economic importance to be able to product shafts and bearings separately and to assemble these on the job. The question, of course, that is always raised is: What will be the expected rejection of such assemblies because of failure to satisfy the clearance specification?

From the theory of the previous section we see that this question can be answered readily, at least if we assume that radii of bearings and shafts are normally controlled with standard deviations σ_1 and σ_2 respectively. Under these conditions the difference $\rho_1 - \rho_2$ between any bearing and shaft chosen at random will be distributed normally about a mean value $\bar{\rho}_1 - \bar{\rho}_2$ with standard deviation

$$\sigma = \sqrt{\sigma_1^2 + \sigma_2^2}.$$

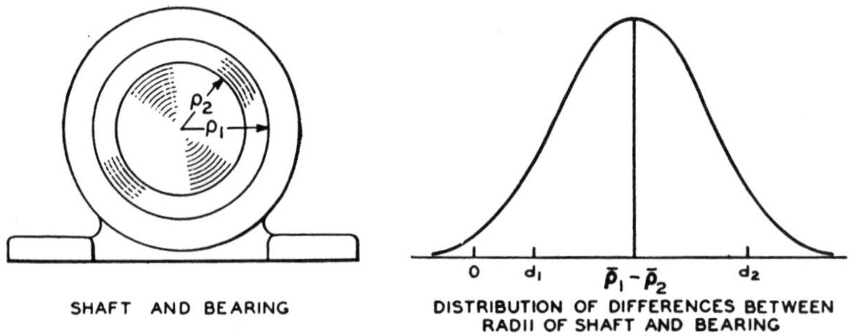

FIG. 3.—HOW MANY REJECTIONS SHOULD WE EXPECT IN ASSEMBLY?

Hence, the probability of a random assembly being rejected because the clearance fails to come within the required limits is given by

$$1 - \int_{z_1}^{z_2} \frac{1}{\sqrt{2\pi}} e^{-z^2/2} dz,$$

where

$$z = \frac{(\rho_1 - \rho_2) - (\bar{\rho}_1 - \bar{\rho}_2)}{\sigma}$$

$$z_1 = \frac{d_1 - (\bar{\rho}_1 - \bar{\rho}_2)}{\sigma}$$

$$z_2 = \frac{d_2 - (\bar{\rho}_1 - \bar{\rho}_2)}{\sigma},$$

and the value of the integral can be read directly from Table A.

C. *Example 3.*—We shall now consider a problem involving maximum control. Many instances arise in production where materials must be covered with protective coatings. Of such are the various kinds of platings, nickel, chromium, zinc, etc. In other instances we have coatings of paper or lead.

In practically every instance of this kind it is very desirable to maintain a uniform coating that is never less in thickness than some prescribed value. It is obviously desirable from the viewpoint of saving to reduce the variability to a minimum. Table 3 gives an observed distribution of one such kind of

TABLE 3.—DO THE VARIATIONS IN THICKNESS INDICATE A POSSIBLE SAVING?

Thickness in Inches	Number of Observations	Thickness in Inches	Number of Observations
0.125	2	0.131	20
0.126	12	0.132	5
0.127	21	0.133	3
0.128	18	0.134	0
0.129	33	0.135	3
0.130	33		

coating supposed always to be more than 0.124 inch in thickness. The histogram in Fig. 4 shows this distribution. What

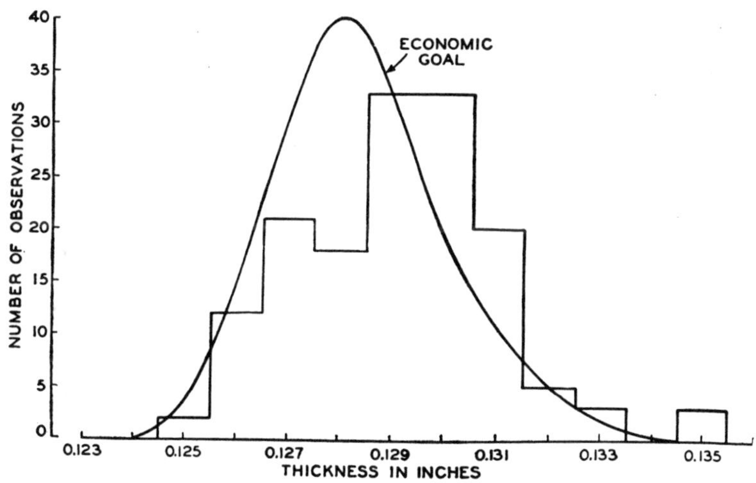

FIG. 4.—HOW MAXIMUM CONTROL SAVES MONEY.

does the theory of maximum control tell us about the uniformity of coating? In the light of the previous section the lack of smoothness in this distribution is indicative of the presence of assignable causes of variation which can be removed. In fact, an investigation revealed assignable causes of variation, and on removing these, the resulting quality approached the distribution shown by the smooth curve of Fig. 4, representing the state of maximum control for this particular kind of coating. By attaining this state of maximum control, it is apparent that the average thickness of coating is materially reduced without increasing the probability of obtaining a defective thickness.

Not only does control lead to a saving of material in such cases but it also leads to a more uniform product because as shown in Chapter XXIV of Part VII, it is practically impossible to sample for protective purposes unless the quality is controlled.

APPENDIX II

Presentation of Original Experimental Results Useful in Obtaining an Understanding of the Fundamental Principles Underlying the Theory of Quality Control

The six tables in this appendix give in detail the results of 4,000 drawings from each of the three experimental universes referred to in the text. Tables A, B, and C give the original drawings divided into groups of four in the order in which they occurred. Tables D, E, and F give various statistics for these samples of four. It should not be inferred that these statistics are arranged to correspond to the samples as this is not always the case. We have made extensive use of these data in our discussions of the theory of quality control, and it is advisable to reproduce these data if for no other reason than that the reader may wish to carry out for himself computations similar to those referred to throughout the text.

There is, however, a far more important reason for presenting these experimental results. It will have become apparent by this time that statistical theory rests upon a fundamental natural law—the law of large numbers. In the last analysis we must always appeal to experimental evidence to justify our belief in such a law and to give us a feeling for its physical significance. For example, in the discussion of the theory of statistics, we always have to talk about doing something again and again under *the same essential conditions;* or, as we have said, under a controlled condition where the *chance cause system is constant.*

We have used these data in various places throughout the book to illustrate a controlled phenomenon. In particular we

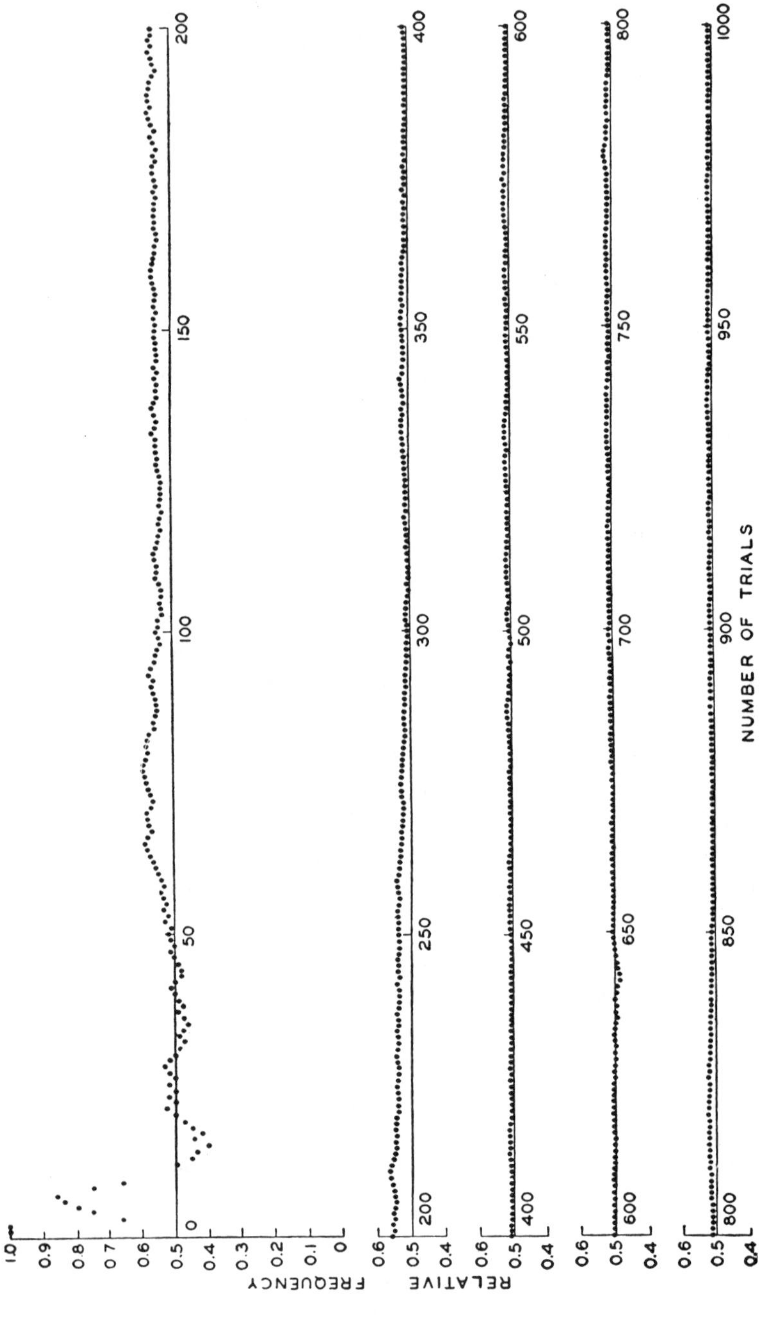

FIG. 1.—STATISTICAL APPROACH TO A LIMIT.

have shown how they can be used in checking the results of the mathematical theory of distribution, and in certain other instances, in indicating the probable character of some distribution function not yet determined *a priori*. Most of this discussion was limited to the statistics of samples of four. Often, of course, we wish to investigate in a similar way the nature of the distribution functions for sample sizes other than four. This can readily be done for the three types of universes through the use of the data in Tables A, B, and C.

These data have been used in many ways other than those mentioned in the text. For example, they have been found to be of great use in the experimental determination of the correlation between the average and range, which correlation is sometimes required in the establishment of an efficient inspection method where it is not feasible for one reason or another to calculate the standard deviation.

In this connection it is perhaps worthwhile to illustrate the use of these data in indicating in a somewhat more concrete manner than was done in the text the nature of the statistical limit involved in the statement of the law of large numbers. For example, suppose we consider a thousand drawings from any one of the universes, let us say the normal one. It will be recalled that half of the 998 chips were of one color [1] and half of another. If we let p represent the ratio of the number of chips observed to be of one color in a series of n drawings to the number n of drawings, then this fraction p should obey the law of large numbers and approach $\frac{1}{2}$ as a statistical limit; that is,

$$\underset{n \to \infty}{Ls}\ p = \tfrac{1}{2}.$$

Fig. 1 shows the statistical approach of the fraction p in one such series of 1,000 drawings.

Obviously, as a result of the first drawing, p will be either zero or unity. In fact, p will continue to remain zero or unity until a chip is drawn which is of a color different from that of

[1] Colors used instead of plus and minus.

the first one drawn. Thereafter p will never become equal to 0 or 1, but will always lie somewhere within this range. In the definition of a statistical limit, it was pointed out that there is no value of n such that for n greater than this value, the absolute value of p always becomes and remains less than some preassigned quantity—characteristics which belong to a mathematical limit.

The experimental results shown in Fig. 1 illustrate how the fraction p oscillates back and forth. A student of the theory of control can well afford to carry out similar tests of this nature until he has gained a clear picture of the significance of the statistical limit.

TABLES

TABLE A—4,000 drawings from a normal universe consisting of 998 approximately identical chips marked as indicated in Table 22 of the text.

TABLE B—4,000 drawings from a rectangular universe of 122 approximately identical chips marked as indicated in Table 28 of the text.

TABLE C—4,000 drawings from a right triangular universe made up of 820 approximately identical chips marked as indicated in Table 28 of the text.

TABLE D—Observed distribution of arithmetic mean $\overline{X}$, median, $\frac{\text{Max.} + \text{Min.}}{2}$, mean deviation μ, standard deviation σ, and ratio $z = \frac{\overline{X}}{\sigma}$ for 1,000 samples of four from the normal universe.

TABLE E—Observed distribution of arithmetic mean $\overline{X}$, standard deviation σ, and ratio $z = \frac{\overline{X}}{\sigma}$ for 1,000 samples of four from the rectangular universe.

TABLE F—Observed distribution of arithmetic mean $\overline{X}$, standard deviation σ, and ratio $z = \frac{\overline{X}}{\sigma}$ for 1,000 samples of four drawn from the right triangular universe.

TABLE A.—DRAWINGS FROM NORMAL UNIVERSE

1.7 .2 1.4 .5	.3 .3 .4 .4	.4 .4 .1 .4	-1.8 -.9 -.6 1.7	.5 -.7 .8 1.0	-1.1 .7 .1 -.3	-.7 1.5 -.4 .7	.3 -1.8 -.1 1.3	-.5 -.8 .7 .3	-.1 .2 0 -1.7	1.0 -1.2 0 -1.9	-.9 -1.2 .6 .4	-.4 .5 .1 -.1	2.2 -.1 -.9 -1.2	-.4 -1.0 0 -1.0	-1.1 -2.9 0 0	-.2 .4 .9 -1.5	-.1 -.5 -.6 0	-.9 .7 .2 -.5	-.6 -.8 -1.4 .5	-.2 .9 -.7 -.9	1.1 .2 1.6 -1.8	-1.6 -.7 1.1 1.2	.2 -.2 1.6 -.3	1.2 .4 -.8 .4
-1.0 .8 -.3 .2	0 -1.6 .7 1.3	-.2 -.1 .2 .5	.5 0 .7 -.4	2.1 -1.7 1.5 2.5	.4 -1.1 -1.9 -1.4	.2 -.2 1.1 1.0	-1.6 .1 -1.0 .5	-.5 1.4 -.1 -.3	-1.2 -.8 -1.0 .3	-.9 .1 .9 -.5	-1.3 1.4 2.4 -1.7	.6 1.8 -1.1 1.1	-.5 .1 .8 0	.5 -.9 -1.0 .4	-.9 -.8 1.4 -1.1	.9 -.8 -.6 -.1	1.0 1.4 -.6 -1.2	-.7 -.5 1.6 -.1	-.7 .7 1.4 .4	.6 2.2 0 -.2	.5 -.7 -1.9 -2.5	.3 -1.5 1.0 -.1	-1.2 0 -.8 -.5	-.7 0 -1.0 -1.1
-2.3 .2 .6 .8	-.1 0 .9 .1	.6 -1.8 .4 -.5	.6 .7 .9 .2	.8 -2.1 -.5 .9	-1.9 1.4 -.1 -.1	.1 -1.2 .1 -.5	-.8 1.7 -1.8 -.3	-.1 -.6 .2 1.4	1.2 -.4 .2 -.3	-.1 1.0 1.3 -.1	-.7 -.8 -.7 .9	.4 -.3 2.2 -.2	-.3 1.0 -.7 -.6	.4 .8 -1.4 -.2	.9 -1.1 .9 .2	1.2 -.5 -.5 1.2	0 -.5 .8 .9	1.3 -.8 -2.0 -.2	-1.3 .1 -2.0 -1.4	1.0 1.9 .8 .7	-.8 .9 -.4 -1.2	0 .6 .4 -1.2	1.1 .7 -.3 .2	-2.5 -1.0 1.3 -.4
.8 -.4 .8 -.5	-.3 .8 1.0 .3	-1.0 -.7 -.2 .5	-.1 -.1 .4 -.1	-.5 .5 .7 1.2	1.2 2.9 .8 -.2	-.6 .2 -.8 -.8	.8 1.0 .1 2.2	-.8 2.2 .3 -.3	1.6 .2 -1.0 2.0	-.3 -.1 -.6 -1.5	.1 -.4 .4 .5	.2 1.6 0 .2	.5 -1.0 .4 1.6	2.5 -.5 .3 2.4	-.8 1.6 2.2 1.2	-1.6 -.6 -2.8 1.3	.6 2.2 -1.1 2.0	-.1 -.9 -1.3 -2.1	.3 .1 .2 -1.2	2.2 .4 -1.3 -2.5	-.7 1.1 -.9 -.1	-.2 -.8 1.5 -.9	.2 -.3 -1.4 0	-.7 -.7 -.3 .6
.3 -.4 .1 -.2	-.6 2.0 1.5 -.2	.3 -.4 -.1 0	1.2 -.4 1.0 .3	-.5 -1.4 1.4 .9	-1.8 1.5 .6 -.3	.7 -1.1 1.7 -1.6	1.2 2.2 -.6 -.5	-.5 -.9 0 -.9	-1.9 -2.7 -.5 -.1	-1.3 2.3 -2.2 -1.0	1.4 .5 -.7 .9	-.7 .5 .5 1.9	-1.8 .8 .1 .7	2.3 .8 .7 .3	.1 .6 .5 1.6	-.4 -1.0 .0 1.7	-.5 1.4 .4 1.7	-.4 .6 -.7 -1.0	.7 -.1 .6 .1	.4 -.3 1.0 .8	.9 .2 .1 -.2	-.2 1.0 -1.3 -.1	1.8 .4 -.6 -.6	-.3 .4 1.0 -.2
.4 -.9 .6 .5	-.6 -.7 1.0 -.3	1.5 -.6 .3 -.3	.1 -.2 -1.3 .3	0 1.2 -1.0 .2	1.0 .3 -1.9 .8	.7 .2 -1.8 .8	-1.6 .1 -1.5 -2.7	-1.9 -.4 .3 1.2	.5 .2 .8 1.2	0 -1.6 -1.5 .8	-.9 -.3 .6 -.2	-.5 1.1 -1.3 -.4	-1.5 -.8 -.8 -.7	-1.5 .3 -.9 .3	.1 -.4 .9 0	-2.6 -3.0 -.7 .9	.7 -2.2 0 -.7	-1.0 1.7 .7 -.2	-.5 -1.5 .7 -.7	-.2 .7 1.9 .8	0 -.5 -.2 .9	1.3 1.4 1.3 -.8	.5 -1.7 -1.2 -1.3	-.3 -.6 .4 .2
-1.1 -1.1 1.2 -.9	.5 .5 -.2 -.4	.8 .5 -.6 1.0	1.3 -2.6 -.2 -.9	-1.6 .4 -1.0 0	.3 -1.5 0 -1.8	0 -.3 1.0 -.6	-.2 -.1 1.7 1.1	.7 -.4 -.6 -1.6	2.2 -1.6 -1.5 -.2	1.5 -.4 .6 -.7	.6 -.7 -1.5 -1.8	1.1 .2 .3 .3	.1 -.3 -1.1 2.5	1.1 .1 -.6 0	1.9 1.3 -1.1 -.7	-1.2 -.6 -.4 -.1	1.1 .8 -2.0 1.9	.6 -.2 .3 2.1	-.9 .1 -.6 -1.4	1.3 0 -.8 -.1	-.3 1.1 1.2 -.7	.5 -.2 1.1 1.8	1.8 1.7 -.3 1.3	-.1 .4 -.4 .6
-.9 -.3 .6 0	-.4 1.3 .1 -.1	.8 .1 -.3 .8	-.9 -.1 .3 -2.1	-1.0 -1.0 .1 1.4	.3 -.4 .3 1.4	2.0 -1.1 -2.3 .1	.2 -.9 -.2 -.3	.7 -.1 -.3 -.1	-.2 -.7 -.1 -1.8	2.1 .6 1.5 1.1	-1.3 .5 -1.8 -.3	1.1 -1.1 .9 .6	.2 .5 -.6 -.1	.3 .2 .1 .1	1.1 -1.3 1.5 0	.3 -.1 -.8 -1.1	1.0 .6 -1.1 .7	-.5 1.3 1.2 -1.7	1.3 .4 -.3 -1.0	.3 -.6 1.9 -.9	.1 .2 .5 .4	-.9 .3 -.1 1.4	-2.1 3.0 .8 -.1	-1.1 .5 .1 .3
2.0 1.1 -1.8 -.8	-.9 2.0 -.1 .9	.4 .9 .2 .1	-.9 1.0 -1.0 -1.8	-.7 .1 .9 .8	.2 -1.9 .8 -.3	-.7 -1.2 .2 .2	-.8 .2 2.4 1.2	-.5 -.6 0 1.1	1.4 .7 1.7 .6	.4 -.3 1.8 1.1	-1.0 .4 -.6 -.1	-.9 -.2 .3 -.4	-1.4 .5 .2 .5	-1.4 .4 -1.4 1.1	.3 -1.8 -1.0 .6	0 -1.0 -1.0 -.9	.4 -.4 -.1 1.5	-.5 -.6 1.1 .7	-.9 -.5 .5 -.4	-.1 .2 .1 1.0	-.2 -.9 -.6 .1	-.2 -1.0 1.3 -.3	-1.0 -.1 .1 -.2	1.1 -1.9 -.1 1.5
.1 -.3 -.8 .1	.8 .4 1.6 .7	-1.2 1.1 -2.2 -2.0	.5 -.5 .9 1.9	.1 -.7 1.1 -.5	.7 -.4 -1.0 .5	-3.0 1.1 1.0 .7	.4 -1.5 -.1 -.9	.7 -.1 .4 -.6	-1.4 .6 0 -1.7	.7 1.6 .2 -.3	.5 .6 -1.1 2.8	.6 .5 .2 1.0	1.7 -.5 1.3 .2	.8 -.3 1.1 .5	-.2 .3 -.6 -2.0	.1 -1.5 .2 .5	-.2 -.8 -.3 -1.3	.7 -.6 .5 .6	-.6 .8 -1.7 -1.3	.8 1.4 -.5 -1.1	-1.0 -1.0 -.1 .6	.4 -.9 -.2 1.2	1.0 .1 -1.0 .5	1.2 -.7 1.4 .4

-.6	.6	.9	.6	-1.9	1.6	-.2	.9	.7	-.9	.2	.2	.3	-1.9	1.4	1.2	-3.0	.3	-.5	.7	1.4	-.5	-.8	-.7	.1
-1.4	.5	.5	0	.4	-.8	.4	.6	-.2	0	.3	-.8	.7	0	.2	.6	.6	-1.3	-.2	-.4	-.3	.4	-.5	-1.3	.5
-1.4	-.4	0	-.8	-.5	-.6	1.8	0	.5	.3	.2	.7	-.2	-1.1	.5	.7	1.2	-.2	-1.7	.3	-1.4	-1.7	-1.6	-1.2	-1.6
-.8	-.7	.4	-1.4	.3	.3	-1.1	.3	.6	1.6	.9	-.3	2.0	0	.1	-1.1	-.5	-.2	.6	-.4	-.7	.4	0	.8	1.5
.5	0	-.1	-1.0	0	-1.5	.1	.8	1.9	-.5	0	.8	-.3	-.5	1.3	.3	-.4	1.1	-1.8	0	-1.1	.7	2.2	.4	-.7
.5	-.4	-1.1	.7	-.4	-1.0	-.4	-1.1	-.4	-.3	-.7	-1.3	1.5	.1	-.8	-.9	.7	-.2	-.6	-.7	-.1	.7	-1.4	.4	-1.1
-.3	-1.1	-2.7	.6	-.4	.2	1.1	.2	.8	-1.7	.4	-1.1	-.1	1.7	1.7	.6	1.0	1.1	-.4	1.9	-.9	2.9	.1	1.3	-1.4
0	.3	-1.0	-1.0	1.8	.5	-1.2	.3	2.1	2.0	.2	-.4	1.4	.2	.9	.1	-1.2	.9	-.4	.7	.9	.3	1.7	-1.3	.7
-.3	1.7	-1.8	-2.5	2.8	-.2	-.2	-1.2	2.5	.6	0	0	-.5	-1.0	.5	2.0	.3	-1.0	-1.2	-.6	-.6	-2.5	2.5	.7	.5
-1.3	1.0	.5	1.0	-.9	1.3	-.6	-1.0	.8	-.4	.1	0	0	-.1	-.3	.9	2.1	-.7	.4	1.3	1.4	-.2	.8	1.0	.8
0	1.2	.9	-1.2	-.7	-.1	-1.0	-.8	1.3	.6	1.2	.6	-1.1	-1.1	.2	.8	-.1	-.1	-.6	.4	-1.4	1.1	1.6	-1.4	-.6
0	-1.4	.9	2.3	.1	2.1	.4	-1.0	1.0	.5	.3	-.1	-.3	1.1	1.7	-1.1	-.6	.4	-2.2	-1.0	-.7	.6	-.5	-.1	-.6
-.4	.4	-.4	-.3	-.2	1.7	.4	-.3	-2.0	-.9	.5	-.4	.5	1.6	-.3	0	2.2	.1	-.2	1.8	-.2	-1.4	-.6	-1.3	-2.2
.8	-.1	1.2	-1.0	-.7	2.7	-.2	.2	-1.1	.2	1.0	2.3	-.4	.2	-.3	-1.0	.3	2.1	-.4	1.1	1.8	.8	-.4	.3	-1.3
-1.3	-.1	-.3	.8	.5	.4	-.5	-.2	-2.3	.1	-1.0	.6	-.8	0	0	-1.7	1.1	1.2	-.1	-1.8	.1	-2.3	-.1	-.3	0
.3	-.7	-.7	-.2	-.5	.3	.3	1.1	1.9	-.9	-.8	.3	3.0	.8	1.1	1.8	-.7	-.1	1.0	-.4	2.8	0	.2	1.4	.9
.9	-.9	.5	1.8	.1	1.3	.9	-1.3	.6	-.8	1.0	-.6	-.4	-1.1	.8	-1.2	.9	1.0	.1	.4	.6	1.0	1.3	-.4	-1.0
-1.3	.1	-.4	.5	-.2	-.4	-1.0	.8	-1.1	-1.1	-1.9	1.7	-1.0	1.0	.8	-.4	.6	-1.9	-.7	-2.6	.1	-1.0	1.2	-2.0	-.2
-.4	-.4	.3	-1.0	-.4	-1.6	1.9	.8	-.3	-1.1	1.1	.6	-.5	.5	.3	.7	.3	-1.1	0	.5	-1.7	1.6	-.4	-.1	1.1
2.1	.6	-.4	-2.6	1.2	1.7	.2	-.3	.4	1.6	.4	-.1	1.2	-1.2	1.4	-1.8	-1.2	.4	1.5	-.4	1.0	-.6	.1	-.5	.5
.9	-.6	-1.4	1.8	-.6	-.5	-.1	-.1	.9	.6	.3	-1.0	1.4	1.4	.6	2.2	0	.7	-1.5	0	-.7	-1.4	.7	1.4	1.0
.4	.6	-.1	-1.2	-.1	-.8	-.8	2.1	-.1	.9	-.8	.1	-.3	0	-1.1	.6	-.8	-2.4	-.2	-.9	-1.3	.1	.1	-.5	-1.0
1.3	.4	1.4	1.0	1.2	.7	.2	.6	-1.6	1.9	-.2	-1.2	.8	-.6	-.7	-1.7	.2	-1.7	1.2	-1.8	.8	-.3	.2	-.4	-1.1
-.8	.8	-1.0	.1	.3	1.1	0	.2	-.7	1.7	-.1	.7	.1	-.2	.7	-.3	1.7	.1	.7	-.3	0	-.5	-.4	-.5	.4
-.7	1.5	.5	1.0	-.6	-1.5	.8	.9	-.5	-2.0	-.5	.1	.6	-.1	1.0	-.3	-.2	.1	-.3	2.7	.3	.1	.2	1.7	1.5
.5	.6	.4	-.5	.3	-.4	.9	-.1	1.3	-.2	.4	-1.4	.2	1.4	-.3	-.6	.9	-.9	-1.2	.2	-.3	-1.1	-.6	.7	-2.6
.1	-1.1	.5	1.4	.9	-.9	.5	-.7	-.3	-.9	1.1	-2.0	-1.4	0	-1.8	.3	.2	-.3	1.3	-1.1	.3	1.5	.1	-1.8	-.4
-.3	.6	0	-.1	.1	.5	-.6	-.1	-.6	.2	.7	0	-.3	1.3	1.1	-.6	0	-.8	.6	-.4	-1.1	-1.1	.8	-1.3	-1.2
-.9	-.5	0	1.0	.2	1.3	.6	.4	-.4	-.3	-.3	-.8	.7	-1.0	1.0	.1	-.6	.6	-2.1	0	.1	.9	-.2	1.0	.7
.1	1.1	1.8	-1.1	.1	1.2	-.7	2.3	-1.6	.5	-.3	-1.3	-.2	1.4	.6	.5	.3	.1	1.8	.7	-.2	-1.9	.2	-.2	.2
-.1	.4	-1.3	.2	1.2	-.9	-.8	1.2	-1.3	-1.4	-.2	-1.2	.5	.3	1.7	.5	.9	1.5	.9	.8	-.8	1.9	1.5	-.2	-.6
-.1	-.2	-1.2	-.4	.7	1.8	0	0	.9	.9	2.6	-.4	-.1	.6	.5	-.9	.4	.4	-.5	.3	-.4	.8	1.8	1.0	-.9
.3	-.2	1.0	1.2	.9	.6	1.5	-1.0	-1.1	-.5	2.5	-1.8	.8	1.4	.9	-.2	-1.0	-.6	-1.0	.1	.9	1.0	-.4	-.4	-.1
-.6	-.1	1.0	1.8	-.1	.3	1.5	.3	-.4	-.1	.5	-.3	-.2	1.4	-.4	.7	-.1	0	-1.0	.2	.1	-.6	0	-2.2	-.4
.7	1.3	.1	-1.2	.4	0	.9	-1.2	.9	1.5	-.3	1.5	.3	-.4	.8	.4	.6	-.5	.6	-.8	-2.5	.2	-.1	1.5	-.2
.4	-.2	1.0	1.4	-.2	0	.4	1.5	.7	.3	-2.3	.9	-.9	.9	-.7	1.5	-.6	-.8	-1.8	-.1	1.1	-.5	-.7	0	.4
-.7	2.2	-1.0	-.1	-.3	-.7	1.3	-.2	.2	.9	.1	-1.8	-.2	-.6	-.5	-.2	.8	-.4	1.5	.6	-.4	-.5	.2	-1.0	0
.4	-.3	.8	-.6	-.6	1.2	2.0	.6	-.1	1.6	.9	-1.3	1.7	.8	-.4	.5	-.9	-.3	-1.1	1.1	-.3	-1.6	-2.4	1.1	-.6
.5	-.4	-.3	2.3	-.6	-.5	.4	0	.6	-1.2	-.2	-.4	-1.3	1.1	-1.7	1.4	1.0	-.7	0	1.5	1.2	-.4	-.3	-.2	1.1
.6	-.9	-.6	.4	-.7	.1	-.4	1.1	-.3	-.6	.3	-1.1	-1.6	1.3	.4	-.5	-.4	-.3	.7	-.4	-.1	1.1	.6	.2	1.4

TABLE A.—DRAWINGS FROM NORMAL UNIVERSE—(CONTINUED)

.9 .5 -.9 1.0	1.4 2.7 .5 -1.0	-.9 -1.6 0 -.5	-1.2 -2.3 -1.0 1.1	-.7 .4 1.1 1.4	0 -.3 .4 -.1	2.2 -1.2 .4 .1	-.6 -.1 -.5 -1.1	0 -.9 -.5 .1	1.6 -1.1 1.0 .1	.9 -.4 -.2 -.7	.1 1.2 .2 -.2	.6 .1 0 1.6	.1 1.2 -.7 .7	2.7 -.8 1.7 .6	.4 0 .1 .5	.5 -.5 -.6 0	1.9 1.6 -.7 -1.5	1.5 .6 .8 .4	1.3 .6 -.2 -1.7	.3 -.8 -.8 -1.4	-2.0 -.5 -.4 1.9	.1 .2 1.9 -1.3	.1 -2.3 -.8 -1.0	-.1 -.8 2.6 .1
-1.5 -.5 -1.2 1.4	.2 -.5 .6 1.8	.7 -.8 .9 1.9	1.4 -1.1 -.1 -.7	0 .8 -1.5 -1.8	2.0 -.8 1.7 -1.7	1.1 .1 .9 1.0	-.6 1.1 1.0 .4	.5 -.8 -.5 1.2	.7 -.6 -.7 .9	-1.1 .6 -1.2 1.7	-.4 .6 1.0 .1	.2 -.4 -1.3 .3	-.4 0 -.3 -1.7	.6 2.3 .7 .4	-1.4 -2.3 -1.5 -.5	-1.5 .2 1.1 .1	2.2 -.6 .2 0	.7 -2.4 1.2 1.5	.6 1.3 1.3 -1.6	1.4 .9 -.3 .7	.7 .6 -1.0 1.0	-.4 .8 -1.5 -.8	-1.6 1.6 1.3 .3	-.3 .3 -.8 .3
-.2 .8 -.5 .5	-.9 -.6 .4 .8	1.3 .8 1.8 -.8	-.9 -1.3 -1.2 .1	-.2 .5 -.8 -1.4	-.4 .6 -1.8 .1	2.0 -.8 -.9 1.5	.6 .4 -.4 -1.8	.3 .4 -1.9 .8	.1 -.9 -.8 -.3	-.3 2.1 -.7 .2	-.7 1.4 -.7 -1.8	1.6 1.1 -1.1 -.8	.2 1.2 -.4 -.2	.3 .1 -.4 -1.5	-.5 -.5 -2.0 -1.8	-.6 -1.3 .3 -1.2	-.1 .7 -2.1 -2.1	1.6 .2 1.6 1.3	-.5 -.2 -.9 -2.4	-.8 -.6 -.6 -.1	1.6 .2 -1.2 -.9	1.7 2.8 -1.6 -.9	.1 0 -.5 -2.4	-.2 -.7 -1.4 .5
-.2 .1 .7 -.5	-.1 -.3 -1.3 .9	-1.1 .7 -.3 -.6	.3 .8 -1.7 .2	.3 .4 1.0 -.2	.5 -.5 .6 1.1	-.4 .2 .6 .3	1.3 .3 .7 1.5	0 1.0 1.6 -.2	.1 -.4 -1.2 .6	.7 .5 -.5 -1.4	-.2 -1.5 .9 .7	-2.0 .2 .2 .7	-.2 -1.4 .2 .2	-1.0 -.1 -2.6 -.7	0 0 -.2 -.6	-1.3 -.6 -.5 .5	-1.4 -1.1 1.0 -1.8	0 -.6 .9 1.1	-.9 .1 1.1 -.3	.1 -1.6 -.2 -.1	.8 -.9 0 -.4	.2 1.5 -.5 -.2	.1 -3.0 -.9 -.4	1.1 .4 1.5 .2
1.3 -.2 -.4 .6	-.3 -.7 -.9 -.5	-.2 1.1 1.4 .4	-.5 .5 1.8 1.2	-.7 .2 -.4 -.9	0 -.8 .9 2.2	1.1 -.9 1.4 -1.3	1.1 .8 -.4 .6	-.5 -.7 -1.4 .8	-.5 -.3 -1.3 1.2	-.6 -.8 .9 -.7	-.3 -.5 -.7 .5	.4 -1.9 .6 -.2	-1.7 .5 2.0 -1.8	-1.0 1.7 -.1 .9	-.4 .7 -.2 -.9	-.2 .3 -1.3 1.5	-1.2 .3 -1.3 .9	.1 .7 0 0	1.5 -.3 -.5 -.2	-.4 .7 -2.6 .2	.3 .4 0 -.1	-1.5 -2.2 -.7 -.1	-.7 .5 -2.1 0	-.5 -.4 2.8 .9
.9 .5 .5 -1.1	-.6 1.1 1.4 -.2	1.8 1.2 -1.0 -.8	.7 1.8 -.7 -1.6	-.4 -.2 1.6 .4	-.6 -.2 .5 2.1	.9 1.0 .2 .3	-.1 -2.9 2.1 .1	.6 .7 -1.1 -.6	-.4 -.2 -.6 -1.5	-.8 -.5 .6 .2	.1 2.5 1.1 .4	.7 .6 -.7 -.2	-.3 0 .5 -.1	0 .7 .2 -.2	.9 -.7 -1.6 -2.5	.6 2.1 .9 -.6	.7 .6 2.2 .2	1.7 -1.9 .4 .6	-.4 -.7 -1.6 -.4	.3 -1.2 -1.3 -.5	1.0 -1.6 -.4 -.7	-.6 -1.2 -1.0 -.4	-.7 -2.1 .4 .2	-.4 2.0 -.4 -.2
1.5 -.5 .4 -1.0	1.7 -.3 .9 -1.4	.7 -.8 1.0 -.5	-1.1 2.3 -.8 -.8	.5 1.8 .6 1.1	.4 -1.1 -2.2 -.4	-.7 -1.0 .2 -.9	-.8 .4 -.9 .1	1.8 -1.6 -1.0 -1.2	0 -1.6 3.0 -.4	-.8 -.8 1.1 -2.0	2.1 .1 .1 2.3	.2 1.1 -.7 1.7	-1.7 1.7 -1.3 .5	.1 .5 -.7 .6	-.7 -.3 1.4 -.5	.5 .5 .7 -.7	-.1 -1.0 1.4 .4	-.3 .1 -1.4 1.2	.9 .6 -.9 .8	.4 .3 -.6 0	.2 2.1 .7 .9	-.1 -.7 -.6 1.1	2.2 -.9 1.3 -.9	-1.8 -.9 .9 .9
1.1 -.2 .7 -.2	-.1 -.8 .6 -.1	.6 .2 1.0 2.3	-.9 1.0 .3 -.8	.1 1.0 1.2 -1.4	-1.4 -.1 1.1 -.7	1.3 .3 -.4 .2	-.8 .6 .2 1.1	1.5 .3 .6 -1.4	-.3 1.0 .9 -.1	-.3 -1.5 -.6 -.7	-.5 .5 1.2 -.2	.1 1.6 .7 -.3	.8 .7 .7 2.2	.8 -2.2 1.2 .9	.3 .4 2.0 -1.3	.7 .7 -.7 .5	-.1 -.9 .2 .1	.5 .2 -.1 1.9	.6 -.5 -1.1 -.6	-1.1 -.5 -.7 1.2	1.0 -1.0 -.9 .3	.5 -.7 -.6 -.9	.8 -.5 -.6 -.3	-.9 -1.0 .1 -1.9
-.1 .4 -1.5 .1	.2 .3 1.2 -.6	.7 -1.3 1.6 .9	-1.2 1.2 -.1 -1.7	.8 2.6 1.0 1.2	-.5 .8 -.2 -.9	1.3 .3 -1.4 .4	-.3 1.1 -1.2 -1.4	-.7 -.4 .9 .6	-.6 -.3 -.6 .3	0 .8 -.6 .1	1.0 -.7 -.5 .5	-.1 -.9 .9 -.4	-.2 .1 .1 -1.5	-1.2 -.3 .4 -1.2	-.6 -1.6 -1.4 -.9	1.0 -.4 .8 -1.3	.4 .4 -.9 0	2.7 -.1 .5 0	.8 -1.3 1.1 0	-1.3 .6 -1.2 1.4	.9 .2 .5 .4	1.1 1.9 .8 -1.3	1.7 -.4 1.9 -.7	.8 -1.0 1.7 .9
-1.0 -.1 .1 -.1	-2.2 -.4 .1 1.5	.6 .5 -.3 -.7	-.7 -1.2 1.6 -.2	.1 .4 -1.3 -.4	.6 -.8 -.9 2.3	.7 -1.5 .2 1.6	-.9 .4 -.2 .8	.6 .7 .3 .2	-.9 1.6 -1.2 -.9	.4 -1.4 -.9 1.2	-.9 -.8 -.6 -1.1	.2 -1.2 .1 -.4	1.4 1.9 .4 .2	-1.1 1.3 -.7 -1.8	1.3 2.0 -1.7 1.5	.8 -.7 1.6 -.3	.7 .2 -.8 .4	.8 .1 1.6 -1.2	.3 -1.8 -2.5 -1.4	-.2 -1.8 -.4 .8	-.4 -1.1 -1.1 .2	.6 -.2 -.7 .4	.6 -1.4 1.5 -1.9	-.6 -.3 .2 1.1

.6	0	-.6	-2.5	-.7	-1.7	.7	1.7	-1.0	-.8	-.6	.5	2.5	-.2	.5	.6	1.4	.6	.1	.9	-.2	.2	.1	.3	-1.0
-.2	-.4	.5	.7	.2	-.7	.8	-.3	.1	-.4	-.3	1.0	-.1	.2	-.3	.8	.9	1.3	.1	-1.4	.6	1.2	-1.2	.9	.5
1.1	1.1	-.2	1.2	-.7	-1.3	-1.5	.6	-.6	2.1	-.2	.5	-1.5	.9	2.4	-.2	-.4	.3	1.1	1.5	.6	1.1	1.1	.5	2.2
-2.0	-.7	-1.6	-.5	-.6	-.2	1.1	1.5	.4	-.8	1.4	-.8	-.1	-1.2	1.3	.1	-.9	-.1	.6	.1	.4	-.2	2.2	1.0	-.6
-.9	1.4	-.7	-1.8	-.1	.5	-2.3	1.4	.9	-.4	-.8	-.6	-.2	.9	1.9	1.0	-2.9	-1.0	-.4	-1.7	.3	1.3	-1.5	.5	.1
1.6	.2	-1.9	-.7	1.6	-.3	.4	-.4	.3	0	1.2	-.2	-.5	-.1	.6	0	1.1	.6	1.0	.2	1.3	-.4	-.2	-1.3	1.1
2.5	.8	1.8	-.4	-1.1	-1.9	-.9	.6	-1.9	1.1	.9	.7	-.2	-.4	-1.9	1.7	-.2	1.7	.6	-.3	0	-.1	.5	-.6	-.4
-.1	.1	2.8	.4	-1.4	-1.0	-.8	-.5	-.6	-.6	-.3	-.2	-1.0	1.1	0	.2	2.3	0	1.6	-.7	1.1	1.9	-.1	-.2	1.7
-.8	-.6	1.4	.7	0	.9	-.1	-.3	-.5	-.5	.7	-.9	-2.0	-.6	-1.0	-1.5	-1.1	1.3	2.4	.1	.8	-.6	-1.4	-.7	.7
.1	-1.1	-.4	-.8	-.8	-.4	0	-.9	.8	2.3	.8	.2	.5	-.5	.4	-.6	-.2	0	.3	-.1	.4	1.6	-.7	.2	-.6
-1.3	-.9	0	-.9	-.1	-1.1	.7	-.5	-.5	-1.0	-2.2	-.2	-.9	-1.5	-.5	-1.1	-.2	-.5	-.8	.3	.3	.5	.4	.4	1.3
.9	-1.3	.2	-1.0	.7	.1	.8	.4	-.5	.7	-.5	0	.8	1.3	-.6	-.1	0	-.3	-.2	-2.1	.8	-.5	1.7	-.2	1.3
-1.4	-.2	.5	.5	-.3	-.2	-1.1	.4	1.2	.2	-1.2	.5	-1.8	1.0	-.4	-.4	0	-.3	.4	-.9	-.5	1.0	.8	6	-.4
-.4	.4	.7	.6	.4	-.4	.4	.4	.2	-1.1	-.2	-2.2	.2	.8	-.9	2.2	1.1	1..3	0	-.2	-1.4	1.4	.7	1.4	-.8
.5	-1.0	.6	1.0	-.9	.5	-1.0	.4	.8	-1.7	-.7	0	-.1	-1.1	-.1	-.4	-1.0	.8	1.4	-.1	1.8	1.9	-2.2	1.5	1.0
.6	.6	1.2	0	-1.0	1.4	-1.6	.9	-.4	1.7	.3	1.0	-.4	.5	-2.3	1.3	-.4	-.6	-.5	-.2	2.0	2.1	-.3	1.7	..5
-.1	.3	-.4	-.4	.6	-.6	.5	-1.5	-.4	.3	2.1	-.1	-.1	1.1	.7	.2	1.1	-1.5	.5	-.3	-.1	-.6	0	.9	1.0
-.4	-1.0	1.0	.6	-.2	1.8	-.3	1.4	-.7	.3	-.1	-.6	-1.2	-.5	-.8	.4	-1.0	.1	-1.2	-.4	.5	.6	-.7	1.4	.7
-1.8	-.2	-.8	-1.1	-1.5	.9	-1.0	0	-.2	.7	-.4	0	1.4	-1.2	2.3	-.3	-1.2	.6	1.6	-1.2	1.0	1.4	.6	1.1	-.7
1.1	.5	-1.0	.8	-.8	.2	.6	-.2	.4	-.7	.7	-1.1	-.4	.8	-1.5	-.7	1.5	0	-.2	.3	-.1	1.2	-1.2	-.5	1.4
-.9	-1.5	-.3	1.0	.5	-.8	-1.6	-1.1	-.1	.7	1.7	-.1	1.9	.3	0	.5	0	-.4	-1.6	.3	-1.8	.2	-.1	1.1	0
.2	1.8	1.1	.1	-.7	-.6	.7	.2	.1	.2	-.6	.7	-.1	2.6	-.2	.9	1.5	-.1	-1.1	-.1	-.7	0	.4	-1.1	-1.1
-.9	1.0	.8	-.1	1.1	.4	-.6	1.0	.8	.4	.4	-.7	.5	.8	0	.3	-.6	.9	.1	-.7	-1.3	-1.8	.5	.6	1.6
.7	.4	-.3	.2	-.9	-.2	-.4	-.7	-.2	.5	-.4	2.3	.5	.3	.4	-.1	2.5	-.1	.3	1.0	-.7	-.1	-1.2	-1.5	-1.5
-.6	.4	-1.0	-.4	.2	.7	-1.1	-1.0	.3	0	1.3	-.8	-.3	.3	.5	1.9	-2.4	.2	-2.0	-.4	.3	.7	2.0	-.3	-1.3
-.4	-1.4	-1.7	-1.6	.8	-.3	-.6	0	0	-1.5	1.2	.2	.9	.2	-.6	1.1	1.3	.5	-.2	.2	-.8	1.1	-.4	.7	.8
-.6	.1	0	2.2	.8	-.7	.9	-.1	.9	.9	-1.1	-.4	.5	-.7	1.0	-.2	.3	-2.7	.9	1.6	.7	.3	-2.2	-1.8	1.3
-.9	1.2	-.5	1.8	1.3	1.3	-.4	.7	.4	-.3	-.3	-1.0	-.1	-.4	-.2	-.1	.7	1.7	-1.0	.7	-.5	-1.4	-.4	-1.2	.3
.7	.2	-.9	1.2	-.1	.3	-1.0	-.2	-2.4	-.2	.1	-1.1	.1	0	2.4	.3	-.3	.2	.5	1.5	.8	-.4	-.3	1.8	1.0
-.5	-.5	.9	-.3	-1.2	-.7	1.2	.7	.9	-1.5	.8	.5	.9	-.8	-1.7	1.0	1.9	.9	-.8	.7	0	-2.0	1.1	-1.0	.7
-.5	.5	-.6	-.4	.2	-.7	-.4	-.8	.6	-.2	.4	.6	1.0	-.8	-.3	-.4	-.2	.8	.7	-.4	-.1	-.8	.3	.1	-2.0
-.6	0	-.5	-1.6	-.5	-.4	.4	.8	0	-.5	.6	.1	1.5	-1.7	.1	.4	-1.2	-.6	-2.8	.4	-.3	-1.2	.6	-1.0	.7
.4	1.3	-.6	.7	-1.8	.1	.1	1.0	.4	-2.2	1.2	1.2	-2.2	-.2	0	-.7	1.5	-.2	.4	.2	-.5	-.4	-.1	-1.0	-.4
.2	.6	-.2	.5	-.8	0	-.3	-.2	-.8	-1.5	.4	.9	-.7	-.7	-.9	1.2	1.5	-.4	1.5	-.1	-.3	.5	.8	.9	0
.5	-1.3	-1.2	-1.2	-.2	1.0	.5	1.3	-1.4	-.1	-.2	-2.0	-1.5	.8	.5	.1	.6	.8	.9	-.6	-1.2	.2	0	1.5	-.2
-1.1	.7	.6	-.8	-.5	1.4	-.7	.5	-.3	.3	1.0	1.4	-1.3	.5	.8	-.1	-.5	1.5	.4	.4	1.1	-1.2	-.5	.4	-1.4
.1	-.8	-.3	1.0	.7	.8	-1.3	.1	-.4	.3	.1	-.3	.1	-.1	-.4	.1	-.7	2.1	.4	-2.3	-.5	-1.7	-.4	.2	1.2
-.8	-1.1	-.5	0	-.3	-.6	.4	-.8	.1	.4	.1	-.2	.1	-1.0	-.3	-.2	-.2	1.2	.3	.7	2.1	.5	-.1	.2	-.6
-1.2	1.3	-.3	-.4	2.8	-.2	.1	.3	0	-2.6	0	1.8	.9	.8	0	-1.0	-.8	-1.6	-.3	1.4	.6	-.5	.7	.1	-.9
-.5	-.2	-.4	1.2	1.8	-.5	.9	-1.0	0	1.5	.2	-2.6	-.6	-.6	.4	-.5	-.4	-.1	-1.6	1.3	2.4	-1.9	-.9	.8	-.7

TABLE B.—DRAWINGS FROM RECTANGULAR UNIVERSE

-.7	-2.5	1.7	.8	.9	-1.9	-2.3	-1.2	-3.0	-2.1	1.8	-2.7	-.8	2.7	-1.2	-.1	-2.9	2.1	.2	1.7	-.7	2.4	-1.6	1.5	3.0
-1.4	2.2	2.1	-2.7	-.5	1.0	.7	1.8	2.5	1.1	-.1	-1.2	-1.1	1.2	-2.4	-2.8	.7	1.0	2.2	-.6	.3	1.2	-.2	1.7	-1.0
.5	2.7	1.8	3.0	-1.2	2.4	-.5	-1.5	1.8	-.2	-.8	-1.3	-2.8	-2.8	1.2	-1.3	.8	.8	-.1	-.5	-.4	2.7	1.1	-2.3	.6
1.5	.2	1.3	.8	.2	1.7	-2.6	.3	.4	-.6	2.5	-1.2	-1.5	-.3	-1.6	2.7	-1.0	.4	-2.3	-1.3	2.9	.9	2.5	.5	-1.7
-.8	2.1	-2.0	1.4	3.0	2.7	-1.7	.7	-.1	-2.1	-1.8	-2.2	.5	-2.3	-1.2	-2.6	3.0	-2.3	-1.4	2.0	-.7	1.4	1.5	1.5	-.1
3.0	2.5	-1.2	-.6	-.7	2.1	2.4	1.7	-.6	2.1	2.6	.2	1.5	1.6	-1.0	.6	-.6	1.4	2.8	-1.8	-.5	-1.1	1.7	-2.0	.9
1.1	-2.7	-.5	-.4	2.0	-1.0	-2.3	-.9	-2.2	-.4	3.0	-.7	.3	-1.1	.1	-1.1	1.0	-1.2	2.1	.1	.8	-2.1	-2.9	1.6	1.1
-.8	-.5	-2.6	1.0	1.7	-1.8	-1.4	-1.4	1.5	-2.2	.3	1.0	2.2	1.8	1.4	1.9	.9	.8	2.5	-2.8	.6	-2.9	1.3	.6	2.7
2.2	1.1	-.6	.7	-.7	-1.7	.5	2.4	1.8	-1.2	2.2	-.3	-1.4	-.2	-.8	-1.2	3.0	-2.8	.8	.4	1.0	-.8	-.2	1.2	-1.1
.2	1.5	-1.7	.9	-2.0	2.9	.2	1.1	.7	2.8	-2.3	-.1	1.5	-2.1	-2.7	2.5	-.8	-1.1	1.9	-1.6	1.1	2.2	-2.3	2.2	-2.6
1.2	1.0	2.8	-.9	-2.6	1.5	-2.5	-2.6	1.3	1.3	-2.9	-2.7	-2.4	1.8	-.9	2.3	.3	-3.0	-.2	-.3	.5	.8	1.3	-2.8	-1.4
-.7	.3	-2.9	.4	-1.5	-.9	-1.5	2.7	1.3	.5	.3	-2.3	1.9	-.1	2.8	-.3	-1.5	2.1	-1.7	-.5	1.6	.6	2.2	-2.5	1.0
2.2	.2	-1.8	2.4	-2.9	1.9	2.3	-2.0	1.6	.2	-2.8	-1.8	-2.0	1.9	1.3	.7	-1.5	-1.5	-.9	.2	-2.3	-2.6	1.7	2.8	.2
1.6	3.0	2.9	3.0	2.8	-1.1	-3.0	.6	1.1	2.9	-1.8	-2.6	-.2	-.1	3.0	1.0	-1.8	-2.5	-.7	2.2	-2.9	-1.3	-.9	2.8	2.2
3.0	2.5	-2.8	-1.1	-1.0	-2.9	1.1	.8	.6	-2.6	-1.3	-2.2	-2.4	-1.7	2.2	.9	-2.0	.9	.2	2.7	-2.5	.6	1.5	2.4	-.1
-1.8	-.4	2.3	1.1	-1.5	-1.7	-.5	-1.0	-2.6	2.9	.9	-2.4	.2	.5	1.2	2.7	2.3	.2	.9	.5	.8	-2.7	-2.3	-1.1	2.3
1.7	-.7	2.4	-1.6	1.5	3.0	-.8	2.1	.8	-1.9	.1	-1.7	.7	-1.3	2.0	-.5	1.7	-2.9	1.0	-.4	-.7	-.1	.5	-.5	-.6
-.6	.3	1.2	-.2	1.7	-1.0	3.0	2.5	2.7	1.8	-.7	2.2	1.1	-.8	2.2	1.0	.6	.1	2.0	-1.9	.7	.4	1.6	2.8	-1.9
-.5	-.4	2.7	1.1	-2.3	.6	1.1	-2.7	2.1	.6	1.1	1.1	2.8	-1.8	.7	-2.5	1.8	2.6	-1.6	2.7	-1.7	2.3	-2.2	-1.9	-.4
-1.3	2.9	.9	2.5	.5	-1.7	-.8	-.5	-.9	-.9	-2.2	.1	.1	-.8	-3.0	1.7	2.1	1.1	-2.5	-3.0	-2.1	1.9	-1.6	1.7	2.7
-.7	-1.6	2.4	.8	3.0	-2.5	-1.1	-2.8	-2.1	.2	.4	1.2	2.1	3.0	2.4	-2.0	-3.0	2.8	1.2	.6	-2.4	1.3	.1	2.1	.3
-2.3	2.0	2.1	-1.9	-2.3	.1	1.3	2.1	.9	-1.5	.1	-1.8	1.0	-.4	1.9	-1.1	1.7	1.2	.7	1.0	-.1	-.9	.5	1.0	-.7
-.4	-.6	-2.1	.3	-.2	1.5	-.5	-1.6	-2.9	1.5	2.5	-2.3	.4	.4	-2.5	-1.6	-1.4	-2.6	-.8	-.9	1.7	-1.9	.2	1.8	-2.9
-.5	2.0	-2.2	2.5	2.1	.2	-.2	2.7	.1	2.4	-1.2	.8	1.7	1.6	-3.0	1.5	-.5	-2.7	2.8	2.2	2.8	-.2	-.3	1.1	.5
-2.7	1.7	-.4	-2.9	2.3	-1.0	2.9	.4	3.0	-2.6	1.4	1.4	-1.9	-1.9	-2.8	-2.7	-1.1	.8	2.0	-.8	1.1	-.5	.5	2.8	.8
1.3	-2.0	-1.7	-.3	1.3	-1.5	1.2	2.3	1.5	.7	.7	2.7	2.7	-.3	-2.9	1.2	-2.2	2.5	.1	2.7	2.5	-1.0	.8	-3.0	-.7
-2.3	2.7	-2.1	.4	-2.0	2.2	.5	-.4	.4	2.3	-.6	-2.3	-2.3	1.5	2.0	2.9	2.7	-.6	2.1	-2.9	-2.4	-3.0	2.2	-2.2	.2
1.3	-1.1	2.5	.3	.8	-2.4	-.2	-.8	1.5	-2.4	1.2	2.9	.4	-1.7	2.7	-2.6	-2.8	.8	-.9	1.5	-1.5	1.5	-1.0	2.8	-.9
2.1	.4	.7	-1.6	.8	2.0	-1.8	-1.3	-2.6	-1.8	-1.0	-.8	-.3	-1.3	-.4	1.8	1.4	-.3	3.0	.4	-.7	-1.0	-1.6	1.2	-2.8
1.7	-2.6	2.8	1.3	.9	-.1	-1.6	-2.5	-1.0	-.8	-2.9	-3.0	1.0	-2.4	2.2	-2.7	.3	1.2	2.2	-2.6	-2.9	-.1	-2.0	-2.1	-.9
-.1	.1	-.8	-1.1	1.5	-2.8	1.8	-.1	1.3	2.4	-1.9	-1.2	1.7	-.7	-.3	2.4	.1	1.1	-1.2	-.9	.9	.2	.9	-2.1	-.2
-.3	-1.9	2.9	-1.8	-2.4	-2.7	.8	-2.9	-.6	2.7	-.3	-.8	2.3	.8	.5	2.1	.1	2.9	2.3	-2.5	-.8	-1.6	1.5	1.4	.5
-2.6	-2.2	-1.3	-.1	.5	-3.0	2.5	-1.1	-.8	-1.1	-.2	-.7	-.9	-.3	1.6	.9	.1	1.7	2.7	-.6	2.3	2.7	.1	-.2	-1.0
.6	.2	2.2	2.0	-2.7	2.2	-3.0	.5	-1.2	-1.0	1.3	2.8	-1.9	.4	2.4	-1.5	.9	-2.6	-.1	.6	-.3	1.5	2.9	-1.5	-1.8
-1.9	1.5	-.9	.7	.2	1.4	2.0	-.9	-2.4	-2.4	2.3	-1.1	-2.4	.7	2.5	3.0	2.9	2.8	.5	2.8	2.7	-2.3	2.2	3.0	-2.5
-.5	.7	2.5	-.8	2.0	2.0	-1.7	-2.0	-1.6	.8	-.2	-1.4	2.9	2.1	1.6	-1.8	-2.8	-1.3	.9	-3.0	.7	2.8	-2.2	-.4	.3
-.5	.9	-.4	2.0	.9	.2	-1.7	1.6	1.1	-.2	1.8	2.6	-.7	-2.3	2.5	-2.0	-.9	2.7	.9	-.6	1.8	-2.1	-.5	-1.0	-3.0
-.2	-.4	-2.9	2.1	1.8	-.7	-1.3	-2.9	2.1	1.6	1.0	1.4	-.8	1.1	-1.1	-.1	2.9	1.5	-1.5	1.3	-3.0	-1.2	-1.6	2.8	1.1
.5	-2.9	-2.1	1.0	2.4	1.7	.4	-.3	3.0	.3	-.6	-1.8	-.3	-.1	-2.8	-1.0	2.8	.8	.3	-2.4	-1.9	1.6	-.3	-1.9	2.0
-1.3	.4	.5	.8	.7	.2	1.6	-1.9	2.5	-1.5	-.4	.8	2.4	-2.6	-2.3	3.0	-.8	-.7	-.5	2.9	-2.2	1.8	-2.3	1.1	-2.1

1.2 .4 -1.9 2.9	-1.1 1.5 -.2 .6	.2 2.5 -2.7 3.0	-.1 .7 -.4 -2.1	-2.2 -1.8 -2.2 .9	-.6 2.0 3.0 .7	.4 2.7 1.4 -1.8	-2.1 2.9 -.7 -.3	2.0 2.7 -.1 -.3	.4 -2.8 1.9 -2.9	-1.2 -.3 -2.4 -2.7	-1.4 -.4 1.0 .1	-1.1 -1.6 1.3 -.9	-1.0 -1.3 -2.1 .7	-1.1 1.2 .7 .3	1.7 -2.8 .7 -.4	.1 -1.5 .9 2.5	2.2 1.1 -.5 -.6	-2.9 -.9 2.3 2.4	.3 1.3 -1.3 -.8	2.3 2.4 -1.6 2.2	-2.5 -.8 -.5 2.8	-1.9 2.5 -2.7 2.0	-.4 -1.1 -2.5 -2.6	.2 -.5 1.6 2.5
.9 -2.7 2.0 2.7	2.2 -.6 -.1 1.1	1.6 -1.8 2.1 1.8	1.6 -1.5 -.7 -2.7	-1.4 .3 .8 -2.3	-1.3 .9 -.9 2.7	-.8 -1.1 1.4 2.7	-.5 -2.0 -2.3 -.1	2.5 1.2 -.9 1.4	-2.8 -2.2 -2.0 2.0	-.8 2.1 2.6 -.4	2.9 .1 .6 1.4	1.4 1.3 2.6 -3.0	-2.9 -.5 2.0 3.0	2.3 .5 1.9 .6	.6 2.3 .5 -1.8	1.9 2.0 -2.8 -.9	2.6 -.8 .5 1.0	1.2 .2 2.4 .2	2.6 .6 1.5 2.2	1.9 .6 -1.5 -2.0	1.5 -.1 -2.3 -1.4	1.7 -2.3 2.5 2.6	1.5 -2.6 1.4 -1.0	-2.6 -1.6 -2.1 1.6
.9 -1.8 .2 2.4	.8 2.0 -2.1 1.0	2.1 .4 2.5 1.7	.2 1.0 2.9 3.0	-1.0 -.4 2.6 1.5	2.3 -.7 1.1 .9	.8 2.6 2.6 -.6	-.6 1.4 1.0 2.2	-.4 1.3 2.5 -1.0	.2 -.7 .4 -2.0	-.9 -1.6 3.0 -.6	-1.5 1.0 2.6 .4	-1.5 -1.5 2.0 -1.0	-1.2 .9 2.0 2.7	-.7 .7 .9 -1.9	-.7 2.1 2.8 1.2	.4 -1.9 2.8 2.6	.1 1.8 -.9 -1.6	-1.9 -.9 1.7 2.9	-2.7 2.8 -.2 .4	1.0 .9 -2.2 -.5	-.2 -.8 -2.5 2.7	.4 -.9 -2.7 1.3	2.1 1.8 -2.6 -.8	-.3 -2.5 -1.0 -2.5
-1.6 -.2 2.5 -2.7	-2.3 .2 -.1 2.6	1.0 1.2 -2.7 -1.1	1.7 -2.6 1.0 .8	-1.9 -2.2 2.8 1.3	-2.7 2.9 2.9 1.1	-1.6 1.5 -1.1 2.4	.7 -1.3 2.1 -1.0	.2 -.7 -1.5 -2.0	2.0 -2.0 2.5 -.2	-2.9 -.4 1.4 -2.7	-3.0 1.9 -1.6 1.6	-2.3 -1.5 -2.3 19	1.3 .7 -2.4 -.8	2.2 1.5 -1.2 -2.2	-.2 2.9 1.0 -.6	2.0 -3.0 .1 1.8	2.3 -2.6 -1.9 -1.7	1.3 -2.4 -2.9 1.7	-1.6 -2.2 2.7 2.1	-1.4 -2.9 -.9 -2.1	-.7 -1.3 -1.2 1.2	.4 -2.7 2.8 2.2	1.7 -2.3 1.8 3.0	1.2 2.4 -.1 -1.4
-1.3 -2.5 2.7 2.4	-.1 -1.4 -1.9 2.7	-.8 2.0 .2 -1.9	1.9 2.2 .4 1.7	-.3 1.4 .3 -1.6	2.6 1.1 1.1 .1	-1.7 1.6 2.6 -1.1	1.6 -1.9 1.8 -.2	-2.9 2.7 -2.9 2.8	-3.0 2.0 -1.7 -.7	-.3 -1.2 2.8 -1.1	-2.2 .8 2.2 -.3	-2.6 2.3 2.2 -2.4	-2.8 -3.0 -1.9 .2	2.3 2.2 -1.5 -1.0	.3 -.1 -2.1 2.5	2.5 -.3 -1.3 2.3	1.8 -2.6 -.1 -.1	-1.2 2.4 -1.3 -1.5	1.5 -.3 -1.6 -1.0	-3.0 -2.6 -.5 2.8	1.7 -2.4 -.1 2.9	2.0 -1.5 .4 -2.5	.7 -2.4 .3 2.6	.8 .3 -2.4 -2.3
-.8 -2.9 1.1 -1.6	2.0 1.2 -1.6 .1	-2.5 -1.3 1.2 1.4	.7 -1.0 -2.5 -2.7	.4 -.7 .2 -.5	.1 .2 2.2 .6	2.3 -.6 -1.6 1.7	-1.5 .6 -2.7 -1.7	.7 .3 -.9 .3	.2 -.5 -.4 -2.1	1.8 -.1 2.8 -2.0	2.3 3.0 2.9 2.1	3.0 -1.3 -2.6 .2	2.8 -.4 2.7 2.4	-2.2 .4 -2.5 -2.6	-1.0 -1.2 .7 1.3	.6 -1.9 -.3 -.6	-.2 -.6 -.1 1.8	2.0 -2.1 .9 2.4	-.3 2.7 -2.9 2.1	.6 -1.9 -1.8 1.2	1.6 1.3 -.6 -.7	2.2 -1.7 -2.9 -.2	.2 -.4 2.5 .9	-.7 1.7 1.2 1.7
1.9 -.1 .6 .1	-.1 -2.7 .4 -.9	2.0 .9 -1.1 1.6	2.8 1.9 -2.9 .1	-.4 1.9 -2.7 -1.5	-1.4 -2.3 -.6 -2.1	2.4 1.1 -1.8 -.1	-2.7 .2 -2.1 -2.8	1.2 1.6 1.4 -1.0	.5 1.8 -2.0 .5	-2.2 -3.0 -2.5 .5	-.2 -1.5 1.5 .7	-.8 .5 1.0 2.6	1.8 2.5 2.9 1.7	2.9 2.9 -1.6 .4	2.7 -1.3 -2.2 -2.0	1.6 .3 -.6 -1.0	-.7 1.3 2.0 -1.1	-.9 2.0 -2.6 -1.2	2.0 1.7 1.5 -2.9	-.1 -1.6 -.4 1.4	-2.9 -1.9 .8 2.4	-.4 2.4 .6 1.5	-1.6 1.1 .8 .2	-2.0 -.2 1.2 1.6
.4 -2.7 1.8 -.4	-1.6 1.4 -.4 -2.1	-1.2 -1.8 -2.4 1.7	-1.3 -.7 2.6 -2.6	1.3 1.7 1.1 1.3	-.2 -1.3 2.1 2.5	1.7 1.5 -3.0 .6	1.1 .3 -2.3 -3.0	-.5 -.8 .8 -1.0	3.0 1.9 2.4 -3.0	.5 -2.6 1.5 3.0	2.2 -2.6 -1.7 .9	-2.3 -1.5 -2.7 -.5	-.8 2.5 -2.1 2.2	.9 -.7 .6 1.7	-1.5 2.3 -2.6 2.5	1.8 -2.8 1.4 3.0	-2.1 -2.4 -.4 -1.4	1.6 -.7 2.7 -1.8	1.0 1.3 2.6 1.6	-1.3 -1.1 -2.9 2.7	-.3 1.7 .4 -1.7	-.9 -2.4 -1.0 -.1	-1.6 2.7 .3 -1.6	2.8 1.0 -2.9 -1.2
2.7 2.1 -1.9 .7	-2.4 -1.6 2.6 -1.7	-2.0 -2.2 2.4 -.4	.2 1.8 -1.6 1.8	2.2 2.2 -2.6 2.1	2.9 2.3 -.2 1.3	.5 2.6 -3.0 .9	-2.4 1.7 -.6 -.6	-2.1 -2.3 2.6 -.8	.4 -.3 2.9 -2.3	-3.0 -2.2 2.2 -.8	.1 1.2 -1.7 1.5	-2.8 1.4 -2.5 -2.0	1.3 .5 -2.3 1.9	1.0 2.0 -2.8 2.7	2.9 -1.9 -2.8 .2	2.3 -1.3 .9 2.2	-2.0 -1.9 -3.0 2.2	-1.1 -.6 .3 -2.2	-2.4 -2.3 -1.5 -2.1	-2.5 -1.6 -1.1 2.1	-2.0 .5 1.8 3.0	1.9 -1.7 .6 -1.0	1.1 2.5 -.5 1.5	-2.7 2.5 -1.4 .1
1.5 2.4 .5 -2.8	1.5 .4 1.7 -1.4	-.8 -2.9 .2 -.8	-.9 .6 -2.4 1.3	1.5 1.8 -2.1 1.2	2.5 2.8 .5 1.8	-1.7 -.4 -2.8 1.2	2.1 -3.0 -2.4 -1.8	-.7 1.9 1.3 -2.9	-1.5 1.2 1.7 -.5	-2.7 1.8 -1.1 -.5	1.5 .8 2.0 3.0	.9 .1 -.7 .9	2.6 -1.4 .2 2.0	.5 1.5 1.0 2.6	.4 -1.7 -1.9 1.0	.3 -2.2 1.1 -1.1	1.2 -1.3 1.6 .5	-.6 -1.9 .9 -.9	-3.0 1.8 2.8 -1.6	2.2 -1.8 .3 2.9	1.3 -2.0 .9 -2.5	-1.8 -.5 1.1 1.9	.7 -.6 -1.3 -2.3	.4 -.1 1.3 -.7

TABLE B.—DRAWINGS FROM RECTANGULAR UNIVERSE (*Continued*)

-2.0	3.0	.5	-1.7	-.4	-.4	2.8	-1.2	-3.0	1.5	-1.4	-2.0	.3	1.6	-2.7	-1.4	1.3	1.7	1.2	1.1	2.9	1.0	-1.8	-3.0	-2.4
-.1	2.0	-2.4	2.2	-2.7	2.8	-1.5	-.1	-1.2	-2.2	-.9	.8	2.3	-2.7	-.4	1.7	-2.6	-1.3	-2.3	-1.0	2.4	2.2	1.9	-.3	-2.8
.6	-1.8	1.8	.6	-.1	-2.9	2.0	-2.7	-.1	1.5	-.7	-2.7	.7	1.5	-3.0	.1	-1.2	-3.0	.9	-1.1	-1.1	-.1	2.7	1.4	-1.3
-2.3	-2.9	-.5	2.9	-1.7	1.7	2.2	.2	3.0	.3	-1.1	2.5	-1.4	-.2	-1.1	1.0	.2	.7	2.1	2.0	-.4	-.4	1.7	1.8	1.7
1.4	-3.0	-.6	-1.4	1.3	-2.9	-1.0	1.3	-1.0	-.6	-.8	-.8	2.8	-.7	2.0	1.6	-.8	1.8	-1.1	2.9	2.4	-.6	2.8	-.5	2.7
3.0	.0	-2.4	-.5	1.5	2.0	-1.3	1.9	-1.3	1.8	1.9	2.1	2.9	.3	.7	-2.1	.3	2.2	-.2	1.6	-2.4	-1.1	.6	-2.1	-2.0
1.3	-2.4	-1.7	0	.2	2.5	-1.6	-1.3	1.1	2.6	1.3	1.9	-1.9	.5	0	2.8	-.4	-.8	-.9	1.6	.2	1.4	1.8	-.7	-1.1
3.0	-2.0	-3.0	-2.5	-2.0	-2.0	2.7	1.7	-.1	-.6	-1.2	1.6	2.6	-1.3	-.3	.5	-.8	2..6	2.6	.3	1.1	-.5	1.7	-2.6	2.0
0	-1.5	-1.1	-2.4	1.7	-.1	.6	.9	1.1	1.7	1.9	-1.6	-3.0	2.0	-.5	-1.7	-1.3	2.7	-1.6	2.1	2.1	2.9	2.6	-.6	-2.7
-.2	2.1	.6	-1.0	0	-.2	2.3	.1	-2.8	-2.7	-1.3	-.7	-.4	-.1	2.5	-.3	-.6	1.2	2.3	1.1	-1.6	-1.5	1.4	-2.5	.5
-1.6	1.5	-1.2	-.9	-2.9	-.1	3.0	-2.5	-2.3	-1.8	1.0	-2.5	1.5	1.2	-.2	-1.3	2.8	.3	-1.8	-.9	-2.9	.8	.8	1.6	1.2
1.7	-1.4	-.7	2.9	3.0	.8	1.3	-.9	2.2	.3	-2.4	-2.4	2.2	-.7	.6	-.1	.5	1.9	1.4	1.8	-1.5	-.2	.4	2.5	-.4
-1.7	-.6	-2.0	-2.1	-.3	-2.2	1.9	-.8	.9	3.0	-.7	1.6	-.9	-1.7	.9	2.6	1.6	2.6	.5	2.1	.4	-2.5	-.5	-2.8	2.5
1.2	2.1	-1.0	-.3	-2.1	-2.3	-.3	-1.9	.3	2.7	-.6	2.5	.6	2.5	-2.5	.4	-1.0	-1.5	.3	1.7	2.8	1.9	1.3	-.1	2.0
.7	.8	-.8	1.8	.1	-2.4	.9	2.0	2.5	-2.4	-1.3	-2.4	1.4	1.8	2.7	2.2	-1.7	2.3	-1.0	-1.0	-.4	-1.3	.1	2.8	1.8
1.7	-1.4	.5	2.7	-.3	-3.0	-.2	-2.7	3.0	-1.3	-.9	-1.6	1.3	2.0	2.5	-1.1	2.6	-1.1	.8	.8	.3	-.8	1.7	-1.4	-2.9
-1.8	-.1	-.7	2.8	-1.9	1.6	-1.3	1.5	.5	-.3	.1	2.9	0	-.7	-.4	-.5	-.7	-2.8	.4	-2.5	-2.8	-.5	1.0	-.5	-3.0
-2.1	2.1	-1.4	.4	-2.8	-1.2	-.3	.8	-2.1	.6	.4	1.1	1.6	-2.8	-.5	-.1	.4	-2.9	2.8	-1.0	-.2	-2.2	1.7	-1.7	-.4
-1.1	1.3	.5	1.9	1.3	.6	-1.3	-2.5	-2.3	-2.7	2.6	.7	-1.1	2.2	-2.3	-1.1	-2.9	.6	.4	1.1	.3	-2.3	1.3	1.4	1.5
1.2	2.5	1.9	-1.7	2.7	-2.6	1.4	-2.4	-.7	2.9	1.3	2.3	.5	-1.6	.9	.8	-1.4	-2.6	2.2	1.1	-.2	2.0	2.9	1.6	2.4
1.8	2.0	.5	-1.4	2.7	-1.4	-1.7	-1.3	-3.0	1.6	.3	-1.8	-.5	-2.7	1.9	2.7	1.2	-2.7	2.8	1.9	2.5	1.7	-.1	-1.6	-2.1
-2.7	2.9	-2.1	-.7	-.8	-.2	2.1	-.6	.9	-.5	-.7	-1.4	-.8	-.1	2.7	2.8	1.2	2.5	-2.3	1.6	-2.1	1.6	-2.0	.9	-1.4
2.2	-1.0	-2.6	-.8	-.7	-1.9	-.6	-2.9	-1.8	-2.3	-1.9	-2.6	.6	2.5	1.3	-2.4	-2.8	-2.5	1.5	2.2	-1.9	3.0	1.2	-2.8	.9
2.2	-2.3	-.7	-2.9	-2.1	-2.2	-2.6	1.4	-.6	.6	-2.1	-1.3	-.6	2.6	-2.8	-1.9	-1.9	-.8	3.0	.5	-2.4	-2.1	-2.2	-2.1	2.5
.2	1.6	2.5	1.2	0	-.7	-2.1	2.9	-2.6	-2.0	.5	-3.0	.6	2.6	-1.3	-1.9	-1.3	-2.1	2.9	-1.2	.3	.1	-1.8	-1.4	2.6
-.6	.7	-1.5	.1	-2.9	-.9	2.4	-2.7	1.6	-1.4	.1	2.6	-2.6	-2.1	-1.0	1.8	2.0	-.9	2.6	1.5	-1.1	-.2	-.8	-2.0	-.2
2.4	1.5	.4	.9	-.1	2.1	.7	2.9	-.1	1.4	1.8	1.9	1.3	-.9	-2.1	-2.5	2.6	2.1	2.1	-2.1	-2.8	2.3	-.3	2.3	-2.3
1.4	-1.3	-2.2	-.8	-.3	.6	2.6	2.1	-2.9	-2.3	-.9	1.7	-1.9	.2	2.7	.5	2.6	2.5	-.7	2.2	.3	.4	-2.7	.6	-1.4
-.7	-2.5	-.2	-.4	-.8	2.1	-.7	.2	-1.5	-3.0	2.8	-2.1	-1.4	-1.1	-2.5	-1.7	.2	.2	-.4	2.5	2.3	.5	-.9	-1.9	2.5
1.4	.6	-.6	-1.4	-.4	.5	3.0	-.2	.5	-2.1	-.6	-.4	-1.0	-2.1	1.2	2.6	.8	1.8	2.4	-1.0	-2.3	1.7	.2	-2.4	1.1
-2.3	2.3	-.3	1.2	-1.4	-2.6	-2.6	-2.7	2.0	1.8	-2.6	-2.2	.2	-1.1	-1.1	-2.2	-2.6	-.8	-2.3	-3.0	-.9	1.3	-.9	.2	-3.0
-1.0	-1.5	-2.0	-.5	-2.2	-1.4	2.8	-2.6	1.8	-2.6	1.6	-1.1	1.7	-.2	-1.9	.7	-1.8	-.4	1.2	1.0	2.0	-1.6	0	-1.6	2.4
.6	-2.6	-2.2	-2.0	.7	.3	1.3	.6	2.2	-1.0	-2.0	1.4	.4	2.7	.1	.9	-1.4	-.2	-2.0	2.4	-1.7	-1.9	2.0	-.4	.2
2.2	-2.7	-2.7	-.7	-3.0	-1.1	-1.1	-1.6	-2.9	.5	-1.5	2.6	-.4	-1.5	1.7	.8	1.6	-.9	.1	2.6	2.9	1.5	-2.5	-1.6	1.9
-.5	-.6	-.1	-2.2	0	-2.2	1.2	1.8	1.6	-2.1	-1.0	-2.4	.3	3.0	.4	-1.4	1.7	.6	.7	1.3	-.3	2.8	2.5	2.0	.2
.4	-1.0	-2.5	-.3	-1.4	.7	-1.1	2.2	.6	2.4	-2.1	-2.4	1.3	2.8	-1.6	.8	1.3	-3.0	1.8	2.4	1.2	-1.7	1.9	.4	2.9
1.0	.6	-.5	2.3	2.3	.4	1.0	1.9	2.4	1.5	-.2	1.7	-.8	1.7	-3.0	-1.6	-2.2	.7	-1.8	-2.0	2.0	-2.5	2.7	-1.0	.2
-1.4	2.1	-3.0	2.6	-1.9	-1.5	2.1	-2.8	-2.0	-1.9	-1.0	-1.4	-.9	-.9	-1.1	1.8	1.0	-2.4	-.9	-.3	1.1	.6	1.0	-3.0	1.1
-.2	1.7	1.9	1.7	1.6	2.5	1.3	-2.7	-.5	.5	1.2	-1.9	1.3	-1.6	-2.2	3.0	-1.6	2.7	-2.6	1.7	3.0	-1.0	-1.5	2.9	-.2
-2.9	-.4	-1.6	-1.1	-.2	1.9	1.0	-2.3	.3	1.5	1.5	-1.6	1.7	1.8	1.2	1.2	2.3	.6	-1.3	-2.7	-2.9	-2.8	1.1	-.1	.3

2.0 -.3 -.9 .4	1.8 -1.8 -2.8 .4	1.4 .2 -.8 -.6	2.1 -.2 .9 -.3	1.4 -2.2 -.3 -.8	-.1 -.2 .4 2.5	2.3 .9 .5 -1.6	1.8 -1.8 -.8 -2.1	-2.8 2.2 -1.0 -.3	2.2 1.9 -1.3 .7	1.6 -1.8 -.3 2.3	-.6 -2.0 1.2 .7	-2.0 .2 2.7 -1.1	-2.1 2.3 -2.7 -1.2	2.3 -1.2 1.6 0	-2.2 .5 .9 -1.2	2.8 -.4 -1.4 -1.4	1.8 -2.8 2.2 2.7	-1.6 1.5 -1.4 2.7	-1.6 -2.8 -2.9 .2	.4 .2 -2.6 .2	.7 -2.4 .6 -1.6	-.6 -2.3 -2.3 -1.1	2.0 -.2 1.1 -.7	-.2 1.2 -.7 2.6
-2.6 -.4 -2.7 -1.9	-1.4 -1.9 -.5 -1.5	-2.7 -2.1 1.0 .2	-1.6 -1.5 -1.2 1.7	1.3 1.1 -1.5 2.1	-2.0 2.3 2.1 -1.8	-.8 0 -.4 .9	-2.4 .3 -1.9 1.1	-.6 1.7 -2.9 1.7	-2.3 -2.9 2.0 -2.1	-1.2 1.2 .2 1.3	-1.4 .2 .3 -2.7	.8 1.0 -1.3 -1.7	2.0 -.8 -2.8 -2.5	1.8 2.8 -1.6 2.1	1.4 -2.1 1.9 -.5	-1.6 1.5 -1.3 2.1	-.1 2.4 -1.1 -1.0	-3.0 -1.7 1.4 -.8	2.0 -2.6 -.4 -.3	.9 .3 -.7 .3	-2.3 -.3 2.3 -2.1	.7 1.0 -2.1 -1.9	-2.9 2.0 -1.2 1.2	-1.9 -2.0 -1.5 -1.6
0 -1.0 -2.3 .3	-.6 2.1 .7 3.0	2.8 3.0 -1.4 1.5	1.1 .4 -1.2 2.2	2.1 2.6 1.1 -.6	1.9 -.4 -2.6 -.2	.8 -3.0 1.5 1.4	2.3 2.0 .2 -1.7	-.2 1.8 -1.9 1.2	-1.4 .3 1.7 -1.0	-1.8 -2.1 -1.6 -2.3	2.1 -1.9 -1.1 -.4	-.8 .3 .3 .4	-2.2 -.9 -2.6 -2.9	.2 1.7 -.2 2.0	0 2.3 1.4 -2.8	1.4 -2.5 -3.0 1.0	-3.0 -1.4 -3.0 -.3	-.2 .8 -.3 2.9	-.1 -2.1 2.2 .2	2.2 -2.9 -1.8 1.6	-1.0 0 2.0 1.1	.8 -.4 -2.1 .1	1.3 -.9 -.9 -2.6	2.9 .3 1.3 1.9
-2.5 -2.6 .2 -2.8	-.3 -1.2 1.3 1.3	1.0 .2 -.3 2.0	.6 -2.5 -3.0 -2.5	2.3 -2.7 2.3 3.0	.1 1.9 -2.2 -1.9	2.5 1.0 -3.0 -2.5	1.0 -1.6 -2.9 -2.4	-2.2 -1.9 -2.7 -3.0	2.5 -1.3 1.0 -.3	-.6 .7 2.7 .8	-1.1 0 .3 -3.0	1.4 -2.2 -1.4 1.5	2.5 -2.5 -1.8 .3	.9 1.4 .8 1.3	1.1 -.8 -1.0 -1.0	-.5 -1.5 -1.9 1.2	-2.1 2.6 2.3 -.4	-1.3 -1.1 .1 .7	1.5 -1.6 -1.1 -1.3	2.9 -1.1 1.6 -.7	1.3 -1.2 -2.3 2.3	-.7 -2.3 -2.4 .6	-1.3 2.4 2.8 2.4	1.6 -.8 .6 -2.2
-.6 2.0 .9 .8	-2.4 -2.1 2.6 .8	2.2 .1 1.8 1.2	-2.6 -2.7 -1.1 -.4	-2.7 -.9 2.9 -.5	1.8 -2.9 -2.8 -2.3	2.3 -.2 2.9 -2.0	-1.6 -2.3 -2.6 -.6	1.4 -1.6 .6 -.8	-1.6 1.1 2.9 2.4	-.2 2.0 -2.6 .7	1.6 -.1 -1.1 -.3	.7 -3.0 -1.0 1.6	.3 .1 -3.0 2.9	-1.7 -.5 .9 2.8	-2.9 -1.1 1.7 -1.6	2.0 .6 -2.8 -2.5	-1.3 2.6 .3 -2.9	2.3 -.7 1.3 -2.6	.8 2.9 -1.2 -2.7	-.8 -.9 -1.2 -.8	-1.3 0 1.7 -2.7	-2.0 .4 -1.5 1.7	2.5 1.0 2.8 -.3	2.8 2.5 -.2 -.2
-2.5 1.8 1.6 1.1	1.2 .5 -.1 .7	-.1 -1.0 -1.1 .8	.7 .3 0 1.2	.8 -2.9 .9 1.5	2.7 2.4 2.6 -2.8	-.1 1.5 1.0 -.5	.6 .3 -1.6 -1.3	-1.9 -3.0 2.3 0	-2.3 -.4 -1.2 -1.5	.2 -2.7 1.8 1.1	-2.6 -.3 -1.5 .3	1.1 -2.5 1.4 .2	-1.7 -1.2 1.9 2.5	1.2 -1.2 -.7 -2.6	2.0 .3 2.0 1.3	-1.3 2.7 -1.3 -2.3	2.9 2.0 1.6 -2.7	-.3 -1.1 -1.4 .5	-1.1 -1.9 -.1 .5	-1.4 -2.4 .5 1.4	.6 1.1 -1.8 1.0	0 -1.3 -2.2 -2.0	-1.9 -3.0 -2.7 .9	-1.0 1.4 1.3 3.0
.3 2.9 .6 1.9	2.7 -1.0 1.7 1.6	2.9 1.4 1.9 .1	1.7 2.0 2.2 -2.1	-1.1 1.3 -1.0 -.7	.6 1.9 .4 2.7	-1.8 -2.5 -.8 -2.8	1.4 -1.6 -2.4 -.7	-2.9 1.8 1.3 .6	-1.1 2.9 1.6 2.6	-2.7 -1.6 -.7 -1.8	2.4 2.2 .9 0	-1.8 -.3 -2.6 -2.2	-1.3 -3.0 -2.4 -2.9	-1.2 -2.9 .3 0	-2.1 1.0 1.1 -2.1	3.0 1.9 -2.0 2.7	.5 -.8 -2.3 -2.5	1.4 -2.9 .5 -2.8	-.1 -2.9 -1.4 .2	.3 .6 2.5 2.8	.3 .7 2.2 2.5	-1.7 -2.9 -1.4 -.5	-.8 -2.9 -2.6 -1.7	1.7 -2.9 1.9 1.9
-.8 -1.0 .8 -2.6	0 .8 -2.3 -.6	-2.8 1.5 .8 2.9	2.5 -.2 2.5 .1	.8 -2.8 -1.7 -2.3	-1.5 -2.9 -1.0 2.0	.6 -1.1 -1.8 -.8	-1.5 1.2 -.5 2.0	-2.5 1.4 -.7 2.0	-.3 -.1 1.2 1.3	2.7 -3.0 -.9 -3.0	-2.5 -1.9 2.1 -1.1	0 -.9 1.1 .6	-2.5 1.2 -2.3 -2.9	-.3 2.3 -2.0 -2.4	-1.9 -1.8 3.0 -1.5	.6 -2.4 -1.2 2.4	-1.0 -1.3 -.2 -.2	-1.0 .5 1.1 -.3	2.7 -.8 -2.2 -1.0	2.9 1.7 1.4 1.5	-3.0 -.2 3.0 -1.2	.5 -.4 -.2 -2.0	-2.9 2.0 1.6 -.9	.4 -.9 -3.0 2.4
1.1 1.9 2.8 -.5	1.4 2.8 -1.3 -.2	1.1 -2.2 -.4 -.7	1.4 .5 2.2 1.8	-2.5 .4 -2.0 -1.1	-.8 -.2 1.4 .8	1.0 -1.8 2.0 -1.8	2.5 -.4 .4 -1.0	.1 1.2 -.2 1.2	-2.3 2.8 -1.5 -.8	-.4 -1.6 -1.6 .5	2.9 1.8 -1.5 -2.5	1.0 -.1 .4 -.8	.3 1.8 1.2 .1	.9 2.2 -1.4 2.1	2.7 -.3 -2.1 -1.6	-2.0 .1 -1.8 3.0	-2.0 -1.7 2.1 -1.4	-1.8 .5 -.4 .7	-.4 1.0 -.1 -1.6	-.6 -1.3 -.6 2.4	1.3 -1.8 2.7 .1	-2.4 -1.8 1.5 1.5	-1.3 -1.5 -2.0 -2.6	-2.6 3.0 1.6 -.9
-.9 -1.6 -1.2 -2.3	-2.5 -.2 2.7 2.1	.1 -2.2 -2.6 -.4	-.9 .3 1.8 -2.7	-.6 -2.6 -2.9 0	1.1 -2.0 -2.4 2.4	-1.5 3.0 2.4 -2.4	2.2 .2 -1.7 0	1.2 1.4 1.4 1.5	.6 -.9 -2.7 -2.3	1.3 -1.1 -.3 .5	2.9 -1.0 -.7 .3	3.0 .6 2.7 -.3	-1.6 1.4 -1.5 -1.0	3.0 -1.2 -1.4 -.8	1.2 -.4 -2.1 -1.1	-2.8 -.3 .1 2.8	.1 -2.2 2.9 2.4	.2 -.4 -2.4 2.7	-1.3 2.6 -1.4 -.1	1.1 1.4 1.2 -.9	-1.8 .1 -1.4 -.1	1.8 -1.1 1.3 -2.5	-1.2 -1.8 .2 -.8	-.9 .9 -1.9 .3

TABLE C.—DRAWINGS FROM RIGHT TRIANGULAR UNIVERSE

-1.1	1.7	.1	.1	.7	-.8	.8	1.4	-1.1	1.3	-.2	-.6	1.5	-.1	-1.0	-1.0	-1.0	-1.1	.1	-.7	.4	.2	.6	.3	1.2
-.1	-.8	-.4	-1.1	-.5	1.7	-.8	.6	-.7	-1.3	-1.2	.5	.6	.5	1.4	-.8	1.5	.3	.5	.8	.7	-.2	.5	.2	1.0
-.2	0	-.6	1.4	.6	-.3	-.1	-1.1	1.4	-.4	.5	1.4	-1.0	-.8	-1.2	.3	.2	-.6	-1.0	.8	-.8	.4	.7	.4	-.2
1.4	.1	1.9	-.7	2.0	.8	-1.7	-.7	.2	1.2	1.4	-1.2	-1.1	1.8	.1	1.6	-1.1	.4	.5	0	.5	-1.1	-.8	-1.1	1.3
.5	.1	.5	0	.2	.5	1.2	.5	-.7	0	-.7	.7	1.9	.1	-1.3	-1.3	1.3	.3	1.8	-1.1	1.8	1.9	-.1	0	-1.0
0	.7	-.8	.3	-1.2	1.3	.5	-.6	.4	0	.4	-1.1	-.6	.3	1.2	.7	1.5	1.4	1.3	1.3	-.8	1.4	1.0	1.5	1.3
.4	.6	-1.0	1.0	-1.3	.9	-.3	.2	.8	.4	-1.1	1.4	.5	1.7	-.2	1.1	-.5	.9	-.8	.8	1.3	.6	-1.1	2.0	1.6
-1.0	-.8	0	1.5	-.3	-.2	.8	.9	.4	-1.1	0	-.6	.4	-.8	-1.2	1.3	-1.1	-1.2	-.7	-1.3	-.6	-.7	1.5	-.6	-1.0
1.6	.4	-1.3	.1	.4	.6	-1.1	-.3	-1.3	-.6	1.6	.3	-.9	1.0	-1.0	-1.1	2.3	-1.1	2.2	-1.2	.7	-.7	-1.3	1.5	-1.0
-1.0	1.5	.3	-1.0	-1.2	-1.2	-1.1	2.2	-1.1	1.4	-1.0	.3	-1.2	.1	-.9	.9	1.7	1.5	1.1	-.1	-.3	.7	-1.1	0	-1.3
-.3	-1.1	1.3	.6	-.7	-.4	-1.0	-.4	1.3	-.8	-.5	-.1	.1	-.3	.3	-1.1	-.3	.4	.2	1.4	1.4	1.4	-.1	-.6	-.2
1.3	.5	.3	1.6	1.4	-.4	1.5	-.2	-1.3	-1.2	-.8	1.2	-.8	0	-.5	1.5	.2	-.6	-.4	.7	-1.2	-1.2	1.3	-1.1	1.3
-.6	.1	-.6	2.0	-1.0	-.9	-.3	2.3	-1.1	.1	.7	2.0	-.8	-.6	-.9	-.9	-.4	2.2	-.1	-1.0	-1.2	-.3	-1.0	-1.3	1.9
.8	-.8	1.2	-.9	1.9	1.0	1.4	-.6	1.8	-.6	-1.0	-.9	-1.2	-.4	-.6	1.9	-.6	.1	-1.1	-.3	-1.2	1.7	1.8	1.6	-.2
-1.5	1.5	.4	.7	-.8	-1.2	2.1	0	.2	-1.2	1.1	.6	1.7	-1.1	-1.3	-.6	2.3	-.7	-.4	1.9	1.7	-1.2	-1.1	-1.0	-1.0
1.4	2.1	2.3	1.3	1.2	1.7	-.8	1.6	-.3	1.7	1.9	1.2	.9	1.8	1.6	-1.0	-.1	.3	1.8	0	-.2	-.6	-.2	-.5	-1.0
1.5	.3	.2	.6	-.4	.7	.5	.3	0	-1.3	-.2	1.9	-.6	-.6	.5	-1.1	.3	-.1	1.6	.1	-.3	.6	-1.0	-.9	.1
.1	-.5	-.1	.8	1.0	.8	.6	-.2	-.5	0	.7	.4	.4	.1	1.0	.2	-1.1	.1	.4	-.1	-1.2	-.9	-.8	.1	1.4
.1	.3	-1.2	-.6	.9	-.6	-.8	-.7	-.8	-1.0	-.8	-1.0	.8	-1.3	.2	-.4	.1	-1.3	1.3	-.3	.3	-.7	.5	.5	.4
.8	-1.1	.2	.8	0	-.4	-.5	-1.0	.5	-.5	-.6	.1	-.6	-.3	-.4	.3	.2	.6	1.8	-1.3	-.9	-.4	-.5	-1.0	.7
-1.0	-1.0	-.7	0	.1	-.5	.4	-1.1	.3	-.1	.4	-.8	.3	-1.0	-.6	-.1	-.2	-1.0	-1.1	-.5	-1.2	-.4	-1.2	.2	-.5
.1	-.7	-.4	-1.1	1.4	.4	-1.1	-1.3	-.6	-.9	-1.0	-.8	-.5	.2	-.5	1.2	2.1	-.1	1.5	1.6	-.5	1.4	1.4	1.4	-1.7
-1.2	-.9	.6	-.6	.3	1.0	-.2	-.9	-.4	.6	-.3	-.7	-.6	-.1	.9	-.1	.4	-.7	-.6	-.2	-1.3	-1.1	-.4	-1.2	-.6
-1.0	.3	-.4	-1.3	.1	-.2	-.8	.2	-1.2	-.6	-1.1	.7	-1.2	-.5	.1	0	-.5	1.6	-.3	-1.0	1.3	-1.2	.2	-1.1	-.9
.6	.7	-.1	.2	.3	-.4	-.7	-.3	.9	-.4	-.9	-.2	1.4	.4	-1.2	-1.1	-.1	.4	-.1	-.7	1.1	-1.3	-.7	-.4	0
-1.2	0	-1.3	.3	-.8	-1.3	.5	-1.3	.2	-.7	.2	.2	1.1	-1.3	-.5	0	-.7	0	-1.2	.4	.2	-.2	.1	-.2	-.2
-.8	1.2	-.8	-.9	.4	-.2	-.6	-.1	1.1	-1.0	.8	-.2	.5	-1.2	-.1	0	-.1	.6	-.3	.2	-.1	-1.0	.3	-1.2	-1.1
-1.1	.3	-.6	-.4	-.1	-.1	.3	-1.0	-.1	.3	1.2	1.6	.3	-.4	-.1	-.4	-1.2	-.5	-.7	-.1	.6	-.4	-.8	-1.3	-1.0
-.1	.2	.8	-1.0	-.1	.4	.2	1.0	-1.3	-1.0	-1.2	-.6	.8	-1.3	.1	-.1	.3	1.7	-.8	-1.3	-1.2	-.4	-1.1	-.1	1.3
-1.1	0	.3	-.3	-.6	-.8	.5	1.1	-1.3	-.1	-.8	-1.3	1.7	.4	.2	.6	-.1	2.5	-1.1	-.8	2.3	.2	1.3	1.9	-1.0
-.3	-.6	-.4	-.8	-.6	-.4	1.2	.5	.7	1.5	.6	1.6	1.1	-.8	-.8	-.7	-1.0	1.0	1.9	-1.1	-1.1	-.5	0	-.4	-.8
-1.2	.6	.4	.2	-1.3	-.1	2.2	-1.2	1.3	-1.1	1.3	1.0	-1.0	.2	.3	-.2	-.2	-.7	-1.0	-1.0	-.9	-.7	-.8	-.2	1.1
-.4	-.4	-1.0	-.1	-.4	-.6	-1.0	.9	.9	-.8	1.0	.1	-1.3	-1.3	0	.5	-.8	-.2	-.6	.9	-.6	1.1	-.2	2.0	-.5
.3	-1.0	-.4	-.3	-.9	1.1	-.4	.9	-.9	.8	-.9	1.0	-1.2	-.8	.3	-1.1	-.7	-.3	.6	-.9	-.3	-.3	-.1	1.0	-.1
.6	.9	-.4	1.4	.5	1.2	.8	-.9	-.5	-.2	.2	-.9	-.3	-.7	.4	-1.3	.9	-.3	-1.0	-.7	0	-.8	-1.2	.1	-1.2
1.5	.6	.7	.5	-1.2	0	.8	-.8	.9	1.0	.7	.1	.6	.6	1.8	-1.1	-.9	1.5	-1.2	-.3	1.2	-.1	.7	1.2	.7
.2	.2	.8	-.2	1.0	.4	-1.2	.7	-.4	1.1	-.2	.6	.8	0	.9	-1.3	.1	-1.1	-.8	-1.0	-.7	.4	-.7	-.9	.4
-.9	-.9	-.9	-1.0	-.9	-.5	.7	-1.0	.6	.3	-1.0	1.7	-1.1	1.4	.5	.4	-1.2	.5	.8	-.2	-.1	-1.3	-1.2	.8	-.8
1.0	1.0	0	0	.1	.9	-1.2	-1.2	-1.3	1.5	.5	.2	-.7	-.5	-.5	.3	.5	.5	.9	.7	.4	-.7	.5	-.8	.9
-.4	-.7	-1.1	.9	-.3	-1.0	.2	.2	.2	-.4	.9	2.1	.4	1.0	-1.0	.2	.4	.6	0	.2	-1.3	-.1	0	.3	-.6

.8	.4	.8	−1.0	1.2	1.4	1.1	.5	.6	.6	.8	.6	.1	−1.0	−1.1	−.5	−1.2	−1.0	1.0	.4	−.6	1.0	−.2	0	.5
−.9	−1.3	−1.0	.1	1.7	.6	.6	−1.3	.2	−1.1	.8	−1.3	.7	.7	.6	−1.3	−1.2	.2	.5	−.2	1.2	−.7	.9	−.7	−1.3
−1.3	.5	.7	.8	.7	1.9	−.7	−.2	−1.2	.2	−.5	.4	.5	.9	−.5	.4	.7	.9	−.1	1.7	−.6	−.8	−.6	0	−1.3
.5	.4	.2	.3	−.1	.1	−.7	.1	−.6	−1.2	−1.1	−.2	−1.2	−.1	.8	.6	.6	.4	−.9	1.2	.2	0	−.9	1.1	−.6
−1.3	.1	−.9	−.7	1.1	−1.1	−.2	−.2	1.6	.4	.6	−.7	−.4	.9	−.2	−1.2	.9	1.2	.7	.6	1.9	1.4	.7	1.2	−1.0
−.7	.6	−.1	−.9	.4	.7	.4	.6	−.2	−.6	−1.2	−.1	.5	−.9	1.6	.4	−.6	1.5	1.0	−1.2	2.2	1.1	−1.1	.2	.8
−.2	−.5	−1.2	−1.1	−.6	−.5	.3	−.4	.8	1.2	−.3	.8	−1.3	−.4	1.6	.6	.5	1.2	−.4	−.7	.5	−.4	−.3	−.6	−.5
.5	1.3	.6	.7	−.7	−1.0	1.6	−1.2	0	−.6	−.4	−1.0	−1.1	−.5	−.3	−.5	1.2	−.3	−.8	.3	.4	−.2	−.4	−.1	−.2
.3	−1.3	−.4	−.7	−1.0	−.5	−.3	−.9	.8	−.5	.9	−.9	−.4	−.3	.5	−1.0	.6	−1.3	−.6	−1.3	.5	−.1	0	.4	−.9
.9	−.2	.7	.9	.5	.1	.4	−1.3	−.2	.2	.2	.8	−.4	−.1	−1.2	−.7	−.9	.4	.6	−.4	−.4	−.3	−.3	.4	.7
−.8	.4	0	.3	−1.2	−.5	−.6	.4	0	−.8	−.8	.1	1.0	1.4	−1.0	−1.2	−.6	−1.1	−1.1	−.5	.5	−1.2	−.1	.1	−.1
−.1	−1.0	1.3	−.8	−.1	1.2	−1.3	−.3	1.5	.9	−.5	−.8	−.7	−.3	−1.0	.5	−1.1	−.8	−.6	.4	1.3	−.2	−1.1	−1.2	.7
1.2	.4	−1.0	−1.1	.7	.3	.5	.3	.1	−.6	.7	.5	−.1	−.7	.3	.6	.6	.5	−.9	−.3	0	.7	1.1	−1.0	.3
.3	−1.2	.4	.5	−.7	.5	.4	−1.2	−.1	−.1	−.4	1.9	.4	0	−.1	.3	−1.0	−.8	−.7	−.9	−.4	.1	1.7	−1.0	−1.3
−.4	.4	.4	.5	.6	−1.1	−1.1	.4	−1.0	.5	1.2	.3	−1.2	1.6	−.6	−.5	−.4	−.4	.3	.7	.6	−.9	.1	−.5	−.6
1.2	−1.1	−1.2	−.7	.9	−.6	−.2	−.2	.6	1.0	−.3	1.4	−1.0	1.2	−1.3	−1.0	.3	.8	−1.3	−.4	−1.0	−.7	.2	.6	−.4
.2	−1.2	.5	.7	−.8	1.3	−.6	−1.3	−1.2	.2	−.1	.2	.3	−.8	1.2	−.5	−.1	−.6	.1	0	−.2	1.7	1.0	1.3	−.2
.7	.5	−.2	−.3	.7	1.0	−1.2	−.6	−1.1	−.5	−.6	.3	.3	−.6	.2	−1.0	−.6	.2	−.4	.1	1.1	.2	−.5	−.2	.6
−1.0	.1	−1.2	−1.0	.3	−.3	−.5	−.7	.5	1.2	.6	−.7	−.1	.2	1.2	−.2	−.3	0	−.7	−.9	−.5	.4	−.6	.1	.1
−.7	−.3	.1	.3	−1.0	−.4	.5	.4	−.5	−.5	−.7	.3	−.7	.2	.3	0	−1.1	−.8	.3	−.2	.4	.3	−.4	−.3	1.4
−1.1	−.9	.2	.5	1.1	.4	−.4	−.3	.2	−.1	.6	.4	−1.2	.1	.2	.2	.3	−.1	−.3	−.6	.6	−1.1	−.3	0	−.1
.5	.7	1.5	1.5	.3	.3	−1.0	−.9	−.8	.4	1.6	.6	−.6	1.1	−.1	−.8	1.3	−.7	−1.1	−.4	1.4	−.9	−1.3	−1.1	.9
−.4	−.5	−.1	1.6	1.1	−.1	0	−1.3	−.7	−.6	1.1	1.0	−.2	.4	.6	−.5	.8	−1.1	−1.3	.2	.5	−1.0	−1.2	−.1	1.0
−.7	−.2	0	−.1	−.6	−.6	−.1	−.4	.1	−.3	.6	0	−1.0	.7	−.4	−.2	.9	−.4	−.9	−.8	.4	−.1	−1.2	−1.0	0
2.5	−.8	−.3	.7	.6	1.8	1.8	.2	0	−.3	−1.0	−.6	−.6	.8	2.2	−.1	−1.0	.1	1.7	−.6	−.6	−.8	−.1	.4	−.7
−.5	2.2	−.4	1.8	−.4	−1.2	.4	−1.1	−1.3	−.4	−1.1	−.3	−.7	.8	−.6	−1.2	−.3	2.0	.3	2.0	−.5	−.4	−.3	.1	−1.1
−.5	−.1	1.5	0	1.7	.4	−1.2	1.9	−.6	1.8	−1.3	−.6	−.5	.7	1.0	1.7	1.5	−1.0	2.1	1.5	−.2	−.7	−.4	.2	−1.1
2.2	1.9	2.6	−1.2	−1.3	0	.4	−.9	1.7	2.6	−1.1	−.5	−.7	.8	2.4	1.8	2.0	1.6	−.9	2.4	−.2	−.4	−.5	0	−.9
1.0	−.8	−.8	−.1	−.5	.9	2.0	.2	−.8	−.3	−.3	−1.0	.1	−.8	−.8	−.3	−.8	.1	1.9	2.3	−1.3	−1.2	2.1	−.8	2.1
.8	−1.0	−1.0	0	−.8	−1.2	−1.2	−1.2	1.6	−.6	−.8	−1.0	−.2	−.4	−.7	0	.4	−1.1	−.1	−.4	−1.2	−1.3	.2	−1.3	1.9
1.2	−1.0	−.6	−.3	−.7	.6	1.3	2.0	−.7	−.6	−.6	−.5	−.3	−.9	−.3	1.9	2.3	−.6	−.6	−.8	1.8	−.3	.8	1.7	1.0
.8	−1.2	−.8	−.4	−.4	2.0	−.3	.2	2.4	−.1	−.5	−.6	.2	−.9	−.6	−1.2	−.2	2.0	−1.2	.3	−.2	1.8	−1.0	1.9	−1.1
.6	−.1	−.9	−1.3	−.3	−.3	−1.1	1.3	.4	−.1	1.3	−.2	−.7	−.6	−.8	−1.1	−.7	−.9	−.9	.2	−.2	.4	−.6	.8	−.3
.5	−.1	.1	−.2	−.5	−.2	−.5	1.3	−.8	−1.3	1.3	.4	−1.1	−.1	−.7	−.6	−.4	−1.0	−.6	−.6	−1.0	1.1	.1	.6	−.7
1.2	.6	−.7	−1.0	−.6	−.1	.1	.1	−.7	−1.3	.7	−.1	−.5	−.5	−1.3	−1.1	−1.0	−.7	−1.2	.5	−.8	.8	−.5	.6	−.1
.1	−.5	−1.0	−1.1	.5	.8	.1	.5	.4	−.1	.8	.4	−.8	0	−1.2	−1.2	−.9	−.4	−1.2	−.3	−.8	1.1	.1	.1	0
.5	.5	−.3	.1	.7	−.6	−1.0	−.3	−.1	−.9	.7	.1	−.8	−.6	0	−.5	−.1	−.7	0	−1.1	−.4	0	.3	−.4	−.2
1.2	.6	−.2	−.2	.6	−.6	−.4	−.2	0	−.2	.5	.8	−1.1	−.3	.7	.1	.5	−.6	−.7	−1.0	−.3	−.8	.3	−.4	−.4
.6	.4	.4	−.5	1.0	−1.2	−.2	−.1	−.5	−.8	0	.3	−.4	−.8	.4	−.7	−.4	−.8	−.7	−.3	−.4	0	−.5	−1.2	−1.0
1.1	1.1	.1	−.6	.3	−1.2	−1.0	−.9	−.8	−.1	.8	0	−1.2	−1.1	−.1	−.5	−.2	.1	−.9	−1.2	.5	−.4	−.5	−1.2	−.6

TABLE C.—DRAWINGS FROM RIGHT TRIANGULAR UNIVERSE.—(*Continued*)

1.1	1.3	1.7	1.8	1.8	-.8	1.1	2.0	1.4	-.9	-1.3	-.8	.5	.1	0	.3	.5	.5	-1.0	0	1.2	-1.0	-1.2	1.5	-.8
1.2	-1.0	-.1	1.3	1.3	1.6	-.9	.2	-1.0	-.6	1.1	0	1.5	-.6	1.1	.5	-1.2	-1.2	1.4	2.4	.2	-.1	-.9	0	1.6
-.4	-1.1	1.8	-.6	.5	.3	.7	1.6	-.3	1.2	-.3	1.6	-.9	-1.3	-.3	-1.3	-.3	1.2	.7	1.0	.4	-.2	-.3	-.9	-.7
-1.2	1.2	-.6	-.4	-.6	1.2	-1.3	-.4	1.0	1.5	.8	1.3	.2	1.1	-1.3	1.1	1.2	-.6	-.8	.6	2.6	1.4	1.2	-.5	.1
1.1	-.5	1.4	0	-1.1	1.2	-.7	-.6	1.4	2.0	1.2	-.8	.2	-1.1	-1.2	-.6	.5	-1.3	-1.2	2.0	.4	-.5	1.1	1.0	1.2
-1.3	1.2	.2	1.2	-1.1	-.4	1.5	1.3	-1.0	0	-.9	-.6	-.5	.4	1.2	1.8	-.1	1.1	-.7	0	.5	-1.3	-.6	1.4	-.8
-.7	-1.2	-.4	-1.2	.1	2.0	-.9	-1.1	-.5	-.4	-1.2	-.5	-1.3	-1.0	.3	.5	1.8	-.8	.9	-.2	1.0	.5	.6	-.9	.8
-.5	-.9	-1.0	-1.1	1.3	1.2	-.7	-1.1	-.6	-.3	-.8	1.6	1.1	1.3	-.9	.3	-.6	-.2	1.1	2.1	-1.3	0	-1.2	-.1	-1.1
.7	1.0	1.6	-1.0	.2	-1.0	-.9	-1.2	-.3	-.3	-1.3	1.1	.4	1.0	-.3	1.2	-1.3	-.9	-.2	1.4	-.3	-.6	-1.0	-.5	-1.0
1.3	-1.0	-.3	-.7	1.2	.2	.8	0	-1.3	.5	-.1	.4	-1.2	.3	1.1	.5	1.0	-.6	1.4	-.1	-1.1	-.5	1.3	1.8	-1.0
1.0	.4	-.7	1.3	-1.1	-1.1	.1	-2.3	1.0	1.6	1.0	-1.2	.4	-.3	.4	-.9	-.7	0	-.1	-.4	1.2	1.1	-.3	.2	1.3
-1.0	1.3	1.3	.3	-1.0	1.2	1.4	-1.1	-.1	-.7	-.1	0	1.1	-1.3	-1.2	-1.1	-.4	1.4	-.9	-.9	-.9	-1.2	-.9	-.5	-.4
-1.1	1.7	-.3	1.6	-1.0	1.2	-1.3	1.0	.9	.4	.6	.9	.6	1.5	1.0	-.6	1.1	-.6	-.1	.3	1.1	1.3	-.8	.3	-.7
-.6	-.6	-.8	.4	1.3	-1.0	-.9	1.5	1.4	-1.0	-1.2	.6	-1.3	-.1	-.1	.6	-.1	-.6	1.6	1.2	1.7	-.9	.3	1.0	.6
-1.0	-.5	1.5	-.2	-1.0	-1.0	-1.1	-.5	-.4	.8	1.0	-1.3	-.4	1.8	1.1	.2	0	1.6	-.6	-.4	-.3	-.6	1.4	.1	1.5
1.2	-.1	-.4	-.7	.5	-1.1	1.0	-.7	-.8	1.2	-.6	-.5	.9	-.4	2.1	1.6	2.1	.6	1.0	1.8	-.5	.2	-.5	-1.2	.8
-1.0	-.2	0	-.6	2.3	2.0	.3	1.7	.5	-1.1	.8	-.7	-.5	1.1	-.3	-.1	-.7	-.8	0	1.2	-1.3	1.9	-1.1	1.7	.2
-.1	-.1	-.5	-1.1	-.6	-1.1	-1.2	-1.1	-.4	-.1	-.4	.3	-.3	-1.3	2.1	2.2	.7	.6	.1	-.4	1.8	-1.2	1.1	-.5	1.2
-.2	-1.0	.4	2.0	-.8	-.8	1.8	-1.0	.8	.1	.1	-.5	.5	-.6	-1.0	-.9	-.5	2.3	1.8	2.4	.8	.7	1.9	.7	.5
-.5	-.5	.3	1.2	-.6	-.5	1.0	-1.3	.6	-.7	.6	.5	.7	1.8	.6	.6	2.4	.2	-1.3	-.7	1.0	1.1	-1.2	1.0	-1.0
1.4	1.6	-.3	-.8	-1.1	.2	-.7	-.7	-.8	.6	1.5	-.9	.1	-.8	-1.1	-1.2	.1	1.1	-1.3	.3	.4	-.8	-.1	-1.2	-.4
-.8	.9	1.1	-.2	-.5	.1	-.3	1.1	-1.1	2.4	-.4	-1.3	-.3	-1.0	-1.3	1.1	-1.0	.2	.9	.4	.5	2.1	-.6	-1.2	0
.7	-.1	-1.1	1.4	1.1	.6	-.7	-.7	.6	.5	-.1	-1.0	-.3	-.5	1.0	-1.0	1.0	-1.2	.8	-.5	-.1	-.6	-.8	-.1	-.8
0	-.6	-.6	-.7	-.6	2.3	1.5	-1.1	-1.3	.7	-.2	.6	1.6	.9	-1.1	-.2	-1.3	.1	.8	-.2	-.4	1.2	.3	-.5	.3
1.1	-.8	-.5	-.7	.1	-1.0	-.3	-.8	-.2	-.5	0	-.1	-.1	-.2	.9	-1.0	-.5	-.5	-1.0	-1.0	-.8	.4	-1.1	.2	-1.0
-.3	2.1	.1	.7	.3	-.7	-.2	.3	-.7	0	-.2	-1.2	-.5	-1.1	2.3	-.6	-.1	-.7	-.2	-1.0	.6	-1.0	-1.0	.5	-.4
-.7	-1.0	-.7	-.1	.7	.3	-.7	.2	.4	-.7	-.6	-1.1	-.5	-1.3	1.3	-1.0	.9	.7	.4	.4	-.5	-.3	.3	-.2	-.9
-.8	1.4	-.1	-.3	1.5	-.7	-1.3	-.1	.3	-1.1	.5	-.6	-1.2	.1	.9	.4	-.4	.1	-1.0	-.7	-.6	-.7	-.9	-.4	-.1
-.8	.6	.1	-.5	-.2	.3	-.2	.6	-.4	1.2	-.7	-1.0	.1	-.3	-.5	1.1	-1.0	.1	-1.3	-.2	-.2	-1.2	.7	.1	0
.1	.9	-.4	.6	-1.0	.6	.1	-.8	-1.1	.5	.2	-.8	-.3	.6	-1.0	1.0	-.5	-.4	-.4	-1.1	-1.1	-.3	1.6	-.7	.2
-.5	.4	-.2	.9	.1	.3	-1.3	.3	-.3	.7	-.3	-.4	-.5	-.1	-.8	.6	-.1	-.3	-1.2	-.8	-.5	-.5	1.4	-.1	-.6
-.8	-.5	-1.3	.3	.4	-.8	-1.0	-.8	-1.2	.3	-.7	-1.3	-.4	.2	-.1	1.5	-.6	-.8	-1.3	-.2	-.4	-.9	1.4	-.8	.3
-.8	-.9	1.2	-.5	-.9	1.1	-.3	-1.2	-.4	.9	0	.6	.7	-1.3	1.3	.3	1.5	-1.2	-.9	.1	1.3	-.4	-.4	.6	-.5
-.3	1.4	1.2	-.8	.9	0	-1.1	-.6	.6	-1.2	-1.0	-.8	1.4	.1	-.1	1.8	0	-1.3	1.2	1.8	0	-.7	.5	2.5	-.5
-1.2	1.4	-.3	1.4	.3	-1.0	-.1	.9	.2	-.5	-.8	1.3	-.7	.8	-.7	-.3	-.5	-.8	-.4	-.3	.1	.2	-.2	.4	.4
1.0	-.2	-1.1	1.3	-1.2	-.1	1.0	-.2	1.7	-.2	1.1	.3	-.1	-1.2	-.8	-.1	-.6	.8	-.8	.2	-.8	1.4	1.7	1.3	1.6
0	1.0	-1.1	-.3	.2	0	.1	-.1	-.7	-1.0	1.1	1.3	1.6	1.4	-.2	1.6	.9	-1.2	-.2	1.7	-1.1	1.1	1.1	-.9	-.3
-.3	-1.0	-1.3	-.5	1.4	-.7	1.0	-1.3	-.5	-.4	-.2	-.3	1.3	-.1	1.0	1.0	-1.2	.5	-1.0	1.3	.5	1.2	-1.0	.6	-.6
-1.3	.2	-1.1	1.6	.7	1.4	-1.1	.8	.8	.9	-1.0	-.9	-.6	2.0	0	-.5	-.9	-1.2	.7	1.2	-.5	.4	1.0	.8	1.3
.8	-1.1	.8	-.3	-.9	.5	-.6	-1.0	-1.3	-1.2	-.8	1.1	1.5	.6	-1.1	1.3	.5	.9	1.1	-.4	1.0	-.9	.6	-1.3	1.5

-.7	1.3	1.4	-.6	1.6	1.4	.9	-.1	.5	-.7	-1.1	.8	2.2	-1.1	1.8	-.4	1.1	-.4	-1.3	-.7	1.3	-1.3	1.0	.5	.2
-.3	1.2	-.6	.9	.2	-.6	0	.7	.4	.1	-.3	1.0	.2	.7	-.2	-.9	-.3	-.7	.7	1.3	-.7	0	2.0	1.2	-1.1
1.4	.5	-.5	-1.1	-.4	-.6	-.3	-.9	1.2	-.7	.9	2.2	.4	-1.3	.3	-.6	-.6	-1.0	-.9	-.6	.6	-1.1	.7	.2	.9
1.3	-.8	.1	-.4	.3	.5	-1.1	-1.3	2.4	1.3	-.7	.2	.4	-1.2	.2	1.1	-.9	1.0	-.7	.6	-.5	.7	0	-.8	.1
-.6	1.3	-.9	.6	1.5	.7	-.1	-.8	-.1	-1.0	-.3	.4	-.9	.8	-1.1	.9	.2	.1	-.9	8	-1.3	.4	1.5	.8	1.0
-.8	.2	0	1.2	.9	.1	-1.1	.2	-1.1	-.4	.9	.7	-.7	-.8	.9	-.5	1.2	1.1	.6	.6	.7	-1.2	1.6	-1.2	-.9
.1	-.7	1.1	-.5	.2	-1.3	.9	-.8	.9	0	-.1	-.9	1.1	-.4	.5	-1.1	-.3	.6	-1.3	-1.1	.7	.8	1.6	.7	1.1
1.2	0	-.1	-.8	-.5	-.5	.3	1.2	-.4	1.0	-1.1	-1.3	.8	1.2	.1	.4	1.7	-.9	.7	-1.2	-.8	.8	-.4	-.3	0
-1.2	-1.0	-.2	1.9	-.9	.3	1.9	2.1	1.9	1.1	2.0	-1.3	-.5	2.0	-.3	2.5	2.1	-.1	2.0	2.5	1.3	1.1	1.1	2.3	-.4
-.6	-1.0	2.0	-.4	2.0	2.2	1.0	.8	-1.0	-1.1	.5	2.0	2.0	.8	-1.2	.5	-1.2	-1.2	-1.2	.4	2.2	-1.2	2.3	1.5	-1.1
-1.2	-.8	-1.2	-1.3	-.4	.2	.8	-.9	.2	.8	-1.3	.7	-1.3	-.7	.9	-.8	-.1	2.1	.1	-.1	-1.1	-1.3	1.2	.8	2.3
2.0	2.2	-1.2	-.8	-1.2	-1.0	-1.3	-1.1	2.3	2.2	-.6	.3	.3	-1.3	2.1	-.8	-.1	-1.1	-1.3	-.8	-1.0	2.1	-1.1	-1.1	-.7
2.1	2.3	2.2	-.3	.6	.8	2.6	2.4	-1.3	.4	-.3	2.3	2.2	-1.1	-1.1	-.9	-.5	-1.3	-.9	-.5	-.7	-.3	1.1	-1.2	1.6
-1.2	.1	-1.2	-1.2	2.1	-1.3	2.2	1.4	.6	.2	-1.1	-1.0	-1.3	2.4	-1.1	-.7	2.2	1.7	-.7	2.5	-1.3	-1.3	1.6	1.9	.7
-1.0	-.1	-.1	2.2	.8	2.1	-.1	-1.1	2.2	-1.3	2.4	-.6	-1.3	-.8	-1.3	2.1	-.8	-.8	-1.3	-.2	1.7	-.8	-1.1	1.3	-.9
-1.3	-1.1	-.2	-.1	-1.3	.2	-.9	-.8	-.1	2.2	-.8	-1.2	-.8	-1.1	1.7	-.9	0	-1.3	1.7	.1	-1.2	1.7	2.0	-.7	2.2
-.2	.7	-1.3	-.9	.1	.5	-.8	-1.3	.2	-.2	0	-.4	-1.1	-1.3	-.2	-.7	-.5	-.6	-.7	.3	-1.3	-.8	.4	-.9	-.7
-1.2	-.3	-.8	.5	2.0	1.4	.5	-.9	0	1.1	-.4	-1.2	-.7	-1.2	.8	.5	-.9	-.7	0	-.7	-.9	-1.0	-.8	-1.0	-1.0
-.5	1.9	0	-.4	-.2	0	1.4	0	1.5	-.8	-.6	-.3	-.2	-.1	-.4	-.1	-1.1	-.6	-.9	-.5	-1.1	.2	-.4	0	.2
1.0	.1	-.9	1.3	-.1	-.8	-.3	.9	-.7	-1.1	-1.2	0	.1	-.4	-.2	-.3	.1	.5	-1.2	-.9	-.1	-.6	-.8	-1.2	-.9
-1.2	-1.1	-1.0	.7	.2	-.1	.3	.1	.6	.2	.9	-.7	1.4	-1.0	2.3	2.3	-1.0	2.5	-1.0	-1.3	-2.3	-.4	-1.1	-1.2	.4
-.1	0	.1	-.4	.1	-1.2	.5	-1.2	-.6	-1.1	.4	.5	.7	-.9	-.5	.4	-1.0	0	2.5	2.3	.5	-1.3	2.5	-.7	-1.3
-.2	0	.3	-.4	-1.1	0	.2	-.8	.7	-.6	-.2	0	.6	2.4	-1.2	1.1	2.6	-1.1	.6	1.4	1.5	2.5	-.4	2.6	-.9
.1	.2	-.7	.9	0	.1	1.5	0	-.1	.1	-.4	-.8	1.9	-1.1	.3	-1.3	-1.0	-.6	-1.1	-.6	-.5	-.9	-1.3	.4	2.5
-.2	1.5	-.7	-.8	-1.2	1.0	-.3	-.9	-.5	-.5	1.5	.8	-.7	1.0	2.0	-1..0	-1.0	0	1.7	-1.3	-.3	2.2	1.7	-.1	1.6
-1.1	1.4	-1.1	1.6	.9	1.3	.9	1.3	2.0	2.0	.7	1.5	1.8	1.6	.5	1.8	.5	-1.1	-1.1	1.5	1.5	.7	-.8	1.1	-1.2
1.8	-1.0	1.4	-.3	1.3	.3	1.2	-1.2	1.4	-.4	-1.0	-1.0	.5	-1.2	1.4	.7	-1.2	1.0	.3	.1	-1.3	-.1	-1.1	2.6	-1.2
.5	0	1.4	1.7	-1.0	-1.2	-1.3	.3	-.1	.9	.8	.4	1.1	0	-.8	-.2	1.6	1.7	-.7	-.9	0	-.6	.2	-.2	0
-.8	.1	-.5	1.5	1.8	-.5	-.6	-1.0	-.3	1.8	-1.2	-.8	-.2	-1.0	-.6	-.6	-.6	1.0	.6	1.5	-.8	.5	1.4	1.6	1.7
-1.1	-.4	-.1	-1.3	-.5	-1.3	-1.2	-.4	-.9	-.7	-.9	-1.0	1.7	-1.3	1.5	1.9	-1.3	1.9	.3	-.5	1.7	2.2	.2	-1.3	1.4
1.7	-1.0	1.6	-.8	0	1.5	.8	1.8	1.9	-.9	1.6	-1.3	-.9	-.5	-1.3	-.9	-1.1	-.9	-.9	.2	1.5	-.7	-1.1	1.2	1.3
0	1.8	-1.2	-.3	-1.0	.3	1.6	-.8	-.6	-1.0	-1.0	1.5	-1.1	1.5	-.7	-.2	1.5	.1	1.9	-1.3	-1.2	1.8	1.8	0	-1.2
-1.3	-.3	.1	-.8	.4	-.4	1.7	1.5	2.1	1.9	1.7	2.2	.5	1.0	1.7	1.2	1.8	-1.3	-.4	-.4	-1.0	2.0	.6	-1.2	-.7
-1.3	1.6	-.8	.1	-.2	.1	2.0	1.0	.7	1.6	1.1	1.6	1.5	-1.1	.6	-1.5	.4	1.4	-.1	-.1	1.5	-.6	1.8	1.5	-.4
1.6	-1.3	.5	.5	.7	-.8	.8	.8	2.0	-.8	.8	-.5	-.6	1.6	-.5	.5	.1	-.1	-1.2	-1.2	-1.2	-.7	-.9	-.9	2.0
.6	.6	.2	.2	-.6	-.9	.7	-1.2	-.6	-.7	-1.0	-.2	2.1	.1	-1.0	.2	-.9	-.5	1.5	1.5	-.2	.2	.6	.7	1.2
-1.0	-1.2	1.7	1.4	-.4	-1.1	-1.0	1.5	.9	1.6	1.7	-1.2	-1.0	1.6	.2	.8	.3	.1	.5	-.6	.2	.4	-1.3	0	-1.5
-1.0	1.5	-.6	-.6	2.3	1.6	0	-.6	-.5	-.2	-.5	1.4	1.8	-1.2	1.3	-1.1	1.3	1.1	-.4	0	.8	.1	.6	-.8	-1.3
1.7	-1.1	-1.0	-.6	-.1	-1.0	.8	.6	-.4	1.6	-.9	.3	1.3	1.1	1.7	-.5	-.5	.5	1.5	-1.3	-1.0	1.1	-.7	.7	-.5
-.9	-1.2	-.3	-1.5	.2	-.5	1.7	-1.2	2.2	-1.2	1.9	1.6	-.7	-.1	-1.1	-.2	-.6	-.8	.9	.6	-1.1	-.8	-.1	-1.2	.5

Table D.—Statistics for Drawings from Normal Universe

Sample Number	$\bar{X}$	Median	$\frac{\text{Max.} + \text{Min.}}{2}$	μ	σ	%	Sample Number	$\bar{X}$	Median	$\frac{\text{Max.} + \text{Min.}}{2}$	μ	σ	%
1	.950	.950	.950	.600	.618	1.537	101	-.050	-.050	-.050	.250	.268	-.187
2	.350	.350	.350	.050	.045	7.778	102	.675	.650	.700	1.075	1.098	.615
3	.325	.400	.250	.113	.130	2.500	103	-.050	-.050	.060	.200	.249	-.201
4	-.400	-.750	-.050	1.050	1.290	-.310	104	.525	.650	.400	.575	.630	.833
5	.400	.650	.150	.550	.660	.606	105	.100	.200	0	1.050	1.111	.090
6	-.150	-.100	-.200	.550	.655	-.230	106	0	.150	-.150	1.050	1.218	0
7	-.275	.150	.400	.825	.873	-.315	107	-.075	-.200	.050	1.275	1.336	-.056
8	-.075	.100	-.250	.875	1.119	-.067	108	.575	.350	.800	1.125	1.179	.488
9	-.075	-.100	-.050	.575	.602	-.125	109	-.576	-.700	-.450	.325	.370	-1.554
10	-.400	-.050	-.750	.650	.758	-.528	110	-1.300	-1.200	-1.300	1.000	1.049	-1.239
11	-.525	-.600	-.450	1.025	1.108	-.474	111	-.550	1.150	.050	1.425	1.704	-.323
12	-.275	-.250	-.300	.775	.785	-.350	112	.525	.700	.350	.625	.776	.676
13	.025	0	.050	.275	.327	.076	113	1.550	.500	.600	.675	.920	.596
14	0	-.500	.500	1.100	1.332	0	114	-.050	.400	-.850	.875	1.045	-.478
15	-.600	-.700	-.500	.400	.424	-1.415	115	1.025	.750	1.000	.638	.760	1.348
16	-1.000	-.550	1.450	1.000	1.185	-.844	116	.700	.560	.750	.450	.552	1.267
17	-.050	.100	-.200	.700	.820	-.061	117	.075	-.200	.350	.813	1.003	.073
18	-.300	-.500	-.300	.250	.255	-1.176	118	.750	.900	.600	.800	.867	.865
19	-.125	-.150	-.100	.575	.618	-.202	119	-.375	-.550	-.200	.488	.602	-.623
20	-.575	-.700	-.450	.538	.687	-.837	120	.325	.350	.300	.325	.335	.970
21	-.225	-.450	0	.575	.698	-.322	121	.475	.600	.250	.425	.497	.956
22	.275	.650	-.100	1.075	1.299	.212	122	.250	.150	.350	.325	.402	.622
23	0	.200	-.200	1.150	1.193	0	123	-.150	-.150	-.150	.600	.814	-.184
24	.325	0	.650	.638	.760	.428	124	.250	-.100	.600	.850	.983	.254
25	.300	.400	.200	.550	.714	.420	125	.225	.100	.350	.475	.522	.431
26	-.075	.050	-.100	.575	.661	-.113	126	.150	.450	-.150	.525	.610	.246
27	.100	.350	-.150	.900	1.084	.092	127	-.150	-.450	.150	.575	.680	-.221
28	.100	.050	.150	.250	.274	.365	128	.225	0	.450	.675	.804	.280
29	.200	.250	.150	.400	.430	.465	129	-.275	-.050	-.600	.513	.618	-.445
30	1.100	1.800	.400	1.400	1.660	.663	130	.100	.100	.100	.600	.781	.128
31	-1.000	-1.250	-.750	.700	.857	-1.167	131	.050	.550	-.450	.975	1.154	.043
32	.025	0	.050	.625	.756	.035	132	-.025	.450	-.500	.888	1.050	-.024
33	-.500	-.450	-.550	.800	.840	-.595	133	-1.425	-1.550	-1.300	.763	.998	-1.427
34	.125	-.200	.450	.638	.750	.167	134	.200	-.050	-.350	.950	1.134	.176
35	-.675	-.900	-.450	.488	.581	-1.161	135	.675	.650	.500	.325	.370	2.830
36	-.100	-.200	0	.600	.678	-.147	136	-.575	-.750	-.400	.975	1.015	-.566
37	.200	.050	.350	1.700	1.742	.115	137	-.200	-.250	-.150	.400	.534	-.375
38	.600	.850	.350	.850	1.069	.562	138	-.275	-.450	-.100	.688	.867	-.317
39	.100	.050	.150	.350	.464	.216	139	-.950	-.800	-.400	.275	.319	-2.978
40	-.250	-.250	-.250	.700	.701	-.336	140	-.450	-.300	-.600	.750	.779	-.578
41	-.350	-.850	.150	.875	1.015	-.344	141	.150	.050	.250	.375	.471	.318
42	-.150	-.350	.050	.550	.657	-.228	142	-1.350	-1.650	-1.050	1.450	1.563	-.864
43	.150	.200	.100	1.050	1.080	.139	143	-.550	-.350	-.850	.900	1.074	-.512
44	.075	-.300	.450	.763	.907	-.083	144	.300	.250	.350	.900	1.007	.298
45	.450	.550	.350	.600	.756	.594	145	-.500	-.600	-.400	.600	.787	-.635
46	.650	.300	1.000	.775	.942	.690	146	.800	.750	.850	.550	.745	1.074
47	-1.150	-1.300	-1.000	1.050	1.151	-1.000	147	.050	-.100	.200	.425	.522	.096
48	-.075	.100	-.250	.725	.912	-.082	148	.800	1.300	.300	.800	.925	.865
49	-.625	.650	.600	.375	.438	-1.426	149	-.925	-1.250	-.600	.713	.844	-1.096
50	-.700	-.850	-.550	.350	.430	-1.627	150	-.275	-.350	-.200	.238	.295	-.932

51	-.175	.400	-.750	1.063	1.246	-.140	151	-.475	-1.000	.050	.838	.971	-.489
52	.225	.050	.400	.338	.396	.568	152	.100	.150	.050	.400	.406	.246
53	-.325	-.050	-.600	.825	.947	-.343	153	.425	.650	.200	.513	.618	.688
54	.600	.650	.350	.200	.255	.235	154	-.600	-.550	.650	1.150	1.402	-.428
55	-.225	.150	-.600	1.075	1.215	-.185	155	-.550	-.500	-.600	.750	.792	-.694
56	-.175	-.100	-.250	.863	1.168	-.150	156	-.750	-.750	-.750	.900	.912	-.822
57	-.375	-.200	-.550	.475	.536	-.700	157	.025	-.150	.200	.488	.602	.042
58	-.300	-.550	-.050	1.000	1.275	-.235	158	.625	.500	.750	.775	.804	.777
59	.225	.050	.400	.588	.736	.306	159	-.475	-.500	-.450	.625	.817	-.581
60	.175	-.050	.400	.525	.634	.276	160	-.275	-.850	.300	1.275	1.531	-.180
61	.525	.450	.600	.625	.634	.828	161	.250	.100	.400	.800	.867	.286
62	-.325	-.700	.050	.613	.709	-.459	162	-.850	-1.100	-.600	.800	.928	-.916
63	.525	.100	.950	.838	1.003	.524	163	.475	.300	.450	.313	.363	1.309
64	-.150	-.450	.150	-.150	.680	-.221	164	.300	-.100	.700	1.100	1.342	.224
65	-.100	.100	-.300	.700	.851	-.120	165	.150	.050	.250	.475	.610	.246
66	.225	.550	-.450	.675	.817	.275	166	.350	.300	.400	1.250	1.275	.275
67	.350	.350	.350	.850	.850	.412	167	-.575	-.500	-.550	.325	.402	-1.430
68	.300	.400	.200	.550	.579	.518	168	.450	.950	-.050	1.225	1.470	.306
69	.425	-.500	-.350	.975	1.188	-.358	169	.700	.450	.950	.700	.857	.816
70	-1.150	-1.350	-.950	.625	.769	-1.495	170	-.700	-.750	-.650	.450	.543	-1.289
71	1.100	.900	.600	.400	.474	2.320	171	.100	-.050	.250	.600	.758	.132
72	-.375	-.600	-.150	.638	.789	-.475	172	.325	.400	.250	.825	.838	.288
73	-.050	.200	-.300	.575	.698	-.072	173	.800	.800	.800	.650	.738	1.084
74	.425	.450	.400	.475	.526	.808	174	1.125	1.500	.750	.713	.844	1.333
75	-.650	-.700	-.600	1.100	1.361	-.478	175	-.175	-.250	-.100	.325	.377	-.464
76	.175	.200	.150	.625	.626	.279	176	-.150	-.150	-.150	.450	.540	-.278
77	.450	.550	.350	.450	.502	.896	177	.225	0	.450	.538	.646	.348
78	-.350	-.450	-.250	.500	.567	-.618	178	.350	.450	.250	.450	.471	.743
79	.025	-.100	.150	.188	.217	.115	179	-.700	-.500	-.900	.800	.917	-.763
80	.475	.600	.350	.488	.618	.768	180	-.125	-.450	.200	.875	.988	-.126
81	1.175	1.000	1.350	.875	1.119	1.055	181	.400	.300	.500	.500	.644	.621
82	-.500	-.700	-.800	.550	.412	-1.215	182	-.325	-.500	-.150	1.375	1.588	-.205
83	1.025	.900	1.050	.588	.756	-1.356	183	-.500	-.250	-.350	.300	.394	-.761
84	.350	0	.700	.925	1.137	.308	184	.050	-.100	.200	.325	.383	.130
85	.700	.900	.300	1.100	1.187	.590	185	-.700	-.450	-.850	.550	.675	-1.037
86	-.625	-.450	-.700	.438	.836	-1.166	186	1.325	1.300	.750	.475	.550	2.409
87	.150	.250	.500	.300	.349	.430	187	-.725	-.800	-.650	.825	.890	-.814
88	.500	.200	.800	.550	.641	.781	188	.375	.750	0	.738	.870	.431
89	.375	.450	.300	.688	.928	.406	189	0	.050	-.050	.350	.406	0
90	1.175	1.350	1.000	1.275	1.306	.899	190	.175	.150	.100	.750	.084	2.082
91	1.050	1.400	.700	1.175	1.125	.938	191	.325	.550	.100	.975	1.087	.299
92	-.925	-1.100	-.750	1.275	1.502	-.616	192	-.425	-.450	-.400	.525	.554	-.767
93	.925	1.300	.550	1.175	1.321	.700	193	.300	.650	-.050	.700	.822	.365
94	-1.100	-1.100	-1.000	.600	.721	-1.527	194	.075	.350	-.200	1.175	1.250	.060
95	-.150	.150	.100	.525	.610	-.246	195	.100	.050	.150	.750	.851	.117
96	-.300	-.450	-.150	1.600	1.771	-.169	196	.175	-.150	.500	.925	1.089	.161
97	-.150	-.400	.100	.650	.779	-.198	197	.300	.800	.200	.150	.158	.190
98	.100	-.500	.300	.900	.962	.104	198	.175	.100	.260	.675	.829	.211
99	-.375	-.150	-.600	.513	.618	-.606	199	-1.100	-1.100	-1.100	1.450	1.518	-.725
100	-.275	-.500	-.050	.438	.551	-.518	200	-.050	.200	-.300	.525	.622	-.804

TABLE D.—STATISTICS FOR DRAWINGS FROM NORMAL UNIVERSE—(*Continued*)

Sample Number	$\bar{X}$	Median	$\frac{\text{Max.} + \text{Min.}}{2}$	μ	σ	%	Sample Number	$\bar{X}$	Median	$\frac{\text{Max.} + \text{Min.}}{2}$	μ	σ	%
201	.125	.150	.100	1.425	1.502	.083	301	-.400	-.150	-.650	.450	.534	-.749
202	.475	.400	.550	.975	1.087	.437	302	.625	1.100	.150	1.013	1.198	.522
203	.400	.300	.400	.250	.308	1.298	303	.125	.700	-.650	.963	1.124	.111
204	-.675	-.950	-.400	.838	1.028	-.656	304	-.100	-.100	-.100	1.750	1.866	-.054
205	.275	.450	.100	.575	.642	.428	305	-.325	-.300	.950	1.125	1.477	-.220
206	-.300	-.050	-.550	.800	1.002	-.299	306	.775	.600	.950	.925	.968	.801
207	-.375	-.250	-.500	.575	.602	-.623	307	-.350	-.400	-.300	.450	.517	-.677
208	.750	.700	.800	1.050	1.185	.633	308	-1.000	-1.000	-.200	.100	.141	-.709
209	0	-.250	.250	.550	.675	0	309	.300	1.050	-.450	1.400	1.641	.183
210	1.100	1.050	.550	.450	.464	2.371	310	.325	.550	.100	.363	.421	.772
211	.750	.750	.750	.700	.782	.959	311	.400	.200	.600	.400	.474	.844
212	-.325	-.350	-.300	.475	.526	-.618	312	.125	0	.250	.238	.277	.451
213	-.300	-.300	-.300	.350	.430	-.698	313	-.475	-.400	-.550	.325	.402	-1.182
214	-.050	.350	-.450	.675	.789	-.634	314	-.275	.550	0	.775	.884	-.312
215	-.325	-.500	-.150	1.075	1.103	-.294	315	-.525	.350	.700	1.050	.736	-.713
216	-.475	-.350	-.600	.925	.973	-.488	316	.650	.850	.450	.875	1.115	.583
217	-.725	-.950	-.500	.363	.421	-1.722	317	.425	.100	.750	.838	1.018	.418
218	.350	.150	.550	.600	.722	.485	318	-.350	-.400	-.300	.500	.540	-.648
219	.175	.100	.250	.725	.740	.240	319	-.900	-.900	-.900	.800	.943	-.954
220	-.325	-.450	-.200	.413	.512	-.635	320	.025	-.100	.150	.825	.896	.028
221	.300	.150	.450	.350	.418	.718	321	-.325	-.650	0	.863	1.042	-.312
222	-.400	-.400	-.400	.350	.381	-1.050	322	-.250	.200	-.700	1.125	1.379	-.182
223	-.050	-.250	.150	.675	.838	-.060	323	1.100	1.200	1.000	.950	1.102	.998
224	-.300	-.150	-.450	.350	.418	-.718	324	.050	.300	-.200	.800	.928	.054
225	.150	.500	-.200	1.150	1.321	.114	325	.025	-.050	.200	.625	.634	.039
226	-.225	-.100	-.350	.325	.370	-.608	326	-.150	-.050	-.250	.700	.789	-.190
227	.875	.750	.600	.363	.444	1.971	327	-.125	-.100	-.150	.288	.390	-.320
228	-1.075	-1.600	-.550	1.088	1.309	-.823	328	-.050	-.350	.250	.625	.736	-.680
229	.700	.700	.700	.700	.860	.814	329	-.175	-.250	-.100	.488	.642	-.273
230	0	-.200	.200	.600	.700	0	330	-.225	-.350	-.100	.375	.455	-.495
231	-.050	.050	-.150	.650	.687	-.073	331	1.275	1.050	1.150	.925	.991	1.287
232	-.050	.850	-.950	1.475	1.710	-.029	332	0	.050	-.050	.350	.367	0
233	-.525	-.500	-.550	.675	.729	-.720	333	.200	0	.400	.450	.552	.362
234	.100	.150	.050	.450	.495	.202	334	-.875	-1.550	-.700	1.388	1.662	-.526
235	-.625	-.700	-.550	.925	.955	-.654	335	-.375	-.400	-.350	.525	.526	-.713
236	.550	.450	.650	.600	.701	.784	336	-.075	-.150	0	.825	.847	-.089
237	.700	.550	.850	1.050	1.387	.505	337	.700	.450	.950	.800	.992	.700
238	.575	.550	.400	.225	.286	2.010	338	.575	.050	1.200	1.213	1.477	.389
239	.675	.750	.600	.825	.873	.778	339	.650	.500	.800	.550	.622	1.045
240	.525	.650	.400	.425	.522	1.006	340	.125	-.150	.400	.488	.576	.217
241	-.625	-.400	-.850	.688	.856	-.730	341	-.225	-.500	.050	1.125	1.316	-.171
242	-.175	.150	-.500	.663	.779	-.225	342	.725	.700	.850	.925	1.064	.682
243	-.650	-.550	-.550	.400	.438	-1.484	343	.825	.650	1.000	.825	.887	.930
244	.300	.550	.050	.450	.524	.572	344	.075	-.150	.300	.463	.545	.138
245	-.700	-.950	-.450	.800	.951	-.736	345	.175	.350	0	1.275	1.390	.126
246	.510	.150	.150	.950	.996	.151	346	1.125	.950	1.300	1.175	1.231	.914
247	-.375	-.550	-.200	.625	.672	-.558	347	-.725	-.700	-.750	1.125	1.202	-.603
248	.125	.100	.150	.675	.773	.162	348	-.225	-.250	-.200	.275	.303	-.742
249	.150	.300	0	.600	.736	.204	349	.025	0	.050	.825	.978	.026
250	.575	.800	.350	.725	.826	.696	350	-.650	-.650	-.650	1.100	1.189	-.547

251	-1.050	-1.100	-.400	.350	.356	-2.950	351	.325	.250	.400	1.175	1.289	.252
252	0	.050	-.050	.550	.561	0	352	-.150	-.150	-.150	.500	.559	-.268
253	.450	.450	.450	.250	.319	1.411	353	0	-.050	.050	.400	.406	0
254	-.400	-.400	-.400	.700	.762	-.525	354	-.325	-.250	-.400	1.475	1.645	-.198
255	-.425	-.100	-.750	.775	.920	-.462	355	.175	-.050	.400	.513	.618	.283
256	.125	-.150	.400	.825	.947	.132	356	.250	.450	.050	1.250	1.328	.188
257	.225	.100	.350	.875	1.055	.213	357	.500	.550	.450	.900	1.056	.475
258	.450	.450	.450	.300	.335	1.344	358	0	.250	-.250	.800	.875	0
259	.400	.550	.250	.300	.354	1.130	359	-.100	.050	-.250	.600	.667	-.150
260	.250	.150	.350	.700	.896	.279	360	-.350	-.950	.250	.975	1.132	-.309
261	.400	.250	.350	.250	.292	1.370	361	.150	.700	-.400	1.025	1.213	.124
262	-.050	-.050	-.050	.500	.559	-.089	362	.400	.250	.550	.750	.863	.463
263	.700	.500	.900	.650	.815	.859	363	-.175	-.450	.100	.688	.826	-.212
264	-.750	-.550	-.950	.750	.801	-.936	364	-.200	-.300	-.100	.950	.967	-.207
265	.550	.380	.650	.425	.512	1.075	365	.825	.800	.550	.288	.390	2.118
266	.350	.650	.050	.725	.867	.404	366	-.675	-.800	-.550	.825	.936	-.721
267	-.425	.050	-.900	1.325	1.607	-.264	367	.150	.450	-.150	.675	.807	.186
268	-.350	-.200	-.500	.475	.585	.598	368	-.550	-.650	-.450	1.250	1.269	-.434
269	-.450	-.350	-.550	.650	.826	-.545	369	.275	.050	.400	.638	.798	.282
270	.050	-.050	.150	.450	.471	.106	370	-.525	0	-1.050	1.038	1.247	-.421
271	-.250	-.500	0	.825	1.030	-.243	371	0	.350	-.350	.850	1.032	0
272	-.350	-.050	-.650	.750	.861	-.463	372	.250	.200	.300	1.050	1.080	.251
273	-.725	-.650	-.800	.475	.581	-1.248	373	.550	.650	.450	.700	.722	.762
274	-.600	-.950	-.250	.700	.840	-.714	374	-.750	-.450	-.950	.625	.736	-1.019
275	.125	.300	-.050	.875	1.119	.112	375	.100	.150	.050	.700	.784	.128
276	.175	.250	.100	.325	.542	.512	376	.450	.650	.250	.650	.789	.570
277	-.300	-.200	-.400	.450	.524	-.572	377	.300	.500	.100	.450	.539	.553
278	-1.225	-1.050	-1.300	.738	.936	-1.308	378	-.175	-.200	-.150	.825	.826	-.211
279	-.275	-.550	0	.925	1.076	-.255	379	.250	-.400	-.700	.775	.909	.275
280	.425	.550	.300	.975	1.114	.382	380	-.450	-.400	-.500	.800	.826	-.545
281	.200	.100	.300	.550	.660	.303	381	-.100	-.150	-.050	.700	.834	-.120
282	.125	.100	-.050	.775	.795	.157	382	.050	.250	-.150	.575	.701	.071
283	-.175	-.050	-.300	.313	.377	-.464	383	1.100	1.350	.850	.900	.997	1.105
284	.700	.400	1.000	.700	.846	.828	384	-.125	-.400	.150	1.063	1.339	-.093
285	-.375	-.400	-.350	.775	.909	-.412	385	-.025	.100	-.150	.338	.415	-.060
286	1.275	1.300	.650	.525	.540	2.360	386	-.500	-.750	-.200	.700	.822	-.608
287	-.200	-.150	-.250	.300	.394	-.508	387	.625	.650	.600	.825	.829	.754
288	-.350	-.450	-.250	.750	.782	-.448	388	.375	.150	.600	.663	.811	.462
289	.500	.450	.550	.600	.652	.766	389	.775	1.100	.450	.788	.952	.814
290	.150	-.100	.400	.625	.753	.199	390	.025	.200	-.150	.463	.563	.044
291	-.125	-.050	-.200	.775	.789	-.158	391	.025	.150	-.100	.825	.879	.028
292	.200	.150	.250	1.200	1.416	.141	392	.275	.100	.450	.713	.905	.304
293	.725	1.000	.450	.463	.540	1.343	393	-.825	-.800	-.850	1.225	1.268	-.650
294	-.800	-.500	-.700	.500	.583	-1.372	394	.050	.250	-.150	.900	1.026	.049
295	.475	.350	.600	.825	.960	.495	395	-.750	-.600	-.900	.600	.687	-1.092
296	-.300	-.500	-.100	.700	.787	-.383	396	-.300	-.350	-.250	.700	.784	-.385
297	1.150	.700	1.300	.875	1.022	1.125	397	-.525	-.400	-.650	.438	.550	-.955
298	.650	.900	.400	1.300	1.415	.459	398	.150	.150	.150	.300	.390	.383
299	.200	.400	0	.750	.941	.213	399	0	-.450	.450	.700	.809	0
300	-.625	-.900	-.350	.663	.804	-.778	400	-.175	-.300	-.050	.875	.901	-.194

TABLE D.—STATISTICS FOR DRAWINGS FROM NORMAL UNIVERSE—*(Continued)*

Sample Number	$\overline{X}$	Median	$\frac{\text{Max.} + \text{Min.}}{2}$	μ	σ	%	Sample Number	$\overline{X}$	Median	$\frac{\text{Max.} + \text{Min.}}{2}$	μ	σ	%
401	-.100	-.100	-.100	.400	.447	-.224	501	.375	-.200	.050	.375	.760	.493
402	.400	.600	.200	.750	.941	.425	502	-.750	-.700	-.800	.500	.585	-1.305
403	.350	.450	.250	.175	.205	1.707	503	-.850	-1.100	-.600	.975	1.229	-.692
404	.500	.450	.550	.700	.718	.696	504	.550	.750	.350	.700	.807	.682
405	.175	.200	.150	.425	.536	.326	505	0	-.050	.050	.200	.255	0
406	-.575	-.650	-.500	.625	.733	-.784	506	.375	.250	.500	.925	1.213	.309
407	.400	.650	.150	.500	.596	.671	507	-.575	-.550	-.500	.275	.356	-1.616
408	0	-.100	.100	.450	.574	0	508	-.325	-.250	-.400	.363	.402	-.808
409	-.025	-.400	.350	.663	.773	-.323	509	.400	.550	.250	.900	1.017	.393
410	-.725	-.550	-.900	.725	.835	-.868	510	-.100	-.300	.100	.500	.503	-.199
411	.425	.550	.300	.475	.589	.721	511	.325	.150	.500	.438	.526	.618
412	-.825	-.700	-.950	.875	.901	-.916	512	.575	.350	.800	.525	.634	.906
413	-.225	-.050	-.400	.625	.750	-.300	513	.325	.400	.250	.625	.708	.459
414	.650	.650	.650	.700	.701	.927	514	1.050	1.150	.950	1.150	1.289	.815
415	0	.350	-.350	1.050	1.177	0	515	.250	.250	.250	.200	.205	1.219
416	-.300	-.450	-.150	.300	.367	-.817	516	-.150	-.250	-.050	.400	.438	-.342
417	.225	.100	.350	.338	.415	.542	517	.325	.450	.200	1.475	1.457	.223
418	-.475	-.550	-.400	.375	.402	-1.182	518	.825	.700	.550	.338	.415	1.988
419	.100	.150	.050	.850	.941	.106	519	0	.200	-.200	.950	1.116	0
420	.350	-.100	.800	1.175	1.432	.244	520	-.675	-.800	-.550	.488	.614	-1.099
421	-.200	0	-.400	.500	.574	-.348	521	-.250	-.450	-.050	1.075	1.393	-.179
422	-.150	-.500	.200	.950	1.071	-.140	522	.225	.150	.300	.838	1.134	.198
423	.125	.150	.100	.375	.497	.252	523	-1.000	-.900	1.100	.650	.857	-1.167
424	-.175	-.300	-.050	1.375	1.431	-.122	524	.450	0	.900	1.075	1.286	.350
425	-.675	-.800	-.550	1.225	1.482	-.456	525	-.450	-.850	-.050	.925	1.128	-.399
426	-.250	-.100	.250	.325	.383	-.652	526	.525	.400	.650	.675	.835	.628
427	.200	.100	.300	.550	.612	.327	527	.675	.800	.550	.738	.965	.699
428	-.175	-.600	.250	1.075	1.249	-.112	528	.900	.950	.850	1.150	1.347	.668
429	-.075	-.100	-.050	.675	.773	-.097	529	-.125	-.400	.150	.775	.950	-.132
430	.550	.450	.550	.400	.438	1.255	530	-.625	-.750	-.500	1.025	1.068	-.585
431	.850	1.250	.450	.875	1.035	.821	531	.300	.450	.150	1.550	1.586	.189
432	-.225	-.350	-.100	.525	.567	-.397	532	.775	.950	.500	.338	.396	1.958
433	.975	.800	1.150	.775	.879	1.109	533	.475	.700	.250	.575	.676	.703
434	-.600	-.850	-.350	.850	.972	-.617	534	.100	0	.200	.750	.797	.126
435	-.075	.100	-.250	.775	.879	-.853	535	.075	.050	.100	.725	.729	.103
436	.450	-.250	1.150	1.075	1.242	.362	536	0	.250	.250	1.150	1.217	0
437	-.925	-1.000	.407	-.925	.356	-2.598	537	.325	.350	.300	.475	.526	.618
438	.225	.200	.470	.375	.383	.587	538	-.300	-.100	-.500	.550	.636	-.472
439	.325	.450	.846	.675	.864	.376	539	-.600	-.350	-.850	.550	.652	-.920
440	.950	.800	.501	.400	.471	2.019	540	1.000	.650	.950	.650	.758	1.319
441	.050	.300	.595	.475	.572	.087	541	-1.425	-1.450	-.900	.475	.638	-2.233
442	.250	.350	.533	.425	.540	.463	542	-.025	.150	-.200	.738	.936	-.027
443	.650	.500	.533	.425	.522	1.245	543	.450	.100	.800	.850	1.052	.428
444	.025	.200	1.661	1.325	1.475	.017	544	.250	.950	-.450	1.330	1.556	.161
445	.450	.500	.376	.300	.319	1.411	545	.400	.950	-.150	1.000	1.190	.336
446	-.325	.300	.345	.275	.327	-.994	546	.675	.800	.550	.488	.618	1.092
447	.425	.850	1.458	1.163	1.410	.301	547	.325	.650	0	.663	.779	.417
448	.825	.850	1.034	.825	.844	.978	548	.475	-.600	-.350	.675	.835	-.569
449	.400	.400	.752	.600	.600	.667	549	.400	.800	0	1.050	1.251	.320
450	-.150	-.200	.752	.600	.634	-.237	550	-.125	0	-.250	.425	.460	-.272

451	.200	.350	.501	.400	.485	.412	551	.150	.150	.150	.500	.522	.287
452	.200	-.150	.689	.550	.636	.314	552	-.075	-.100	-.050	.675	.698	-.107
453	.775	1.000	.424	.338	.390	1.987	553	.775	1.050	.500	.788	.976	.794
454	.800	1.300	1.253	1.000	1.175	.681	554	-.825	-1.050	-.600	.463	.554	-1.490
455	.250	.150	.501	.400	.438	.571	555	-.475	-.500	-.450	.625	.705	-.674
456	.225	.150	.282	.225	.249	.904	556	-.375	-1.500	-.600	.725	.896	-.419
457	1.075	1.200	.533	.425	.460	2.338	557	.450	.350	.550	1.300	1.312	.343
458	-.100	-.350	1.253	1.000	1.089	-.092	558	-.300	0	-.600	.800	.943	-.318
459	.025	.150	.971	.775	.817	.306	559	-.100	.350	-.550	.900	1.056	-.095
460	.300	.100	.752	.600	.748	.401	560	-.475	-.550	-.400	.375	.402	-1.182
461	.100	.100	1.755	1.400	1.720	.058	561	.325	-.050	.700	.888	1.073	.303
462	.075	.300	1.410	1.125	1.262	.595	562	-.450	-.700	-.200	.925	1.158	-.389
463	0	.050	.689	.550	.628	0	563	.200	.150	.250	1.150	1.168	.171
464	.825	1.150	.768	.613	.736	1.121	564	.200	0	.400	.500	.616	.325
465	.150	.200	.877	.700	.709	.212	565	-.375	-.150	-.600	.575	.698	.537
466	.600	.500	.627	.560	.612	.980	566	-1.200	-1.150	-.750	.700	.704	-1.200
467	-.275	-.350	.658	.525	.597	-.461	567	-.700	-.900	-.500	.550	.636	-1.100
468	-.475	-.550	.298	.238	.295	-1.610	568	-.900	-1.100	-.700	1.200	1.233	-.730
469	-.800	-1.000	.877	.700	.872	-.918	569	1.175	1.450	.600	.488	.576	2.040
470	-.150	0	.407	.325	.390	-.385	570	-1.000	-.700	-1.100	.700	.846	-1.182
471	-.100	.500	1.504	1.200	1.435	-.070	571	-.525	-.600	-.350	.213	.259	-2.028
472	.025	-.150	.721	.575	.642	.039	572	-.075	-.350	.200	.975	1.099	-.068
473	-.300	-.250	.313	.250	.274	-1.095	573	.500	.400	.600	1.800	1.810	.276
474	-.275	-.200	1.285	1.025	1.318	-.209	574	-.700	-.250	-1.150	.850	1.007	-.695
475	-.075	-.150	.298	.238	.295	-.254	575	-.450	-.450	-.450	.600	.694	-.648
476	.200	.450	.564	.450	.524	.382	576	.025	-.050	.100	.375	.444	.056
477	.150	-.350	1.285	1.025	1.205	.124	577	-.200	-.200	-.200	.600	.781	-.256
478	-.275	-.450	.674	.538	.669	-.411	578	-.325	-.450	-.200	.525	.657	-.495
479	.500	.150	1.128	.900	1.098	.455	579	-.100	.250	-.450	.800	.951	-.105
480	-.550	-.600	.157	.125	.148	-.374	580	.525	.650	.400	.425	.476	1.102
481	.025	-.200	.783	.625	.740	.338	581	.425	.550	.300	.463	.581	.731
482	.825	.850	1.034	.825	.907	.910	582	.175	.250	.100	.288	.363	.482
483	.375	.300	.627	.500	.512	.732	583	.950	1.000	.600	.450	.476	1.996
484	.100	.050	.376	.300	.339	.295	584	.600	.500	.700	.700	.735	.816
485	.175	.150	1.347	1.075	1.123	.156	585	-.225	-.150	-.300	.575	.665	-.338
486	.275	.200	.407	.325	.402	.684	586	-.175	0	-.350	.775	.841	-.208
487	-1.150	-1.200	.501	.400	.502	2.291	587	-.025	.250	-.300	.825	.947	-.026
488	-.350	-.750	1.379	1.100	1.293	-.229	588	-.225	.200	-.650	.888	1.045	-.215
489	.650	.950	.783	.625	.743	.875	589	-.300	0	-.600	550	.656	-.457
490	-.550	-.450	.721	.575	.750	-.733	590	-1.000	-.850	-1.250	.750	.925	-1.189
491	.300	.150	.815	.650	.731	.410	591	-.200	-.100	-.300	.200	.245	-.816
492	.125	.200	.971	.775	.798	.157	592	-.475	-.550	-.400	.488	.642	-.740
493	-.425	.350	.173	.138	.164	-2.590	593	-.825	-1.250	-.400	.913	1.083	-.762
494	.275	.350	1.034	.825	.955	.288	594	.350	.450	.250	.650	.687	.510
495	.700	.850	.752	.600	.711	.984	595	0	-.100	.100	.600	.728	0
496	.100	-.200	.689	.550	.644	.155	596	-.450	-.150	-.750	.575	.672	-.670
497	.350	-.450	1.347	1.075	.960	.365	597	-.125	-.200	-.050	.525	.622	-.201
498	-.475	-.050	1.207	.963	1.156	-.411	598	.250	0	.500	.625	.763	.328
499	.025	0	.783	.625	.756	.331	599	-1.050	-.650	-1.450	.975	1.180	-.890
500	.475	.550	.971	.775	.811	.686	600	.800	.750	.650	.500	.524	1.527

TABLE D.—STATISTICS FOR DRAWINGS FROM NORMAL UNIVERSE—(*Continued*)

Sample Number	$\bar{X}$	Median	$\frac{\text{Max.} + \text{Min.}}{2}$	μ	σ	%	Sample Number	$\bar{X}$	Median	$\frac{\text{Max.} + \text{Min.}}{2}$	μ	σ	%
601	.325	.200	.450	.625	.676	.481	701	-.275	0	-.550	.613	.729	-.377
602	-.600	-.600	-.300	.200	.224	-2.679	702	.275	.250	.300	.475	.636	.431
603	.675	.750	.600	.575	.622	1.085	703	.475	.800	.150	.888	1.078	.438
604	.750	.850	.650	.750	.856	.876	704	-.450	.650	-.260	1.000	1.114	-.404
605	-.450	-.550	-.350	.350	.415	-1.085	705	1.400	1.111	.900	.600	.707	1.980
606	.575	.450	.700	.975	1.114	.516	706	-.200	-.350	-.050	.500	.628	-.318
607	.075	.100	.050	1.175	1.188	.063	707	.150	.350	-.050	.775	.976	.154
608	.525	.700	.350	.463	.563	.932	708	-.450	-.750	-.150	.850	.986	-.456
609	-.450	-.600	-.300	.625	.795	-.566	709	.100	.100	.100	.650	.667	.150
610	-.225	-.400	-.050	.713	.904	-.249	710	-.300	-.450	-.150	.300	.367	-.817
611	-.300	-.650	.050	.600	.696	-.451	711	.075	.050	.100	.375	.497	.151
612	-.250	-.400	-.100	.375	.455	-.549	712	.075	0	.150	.675	.701	.107
613	-.275	.100	-.650	.813	.983	-.280	713	-.125	-.250	0	.525	.657	-.190
614	-.250	-.600	.100	1.500	1.591	-.157	714	-.375	-.050	-.700	.563	.661	-.567
615	.375	.400	.350	.925	1.018	.368	715	-.575	-.750	-.400	.625	.672	-.856
616	-.200	-.300	-.100	.450	.579	-.345	716	-1.125	-1.150	-.500	.375	.396	-2.840
617	.750	.050	.100	1.050	.675	1.111	717	.025	.200	-.250	.875	.934	.027
618	-.325	-.450	-.200	.925	.950	-.342	718	-.025	.200	-.250	.438	.531	-.047
619	.200	.050	.350	.250	.292	.685	719	.775	.250	1.300	.963	1.135	.683
620	.125	-.250	.500	.688	.801	.156	720	.150	.400	-.100	.800	.928	.162
621	-.525	-.100	-.950	1.038	1.260	-.417	721	-.125	-.300	.050	1.125	1.160	-.108
622	.150	.150	.150	.200	.205	.732	722	.500	.450	.350	.200	.255	1.960
623	-1.125	-1.100	-1.050	.725	.795	-1.415	723	.625	.950	.300	.963	1.181	.529
624	-.575	-.350	-.800	.825	.978	-.588	724	.625	.650	.600	1.175	1.181	.529
625	.700	.250	1.150	1.100	1.332	.588	725	.600	.850	.350	.800	.987	.608
626	.200	.500	-.100	.650	.768	.260	726	-.275	-.100	-.450	.363	.427	-.644
627	.425	.450	.400	.825	.844	.504	727	-.250	-.150	-.350	1.050	1.324	-.189
628	.300	.200	.400	1.200	1.221	.246	728	-.025	-.100	-.050	.525	.545	.046
629	.050	0	.100	1.200	1.301	.384	729	-.125	-.450	.200	.863	1.061	-.118
630	.350	.100	.600	.650	.779	.449	730	-.300	-.150	-.450	.550	.644	-.466
631	.450	.150	.750	.950	1.031	.436	731	.300	-.100	.700	1.150	1.298	.231
632	.600	.600	.400	.350	.354	1.695	732	.250	.450	.050	.900	1.128	.222
633	.200	0	-.400	1.350	1.780	.112	733	.025	.100	-.050	.575	.642	.039
634	-.100	0	-.200	.750	.771	-.130	734	.450	.450	.250	.200	.205	2.195
635	-.675	.500	-.650	.413	.497	-1.358	735	-.350	-.900	.200	.975	1.132	-.309
636	-.125	-.150	-.100	.525	.554	-.226	736	-.175	-.250	-.100	.975	1.030	-.170
637	1.025	.750	1.200	.775	.926	1.107	737	-.850	-.850	-.250	.150	.179	-4.750
638	.100	.200	0	.550	.579	.173	738	-.325	-.150	-.500	.475	.554	-.587
639	.025	-.050	.100	.238	.295	.085	739	.975	.900	.850	.675	.701	1.391
640	.175	.100	.250	.275	.335	.522	740	-.575	-.900	.100	.938	1.152	-.499
641	-.975	-1.150	-.700	1.075	1.256	-.756	741	.775	1.400	.150	1.238	1.451	.534
642	.750	.750	.750	1.000	.960	.781	742	.350	.250	.450	.850	.907	.386
643	.925	.650	1.000	.638	.760	1.218	743	.125	.300	-.050	.463	.563	.222
644	.200	.500	-.100	1.050	1.310	.153	744	.325	.450	.200	.875	1.028	.315
645	-.775	-.550	-.600	.413	.492	-1.576	745	-1.350	-1.600	-1.100	.825	1.030	-1.310
646	-.675	-.850	-.500	.575	.642	-1.051	746	-.400	.300	-.500	.800	.927	.431
647	-.425	-.550	-.300	.725	.934	-.455	747	-.600	-.750	-.450	.500	.543	-1.105
648	-.800	-.800	-.400	.300	.316	-2.531	748	.025	.100	-.050	.475	.512	.049
649	-.550	-.250	-.850	.850	.986	-.554	749	-.300	-.400	-.200	1.350	1.398	-.215
650	.250	-.300	.800	.875	1.013	.247	750	.100	-.500	.250	.550	.644	.155

651	.100	.050	.250	.850	.951	.105	751	-.125	.200	-.450	.975	1.177	-.106
652	.225	.300	.150	1.075	1.178	.191	752	0	-.200	.200	.550	.682	0
653	.100	.100	.100	.750	.765	.131	753	-.475	-.400	-.550	.625	.760	-.625
654	-.100	-.800	.600	1.200	1.391	-.072	754	-.275	.100	-.650	1.225	1.425	-.193
655	1.000	.850	.650	.450	.515	1.942	755	-.456	-.650	-.250	.325	.377	-1.194
656	-.825	-.750	-.900	.825	.955	-.864	756	-.975	-1.000	-.850	.525	.572	-1.705
657	-.600	-.800	-.400	.400	.474	-1.276	757	.275	.750	-.200	.888	1.035	.266
658	-.300	-.350	-.250	.550	.561	-.535	758	.875	1.050	.700	.725	.795	1.101
659	-.500	-1.100	.100	1.150	1.345	-.372	759	-.275	-.250	-.300	.525	.554	-.496
660	.250	-.200	.700	1.375	1.693	.148	760	.025	-.600	.650	1.038	1.209	.021
661	-.625	-.800	-.450	.863	1.110	-.563	761	.075	-.250	.400	.663	.779	.096
662	1.150	1.100	1.100	1.050	1.052	1.094	762	.300	.500	.100	.550	.667	.450
663	.575	.650	.500	.825	.909	.638	763	.200	-.100	.500	1.150	1.446	.138
664	-.200	-.400	0	1.300	1.375	-.145	764	-.075	0	-.150	.625	.760	-.099
665	.125	.500	-.100	.425	.512	.244	765	.975	.900	1.050	.875	.998	.977
666	-.025	-.400	.350	.713	.833	-.029	766	.325	.350	.300	.375	.596	.821
667	.250	.500	0	.475	.554	.452	767	.250	.250	.250	.900	.954	.268
668	.175	.150	.200	.725	.867	.202	768	.525	.450	.500	.425	.512	1.025
669	-.100	-.100	-.100	.750	.930	-.108	769	.475	.350	.500	.375	.415	1.145
670	.350	.700	0	.625	.721	.485	770	.275	.500	.050	.925	1.087	.253
671	.025	.150	-.100	.325	.390	.641	771	.350	.500	.200	.275	.327	1.070
672	.975	.800	.950	.563	.698	1.397	772	.575	.650	.500	.575	.593	.970
673	-.075	-.350	.200	.588	.716	-.105	773	.550	.600	.500	1.100	1.254	.439
674	.425	.200	.650	1.325	1.363	.312	774	.625	.700	.350	.275	.286	2.360
675	-.225	0	-.450	1.125	1.168	-.193	775	.275	-.050	.600	1.075	1.238	.222
676	.350	.250	.450	.550	.567	.617	776	.775	.750	.800	1.275	1.344	.577
677	-.100	-.100	-.100	.350	.495	-.202	777	.625	.500	.650	.475	.522	1.197
678	1.025	.800	1.050	.638	.789	1.299	778	.500	.550	.450	1.800	1.883	.266
679	-.100	-.250	.050	.750	.791	-.145	779	-.625	-.550	-.700	.625	.789	-.792
680	.225	.550	-.100	1.150	1.026	.219	780	-.250	-.600	.100	1.000	1.171	-.213
681	-.275	-.400	-.150	.775	.918	-.299	781	-.675	-.650	-.700	.775	.884	-.764
682	.350	.250	.450	.475	.610	.574	782	-.900	-.850	-.950	.700	.957	-.940
683	.275	.400	.150	.575	.698	.394	783	.275	.100	.450	.725	.779	.353
684	.375	.400	.350	.575	.581	.645	784	-.325	-.150	-.500	.925	1.055	-.308
685	-.775	-.650	-.600	.365	.444	-1.746	785	.025	-.200	.250	.538	.657	.038
686	.250	.450	.050	.825	1.050	.238	786	.250	.500	.200	.800	.826	.303
687	.250	.150	.350	.600	.657	.381	787	-.075	-.200	.050	.388	.476	-.158
688	.525	.400	.650	.625	.716	.733	788	-.475	-.550	-.400	.275	.327	-1.453
689	1.100	.750	.850	.550	.636	1.730	789	.375	.400	.350	.625	.638	.588
690	.175	.850	-.500	1.188	1.579	.127	790	.150	.300	0	1.100	1.368	.110
691	.350	.350	.350	.850	1.167	.300	791	.725	.600	.850	.625	.676	1.072
692	.300	.600	0	.500	.583	.515	792	.075	.450	-.300	1.625	1.932	.039
693	-.175	0	-.350	.363	.432	-.405	793	.325	.300	.350	.825	.978	.332
694	.625	.350	.900	.638	.766	.816	794	.700	.800	.600	.600	.728	.962
695	-.400	-.550	-.250	.500	.620	-.645	795	-.625	-.500	-.750	.575	.698	-.895
696	-.275	-.600	.050	.738	.879	-.313	796	.675	.700	.650	.525	.540	1.250
697	-.150	-.300	0	.800	.838	-.179	797	.675	.600	.750	.925	.955	.707
698	-.425	-.650	-.200	.463	.545	-.780	798	-.385	-.150	-.500	.588	.729	-.446
699	-.150	-.400	.100	.475	.569	-.268	799	-.400	-.400	-.400	.550	.652	-.614
700	-.925	-.950	-.900	.525	.709	-1.304	800	.625	.600	.650	.775	.823	.759

TABLE D.—STATISTICS FOR DRAWINGS FROM NORMAL UNIVERSE—*(Continued)*

Sample Number	$\overline{X}$	Median	$\frac{\text{Max.} + \text{Min.}}{2}$	μ	σ	%	Sample Number	$\overline{X}$	Median	$\frac{\text{Max.} + \text{Min.}}{2}$	μ	σ	%
801	-.275	-.350	-.200	.775	.844	-.326	901	-.625	-.600	-.250	.138	.179	-3.490
802	-.975	-1.000	-.250	.225	.259	-3.765	902	.075	.250	-.100	.738	.942	.080
803	.300	.100	.500	.550	.671	.447	903	-.800	-.750	-.850	.550	.628	-1.274
804	-.500	-.850	-.150	.600	.696	-.718	904	.500	.700	.300	1.500	1.565	.319
805	-.050	-.050	-.050	.400	.531	-.094	905	.775	.800	.550	.288	.390	1.987
806	-.325	-.400	-.300	.375	.471	-.690	906	.250	.200	.300	.750	.792	.316
807	-.175	-.500	.150	.488	.563	-.311	907	-.300	-.500	-.100	.600	.738	-.407
808	.375	.100	.650	1.125	1.270	.295	908	-.100	-.050	-.150	.450	.604	-.166
809	-.300	.100	-.700	1.050	1.210	-.248	909	.400	.350	.450	.250	.324	1.234
810	-.225	-.100	-.350	.338	.415	-.542	910	-.225	-.150	-.300	.675	.858	-.264
811	-.125	-.150	-.100	.625	.729	-.171	911	.275	.450	.100	.975	1.016	.271
812	.350	.350	.350	.400	.402	.871	912	-.500	-.600	-.400	.400	.458	-1.091
813	-.400	-.200	-.600	1.050	1.125	-.356	913	.250	.200	.300	.450	.476	.525
814	-.425	-.550	-.300	.413	.512	-.830	914	-.150	-.100	-.200	.400	.415	-.361
815	-.325	-.550	-.100	.813	1.016	-.320	915	.175	.150	.200	.575	.618	.283
816	-.825	-.850	-.700	.475	.526	-1.569	916	.675	.500	.850	.825	.873	.773
817	-.375	-.200	-.550	.363	.427	-.878	917	-.025	.500	-.550	1.188	1.416	-.018
818	.125	-.150	.400	.588	.701	.178	918	-.075	.350	-.500	1.313	1.616	-.046
819	.425	.050	.800	.988	1.205	.353	919	-.575	-.600	-.550	.925	1.063	-.541
820	-.450	0	-.900	.825	.963	-.467	920	.525	.450	.600	.625	.733	.716
821	.575	.600	.250	.225	.228	2.521	921	-.075	-.100	-.050	.575	.602	-.125
822	.250	0	.500	.800	.890	.281	922	.175	.500	-.150	.788	.952	.184
823	0	-.150	.150	1.050	1.172	0	923	-.250	-.400	-.100	1.125	1.490	-.168
824	-.075	0	-.150	.375	.421	-.178	924	-.650	-.750	-.550	.850	.944	-.689
825	.675	1.000	.350	.638	.776	.870	925	.275	.550	0	.788	.976	.282
826	-.175	.050	-.400	.725	.807	-.217	926	-.225	-.500	.050	.463	.536	-.420
827	-.050	.100	-.200	.550	.622	-.080	927	.050	.100	0	.300	.363	.138
828	.750	.650	.350	.225	.268	.280	928	-.275	-.550	0	.588	.694	-.396
829	.525	.550	.500	.275	.356	1.475	929	-.275	-.350	-.200	.738	.993	-.277
830	-.450	-.600	-.300	.500	.559	-.803	930	-.400	-.300	-.500	.450	.524	-.763
831	.325	.150	.500	.625	.705	.461	931	-.375	-.550	-.200	.338	.377	-.995
832	-.825	-1.050	-.600	.613	.743	-1.110	932	.050	0	.100	.750	.829	.060
833	.525	.400	.250	.188	.217	2.420	933	.125	.250	0	.625	.661	.189
834	.450	.500	.400	.550	.606	.742	934	-.225	.300	-.650	1.088	1.297	-.173
835	-.225	-.450	0	1.175	1.306	-.172	935	-.600	-.350	-.650	.450	.534	-1.124
836	-.450	-.450	-.450	.500	.559	-.805	936	.475	.500	.350	.225	.259	1.835
837	-.175	.250	-.600	1.013	1.222	-.143	937	.025	.300	-.250	.563	.676	.057
838	-.525	-.250	-.800	.638	.766	-.685	938	.875	.950	.700	.388	.502	1.744
839	.300	.650	-.050	.700	.828	.362	939	-.825	-.800	-.850	.438	.602	-1.370
840	-.925	-.650	-1.100	.688	.844	-1.096	940	.125	-.100	.350	1.138	1.473	.085
841	.675	.450	.900	1.075	1.121	.602	941	.325	.350	.300	.375	.497	.654
842	-.075	-.200	.050	.625	.766	-.098	942	.050	-.250	.350	.925	1.137	.044
843	.300	.250	.350	.750	.778	.386	943	.325	.500	.150	.525	.597	.545
844	.325	.200	.450	.575	.698	.466	944	-.600	-.150	-1.050	1.200	1.394	-.431
845	-.350	-.200	-.400	.275	.319	-1.097	945	.550	.550	-1.050	.550	.680	.809
846	.475	.650	.300	1.425	1.460	.325	946	.100	-.050	.250	.350	.418	.239
847	1.600	1.650	.550	.400	.430	3.720	947	-1.100	-1.000	-.800	.500	.592	-1.858
848	-.250	.200	-.800	1.000	1.205	-.208	948	.425	.450	.400	.425	.507	.838
849	1.300	1.450	.550	.350	.418	3.110	949	-.025	-.450	.400	.975	1.146	-.022
850	.075	.050	.100	.675	.712	.105	950	.100	.700	-.500	1.050	1.219	.082

851	-.300	-.250	.850	.800	1.032	-.291	951	0	.300	-.300	.550	.644	0
852	-.100	.050	-.250	.500	.579	-.173	952	.325	.650	0	.813	.976	.335
853	-.300	-.600	0	.650	.781	-.384	953	-.350	-.400	-.300	.550	.653	-.536
854	-.025	.100	-.150	.725	.769	-.033	954	-.200	-.150	-.250	.800	.815	-.245
855	-.475	-.500	-.450	.675	.773	-.614	955	-.825	-.650	-.800	.488	.602	-1.370
856	.575	.550	.600	.775	.884	.651	956	.625	.550	.700	.575	.614	1.018
857	-.050	.150	-.200	.600	.650	-.769	957	-.100	-.100	-.100	.400	.447	-.224
858	-.075	-.100	-.050	.775	1.028	-.075	958	.650	.750	.550	.500	.567	1.146
859	-.225	-.300	-.150	.325	.402	-.560	959	-.525	-.550	-.500	.575	.661	-.794
860	.150	.300	0	.425	.517	.290	960	-.875	-.800	-.700	.975	1.016	-.862
861	.575	.300	.850	.825	.968	.594	961	.500	.700	.500	.500	.548	1.095
862	-.450	-.350	-.550	.400	.438	-1.027	962	.375	1.050	-.300	1.188	1.383	.271
863	-.075	-.250	.100	.738	.942	-.080	963	-1.425	-1.400	-.750	.425	.536	-2.659
864	.050	.150	-.050	.900	.939	.053	964	.100	.150	.050	.550	.587	.170
865	.175	-.050	.400	1.325	1.461	.120	965	.100	.250	-.050	.550	.644	.155
866	-.100	-.050	-.150	.400	.430	-.233	966	.125	0	.250	.538	.687	.182
867	.100	.050	.150	1.200	1.210	.083	967	.775	1.050	.500	.725	.823	.942
868	-.200	.050	-.450	.650	.784	-.255	968	.425	.300	.550	.725	.769	.553
869	.175	.150	.200	.875	1.021	.171	969	.800	.650	.550	.400	.453	1.766
870	-.400	-.350	-.450	.400	.534	-.749	970	-.025	-.050	-.100	.325	.377	-.066
871	.325	.200	.450	.425	.460	.706	971	-.225	-.400	-.050	.663	.835	-.269
872	.650	.900	.400	.650	.779	.834	972	-.225	-.100	-.350	.575	.650	-.346
873	-.325	-.350	-.300	.625	.683	-.476	973	.050	-.050	.150	.375	.471	.106
874	.725	1.000	.450	.613	.729	.995	974	.450	.650	.250	.750	.923	.488
875	.600	.855	.350	.650	.791	.758	975	-.500	-.300	-.700	.450	.539	-.928
876	-.225	-.350	-.100	.675	.698	-.325	976	-.600	-.650	-.550	.400	.474	-1.266
877	.425	.700	.150	.975	1.217	.349	977	-.200	-.500	.100	.750	.925	-.216
878	.325	.250	.400	.625	.634	.513	978	-.375	-.350	-.100	.075	.084	-4.465
879	.300	.150	.450	.350	.418	.718	979	.450	.500	.400	.650	.669	.673
880	0	-.100	.100	.800	.831	0	980	1.250	1.250	1.250	1.050	1.165	1.075
881	-.300	-.400	-.200	.400	.458	-.655	981	-.125	-.350	.100	.463	.554	-.226
882	-.475	-.500	-.450	.625	.817	-.582	982	.025	.250	-.100	.663	.817	.031
883	-.150	-.250	-.050	.750	.814	-.184	983	-.350	-.350	-.350	.550	.559	-.626
884	.150	0	.300	.325	.390	.384	984	-.075	0	-.150	.163	.192	-.391
885	.450	.450	.250	.150	.179	2.513	985	-.100	.350	-.550	1.250	1.518	-.066
886	.275	0	.550	.775	.904	.304	986	.100	.100	.100	.050	.071	1.408
887	.550	.300	.800	.950	1.125	.489	987	-.325	-.250	-.400	1.138	1.587	-.209
888	.700	.500	.900	.600	.735	.952	988	.125	.100	.150	.388	.531	.235
889	1.000	.550	1.150	.800	.946	1.057	989	-.225	-.350	-.100	.575	.672	-.335
890	.050	0	.100	.175	.217	-.230	990	-.075	-.150	0	.275	.311	-.241
891	.400	.400	.400	.300	.361	1.108	991	-.400	-.350	-.450	.350	.406	-.985
892	.725	.750	1.050	1.150	1.300	.558	992	-.175	-.300	-.100	.438	.550	-.318
893	.075	-.100	.250	.413	.492	.152	993	.400	.550	.250	1.250	1.394	.287
894	-.575	-.500	-.650	.775	.798	-.720	994	-.300	0	-.600	.650	.797	-.375
895	.125	.100	.150	.525	.618	.202	995	.275	1.000	-.450	1.288	1.510	.182
896	-1.125	-1.000	-.550	.425	.460	-2.445	996	1.150	1.350	.950	1.350	1.171	.982
897	-.425	-.050	-.800	.688	.801	-.551	997	-.900	-1.100	-.700	.900	.970	-.928
898	-.100	.150	-.350	.550	.675	-.148	998	-.175	-.230	-.100	.475	.581	-.301
899	-.225	-.250	0	1.075	1.098	-.205	999	.325	.200	.350	.238	.277	1.175
900	-.250	-.550	.050	1.050	1.201	-.208	1000	-.250	-.650	.150	.725	.844	-.296

TABLE D.—STATISTICS FOR DRAWINGS FROM RECTANGULAR UNIVERSE

Sample Number	$\bar{X}$	σ	x	Sample Number	$\bar{X}$	σ	%	Sample Number	$\bar{X}$	σ	%	Sample Number	$\bar{X}$	σ	%	Sample Number	$\bar{X}$	σ	%
1	-.025	1.112	-.022	101	-.175	1.126	-.155	201	-1.100	1.239	-.888	301	.425	1.511	.283	401	.625	.779	.805
2	.650	2.045	.318	102	.525	1.418	.370	202	.050	1.379	.036	302	.650	1.656	.394	402	-.825	1.178	-.704
3	.825	1.542	.535	103	1.800	.765	2.353	203	.625	1.734	.860	303	1.675	.789	2.120	403	.850	1.193	.712
4	.475	2.041	.233	104	.450	1.521	.296	204	.450	1.040	.434	304	1.775	1.209	1.468	404	.475	2.178	.218
5	-.150	.783	-.192	105	.350	1.596	.219	205	0	1.701	0	305	.675	1.445	.467	405	-.675	1.695	-.390
6	.800	1.636	.489	106	.225	1.806	.125	206	.650	2.128	.305	306	.900	1.068	.842	406	-1.600	.667	-2.400
7	-1.175	1.348	-.872	107	.625	1.575	.397	207	-.050	2.352	-.021	307	1.350	1.344	1.004	407	.400	1.548	.258
8	-.150	1.316	-.114	108	.350	2.104	.166	208	-.875	.895	-.978	308	1.000	1.020	.981	408	-1.850	1.213	-1.525
9	.425	2.117	.201	109	1.175	1.381	.851	209	-1.500	.592	-2.530	309	.600	1.384	.434	409	.800	1.049	.764
10	-.450	1.141	-.394	110	-.100	1.412	-.071	210	-.925	1.139	-.812	310	-.525	.947	-.554	410	.200	1.377	.146
11	.850	1.346	.652	111	-.425	1.207	-.352	211	.800	1.061	.754	311	-.025	1.784	-.014	411	-1.800	1.358	-1.330
12	-1.600	.636	-2.516	112	.425	1.434	.296	212	-.100	1.693	-.591	312	.625	1.467	.426	412	.125	1.114	.112
13	-1.550	.763	-2.031	113	1.175	1.003	1.171	213	-.575	2.078	-.277	313	-.500	1.458	-.344	413	.825	1.217	.680
14	.200	2.031	.098	114	-1.175	.415	-2.831	214	.725	.873	.830	314	1.100	1.475	.748	414	2.225	.497	4.480
15	-1.000	1.342	-.745	115	.475	2.087	.228	215	2.025	.426	4.754	315	-.250	1.135	-.221	415	1.150	1.887	.610
16	-.375	2.017	-.186	116	-.075	1.610	-.047	216	.150	1.950	.077	316	1.350	1.312	1.310	416	-.700	1.991	-.352
17	-.600	1.508	-.398	117	1.550	.568	2.728	217	.275	2.047	.134	317	.975	1.908	.510	417	.075	.998	.075
18	1.075	.630	1.706	118	.225	2.024	.112	218	.150	2.185	.069	318	-.150	1.278	-.138	418	.925	.996	.931
19	0	1.595	0	119	-.275	1.858	-.150	219	1.000	1.044	.958	319	.450	1.931	.234	419	-.675	1.672	-.404
20	-.175	1.126	-.155	120	-.650	2.143	-.303	220	-.050	2.095	-.024	320	.075	1.956	.039	420	.575	2.014	.285
21	.525	1.418	.370	121	-.950	1.081	-.879	221	1.350	1.211	1.115	321	-.200	1.298	-.155	421	-.175	1.069	-.164
22	1.800	.765	2.353	122	1.125	1.001	1.124	222	1.175	2.070	.568	322	-.200	1.875	-.107	422	-.400	2.108	-.190
23	.450	1.521	.296	123	-.425	1.540	-.276	223	.750	1.991	.377	323	-.475	1.504	.317	423	1.025	1.040	.985
24	.350	1.596	.219	124	.525	1.836	.286	224	.225	1.677	.134	324	.125	1.936	.065	424	.125	1.047	.119
25	.225	1.806	.125	125	-.050	1.689	-.030	225	-1.250	1.040	-1.202	325	1.575	.958	1.640	425	.150	1.410	.106
26	.625	1.575	.397	126	-.975	.773	-1.261	226	-.375	.646	-.580	326	-.500	1.946	-.258	426	-.225	1.632	-.138
27	.350	2.140	.166	127	.450	1.590	.283	227	-.500	1.461	-.342	327	.100	1.737	.058	427	-.675	1.348	-.500
28	-1.575	.795	-1.981	128	.050	2.203	.023	228	-1.225	1.344	-.911	328	-.400	1.605	-.249	428	-.925	1.574	-.588
29	.350	.865	.405	129	.425	1.571	.271	229	1.475	.580	2.543	329	.225	1.665	.135	429	-.500	1.917	-.261
30	1.500	1.358	1.105	130	.650	2.065	.315	230	1.450	.687	2.111	330	0	2.120	0	430	1.350	.218	6.190
31	.500	1.933	.259	131	-.175	1.452	-.121	231	.350	.862	.406	331	1.050	2.286	.460	431	.775	1.580	.491
32	-.750	1.847	-.406	132	-.125	.884	-.141	232	-.250	1.328	-.188	332	.300	1.690	.178	432	.200	1.893	.106
33	.025	1.240	.020	133	.100	2.348	.043	233	-.875	1.703	-.514	333	.125	1.372	.089	433	-.975	1.717	-.568
34	-.350	1.320	-.265	134	-1.000	1.552	-.644	234	2.175	.698	3.116	334	-1.000	.834	-1.200	434	-.375	.701	-.535
35	-.650	1.741	-.373	135	.650	1.467	.443	235	.050	1.110	.045	335	.575	1.801	.319	435	1.075	2.385	.450
36	1.025	1.929	.531	136	.450	1.328	.034	236	.450	.994	.452	336	-1.150	1.770	-.650	436	.600	2.051	.293
37	-.425	1.188	-.358	137	-.525	1.542	-.034	237	.750	1.609	.466	337	-.275	2.087	-.132	437	-.300	1.933	-.155
38	1.125	.769	1.463	138	1.300	.652	1.962	238	.150	1.312	.114	338	-1.050	1.734	-.605	438	-1.750	.841	-2.080
39	0	1.754	0	139	1.150	1.284	.896	239	-.975	1.538	-.634	339	-.300	1.434	-.209	439	.450	1.958	.230
40	-.175	1.035	-.169	140	-.300	2.463	-.122	240	-.925	2.072	-.446	340	.075	1.827	.041	440	.625	.864	.723
41	-.300	1.071	-.176	141	-.800	1.366	-.586	241	-.025	1.871	-.013	341	.775	1.361	.569	441	.175	2.260	.077
42	1.075	1.279	.841	142	-.800	1.699	-.471	242	1.000	1.851	.540	342	.225	2.003	.161	442	.850	2.188	.389
43	-.325	1.492	-.218	143	-.325	2.393	-.136	243	1.075	1.230	.874	343	-.975	1.920	-.510	443	-1.575	.769	-2.050
44	1.500	1.693	.886	144	.975	1.285	.759	244	-.200	.900	-.222	344	-.575	2.087	-.277	444	.450	1.787	.257
45	-.625	1.839	-.340	145	.725	1.108	.654	245	.300	1.991	.151	345	.250	2.171	.175	445	1.625	.602	2.700
46	.050	.658	.076	146	.500	1.969	.254	246	-1.325	1.848	-.717	346	-1.825	.753	-2.430	446	-.650	2.056	-.316
47	-1.175	1.618	-.726	147	-.425	1.165	-.365	247	.025	1.706	.015	347	-.500	1.007	-.470	447	.025	1.228	.020
48	.400	1.911	.209	148	-.125	.286	-.437	248	-1.175	.817	-1.438	348	.675	2.139	.318	448	-1.100	.828	-1.330
49	.425	1.453	.292	149	1.500	.464	3.233	249	.250	2.086	.120	349	1.050	2.001	.524	449	-.050	1.767	-.028
50	1.150	1.004	1.145	150	-.700	1.349	-.519	250	-.500	2.099	-.238	350	.525	1.420	.370	450	-.075	2.160	-.035

51	.725	1.085	.668	151	-.600	1.905	-.315	251	.650	1.727	.376	351	.325	2.268	.144	451	.900	1.772	.508
52	.975	.432	2.257	152	.325	1.934	.168	252	.200	.962	.208	352	-.175	1.785	-.098	452	-.775	1.973	-.393
53	-.600	2.125	-.282	153	-.425	1.802	-.236	253	.750	2.254	.333	353	-.125	1.434	-.087	453	-.550	1.841	-.299
54	.275	.701	.392	154	-.625	1.340	-.466	254	-.475	1.021	-.465	354	1.550	.687	2.256	454	.550	1.403	.392
55	-1.700	.696	-2.443	155	.600	1.595	.376	255	-1.325	1.295	-1.023	355	-.050	1.083	-.046	455	.975	2.065	.472
56	.450	1.841	.244	156	-.675	1.734	.389	256	1.275	1.355	.941	356	1.225	.893	1.372	456	1.575	1.173	1.342
57	-.825	1.232	-.670	157	1.100	1.151	.956	257	.675	1.645	.410	357	.350	1.798	.196	457	.250	2.035	.123
58	.900	2.108	.427	158	.375	1.192	.315	258	-.050	1.830	-.027	358	.325	1.502	.216	458	-.475	1.455	-.326
59	.925	.960	.964	159	1.600	.925	1.730	259	1.075	1.301	.826	359	-.075	2.825	-.027	459	-.650	1.963	-.331
60	.850	1.443	.589	160	-.500	2.080	-.240	260	-.850	2.069	-.411	360	-.850	1.836	-.455	460	.175	1.859	.094
61	-.675	2.050	-.329	161	.675	.779	.866	261	-1.650	.960	-1.719	361	.050	1.626	.031	461	-.950	1.982	-.479
62	-1.350	1.161	-1.163	162	1.175	2.087	.563	262	-.175	.867	-.202	362	.125	1.609	.078	462	.275	1.254	.219
63	-.100	1.840	-.054	163	-.275	2.003	-.137	263	-.575	1.112	-.517	363	-.125	2.376	-.053	463	-1.475	1.684	-.876
64	-.150	1.379	-.109	164	-.600	1.360	-.441	264	-.925	1.021	-.906	364	-1.875	1.268	-1.480	464	.350	1.609	.218
65	-.400	1.996	.200	165	-.250	2.612	-.957	265	.275	.856	.322	365	.500	1.759	.285	465	.725	2.123	.341
66	.825	1.608	.513	166	-.300	2.426	-.124	266	-.200	1.675	-.119	366	.150	1.633	.092	466	-.400	2.194	-.182
67	.250	1.712	.146	167	-.850	2.138	-.398	267	.500	1.442	.347	367	.800	1.640	.490	467	1.025	1.452	.706
68	-1.200	2.043	-.587	168	.875	1.099	.796	268	.550	1.167	.470	368	-.250	1.563	-.160	468	-1.175	1.995	-.589
69	.200	1.325	.151	169	.825	1.275	.647	269	.225	2.234	.101	369	-.400	1.620	-.247	469	-.900	.903	-.997
70	-.500	.718	-.696	170	.125	2.152	.581	270	-.125	1.006	-124	370	-.350	1.163	-.300	470	-2.075	.349	-5.946
71	1.050	.391	2.685	171	-.075	1.965	-.038	271	.225	2.136	.106	371	-.825	2.298	-.360	471	-.775	1.734	-.447
72	.700	1.063	.659	172	-.075	1.601	-.468	272	-.250	1.919	-.130	372	.525	1.998	.265	472	.825	1.855	.445
73	.250	1.704	.147	173	.625	1.137	.550	273	-.025	2.299	-.110	373	-.400	1.733	-.232	473	-.050	1.401	-.036
74	-.475	2.206	-.215	174	.100	2.715	.037	274	-1.650	.934	-1.771	374	.300	1.785	.168	474	1.150	1.081	1.064
75	-1.025	1.297	-.790	175	-.150	.687	-.218	275	.950	1.172	.811	375	-.900	1.461	-.618	475	-.375	1.933	-.194
76	1.250	1.830	.683	176	.850	1.062	.800	276	.725	2.079	.349	376	-1.050	1.450	-.725	476	.400	1.966	.203
77	1.325	1.958	.677	177	-1.000	1.279	-.828	277	.650	1.087	.600	377	.425	1.350	.314	477	.550	1.230	.447
78	.150	2.484	.060	178	1.400	1.544	.907	278	.925	1.584	.584	378	-.300	1.657	-.182	478	-1.075	1.130	-.951
79	1.350	1.572	.859	179	-.800	1.239	-.646	279	-.825	1.571	-.526	379	-1.375	1.366	-1.006	479	-.350	1.426	-.245
80	-.650	2.110	-.308	180	.200	1.525	.131	280	-.650	1.254	-.518	380	-.150	.461	-.325	480	.600	1.573	.381
81	-.950	1.768	-.537	181	-.900	1.994	-.451	281	.350	1.590	.221	381	.775	.844	.941	481	1.900	.886	2.146
82	-.025	1.984	-.013	182	-.200	1.543	-.130	282	.550	1.572	.350	382	.450	1.604	.281	482	-.925	1.492	-.620
83	-.400	1.158	-.345	183	-1.700	1.095	-1.553	283	-1.225	.942	-1.300	383	-1.325	1.201	-1.102	483	-1.275	1.994	-639
84	.175	1.641	.107	184	-.725	1.388	-.522	284	1.050	1.230	.854	384	.100	.600	.166	484	-.100	1.881	-.053
85	.850	2.277	.373	185	.625	1.960	.319	285	-1.250	1.899	-.659	385	-.700	.851	-.821	485	.225	1.287	.175
86	-1.250	1.354	-.923	186	-1.525	.976	-1.563	286	.875	1.492	.586	386	.625	1.859	.341	486	-.625	1.615	-.387
87	-2.250	.296	-7.601	187	-1.450	.910	-1.593	287	1.250	1.059	1.182	387	2.575	.383	6.710	487	1.825	.801	2.278
88	-1.100	1.118	-.984	188	1.175	.968	1.214	288	.575	2.126	.271	388	-.175	2.084	-.084	488	.300	.663	.452
89	.150	1.291	.116	189	-.900	1.155	-.779	289	.400	2.292	.175	389	1.875	1.322	1.420	489	.850	1.571	.541
90	1.925	.733	2.626	190	.500	1.042	.480	290	1.325	.789	1.660	390	-1.725	1.236	-1.420	490	1.400	.778	1.799
91	1.325	.801	1.654	191	.900	2.089	.451	291	.400	1.458	.276	391	-.050	1.074	-.047	491	-.550	1.270	-.433
92	-.750	1.770	-.424	192	.475	.540	.880	292	.050	2.016	.025	392	-.550	.896	-.612	492	-.475	1.270	-.374
93	-.725	1.346	-.539	193	1.225	1.134	1.080	293	.825	1.217	.682	393	.225	.928	.243	493	.500	1.111	.450
94	-.125	.722	-.173	194	1.575	1.632	.965	294	1.000	.906	1.100	394	.800	1.762	.455	494	-.625	1.003	-.625
95	1.400	1.070	1.310	195	-1.400	1.239	-1.130	295	1.725	.760	2.270	395	.400	2.211	.182	495	0	2.579	0
96	-1.725	1.474	-1.170	196	-.875	1.350	-.648	296	-.250	1.579	-.159	396	-.475	1.392	-.342	496	.900	1.826	.493
97	-1.500	1.332	-1.126	197	-.625	.715	-.874	297	-.575	1.431	-.400	397	.400	1.056	.380	497	-.575	1.690	-.340
98	0	1.676	0	198	-.300	1.522	-.197	298	1.125	2.008	.560	398	.650	1.903	.342	498	.175	1.431	.122
99	1.725	1.639	1.052	199	-.400	1.701	-.235	299	-.175	1.721	-.102	399	.800	1.084	.740	499	-.875	1.092	-.801
100	0	1.595	0	200	-.850	1.230	-.691	300	-1.175	1.341	-.717	400	.975	.988	988	500	.225	.733	.307

TABLE D.—STATISTICS FOR DRAWINGS FROM RECTANGULAR UNIVERSE

Sample Number	$\bar{X}$	σ	x	Sample Number	$\bar{X}$	σ	%	Sample Number	$\bar{X}$	σ	%	Sample Number	$\bar{X}$	σ	%	Sample Number	$\bar{X}$	σ	%
501	-.950	1.230	-.772	601	-.950	1.293	-.735	701	.675	.973	.694	801	-.750	1.016	-.739	901	1.425	1.043	1.365
502	.075	2.481	.030	602	1.450	.994	1.459	702	-1.725	.936	-1.843	802	1.300	1.369	.950	902	1.250	1.368	.914
503	-.150	1.534	-.098	603	.075	1.254	.060	703	-1.875	1.040	-1.803	803	1.475	1.757	.840	903	1.575	1.008	1.562
504	1.000	1.768	.565	604	.850	1.704	.499	704	-1.300	.815	-1.595	804	.625	1.233	.505	904	.950	1.770	.536
505	-1.225	1.043	-1.175	605	-.175	2.253	-.078	705	-.925	1.417	-.653	805	1.300	1.223	1.062	905	-.375	.978	-.384
506	.300	2.176	.138	606	-.400	1.619	-.247	706	-.575	1.152	-.499	806	-.325	1.593	-.204	906	1.400	.946	1.480
507	1.375	1.686	.845	607	-.375	1.103	-.340	707	.075	1.176	.064	807	.175	1.853	.094	907	-1.975	.769	-2.568
508	-.950	1.137	-.839	608	-.650	1.817	-.358	708	.750	1.479	.507	808	.700	1.602	.437	908	-.825	1.418	-.581
509	-.325	2.181	-.148	609	-1.150	1.135	-1.013	709	.375	1.975	.190	809	.225	1.425	.158	909	.200	1.840	.109
510	.275	1.511	.183	610	.125	2.005	.062	710	-.025	1.698	-.015	810	-.100	1.214	-.082	910	1.500	1.576	.952
511	-1.025	.259	-3.951	611	1.150	.986	1.166	711	-1.650	.439	-3.759	811	-1.950	.269	-.725	911	-1.700	.711	-2.390
512	-.350	2.103	-.166	612	1.750	.887	1.973	712	-.200	2.241	-.089	812	-.325	1.497	-.286	912	1.375	.981	1.401
513	.475	1.316	.365	613	.250	.971	.257	713	.400	.604	.662	813	.050	.492	.102	913	-1.725	.870	-1.981
514	.050	1.742	.029	614	-.725	1.846	-.393	714	1.750	1.879	.931	814	-2.150	.763	-2.810	914	-2.400	.675	-3.558
515	-1.800	1.084	-1.781	615	-.575	1.139	-.505	715	.150	1.176	.128	815	.925	.942	.982	915	-.950	1.258	-.755
516	.350	1.159	.310	616	-.225	.691	-.326	716	.275	.968	.284	816	.225	1.929	.117	916	-.525	1.575	-.333
517	-.575	1.467	-.393	617	-1.150	1.197	-.961	717	.800	1.279	.626	817	-.775	1.988	-.390	917	1.400	2.004	.699
518	-.475	1.814	-.260	618	-1.925	1.462	-1.317	718	-.875	1.337	-.654	818	-1.925	1.143	-1.682	918	-1.275	1.217	-1.098
519	.475	1.662	.286	619	1.450	1.071	1.354	719	.150	1.383	.108	819	.800	1.287	.621	919	-.950	1.927	-.492
520	.250	1.339	.187	620	-.325	1.520	-.214	720	2.175	.512	4.248	820	.050	1.524	.033	920	-1.050	1.226	-.858
521	.950	1.727	.550	621	-.725	1.215	-.597	721	.525	1.712	.307	821	-.225	2.171	-.104	921	1.550	1.110	1.399
522	.675	1.023	.660	622	-.750	1.741	-.431	722	.175	2.029	.086	822	.525	1.130	.471	922	1.425	.942	1.510
523	1.125	1.730	.650	623	1.725	.722	2.389	723	.975	2.019	.483	823	-.400	1.070	-.374	923	-1.625	.828	-1.895
524	-.025	1.890	-.013	624	.200	1.369	.146	724	.100	1.308	.076	824	-.775	1.385	-.560	924	-2.000	.822	-2.430
525	-1.200	1.762	-.681	625	.125	2.068	.060	725	1.300	1.155	1.126	825	1.600	.943	1.699	925	.650	2.051	.292
526	2.175	.826	2.633	626	.875	2.070	.423	726	-.875	1.445	-.606	826	-1.925	1.232	-1.561	926	-.900	1.204	-.747
527	-1.850	1.126	-1.643	627	.400	2.125	.188	727	1.000	.977	1.023	827	.275	1.073	.256	927	-.525	1.139	-.461
528	-1.925	.893	-2.156	628	-1.225	1.215	-1.008	728	-.800	1.793	-.446	828	.725	.870	.833	928	.600	2.104	.284
529	-1.100	.951	-1.157	629	-1.450	.879	-1.650	729	1.475	1.365	1.081	829	-1.850	1.429	-1.295	929	1.225	1.279	.959
530	.250	1.390	.180	630	-.225	1.777	-.127	730	.450	1.635	.275	830	1.225	2.284	.536	930	-1.500	1.384	-1.081
531	-.100	2.378	-.042	631	-1.425	.763	-1.868	731	.825	1.545	.534	831	-.525	1.656	-.317	931	-.850	1.787	-.476
532	-.300	1.745	-.172	632	-.700	1.765	-.397	732	1.350	.450	3.000	832	-.500	2.318	-.216	932	-.775	.873	-.889
533	.900	1.288	.699	633	-.850	1.544	-.551	733	-1.475	1.958	-.753	833	-1.475	1.502	-.982	933	.300	1.377	.218
534	-.325	.934	-.348	634	-1.125	1.445	-.779	734	.050	1.588	.031	834	-2.450	.427	-5.745	934	.050	1.781	.028
535	.800	1.428	.560	635	-.150	1.447	-.104	735	.400	1.389	.288	835	.475	1.425	.334	935	.525	.729	.721
536	.300	1.325	.226	636	-1.100	.970	-1.134	736	.375	1.021	.367	836	.900	1.177	.766	936	-1.050	2.329	-.451
537	1.200	1.168	1.027	637	-1.775	.512	-3.467	737	-.800	1.455	-.550	837	-.950	1.293	-.735	937	-.850	1.774	-.479
538	1.600	2.024	.791	638	-.425	.471	-.902	738	.325	1.184	.274	838	-.175	1.650	-.106	938	.200	.745	.268
539	-.300	.735	-.408	639	.575	2.179	.264	739	.250	1.521	.164	839	-.375	1.954	-.192	939	-1.625	1.645	-.989
540	.600	.886	.677	640	.775	2.123	.365	740	-1.275	1.580	-.807	840	1.100	.255	4.320	940	-.600	1.851	-.324
541	.700	1.810	.387	641	.300	2.457	.122	741	1.100	1.688	.652	841	-.425	.884	-.481	941	-.550	2.055	-.267
542	-.425	.449	-.947	642	-.575	1.803	-.319	742	-.125	1.846	-.068	842	-.675	1.197	-.504	942	-.150	1.819	-.024
543	1.300	1.221	1.065	643	-.875	2.084	-.420	743	.400	1.821	.220	843	.600	1.948	.308	943	-.675	.487	-1.387
544	.100	1.482	.067	644	1.250	2.129	.587	744	-1.650	.634	-2.603	844	-.400	.831	-.481	944	.075	.795	.094
545	1.600	.919	1.741	645	1.550	.642	2.414	745	-.825	1.699	-.486	845	-.625	1.239	-.505	945	-.325	1.827	-.178
546	.325	1.757	.185	646	-.975	2.014	-.484	746	.800	2.239	.357	846	.675	1.647	.409	946	1.875	.602	3.115
547	-.200	.951	-.210	647	1.050	1.901	.552	747	-1.425	1.353	-1.053	847	.025	1.851	.014	947	-.350	2.179	-.161
548	1.725	.779	2.214	648	.775	1.404	-.552	748	.825	1.502	.549	848	-1.200	1.239	-.970	948	-.525	.915	-.574
549	-1.475	.895	-1.648	649	-1.400	1.395	-1.004	749	-.300	2.125	-.141	849	1.575	1.669	.945	949	-.050	1.986	-.025
550	.400	1.991	.201	650	-.025	1.832	-.014	750	.350	.466	.751	850	-.200	1.435	-.139	950	-.275	1.964	-.140

TABLE D. — STATISTICS FOR DRAWINGS FROM RECTANGULAR UNIVERSE

Sample Number	$\bar{X}$	σ	x	Sample Number	$\bar{X}$	σ	%	Sample Number	$\bar{X}$	σ	%	Sample Number	$\bar{X}$	σ	%	Sample Number	$\bar{X}$	σ	%
551	-.025	1.171	-.021	651	.850	1.143	.744	751	.300	1.084	.276	851	.775	.923	.830	951	1.325	1.213	1.091
552	.175	1.639	.107	652	.625	1.165	.536	752	-.600	1.806	-.333	852	-.275	2.078	-.132	952	.675	1.558	.433
553	-.600	.718	-.836	653	-.200	1.826	-.110	753	.050	.865	.058	853	1.325	.792	1.671	953	-.550	1.172	-.469
554	-.350	1.968	-.178	654	.350	.776	.451	754	.625	.973	.642	854	-1.700	.982	-1.731	954	1.475	.630	2.341
555	.450	2.207	.204	655	-.825	1.203	-.686	755	.475	1.287	-.369	855	-.300	2.025	-.148	955	-1.300	1.102	-1.180
556	.100	.406	.246	656	.275	1.201	.229	756	.650	1.092	.596	856	-1.550	1.947	-.796	956	.300	.854	.351
557	1.800	.919	1.960	657	.900	1.883	.478	757	.525	1.397	.375	857	.750	1.968	.380	957	-.150	1.687	-.089
558	-.625	1.240	-.504	658	1.300	2.332	.557	758	-.725	1.535	-.472	858	-1.775	.769	-2.310	958	-.375	1.324	-.283
559	-.450	2.143	-.210	659	-1.000	1.853	-.540	759	-.475	1.794	-.265	859	-1.000	1.170	-.085	959	.575	.634	.908
560	-.625	1.728	-.362	660	-1.075	1.465	-.734	760	.875	1.375	.636	860	1.200	1.745	.688	960	-.450	1.950	-.230
561	-.200	1.725	-.116	661	.375	.968	.387	761	.450	1.610	.279	861	-.250	1.630	-.015	961	-.775	.884	-.877
562	-1.800	.725	-2.483	662	.800	2.219	.361	762	-.175	1.242	-.141	862	.025	.933	.025	962	.175	2.238	.078
563	.075	2.014	.037	663	-.650	1.638	-.397	763	-.050	1.770	-.013	863	-.425	1.756	-.242	963	.125	.661	.189
564	.600	1.061	.566	664	-.050	1.733	-.029	764	-.925	1.937	-.478	864	.075	2.091	.056	964	.850	.687	1.238
565	.600	1.168	.514	665	-.425	1.848	-.230	765	.675	1.366	.494	865	.375	1.675	.224	965	.950	1.450	.655
566	-.850	.669	-1.271	666	-.525	1.750	-.300	766	-.500	1.259	-.397	866	-.975	1.678	-.581	966	-.325	1.866	-.174
567	.350	1.553	.225	667	1.475	1.621	.910	767	-.100	1.723	-.058	867	-.675	2.039	-.331	967	-.175	2.008	-.087
568	1.525	.884	1.725	668	.400	1.952	.205	768	.975	2.203	.810	868	-.325	2.033	-.160	968	-.750	1.659	-.452
569	.075	1.805	.042	669	1.725	1.429	1.207	769	.300	1.851	.162	869	.075	1.885	.040	969	-.250	.986	-.282
570	1.025	1.169	.877	670	.100	1.796	.056	770	-1.775	1.250	-1.420	870	-.050	2.108	-.024	970	-.275	.926	-.297
571	-.975	1.859	-.524	671	-.825	1.275	-.647	771	-.450	1.244	-.361	871	-.925	.164	-5.640	971	-.025	1.429	-.018
572	.500	1.608	.311	672	.650	.976	.666	772	-.675	1.355	-.499	872	-.575	1.624	-.354	972	.575	1.651	.166
573	1.300	.831	1.562	673	-1.400	.925	-1.514	773	-1.575	.746	-2.111	873	-.350	1.484	-.236	973	-.300	1.812	-.165
574	.250	1.947	.128	674	-.125	1.699	-.074	774	.550	1.064	.517	874	1.500	1.243	1.209	974	-1.850	.502	-3.681
575	-.350	1.471	-.238	675	-.325	1.846	-.176	775	.725	1.287	.563	875	1.225	1.429	.859	975	.275	2.170	.127
576	.475	1.305	.365	676	-.650	1.328	-.489	776	-1.900	.919	-2.348	876	.500	1.751	.285	976	-1.500	.524	-2.861
577	.225	1.339	.168	677	-.275	1.861	-.148	777	-1.325	.512	-.934	877	.575	.466	1.231	977	.525	2.055	.256
578	-.825	.890	-.927	678	-.775	.722	-1.073	778	-.900	1.541	-.583	878	-.350	.770	-.455	978	-1.275	1.148	-1.110
579	.525	1.866	.283	679	-.275	.936	-.294	779	-.650	1.365	-.476	879	.550	.450	1.220	979	-.375	1.648	-.228
580	-.650	.853	-.682	680	-1.200	.678	-1.770	780	.750	1.352	.554	880	.075	1.738	.043	980	-1.525	1.248	-1.221
581	-2.475	.311	-7.958	681	-.350	1.795	-.195	781	.150	2.052	.073	881	-.125	2.326	-.048	981	-.225	2.033	-.111
582	.575	.898	.640	682	.625	2.373	.263	782	-.075	.630	-.119	882	.475	.307	.588	982	.375	2.356	.175
583	-.850	1.778	-.478	683	-1.325	1.333	-.994	783	-.725	1.464	-.495	883	-.500	.962	-.519	983	.175	1.383	.126
584	1.650	1.128	1.463	684	.700	1.395	.502	784	-.025	1.907	-.013	884	-.650	2.013	-.305	984	1.375	.109	13.620
585	.500	2.384	.210	685	-1.475	1.917	-.769	785	-1.325	1.942	-.682	885	-1.350	.680	-1.985	985	-1.325	1.297	-1.041
586	-.875	.268	-3.265	686	.300	2.071	.145	786	.375	1.006	.371	886	.100	1.713	.079	986	.100	.894	.112
587	.025	2.069	.012	687	-1.450	.743	-1.952	787	-.900	1.239	-.726	887	-1.025	1.117	-.919	987	.375	1.535	.244
588	.600	.919	.653	688	-.125	1.207	-.104	788	-.300	1.210	-.248	888	.050	1.537	.033	988	1.500	1.391	1.079
589	1.150	1.665	.691	689	-1.125	.672	-1.674	789	-1.025	1.906	-.539	889	.375	1.846	.203	989	-.675	1.219	-.564
590	.900	2.083	.432	690	-1.075	1.404	-.766	790	1.275	1.699	.751	890	-.825	1.361	-.605	990	-.100	1.803	-.055
591	1.025	1.481	.692	691	-.150	1.929	-.078	791	.175	1.590	.110	891	1.400	.696	2.018	991	-.600	1.202	-.499
592	.375	1.778	.211	692	-.850	1.396	-.609	792	.175	1.642	.107	892	-.550	1.920	-.286	992	-.050	1.986	-.025
593	.575	1.883	.305	693	.200	.990	.202	793	.050	1.412	.035	893	.950	2.159	.441	993	.800	2.029	.394
594	.150	.687	.218	694	.225	1.764	.128	794	-1.025	1.604	-.640	894	-.575	.740	-.779	994	.025	1.820	.014
595	.900	1.194	.754	695	-.125	2.073	-.060	795	-.325	1.627	-.199	895	-.650	.921	-.705	995	-.050	1.613	-.031
596	.775	1.209	.641	696	.275	1.942	.142	796	.200	.574	.348	896	-.475	1.502	-.316	996	.700	.930	.754
597	-.675	1.610	-.419	697	.475	1.274	.373	797	-.600	1.847	-.325	897	.225	1.184	.190	997	-.800	.815	-.981
598	.650	.887	.733	698	-.400	.505	-.792	798	-.575	1.431	-.400	898	-1.375	.861	-1.596	998	-.125	1.756	-.071
599	-.375	2.067	-.181	699	-1.425	.981	-1.453	799	-.225	1.942	-.116	899	-1.675	1.540	-1.087	999	1.175	1.425	.825
600	.850	2.180	.390	700	.750	2.234	.336	800	-1.750	.206	-8.500	900	-.900	.728	-1.232	1000	-.400	1.082	-.370

TABLE F. — STATISTICS FOR DRAWINGS FROM RIGHT RECTANGULAR UNIVERSE

Sample Number	$\bar{X}$	σ	%	Sample Number	$\bar{X}$	σ	%	Sample Number	$\bar{X}$	σ	%	Sample Number	$\bar{X}$	σ	%	Sample Number	$\bar{X}$	σ	%
1	0	.895	0	101	.625	.580	1.078	201	.500	.682	.733	301	.075	.617	.122	401	.925	1.422	.650
2	.025	1.021	.024	102	-.250	.590	-.424	202	.025	.762	.033	302	-.525	.668	-.787	402	.800	1.258	.636
3	.500	.885	.566	103	-.225	.575	-.391	203	-.275	.618	-.445	303	.400	.652	.613	403	.850	1.262	.674
4	-.175	1.033	-.169	104	.400	.587	.681	204	.375	.661	.567	304	-.075	.708	-.106	404	.325	1.089	.298
5	.700	.886	.790	105	.375	.593	.633	205	-.500	.643	-.776	305	-.450	.686	-.655	405	.150	1.118	.134
6	.350	.971	.360	106	.125	.633	.197	206	.425	.755	.563	306	-.450	.610	-.738	406	.250	1.070	.234
7	-.450	.918	-.490	107	-.050	.610	-.082	207	.050	.179	.064	307	-.525	.640	-.820	407	.350	1.062	.330
8	.050	1.010	.049	108	-.400	.380	-1.050	208	.025	.875	.029	308	.525	.675	.776	408	.025	1.190	.021
9	-.050	.961	.052	109	-.200	.495	-.404	209	.100	.815	.123	309	-.050	.657	-.076	409	-.050	1.110	-.045
10	.200	1.098	.182	110	-.700	.494	-1.430	210	.200	.735	.272	310	.050	.656	-.076	410	.925	1.308	.708
11	.125	.950	.132	111	-.225	.575	-.391	211	.250	.723	.346	311	-.200	.695	-.288	411	1.125	.112	-1.005
12	.025	1.001	.025	112	.350	1.035	.338	212	.075	.671	.112	312	-.125	.661	-.189	412	-.500	.123	-4.065
13	0	1.099	0	113	0	.616	0	213	-.550	.770	-.714	313	.175	.712	.246	413	-.625	.083	-7.539
14	.350	.955	.366	114	-.525	.512	-1.030	214	-.550	.695	-.791	314	-.675	.683	-.989	414	.775	.045	17.338
15	-.175	1.035	-.169	115	.325	.507	.641	215	.625	.694	.901	315	-.600	.660	-.910	415	1.250	1.195	1.050
16	.025	1.035	.024	116	-.250	.559	-.447	216	-.750	.725	-1.035	316	-.400	.720	-.555	416	.550	1.260	.436
17	-.100	1.056	-.095	117	-.125	.567	-.220	217	-.375	.739	-.509	317	-.700	.660	-1.061	417	.550	1.238	.444
18	-.250	.627	-.399	118	-.475	.540	-.880	218	.175	.766	.228	318	-.425	.686	-.679	418	.675	1.199	.563
19	.075	.694	.108	119	.025	.614	.041	219	1.275	.536	2.379	319	-.550	.698	-.788	419	-.450	.602	-.748
20	.800	1.185	.675	120	.225	.626	.359	220	-.400	.539	-.742	320	-.250	.701	-.355	420	.475	.601	790
21	.200	.604	.332	121	-.525	.576	-.911	221	.075	.683	.110	321	1.325	1.156	1.146	421	-.375	.179	-2.095
22	-.175	.576	-.304	122	-.350	.577	-.607	222	-.025	.705	-.035	322	-.450	.439	1.025	422	-.575	.179	3.212
23	.225	.618	.374	123	-.450	.577	-.780	223	-.200	.675	-.296	323	-.375	.432	-.868	423	-.325	.148	-2.196
24	-.050	.610	-.082	124	-.325	.641	-.507	224	1.075	.672	1.600	324	-.075	.661	-.083	424	.175	.148	1.183
25	.825	.603	1.370	125	.650	.482	1.349	225	-.275	.685	-.403	325	.100	.662	.151	425	-.950	.166	-5.723
26	-.025	.592	-.042	126	-.775	.510	-1.520	226	-.025	.708	-.035	326	.575	.672	.855	426	.950	.141	6.725
27	.150	.593	.253	127	-.575	.515	-1.115	227	-.100	.758	-.132	327	-.375	.776	-.483	427	-1.000	.141	-7.092
28	-.325	.622	-.522	128	-.225	.492	-.457	228	-.300	.758	-.396	328	-.350	.752	-.466	428	-.800	.141	-5.650
29	.700	.587	1.193	129	-.750	.503	-1.495	229	-.075	.675	-.111	329	-.200	.872	-.229	429	-.200	.158	-1.265
30	-.650	.627	-1.037	130	.475	.538	.885	230	-.025	.691	-.036	330	.375	.630	.595	430	-.600	.158	-3.800
31	.625	.552	1.132	131	.175	.575	.304	231	-.050	.742	-.067	331	-.225	.653	-.345	431	.575	1.150	.500
32	.550	.550	1.000	132	-.425	.576	-.738	232	-.375	.844	-.444	332	-.100	.635	-.157	432	.430	1.267	.355
33	.250	.550	.455	133	-.775	.580	-1.336	233	-.325	.796	-.408	333	-.175	.634	-.276	433	.300	1.136	.264
34	.250	.548	.456	134	-.475	.536	-.886	234	-.225	.716	-.314	334	-.100	.578	-.173	434	.625	1.410	.445
35	-.175	.558	-.313	135	-.250	.568	-.440	235	.625	.733	.853	335	.200	.930	.215	435	-.400	.212	-1.887
36	-.350	.585	-.600	136	-.500	.604	-.828	236	.050	.722	.069	336	.300	.675	.444	436	-.550	.180	-3.056
37	.100	.998	.100	137	-.400	.636	-.629	237	1.150	.775	1.480	337	-.775	.228	-3.399	437	.550	.890	.618
38	-.500	.534	-.936	138	-.250	.742	-.342	238	-.475	.653	-.727	338	-.050	.230	-.242	438	.325	.896	.363
39	.150	.550	.273	139	.475	.758	.626	239	.875	.586	1.492	339	-.750	.206	-3.641	439	-.375	1.010	-.371
40	-.025	.596	-.042	140	-.025	.760	-.033	240	-.425	.596	-.713	340	-.600	.187	-3.220	440	1.025	.653	1.570
41	.450	1.030	.437	141	.250	.550	.455	241	-.100	.695	-.144	341	-.150	.634	-.236	441	.100	1.129	.089
42	.300	1.123	.267	142	.450	1.002	.449	242	-.050	.680	-.074	342	-.125	.621	-.208	442	.425	1.160	.366
43	.350	.976	.359	143	-.050	1.010	-.049	243	.125	.712	.176	343	.025	.650	.038	443	.100	1.177	.085
44	.400	1.160	.344	144	-.125	.975	-.128	244	.225	.687	.328	344	-.650	.595	-1.091	444	0	1.162	0
45	.075	1.148	-.066	145	-.025	.843	-.029	245	-.175	.602	-.291	345	-.225	.580	-.388	445	.350	1.193	.294
46	.425	1.141	.372	146	-.425	1.043	-.407	246	-.425	.638	-.666	346	-.200	.583	-.343	446	-.225	1.245	-.181
47	.800	.981	.815	147	-.325	1.042	-.312	247	-.425	.638	-.668	347	-.200	.640	-.313	447	-.250	1.245	-.201
48	.325	1.006	.323	148	0	.950	0	248	-.350	.650	-.539	348	.775	.659	1.750	448	.525	1.117	.470
49	.725	1.060	.685	149	-.175	1.064	-.164	249	-.150	.723	-.207	349	-.475	653	-.728	449	.375	1.435	.262
50	.125	1.244	.100	150	-.075	1.034	-.073	250	-.025	.701	-.036	350	-.400	.644	-.621	450	.975	1.268	.769

51	.400	1.081	.370	151	-.625	.722	-.866	251	-.350	.772	-.454	351	-.200	.682	-.293	451	.600	.394	1.523
52	.325	.928	.350	152	.550	.439	1.255	252	0	.752	0	352	-.225	.630	-.357	452	-.025	.396	-.063
53	.150	.930	.161	153	-.700	.405	-1.750	253	.175	.718	.244	353	-.200	.628	-.319	453	-.625	.441	-1.420
54	.325	.936	.347	154	-.200	.485	-.412	254	.050	.668	.076	354	-.075	.641	-.117	454	-.900	.418	-2.155
55	-.025	1.006	-.025	155	-.050	.472	-.117	255	.875	.665	1.316	355	-.200	.718	-.279	455	-.175	.409	-.428
56	-.350	.638	-.549	156	-.500	.474	-1.055	256	1.000	.694	1.440	356	.400	.758	.528	456	.050	.439	.114
57	-.425	1.112	-.382	157	-.125	.530	-.236	257	.175	.779	.225	357	-.450	.610	-.738	457	-.350	.496	-.706
58	.325	1.081	.300	158	-.675	.490	-1.375	258	-.225	.669	-.336	558	-.550	.610	-.902	458	.800	.520	1.540
59	-.600	1.100	-.545	159	.525	.490	1.070	259	-.250	.697	-.358	359	-.575	.675	-.850	459	-.175	.576	-.304
60	-.300	1.005	-.299	160	-.450	.492	-.915	260	-.375	.789	-.475	360	.100	.696	.144	460	-.700	.600	-1.167
61	-.175	1.040	-.168	161	.325	.792	.410	261	0	.826	0	361	-.200	.490	-.408	461	1.025	.276	3.710
62	.425	.476	.893	162	.350	.740	.473	262	-.125	.737	-.169	362	.025	.421	.059	462	.125	.277	.451
63	-.700	.485	-1.443	163	.825	.443	1.820	263	.025	.740	.034	363	-.050	.409	-.122	463	-.775	.215	-3.580
64	.200	.485	.413	164	-.625	.687	-.909	264	.125	.750	.167	364	-.250	.455	-.550	464	-.300	.200	-1.500
65	-.525	.515	-1.020	165	-.475	.448	-1.060	265	-.050	.783	-.064	365	.725	.476	1.523	465	-1.000	.255	-3.922
66	.050	1.169	.043	166	-.375	.449	-.835	266	-.200	.758	-.264	366	-.425	.377	-1.127	466	-1.000	.244	-4.260
67	.975	1.058	.921	167	-.525	.458	-1.150	267	-.275	.926	-.297	367	-.525	.376	-1.398	467	-.750	.229	-3.275
68	.050	.996	.050	168	.125	.438	.285	268	.125	.698	.179	368	-.300	.413	.729	468	-.750	.229	-3.275
69	.775	.981	.790	169	-.575	.421	-1.368	269	.125	.708	.177	369	-.175	.396	-.442	469	-.975	.249	-3.916
70	.200	.967	.207	170	-.050	.415	-.121	270	.775	.729	1.063	370	-.250	.394	-.638	470	-.050	.426	-.117
71	.150	.986	.152	171	.450	.450	1.000	271	.050	.740	.068	371	.200	.611	.327	471	-.700	.300	-2.333
72	.050	1.089	.046	172	-.725	.440	-1.650	272	-.125	.718	-.174	372	.650	.608	1.075	472	.850	.283	3.010
73	-.300	1.030	-.291	173	-.275	.480	-.570	273	-.200	.680	-.294	373	-.125	.653	-.191	473	-.225	.318	-.708
74	-.050	.975	-.051	174	-.775	.482	-1.610	274	.100	.644	.155	374	.225	.636	.353	474	.525	.259	2.027
75	-.300	1.008	-.298	175	-.575	.482	-1.193	275	-.675	.736	-.917	375	.475	.606	.784	475	-.275	.268	-1.026
76	.025	1.141	.022	176	-.675	.482	-1.400	276	-.425	.660	-.644	376	-.425	.585	-.726	476	.850	.300	2.840
77	.725	1.140	.637	177	.050	.433	.115	277	.375	.660	.568	377	-.225	.588	-.383	477	.650	.296	2.440
78	.825	1.064	.775	178	.275	.432	.637	278	.400	.702	.570	378	.400	.644	.621	478	0	.220	0
79	.775	1.071	.724	179	-.475	.466	-1.019	279	-.500	.707	-.707	379	.875	.708	1.235	479	-.300	.274	-1.095
80	.325	1.249	.261	180	-.650	.427	-1.522	280	.050	.743	.067	380	.475	.701	.677	480	.650	.250	2.620
81	.150	1.230	.122	181	-.225	.432	-.545	281	-.475	.715	-.663	381	0	.393	0	481	-.900	.300	-3.000
82	.600	1.187	.506	182	1.025	.769	1.333	282	.525	.661	.794	382	-.375	.390	-.962	482	-.650	.342	-1.905
83	.825	1.169	.702	183	.350	.923	.380	283	-.300	.640	-.469	383	-.725	.400	-1.313	483	-.375	.310	-1.210
84	.150	1.059	.142	184	.150	1.170	.128	284	.550	.712	.773	384	-.300	.453	-.662	484	-.350	.319	-1.095
85	0	1.084	0	185	-.175	1.043	-.168	285	.100	.755	.132	385	-.150	.364	-.412	485	-.500	.353	-1.435
86	.675	1.060	.637	186	-.025	1.030	-.025	286	-.325	.638	-.510	386	.975	.415	2.349	486	.500	.308	1.625
87	.725	1.060	.685	187	.175	1.171	.149	287	-.250	.686	-.364	387	.500	.361	1.385	487	.300	.308	.975
88	.150	1.193	.126	188	.650	1.009	.645	288	-.575	.705	-.815	388	-.750	.384	-1.953	488	-.875	.312	-2.715
89	-.075	1.120	-.068	189	-.375	.701	-.534	289	-.225	.676	-.333	389	.575	.381	1.505	489	-.700	.291	-2.410
90	-.300	1.125	-.267	190	-.050	.438	-.114	290	.775	.844	.918	390	.075	.370	.203	490	.250	.320	.781
91	-.150	1.190	-.126	191	-.100	.464	-.216	291	-.175	.722	-.242	391	-.325	.370	.878	491	-.400	.300	-1.333
92	.300	1.168	.257	192	-.250	.471	-.531	292	.500	.682	.733	392	.825	.353	2.340	492	-.050	.335	-.149
93	.475	1.064	.446	193	1.125	1.180	.955	293	.900	.702	1.280	393	-.575	.370	-1.554	493	-.500	.354	-1.412
94	.050	1.060	.047	194	-.250	1.246	-.201	294	.125	.746	.168	394	-.900	.374	-2.406	494	-.575	.339	-1.699
95	.150	1.074	.140	195	1.050	.187	-5.620	295	-.250	.730	-.343	395	-.400	.375	-1.070	495	-.900	.353	-2.543
96	-.225	1.184	-.190	196	-.225	1.462	-.154	295	1.250	.808	1.550	396	.725	.396	1.830	496	-.150	.378	-.397
97	-.100	1.089	-.092	197	-.350	.335	-1.045	297	.475	.770	.618	397	-.775	.392	-1.975	497	-.300	.332	-.904
98	-.125	1.110	-.112	198	-.150	.929	-.161	298	-.275	.642	-.428	398	-1.000	.406	-2.463	498	-.100	.400	-.250
99	-.300	1.134	-.265	199	.300	.930	.323	299	.175	.651	.271	399	-.550	.501	-1.099	499	-.800	.400	-2.000
100	-.075	1.170	-.063	200	.150	1.055	.142	300	-.225	.657	-.342	400	.450	.503	.895	500	-.550	.295	-1.860

TABLE F. — STATISTICS FOR DRAWINGS FROM RIGHT TRIANGULAR UNIVERSE — (*Continued*)

Sample Number	$\bar{X}$	σ	%	Sample Number	$\bar{X}$	σ	%	Sample Number	$\bar{X}$	σ	%	Sample Number	$\bar{X}$	σ	%	Sample Number	$\bar{X}$	σ	%
501	-.175	1.030	-.173	601	-.450	.449	-1.002	701	-.325	.829	-.392	801	-.250	1.115	-.224	901	.250	1.059	.236
502	.100	1.152	.087	602	-.450	.350	-1.286	702	.425	1.005	.423	802	-.150	1.359	-.110	902	.475	1.035	.457
503	.700	1.065	.657	603	.050	.350	.143	703	.250	.991	.252	803	-.150	1.310	-.115	903	.250	1.160	.216
504	.525	1.043	.503	604	.375	1.270	.295	704	.350	1.006	.348	804	-.150	1.225	-.125	904	.550	1.113	.483
505	.750	.907	.827	605	.075	1.285	.058	705	-.225	.858	-.262	805	-.125	1.260	-.099	905	0	1.120	0
506	.575	.920	.625	606	-.100	1.225	-.082	706	0	.744	0	806	.425	1.145	.371	906	.350	.965	.363
507	-.100	1.020	.098	607	.475	1.103	.431	707	-.125	.750	-.167	807	.600	1.177	.510	907	.125	.995	.126
508	.850	1.030	.825	608	-.425	1.230	-.346	708	-.275	.764	-.360	808	.225	1.310	.172	908	-.125	.996	-.125
509	.275	.965	.285	609	.375	.409	.818	709	.525	.766	.685	809	.850	1.328	.640	909	.700	1.032	.678
510	.300	1.061	.283	610	-.450	.476	-.945	710	-.250	.757	-.330	810	.750	1.193	.629	910	.500	1.027	.487
511	.075	.950	.079	611	.275	.465	.591	711	-.175	.825	-.212	811	.150	1.246	.120	911	.500	.919	.544
512	.525	.973	.540	612	-.100	.510	-.197	712	.350	.757	.462	812	.075	1.250	.060	912	.425	.912	.466
513	.325	.865	.380	613	.100	.510	.196	713	.320	.795	.403	813	.125	1.220	.102	913	.675	.915	.737
514	-.175	.887	-.197	614	.250	1.250	.200	714	-.400	.886	-.451	814	.200	1.290	.155	914	.350	1.062	.330
515	-.125	.855	-.146	615	-.150	1.081	-.139	715	.350	1.159	.302	815	-.075	.836	.089	915	.375	1.242	.301
516	.775	1.050	.736	616	.150	.886	.169	716	.450	1.141	.394	816	.425	.823	.516	916	.350	1.350	.259
517	.325	1.042	.312	617	.050	.895	.056	717	.475	1.234	.385	817	.100	.840	.119	917	.175	1.198	.146
518	-.025	1.148	-.022	618	-.025	.934	-.027	718	.575	1.119	.514	818	-.625	.844	-.741	918	-.075	1.327	-.057
519	.400	1.056	.379	619	.075	1.008	.074	719	.150	1.101	.136	819	-.225	.842	-.268	919	-.100	1.332	-.075
520	.050	1.081	.046	620	1.000	.882	1.135	720	.625	1.252	.499	820	.450	.801	.562	920	.500	1.221	.410
521	1.100	.943	1.168	621	.575	1.145	.502	721	.150	.750	.200	821	.350	1.435	.244	921	-.025	1.000	-.025
522	.025	.865	.288	622	.625	1.135	.550	722	.125	.804	.155	822	.175	1.470	.119	922	.550	1.060	.519
523	-.300	.925	-.325	623	.175	1.351	.129	723	.400	.821	.476	823	.875	1.234	.709	923	0	1.090	0
524	.025	.908	.028	624	.725	.795	.912	724	1.200	.822	1.460	824	.875	1.250	.700	924	.850	1.130	.751
525	.050	.961	.052	625	.225	.795	.283	725	.250	.862	.290	825	.025	1.337	.018	925	-.200	1.148	-.174
526	-.350	.888	-.394	626	.325	.817	.398	726	-.200	.750	-.266	826	-.350	1.419	-.247	926	-.050	1.087	-.046
527	-.350	.885	-.395	627	.450	.854	.527	727	-.225	.873	-.258	827	.300	1.241	.242	927	.075	1.045	.072
528	.050	.887	.056	628	-.225	.815	-.276	728	-.675	.855	-.790	828	.175	1.246	.140	928	-.050	1.031	-.048
529	-.275	.973	-.283	629	-.075	.880	-.085	729	.125	.855	.143	829	.150	1.254	.120	929	-.225	1.057	-.213
530	-.200	.995	-.201	630	-.275	.826	-.333	730	.350	.838	.418	830	.550	1.213	.454	930	.175	1.045	.167
531	1.000	.870	1.149	631	.800	.886	.903	731	.300	.765	.392	831	.450	1.220	.369	931	0	1.032	0
532	-.200	.985	-.203	632	-.050	.910	-.055	732	-.150	.789	-.190	832	.950	1.484	.640	932	.150	1.109	.135
533	-.375	.988	-.380	633	-.350	.853	-.411	733	.400	.822	.487	833	.475	1.470	.323	933	-.100	1.118	.089
534	-.175	.928	-.188	634	-.650	.741	-.875	734	-.425	.766	-.555	834	.350	1.265	.276	934	.025	1.103	.023
535	.325	.978	.332	635	1.050	.783	1.341	735	-.425	.820	-.518	835	.375	1.280	.293	935	-.200	1.160	-.172
536	-.425	.950	-.448	636	.200	.758	.264	736	-.225	.820	-.274	836	.050	1.387	.036	936	-.375	1.145	-.328
537	-.075	.972	-.077	637	-.400	.895	-.446	737	.300	.926	.324	837	-.125	1.417	-.088	937	-.400	1.110	-.323
538	-.125	.884	-.142	638	.275	.781	.352	738	.950	.901	1.054	838	-.300	1.455	-.206	938	-.125	1.105	-.113
539	-.100	1.062	-.100	639	-.350	.743	-.471	739	.975	.795	1.226	839	-.150	1.477	-.102	939	-.325	1.091	-.298
540	-.150	.960	-.156	640	-.625	.942	-.663	740	-.075	.746	-.101	840	-.450	1.243	-.362	940	.375	1.040	.361
541	.500	.857	.583	641	-.325	.904	-.360	741	.850	.805	1.065	841	-.100	1.270	-.079	941	.050	1.097	.046
542	.400	.897	.446	642	-.300	.912	-.329	742	-.175	.892	-.196	842	.225	1.176	.191	942	-.375	1.112	.337
543	-.250	.844	-.296	643	.300	.897	.334	743	.050	.825	.061	843	-.250	.959	-.262	943	.225	1.290	.174
544	.525	1.040	.505	644	.025	.993	.025	744	.300	.926	.325	844	.150	.814	.184	944	-.300	1.172	-.256
545	.475	.993	.478	645	.975	1.455	.687	745	0	.367	0	845	.950	.800	1.190	945	.475	1.188	.400
546	-.025	1.028	-.024	646	.150	.864	.175	746	.100	.367	.272	946	-.025	.821	-.031	946	-.175	1.139	-.154
547	.300	1.309	.229	647	-.325	.665	-.490	747	.475	1.219	.390	847	.450	.836	.538	947	-.625	1.110	-.565
548	.900	1.180	.763	648	-.025	.918	-.027	748	-.300	.430	-.698	848	.425	.844	.504	948	.900	1.195	.752
549	.575	1.130	.508	649	.350	.907	.386	749	-.750	.470	-1.590	849	-.200	.913	-.219	949	.325	1.303	.249
550	.375	1.132	.331	650	.025	.991	.025	750	-.225	.415	-.542	850	.475	.934	.510	950	.900	1.170	.770

551	.800	1.164	.687	651	.500	.892	.561	751	-.175	.760	-.230	851	.575	.852	.675	951	-.225	.795	-.283
552	-.100	.384	-.260	652	.425	.884	.482	752	.425	1.349	.315	852	.560	.838	.657	952	.600	.830	.725
553	.150	1.074	.140	653	.475	.991	.479	753	-.300	.380	-.950	853	.100	.797	.125	953	-.750	.472	-1.589
554	0	.484	0	654	-.025	.904	-.028	754	-.100	.510	-.196	854	-.300	.738	-.407	954	.125	.845	.148
555	0	.485	0	655	-.175	.944	-.185	755	.650	.536	1.213	855	.425	.728	.585	955	.450	.900	.500
556	.175	.482	.363	656	-.175	.945	-.185	756	-.525	.492	-1.067	856	.175	.838	.209	956	.275	.796	.346
557	-.300	.560	-.536	657	.350	.856	.409	757	-.625	.430	-1.450	857	-.125	.715	-.175	957	.200	.834	.240
558	1.300	.560	2.320	658	-1.150	.814	-1.413	758	-.100	.441	-.227	858	-.400	.768	-.522	958	-.325	.850	-.382
559	.525	1.028	.511	659	-.175	.815	-.215	759	-.050	.438	-.114	859	1.125	.798	1.410	959	.250	.820	.305
560	.500	1.255	.398	660	1.050	1.101	.954	760	.275	.881	.312	860	-.575	.396	-1.452	960	0	.818	0
561	-.125	.813	-.154	661	-.075	.396	-.019	761	-.300	.748	-.401	861	-.550	.432	-1.272	961	.650	1.006	.646
562	075	.834	.090	662	-.725	.475	-1.525	762	1.050	.727	1.443	862	-.475	.444	-1.070	962	.775	1.150	.674
563	.175	.844	.207	663	-.560	.415	-1.350	763	.800	.810	.986	863	-.475	.460	-1.033	963	.875	1.035	.855
564	-.075	.844	-.089	664	-.625	.530	-1.270	764	-.725	.826	.878	864	-.750	.512	-1.465	964	.400	1.015	.394
565	0	.851	0	665	1.350	.572	2.360	765	.525	.765	.685	865	0	.424	0	965	.200	1.040	.192
566	-.075	.960	-.078	666	-.550	.571	-.963	766	-.200	.770	-.260	866	-.150	.433	-.346	966	.100	.993	.101
567	-.350	.844	-.415	667	-.025	.553	-.045	767	-.175	.765	-.229	867	-.600	.458	-1.310	967	.350	.966	.362
568	-.025	.884	-.028	668	-.100	.548	-.183	768	-.275	.765	-.360	868	-.350	.480	-.730	968	-.125	.981	-.127
569	.050	.838	.060	669	-.450	.589	-.765	769	-.550	.753	-.730	869	-.700	.441	-1.590	969	-.050	.981	-.051
570	0	.857	0	670	-.575	.576	-.998	770	.150	.838	.179	870	-.450	.456	-.986	970	-.050	.981	-.051
571	-.275	.901	-.305	671	-.325	.545	-.596	771	.175	.683	.256	871	-.850	.456	-1.864	971	-.225	1.064	-.211
572	-.300	.850	-.352	672	-.400	.524	-.875	772	-.425	.816	-.520	872	-.550	.454	-1.212	972	.225	1.083	.208
573	-.225	.920	-.245	673	-.675	.565	-1.195	773	.925	.718	1.290	873	-.400	.489	-.818	973	.525	.958	.548
574	.225	.945	.239	674	.025	.349	.072	774	.275	.718	.373	874	-.775	.460	-1.684	974	.025	1.115	.022
575	-.275	.993	-.277	675	-.600	.367	-1.635	775	.025	.719	.035	875	-.600	.474	-1.270	975	.525	1.115	.470
576	-.375	.928	-.404	676	-.500	.367	-1.362	776	-.025	.732	-.032	876	-.350	.503	-.696	976	-.300	1.151	-.260
577	.125	.927	.135	677	.350	.521	.672	777	.200	.716	.279	877	-.225	.512	-.439	977	-.500	1.155	-.433
578	0	.886	0	678	-.450	.521	-.865	778	.025	.709	.032	878	-.325	.540	-.602	978	-.050	1.040	-.048
579	.275	.858	.321	679	.325	.520	.625	779	.125	.810	.154	879	.200	.604	.332	979	-.275	1.050	-.274
580	-.050	.990	-.505	680	-.175	.520	-.336	780	.525	.750	.700	880	-.200	.524	-.382	980	.500	1.060	.472
581	-.475	.968	-.491	681	.100	.534	.187	781	-.250	.740	-.338	881	.300	.524	.573	981	-.250	1.092	-.229
582	-.575	.920	-.625	682	-.600	.570	-1.053	782	0	.728	0	882	.625	.517	1.209	982	.375	.995	.388
583	.325	.945	.348	683	-.175	.633	-.276	783	-.050	.829	-.060	883	-.475	.545	-.872	983	.075	1.047	.072
584	.375	.895	.419	684	-.750	.403	-1.860	784	-.175	.719	-.243	884	.150	.532	.282	984	.550	1.102	.499
585	.350	.827	.423	685	.675	.406	1.671	785	-.100	.728	-.137	885	-.350	.532	-.658	985	.450	1.203	.374
586	-.150	.879	-.170	686	-.375	.254	-1.455	786	-.100	.720	-.139	886	.175	.512	.342	986	.550	1.238	.445
587	-.075	.880	-.085	687	-.875	.327	-2.680	787	-.275	.845	-.326	887	-.250	.532	-.469	987	.525	1.125	.477
588	-.050	.868	-.058	688	-.025	.356	-.070	788	.075	.887	.085	888	1.150	.528	2.180	988	.350	1.218	.288
589	.700	.958	.730	689	.100	.339	.295	789	.200	.825	.243	889	-.150	1.470	-.119	989	.350	1.087	.322
590	1.025	.779	1.316	690	-.600	.339	-.177	790	.100	.748	.134	890	.225	1.310	.172	990	.525	1.087	.483
591	.450	.792	.568	691	1.050	.319	.329	791	-.075	.775	-.097	891	.625	1.300	.481	991	-.250	.687	.364
592	.775	.898	.863	692	-.450	.450	-1.000	792	.700	.791	.885	892	-.100	1.560	-.064	992	.125	.763	.164
593	.250	.986	.254	693	-.350	.320	-1.090	793	.225	.738	.305	893	.200	1.361	.145	993	.225	.691	.326
594	.475	.868	.547	694	-1.050	.378	-2.778	794	-.225	.885	-.254	894	.250	1.460	.171	994	.625	.691	.904
595	.725	.841	.862	695	-.575	.390	-1.474	795	-.225	.928	-.242	895	.450	1.457	.309	995	-.325	.705	-.461
596	.500	.927	.539	696	-.550	.335	-1.642	796	-.175	.893	-.196	896	-.200	1.401	-.143	996	-.275	.803	-.342
597	0	.851	0	697	-.725	.350	-2.675	797	.200	.825	.243	897	-.025	1.492	-.017	997	.200	.682	.293
598	.100	.850	.117	698	1.275	.342	3.728	798	1.075	.853	1.260	898	-.075	1.520	-.015	998	-.375	.705	-.533
599	.050	.795	.063	699	-.375	.383	-.979	799	0	.815	0	899	.275	1.462	.188	999	-.325	.733	-.443
600	.450	.856	.526	700	-.025	.348	-.072	800	.300	.815	.368	900	.175	1.482	.118	1000	.050	1.050	.048

APPENDIX III

A Bibliographic Guide with Suggestions for Study in the Further Development of a Scientific Basis for the Economic Control of Quality of Manufactured Product

As stated in the preface, the present book is but an *initial* step toward the formulation of a scientific basis for securing economic control. Much remains to be done. In presenting a list of references for further study, an attempt has been made to include those suggestive of what appear to be profitable lines of further development.

Throughout the book we have had occasion to give many specific references. The object of the present bibliography is to suggest references of a more or less general nature to be read in connection with each of the seven parts. It is hoped that in many instances these references will be suggestive of work which may be profitably done in extending the theory of quality control, particularly in the direction of the development of improved ways of securing good data through the more thorough application of the scientific method.

References for Parts I and III

1. *Exact and Statistical Laws*

In Parts I and III the rôles of exact, empirical, and statistical laws in helping us to do what we want to do are touched upon.

The recent book, *A History of Science*, C. D. Whetham, 2nd edition, Macmillan Company, New York, 1930, gives an interesting and up-to-date survey of the results of human effort in establishing laws of nature. To get a more exact picture, however, we must turn to some such book as *Introduction to Theoretical Physics*, A. Haas, 2nd edition, Constable & Company, London, Vol. I, 1928, Vol. II, 1929; or the book of the same title by L. Page, D. Van Nostrand Company, Inc., New York, 1928.

With the development of the atomic structure of matter and electricity, it became necessary to think of laws as being statistical in nature. The importance of the law of large numbers in the interpretation of physical phenomena will become apparent to any one who even hastily surveys any one or more of the following books: *Statistical Theories of Matter, Radiation, and Electricity*, K. K. Darrow, The Physical Review Supplement, Vol. I, No. 1, July 1929, also published in the series of Bell Telephone Laboratories' reprints, No. 435; *Introduction to Statistical Mechanics for Students of Physics and Physical Chemistry*, J. Rice, Constable & Company, Ltd., London, 1930; *Statistical Mechanics with Applications to Physics and Chemistry*, R. C. Tolman, Chemical Catalog Company, New York, 1927; *Kinetic Theory of Gases*, L. B. Loeb, McGraw-Hill Book Company, New York, 1927; *The Kinetic Theory of Gases*, E. Bloch, Methuen & Company, Ltd., London, 1924; *Introduction to Modern Physics*, F. K. Richtmeyer, McGraw-Hill Book Company, New York, 1928; *Modern Physics*, H. A. Wilson, Blackie & Son, Ltd., London, 1928; *Introduction to Contemporary Physics*, K. K. Darrow, D. Van Nostrand Company, Inc., New York, 1926; and *Atoms, Molecules and Quanta*, A. E. Ruark and H. C. Urey, McGraw-Hill Book Company, New York, 1930.

One cannot return from even a brief excursion into the field of modern physics and chemistry without having caught a glimpse of the importance of the concept of the statistical limit in all of the latest developments. Even in this field of exact science *nothing is exact*. In the last analysis the influence of chance causes is felt. Almost the only things that appear to be constant are distribution functions or statistics of these functions—and this constancy is only in the statistical sense. For example, one interested in the specification of quality of materials need read only Chapter III of *The Physics of Solids and Liquids*, P. P. Ewald, Th. Pöschl and L. Prandtl, Blackie and Son, Ltd., 1930, to see how far we are from being able to explain some of even the simplest mechanical properties in terms of atomic physics.

2. *Empirical Laws*

To contrast the way in which the so-called exact and statistical laws enable one to predict with the way in which an empirical law does, the recent excellent book *Business Cycles*, W. C. Mitchell, National Bureau of Economic Research, New York, 1927, should prove to be of interest. The author of this book discusses in a critical manner the very extensive amount of work that has been done in trying to develop a rational basis for predicting cyclic movements with a net result that is not so very encouraging. Even a casual reading of this book must impress one with the serious hopelessness of trying to predict the future in terms of the past when the *chance* cause system is not constant. In the present state of the scientific method of induction, it appears that empirical relationships such as time series give little basis for prediction. This conclusion is consistent with that so admirably presented in a recent paper by S. L. Andrew in the *Bell Telephone Quarterly*, Jan., 1931, and also with conclusions set forth in the recent book *Business Adrift*, by W. B. Donham, Dean of the Harvard Business School. Such reading cannot do other than strengthen our belief in the fact that control of quality will come only through the weeding out of assignable causes of variation—particularly those that introduce lack of constancy in the chance cause system.

3. *Frequency Distribution Functions*

In Part III we considered very briefly the problem of determining the kind of frequency distribution function or functions that we might expect controlled quality to follow. In this connection we touched upon the philosophy of frequency curves as laws of distribution.

Two systems of curves were mentioned in particular, namely, the Pearson and the Gram-Charlier systems. Although we have not had occasion to make much use of these functions as such, a serious student of control of quality will find it greatly to his advantage to read some of the original memoirs dealing with these two systems of curves. Those of Pearson are naturally available in English and cannot help but prove stimulating. The more formal part of Pearson's work in this field has been summarized by Elderton in the interesting book, *Frequency Curves and Correlation*, second edition, Layton, London, 1928. T. L. Kelley, a former student of Pearson, also has much of interest to say about this system of curves in his book, *Statistical Method*, Macmillan Company, New York, 1923.

Very interesting and stimulating accounts of the significance of the Gram-Charlier series have been given by Arne Fisher, *Mathe-*

matical Theory of Probabilities, 2nd edition, Macmillan Company, New York, 1922; by F. Y. Edgeworth in a series of articles referred to in his article *Probability* in the 13th edition of the Encyclopedia Britannica; and by T. N. Thiele, *Theory of Observations*, London, 1903. J. F. Steffensen in *Some Recent Researches in the Theory of Statistics and Actuarial Science*, Cambridge University Press, 1930, makes some very interesting and pertinent remarks on the theoretical foundation of certain types of frequency curves.

It is of particular interest to note the way in which Edgeworth arrives at the Gram-Charlier series as a method of expressing the results of the joint action of a complicated system of causes. Of course, the Pearson system can be given somewhat similar causal interpretation although great emphasis has not been laid upon this point by many of those writing about the Pearson system.

The sythentic building up of a frequency curve in terms of the effects of component groups of causes forms a basis, as we have seen, for our discussion of the necessary and sufficient conditions of maximum control. We have emphasized the significance of the fact that, as the number of causes of variability is increased, we seem to approach closer and closer to what we have termed the point (0, 3) of maximum control in the $\beta_1\,\beta_2$ plane.

In this connection *The Behavior of Prices*, F. C. Mills, National Bureau of Economic Research, Inc., New York, 1928, should prove interesting reading, particularly that part having to do with the march of the β's back to normalcy, as he puts it.

4. *Probability*

Probability and its Engineering Uses, T. C. Fry, D. Van Nostrand Company, New York, 1928, and *An Introduction to Mathematical Probability*, J. L. Coolidge, Oxford University Press, New York, 1925, contain interesting discussions of the meaning of probability and the difficulty involved in defining it.

5. *Quality Control*

The only book touching upon the subject of quality control in anything like the sense of the present text is that by Becker, Plaut, and Runge, referred to in Chapter I of Part I.

References for Part II

1. *Economics*

The problem of economic control of quality in its broadest sense is, as we have seen, that of doing what we want to do within limits which are economical. To do this, we must establish *economic standards* of quality. A brief outline of the economic considerations which must be taken into account in attempting to establish such standards of quality is given in an interesting article, "Standard Quality," G. D. Edwards, *Bell Telephone Quarterly*, Vol. VII, pp. 292–303.

For example, in establishing such a standard, we must consider the relationship between cost and value. Value, however, is not so easily defined in a way that will cover all of the prevalent concepts of this term. To attempt to do so leads us into difficulties touched upon in our discussion of the definition of quality.

Naturally, value in some way or other depends upon the degree to which a given quality satisfies human wants; but, in turn, human wants are not constant even for the same person. Furthermore, the degree to which a thing having several quality characteristics tends to satisfy the human wants of even a single person is to a large extent a complicated and unknown function of the magnitudes of the physical characteristics of the thing. Even assuming that the value determined on the basis of the wants of a single person is a constant, it is apparent that the values for different people differ among themselves so that, in the last analysis, value, if it can be expressed quantitatively, is presumably a frequency distribution function.

A brief, terse exposition of the fundamental economic problems involved in attaining a dynamic measure of value will be found in the *Mathematical Introduction to Economics*, G. C. Evans, McGraw-Hill Book Company, New York, 1930. Having obtained a picture of the complicated nature of this problem, one may feel inclined to despair of its solution. However, for some time to come, it is likely that we shall not get away from the desire on the part of all of us to find some measure of quality which is common to all qualities.

In our discussion of economic control, we left out any detailed consideration of this problem of finding an adequate measure of value, even though such a measure apparently would serve a very useful purpose. We started with the tacit assumption that when such a measure of value can be found, it will have two characteristics: it will be a statistical quantity, and it will be statistically related to the measurable quality characteristic of the product.

Beginning at this point, we have shown, particularly in Part I, that certain economic advantages can be attained in the production of a controlled quality. This means, of course, as previously stated, that the quality standard is some frequency distribution function. We emphasized the importance of at least two characteristics, namely, the average $\bar{X}$ and the standard deviation σ of this function. To insure that the specified parameters in a given case are economic standards would require a consideration of the fundamental problems involved in establishing measures of value already referred to. In such cases we must choose standards which to the best of our knowledge at the present stage of the development of the subject appear to be reasonable estimates of economic standards.

2. *Texts on Statistical Theory*

The ninth edition of Yule's *An Introduction to the Theory of Statistics*, C. Griffin & Company, Ltd., 1930, should prove to be a veritable storehouse of knowledge in respect to many of the things discussed in Part II. This is particularly true in respect to measures of central tendency, dispersion, and correlation. As supplementary reading for the more technical part of the discussion, *Mathematical Statistics*, H. L. Rietz, Open Court Publishing Company, Chicago, 1917, should prove of great value, particularly in connection with the consideration of the analytical aspects of correlation. A. L. Bowley's *Elements of Statistics*, Chas. Scribner's Sons, New York, 1926—in particular the second volume—contains much of interest in regard to the point binomial and the second approximation (23). *The Mathematics of Statistics*, R. W. Burgess, Houghton Mifflin Company, New York, 1927, will be found helpful as a general elementary text. It also contains references to several elementary books dealing with statistical methods and their application in other fields such as economics. Two of these should be mentioned here: *Statistical Methods Applied to Economics in Business*, F. C. Mills, Henry Holt & Company, New York, 1924, and *Principles and Methods of Statistics*, R. E. Chaddock, Houghton Mifflin Company, Boston, 1925. Attention should also be called to the recent book, *The Mathematical Part of Elementary Statistics*, B. H. Camp, D. C. Heath & Co., New York, 1931.

3. *Curve Fitting*

In connection with our discussion of the derivation of empirical formulas to represent relationships, the little book, *Empirical Formulas*, T. R. Running, Wiley & Sons, New York, 1917, is of interest. The method of moments is discussed in some detail in Elderton's book, *Frequency Curves*, previously referred to. The method of least squares is admirably treated in the *Calculus of Observations*, E. T. Whittaker and G. Robinson, 2nd edition, Blackie & Son, London, 1926.

References for Part IV

In 1922, R. A. Fisher presented in *The Philosophical Transactions of the Royal Society* in London an article, "The Mathematical Foundations of Theoretical Statistics," in which he characterized three fundamental problems, namely, specification, distribution, and estimation. At least the first nine paragraphs of this paper should be read by any one interested in the application of statistical theory in the control of quality. In Part IV, we are particularly interested in the theory of distribution which has been developed to a marked extent during the last few decades at the hands of R. A. Fisher, "Student," J. Neyman, L. Isserlis, A. E. R. Church, V. J. Romanovsky, J. Wishart, E. L. Dodd, B. H. Camp, H. Hotelling, Karl Pearson, E. S. Pearson, L. H. C. Tippett, P. R. Rider, A. A. Tchouproff, A. A. Markoff, M. Watanabe and E. Slutsky.

Perhaps one of the best ways for a newcomer to orientate himself in this field of investigation is to read the excellent "Report on Statistics" by H. L. Rietz, published in the *Bulletin of the American Mathematical Society*, October, 1924, pp. 417–453. References to later work of the men mentioned in the previous paragraph and others on the theory of distribution will be found in the bibliographies of the books by Yule, Rietz, and Kelley, already referred to. In connection with the discussion of Tchebycheff's theorem, one of the most interesting articles is that of A. A. Tchouproff, "Asymptotic Frequency Distribution of the Arithmetic Means of n Correlated Observations for Very Great Values of n," *Journal of the Royal Statistical Society*, Vol. LXXXVII, 1925, pp. 91–104. This article gives detailed references to the work of Watanabe, Markoff, Slutsky, and others touching upon this same problem.

A recent paper, "British Statistics and Statisticians Today," H. Hotelling, *Journal of the American Statistical Association*, June,

1930, pp. 186–190, gives an interesting brief account of what is going on in England today in the development of statistical theory. If one is interested in tracing the development of the theory of distribution or, in fact, any part of statistical theory back through the ages, *Studies in the History of Statistical Method*, Helen M. Walker, Williams & Wilkins Company, Baltimore, 1929, will be found helpful. Perhaps our best general source of information on the important work of the Scandinavian School of statisticians is the book by Arne Fisher previously mentioned.

References for Parts VI and VII

1. *Estimation*

Two fundamental statistical problems are touched upon in Parts VI and VII. One is that of going from a random sample of size n to its universe.

Today there are in the literature the following three general methods of going from a sample to its universe:

(*a*) The *a posteriori* method.
(*b*) The method of maximum likelihood.
(*c*) The empirical method.

To mention these three in the same breath in the presence of a group of statisticians is almost certain to start an argument, for there is a wide divergence of opinion as to the comparative validities of these methods.

For this reason, the reader will find it advantageous to consider in some detail the original memoirs dealing with these separate methods. The *a posteriori* method is tied up with the theory of causes and the name of Bayes. The recent important article, "Frequency Distribution of the Unknown Mean of a Sampled Universe," E. C. Molina and R. I. Wilkinson, *Bell System Technical Journal*, Vol. VIII, pp. 632–645, October, 1929, should prove an interesting starting point for the consideration of this method, although the reader will doubtless wish to read other original memoirs referred to in connection with the discussion of Bayes' theorem in the general bibliographies mentioned in a previous paragraph.

The method of maximum likelihood is tied up largely with the work of R. A. Fisher, starting primarily with his article in the *Philosophical Transactions* previously mentioned.

A recent article, "On the Use and Interpretation of Certain Test Criteria for Purposes of Statistical Inference," E. S. Pearson and J. Neyman, *Biometrika*, XXA, pp. 175–240, 1927, and XXA, pp. 263–294, 1928, is perhaps the best critical discussion of the available methods of solving the problem of estimation. It should certainly be read by any serious student of this subject.

The third edition of *Statistical Methods for Research Workers*, R. A. Fisher, summarizes most of the detailed methods of estimation developed by him. It is a book of particular value to scientists and engineers, although one must keep in mind the serious limitations of all methods of estimation based upon small samples as noted in the text and discussed in such references as that of Pearson and Neyman.

It is of interest to note that a divergence of opinion is expressed in the literature as to the usefulness of the theory of the so-called small sample. Perhaps most of the critical remarks are based upon the assumption that this theory is to be used as the basis of estimation, and that it may give the impression that we can replace large samples by small ones. In the first place, a careful reading of the available literature does not reveal any specific suggestion to substitute small samples for large ones. In the second place, it should be noted that the application of small sample theory used in this text is required in handling large numbers of data in a *rational* way by breaking them up into rational subgroups. In this work the distribution theory for small samples plays a prominent rôle.

In general the problem of estimation presents the universal difficulties involved in all induction. If one reads such a book as *A Treatise on Probability*, J. M. Keynes, Macmillan Company, New York, 1921, he may feel at first very much discouraged, because his attention will have been directed to many of the serious difficulties involved in the application of probability theory. A useful tonic in such a case is to read any one or more of the following books: *The Nature of the Physical World*, A. S. Eddington, Macmillan Company, New York, 1928; *The Logic of Modern Physics*, P. W. Bridgman, Macmillan Company, New York, 1928; *The Analysis of Matter*, Bertrand Russell, Harcourt, Brace & Company, Inc., New York, 1927. At least, these three books should prove to be a tonic, if it is true that misery loves company. Certainly the serious difficulties involved in the interpretation of physical phenomena are common in all fields, and the discussions in these books show how much we must rely upon the application of probability theory even in an "exact" science.

2. *Detecting Lack of Control*

The second fundamental statistical problem is that of determining whether or not a given set of data comes from a constant system of causes, or more generally it is the problem of dividing the universe of objective values into rational subgroups schematically represented in Fig. 144. In our discussion of ways and means for detecting lack of control, we have pointed out again and again the necessity of subdividing the data into rational subgroups. To do this requires the exercise of human judgment.

In the last analysis we must depend upon the use of scientific method—that is, upon human intuition, imagination, reasoning, and knowledge. It is perhaps only through the application of this general method that we can hope to attain good data, one characteristic of which is that they be subdivided into rational subgroups. It may be of interest, therefore, to sketch briefly a course of reading which will be found helpful to the student in the application of scientific method to the further development of the theory of quality control. To do so necessarily takes us into the fields of psychology, philosophy, and logic; into the field of psychology because we must get some sort of picture of the way the mind works; into the field of philosophy because we need some hypothesis as to the nature of reality and the function of laws, theories, and causal explanations; into the field of logic because it presents what we know about the formal methods available in the theory of deduction and induction.

How do data depend upon the mind? What is the effect of factual experience and the effect of reasoning upon an observer? These are important questions. What we sense through any one of our senses depends partly upon previous use of these senses. Thus a child looking at a straight stick extending beneath the surface of a pool of water sees a bent stick. Similarly, the first time one sees what is shown in Fig. 131, he sees the length of the line (*a*) to be different from that of line (*b*), although they are of the same length. In this way, factual experience influences what we sense through any one of our senses.

Perhaps more important, however, is that the mental experience involving reasoning influences to a marked extent what we sense. One looking at a line AB, Fig. 1, and thinking of the points on the line, sees those points in an entirely different way after he has tried to place such points as $\sqrt{3}$ and π on that line.

Almost every day one hears of some physical discovery which has been influenced by a conceptual theory. A trained experimentalist who is at the same time familiar with the current theory or theories having to do with the phenomena which he is investigating will, in many cases at least, be able to get better data for the particular purpose in hand than he would be if he did not know the theory.

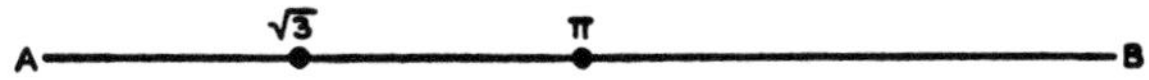

FIG. 1.

In this same connection, it is important to note some of the applications of the theory of frequency curves in assisting one to break down an observed set of data into rational subgroups or to indicate in ways other than those described in the text whether or not this can be done. For example, the fact that an observed point in the $\beta_1\,\beta_2$ plane is in the neighborhood of (0, 1.8), Fig. 2, is consistent

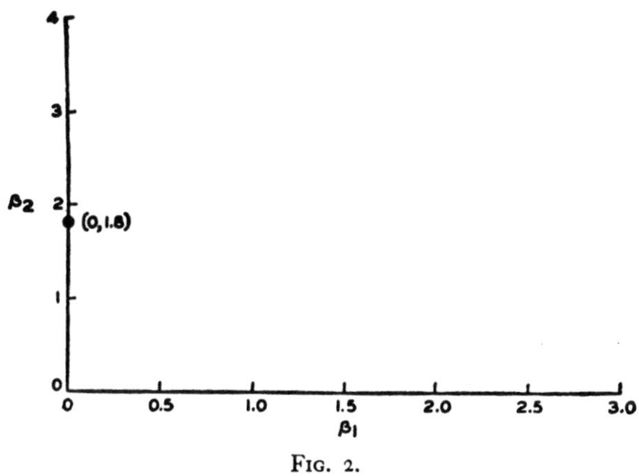

FIG. 2.

with the hypothesis that the observed set of data came in approximately equal proportion from, let us say, *m* rational subgroups. In a similar way, an observed value of skewness may be consistent with some rational hypothesis in respect to the causes of variation. In other words, an observed set of statistics can be suggestive of a working hypothesis in much the same way that a rough plot of an observed frequency distribution may be suggestive in the sense indicated by E. B. Wilson in his article, "The Development of a Frequency Function and Some Comments on Curve Fitting," *Proceedings of the National Academy of Sciences*, Vol. 10, 1924, pp. 79–84.

Another very important use of the knowledge of the theory may be that of detecting mistakes in computation. For example, if one found a point (β_1, β_2) below the line $\beta_2 - \beta_1 - 1 = 0$, Fig. 3, he would know that a mistake had been made because, as was originally shown by Pearson, it is not possible for a frequency distribution function to have a point in this area.

Broadly speaking, we see again why it is so necessary in the control of quality of manufactured product to have data accumulated by someone acquainted with the available factual and conceptual expe-

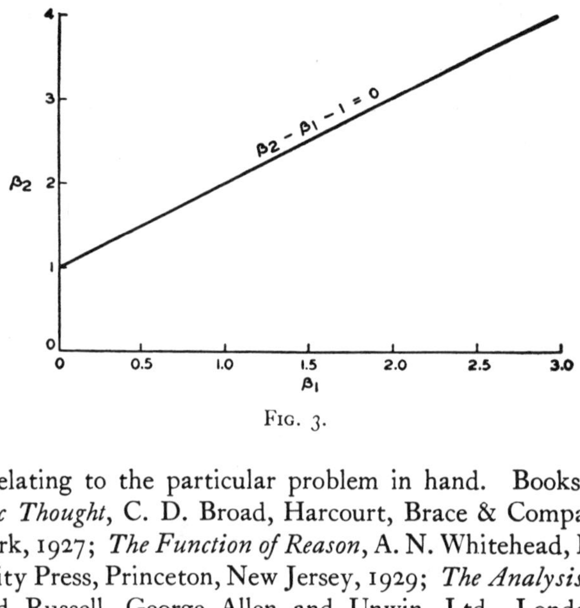

Fig. 3.

rience relating to the particular problem in hand. Books such as: *Scientific Thought*, C. D. Broad, Harcourt, Brace & Company, Inc., New York, 1927; *The Function of Reason*, A. N. Whitehead, Princeton University Press, Princeton, New Jersey, 1929; *The Analysis of Mind*, Bertrand Russell, George Allen and Unwin, Ltd., London, 1922; *Conflicting Psychologies of Learning*, H. B. Bode, D. C. Heath & Company, New York, 1929; *The Principles of Psychology*, William James, Henry Holt & Company, New York, 1890; *The Revolt Against Dualism*, A. L. Lovejoy, W. W. Norton & Company, Inc., New York, 1930; and *Human Learning*, E. L. Thorndike, The Century Co., 1931; contain much of interest in this connection.

Having seen what an important part conceptual experience may play in taking data, one is likely to become more interested in formal logic. The meaning of the laws of thought and the application of syllogistic reasoning take on a new interest. For example, a fundamental understanding of the theory of control tacitly involves such mathematical concepts as function, limit, continuity, and so on, developed to a degree of refinement which comes from the study of the discussion of these subjects in such a book as G. H. Hardy's *Pure Mathematics*, Cambridge University Press, London, 1928.

Perhaps of even greater interest, however, is the consideration of what we mean by *judgment* and *common sense*—two things which we find we must use so often in experimental work of all kinds. One soon finds that there is a considerable divergence of opinion in respect to such matters as will be evidenced by a more or less systematic browsing in the following treatises on logic. *Elementary Logic*, A. Sidwick, Cambridge University Press, London, 1914; *Principles of Logic*, H. W. Bradley, Vol. I and Vol. II, 2nd Edition, Oxford University Press, London, 1922; *An Introduction to Logic*, H. W. B. Joseph, 2nd Edition, Oxford University Press, London, 1922; *Formal Logic*, J. N. Keynes, 4th Edition, Macmillan Company, Ltd., London, 1928; *Logic*, W. E. Johnson, Cambridge University Press, London, Vol. I, *Logic, General*, 1921; Vol. II, *Logic Demonstrative Inference: Deductive and Inductive*, 1922; Vol. III, *The Logical Foundation of Science*, 1924; *The Logic of Discovery*, R. D. Carmichael, The Open Court Publishing Co., Chicago, 1930; *Rational Induction*, H. H. Dubs, The Chicago University Press, Chicago, 1930; and *Scientific Inference*, Harold Jeffreys, Macmillan Co., New York, 1931.

It will be noted that the application of the formal scientific method in discovery involves a human choice at every step. For example, in the discovery of a functional or statistical relationship, the following choices must be made:

1. Choice of data.
2. Choice of functional form.
3. Choice of number of parameters, at least in certain cases.
4. Choice of method of estimating parameters.

To a certain extent this field of choice is a kind of methodological No-Man's Land.

History of science shows, however, that the discoverers of the past have, in general, been those broadly trained in the particular field of discovery of their choice. They have been those familiar with the status of experimental and theoretical results in their particular field. The importance of theory in helping one to choose the right thing to be discovered is illustrated by the fact that several elements in the periodic table have been looked for and found because their existence was suggested by the blank spaces. So it is that many of the discoveries of science have been suggested by theory.

Furthermore, it is of interest to note that important discoveries have usually come only after the investigator has surrounded himself for a considerable period of time with the facts bearing upon the subject and during this period has kept these more or less constantly in mind. It is true, however, history also indicates that many of these discoveries have only come after the investigator has dropped the search for a time more or less completely from his conscious consideration. In all cases, however, it appears that preliminary conscious attention to the facts in hand is essential.

Coming now to the more or less formal treatment of scientific method, the following books will be found helpful in something like the order listed: *The Foundations of Science*, H. Poincare, The Science Press, New York, 1929; *The Principles of Science*, W. S. Jevons, Macmillan Company, Ltd., London, 1924; *Essentials of Scientific Method*, A. Wolf, Macmillan Company, New York, 1927; *Scientific Method*, A. D. Ritchie, Harcourt, Brace & Company, New York, 1923; and *Physics, The Elements*, N. R. Campbell, Cambridge University Press, London, 1920, together with Vol. III of Johnson's *Logic* noted in the previous paragraph.

Books such as the *Quest for Certainty*, John Dewey, Minton Balch Company, New York, 1929; and in particular, A. N. Whitehead's *Process and Reality*, Macmillan Company, New York, 1930, contain much of interest. Just as a simple example, it is necessary for us to think of a quality characteristic as an entity in the sense adopted by Whitehead if it is to be general enough to be of use in the many practical problems that arise in the interpretation of a sample.

Other References

1. *Errors of Measurement*

It is assumed that the reader has available one or more of the following books on the discussion of the errors of measurement: *The Combination of Observations*, David Brunt, University Press, London, 1917; *The Calculus of Observations*, E. T. Whittaker and G. Robinson, Blackie & Son, London, 1924; *The Theory of Measurements*, A. D. Palmer, McGraw-Hill Publishing Company, New York, 1930; and

The Theory of Measurements, L. Tuttle and J. Satterly, Longmans, Green & Company, New York, 1925.

Brunt's book contains, in addition to the ordinary discussion of the theory of errors, an interesting introductory chapter indicating various ways of developing the normal law. The book by Tuttle and Satterly gives a particularly good elementary discussion of many things which must be considered in correcting data for errors of measurement. Palmer's treatise is of particular value in outlining things which must be considered in planning physical measurements so as to reduce the errors of measurement to a minimum.

2. *Tables*

Of course, every one needs a table of squares, reciprocals, and square roots such as that of Barlow published in revised form by E. and F. N. Spon, Ltd., London, 1930, and a table of logarithms such as those of Vega published by D. Van Nostrand Company, New York, 1916. In addition to these, any one interested in the theory of quality control will find much use for Pearson's *Tables for Statisticians and Biometricians*, published by the Cambridge University Press, London, 1924. The second volume of these tables which is now in the process of preparation is supposed to contain the tables which have appeared in *Biometrika* since the publication of the first volume in 1924. In a way, the promised second volume will be even more helpful than the first. The books by Fry, Arne Fisher, and R. A. Fisher contain many useful tables. For a more complete bibliography, the reader is referred again to that of Yule.

3. *Magazines*

Without question, one magazine which has been found most useful in our study of quality control has been *Biometrika*, edited by Karl Pearson and his son Egon Pearson, and published by the Cambridge University Press, London. It has carried many of the important papers of "Student," R. A. Fisher, L. H. C. Tippett, J. Neyman, J. O. Irwin, Karl Pearson, E. S. Pearson, J. Wishart, and their associates. The *Skandinavisk Aktuarietidskrift*, Stockholm, contains many important articles in English as well as in foreign languages. The same is true of *Metron*, an international review of statistics published in Rome, Italy.

The Journal of the American Statistical Association, New York, contains many discussions of the applications of the more elementary theory of statistics in the field of economics. The same can be said of the *Journal of the Royal Statistical Society*, London, although this Journal has also published several important articles on the theory of statistics. Both of these Journals are of value because of their reviews of current literature. The *Annals of Mathematical Statistics* is a Journal recently started in cooperation with the American Statistical Association. It is devoted to both theory and application of mathematical statistics.

A glance at any of the complete bibliographies previously referred to will show that important articles have appeared in many other journals than those listed here.

4. *Mathematics*

It is assumed, of course, that the student of the theory of control is equipped with elementary texts up to and including differential and integral calculus. For a more complete treatment than is ordinarily given in any elementary text, the following books are suggested. In questions involving purely algebraical manipulation as in the discussion of the multinomial theorem, the student will find *Algebra*, G. Chrystal, Vol. I and Vol. II, 5th Edition, A. and C. Black, Ltd., London, 1920, of great help. For a discussion of the subject of symmetric functions and related topics of interest in the application of the method of moments and the use of semi-invariants, M. Bôcher's *Introduction to Higher Algebra*, Macmillan Company, New York, 1921, will be helpful. *Advanced Calculus*, W. F. Osgood, Macmillan Company, New York, 1925, treats in sufficient detail for most purposes the analytical methods required for an understanding of the mathematical theory found in most articles on the subjects of specification, distribution, and estimation. Two excellent books on the mathematical theory of statistics are: *Statistique Mathématique*, G. Darmois, Gaston Doin et Cie., Paris, 1928, and *Statistique Mathématique*, Charles Jordan, Gauthier-Villars et Cie., Paris, 1927.

5. *Graphical Methods*

We have neglected to consider in any great detail the important problem of presenting the results of quality control studies in a way to be of greatest service even though so much depends upon a thought-

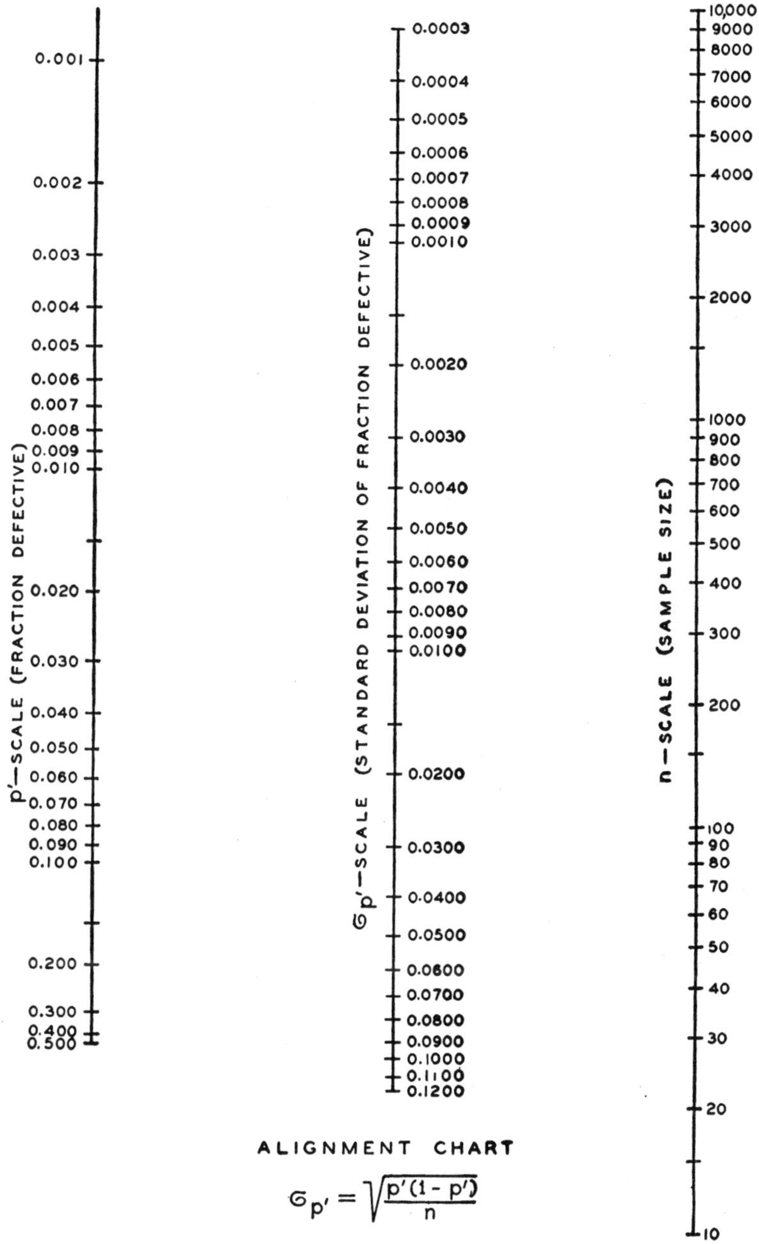

ALIGNMENT CHART

$$\sigma_{p'} = \sqrt{\frac{p'(1-p')}{n}}$$

FIG. 4.

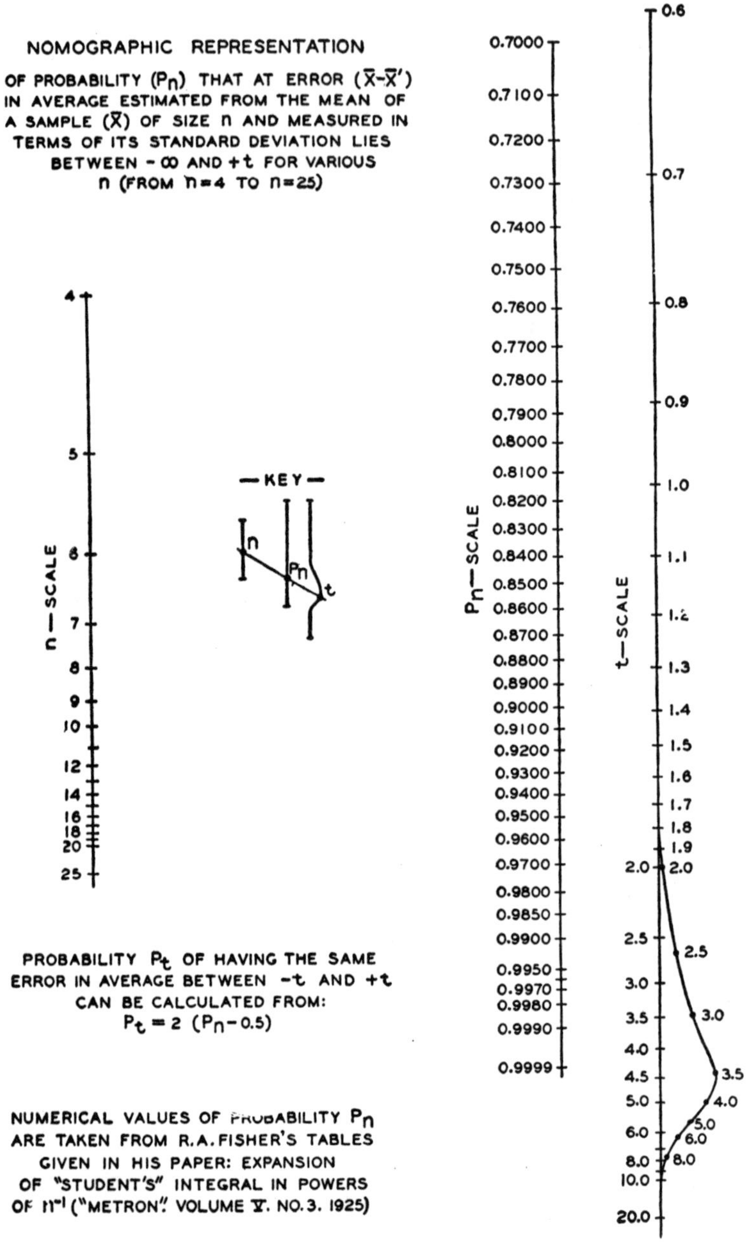
NOMOGRAPHIC REPRESENTATION
OF PROBABILITY (P_n) THAT AT ERROR ($\bar{X}-\bar{X}'$) IN AVERAGE ESTIMATED FROM THE MEAN OF A SAMPLE ($\bar{X}$) OF SIZE n AND MEASURED IN TERMS OF ITS STANDARD DEVIATION LIES BETWEEN $-\infty$ AND $+t$ FOR VARIOUS n (FROM n=4 TO n=25)
n—SCALE
4
5
6
7
8
9
10
12
14
16
18
20
25
—KEY—
n
P_n
t
P_n—SCALE
0.7000
0.7100
0.7200
0.7300
0.7400
0.7500
0.7600
0.7700
0.7800
0.7900
0.8000
0.8100
0.8200
0.8300
0.8400
0.8500
0.8600
0.8700
0.8800
0.8900
0.9000
0.9100
0.9200
0.9300
0.9400
0.9500
0.9600
0.9700
0.9800
0.9850
0.9900
0.9950
0.9970
0.9980
0.9990
0.9999
t—SCALE
0.6
0.7
0.8
0.9
1.0
1.1
1.2
1.3
1.4
1.5
1.6
1.7
1.8
1.9
2.0
2.5
3.0
3.5
4.0
4.5
5.0
6.0
8.0
10.0
20.0
PROBABILITY P_t OF HAVING THE SAME ERROR IN AVERAGE BETWEEN $-t$ AND $+t$ CAN BE CALCULATED FROM:
$P_t = 2\ (P_n - 0.5)$
NUMERICAL VALUES OF PROBABILITY P_n ARE TAKEN FROM R.A. FISHER'S TABLES GIVEN IN HIS PAPER: EXPANSION OF "STUDENT'S" INTEGRAL IN POWERS OF n^{-1} ("METRON" VOLUME V. NO. 3. 1925)

Fig. 5.

ful and artistic layout of the graphical presentation. In this connection, *Layout in Advertising*, W. A. Dwiggins, Harper & Bros., New York, 1928, should prove to be suggestive.

In closing, we should note that in the application of the method of control, it is sometimes advisable to substitute nomograms for tables in shop practice. For example, Fig. 4 gives a nomogram which enables one to read off the standard deviation σ in terms of a given sample size n and probability p'. In a similar way, Fig. 5 presents in graphical form the very complicated table of "Student's" integral. For a discussion of this nomogram and of the application of nomography in this way, see the paper by V. A. Nekrassoff, "Nomography in Applications of Statistics," published in *Metron*, Vol. VIII, 1930, pp. 95–99.

INDEX OF NAMES

[The numbers refer to pages]

INDEX OF SUBJECTS

[*The numbers refer to pages*]